TELEVISION AND RADIO IN THE UNITED KINGDOM

Television and Radio in the United Kingdom

Burton Paulu

University of Minnesota Press · Minneapolis

Published by the University of Minnesota Press,
2037 University Avenue Southeast, Minneapolis MN 55414
Printed in Hong Kong

Library of Congress Cataloging in Publication Data

Paulu, Burton, 1910–
    Television and radio in the United Kingdom.

    1. Broadcasting—Great Britain—History. I. Title.
PN1990.6.G7P3   384.54'0941   80–20870
ISBN 0–8166–0941–1

To Sarah Leith
Nancy Jean
and
Thomas Scott

Contents

Preface

My first contacts with British broadcasting came during World War II, when I worked in London and Luxembourg with the radio branch of the United States Office of War Information. There I quickly learned that most Americans had little knowledge or understanding of broadcasting abroad, and that there were no books to provide them with impartial accounts of the British or other foreign systems.

After doing graduate work in the late 1940s with Charles A. Siepmann, a former BBC employee who was both an admirer and critic of the British system—and a really outstanding teacher, I took advantage of a Fulbright grant in 1953–4 to write *British Broadcasting: Radio and Television in the United Kingdom*. Its sequel, *British Broadcasting in Transition*, published in 1961, examined the effect of competition on the British system.

Then I turned my attention to Europe, completing *Radio and Television Broadcasting on the European Continent* in 1967, and *Radio and Television Broadcasting in Eastern Europe* in 1974. The years spent studying and writing about continental—especially East European—broadcasting gave me a better understanding and increased appreciation of the British system, and led to the present volume which, however, is more tnan a rewriting and updating of my two previous books on the subject, even though it draws upon them in various ways. Since they were written, the world has changed, Britain has changed, and I have changed, so that this book is new in most respects, even though cast in the format of the first one.

This study involved a three months' visit to the United Kingdom in the late spring and early summer of 1976, as well as a month in London in the autumn of 1978. Thanks are due to the University of Minnesota for providing a quarter's leave in 1976 (the month in 1978 came after retirement had eased my administrative schedule), and for grants from the Office of International Programs, the McMillan Fund of the College of Liberal Arts, and the Graduate School. In the United Kingdom I benefited from excellent treatment by both the BBC and the IBA, which provided library facilities, some office space, staff consultation, and much friendly and enjoyable hospitality. Most of the manuscript was read by one or more experts from both organizations, who supplied useful information and eliminated many errors. At the BBC a splendid schedule was set up by Stephen Kanocz, Senior Liaison Officer, International Relations, while at the IBA there were Bernard Sendall, former Deputy Director General; Colin D. Shaw, Director of Television; and Michael Gillies, Television Administrative Officer, the latter of whom served as liaison person with the IBA and its programme companies during my 1978 visit to London.

Here at home I am indebted to two graduate student assistants (Ray Olson and

Kristi Wermager), three typists (Margaret Mattlin, Marybeth Casey, and Randi Vagle), my patient wife (Frances B. Paulu), and to my faithful Bedlington dogs (Lancelot II and Lancelot III), who successively kept me company in my study during many hours as I read, typed, dictated, and corrected manuscripts. But what is said here is all mine, and no one else assumes any responsibility for it.

Minneapolis, Minnesota   BURTON PAULU
May 1980

1 Introduction

Britons and Americans often discuss each other's broadcasting—and in the process usually reveal more opinions than understanding. Unfortunately, the purpose of most such exchanges is to prove that one or the other system is 'better', rather than to share knowledge on the assumption that broadcasting merits serious discussion. From such debates, neither country learns much about the other's broadcasting.

Americans tend to go to extremes in their references to British broadcasting. Admirers of London productions often base their judgements on the exceptional British programmes occasionally carried by American stations, forgetting that these are atypical. (Many Americans, incidentally, credit all such programmes to the British Broadcasting Corporation, not realizing that some of the best are produced by the Independent Broadcasting Authority's commercially supported companies.)

Other critics go to the opposite extreme, contending—erroneously—that British broadcasting is elitist, and that its programmes are mandated by the government without consideration for audience preferences. Many British commentaries on American broadcasting are equally uninformed, concentrating on its inadequacies, especially its excessive commercialism and poor programme balance; overlooking entirely its many superb programmes.*

Many of the cultural and political similarities of the United Kingdom and the United States are reflected in their broadcasting. Both countries are democratic, and both are dedicated to freedom of expression. They share many cultural traditions as well as the same language. Both regard it as essential that there be no government control of broadcasting content. The fact that one of Britain's broadcasting organizations is commercially supported, as are most American networks and stations, suggests another similarity, although British commercial television operates in a very different way from its American counterpart.

Any attempt to equate the BBC with America's public (educational) broadcasting service is fatuous, even though both are non-commercial. The BBC is a monolithic national organization offering a complete range of programmes, whereas America's public stations are independent of each other, and local. Furthermore, having been set up to redress the imbalance of commercial programming, and having limited resources, the latter provide balance rather than

---

* Throughout this book, the British Broadcasting Corporation is referred to as the BBC or the Corporation, and the Independent Broadcasting Authority as the IBA or the Authority. Before it was authorized to operate radio as well as television stations in 1972, the IBA was officially the Independent Television Authority (ITA), while its television programme service, then and now, is identified as Independent Television (ITV).

full-range services. Finally, the BBC is much better supported than is American public broadcasting.

Controlled competition is the keynote of the British system, whereas American commercial broadcasting is marked by less control and much more competition. The United Kingdom has found a way to regulate broadcasting without materially affecting the programmers' freedom to deal with important controversial issues. Meanwhile, in the United States, a system has grown up which has the effect of limiting public service in many basic programme areas, while putting off its critics in the name of First Amendment freedom.

It would be absurd, of course, to suggest that any country should adopt the exact pattern of broadcasting developed by another one. A broadcasting system grows out of its environment, and cannot be described or appraised apart from its national setting. Nevertheless, a knowledge of British broadcasting can be helpful to Americans, and can provide them with perspective as they appraise the strengths and weaknesses of their own system.

Radio broadcasting developed in both the United Kingdom and the United States in the early 1920s. Britain's first broadcasting agency was the British Broadcasting Company, created in 1922 as the sole authority to broadcast. This was a private company made up of radio manufacturers, deriving its income from licence fees paid to the government by the owners of radio sets and from royalties on the receiving equipment sold by its members. It was succeeded in 1927 by the present British Broadcasting Corporation.

The new British Broadcasting Corporation had three distinctive features: it was a public corporation; it was non-commercial; and it was a monopoly. It still is public and non-commercial, but it lost its television monopoly when the ITA went on the air in 1955, and its radio monopoly with the advent of the IBA in 1972. Controlled by its own Board of Governors, the Corporation is highly independent of the government, despite support by Parliamentary grants based on the yearly licence fees paid by all television set owners. (Radio licences, first required in 1922, were discontinued in 1971.) The BBC is prohibited from doing commercial broadcasting.

With some 26,600 employees, the BBC is second in size only to that of the Soviet Union among world broadcasting organizations. The Corporation is a complete broadcasting entity in itself, unlike the Independent Broadcasting Authority, which is legally obliged to contract with programme companies to produce its programmes. The BBC now operates four nationwide radio networks: Radio 1, essentially a popular music service; Radio 2 (formerly the Light Programme), featuring light entertainment, sports, and middle-of-the-road music; Radio 3 (succeeding the Third Programme), with classical music, significant drama, and serious talks and discussions; and Radio 4 (descended from the Home Service), a general-purpose network carrying the major radio newscasts, some music, much drama and entertainment, many talks, and education for young and old. Since 1967 the BBC also has operated some local radio stations. Service for overseas audiences—External Broadcasting—is another of the Corporation's assignments.

After some years of experimentation, the BBC inaugurated the world's first permanent high-definition television service in 1936. Following a World War II hiatus, telecasting was resumed on 7 June 1946, and a second network began in 1964. BBC 1 now provides a general service, while BBC 2, although carrying some light entertainment, sports, and other programmes of high audience appeal, is more specialized and intellectual in nature.

In the United Kingdom, the tradition was early established for government committees periodically to survey broadcasting and advise on future policies. The three most recent of these surveys were the Beveridge Committee appointed in 1949, the Pilkington Committee in 1960, and the Annan Committee, first appointed in 1970 but not active until 1974.

The Beveridge Committee, after a very thorough examination of all aspects of British broadcasting, recommended in 1951 the continuance of the BBC monopoly, although with certain procedural changes. For a number of reasons, however, the government postponed action, and the ensuing delay provided the advocates of commercial television with an opportunity to campaign for a supplementary service. Thereafter, intensive debates both in and out of Parliament culminated in the creation in 1954 of another public corporation, the Independent Television Authority, something like the BBC, but entirely separate from it, to select and regulate privately owned companies which presented programmes over transmitters the ITA owned and operated. These contractors pay the IBA, as it now is called, for broadcasting rights, meeting their costs from advertising revenues. The IBA provides Britain with its third television service, and when it commences operations, probably in 1982, will also be responsible for the fourth service. The same basic pattern also applies to the local radio stations administered by the IBA since 1972.

Between 1952 and 1972 the ITA came under attack in a series of inquiries, of which the most important was by a committee appointed in 1960, chaired by Sir Harry Pilkington, which surveyed the work of both the BBC and the ITA. Its report, issued in 1962, praised the BBC highly, but was very critical of ITA programme quality, balance, and high profits. Although the government did not adopt all of the committee's recommendations, it did follow the suggestion that the BBC, rather than the ITA, be given a second television channel. As a result of this and other criticism, the Authority engaged additional personnel and began to supervise its output more closely, while the government imposed an annual levy on programme company profits, above and beyond the normal taxes paid by all commercial enterprises.

Despite the strong opposition to the original proposal to introduce competitive television, and subsequent debates about the operation of the IBA, Independent Broadcasting clearly is accepted, and it is reasonable to assume that in the future, Britain will continue to be served by both the IBA and the BBC. The assignments given to both the Pilkington and Annan committees assumed the continuation of the two groups.

The most recent inquiry into British broadcasting was conducted by a committee headed by Lord Annan, Vice-Chancellor of the University of London. The committee's 522-page report was issued in March 1977, and some of its 174 recommendations and many comments are referred to in this book. Among other things, the committee proposed giving the fourth television channel to a new Open Broadcasting Authority, with financing to come partly from advertising and partly from educational grants. The committee also favoured a new authority to take over the local radio stations from both the BBC and the IBA, and recommended creating a Public Enquiry Board which would hold public hearings every seven years on broadcasting performance.

These and some of the committee's other proposals generated strong reactions, and the BBC, the IBA, and many groups and individuals wrote and spoke on the subject. The Labour Government, which had appointed the Annan Committee, indicated in July 1978 that it would follow most of these recommendations, but when the Conservatives returned to power in May 1979, they announced that the fourth television channel instead would go to the IBA. After much discussion, this was the subject of legislation passed by the House of Commons in 1980.

Although it no longer can be said that 'the sun never sets on the British Empire', the United Kingdom is still a going concern, with not only a great past but also a promising future. The United Kingdom ceased to be a major military power after World War II, and has suffered serious economic setbacks in recent years. Yet it remains important in world councils because of its intellectual achievements. Former Senator William Fulbright, who was a lawyer and educator before becoming first a congressman and then a senator, described the situation very eloquently when he said:[1] 'Britain has bequeathed a great legacy to much of the world, the legacy of her own experience in constitutional government, peaceful evolution, and the orderly accommodation of diverse interests within the society.' Britain continues to produce outstanding political leaders, writers, and scientists, and has shown remarkable flexibility in adapting to its current problems. Many contemporary British institutions deserve study, therefore, if not emulation, and one of them is broadcasting.

This book surveys and appraises the salient features of British broadcasting, describing the system and judging its performance. It does not, however, deal with such non-broadcast uses of radio and television as cable distribution and closed-circuit television. These are extensive and important enough to deserve a separate study. Furthermore, broadcast radio and television provide more than enough for treatment in a single volume.

Successive chapters here deal with the constitutions of the BBC and the IBA; their economic bases; physical plants and electronic facilities; personnel; radio and television programmes; audience reaction; and the external broadcasting done by the BBC for reception abroad. In covering the subject extensively, I accept the judgement of the late Director-General of the BBC, Sir Charles Curran, who wrote about 'the impossibility of separating out any one strand . . . from another. . . . The evolution of broadcasting and its continuing operation . . . did indeed present itself as a seamless robe.'

But a word of warning is in order. Broadcasting constantly evolves and changes. Even if correct when written, some of what follows may be altered by publication date, and greatly changed thereafter.

2 Constitution of the BBC: Historical Development

The United Kingdom of Great Britain and Northern Ireland includes England, Wales, Scotland and Northern Ireland. Its total area—94,209 square miles—is approximately that of the American state of Oregon, although its population of 56 million is one-fourth that of the United States.

Despite the country's compactness, however, its several sections manifest intense degrees of independence. One would expect Northern Ireland to be affected by the many years of conflict between Ireland and Great Britain, as well as by its own long and bitter internal feuds. But Scotland too insists on its cultural uniqueness and periodically proposes administrative devolution, while Wales raises broadcasting problems by insisting on having programmes in Gaelic. Even the various sections of England show strong regional variations, one aspect of this being the wide range of spoken English encountered in different parts of the country.

Of the two broadcasting organizations authorized by the British government, the BBC is the basic one. It was first; and when in 1953 the government announced its intention of setting up the ITA, it stated that 'the BBC would continue to be the main instrument of broadcasting in the United Kingdom.'[1] Both the Pilkington and Annan Committees agreed; and although the Independent Television Companies Association challenged this statement 'so far as television is concerned' on the grounds that the 'BBC does not command a majority of viewers, and a national service is better provided from regional bases such as ITV's,' the subsequent government White Paper supported the recommendation of the Annan Committee that the BBC 'should continue to be the main national instrument of broadcasting in the United Kingdom'.[2]

THE EARLY YEARS OF BRITISH BROADCASTING

Radio broadcasting developed during the last decade of the nineteenth century, following the pioneering work of the Italian, Guglielmo Marconi (1874–1937), and the Russian, Alexander Stepanovich Popov (1859–1905). Both built upon scientific foundations laid by others, and achieved break-throughs at about the same time, 1894 being claimed as the date when Marconi, and 1895 when Popov, invented radio.[3]

In both Britain and the United States, radio amateurs were active preceding World War I, although required by both governments to cease their activities during hostilities. Following the Armistice, however, the amateurs renewed their work, and there soon was great demand for entertainment programmes. This led to the formal inauguration of regular broadcasting in Britain on 23 February 1920, by the Marconi Company, from a station in the London area. Other stations soon followed.[4]

Although radio fans responded enthusiastically, the Post Office, which then discharged the technical regulatory functions now assigned to the Federal Communications Commission in the United States, disapproved of these broadcasts, fearing that they would interfere with point-to-point messages. Therefore, broadcasting for the general public was developed against the wishes of the government departments concerned, and in the almost complete absence of any wide appreciation of its social potentialities.

In the United Kingdom, as in the United States, the manufacturers of receiving sets provided leadership in the early development of broadcasting, hoping thereby to stimulate the sale of receivers. Set owners also supported it, since they wanted more programmes of music and entertainment. As a result, the British Post Office in May 1922 called a meeting of interested manufacturers of wireless sets and began the discussions which led to the creation later that year of the British Broadcasting Company.

The British Broadcasting Company was incorporated on 15 December 1922, and received its licence to broadcast on 18 January 1923.[5] Although it differed in some important respects from the later British Broadcasting Corporation, it influenced both the legal structure and programming policies of its successor.

The Company, unlike the Corporation, was a privately owned commercial organization made up of the manufacturers of broadcasting equipment.[6] Its funds came from three sources: the original stock; royalties on the receiving sets sold by members; and a portion of the proceeds from the sale of broadcast receiving licences. All British Broadcasting Company members agreed to sell no receivers or parts unless made of British components by company members, and to pay the company royalty on all sales. At the same time, each owner of a set had to purchase annually a ten-shilling licence from the Post Office, and the government agreed to issue licences only to people using receivers made by members of the company. In return for the financial risks of setting up the broadcasting service, therefore, the manufacturers were guaranteed protection against foreign competition.

The company was to establish eight broadcasting stations in different parts of the British Isles, and to provide 'a programme of broadcast matter to the reasonable satisfaction of the Postmaster General'. In addition to many requirements regarding technical operating standards, the licence contained several important programme provisions, the first of which was later incorporated into the licences of the British Broadcasting Corporation: 'The Company shall if so requested by any Department of His Majesty's Government . . . transmit . . . any communiqués, weather reports or notices issued thereby as a part of any programme or programmes of broadcast matter.'[7]

There were two limiting clauses: one pertaining to news and the other to commercial programmes. In response to requests from the press, which even in

1922 was concerned over the possible effects of broadcasting on newspaper circulation, the licence provided

> that the Company shall not broadcast any news or information in the nature of news except such as they may obtain on payment from one or more of the following news agencies, viz., Reuters', Ltd., Press Association, Ltd., Central News, Ltd., Exchange Telegraph Company, Ltd. or from any other news agency . . . approved . . . by the Postmaster General.

It also ruled against direct advertising by stipulating that the company should not,

> without the consent in writing of the Postmaster General receive money or other valuable consideration from any person in respect of the transmission of messages by means of the licensed apparatus, or send messages or music constituting broadcast matter provided or paid for by any person, other than the Company or person actually sending the message.

The latter clause was interpreted by the British Broadcasting Company as excluding the broadcasting of advertisement but not of 'sponsored programmes'—those in which an advertiser supplied a programme in return for a mention of his product on the air (see below, pp. 24, 49).

Finally, it should be observed that the British Broadcasting Company in effect—though not legally—had a monopoly on broadcasting in the United Kingdom. The Postmaster-General might have licensed other broadcasting agencies had he chosen to, but he did not, so that monopoly was introduced at the very outset.

THE BROADCASTING COMMITTEES

A few months after it took to the air, so many weaknesses developed in the financial structure of the British Broadcasting Company that, on 24 April 1923, the Postmaster-General appointed a seven-man investigating committee to review its status.[8] Headed by Major-General Sir Frederick Sykes, the committee's members were drawn from Parliament, the Post Office, the press, the radio manufacturers, and the Company. Although the problems of the Company were its first concern, the committee was also instructed to consider 'broadcasting in all its aspects', and was asked to make recommendations for its future development.

First among the reasons which led to the committee's appointment was the breakdown of the company's financial basis. People were building their own sets out of imported materials. They then either took out experimenters' licences—which did not require the use of British Broadcasting Company parts or sets—or else evaded the law by purchasing no licences at all. The Company thus lost money on both set royalties and licence fees. The Sykes Committee also had political problems to solve: the Beaverbrook newspapers had taken the lead in condemning the Company as a monopoly to enrich the six large firms, while there were complaints from small manufacturers that they were being forced to join an organization run to their disadvantage by their large competitors.

After thirty-four meetings, in the course of which it examined thirty-two witnesses and received memoranda from exponents of all points of view, the committee issued a report on 19 August 1923, which set forth recommendations for both the immediate and long-range development of British broadcasting.[9] Most of its proposals were accepted. The government issued a single licence at 10 shillings to cover all types of radios. The system of royalties was dropped, as was the ban on foreign receivers. In response to its critics the Company included radio dealers as well as manufacturers among its members, and gave the smaller stockholders more influence in its affairs. Thus modified, the British Broadcasting Company had its licence extended to 31 December 1926.

Looking to the future, the Sykes Committee forecast the eventual replacement of private by public operation. Noting that 'broadcasting holds social and political possibilities as great as any technical attainment of our generation', it went on to say:

> For these reasons we consider that the control of such a potential power over public opinion and the life of the nation ought to remain with the State, and that the operation of so important a national service ought not to be allowed to become an unrestricted commercial monopoly.[10]

But the Company was to be independent of the government:

> If a Government Department had to select the news, speeches, lectures, &c., to be broadcast, it would be constantly open to suspicion that it was using its unique opportunities to advance the interests of the political party in power; and, in the endeavour to avoid anything in the slightest degree controversial, it would probably succeed in making its service intolerably dull.

To draw up plans for the permanent structure of British broadcasting, the government appointed another committee on 20 July 1925. Under the chairmanship of the Earl of Crawford and Balcarres, this group was to 'advise as to the proper scope of the Broadcasting service and as to the management, control and finance thereto after the expiry of the existing licence of 31st December 1926'.[11]

Although the BBC was a private commercial company, its Managing Director, John C. W. Reith (see below, pp. 9, 135–6) was already regarding it as a public corporation. In his book, *Into the Wind*, he stated: 'The BBC should be a public service not only in performance but in constitution.'[12] He circulated a memorandum to the committee's members in November 1925 to 'show the desirability for the conduct of Broadcasting as a Public Service, for the adoption and maintenance of definite policies and standards in all its activities, and for unity of control'. In this paper Reith expressed one of the ideas he was the reiterate in later years: 'He who prides himself on giving what he thinks the public wants is often creating a fictitious demand for lower standards which he will then satisfy.'

The Crawford Committee, even at the early date of 1925, saw the importance of freedom from government, since it wrote that 'a public corporation [would be] the most appropriate organisation' to run broadcasting because it 'would enjoy a freedom and flexibility which a Minister of State himself could scarcely exercise in arranging for performers and programmes, and in studying the variable demands of public taste and necessity'.[13] Although 'the State, through Parliament, must retain the right of ultimate control, ... The ... [Corporation] should ... be invested with the maximum of freedom which Parliament is prepared to concede.'

The committee's recommendations led to the Charter and Licence which created the BBC and authorized it to broadcast for ten years from 1 January 1927.[14] Broadcasting became a monopoly, financed by annual fees on radio receivers, and administered by an independent public corporation. These three principles determined the BBC's structure until its monopoly was ended in 1954 by the creation of the ITA. Reith became the first Director-General of the new corporation, a position he retained until 1938. (Reith became Sir John Reith in 1927, and Lord Reith in 1940.)

Certain changes have been made periodically in the BBC's status, usually following investigation by a prestigious non-partisan government-appointed committee as the current charter and licence came up for renewal. As the first 10-year licence period drew to a close, a committee headed by Lord Ullswater was appointed on 17 April 1935.[15] One of its members was Clement R. Attlee, MP, whose reservations to the final report presaged some future trends. (Attlee later was Prime Minister, from 1945 to 1951.)

Attlee's reservations are worth noting. Writing as a Labour MP, he commented that 'it is undesirable that the Governors should be drawn solely from persons whose social experience and background is that of the well-to-do classes'[16] (see below, pp. 133–4). Furthermore, because the members of the Board of Governors were too old, 'with a consequent over-emphasis on the outlook of the past', he recommended retiring them at the age of 60. He complained about the Corporation's attitude toward employee unions, and above all took exception to the way 'the broadcasting system was used by the Government' during the General Strike of 1926: this 'created in the minds of a very large section of the community grave suspicion which has prejudiced the Corporation ever since. The B.B.C should have sufficient independence to resist being made the instrument of one side in a national controversy.' Finally, he stated that during the general election of 1931 the government was favoured in the allocation of broadcast time.

The subsequent parliamentary debate led to no changes in the government's proposals, so that the Charter and Licence were renewed and the BBC's life assured until 31 December 1946. But the BBC's historian remarked: 'The Ullswater Report suggested no drastic changes in the life of the BBC, but it hinted, for those who had eyes to read and ears to hear, that one day drastic changes might come.'[17] In 1946, both Charter and Licence were further extended to 31 December 1951, without inquiry, on the grounds that the dislocation resulting from the war made considered judgement impossible at that time.

The Beveridge Committee, appointed in 1949, conducted what was by far the most exhaustive examination of British broadcasting up to that time. Although it raised far more questions about basic theories than had any of its predecessors, this committee also recommended the extension of the BBC's Charter and Licence on the same fundamental basis as before.[18] But the Labour government did not issue the new Charter and Licence before going out of office in October 1951, and since the new Conservative government had its own ideas about broadcasting, especially in regard to television, it gave the BBC only a six months' extension while permanent policies were debated within party councils. These were announced in May 1952 as the continuation of radio broadcasting as before, with the addition of 'some element of competition' in television, and it was understood—though not so stated—that the new service was to be commercially supported.[19] However, the new government proposed no basic changes in the BBC itself, and the Charter and Licence accordingly were extended for another 10-year period, effective from 1 July 1952.[20]

In view of the subsequent introduction of competitive commercially supported television, notice should be taken of the minority report submitted by Beveridge committee member Selwyn Lloyd, MP, who maintained that 'all this actual and potential influence should [not] be vested in a public or private monopoly'.[21] The BBC had too much power, he said, and he mentioned with particular displeasure Lord Reith's paper to the committee which declared that 'it was the brute force of monopoly that enabled the BBC to become what it did'. Selwyn Lloyd remarked: 'I do not like this "brute force of monopoly", and I am afraid that its dangers in regard to this medium of expression are both insidious and insufficiently appreciated by the public.'

During the subsequent debate in the House of Commons, Selwyn Lloyd actively supported the creation of the ITA. (For a review of the debate which led to the creation of the Independent Television Authority in 1954, see below, pp. 61–3).

On 13 July 1960, a committee chaired by Sir Harry Pilkington was appointed to:

consider the future of the broadcasting services in the United Kingdom . . .; to advise on the services which should in the future be provided . . . by the BBC and the ITA; to recommend whether additional services should be provided by any other organization; and to propose what financial and other conditions should apply to the conduct of all these services.[22]

The continued existence of both BBC and ITA was assumed, although the committee was authorized to recommend the creation of additional broadcasting organizations. On the same day the committee was appointed, the expiration dates of the BBC's Charter and Licence were extended to 29 July 1964, to coincide with the expiration of the Television Act of 1954, which served as charter and licence for the ITA.[23]

The committee had many meetings—seventy-eight of its entire membership and forty-three meetings of sub-groups—and received 852 memoranda and papers along with many letters from 'individual members of the general public'. Its report, made on 5 June 1962, ran to 302 pages with 1268 pages of supplementary material. Briefly, the members were very enthusiastic about the BBC, but harsh in judging the ITA. (The sections of the report dealing with Independent Television are reviewed on pp. 82–3 below.) Although noting some charges of excessive violence and programme triviality, along with complaints about the Corporation's services in Scotland, Wales, and Northern Ireland, the committee nevertheless felt that there was a 'sense of responsibility underlying the programming policy of the BBC', for which reason no fundamental changes were recommended in its constitution or organization.[24] The Committee suggested more autonomy for the National Broadcasting Councils of Scotland and Wales, as well as the development by the BBC (but not the ITA) of some local radio stations. Most important, though, was its recommendation that the BBC provide a second television service, whereas 'so long as Independent Television is constituted and organised as at present, it should not provide any additional services of television'.

The BBC, of course, was delighted with the report. In the words of Sir Hugh Greene, then Director-General: 'the BBC emerged from . . . [the Pilkington inquiry] more successfully than we had imagined in our wildest dreams. . . . Everything was there that we had hoped for, or very nearly everything.'[25] But the ITA's reaction was one of dismay—and this was not the last time in the decade that a report would condemn it.

Only a few portions of the report were accepted by the government, but the issues raised relative to the ITA initiated a series of discussions which carried over into the deliberations of the Annan Committee. Because of the complexity of the proposals, the government issued two White Papers in response to the report, one in July and one in December 1962. The most important recommendation was that a second BBC television service be started in London in mid-1964 and extended to the rest of the country 'as rapidly as possible'.[26] No additional nation-wide radio network services were recommended, but the government did accept the suggestion that local radio stations be set up by the BBC. About another ITA television service, the second White Paper stated: 'While the government does not propose to authorize a second independent programme in the near future, it does not dismiss the possibility of doing so later'.[27] The government then provided a new Charter and Licence to run for 12 years until 31 July 1976. When the appointment of the Annan Committee was announced in 1974, the Charter and Licence of the BBC and the legislation constituting the IBA were extended to July 1979.

Broadcasting—especially television—was widely discussed during the latter 1960s and early 1970s. Much, although not all of this, pertained to Independent Television, there being particular concern about its programme quality and balance, and the large profits made by its programme companies. In 1971, a select committee of the House of Commons, appointed to examine the reports and accounts of various 'nationalised industries', included the ITA in its purview. One of its recommendations was for 'a full ranging enquiry at the earliest opportunity to consider broadcasting after 1976'.[28]

In 1970, the Labour Government had announced plans to appoint such a committee, headed by Lord Annan, Provost of University College, London, but before the other members of the committee were named, the Conservative Party came into power, and decided in March 1973 that 'a full ranging enquiry [is] undesirable now'.[29] It did, however, 'commission an independent study of the coverage of the broadcasting services in Scotland, Wales, Northern Ireland and rural England'.

On 10 April 1974, after Labour returned to power, the committee was reactivated again, with Lord Annan as chairman, and on 12 July the other members were named.[30] The committee was

> to consider the future of the broadcasting services in the United Kingdom . . .; to consider the implications for present or any recommended additional services of new techniques; and to propose what constitutional, organisational and financial arrangements . . . should apply to the conduct of all these services.

The terms of reference, however, excluded the Channel Islands, the Isle of Man, and the BBC's External Services. The charge did not say so, but it was understood that both the BBC and IBA would be continued, although there was no prohibition against the creation of additional broadcasting organizations.

Before it reported some 3 years later in March 1977, the full committee held forty-four meetings, while subcommittees had twenty-eight meetings. Twenty-five days were spent receiving evidence in London, Edinburgh, and Cardiff. Some members paid visits to Canada, West Germany, the United States, France, New Zealand, and Israel, and a number of studies were conducted especially for the committee. Several thousand letters were received, and memoranda reached the committee from nearly 750 organizations and individuals.

The committee's 522-page report included much information, provided many comments about all aspects of British broadcasting, and concluded with 174 recommendations. Most widely discussed of these was the recommendation that the fourth television channel be turned over to a new Open Broadcasting Authority, to be operated 'as a publisher of other organisations' programmes', and supported by a combination of advertising and grants. This recommendation pleased the BBC, which had made a similar proposal itself, but it greatly disappointed the IBA, which was counting heavily on having a second television channel of its own.

'Broadcasting', said the committee, should continue to be provided as public services, and continue to be the responsibility of public authorities, . . . [with independence] of Government in day-to-day conduct of their business'. There should be a Broadcasting Complaints Commission 'to consider complaints against all the broadcasting authorities or misrepresentation or unjust or unfair treatment of broadcast programmes', along with a Public Enquiry Board to hold public hearings every seven years 'on the way each Broadcasting Authority has discharged its responsibilities'.

The BBC should 'continue to be the main national instrument of broadcasting', and should maintain its unitary structure, although some members of the committee wanted it divided into smaller units. There was agreement all around that the Corporation should continue to be financed by the revenue from broadcast receiving licences, and general opposition to support by advertising or government grants. The Independent Broadcasting Authority should be renamed the Regional Television Authority, and be responsible only for a single television service. The

IBA and BBC local radio stations should be assigned to a new Local Broadcasting Authority, with support for all to come mainly from advertising revenue. The most controversial of the committee's recommendations was that the fourth television channel—or network—should be assigned to a new Open Broadcasting Authority (OBA), and should be financed by a combination of advertising, sponsorship, and grants from educational sources. However, the OBA was not to begin operations 'until the nation's economy' could support a high level of service.

Reaction to the report was both extensive and intensive. The BBC, the IBA, and the Independent Television Companies Association, issued long formal statements, supportive of their respective interests. There was a tremendous amount of newspaper discussion: a BBC compilation of press coverage filled a volume half an inch thick.

In May 1978, the Labour Government issued a White Paper accepting many of the Annan Committee's proposals, including the assignment of the fourth channel to a new OBA, and adding a proposal for 'separate Service Management Boards for each of the three [BBC] services', that is, for radio, television, and external broadcasting. About half the members of each board would be appointed by the Home Secretary from outside the Corporation's staff. It was intended that 'many of the management functions' assigned to the Board of Governors would be delegated to these boards, a procedure rationalized as enabling the Board of Governors to 'concentrate on their supervisory and public accountability role'. But this proposal was roundly condemned by the BBC, the IBA (the Boards were to have no control over it, but perhaps the IBA saw a possible future relationship), and the press as containing a potential for government control. However, the new Conservative Government that came in following the May 1979 election negated the White paper, assigned the fourth channel to the IBA, and dropped the Service Boards proposal (see below, pp. 85–6, for details on the fourth channel and the IBA).

THE DEVELOPMENT OF THE MONOPOLY

Monopoly, from the very outset one of the fundamental features of British broadcasting, was introduced for a variety of reasons.[31] Historically, telephone and telegraph services in Britain, as in almost all European countries, were a monopoly of the government Post Office, and so it seemed natural that broadcasting also should be a monopoly. Then there were technical factors. Because of a shortage of broadcast frequencies, all Europe favoured monopoly operation, under the assumption that it would facilitate the allocation of channels. Peter Eckersley, the first Chief Engineer of the British Broadcasting Company, wrote: 'The BBC was formed as the expedient solution of the technical problem; it owes its existence solely to the scarcity of wave-length.'[32] Furthermore, the British Post Office was under great pressure from the armed services to limit the assignment for frequencies of broadcasting. Radio manufacturers, anxious to put a number of stations on the air quickly, also favoured monopoly, because the Marconi Company was unwilling to share with others the many essential patents it held.

Even in the early 1920s, the press feared the effects of commercial radio on its revenues, and therefore opposed broadcast advertising. Consequently, it favoured licence-fee support; and since the easiest way to collect and distribute such funds was with one collection agency—the Post Office, and a single recepient—the BBC, monopoly seemed the course to follow.

Although politicians then had little interest in broadcasting, they realized that in the future it might have great political value, and so none of them wanted radio to fall into the hands of their opponents. Accordingly, the three parties— Conservative, Liberal and Labour—were prepared to assign broadcasting to a single public corporation which neither the government nor any of them could easily control.

America's frequency allocation problems also were a factor. Until the creation of the Federal Radio Commission in 1927, the United States government lacked statutory authority to assign stations to specific frequencies and to determine their power, with resulting chaos on the American air. For many years this was one reason the British were disposed to question the merits of the American system; commercialism, of course, was another one.[33] F. J. Brown, assistant secretary at the Post Office, recently had observed American broadcasting, and jumped to the conclusion that the presence of many competing stations—rather than inadequate legislation—caused the trouble, and recommended strongly against licensing more than one company. As the Post Office Official most directly concerned with broadcasting, and as a member of the Sykes Committee, he was very influential.

The factor which later became the main argument of monopoly supporters was introduced by Percy Scholes, the well-known British musicologist, who, following a trip to the United States in 1925, reported to the Sykes Committee that competition among America's stations was lowering programme standards, at the same time that advertising was gaining the upper hand.[34] Moreover, Post Office officials, confronted by twenty-four applicants for licences, persuaded them to form one company in order to avoid the unpleasant task of choosing among them.

No list of reasons why British broadcasting developed as a monopoly would be complete without reference to John Reith.[35] Able, ingenious and self-righteous, Reith combined sincerely-held beliefs about the social obligations of broadcasting with the conviction that monopoly was the only way those objectives could be achieved. He told the Sykes Committee on 14 June 1923: 'There is a very great advantage in having a uniform policy of what can or cannot be done in broadcasting', and in 1949 referred to the 'brute force of monopoly' as the basic reason for the success of British broadcasting.

Despite all this, the British Broadcasting Company was never guaranteed a monopoly.[36] In fact, in the Supplementary Agreement issued in 1923 following the Sykes Committee report, the government expressly reserved the right to license additional stations.

The Crawford Committee, appointed in 1926 to advise on the permanent structure of British broadcasting, recommended a monopoly, principally in the belief that competition for listeners would force down programme standards. In the absence of any opposing views, the case for monopoly—supported by wireless associations, newspaper publishers, and educators—impressed the committee so much that it dismissed the whole matter in a single sentence: 'It is agreed that the

United States system of free and uncontrolled transmission and reception, is unsuited to this country, and that Broadcasting must accordingly remain a monopoly . . .'[37]

Reith wanted the Charter of the new BBC, which took effect on 1 January 1927, to guarantee the Corporation a monopoly, but the Post Office refused, although it agreed to omit reference to any right of licensing other broadcasting authorities.[38] Accordingly although neither its Charter nor Licence specifically said so, the BBC, which began operations on 1 January 1927, was assumed by all concerned to be a monopoly, a decision strongly supported by the articulate public of the day.[39]

When the first Licence was up for renewal, the advantages of monopoly seemed so obvious they were not even discussed. The Ullswater Committee, appointed in 1935, wrote a 55-page report scrutinizing many aspects of the Corporation's work, but, in the words of one of its members, took 'for granted the principle that there should be a Government monopoly'.[40] Parliament and the public agreed, although in later years the monopoly was widely criticized for many reasons both by interested and disinterested critics, and in the 1940s former employees as well as outside observers began to write books critical of the BBC, most of which devoted at least some space to the question of monopoly.[41]

The first actual breach of the monopoly was by the American Forces Network, established in London in July 1943 to serve American military personnel stationed in Britain—and the BBC had to be pressured before it would agree to admit the AFN.[42] AFN programmes originated in its own studio centre in London and were broadcast only by low-powered transmitters at the forty or fifty principal American camps. Since the AFN output consisted mainly of popular music and comedy shows (without commercials) from all four American networks, they had great appeal for those British teenagers who could hear them. Critics of the monopoly, and advocates of commercial broadcasting, frequently cited the AFN as a model for Britain to follow, which undoubtedly was one of the reasons the BBC opposed the AFN in the first place.

After the war, monopoly had to be defended against critics in both political parties, especially during the parliamentary debates in 1946 on the propriety of renewing the 1937 Charter and Licence without the customary investigation.[43] For example, Sir Frederick Ogilvie, who succeeded Reith as Director-General from 1938 to 1942, wrote to *The Times*—the standard way to air opinions on serious subjects in Britain—commenting on the 1946 White Paper which had announced the government's intention of extending the BBC's licence without an inquiry. In his letter, published on 26 June 1946, Sir Frederick said that, as he saw it, the question was 'not a matter of politics, but of freedom.'[44] Pointing out that 'Freedom is choice', he argued: 'In tolerating monopoly of broadcasting we are alone among the democratic countries of the world.'[45]

Thereafter, a series of public opinion polls indicated increasing support for both a second television service and for ending the monopoly.[46] Taken together, these polls indicated that since the middle 1940s there had been a fairly even division of opinion as to the desirability of continuing the BBC monopoly or of supplementing it with commercial broadcasting paid for by advertisers. For the most part, the upper classes (who, of course, were in a numerical minority) opposed both monopoly and commercial broadcasting; the lower classes, on the other hand, favoured commercial broadcasting. It was generally agreed that competition would improve programmes, and that if there were commercial stations, the BBC ought not to run them. There was a strong desire for a good television service, but an even division of opinion on the desirability of commercial television as such. Therefore, when the ITA came into being in 1954, it was not in answer to an overwhelming demand for competitive commercial broadcasting; but on the other hand, it did not come into existence against the wishes of a large majority.

THE MONOPOLY DEBATE

The arguments for and against monopoly have remained the same ever since the founding of the British Broadcasting Company in 1922, although their emphasis has varied depending upon the occasion.[47] As was observed above (pp. 13, 14), one of the original arguments was that the limited number of frequencies required that all stations be controlled by a single authority so that maximum coverage might be secured with minimum interference—a problem that affected monopoly operation on the Europen continent too. Although a case could be made for this, there was one good counter-argument, which was hardly ever advanced: a regulatory agency could assign frequencies as does the American Federal Communications Commission, the stations then being operated and programmed competitively.

Another argument pertained to finance: it would be difficult if not impossible to divide licence fees among several competing broadcasters whose coverage areas might overlap, and whose programme resources, skills, and costs might vary. But this ignored the possibility of supplementary commercial revenue, although the Sykes Committee in 1923 recommended for radio, and the Selsdon and Ullswater Committees in 1935 and 1936 recommended for television, such additional support.

More widely questioned was the claim that monopoly ensured greater efficiency of operation than did a competitive system. The opposite view also was put forth: the absence of competition leads to complacency and inefficiency, and there would be more imaginative programming if several licensees had to compete for audiences. In later years, it also was charged that the BBC had grown to unwieldy size, and that there would be better broadcasting if it were broken up into several competing organizations.

But the principal argument in favour of monopoly was always that it ensured a better balanced programme service, and would maintain higher standards than would a competitive system. This point usually involved the merits of competitive commercial broadcasting too, since the alternative to a licence-fee-supported monopoly was assumed to be competitive commercial broadcasting. BBC spokesmen, early and later, provided the most complete statements of this position. Lord Reith, the Corporation's influential first Director-General, pressed it in the early days and again in retrospect a quarter of a century later when he wrote in his memoirs: 'It was, in fact, the combination of public service motive, sense of moral obligation, assured finance, and the brute force of monopoly which enabled the BBC to make of broadcasting what no other country in the world has made of it.'[48]

He reinforced this in a statement to the Beveridge Committee:

> It was the brute force of monopoly that enabled the BBC to become what it did; and to do what it did; that made it possible for a policy of moral responsibility to be followed. If there is to be competition it will be of cheapness not of goodness. The usual disadvantages and dangers of monopoly do not apply to Broadcasting; it is in fact a potent incentive.[49]

Strategically the phrase 'brute force of monopoly' proved unfortunate, and it was quoted with effect by the opponents of monopoly in the 1952 and 1953 parliamentary debates on commercial television.[50] There was reference above to the comment by Selwyn Lloyd, one of the members of the Beveridge Committee: 'I do not like this "brute force of monopoly"'.[51]

The BBC's memorandum on 'Monopoly and Competition in Broadcasting', presented to the Beveridge Committee in May 1950, remains the most complete exposition of this rationale for monopoly. The Corporation stated that, even if arguments based on shortage of frequencies and on financing were eliminated, monopoly still could be justified by 'the crucial test . . . of standards', which it described as 'the purpose, taste, cultural aims, range, and general sense of responsibility of the broadcasting service as a whole'. The memorandum then elaborated:

> Under any system of competitive broadcasting all these things would be at the mercy of Gresham's Law [the tendency of bad money to drive good money out of circulation]. . . . The good, in the long run, will inescapably be driven out by the bad. . . . And because competition in broadcasting must in the long run descend to a fight for the greatest possible number of listeners, it would be the lower forms of mass appetite which would more and more be catered for in programmes.[52]

The BBC also argued that, because its survival does not depend on obtaining a maximum audience, a monopoly can maintain a better balanced schedule than can competitive services. It can meet all the nation's broadcasting needs, and particularly can provide programmes for minority as well as majority groups, scheduling them at convenient listening hours. It can strive over a long period to improve public taste. Finally, it can minimize broadcasts of wide popular appeal but no social value, and can omit positively harmful programmes entirely from the schedule.*

* On 30 September 1977, *The New York Times* (p. c28) carried an article about ABC TV's current leadership of NBC and CBS in audience ratings, which quoted the President of CBS TV to the effect that ABC was winning its prime time ratings with 'junk'. After referring to several popular ABC programmes he was quoted as saying: 'They're all clever and well done, but they are like junk food. It's just like going into a fast food restaurant and getting a cheeseburger, fries and a shake rather than a responsible restaurant that provides you with nourishment'. He went on to suggest that ABC's success would force down the level of all network programming.

The most important argument against monopoly has been that it constitutes a potential if not real threat to freedom of speech, the more so in view of the closeness of the BBC to the British government. Some critics disapproved on general principles any sort of broadcasting monopoly. Others cited specific instances in which they alleged freedom of expression had been curtailed by the Corporation. Still others claimed that the BBC, in order to avoid government interference, was too timid in treating controversial issues, thereby depriving the public of vital information.

In reply, the Corporation admitted that there were provisions in its charter that made it appear subservient to the government, but vigorously denied that it was so in fact. Actually, it said, the British two-party system ensured a political balance in its programmes; furthermore, successive parliaments had reiterated that the BBC should remain free from government controls.

Another argument against monopoly was that dictation by the BBC of the nation's programmes was wrong. Let the people decide for themselves by choosing freely among several competing systems rather than having the nature and proportions of their broadcasting fare determined for them. Specifically, it was often charged that the BBC overprovided for minority cultural groups, and was unresponsive to demands for certain popular programmes.

In reply the BBC pointed to its many popular entertainment programmes, at the same time emphasizing its obligation to upgrade public taste over the long run by always doing some programming for minority groups, and trying to raise the level of popular taste so that these minorities might become majorities. It is remarkable that this argument was not met with denials that the BBC had succeeded in improving public taste, since there was considerable evidence that the planned programme balance had no long-term effects on audience preferences.

Throughout the years, broadcasting in the United States was cited by both sides to prove their arguments—and it was more damned than praised in the process. Competition and commercialism were the two main features singled out for comment. In the United States in the middle 1920s, confusion prevailed in the allocation of frequencies. Later there were references to the lower cultural level of American broadcasting, its real or imagined lapses from good taste in both programmes and commercials, its exorbitant production costs, and its allegedly irresponsible handling of news and current affairs programmes. On the other hand, justification for ending the monopoly and introducing commercial broadcasting was found in the American system's greater responsiveness to audience interests, its ingenuity in programme development, its more adequate financing, and its allegedly more complete coverage of news and controversial issues.

Self-interest usually determined the line-up of groups favouring and opposing monopoly. At first, the two major political parties, Conservative and Labour, as well as the minority Liberal Party, all favoured the monopoly. In the commercial television debates of 1952, however, the Conservative Party supported the ITA and the Labour and Liberal Parties opposed it. The press in the main supported monopoly, partly because a non-commercial monopoly would not compete for advertising revenue. But once commercial broadcasting became a reality, newspapers were among the major stockholders in the programme companies (see p. 78, below).

Government departments usually supported monopoly, as did the BBC itself, and the Corporation was effectively seconded by its various advisory councils and committees. Finally, monopoly was advocated by many of those individuals and institutions accepted as the traditional guardians of public welfare and morality. Their support was based on the belief that competition would lower programme standards, although some of them also may have felt that their personal tastes would be better served by the BBC than by competing stations, especially if the latter were commercially supported. Among this group stood the churches, particularly the influential Church of England; the leading educators and educational organizations; and a great many people of artistic and intellectual inclination. However, the Catholic Church, which felt that it did not receive sufficient time on the BBC, was inclined to favour the legislation creating the ITA.

The opposition to monopoly, which developed in strength only after World War II, enlisted in its ranks a varied assortment of people and organizations. The Conservative Party's opposition resulted from the tangled skein of circumstances and issues described elsewhere (see below, pp. 57, 59–60). Some liberal intellectuals opposed any sort of broadcasting monopoly as a potentially dangerous concentration of power. Many less sophisticated people opposed it in the belief that a competitive system would give them more programmes to their taste. For reasons of personal gain, some advertising agency executives opposed the monopoly, although others supported it, preferring to work in the older media with which they were already familiar. Finally, opposition to the monopoly came from some of the individuals and organizations the BBC inevitably had displeased or alienated at one time or another during its long regime as the United Kingdom's only broadcasting organization.*

---

* Periodically through the years it has been proposed that the BBC be made into two or more separate organizations, either (in the early years) because monopoly was undesirable in itself, or because the Corporation allegedly was too large for efficient operation. During 1944, for example, a prestigious British magazine, *The Economist*, ran a series of articles which advocated ending the BBC monopoly. (*The Economist*, **147**, 564–5, 28 October 1944; 597–8, 4 November 1944; 630–1, 11 November 1944; 660–2, 18 November 1944). In 1949, the Beveridge Committee heard proposals for dividing the Corporation along functional lines (i.e. domestic radio, television, External Broadcasting, etc.), with varying plans for licence fee and/or advertising support, and committee member MP Selwyn Lloyd wrote a minority report suggesting a functional breakdown of the BBC with financial support from a combination of licence fee and commercial revenue (Beveridge I, ##154–180; pp. 201–10). But the majority report recommended continuation of the monopoly. The Pilkington Committee of 1960 received proposals for a third television network to be operated by the BBC, the ITA, the two together, or an entirely new agency (Pilkington I ##893–905). The Committee rejected all of them. In 1977, a minority of the Annan Committee favoured dividing the Corporation into two separate agencies, one for television and one for radio. This suggestion was rejected, although the majority report recommended a new Local Broadcasting Authority to operate all the local radio stations (taking them away from the BBC and the IBA), and a new Open Broadcasting Authority for the fourth channel (Annan, ##9.30–0.57; page 480, recommendations 73–103). The Labour Government then in power accepted the latter proposal (*1978 White Paper*,

Britain now has two nationwide organizations—very similar in make-up apart from their means of financial support—offering both radio and television programmes. The two controlling groups, the BBC's Board of Governors and the Independent Broadcasting Authority, are required by the government to maintain high programme standards. Furthermore, the total number of services is limited. There now are three and probably never can be more than six television networks; the four national radio networks all are run by the BBC, and only locally is there radio competition. Therefore, British broadcasting is not competitive in the American sense. In fact, the high quality of its services is possible only because the extent and nature of competition are controlled. British broadcasting is a controlled duopoly, run by two public corporations, both operating under the same strict ground rules laid down by the government.

RELAY EXCHANGES, FOREIGN COMMERCIAL BROADCASTING, AND PIRATE STATIONS

Interesting insights into the issues of monopoly and commercial broadcasting are provided by the BBC's long opposition to radio relay exchanges at home and to commercial stations abroad.[53]

Radio relay exchanges grew up all over Britain in the middle 1920s. These exchanges picked up programmes off the air on high-grade receivers or (in later years) received them by direct line from the BBC. The programmes then were fed by wire to loudspeakers in subscribers' homes. This system of distribution appealed particularly to the lower-income groups, because it required no capital outlay, and was cheaper to maintain than off-the-air receivers. Above all, the exchanges provided interference-free reception from more stations than was possible on most sets, including foreign commercial stations like Radio Luxembourg and Radio Normandy.

By 1930 there were 86 radio relay exchanges with 21,677 subscribers. By 1955, 250 separate firms provided relay service to over a million homes, comprising about 10 per cent of the radio homes of the country, and television exchanges were beginning to pipe programmes to their first subscribers.[54] In 1973 there were some 2000 licensed relay systems with approximately 2.5 million subscribers, representing 13 per cent of all television households. Some of these subscribers, however, received radio only.[55] Except for a few local television experiments, the relay companies are not allowed to originate programmes of their own, being licensed to distribute only programme material from authorized broadcasting stations.

From the very beginning, the BBC itself, other supporters of the monopoly, and the opponents of commercial broadcasting were concerned over the growth of relay exchanges. In 1933 the Corporation pointed with alarm to the fact that the exchanges 'have power, by replacing selected items of the Corporation's

---

##15–24), but the Conservative Government elected in May 1979 changed this and decided that both the BBC and the IBA were to continue operating all their television and radio services as before.

programmes with transmissions from abroad, to alter entirely the general drift of the B.B.C. programme policy'. It further objected that relays might 'discriminate amongst the broadcast talks, relaying those of one political colour and suppressing others'.[56]

In response to representations from the Corporation, the Ullswater Committee in 1935, the Beveridge Committee in 1949, and the Pilkington Committee in 1960 all addressed themselves to the problem of the relay service.[57] Successive governments in the main agreed with the BBC on the necessity of close regulation of relays, and used their licensing powers accordingly. Beginning in 1937, radio exchanges were required to carry a certain minimum of BBC programmes, and this was later amended to include IBA programmes as well. All BBC and IBA television programmes available in an area must be offered by the television relays serving that area. The relay companies are also prohibited from originating any programmes of their own, from relaying from abroad programmes in the English language 'containing political, social or religious propaganda', from 'announcing the result of any sweepstake in connection with a horse race', or from receiving payment for the distribution of any programmes.[58]

The other threat to the monopoly came from the several foreign stations which were established to beam commercial programmes to the United Kingdom. Best known was the high-powered Radio Luxembourg which, beginning in 1933, devoted a good share of its output to commercial programmes in English for British listeners.[59] Also important was Radio Normandy, which operated from the mid-1920s up to World War II. By 1938, approximately 300 British firms were spending £1,700,000 a year on programmes being broadcast by these stations. The strict programme policies of the Corporation in those years provided initial impetus for growth of Radio Luxembourg and Radio Normandy, whose best audiences were on Sundays, when the BBC's schedule was limited to serious and religious programmes, and on weekday mornings, when BBC transmissions usually did not begin until 10.15.[60] After an exhaustive analysis of the evidence, Ronald H. Coase concluded that 'the monopoly was an important factor, perhaps the main factor, leading to a Government policy which had as its aim the suppression of foreign commercial broadcasting designed for listeners in Great Britain'.[61]

The BBC opposed these foreign stations because they upset the programme pattern it had ordained for the British public, and also because it disliked commercial broadcasting in general. The press joined with the BBC mainly because the Luxembourg and Normandy stations competed with newspapers for advertising revenue. The fact that Radio Luxembourg operated on a wavelength not assigned to it by international convention enabled the Corporation to rationalize its objections on technical grounds, but programming and audiences were the underlying considerations.

Successive governments agreed with these BBC criticisms of foreign commercial broadcasting, and tried unsuccessfully to hinder especially the operations of Radio Luxembourg.[62] In 1949 Parliament expressly forbade political broadcasting over foreign stations by candidates for Parliament and, in response to the use of some of the 'pirate stations' by local candidates in the 1960s, the Representation of the People Act 1969 extended this to include 'local government' elections as well.[63]

Radio Luxembourg still broadcasts daily to the United Kingdom with programmes of popular music, light drama, and some American fundamentalist religion. With 1200 kilowatts power on 1440 kilocycles, it puts a strong signal into most of the British Isles. However, the coming of BBC Radio 1, and of the local BBC and ITA stations, reduced Radio Luxembourg's British audience substantially.

In more recent years, Britain was faced with the problem of 'pirate' radio stations broadcasting commercial programmes consisting mainly of recorded popular music from ships or artificial islands located in or near British territorial waters. Motivated by hopes for large and quick returns from small investments, a number of these stations grew up to serve northern Europe in the late 1950s and early 1960s. But the most popular target was the United Kingdom, where stations operated both on the high seas and within British territorial waters.[64]

The pirate stations posed problems for all the countries concerned. They threatened national broadcasting monopolies; they introduced commercial broadcasting to countries that had legislated against it; and by operating on frequencies not assigned by a responsible international agency, they interfered with authorized marine, aircraft, and broadcasting services. In addition, they offered unfair competition to legitimate land-based operations, since they did not comply with those sections of the copyright and performance laws which, in most European countries, required payments, not only to the holders of music copyrights, but also to record manufacturers for the use of their recordings on the air. For this reason, the United Kingdom's record manufacturers were even more opposed to pirate broadcasters than was the BBC.

Getting rid of these stations, however, proved very difficult, despite various international agreements prohibiting such operations.[65] The problem in the United Kingdom was complicated by the need to meet audience demands by providing a replacement service once the pirates were eliminated; and this had to be a daylong popular music programme based largely on recordings.[66] Neither the BBC nor anyone else could provide this without securing 'needle time' (see below, pp. 344–5) from the record companies.

In December 1966, a government White Paper authorized the BBC to develop a continuous popular music programme on one of the frequencies previously used for its Light Programme.[67] Thereafter, on 14 July 1967, approval was given to a law which made it illegal for British subjects to own, operate, supply or advertise on pirate stations, whether located on ships, aircraft or 'structures' on the high seas or within British territory, or to induce anyone else to do so.[68] The government then proceeded to confiscate those pirate stations that did not voluntarily cease operations, and the BBC began Radio 247 (so called because it used the medium wave length of 247 metres to broadcast almost day-long programmes of popular music.) This service evolved into the present BBC Radio 1.

THE FINANCIAL BASIS OF THE BBC*

Another distinctive feature of the BBC is its support by licence fees. The IBA is supported by advertising, but the BBC always has been and is firmly resolved to remain non-commercial. However, the External Services—broadcasts for listeners abroad—are supported by direct Parliamentary grants. The income from the many BBC publications, including the *Radio Times*, the Corporation's programme guide, which carries advertising, is applied to domestic broadcasting, as is that from the sale of BBC programmes abroad by BBC Enterprises.

Anyone who operates a television receiver in the United Kingdom, or who obtains television programmes from a relay exchange, is required by law to purchase a licence annually from the Post Office. As of November 1979, the fee for a monochrome television licence was £12 and for a colour television licence £34. Radio only and combined radio–television licences were abolished on 1 February 1971, and since then only television licences have been issued.

In the United Kingdom, as in most countries supporting broadcasting by the proceeds from licence fees, the government always holds back a portion of the gross revenue to cover collection and, administrative costs, and for a good many years—1927–60—some of the receipts also were retained by the Treasury for general government use.[69] During World War II, the government retained all licence fee payments, and appropriated directly for the BBC, without reference to the receipts. Currently, after discussion between the government and the Corporation to determine the amount to be withheld to cover the costs of collection, and of investigating complaints of interference, the government asks Parliament to appropriate the agreed-upon amount for the BBC's use.[70] This always is done as requested by the government, although there sometimes is debate or discussion of BBC programmes and policies before the broadcasting vote is taken.

Linked with the principle of licence fee support has been non-commercial operation. A number of continental European broadcasting organizations derive funds both from licence fees and advertising, and this has been suggested from time to time for the BBC, but the Corporation is strongly opposed to broadcast advertising. Under all of the Corporation's licences to date, the BBC may broadcast no commercial programmes without government permission and it has never requested such permission. The exact phraseology of the current Licence is as follows:

> The Corporation shall not without the consent in writing of the Postmaster General receive money or any valuable consideration . . . in respect of the sending or emitting, . . . of any matter whatsoever . . . , or and shall not send or emit . . . any sponsored programme.[71]

The decision to support the BBC by an annual tax on receiving sets, and to prohibit commercial broadcasting, was very deliberately taken. The original

---

* This section deals only with the basic principles followed in supporting the Corporation's domestic services. The actual working of BBC finances is taken up in Chapter 7, pp. 100–12.

British Broadcasting Company received its capital and operating funds from the sale of stock, from licence fees, and from royalties on the sale of radio receivers. Commercial advertisements were prohibited except with the Postmaster General's permission, but sponsored programmes were allowed, and eight of them were broadcast in 1925 and one in 1926, the sponsors being various London newspapers. There have been no sponsored programmes since that date, however.[72]

In British usage, a 'commercial advertisement' is a direct sales message inserted into a broadcast over which the advertiser has no control (as in the case of IBA programmes); 'spot announcement' would be the American equivalent. A 'sponsored programme', on the other hand, is 'any matter which is provided at the expense of any sponsor (that is, any person other than the Corporation and the performers) for the purpose of being broadcast and is the subject of a broadcast announcement mentioning the sponsor or his goods or services'.[73]

The Sykes Committee in 1923 recommended annual taxes on receivers as the principal means of support.[74] This proposal was accepted by the Crawford Committee and written into the first and succeeding licences of the British Broadcasting Corporation.[75] Surprisingly, though, John Reith was disturbed about the prohibition of advertising in the Charter: 'Should not the Corporation', he wrote, 'have liberty with regard to advertising as a supplementary source of revenue in case of need?'[76]

The Ullswater Committee in 1935 recommended excluding direct advertising, although accepting the idea of some sponsored programmes, which, it hoped, would 'be limited to the initial stages of television broadcasting'.[77] The Beveridge Committee in 1951 decided against the use of general tax funds, because that might make the BBC more dependent upon the government. It wrote: 'For broadcasting to be dependent year by year on a variable grant . . . would mean that broadcasting would be subject to the decision, which might at times appear the whim, of the Chancellor of the Exchequer.'[78]

Recommending the continuation of licence-fee support, the committee summarized the principal reasons which had been advanced for it through the years. The committee majority wrote:

> Sponsoring . . . puts the control of broadcasting ultimately in the hands of the people whose interest is not broadcasting but the selling of some other goods or services or the propagation of particular ideas. If the people of any country want broadcasting for its own sake they must be prepared to pay for it as listeners or viewers; they must not ask for it for nothing as an accompaniment of advertising some other commodity.[79]

Four of the committee's eleven members dissented on this point, including the chairman, Lord Beveridge. Three favoured some commercial support for the BBC, while strongly opposing competitive broadcasting. One member advocated the introduction of competitive commercial broadcasting. The report stated that on this problem the committee 'found it less easy to reach an agreed conclusion than on almost any other issue that has come before us'.[80]

Although the government committees investigating the BBC all have opposed commercial support for its radio services, the television committees, taking note of the threatened high costs of that medium, regarded advertising with less disfavour. The Selsdon Committee in 1935, Britain's first television committee, thought it 'legitimate, especially during the experimental period of the service', for the Corporation to accept some sponsored telecasts as a way of meeting its operating costs.[81] As was pointed out above, the 1935 Ullswater Committee believed that financial necessity might require some television programmes to be sponsored, but hoped such practices would be limited to the early years of the service.[82]

The Hankey Television Committee in 1943 withheld comment because of unsettled war conditions, but it at least did not oppose sponsored programmes as a possible source of revenue.[83] The decision in favour of commercial support for Britain's alternative television service in 1955, therefore, had some background.

The alignment of individuals and groups on the issue of commercial broadcasting by the BBC closely approximated the division on monopoly, largely because the two were interrelated, the general assumption being that the alternative to a licence-fee-supported monopoly was a competitive commercial system. Of particular interest was the continued opposition of the press to commercial broadcasting. The Sykes Committee wrote in 1923 that the protests it received from the press against radio advertising were

> mainly on the ground that it would seriously affect the interests of newspapers, which rely largely on advertising revenue. They also contend that, while broadcasting in this country remains of the nature of a quasi monopoly, it should not be allowed to compete with newspapers as an advertising medium.[84]

In 1950 the Newspaper Proprietors Association told the Beveridge Committee that it still was 'opposed in principle to the introduction of any system of radio advertising in this country'. Since newspapers are now involved financially in several of the programme companies connected with the Independent Broadcasting Authority, it is interesting to notice the Association's further statement: 'If broadcast advertising is introduced into this country, the newspapers will claim the right, either jointly or individually, to take part in the running of it.'[85] And this, of course, is what happened (see p. 78, below).

Despite actual financial problems in recent years, resulting from an expansion of its operations, inflation, and—more recently—the high cost of colour television, the BBC has continued to expound the virtues of financing its services with the proceeds from licence fees.[86] It told the the Annan Committee in September 1974, that except for licence revenue, there were 'perhaps three main ways of financing the BBC': a Parliamentary grant-in-aid, pay-television, and advertising revenues. The first of these would have the advantage over the licence system in saving over £12 million in collection charges, but nevertheless would be undesirable. The Corporation quoted evidence provided to the Pilkington Committee by the Treasury, which said that if the Corporation were financed from general taxation it 'would be in a position very similar to that of a Government Department and would have to be subject to much the same amount of detailed control'. The Annan

Committee agreed with the Corporation.[87] It is remarkable that during all the discussions of the pros and cons of licence fee support the point has seldom been made that a radio or television licence fee is a regressive tax, bearing more heavily on listeners and viewers with lower incomes.

Advertising, the Corporation told the Annan Committee, which is the alternate choice most often suggested, the BBC 'firmly rejected'. An advertising-supported broadcasting service would bring 'economic pressure . . . towards the programmes which attract the largest audiences. . . . Minority audiences are bound to suffer unless protected in some way, because the times at which they are available to view are not different from those at which the community at large is available'.

A month later the Chairman of the BBC Board of Governors in a public address ascribed the 'autonomy' of the Corporation in part to its 'independent financial basis, derived, of course, from the licence fee'. He emphasized: 'For if government pays the bills, it is readily arguable that *nothing* is outside their competence.'[88]

The Annan Committee reviewed with both BBC and IBA officials the question: 'Does the Government use the licence fee and the levy [on IBA programme company profits] as a lever to exercise control over programme policies?' Spokesmen for both groups replied in the negative, and the Committee commented: 'If there were to be improper pressure, there would be an uproar within and outside Parliament.'[89] But one BBC official pointed out to me that the Corporation's producers and directors are aware of the tensions existing when financial matters are being discussed with the government, and might on their own change the schedule times or nature of some programmes.

Recently, with costs increasing due to inflation and competition with the IBA, and income levelling off as the number of homes with colour receivers is stabilized, the BBC has become increasingly concerned about raising enough money to cover its costs: yet it dislikes the idea of direct treasury grants, fearing that they would lead to government influence. Among the solutions proposed has been indexing the licence fee to living costs, as is done in some continental countries. (Britain's licensee fees are lower than those in most European countries, incidentally.) Director-General Ian Trethowan suggested in January 1979 that the BBC might be funded through increased National Insurance contributions. Since these are made by all employed workers, and are related to their levels of income, such a system would avoid the regressive aspects of the present licence fee system.[90]

3 Constitution of the BBC: Operations

The theories underlying the structure of the BBC are important only as they translate into programme services. Above all is the question of whether or not the freedom from government control envisaged by Reith and his successors has been achieved. This chapter deals with the subject in the context of the Corporation's overall structure; later chapters examine it while reviewing the programmes produced by the organization. Although the BBC is the focal point of the pages that follow, the precedents established by the Corporation before the ITA came on the air now apply to the Authority and its programmes too.

THE BBC AS A PUBLIC CORPORATION

It was decided at the very beginning to set up the British Broadcasting Corporation as a public corporation.[1] John Reith—who already was running the British Broadcasting Company as though it were a public corporation rather than a private company—believed that the permanent BBC 'should be both a public institution and an independent institution, as free as possible from interference both by business and by government'.[2]

The first committee which made proposals for the permanent structure of British broadcasting declared that control of anything so important to the life of the nation should not reside permanently with a commercial company, but 'ought to remain with the state'.[3] But this was not to say that broadcasting should be run by the government. The chief official of the Post Office, Sir Evelyn Murray, wrote in a memorandum to the Crawford Committee in 1925 that

> the Corporation should enjoy a large measure of independence and should not be subject either in general policy or its choice of programmes to the detailed control and supervision of the Postmaster-General, from which would follow the corollary that the Postmaster-General would not be expected to accept responsibility or to defend the proceedings of the Corporation in Parliament.[4]

Thereafter, the Crawford Committee recommended a public corporation to 'act as a Trustee for the national interest', precisely because it believed that 'such an authority would enjoy a freedom and flexibility which a Minister of State himself could scarcely exercise'. It went on to say that, although the State, through Parliament, must retain the right of ultimate control . . . we think it essential that the . . . [Corporation] should not be subject to the continuing Ministerial guidance and direction which apply to Government Offices . . . [The Board of Governors, therefore, should] be invested with the maximum of freedom which Parliament is prepared to concede.[5]

The Crawford Committee further recommended that the BBC should be 'a public corporation', and that it should be set up either by an Act of Parliament or by incorporation under the Companies Acts.[6] As things turned out, the government did make it a public corporation, but rather through the instrument of a Royal Charter, believing that would give it more independence, and more 'status and dignity'.[7]

In the United Kingdom, public corporations include the Port of London Authority, the Central Electricity Board, and the London Passenger Transport Board. A cardinal feature of all these is their relative independence of state control. It is difficult for Americans to understand the relationship between the BBC and the British government. The Tennessee Valley Authority is roughly similar, although its periodic involvement in politics represents a marked departure from the British pattern. The Red Cross, chartered by Congress but independently run by its own Board of Trustees, is perhaps America's nearest equivalent. In a public address, Sir Hugh Greene, former Director General, remarked that although some people had suggested he explain the BBC to Americans by comparing it with the TVA, 'I think it is much safer just to say that we are as strange in the American scene as a kangaroo would be in the English countryside.'[9]

There also is the fact that the relationships of United States government departments and agencies to Congress and the Executive are quite different from those of a British government department (which the BBC, of course, is not) to Parliament. The experiences of America's public broadcasters during the last years of the Nixon administration, when they were subject to various kinds of government pressures, demonstrate the dangers that would be inherent in an American BBC, supported by Congressional appropriations and operated by a Board of Directors nominated by the President. But the imporatnt question is not, how a BBC-type public corporation would operate in Washington, but how it works in London.

THE CHARTER AND THE LICENCE

The existence of the BBC depends upon its Charter and Licence. The former, issued in the name of the Crown by the government in power, creates the BBC as a public corporation. Authority to broadcast, and various accompanying requirements, are provided by the Licence and Agreement, issued from 1927 to 1969 by the Postmaster-General, from 1969 to 1974 by the Minister of Posts and Telecommunications, and since then by the Secretary of State for the Home Department (the Home Secretary). These two documents have been qualified by the various broadcasting committee reports already mentioned, by government White Papers, by statements in Parliament by both government and opposition spokesmen, and by various 'Prescriptions' issued by the Home Secretary acting under the Charter and the Licence.

The BBC also is subject to the Representation of the People Act, in its handling of broadcasts of Parliamentary elections; the Race Relations Act; the Law of Defamation; the laws relating to contempt of court; the Official Secrets Act; the copyright laws; legislation and rulings relative to paying taxes on its income-producing activities (publications, programme sales, interest and rents received); and any applicable regulations pertaining to building construction, housing, sanitary codes, safety laws, etc.[10]

The present Charter is the fifth in the history of the corporation, previous charters having been issued in 1927, 1937, 1947, and 1952. The *1964 Charter* initially was granted for 12 years or until 1976, but due to delays related to the appointment and reporting of the Committee on the Future of Broadcasting under Lord Annan, this was later extended until July 1979.[11] When it was seen that the government could not react quickly to the recommendations of the Committee, the Charter and Licence were extended again until 1982.

The Charter's preamble states that, in view of the 'great value' of broadcasting as a means of 'disseminating information, education and entertainment', the BBC shall 'provide broadcasting services pursuant to such licenses and agreements' as may be issued to it.[12] The 'information, education and entertainment' phrase is somewhat the British equivalent of American broadcasting's famous 'public convenience, interest or necessity' clause as a source of policy guidance.[13] Both phrases have been criticized as vague and unspecific.

In addition to creating the BBC and conferring on it the ordinary powers of corporate bodies, the Charter says:

> The Corporation is hereby authorised, empowered and required to provide from time to time all such broadcasting services and facilities and to do all such acts and things as shall from time to time be required by or under any Licence granted by Our Postmaster-General for the Corporation or any agreement made by Our Postmaster-General with the Corporation.[14]

The BBC is controlled by its twelve Governors, who in strict legal fact *are* the Corporation.[15] They are appointed by the Queen in Council—in effect by the government of the day—for 5-year terms; and they may be dismissed at will. One of them is nominated as Chairman, another as Vice-Chairman, and three others as national governors for Scotland, Wales, and Northern Ireland, respectively. There is no provision for balancing political parties as with the American Federal Communications Commission—of which not more than four out of the seven commissioners may belong to the same political party—although it is assumed that the Board will be non-partisan in make-up. However, there have been frequent complaints that BBC Boards have been predominantly conservative in outlook. A member of the House of Commons must resign his seat before serving on the Board of Governors, and vice-versa, although a member of the House of Lords may be on the BBC Board. No one may serve simultaneously on the BBC Board of Governors and the IBA Authority, although it is quite legal for an individual to serve non-overlapping appointments on the two boards, as two have done: Lord Hill, as Chairman of the Authority and then Chairman of the BBC Board of Governors; and Lady Plowden, as Vice-Chairman of the BBC and then Chairman of the Authority.[16]

To advise and assist the Governors, the Charter provides for a number of national and regional councils and committees; however, the Board retains ultimate control of the Corporation, subject only to the conditions of the Charter and Licence.[17] (Further details about the BBC's committees are provided below on pp. 139–43.) The Corporation also is required to make an annual report and review of its accounts.[18] Finally, the Charter may be revoked whenever the government has 'reasonable cause' to believe that the requirements of the Charter or Licence, or any government instructions issued under their authority, have not been satisfactorily discharged.[19]

The accompanying Licence and Agreement—dated 7 July 1969 (Cmd. 4095)—appear to impose even more stringent controls than does the Charter. First there are the technical requirements: the Corporation may broadcast only over those stations licensed to it by the Secretary of State for the Home Department, who also determines frequencies, power, and technical operating standards.[20] The Licence also outlines arrangements for the Corporation's financial support. For the domestic services, the Home Secretary is to pay the Corporation (out of such funds as Parliament may appropriate) the entire net licence revenue (that is, the gross licence revenue less collection costs), or 'such percentage or percentages thereof as the Treasury may from time to time determine'.[21] Support for the External Services is voted directly by Parliament, under the theory that licence fees collected from the owners of home receivers should not support programmes for overseas audiences. The Licence also in effect prohibits commercial broadcasting by the BBC[22] (see above, p. 23).

An addition to the 1969 Licence was the requirement that the BBC might be required to share towers and other transmitting facilities with the ITA.[23] (A corresponding obligation is laid on the IBA.) In addition, government approval is required before the Corporation may employ aliens; the Corporation is to conform to certain specified labour practices; and it must recognize the right of its employees to join labour unions.

Most important are the several programme requirements.

Unless prevented by circumstances beyond its control, the Corporation shall send efficiently programmes in the Home Radio Service, the Television Services, and the External Services from such stations as after consultation with the Corporation the Postmaster-General may from time to time in relation to those services respectively in writing prescribe.[24]

There is only one specific programme requirement: The Corporation is to broadcast daily 'an impartial account' of Parliamentary proceedings.[25] In addition, whenever so requested by any Minister of Her Majesty's Government, it is to broadcast 'any announcement . . . which such Minister may request', and also, 'whenever so requested by any such Minister in whose opinion an emergency has arisen or continues . . . any other matter which such Minister may request the Corporation to broadcast'.[26] At its option, however, the BBC may indicate that such material 'is sent at the request of named Minister'.

There is also a veto power. The Secretary of State for the Home Department may

> require the Corporation to refrain at any specified time or at all times from sending any matter or matters of any class specified in such notice. . . . The Corporation may at its discretion announce or refrain from announcing that such a notice has been given or has been varied or revoked.

Acting under this clause of the licence, the government has from time to time issued instructions to the Corporation, the current status of which is defined in several 'prescriptions' and in a letter of 19 June 1964, from the then Chairman of the Board of Governors to the Postmaster-General.[27] Taken together, the prescriptions and the letter require the BBC: 'to refrain from expressing its own opinion on current affairs or on matters of public policy' (a stipulation in effect since 1927); to exclude from its programmes material 'which offends against good taste or decency or is likely to encourage or incite to crime or lead to disorder or to be offensive to public feeling'; to 'ensure . . . so far as possible . . . due impartiality . . . in news programmes and programmes dealing with matters of public policy, and also in the treatment of controversial subjects generally'; to broadcast no subliminal messages of any sort; to 'ensure that proper proportions of programmes are of British origin and British performance;' and, 'to exclude from the earlier part of the evening's programmes those which might be unsuitable for children'. The IBA Act of 1973 imposes the same requirements on Authority programmes. As the Corporation put it:

> These are all, strictly speaking, obligations which the BBC has imposed on itself, but their formal communication by the BBC's Chairman to the Minister and the latter's formal acknowledgement of them have invested them with something of the nature of a prescription.

Finally, the BBC's facilities may be taken over by the government whenever a sufficient emergency 'shall have arisen', and the Licence may be revoked if the BBC does not 'send efficiently', or fails to carry out its obligations under either Charter or Licence.[28] To insure that the Licence was a compact between the BBC and the entire government, it did not become operative until approved by the House of Commons.

This list of the powers retained by the government over the BBC would at first appear to run entirely contrary to the recommendations of the many government committees that a public corporation be set up so that the broadcasting authority might 'enjoy a freedom and flexibility which a Minister of State himself could scarcely exercise'. But in the British context, these grants of authority need not necessarily indicate government control.

THE BBC AND THE GOVERNMENT

Any review of broadcaster–government relationships in the United Kingdom inevitably must cite the experiences of the BBC more than those of the IBA. The Corporation has been around much longer; it operates more broadcasting services; and it presents more programmes of the type that might invite government reactions. Nevertheless, since the potential for government control is exactly the same for both organizations, precedents involving the BBC apply to the IBA as well. In fact, IBA officials willingly agree that the battles for BBC independence fought—and usually won—by John Reith and his successors are just as important today for the IBA as for the BBC.

(a) Committee and Government Pronouncements

From the very beginning, it was everyone's intention that the BBC should have the maximum possible amount of independence in programming. Investigating committees and White Papers have restated with variations that description of the relationship between the BBC and the government sketched as ideal by the first Director-General, who had so much to do with creating the BBC as a public corporation. Reith wrote: 'The crucial point to me in 1930 was freedom from political or ministerial or civil service interference directly or indirectly in management as distinct from major policy'.[29] Reith was much concerned lest the government intrude on what he regarded as the BBC's preserve. One of his biographers wrote that 'he was obsessed by the restrictions imposed', and feared 'further encroachments ... by the politicians, the press and other vested interests'.[30] In 1936 the Ullswater Committee spoke in the same vein as did a Labour government ten years later.[31]

In the early 1950s, both Labour and Conservative governments agreed with a similar statement from the Beveridge Committee, while ten years later the Pilkington Report linked the independence of the two organizations to their obligations:

> For, if the need to preserve a traditional independence of the broadcasting organisations calls for constant vigilance on the part of the Government of the day, it demands no less an unremitting discharge by the two public corporations of their responsibilities. The two—the independence and the responsibilities— go together.[32]

The Annan Committee in 1977 wrote that

> the independence of the Broadcasting Authorities from day-to-day control by Government is fundamental to British broadcasting. . . . [Yet], The question remains, and will always remain, how do you reconcile the independence of broadcasters with the Government's ultimate responsibility for broadcasting?[33]

The answer, said the Committee, echoing the words of the Pilkington Committee fifteen years earlier, is 'Parliamentary accountability'.

The BBC and the IBA play a dual role: they must ensure that broadcasting is done in the public interest and is responsible to public opinion,

> particularly as expressed in Parliament. At the same time they exist also to defend the broadcasters from undue pressure from whatever quarter. . . . Parliament has the undoubted right to censure or indeed take even severer measures, against the Authorities if it considers them to have been in grave breach of their duty. But Parliament delegates to the Authorities the duty of judging what is, or is not, in the public interest; and it is to the Authorities that the broadcasters are responsible.

There can be no doubt that successive investigating committees and governments have pledged themselves to respect the operating independence of the BBC—and, in more recent years, of the IBA. But what have been the actual working relationships between the broadcasters and successive governments? In the case of the Corporation, there have been charges and denials that governors have been chosen to reflect the Conservative views of some of the cabinets which selected them, although no governor has ever been dismissed. The percentage of license revenue to be given the BBC has been the subject of extended negotiations with various governments, but there is no evidence that this lever was ever actually used to influence Corporation policy. Neither Charter nor Licence has ever been revoked, although during World War II the Corporation was almost taken over, as the Licence permits in emergency situations.*

The House of Commons Estimates Committee, after surveying the financial affairs of the BBC, wrote in 1969:

> The Powers of the Government over the B.B.C. are theoretically absolute. . . . The most important of these powers is the direct control which the Government possesses over the income of the B.B.C. through prescribing the amount of the licence fee. . . . These powers have an undoubted importance as a form of financial discipline on the B.B.C., but clearly this has not been the only criterion by which Governments have exercised them.

The Committee concluded that long-term policy in regard to expansion sometimes

* In 1963, Gerald Beadle, who first joined the BBC staff in 1923, and remained associated with it until his retirement in 1961, most recently as Director of Television, commented on the financial aspects of BBC–government relationships. As to 'the extent of the Government's control over the BBC', he said that

> in practice its control over day-to-day management and over editorial matters is nil, [but] I have to admit that the government does exercise a broad financial control, which in turn governs the pace of the BBC's development and the scope of its activities. . . . A good understanding between the Treasury and the BBC is essential. However, the controlling hand is there and the question arises as to whether it is used wisely.

He went on to indicate that in the decade after World War II, the government did use its financial powers to delay the development of BBC television. (Gerald Beadle, *Television: A Critical Review*, p. 59.)

has been influenced, if not controlled, by the Government through this financial power.[34]

Then there is the power of the government to initiate and veto broadcasts. When the House of Commons was discussing the BBC's first Charter and Licence in 1926, the Postmaster-General explained that these controls over programmes were intended to have very limited application.[35] About the clause requiring the Corporation to broadcast 'any matter' requested by a government department, he said: 'This is a means of getting publicity for important objects which arise suddenly', such as broadcasts for lost persons, gale and storm warnings, or 'information of an outbreak of foot-and-mouth disease'. He then warned: 'If any Government oversteps the line and goes beyond this, I have no doubt that they will be ... properly brought to book, in the House of Commons.'

The power to veto broadcasts, the Postmaster-General admitted, was 'an overriding discretion', but he thought the force of public opinion, 'not only in this House but outside', would prevent its abuse. As for him, he was going to prohibit only two types of broadcasts: editorializing by the Corporation (a rule still in effect); and 'the broadcast, by speech or lecture, of matter on topics of political, religious or industrial controversy' (a prohibition lifted in 1923 and never reimposed). Summarizing the position of the government, the Postmaster-General said:

> While I am prepared to take the responsibility for broad issues of policy, on minor issues and measures of domestic policy, and matters of day to day control, I want to leave things to the free judgement of the Corporation. I want to make this service not a Department of the State, and still less a creature of the Executive, but so far as is consistent with Ministerial responsibility, I wish to create an independent body of trustees operating the service in the interest of the public as a whole.[36]

In 1931, when Clement Attlee was Postmaster-General, he told the House of Commons 'that I am not responsible for programmes', and that therefore he would not attempt to defend them. In 1933 the House of Commons resolved 'that it would be contrary to the public interest to subject the Corporation to any control by the government or by Parliament other than the control already provided for in the Charter and Licence of the Corporation. . . .'

A more recent example was provided by a House of Lords debate in July 1959 relative to the announced intention of the BBC to broadcast an appeal by the Bishop of Southwark on behalf of the Family Planning Association. After quoting the *1952 White Paper* to the effect that the government accepted the Beveridge Committee's recommendations for the Corporation's independence in programme planning as well as in general administration, the government spokesman added: 'My Lords, that is still the Government's view. The statement endorsed a policy that has been the view of successive Governments over a very long period of years down to the present day. . . . The independence of the BBC is a prized and very valued asset.'

(b) The General Strike of 1926

The BBC has consistently fought off all attempts at government control. One of the first precedents was established during the General Strike of 1926.[37] There were two points of view in the Cabinet. Winston Churchill, Chancellor of the Exchequer, was prepared to resort to almost any extreme to put down the strike, and he and his supporters were anxious to take over the BBC, along with *The Times* newspaper, running it as they did the *British Gazette*, a government publication Churchill edited and managed. The other group—which included Prime Minister Stanley Baldwin—thought it best to leave the BBC at least in a 'semi-independent' state. Reith's role was complicated by the fact that the Crawford Committee was meeting to consider the Company's future at the very time the General Strike took place.

Among the difficult decisions confronting the Company was whether or not to broadcast a statement about the strike prepared by a group of church leaders, despite objections from Prime Minister Baldwin.[38] The Company's first decision was against the broadcast, but several days later this was reversed and the manifesto was aired. In another case, the Company refused to schedule a talk by a Labour or trade union speaker, and Reith said this decision was taken because of government opposition. During the strike, the Company also refused to give air-time to the Archbishop of Canterbury and to Ramsey MacDonald, leader of the parliamentary opposition, again in accordance with government urging.

Reith strongly opposed the commandeering of the Company.[39] He thought consultation between the BBC and the government preferable to a takeover; he maintained that if the BBC became a government organ, the strikers would paralyze the broadcasting service too; and, finally, he argued that the BBC could play a more positive role if it acted with apparent freedom. Nevertheless, he did believe that the Company had to be 'for the government in crisis'. The Cabinet was divided and confused, but Prime Minister Baldwin sided with Reith, and on 11 May, just before the strike ended, the Cabinet formally voted not to take over the Company.

Despite the fact that the BBC was not formally commandeered, it is clear that here, as elsewhere in its history, it accepted government guidance in order to avoid setting the precedent of a takeover or veto. After the strike was over, Reith wrote a long memorandum in which he said: 'There could be no question about our supporting the Government in general, particularly since the General Strike had been declared illegal in the High Court.' He also stated that 'the position was one of extreme delicacy and embarrassment throughout'.

Later Reith wrote that, although 'complete impartiality . . . was, in the circumstances, not to be expected, the BBC had endeavoured to preserve its tradition of accuracy and fair play.'[40] But the leader of the opposition Labour Party, Clement Attlee, believed that it had not done this, and, as a member of the Ullswater Committee, wrote in 1936: 'In my opinion there is no doubt that the way in which the broadcasting system was used by the government of the day created in the minds of a very large section of the community grave suspicion which has prejudiced the Corporation ever since.'[41]

About the affair, the historian of the BBC, Asa Briggs, concluded:

On the whole the programmes were impartial. . . . A perusal of all the news bulletins sent out by the BBC during those hectic nine days suggests that what was included was usually right, although much news was excluded. There was no fabrication, no attempt to twist or to distort. . . . There is little doubt that BBC news assisted the government against the strikers. Above all, it had a steadying effect on opinion. It helped more than any other factor to dispel rumours.[42]

The author of the most complete analysis of the episode, who based his conclusions on material in the BBC's archives, observed: 'There is no doubt from reading through the various memos and numerous expressions of intent that the BBC's coverage was specifically aimed toward a particular end, which was the defeat of the Strike.'[43] His final conclusion was a harsh one:

It has often been assumed that during the General Strike the BBC was able to sustain its independence, even though at times somewhat shakily. The study here shows that such a view is little more than fiction and that there was in effect a clear submission to the wishes of the government.

But in an interview broadcast during the 50th anniversary of the General Strike in 1976, Sir Charles Curran, then the Director-General, pointed out that one must take

into account the practical circumstances in which Reith found himself. The Charter which was about to come into effect had not been approved and, if Reith had gone completely against the government, the Charter might have been forfeit. Now, you may say that is an unworthy kind of pragmatism, but I do not think anybody who has enjoyed the benefits of the Charter since 1927 could possibly say that Reith was wrong in that judgment. And, when you consider that one of the most powerful ministers of the government, Churchill, was totally for commandeering the BBC, I think Reith had everything to gain by keeping himself on the right side of government.[44]

(c) The Veto

The government has never vetoed a programme, although the Corporation once cancelled a broadcast in order to avoid a threatened veto—perhaps in order to maintain its claim that the government has never vetoed a programme. This was in 1932, after the Cabinet had unanimously objected to a scheduled broadcast by an ex-commander of a German World War I submarine. At a meeting of the Postmaster-General, the chairman and vice-chairman of the BBC's Board of Governors, and the Corporation's Director-General, the two governors decided to cancel the programme in order to avoid a veto. Reith himself drafted the explanation 'that the talk was a serious contribution to the elimination of war, but that . . . in view of the Lausanne Conference then sitting, it had been decided to cancel it'. On a later occasion, Reith asked Kingsley Wood, who had been Postmaster-General at the time, whether he would have used his veto, had the

Corporation insisted on broadcasting the talk. 'Not on your life,' he replied, 'I would never have done it.'*

In 1965, Sir Hugh Greene stated in a public address that in the 42½ years during which the Postmaster-General had the authority to

> require the BBC to broadcast or refrain from broadcasting any particular matter, . . . this right has never been exercised in respect of any single programme. This fact alone, in view of the significance and authority we give in Britain to such working precedents, makes it highly unlikely, I think, that it ever would be exercised in face of opposition from the BBC's independent governing body and its Director-General.[45]

But in the same talk, Greene indicated that 'we have to resist attempts at censorship', and mentioned pressures received from various sources.

There were problems again during World War II, since wartime information media everywhere are expected to work closely with their governments. Reith had foreseen this possibility, recognizing that in time of war the 'director-general of the BBC would be responsible to the Minister of Information', although the independence of the BBC would be 'respected as far as possible'.[46] The government clearly was prepared to act against unwanted ideas which might seriously interfere with the war effort. Thus, it banned the *Daily Worker* in 1942.[47] Winston Churchill, consistent with his attitudes during the General Strike, suggested closing down the *Daily Mirror* for 'rocking the boat' and awakening 'class and party dissensions'. He was not too fond of the BBC either. Reith wrote later that 'Churchill spoke with great bitterness: an enemy within the gates; continually causing trouble; doing more harm than good; something drastic must be done about them.'[48] These critical comments from Churchill presaged his support for commercial television in the early 1950s. In a brief for the Ministry of Information dated 1 July 1943, the BBC declared:

> The policy of the Governors is that the microphone is not the place in wartime for persons antagonistic to the war effort and further that the special facilities of the microphone, whatever the speaker desires to say there, should not be accorded to those persons whose words and actions are calculated to hamper the nation in its struggle for life.[49]

Sir Gerald Beadle, writing in 1963, summarized his observations of the wartime BBC, derived from his membership on the Board of Management:

> The Ministry of Information was directing all programmes, which in its own opinion had any bearing on the war effort, and it was even concerning itself with

---

* Reith, *Into the Wind*, pp. 160–61; Beveridge I, p. 8; Briggs II, pp. 129–30. In 1931 a projected series of talks on India in which Winston Churchill wished to take part was cancelled at the request of the Secretary of State for India, who feared the effects of such a series on British–Indian relations; but on this occasion, plans had not advanced to the point of programmes actually being scheduled. (Reith, *Into the Wind*, p. 15.)

internal staff appointments. . . . In the special circumstances of the war, some compromise with the BBC's traditional independence from government was inevitable. . . .'[50]

In 1972 the BBC wrote retrospectively: 'The exigencies of war had necessarily meant some restriction of the BBC's normal liberties. However, although relations with the wartime Government became difficult at times . . . the BBC was never subjected to direct government control, and once the war was over it regained in full its former freedom and independence.'[51]

(d) The Suez Incident

Another episode involving the independence of the BBC came up in 1956, when Gamal Abdel Nasser, President of Egypt, nationalized the Suez Canal. Thereafter, Britain, along with Israel and France, attacked Egypt, although they withdrew after the United Nations Emergency Force entered the conflict. Tensions were high within Britain, since the Cabinet, Parliament, and the nation were deeply divided as to what national policy should be.

Prime Minister Eden insisted that the invasion of Egypt in November 1956 amounted to a declaration of war; that the BBC therefore was obliged to support the government's position; and that otherwise it should be taken over by the government. But after two broadcasts by Prime Minister Anthony Eden and one by Foreign Minister Selwyn Lloyd presenting the government point of view, the BBC insisted on giving air time to Hugh Gaitskill of the Labour Party.[52] There also was the related question of whether the BBC's External Services, which could be heard by British troops in Suez, should report the division of opinion at home, or if it should be made to appear that there was only one point of view. A London news-paper published in 1968 that 'Eden's plan was to control the overseas broadcasts particularly and force the BBC to allow Ministerial broadcasts [by the Prime Minister] whenever he wished without allowing the Opposition the right to reply.'[53]

As the story is told by long-time BBC employee Harmon Grisewood, Prime Minister Eden 'had instructed the Lord Chancellor to prepare an instrument which would take over the B.B.C. altogether and subject it wholly to the Government'.[54] As Grisewood and the BBC saw it:

It was the B.B.C.'s duty to report to the people any opinions about the question which were important enough to affect the outcome. This was bedrock democracy. . . . Despite the P.M., Suez was a Parliamentary issue. It was not a national war; the B.B.C. should not and would not be manoeuvred into acting as though it were.

Finally, after considerable debate, and because the BBC's Board of Governors and all its key staff members supported the position of the Corporation, the Cabinet did not move against the BBC.

In 1972, in the course of a review of its first 50 years, the BBC published an article by Charles Curran, then Director-General, which included the following comments on the Suez episode.

> In 1956 the BBC had to face pressures stronger than any which had threatened its editorial independence in the thirty years since the General Strike. . . . The pressure on the External Services, broadcasting to the world, including the area of conflict, was particularly severe. Against formidable arguments about the national interest, the duty to provide an impartial service was held by the BBC to be paramount, and the pressures were successfully resisted.[55]

(e) Accountability to Parliament

The accountability of the BBC to Parliament is another aspect of its status as a public corporation. There may be—and often is—discussion about the BBC on such occasions as when Parliament votes money to the Corporation or receives its annual report. The issuance of such special documents as the Crawford, Ullswater, Beveridge, Pilkington and Annan Reports, and the periodic government White Papers on broadcasting policy, may also signal parliamentary debate, sometimes at considerable length. On those and other occasions, Parliament may discuss practically any aspect of BBC policies or programmes, thus apprising the Corporation of its ideas on broadcasting.

It is the prerogative of members to ask questions of the Home Secretary about matters of broadcasting policy. But there always have been limits to the subjects about which questions could be put: the corollary of the Corporation's day-to-day operational freedom has been the right of the responsible Minister to refuse to answer questions about details of programmes, appointments, and salaries. Back in 1929, the Speaker of the House of Commons refused to put to the Postmaster-General a question of this sort, because, as he said, 'there is no Minister who has responsibility for the BBC', and it is pointless to 'put questions to Ministers on matters in regard to which they have no responsibility'.[56]

Through the years this policy has been repeatedly reaffirmed. Examples include an incident in 1950, when the Postmaster-General rejected a demand for a parliamentary investigation of BBC television's broadcast of the play *Party Manners*, on the ground that it was traditional to leave 'the governors of the Corporation completely free in day-to-day management, including programme policy'.[57] In 1954 requests from some Members of Parliament for the cancellation of a scheduled repeat broadcast of George Orwell's *1984* were allowed to die for the same reason. (For a description of the latter episode, see below, pp. 323–5.) Again, on 26 January 1955, the Assistant Postmaster-General refused to answer a question about BBC programmes, saying that it had been the policy of successive governments to leave control of programmes to the Corporation, and that he therefore would not even discuss the matter.[58] On 20 May 1974 the Home Secretary, replying to a Parliamentary question, said: 'As the House knows, although I have a general responsibility, I do not issue, and would not wish to issue, directions to the broadcasting companies about particular programmes but no doubt what my right hon Friend has said will be noted.'[59]

The authority of the responsible Minister to refuse to answer questions about the

BBC, therefore, sets up an official barrier between inquisitive MPs and the Corporation. The Home Secretary, acting on Cabinet instructions, could therefore enlarge or decrease the extent of parliamentary influence by his attitude at question time. Regardless of this, of course, any Member of Parliament may still make known his opinions, either by personal communication to the Corporation or through public statements, and the Corporation, as a matter of standard procedure, keeps in touch with parliamentary opinion in every possible way.*

(f) Comment

Are the BBC and the IBA free of government control or influence? There is no question that ultimate policy control resides with the state—but this is true of broadcasting in every country in the world. Since British broadcasters are closer to Parliament than are American broadcasters to Congress, it would appear that, theoretically at least, the BBC and the IBA are less free than American broadcasters. However, in practice, public opinion prevents them from becoming in any sense government mouthpieces. I have discussed this aspect of British broadcasting with officials both in the BBC and IBA, with Members of Parliament from the Labour and Conservative Parties, with broadcasting critics, and many others, all of whom have assured me that, in fact, the British government maintains no control over the programmes broadcast by either organization. After reviewing the evidence the Annan Committee, though referring to 'the dialogue of a Parliamentary democracy', took the position that Parliament would make 'it hot for the Executive if a Minister exceeds the bounds decreed in this case not so much by law as by custom or convention'.[60]

Is the BBC free in its daily operations? The same question is raised about American broadcasting, where there are concerns about congressional and presidential influence over the Federal Communications Commission and the broadcasters, FCC influence on broadcast licensees, broadcaster influence on the FCC, and the influence of sponsors and other pressure groups on broadcasters.†

---

* There have been differences of opinion as to which Minister should represent the BBC in Parliament. Originally it was the Postmaster-General, but the BBC itself urged the Ullswater Committee to recommend a more senior minister, believing that the Corporation's influence thereby would be greater in government circles. However, the Ullswater Committee rejected the proposal on the ground that this might lead to the BBC's being more closely controlled. (*Ullswater Report* #53; *Broadcasting: Memorandum by the Postmaster General on the Report of the Broadcasting Committee, 1935* (Cmd. 5207), #4; Gordon, *The Public Corporation in Great Britain*, pp. 181–2; Reith, *Into the Wind*, p. 187. In 1969, the Minister of Posts and Telecommunications became the responsible minister, and in 1974 this was changed to the Secretary of State for the Home Department (the Home Secretary) (*BBC Handbook 1979*, p. 264). For a recent review of the question of which minister should have responsibility for broadcasting, see *Annan*, ##5.29–5.33.)

† Examples of attempts by American government agencies and the president to influence broadcasting are provided in Paley, *As It Happened: A Memoir*, pp. 310–27. See also Chapter 8, 'Pressures, Censorship, and Self-Censorship', in Gans, *Deciding What's News*, pp. 249–78. For comments from the British side, see Smith, *Television and Political Life*, pp. 14–15.

The standard BBC position was stated by Hugh Greene, Director General from 1960 to 1969, in a talk he gave in New York in 1961:

> On paper, the Government of the day has the power to veto any BBC broadcast. The BBC—and this is the important point—has the right to broadcast that this veto has been exercised. In the whole history of the BBC no Government—not even in war-time—has made use of this power in connection with any particular programme or item and it is now pretty well politically unthinkable that it ever could be made use of.[61]

In my opinion, both of Britain's broadcasting organizations enjoy as much freedom from government influence or control as do those in any country in the world, and a good case can be made that they have more freedom than is permitted anywhere else. Both groups are aware of public opinion generally, and are responsive to cabinet and parliamentary trends. At times they may have given a point here and there in order to avoid a veto, although the examples given would seem well justified. BBC (as well as IBA) insiders have clearly documented the extent of direct and indirect government and party pressure at one time or another.[62] But most such pressures have been successfully resisted and, as reported above, on such really crucial occasions as the General Strike and the Suez crisis, the Corporation, on balance, has come out ahead. Therefore, it is my conclusion that the BBC—and the IBA, which built upon the BBC's traditions in this respect—are to all intents and purposes free from government control. Furthermore, the BBC obviously is free from advertiser control, while the IBA, partly due to its own wishes on the matter and partly because of the constraints placed upon its governing authority, has great freedom from advertiser pressure. In the chapters on programmes, especially those relative to news, current affairs, political broadcasting, and drama, some of these general principles will be examined again in the context of day-to-day operation.

THE BBC AND THE IBA: COMPETITION OR COOPERATION?

When the possibility of setting up another broadcasting organization—especially one that would be commercially supported—was first broached, the BBC was greatly upset, and when the ITA finally did go on the air, Corporation spokesmen were very critical.[63] In 1959, Hugh Carleton Greene, then BBC Director of News and Current Affairs, who became Director-General the next year, told a group of German businessmen that radio and television 'are too powerful in their potential longterm effects for their control to be entrusted to politicians—or business men'.[64] He believed that 'when the object of a broadcasting system—the very reason for its existence—is to sell goods the programmes cannot possibly remain unaffected'.

A former Director of BBC Television spelled this out in direct programme terms which have been reiterated by current management.[65] 'ITV is a branch—and a very important branch—of the sales side of British Industry.' Its task, therefore, is 'to present a programme to the public which will secure a steady predictable audience—an audience which a client can buy in advance with confidence'. Therefore, ITV programmes will 'go for well-tried formulae—things which either the BBC or they or the Americans have devised and built up as popular favourites with big followings'. In contrast, the BBC follows 'a completely different course—not because of any special qualities residing in those who run it—but simply because the BBC has an entirely different way of earning its living'. It therefore will continue to be 'devoted to satisfying the requirements of an educated democracy in the making'.

What then could the BBC do about ITV? Ignore it? Compete? What? BBC spokesmen often claimed that because the two systems had different objectives, they were not really in competition. But the BBC had to compete for viewers, whatever term it applied to the process. As Sir Ian Jacob, Director-General when the ITA came on the air, stated, with real insight:

> It may be argued that the BBC is in a position to ignore the relative size of its audience and that it is not obliged to compete with Independent Television. But, to some extent, it must compete for its audiences, or its audiences will diminish beyond that level at which the Corporation could continue to claim that it is the national broadcasting authority. This is the situation into which the Corporation has been placed by competition.[66]

In 1971, Hugh Wheldon, then Managing Director of BBC Television, observed that if people watched BBC television less and less, they soon would ask, 'Why should we pay this licence?'[67]

In a presentation to the Annan Committee in 1975 on 'Choice in Television', the BBC recalled that when most of the audience chose ITV over BBC television during the first years of the new service, the Corporation realized 'that in the interests of all concerned it had no choice but to fight back'.[68] Otherwise, 'The spectre haunting the BBC was of a reduction to secondary status as a junior partner of ITV', which would put the Corporation in the position of no longer being able to employ the best talent, or of attracting maximum audiences for the programmes it produced.

Grace Wyndham Goldie, reminiscing in 1977, observed that the Corporation had to think of programme quality as well as audience size.[69]

> What could any government reply to a statement which ran 'There seems no difference between the kind of programmes we get from the BBC and from commercial television. If we can obtain programmes like this free, why should we pay licence fees so that the BBC can supply us with exactly the same kind of stuff?' Politically any government in such a situation would find it difficult to enforce the payment of licence fees to the BBC.

The week ITV took to the air, the *Radio Times* cover referred to: 'BBC-TV: The New Pattern'. Initially, the BBC lost heavily in the contest for viewers, getting only 30 per cent of the audience. But by degrees its share of the viewers increased, and in 1980 it was receiving—and was satisfied with—about half of all viewing, the breakdown averaging about 50 per cent ITV, 42 per cent BBC 1 and 8 per cent BBC 2. When the second ITV network is activated, the Corporation will still seek its half of the audience, for which reason it is concerned over the extent to which ITV 2 will be an entertainment channel, i. e., one with high audience appeal. (For further discussion of television audiences, see Chapter 20, 'Audience Research', below.)

The question soon arose, did competition improve Britain's all-around television services or degrade them? Initially, the Corporation forecast that the effect would be negative, and it told the Beveridge Committee in April 1950 that competition would lower levels of responsibility, debase standards, eliminate services for minorities, reduce the number of programmes of educational and cultural nature, and waste resources.[70]

In a paper prepared for the Pilkington Committee in 1961, the BBC, after referring to its earlier submission to the Beveridge Committee, said that the most 'serious' result 'on the debit side was the denial to the public of a planned alternative programme'.[71] The Pilkington Committee received testimony from many sources, both pro and con, and reported a 'widespread' belief that 'the effect of competition had been either mixed, or wholly for the worse'.[72] The Committee concluded that 'the pressure of competition has sometimes caused the Corporation, consciously or unconsciously, to depart in practice from its own ideal of public service broadcasting'.

Inevitably, there are diverse opinions about the effects of competition on the Corporation, most of which pertain to programming. But perhaps most important of all was the impetus the ITA gave to BBC television. After struggling for years to throw off the shackles of control by radio-oriented administrators in Broadcasting House, BBC television took advantage of ITV to press for its own development. Asa Briggs remarked that, beginning in 1954, 'Television for the first time seemed to be winning within the BBC itself.'[73] Eammon Andrews, who won fame as a sports announcer and MC, first on radio and then television, with BBC and later ITV, wrote in 1963:

> People said, and I was one of them, that the best thing that ever happened to the BBC was the setting up of the ITA. . . . In fact, I think the change was there before ITV. The rumour, the threat, was almost sufficient to release forces . . . that were anxious—to gallop down the field of communication without always pulling a coach and four.

But not all observers agreed. In the course of a stimulating examination of what he called *The Least Worst Television in the World* (that is, British television), critic Milton Shulman ascribed any post-ITV improvement in the BBC not to competition, which he thought had depressed the level of the output, but rather to changes resulting from the leadership of Sir Hugh Greene as Director-General and to some of the 'young, fresh talents' who entered the Corporation at that time.[74] The Annan Committee concluded that 'once commercial television was introduced, the kind of broadcasting which both Reith and Pilkington advocated shrivelled'. Yet, it also wrote: 'Severe as some of our criticisms of the BBC have been, they still, in our judgement, give a better all-round service to the public than does ITV.'[75]

But in recent years I have met many BBC officials who agree with me that competition has stimulated improvement, and there was some—perhaps unintended—documentation of this in the Corporation's memorandum on 'Choice in Television', submitted to the Annan Committee in February 1975. Referring to changes in its schedule when ITV went on the air, the BBC stated that some of these helped 'break down a certain remoteness which had developed during the monopoly'. It also said of itself:

> The presentation and promotion of programmes became more professional, with attention paid to the appeal of the network as a whole, as well as to the appeal of individual programmes. [Therefore] The first impact of competition and the changes which it brought about within the BBC's schedules probably improved the BBC's programmes during this period . . . .[76]

With competition came cooperation, some of it required, and some voluntary. The government may require the Corporation and the Authority to 'radiate . . . [certain] broadcast transmissions . . . from a mast, tower, or other installation' belonging to the other.[77] In 1962, the government agreed with the Pilkington Committee that when there is room for only one set of cameras for broadcasting events 'of national interest', they should be those of the BBC, 'the television picture being made available as a right, to the I.T.A.', although when 'practicable', each organization should have its own commentators.[78] Furthermore, the Television Act allows 'the inclusion in the [IT] programmes of relays of the whole (but not some only) of a series of the BBC's party political broadcasts'.[79]

But the BBC always has had reservations about working too closely with its rival. It has distinguished between 'coordination' (which it defines as a reduction in competitive planning), and 'cooperation' (working together in such respects as siting transmitters, sharing pick-up facilities, and consultation in the scheduling of school television.)[80] Because the two broadcasting systems are different, the Corporation told the Pilkington Committee, coordination 'should be no more than a means to an end, which is the provision of the best service to the viewing public'.

However, a BBC–ITV Concordat, and other formal and informal arrangements, have brought the two together on many occasions, to their mutual advantage.[81] They share the same advisory committees for religious programmes and charitable appeals; they confer on trade union problems; they plan school programmes jointly; they have avoided transmitting Welsh-language programmes simultaneously; the government has stated that with the advent of the fourth channel, IBA and BBC Welsh-language broadcasts will be further coordinated; and, in accordance with a recommendation from the Annan Committee, they are endeavouring to develop some joint audience studies. Although highly competitive in sports coverage, each allows the other to use short recorded segments from events covered by the other organization; and during the summer of 1979, after much acrimonious discussion, agreement was reached on television coverage of Football League and some other matches, on a rotating basis which would, among other things, avoid simultaneous transmissions during peak viewing hours (see below, pp. 323–5). At about the same time, the two worked together in presenting a seminar and some lectures during the Edinburgh Festival on the subject of Radio—Art and Utility.

In 1961, six years after the inauguration of ITV, but before the Pilkington Committee report was published, it was my conclusion, after a year's observation on the scene, that British television had been improved by competition.[82] The presence of two separate broadcasting organizations had helped, or at least hastened, the advent of certain improvements. Competition had proved an incentive to the BBC at the same time that it enriched the country's programme service. But I also concluded that competition had improved British broadcasting not only because it provided an alternate channel, but also because the Television Act of 1954 set up a system of 'controlled commercial television' favourable to the regulating agency. Additional viewing during the spring and summer of 1976 and the autumn of 1978, reinforced these earlier conclusions.

Although the ITA did introduce competition to British broadcasting, it was not competition in the American sense. Britain has only two broadcasting organizations, compared to America's three nationwide commercial television networks, four radio networks, and thousands of independently owned stations. Only the IBA seeks advertising money; and since there usually is more demand for air-time than time to sell, earnings usually have been very large. Therefore, Britain's programme companies do not need to compete as bitterly as do their American counterparts.

Most important of all, though, are the legal requirements for high-quality programmes, together with the stipulation that at least some serious programmes must be broadcast during prime-time hours. The BBC, now as always, has every intention of providing a high level of public service. The IBA, after disastrous experiences in the late 1960s and 1970s at the hands of the Pilkington Committee and the House of Commons Committee on Estimates, and the various other buffets it has received, tightened control over its programme companies. Therefore, both BBC and ITA operate under constraints which limit both the amount and nature of their competition. That is one of the main reasons, in my opinion, that Britain is better served by its broadcasters than the Americans are by theirs.

4 The Development of Television in the United Kingdom

The British are proud of their world leadership in television. A Scot working in London was the first person to transmit by radio a picture that moved. Later he was the first man to send a television image across the Atlantic Ocean. But British television's most distinguished 'first' was in the programme field: in 1936 the BBC went on the air with the world's first regular high-definition television programme service.[1]

Basic experiments in television were conducted in several countries following the discovery of the light-sensitive properties of selenium in 1873.[2] The most important early British inventor was John Logie Baird—the prototype of the dedicated and poverty-stricken inventor—who demonstrated the transmission of moving silhouettes by wire in April 1925.

On 27 January 1926 the same ingenious Scot took an important step beyond this when he showed an assemblage of scientists and reporters at the Royal Institution in London that he could, as a London *Times* writer expressed it, transmit through the air not only shadows, but 'the details of movement, and such things as the play of expressions on the face'. On 8 February 1928 Baird broadcast television pictures from London to New York, where they were reproduced on a 2-by-3-inch screen, and in July 1928 he even demonstrated a crude version of colour television.[3]

Television in the 1920s was for the laboratory rather than the home. Baird used a mechanical scanning disc to produce flickering low-definition 30-line pictures at only 12½ frames per second, which revealed little detail to the fans who watched the 5-by-6-inch screens on their early model receivers.[4] Nevertheless, in spite of equipment shortcomings, Baird managed—with difficulty—to set up, in June 1928, Baird International Television, Ltd, and its authorized capital of £7 million was oversubscribed.[5] Radio's history was being repeated: in the United States and the United Kingdom much of the early radio broadcasting had been done by equipment manufacturers in order to stimulate receiver sales; and television's early experimental costs likewise were underwritten by firms wanting to sell sets.

Once television gave promise of emerging from the laboratory to become a mass medium, both the Post Office and the BBC showed interest. In 1926 the Post Office, perhaps disturbed by reports that Baird's money-losing company might be taken over by American inventors, licensed Baird to conduct some experimental transmissions.[6] The next year, Baird transmitted television over a 438-mile telephone line between London and Glasgow, and also gave a demonstration in

Leeds. About the latter, a Post Office official commented: 'The invention has not reached a very advanced stage yet.'

Nevertheless, in June 1929 the BBC agreed to let Baird transmit test programmes over one of its London transmitters. The single transmitter available could be used only when radio programmes were not scheduled, and the output was limited to sound or vision alone, thus requiring the two to be alternated. Yet Tyrone Guthrie, who later was to win international fame as a theatrical producer, wrote an enthusiastic article for the *BBC Yearbook* in 1931 in which he said that he was 'convinced that the future [for broadcast drama] lies along the lines of television', and that in time the new medium would take its place as 'the most popular method of entertainment, and consequently as the most forceful medium of propaganda in the history of the world'.[7]

After much discussion, many differences of opinion, and a successful search for funds, Baird Television Ltd, and the BBC agreed in September 1932 that the BBC would broadcast at least two television programmes each week until 31 March 1934, using the Baird system.[8] All told, there were 76 transmissions in 1932 and 208 the following year.

While Baird was experimenting with mechanical scanners, there were experiments in both the United States and Britain with all-electronic systems, culminating in 1933 in the invention of the ionoscope pick-up tube, which led to the Emitron camera developed in Britain by Electric and Musical Industries, Ltd (EMI), a conglomerate, with ownership links to America's RCA.[9]

After 1932, EMI experiments concentrated on electronic transmissions, and the next year a competitive demonstration led Post Office and BBC observers to conclude that 'the results of the E.M.I. demonstrations were immeasurably superior to those obtained by Baird's and that the E.M.I. equipment was far in advance of its competitor'.[10] Meanwhile, technical advances raised picture definition from 30 to 240 lines for the Baird and 405 lines for the EMI system. All this led to the appointment of a committee to plan for a permanent television service.

THE SELSDON REPORT

On 14 May 1934 the Postmaster-General appointed a television committee consisting of seven members from the Post Office and the BBC, headed by Lord Selsdon, who as William Mitchell-Thompson had been Postmaster-General when the Corporation came into existence in 1927. This group was instructed: 'To consider the development of Television and to advise the Postmaster General on the relative merits of the several systems and on the conditions under which any public service of television should be provided.'[11] Some members were sent to observe developments in the United States and Germany, particularly to report on the all-electronic systems said to be as good as, or better than, the Baird mechanical method then used in London. At home the committee heard from thirty-eight witnesses with many different points of view. In January 1935, it issued the report which laid the basis for Britain's regular television service. The committee dealt with three fundamental problems: technical standards, administrative responsibility, and methods of finance.

The determination of technical standards is prerequisite to the establishment of a television service.[12] If a picture is to be satisfactorily broadcast and reproduced, transmitting and receiving apparatus must be matched in at least a dozen respects. One of the most important of these variables is the number of lines comprising the picture. Other things being equal, the sharpness or resolution increases as more lines are scanned. Another important factor is the number of complete pictures transmitted per second, the flicker diminishing as the frequency is increased.

Ever since 1936, British black-and-white television has used a 405-line standard with 25 pictures per second, although this service will be phased out in the 1980s. Since 1964 it has used a 625-line standard for its UHF broadcasting. Colour was added to the UHF transmissions in 1967. The United States uses a 525-line standard with 30 pictures per second; and most of the rest of the world a 625-line standard with 25 pictures per second, although French television also uses an 819-line standard with 25 pictures per second. But in none of these cases is the actual picture divided for transmission purposes into the full number of lines mentioned, since the number of lines is reduced by about 5 per cent to allow for vertical retrace time. Thus, with the American system, there are 525 lines minus 27, or 498 actual lines, and of European television's 625 lines, 594 are used in actual picture transmission.

In setting technical standards, therefore, the Selsdon Committee had some important decisions to make. If standards were frozen too soon, subsequent technical developments might render the whole system obsolete. On the other hand, until long-term standards were set, the public would hesitate to buy receivers. After careful deliberation, the Committee decided it was too soon to set permanent standards, although it firmly opposed a low-definition system like the Baird 30-line method then in use. There should be, the Committee said, at least 240 lines, with a minimum picture frequency of 25 and possibly even 50 per second. Since the rival Baird and Marconi – EMI systems were competing for selection, the committee recommended that the dispute be resolved by using the two systems alternately, 'in such a manner as to provide an extended trial . . . under strictly comparable conditions'.[13]

Who should run British television? The BBC, the wireless press, the Radio Manufacturers' Association, and the Newspapers Proprietors' Association all advocated turning it over to the BBC. The only considerable voice against this was the General Electric Company, which argued that the BBC might not provide the 'persistence and salesmanship' necessary for developing the new medium, and therefore proposed operation by several 'responsible and substantial companies' supervised by a central television board.[14] This proposal is interesting in view of subsequent complaints that the BBC was too radio-oriented to aggressively develop the new medium.

The Committee considered opening the field to private enterprise, as was done some 30 years later with the ITA, but decided that, because of the 'close relationship which must exist between sound and television broadcasting, we cannot do otherwise than conclude that the Authority which is responsible for the former—at present the BBC—should also be entrusted with the latter'.[15] But there was no real issue here, the selection of the BBC being a foregone conclusion.

Even at this early date, television threatened to be expensive. The problem of finance was twofold: how to pay for the service in its early stages, when no source of revenue related to the ownership or use of sets could be adequate; and how to meet costs in later years. Two sources of funds were considered: advertising and licence revenue. In its testimony, the Newspaper Proprietors' Association hoped there would be no 'forms of advertising by means of what are known as sponsored programmes'.[16] In his testimony, Reith agreed with the committee's already formed conclusion that spot advertising should be ruled out, but was not opposed to sponsorship: 'I have no objection in principle to the sponsor system and we do in fact do something which is near to that, and might do it in the future.'

During the debates in the early 1950s about the creation of the ITA, British critics were much more concerned about sponsored programmes than about direct advertising, fearing that 'sponsorship'—the gift of programmes by advertisers in return for mentions of their names and products over the the air—would give programme control to the advertisers, but in the 1920, and 1930s it was the other way around.[17] The committee, therefore, recommended against 'direct advertisements', but held that 'it would be legitimate, especially during the experimental period of the service', to accept sponsored programmes as a supplemental source of revenue. Indeed there was a little 'sponsoring' as early as October 1936, when a few new cars were 'driven slowly along the terrace of Alexandra Palace . . . halting in turn on a special concrete apron adjoining the ramp on which the television "camera" is manipulated to provide near or distant shots'. However, the new BBC Charter of 1937 forbade sponsored programmes, and the Postmaster-General, in a note to Reith on 15 March 1937, indicated that this prescription was intended to exclude any programmes provided by commercial organizations.

Since licence receipts were to be the principal source of support, the problem was how to raise sufficient money. The committee opposed increasing radio fees in order to pay for television, since only a small percentage of the country's radio licence-holders lived within range of the London television transmitter, and very few of these had television receivers. 'The issue of a special television looker's licence' was likewise disapproved on the ground that, if 'placed high enough even to begin to cover the cost', it might 'strangle the growth of the infant service—while, if it is placed low enough to encourage growth, the revenue must for some time be purely derisory as a contribution towards the cost'.[18] A sales tax on television receivers also was rejected because of the administrative problems encountered in the early 1920s, when attempts were made to support British radio broadcasting that way.

All this led inevitably to the conclusion that, 'during the first experimental period at least, the cost must be borne by the revenue from the existing 10s licence fee'. Since the BBC then was receiving only about 60 per cent of the net licence proceeds, the committee suggested that this gave the Corporation an argument for an increase of its share; and in 1937 the Corporation's share was increased, partly to pay for television, and partly to meet the expenses of the new External Services.[19]

BRITISH TELEVISION FROM 1936 TO 1939

The second phase of British television began on 2 November 1936, when the BBC's first regular service went on the air, and ended on 1 September 1939, when operations were suspended because of World War II.[20]

In the United States, CBS had a low-definition service on the air 49 hours weekly in 1931. The day the World's Fair opened in New York on 30 April 1939, RCA demonstrated 441-line television. The American 525-line system was adopted in 1941.[21]

BBC television was installed at Alexandra Palace, a Victorian building constructed in 1873 for concerts, exhibitions and circuses, and located about 6 miles north of central London. 'Ally Pally', as it often is nostalgically referred to by BBC television pioneers, acquired its twentieth-century claim to fame because it was the highest available building anywhere near central London in which television studios and transmitters could conveniently be installed. Then as now, height was a prime consideration in locating a transmitting antenna, and in the early days it was technically infeasible to separate transmitter and studios. These improvised and inadequate facilities remained BBC television headquarters until the move to Lime Grove in 1950.

In accordance with the Selsdon Committee's recommendations, the Baird and Marconi—EMI systems were alternated experimentally from 2 November 1936, until the first part of February 1937.[22] But the superiority of the latter was immediately apparent, so that the Post master-General announced on 5 February 1937 that henceforth all transmissions would use the Marconi—EMI system. At the same time he assured prospective set purchasers that these standards would not be substantially altered before the end of 1938.[23] As things turned out, they became permanent for British black-and-white television, although beginning in 1964 they were supplemented by a 625-line UHF system, to which colour was added in 1967.

British television was to have slightly less than 3 years' programming experience before World War II put it off the air; yet it accomplished some astonishing things in this short time. Initially it broadcast about two hours a day from 3 p.m. to 4 p.m., and from 9 p.m. to 10 p.m., 6 days a week. There also was an hour of demonstration film from 11 a.m. until 12 noon, and a sound-only relay from one of the two radio networks between 8 and 9 p.m. This schedule was gradually expanded to 24 hours per week by 1939.[24]

Although BBC television programming was necessarily experimental in those years, much creative and imaginative work was done, and some permanent patterns established. From the very beginning there was great emphasis on drama, these early efforts being distinguished by important repertoire, famous casts, and ingenious production. From the studio came both classic and modern plays, and when theatre-owners and unions permitted, direct pick-ups from London theatres, with the greatest performers of the day in the principal roles. Steadily improved production methods were supplemented by experiments with special effects, some of which presaged post-war techniques.[25] All this, it should be noted, was taking place in a daily programme service before the United States did any regular high-definition television at all.

Opera was first broadcast on 13 November 1936, a few days after the opening of the service, and experiments were conducted in which actors mimed the parts before the cameras while singers sang off-screen. There also were ballet, instrumental music, and solo recitals.

On the lighter side were entertainment and sports broadcasts. The tradition of broadcasting circuses was established, along with ring sports, football games, and cricket matches. There were cabarets, fashion parades, cooking demonstrations, and puppet shows.

The acquisition of the Corporation's first mobile unit, cumbersome by today's standards but remarkable then, made possible the world's first real television outside broadcast—the coronation of George VI, on 12 May 1937.[26] This programme stood in the same relation to the new services as did the coronation of Elizabeth II in 1953 to post-war British television. The 1937 broadcast brought the earlier coronation to some 10,000 viewers. When permission was refused for the installation of cameras in Westminster Abbey, it was arranged to televise the procession for 2 hours as it went past Hyde Park Gate, a coaxial cable providing connections between there and Alexandra Palace.

Subsequently, there were outside broadcasts of the tennis matches from Wimbledon (the first television outside broadcasts anywhere to be relayed by radio link), automobile races, the Oxford–Cambridge boat race, the Derby, and other racing events, and of such state occasions as Trooping the Colour. In September 1938 BBC television even had a live pick-up of Chamberlain leaving his plane at London airport, proudly waving the agreement he had just signed with Hitler at Munich.

But despite a promising and ever-expanding programme schedule, British television in these years made only a very slight impression on its potential viewing public. In September 1939 the whole United Kingdom had only about 23,000 sets, most of which were in the London area, since the Alexandra Palace transmitter was the only one on the air. Most British sets had 10-by-8-inch screens or smaller. Picture quality was generally good, since the same definition standards were used then as now for monochrome transmissions, even though there later were great improvements in cameras, transmitters and receivers.

Despite previous government assurances, there still was concern about early obsolescence due to possible changes in transmission standards, for which reason the Postmaster-General announced in February 1938 that these standards would be unchanged until at least January 1941.[27]

In the autumn of 1939 the television industry arranged an attractive display of sets at the Radio Olympia exhibition, and promoted sales with the slogan, 'TV is Here—You Can't Shut Your Eyes to It.' The enthusiasm of the crowds attending indicated that set ownership would have increased substantially if the war had not intervened.

Television was suspended almost everywhere during World War II, because television signals were excellent direction-finders for enemy airplanes, because television staff and equipment had to be used in radio and radar work, and because the frequencies were needed for radar.[28] On 1 September, in view of the tense international situation, the staff was awaiting the word to sign off. At 12 noon the announcer hopefully forecast the next week's transmissions, and introduced an 8-minute Mickey Mouse cartoon, *Mickey's Gala Premiere*, which ended as a caricatured Greta Garbo murmured, 'Ah tink ah go home.'[29] At that moment the order came, and without even a closing announcement, the world's first regular high-definition television service abruptly suspended operations for the duration. Alexandra Palace then became a part of England's radar network, and nothing was done with television until 1945 beyond the assignment of six men to routine maintenance duties.

THE HANKEY COMMITTEE

In September 1943, even with Hitler's *Festung Europa* still intact, the government appointed a committee under the chairmanship of Lord Hankey, 'To prepare plans for the reinstatement and development of the television service after the war', with special reference to technical standards, the extension of television to the rest of the United Kingdom, methods of administration and finance, and 'the development of the export trade' in television equipment.[30] Between October 1943 and its report in December 1944, the committee met thirty-one times, receiving testimony from such varied groups as the BBC, the Ministry of Education, the Board of Trade, the radio and television equipment manufacturers, and the film industry.

The Hankey Committee Report laid the basis for post-war British television, just as the Selsdon Report had done for the period between 1936 and 1939. The determination of technical standards was its first big assignment. In 1944, Britain had only one television transmitter, a limited amount of studio equipment, and about 23,000 home receivers. Since all of this was old and soon would be obsolete, an upward revision in technical standards at that time would have involved much less inconvenience and expense than if made at any later date. The committee called for 'vigorous research work with the aim of producing a radically improved system of Television', because it believed that 'television definition should eventually be of the order of 1,000 lines and that the introduction of colour and stereoscopic effects should be considered'. But nevertheless it recommended that 'the pre-war system of Television on the basis of 405-line definition should be restarted in London . . . as soon as possible after the cessation of hostilities in Europe', with extension to the provinces to follow.[31]

Why was the Hankey Committee willing to freeze British television at what soon became the lowest definition standard in the world? There were two reasons: the adoption of higher standards would have involved a long delay in restarting the service; and, despite some theoretical disadvantages, the 405-line standard in practice could be made to perform at least as well as if not better than, some higher-definition systems. In view of Britain's widespread war damage, a delay of several years would have been necessary before a markedly better system could be put into operation. 'To leave a gap of some years without any television service', the committee wrote, 'would damp interest and seriously retard commercial development of the television industry in this country', as well as for export. Therefore, 'It is most important that there should be no avoidable delay in restarting a television service if this country is to hold a leading position in the television field.'[32]

The committee's major proposals, including those on technical standards, were accepted by the government on 9 October 1945.[33] On 18 June 1946, ten days after the reopening of the service, the Postmaster-General announced that 'the public need have no hesitation in acquiring 405-line television receivers for fear of early obsolescence', and two years later, on 24 August 1948, he stated that, in view of further decisions by the Television Advisory Committee, he could assure the public that there would be no change in technical standards for some years to come.

A NATIONAL SERVICE

Although the question of technical standards was settled indefinitely by the government's acceptance of the Hankey Committee's recommendations, some of the other problems confronting the committee could not be so immediately solved. One of these was the establishment of a national television service, since that involved the construction of transmitters and studios, the procurement of equipment, the recruiting of staff, and the assignment of channels on which to operate the transmitters.

Britain's only pre-war television transmitter was located in London. That was the logical place to begin, since London was the best programme centre, and furthermore offered a potential audience of some 11 million people, constituting almost a quarter of the country's population. But from the very start country-wide service was the ultimate goal. The Television Advisory Committee in December 1938, the Hankey Committee in 1944, and the BBC at all times gave high priority to the development of a national service.[34] But growth of the first of the contemplated networks was disappointingly slow as government allocations of materials were alternately made and withdrawn in response to the fluctuating needs of the export trade and the rearmament programme.

On 9 November 1949, the Postmaster-General approved the BBC's 5 year plan for five high-power and five medium-power stations covering the major population centres. It was hoped to complete this by the end of 1954, but government restrictions on capital investment announced in 1951 delayed the start of construction of the medium-power stations until 1953. Nevertheless, the opening of five additional high-power stations in the major population centres of the country between 1949 and 1952 brought television to 80 per cent of the United Kingdom's population. The addition of three temporary transmitters, activated to bring the coronation in the summer of 1953 to more people, brought television within reach of 85 per cent of the population. Finally, in July 1953, authorization was received to construct five additional medium-and two low-power stations; and in January 1954, five more low-power and one medium-power stations were added. The twenty transmitting stations on the air by 1959, all in Band I—approximately equivalent to Channels 2–6 in American VHF television— brought BBC television to 98 per cent of the population in the United Kingdom. At that time, the proportion of people receiving television service in Britain was equalled only by the proportion in the United States.[35]

Long before completing its first network, the BBC began to plan for a second one. It realized that a second network would represent an improvement in service, and also would relieve some of the pressure under which the Corporation operated in trying to please 50 million people with only one service. Had the BBC been able to get its second network on the air by the early 1950s, it is quite possible that the ITA might never have been set up, since public demand for an alternate service was one of the factors leading to its creation. The 10 year plan which the BBC submitted to the government early in 1953, at the beginning of its new charter period, included a proposal for a second service available to a majority of the population. But the plan was not approved, and the BBC did not get its second network until 1964, almost ten years after the ITA had provided the country with a second service.[36] The ten-year plan also mentioned colour television, although at that time British colour television was still in the laboratory.

ADMINISTRATIVE AND FINANCIAL PROBLEMS

The Hankey Committee also inquired into the problems of administration and support for post-war television. The Selsdon Committee in 1935 had recommended that television be a BBC monopoly, and the Hankey Committee in 1944 agreed:

> We share that Committee's view on the close relationship which must exist between the two services, and we recommend that the post-war television service should likewise be operated by the same authority as is entrusted with the sound broadcasting service, i.e. by the British Broadcasting Corporation.[37]

At that time there was no serious opposition to this procedure, but some sentiment later developed for assigning television to some other agency than the BBC, and also for giving it greater autonomy within the Corporation.

The Beveridge Committee 15 years later heard proposals that television be taken entirely from the BBC for a variety of reasons, among them theoretical opposition to large monopolies and the belief that television would grow more rapidly, and treat its performers more generously, if it were independently run. The committee, however, followed the reasoning of Director-General Sir William Haley, who argued that 'television is an extension of [radio] broadcasting. That is the crucial point . . . [television and radio] are complementary expressions within the same medium. They are parts of one whole.'[38] But the committee recommended that 'within the general framework of the BBC television should enjoy greater autonomy than it has had hitherto'.

Inevitably there was the question of finance. The Hankey Committee held that 'the aim should be to make the television service self-supporting at as early a stage as possible', and suggested a special television licence fee of £1 a year, though conceding that it would be some time before television revenue would cover costs. Even though the BBC's 1937 Licence forbade sponsored programmes, the Committee mentioned them in passing as a possible means of reducing programme costs, but came to no conclusions about them.[39]

When the television service was reopened in June 1946, and the radio licence fee raised from 10 shillings to £1 (then $2.80), a combined radio—television licence at £2 was introduced, the proceeds being divided equally between the two services.[40] In March 1954, this was increased to £3 ($8.40), two-thirds being earmarked for television. But not until 1954–5 was television revenue sufficient to cover costs: in that year, television showed a surplus before taxes of £749,683, although between the end of the war and 31 March 1954, it had accumulated a deficit of £12,427,207. The advent of competition again resulted in a deficit, however, since in 1955–6 television costs exceeded income by £852,845.

AFTER THE WAR

Once it was decided to resume British television in October 1945, much work had to be done in preparation for the inaugural programme which took place on 7 June 1946. The Alexandra Palace studios were in dilapidated condition after 6 years of disuse, and needed many repairs. They remained the centre of British television for 5 years. In 1949 the old Rank Film Studios in London were acquired, and the first of five studios opened on 21 May 1950.[41] (A description of current BBC television facilities is given on pp. 95–7.) The Alexandra Palace studios were re-equipped and used for BBC television news from 1954 to 1969. In 1954, the Shepherd's Bush Empire Theatre was taken over for entertainment programmes with audiences, and the Riverside Film Studios at Hammersmith acquired. This mixture of facilities provided the space for BBC television productions until the Television Centre at White City was ready in 1960.

The new service was officially opened by the Postmaster-General on 7 June 1946.[42] The first programme included the Mickey Mouse film which had concluded the pre-war service, although the very first transmission was a harp recital. On the next day, the Victory Parade was televised.

During the first decade of the post-war service, there were frequent charges that the BBC was essentially a radio-oriented organization, whose leadership lacked interest in television, and accordingly did not vigorously develop the new medium. This criticism peaked in the first half of the 1950s during debates about the proposed new ITA, although it continued long afterwards. In fairness, it must be noted that shortages of funds, material, and power necessarily delayed television's development: people must be housed and fed before they are given television to watch. For example, the entire service was shut down in February 1947 because of national power shortages.[43]

If the limited amount and kind of space devoted to television in the BBC yearbooks between 1947 and 1955 is any indication of the Corporation's regard for the medium, the conclusion must be drawn that the new service did indeed have a low priority.[44] The 1955 *Handbook* devoted only three pages to television, although it made many references to it during paragraphs on 'programmes and programme departments'. But since television then had an output of about 40 hours a week, and was serving 4.5 million people in approximately 3.75 million homes, it is remarkable that most of the references to it during the year preceding the advent of the ITA were in the context of radio programming.

Maurice Gorham, who became the Director of Television in 1946, wrote of his immediate predecessor that he 'wore himself out in three years of battling for television'.[45] Sir Gerald Beadle, Director of Television from 1956 to 1961, wrote:

> Both before, and for several years after the war there was a very strong feeling amongst successive heads of the television service, Gerald Cock, Maurice Gorham and Norman Collins, that television was not being taken seriously enough by the BBC, that it was being treated too much as the Cinderella and as a mere appendage of sound radio.[46]

Gerald Cock, who served as the first director from 1936 to 1939, wrote that John Reith 'was something less than enthusiastic about television', and Beadle heard Sir William Haley, Director-General from 1944 to 1952, say, after seeing his first television demonstration in 1944, that he wouldn't have a television set in his home. But Beadle also pointed out that slow development also was caused by a government decision to limit the Corporation's expansion funds, with the result that, 'at the time of the debates about commercial television the BBC was unfairly accused of going slow in a number of respects'.

The head of television was made a director only in 1950; previously he held the lower status of controller. When he resigned his position as television controller in 1950, Norman Collins complained of the neglect of television, while the former chairman of the Board of Governors, Lord Simon, wrote that although 'four-fifths of the important decisions of the B.B.C. dealt with television . . . the Governors only gave to it one-fifth of their time.'[47] These are important points, since the coming of ITV depended to a considerable extent upon the proselytizing of Collins and others sharing his opinions, who gave as one of their reasons for promoting ITV that unwillingness of the Corporation to adequately support television.

After the coming of the ITA, though, in the middle 1950s, the 'situation began to unfreeze . . . , and the then Director-General, Sir Ian Jacob, a doughty fighter and a bold spender, took the fullest advantage of the easing position and pressed forward with the development of the television service'.[48] So, although the BBC does not bear the entire responsibility for the slow development of television, it surely must shoulder some of the blame. It is dangerous to speculate about how things might have gone had certain preceding events turned out differently, but a plausible argument can be made that, had the BBC pressed the case for television more earnestly—and if it had succeeded in carrying the government of the day with it—there might be no IBA today.

5 The Independent Broadcasting Authority

With the creation of the Independent Television Authority (ITA) in 1954, the BBC faced competition for the first time. The ITA, therefore, was important not only for itself, but also for its influence on the BBC. When set up in 1954, the ITA was authorized to do only television broadcasting, and its programme services, therefore, were known as Independent Television (ITV). When authorized to do radio broadcasting as well , in 1972, its name was changed to the Independent Broadcasting Authority (IBA).

THE POLITICAL BACKGROUND

Commercial broadcasting came to Britain, not spontaneously in answer to widespread public demand, but because a well-organized pressure group took advantage of the temper of the times to end the BBC's television monopoly and to introduce a competitive system supported by advertising.

During World War II, the government set up two committees to study the future of television in the United Kingdom. The official public committee headed by Lord Hankey recommended at the end of 1944 that television be resumed after the war as a BBC monopoly, supported by licence fees[1] (see above, pp. 52–3). The other committee, set up in January 1944, a private off-the-record group of Cabinet members headed by Lord Woolton, who as the post-war rebuilder of the Conservative Party was very important in the creation of the ITA, never made a formal report, partly because its bi-partisan membership of Conservatives and Labourites could not agree on the issues of monopoly and competitive broadcasting. In fact, the doubts of its Conservative members about continuing the BBC's monopoly presaged the later debates on the Television Act of 1954. At any rate, the government accepted the Hankey Committee recommendations in October 1945, and television broadcasting was resumed on 7 June 1946.

With the BBC's Charter and Licence due to expire on 31 December 1946, the Labour government decided that there was insufficient time for the usual inquiry, and so it extended the Corporation's life until 31 December 1952.[2] Parliamentary reaction to this decision, however, revealed the extent to which the Conservative opposition—and especially Winston Churchill—questioned the wisdom of continued monopoly operation without a full-scale inquiry. There also was considerable off-the-record objection within the Labour Party to omitting the investigation. But Churchill's motion to refer the matter to a committee of both houses was defeated 271 to 137.[3]

Although the Beveridge Committee in January 1951 recommended the continuance of the BBC monopoly, the committee received evidence from a variety of sources advocating both competitive and commercial broadcasting.[4] (see above, pp. 9–10, 17). The majority report pointed to the importance, if the BBC monopoly were continued, 'of devising internal as well as public and external safeguards against misuse of broadcasting power'. Selwyn Lloyd, one of the three Parliamentary members, who later became Foreign Secretary in the Cabinets of Prime Ministers Anthony Eden and Harold Macmillan, wrote a minority report strongly opposing any kind of monopoly.

On the item of commercial broadcasting, the committee had more trouble reaching agreement than on any other basic point, and ten of the committee's eleven members signed minority or supplementary reports on the subject. Selwyn Lloyd advocated competitive commercial broadcasting to supplement the BBC; Lord Beveridge and two others proposed the limited acceptance of spot advertising by the BBC, somewhat on the pattern later adopted for the ITA; while six members issued statements strongly opposing any kind of commercial broadcasting.[5]

Government action on the Beveridge Committee's recommendations was delayed by a combination of circumstances.[6] Since the Labour Party was in power, it could easily have rechartered the BBC as a monopoly at that time. But because the Charter and Licence were not due to expire until 31 December 1951, and their extension with no basic changes was taken for granted, there seemed to be no hurry to renew them. Furthermore, the illness and death of Foreign Minister Ernest Bevin on 14 April 1951, led to cabinet changes that caused BBC affairs to be put aside. Not until July 1951, therefore, did the government issue its White Paper commenting on the Beveridge Report. This contained two recommendations which aroused considerable debate in Parliament, resulting in further delay, although neither related to television. Before these matters could be settled, however, and the Charter and Licence renewed, the general election of October 1951 brought a Conservative government into office. Since the Charter and Licence were to expire on 31 December of that year, the new government arranged for a 6 month's extension while permanent policies were debated within party councils.[7]

THE CAMPAIGN FOR COMMERCIAL TELEVISION

In the early 1950s conditions were favourable for the success of a well-organized campaign for commercial television, even though there was little public demand for it, and many of its most ardent supporters were surprised at their eventual success.[8] British Gallup Polls between 1943 and 1953 indicated a fairly even division of opinion on the issues of monopoly and commercial broadcasting. Although there was no overwhelming demand for commercial television, there was sufficient interest—at least in a second service—so that the ITA did not come into existence against the wishes of a majority.[9]

For the most part, the upper socio-economic groups opposed monopoly in theory, although they also opposed commercial broadcasting, which, of course, was one way of ending the BBC's monopoly. The lower groups, on the other hand, favoured commercial broadcasting. But the public wanted a second service, and many people thought the BBC had been too slow in developing television.

The position of the Conservative Party against nationalization and for free enterprise, predisposed it to favour private commercial operations. However, like so many Conservative Parties coming back to power after a socialist regime, it could not return many nationalized enterprises to private control. What is more, some dyed-in-the-wool old-line party members suspected certain BBC employees of left-wing tendencies, or at least assumed that a monopoly like the BBC was basically hostile to free enterprise. This faction joined many new Members of Parliament from the business world in feeling that a commercially supported broadcasting organization would be more apt than the BBC to look at the world as they did. But the party was by no means unanimous in its support of commercial television; in fact, it was split on the subject from the Cabinet down to the lowesst ranks.

The long-time hostility of Winston Churchill to the BBC undoubtedly contributed to the victory of commercial television. Although Churchill never actively supported commercial television, neither did he oppose it in the early stages when by taking a firm position he could easily have squelched the movement. As Chancellor of the Exchequer back in the days of the British Broadcasting Company, he had unsuccessfully advocated taking over the Company at the time of the General Strike in 1926. In the 1930s, he was angry over being denied opportunities to broadcast on such controversial subjects as Indian policy and rearmament (although the parties rather than the BBC were to blame for that). In 1946, he objected to rechartering the BBC without an inquiry. In June 1952 he definitely declared himself, telling the House of Commons that 'the longer I have studied this matter and watched its development in the last few months, the more convinced I am that the present monopoly should not continue'.

Leadership for the movement was provided mainly by individuals who saw financial gains for themselves in a commercial system, although support also came from many disinterested people. Prominent among the proponents were several Conservative back-benchers in Parliament with advertising-agency and electronic-manufacturing connections. Funds for the campaign were provided by equipment manufacturers. There was much lobbying in Parliament.

The most important single exponent of commercial television was Norman Collins, who left his position as Controller in 1950, when he was not promoted to be Director of BBC television. Thereafter, he spent most of four years campaigning for commercial television. It is quite likely that if Collins had stayed with the BBC, Britain might never have had an ITA. Subsequently he became Deputy Chairman of Associated Television, one of the principal programme contractors, and then a director of the ATV Network. (For a brief review of the slowness of the BBC to develop television, see above, pp. 55–6.)

Another very effective worker was Mark Chapman-Walker, then secretary to

Lord Woolton, who was chairman of the central office of the Conservative Party, and head of the informal committee appointed in 1944 to look into the future of British television (see above, pp. 78, 80, 81). It was Chapman-Walker who prepared the original draft of the bill (complete with the non-sponsorship feature), which the Cabinet then rewrote for submission to Parliament. He later became the first managing director of Television West & Wales, the programme company serving the west of England and South Wales.

Gerald Beadle, a long-time Corporation employee, who was director of BBC Television from 1956 to 1961, has emphasized the demand for additional advertising outlets as an important motivation for commercial television.[10] After war-time restrictions on advertising, industry was seeking new ways to tell the public about the 'large range of goods which were becoming available. Television was obviously an excellent medium for this, and industry was not averse to harnessing the television horse to the industrial chariot.'

Advertising agencies were among the most prominent advocates, and much basic planning for the campaign was done by a committee of agency executives formed in 1952, following the encouragement given by the Conservative government's White Paper in May of that year. In spite of this, advertising agencies as a group were divided in opinion. Some opposed commercial television entirely; others wanted straight sponsorship along American lines; while still others liked the idea of commercial television, but feared the American pattern would be too cumbersome, too expensive, and too difficult to operate.

Strongly opposed to commercial television was the group which later came to be known as the 'Establishment', that informal but effective coalition of the British power elite, drawn largely from the upper classes; institutions such as the Church of England, and Oxford and Cambridge universities; along with the major civil service heads, most churchmen and the influential members of the BBC's advisory councils and committees. The vice-chancellors of most leading British universities sent letters to *The Times* opposing commercial television. Many of these people probably opposed the extension of any kind of television. But in addition they felt that competition would force down standards, and they feared that a commercial system would be dominated by advertisers rather than by people interested primarily in public service. A National Television Council was created to expound their views.

Most newspapers opposed commercial television; such publications as *The Times*, the *Manchester Guardian* and the *Observer* taking strong positions. Even a majority of the Conservative press—in spite of Conservative Party advocacy—was against the proposal. But the press was not disinterested, since a commercial television system obviously would provide competition for advertising budgets, and the British press had always opposed commercial broadcasting, whether by the BBC or by foreign stations like Radio Luxembourg. Once the ITA was established, however, most of the principal programme companies were partly owned by newspapers, and with the advent of commercial radio in 1972, their involvement was increased. In 1959, even the *Guardian* became a stockholder in Anglia TV. (For further details on press holdings in programme companies, see below, pp. 76–78.)

COMMERCIAL TELEVISION IN PARLIAMENT

After it had been in office for six months, the Conservative Party issued its first White Paper on broadcasting policy. This began by pointing out that the BBC's various licences did not in themselves establish the Corporation 'as the sole authority for all broadcasting in the United Kingdom'.[11] Rather, the BBC enjoyed the position because successive governments had chosen not to license other broadcasting agencies. The BBC was to continue to operate non-commercially, and was to have first claim on labour and materials in order to establish and maintain a national broadcasting service.

Then came the bombshell: 'The present Government have come to the conclusion that in the expanding field of television provision should be made to permit some element of competition.' Nothing was said about the competitive system being commercially supported, although this was clearly implied. The public was assured that no alternate system would be chartered in haste; Parliament would have the same opportunity to debate the details of competitive television it always had to discuss the BBC's Charter and Licence. In any event, there would be controls and safeguards to ensure a high quality of programmes.

The reaction to this revolutionary proposal was intense, and overnight commercial television became a topic of national discussion. A year and a half—and many debates—later, the government issued another White Paper, which outlined its position in greater detail, advanced supporting arguments, and indicated the general nature of the broadcasting organization it intended to create.[12] The plan was to set up a public corporation something like, but quite distinct from, the BBC, which would license and operate television transmitters. This corporation would sell time to privately financed companies which would provide the programmes, deriving their revenue from advertisements. Both programmes and advertisements would be closely supervised, however, and advertisers would not be allowed to control programme content.

Summarizing its case, the White Paper said:

The policy which the Government recommends to Parliament is designed to achieve three objectives—the first is to introduce an element of competition into television and enable private enterprise to play a fuller part in the development of this important and growing factor in our lives; the second is to reduce to a minimum the financial commitments of the State; and the third is to proceed with caution into this new field and to safeguard this medium of information and entertainment from the risk of abuse or lowering standards. It is the public corporation, with Directors appointed by the Government and free from risk of outside pressure, which will be basically responsible to the Postmaster General, and through him to Parliament, for the standard of new programmes to be shown on the television screens in our homes.

Between the release of the Conservative Party's first White Paper in 1952 and the passage of the Television Act in 1954, the whole subject of commercial television was very thoroughly discussed in Parliament, in the press and at various public meetings. Feeling ran high. For example, the *Manchester Guardian* compared the Lord's debate on the 1953 White Paper to the constitutional struggle of 1911, and Herbert Morrison referred to the House of Commons' discussion as the most important since the war.[13] Two hundred and forty-four Peers voted during the House of Lords debate on 26 November 1953, the largest number voting since June 1948.[14]

During the House of Lord's debate on 22 May 1952, Lord Reith condemned the proposed new service in vigorous language:

> What grounds are there for jeopardising this heritage and tradition [of non-commercial BBC broadcasting]? . . . A principle absolutely fundamental is scheduled to be scuttled. . . . Somebody introduced dog racing into England. . . . And somebody introduced Christianity and printing and the uses of electricity. And somebody introduced small pox, bubonic plague and the Black Death. Somebody is minded now to introduce sponsored broadcasting into this country.[15]

The Commons Debate on the evening of 15 December 1953, at which I was present, was a stormy one, described by *The Times* as 'a scene of noise and confusion seldom seen in the House'.[16] The specific cause of the disorder was a ruling by the Speaker that the failure of the last government spokesman to conclude his remarks before the appointed 10 o'clock hour made a vote on that day impossible. *The Times* wrote that the Speaker's decision was 'announced at the end of a storm of argument, reproach and protest, which again and again moved him to stern criticism of the House'. General public interest was shown by the many letters appearing in the newspapers throughout the period. Although broadcasting policy had never been debated with so much vigour and heat, the arguments used were repetitions or extensions of those which had been advanced for and against monopoly and commercial broadcasting ever since the founding of the British Broadcasting Company in 1922.

The campaign was unexpectedly aided by a serious strategical error on the part of the Labour Party leadership. In June 1952, Labourite Patrick Gordon Walker told the House of Commons: 'We shall certainly not carry on the policy implied in this non-exclusive Licence . . . we reserve our full right to frustrate this retrograde innovation. . . . ' The following year party leader Clement Attlee made the position 'official' by stating that if the Conservative Party allowed television 'to pass into the hands of private profiteers', Labour would have to alter the situation when it returned to power.[17]

The Conservatives enthusiastically seized upon such statements to make commercial television a party issue. Otherwise the Television Act would never have been passed, since there were enough members against it on both sides of the House to defeat it in a free vote, with members released from party control to vote according to their individual convictions. But the Conservatives strictly enforced party discipline, and on 25 March 1954, the bill passed, 296 to 269.[18]

The Television Act of 1954 was not passed in response to wide public demand, or for the reasons given in and out of Parliament in its favour. It was passed because a well-organized out-of-sight campaign took advantage of the atmosphere within the Conservative Party favourable to free enterprise, the pressure for additional advertising outlets at a time when post-war recovery had provided many new things to sell, and the country's desire for a second television service, to garner sufficient votes to create the ITA. Those people close to the movement generally agreed that the public pressure groups and nationwide debates were not decisive, even though often dramatic.

Nevertheless, the nature and source of the opposition left their mark on the unique structure evolved for the ITA. The critics had in mind the BBC's tradition of excellent public service programming; they were afraid that in a commercial system advertisers would control the programmes; they thought that the inevitable competition for audiences would lead to a lowering of standards; and they were sure that competition would result in the neglect of minority interests.*

Therefore, Britain came up with a new pattern, the principal feature of which was the separation of responsibility for programme content and advertising. It is likely that without this and the non-sponsorship provisions, the Television Act would never have passed. The model followed was the press, in which news and editorial material are kept entirely separate from advertising copy, rather than American commercial broadcasting, in which advertisers often provide programmes, or at least participate in their development. The first Director-General of the IBA called this, 'Editorial Television', and the term is a good one.

THE STRUCTURE OF THE IBA

The bill to create the ITA was introduced into Parliament on 4 March 1954, and became law on 30 July 1954. The first ITV programme went on the air in London in September 1955.† All of the bill's basic features survived the debates, although a good many of the 206 amendments introduced (145 by the opposition) were

---

* In November and December 1953, the BBC's top echelon drew up and discussed six counterproposals to the ITV legislation, all of which assumed that the Corporation would become involved in operating the new Authority. But it finally was decided to submit no alternatives, because any plan likely to be accepted would 'make too large a sacrifice of the BBC's principles'. Instead, therefore, an *aide-mémoire* was submitted to the Government on 19 January 1954, which offered arguments against advertisement-supported broadcasting. There also were formal and informal meetings with government leaders concerning various checks and safeguards of concern to the Corporation. Although some of these were accepted, none of them altered the main thrust of the bill (Briggs IV, pp. 947–61; quotation from p. 954).

† Gerald Beadle, a former director of BBC Television (*Television: A Critical Review*, pp. 46–7) believes the British government:

made a mistake in 1954 in allowing the newly-created British Commercial Television Authority to call itself The *Independent* Television Authority. The adjective was intended to imply its independence of the BBC which was factually correct, but outside Britain, especially in America, it was taken to mean independence of the government, with the inevitable implication that the BBC ... was not independent ... and was indeed an incorporated into the final version. Through the years, the basic constitutional features of the IBA have remained the same. However, in response to dissatisfaction with certain aspects of ITV's performance, subsequent legislation has laid down increasingly stringent programme and advertising requirements, and has spelled out more fully the Authority's responsibilities and enforcement powers.

The Television Act 1963 extended the life of the Authority to 1 July 1976; the Television Act 1964 consolidated the Acts of 1954 and 1963; and the Sound Broadcasting Act 1972 changed the Authority's name to IBA and enlarged its functions 'to include the provision of local sound broadcasting services'. The 1964 and 1972 Acts were consolidated by the IBA Act 1973. A supplementary law of 1974 extended the life of the IBA from 31 July 1976 to 31 July 1979; in 1978 this was further extended to 31 December 1981; and the Broadcasting Act 1980 further extended this until 31 December 1996.

The IBA Act of 1973, currently in effect, sets up the IBA to provide 'television and local sound broadcasting services, additional in each case to those of the British Broadcasting Corporation and of high quality, both as to the transmission and as to the matter transmitted'.[19] Except in a few unlikely situations—which have never occurred—all programmes must be provided, not by the IBA itself, but by private companies supported by advertising, which in turn pay the Authority for air-time. However, the IBA and not the programme companies is at all times legally responsible for the service. 'The Authority is thus the architect, the planning board and the day-to-day governing body of the system.'[20]

Corresponding to the BBC's Board of Governors is the IBA itself, consisting of a chairman, deputy chairman, and nine other members, of whom three are selected for their special competence to 'make the interests of Scotland . . . Wales . . . and Northern Ireland, respectively, their special care'.[21] The Authority is expected to be the main interest of the chairman but only a part-time concern of the other members. Members are appointed for not more than 5 years, and may be dismissed at will by the Home Secretary, who is expected to provide information and answer questions in Parliament about the Authority to the same extent as for the BBC. In effect, therefore, the government has the same control over the governing Boards of both organizations. With the ITA, as with the BBC, the government resists attempts at Parliamentary control of programme content. Thus, as early as November 1955, when the Authority had been on the air only 2 months, the Postmaster-General refused to prohibit it from broadcasting a film of a Spanish bullfight, and the next month announced his intention of leaving control of advertising details to the Authority.[22]

---

instrument of government policy, which most Americans were predisposed to believe anyway.

The Annan Committee, which recommended that the name of the IBA should be changed to Regional Television Authority, made the point: 'The title "Independent" has always been open to misinterpretation, and implies that the BBC is in some way the State-controlled broadcasting system, whereas the commercial companies are totally independent of the State' (Annan, #13.43).

As with the BBC, the chairman receives a salary of £17,316 per year, the deputy chairman £4500 per year. All other members receive £2250 per year, plus reimbursement for out-of-pocket costs incurred while transacting IBA business. No one may be a member of the Authority if he is a BBC governor, a member of the House of Commons, or a member of either House of Parliament in Northern Ireland. The desire to safeguard the ITA from industrial pressure underlies an elaborately phrased provision that no Authority member is to have any 'financial or other interest'—particularly 'in any advertising agency', broadcast equipment company or programme company—that is 'likely to affect prejudicially the discharge . . . of his functions as a member of the Authority'.[23] Though not required to do so by law, IBA members do not accept appointments as directors or employees of programme companies for a period of 2 years after serving on the Authority.

The Act empowers the Authority to do most of the things ordinarily done in radio and television broadcasting, including the installation and operation of transmitting facilities, although without the approval of the Home Secretary it is not to 'engage in the manufacture or sale of, apparatus for wireless telegraphy or any other telegraphic equipment'. Such permission has never been sought, however, nor is it likely to be requested.[24] Programmes must normally be provided by programme companies, although the Authority may originate or arrange for the production of some programmes if that is essential 'for securing a proper balance in the subject matter'.[25]

Like the BBC, the IBA is to solicit advice before determining its programme policies.[26] The Authority is authorized to appoint advisory committees, including a general advisory council, and is expressly required to appoint or arrange for the assistance of committees on religion, advertising and education, as well as local committees in each of the areas served by the Authority's radio stations.

The Authority is expected to be self-supporting from the rental payments received from its programme companies.[27] These payments fall into two categories: those designed to cover current IBA operating costs, capital expenditures, and reserve funds; and, the 'additional payments', commonly known as 'the levy', intended to transfer excess profits to the Treasury. In response to the Pilkington Committee's complaint that the Authority was not keeping itself sufficiently informed of public reaction to its programming, the 1963 and subsequent laws have required it to ascertain 'the state of public opinion concerning the programmes (including advertisements)', as well as to encourage 'the making of useful comments and suggestions by members of the public'. Thereafter, these are to be given 'full consideration' by the Authority.[28]

Government review of the IBA is facilitated by requirements for an annual audit and reports, and the stipulation that the Home Secretary may 'at all reasonable times' examine the Authority's 'accounts . . . financial transactions and engagements'.[29] The equivalent of the right of revocation given the government by the BBC's Charter and Licence is found in the provision that the Authority's licence to broadcast 'may be revoked, or the terms, provisions, or limitations thereof be varied, by the Minister . . .'[30]

Clearly, there is a basic difference of approach between the BBC's Charter and

Licence and the several Parliamentary acts involving the IBA. In Programme matters, the BBC documents are very permissive, whereas the laws pertaining to the Authority are prescriptive, setting up a broadcasting system to operate within carefully defined limits. Furthermore, each revision of the law has been increasingly severe, a fact clearly demonstrated by their steady increase in length: the original 1954 act covered 21 printed pages, the 1964 act 37 pages, and the 1973 act 49 pages.

PROGRAMME REQUIREMENTS

Parliament's concern over the performance of a commercial system was clearly shown by the stringent programme requirements in the 1954 and subsequent laws. Whereas the BBC's licence merely requires it to 'send efficiently', the Television Act 1954 and its successors have devoted several pages to programme standards. In fact, many of the things written into the several television acts are a part of the unwritten code of the BBC.

With the IBA, as with the BBC, the government has power to initiate or veto programmes. 'The Minister [the Home Secretary] or any other Minister of the Crown' may 'require the Authority to broadcast . . . an announcement . . . with or without visual images', or he may 'require the Authority to refrain from broadcasting any matter or classes of matter'.[31] However, again as for the BBC, The Authority may state that it is 'doing so in pursuance of such a notice'. The Minister also has power to specify the minimum, maximum or exact hours of broadcasting, although he has not done so for either IBA or BBC since 1972.[32]

Again and again there is emphasis on quality. It is the duty of the Authority 'to provide . . . television and local sound broadcasting services as a public service for disseminating information, education and entertainment', and these must maintain 'a high general standard in all respects'.[33] Although the 1954 law stipulated that programs were to 'maintain proper balance in their subject matter',[34] the Authority's critics complained that the programme companies scheduled 'balance programmes' out of peak viewing hours in order to increase their profits by attracting large audiences with light entertainment during mid-evening periods. Accordingly, this section of the Act now spells out the requirements more exactly: 'It shall be the duty of the Authority . . . to ensure that the programmes . . . maintain . . . a proper balance and wide range in their subject-matter, having regard both to the programmes as a whole and also to the days of the week on which, and the times of the day at which, the programmes are broadcast.' In addition, the Authority is to 'secure a wide showing or . . . hearing for programmes of merit'.[35]

The 1954 Act decreed that nothing should be broadcast 'which offends against good taste or decency or is likely to encourage or incite to crime or to lead to disorder or to be offensive to public feeling', but current legislation goes beyond this, requiring the Authority in addtion, to draw up a violence code, with special reference to children's programmes.[36] Furthermore, in enforcement, the Authority may go beyond the code, and has the power to add additional 'prohibitions or restrictions'.

As long ago as 1927 the Postmaster-General used his veto power over the BBC to forbid editorializing, a prohibition that has remained in effect ever since, so it was not surprising that the original television act forbade editorializing in Authority programmes or publications.[37] The prohibition against editorializing in publications was dropped from the 1964 law, but editorializing on the air by the Authority or its contractors is still forbidden. This was further defined in the 1980 law to exclude 'all expressions of opinion' by the Authority or its contractors 'on matters other than broadcasting which are of political or industrial controversy or relate to current public policy'.

All news must be presented 'with due accuracy and impartiality', and there must be impartiality in treating 'matters of political or industrial controversy or relating to current public policy'. But the law mentions impartiality only in 'matters of political or industrial controversy or relating to current public policy', which suggests that impartiality is not required in artistic, intellectual or scientific areas.[38] Subliminal programmes are prohibited.[39]

The Authority's 'previous approval' is required before its companies may broadcast 'any religious service or any propaganda relating to matters of a religious nature', as well as 'any item . . . which gives or is designed to give publicity to the needs or objects of any association or organisation conducted for charitable or benevolent purposes'.[40] This clause was inserted to prevent individual programme companies from being unduly influenced by organized religious groups.

In response to fears that ITV might be inundated by American films and videotapes, it is the obligation of the Authority to see 'that proper proportions of the recorded and other matter included in the programmes are of British origin and of British performance'.[41] Pressure to limit the amount of foreign material came mainly from two sources: people who feared that British traditions, cultural standards, speech and moral values would suffer from an 'American invasion'; and labour unions and other employee groups, whose main interest was employment for their members. During the parliamentary debates, Labour spokesmen suggested that the allowable amount of foreign material be set at 20 per cent or less, but the government rejected a specific figure as administratively unworkable.[42] In determining national origin, a number of factors are considered.

If a studio is to be used in the production, this must be in British territory. If a film is made by a company, that company must be British and have a majority of British directors. Other relevant factors are the nationalities of producers, writers, actors, composers, musicians and technicians.[43]

The law encourages with television, and requires in the case of radio, the development of local broadcasting. Applicable to both media is the requirement that all stations must carry a 'suitable proportion of matter calculated to appeal especially to the tastes and outlooks of persons served by the station or stations in each area'.[44] Reflecting the constant pressure from Welsh nationalists for programmes in their language, the 1964 law introduced the requirement that 'where another language as well as English is in common use', there must be 'a suitable proportion' of programs in that language.[45] Implementing this, the Authority writes into all contracts the stipulation that programme companies must develop such proportions as it may from time to time specify of their total programme output from local resources, the exact amount depending upon the availability of local material.

There is particular emphasis on localism in radio. After much discussion and long consideration, the government formally announced in a 1971 White Paper that it had decided to introduce 'an alternative service of radio broadcasting', to be run on a commercial basis by the Authority.[46] This recommendation was embodied in legislation approved on 12 June 1972. Among other things, the law stipulates that, since local stations rather than a national network are intended, it is the 'duty of the Authority' to assure itself that broadcasts from its various radio stations 'for reception in different localities do not consist of identical or similar material to an extent inconsistent with the character of the services as local sound broadcasting services'.

Programme companies are forbidden to 'buy' their audiences, since no prize or gift of significant value is to be offered 'which is available only to persons receiving that programme'.[47] In order to prevent the IBA from outbidding the BBC and vice-versa, and getting exclusive rights to 'sporting or other events of national interest', the law states that the Minister may make regulations as to broadcasting rights for such events, subject to Parliamentary approval.[48]

Since the law places responsibility for programme performance entirely on the IBA rather than on the individual programme companies, it provides the Authority with power to enforce both the law and its own rulings as to programme and advertisements. Each revision of the law, in fact, has increased both the Authority's responsibility and its enforcement powers.

The Authority has 'power to do all such things as are in their opinion necessary for or conducive to the proper discharge of their function as described in . . . this act'.[49] Contracts with programme companies 'shall contain all such provisions as the Authority thinks necessary or expedient . . . [for] securing compliance with the provisions of this Act and any restrictions or requirements imposed thereunder in relation to the programmes provided by the programme contractors'.

The Authority complained to the Pilkington Committee that it was uncertain of its right to examine total programme schedules in advance—as opposed to individual items—and so the 1963 law stipulated that programme companies were not to broadcast any programmes unless they constituted a part of a previously approved schedule, 'drawn up in consultation with the Authority . . . for a period determined by the Authority'.[50]

The Authority may give instructions 'either general or specific', as to excluding, including or otherwise changing individual programme items, and it may, 'at any time call for further particulars of a programme schedule submitted to them, or of any item in the programme schedule'. Enforcement is facilitated by the requirement that every contract must give the Authority power to request advance scripts and other details about programmes and advertisements, plus recordings of the material concerned.[51]

ADVERTISING

The law and the regulations for advertising are both severe and strict, as would be expected from the bitter debate which preceded the creation of the commercially supported ITA in 1954. It should be noted that because the British were not used to advertising on radio or television, many of these rules were laid down at the request, not only of Labour, but also of Conservative MPs. In view of the periodic public debates and the criticism of the various committees that have investigated British broadcasting, it is clear that questions have been raised as to how well the Authority has enforced some of these requirements—especially during its earlier years; but currently compliance is the norm and not the exception.

(a) Legal Requirements

First there is law, common and statute, applicable to advertising in all media: over fifty Parliamentary Acts in some way restrict, control or regulate advertising. Then there is the IBA Act, which includes many provisions about broadcast advertising. There also are the regulations promulgated by the Minister in accordance with the Act; the rules and interpretations of the IBA laid down after consultation with its Advertising Advisory committee; and the regulations of the individual programme companies.

Fundamental is the requirement for the separation of advertising and programme content, one of the basic principles of Independent Broadcasting: only spot advertising is permitted, and programme sponsorship is prohibited. The act stipulates that

> nothing shall be included in any programmes . . ., whether in an advertisement or not, which states, suggests or implies . . . that any part of any programme . . . which is not an advertisement has been supplied or suggested by any advertiser; and, except as an advertisement, nothing shall be included in any programme . . . which could reasonably be supposed to have been included therein in return for payment or other valuable consideration to the relevant programme contractor or the Authority.[52]

What happens, therefore, is that several minutes are left free during each programme period for the insertion of commercials. An advertiser may select the time when his advertisement is broadcast, but he has no more control over the adjacent programme than over the news columns on the pages of the newspapers in which he buys space.

This separation of functions is further reinforced by the requirement that 'neither the Authority nor any programme contractor shall act as an advertising agent', as well as by the provision that 'advertisements must be clearly distinguishable as such and recognizably separate from the rest of the programme', and that 'Successive advertisements must be recognizably separate.'[53] In addition to prohibiting an advertiser from declaring or suggesting that he is any way connected with the programme for which he indirectly pays, the law has been interpreted as preventing performers from stepping out of character to give commercials, as is often done in the United States. This rule is applied very strictly.[54] A commercial in which an actor appears out of character in a neutral setting cannot be aired within, or adjacent to, any production in which the actor played a role. According to the circumstances, such timing separations may be fixed at a half-hour or longer. Furthermore, an advertiser cannot insert announcements in newspapers inviting the public to tune to a specific programme on which his commercials appear, although he could refer in a newspaper advertisement to a forthcoming commercial, provided the reference is only to the approximate time it will be broadcast, and not to the programme on which it will appear.

(b) Rules and Regulations

The advertisements that do appear on IBA programme must conform to a formidable set of rules and regulations. A list of requirements is appended to the Act—the Minister may amend these if he considers it necessary—and the Authority must 'consult from time to time with the Minister as to the classes and descriptions of advertisements' which must not be broadcast at all.[55] The Authority is required to appoint and consult with a committee on advertising, which must include representatives of 'organisations, authorities and persons concerned with standards of conduct in the advertising of goods and services (including in particular the advertising of goods or services for medical or surgical purposes)' as well as of 'the public as consumers'. The Authority also must 'appoint, or arrange for the assistance of, a medical advisory panel' to provide advice on advertising relative to medical matters.

To ensure that the programme companies conform to the many rules and regulations in effect, the Authority previews the scripts of almost all commercials before they are recorded, normally examining some 7000 proposed new television advertisements each year. Over half of these scripts are investigated by the Authority, and 20 per cent are returned for changes, although only 2 per cent of the finished films require revision. After summarizing some of the ways in which the IBA checked advertisements, and noting some complaints from advertisers, the Annan Committee wrote: 'on this point, the advertisers' representatives failed to bring tears to our eyes.'[56]

In view of the widespread use of American radio and television for such purposes, it is interesting to notice that British law rules out 'opinion advertising', by excluding advertisements 'inserted by or on behalf of any body the objects whereof are wholly or mainly of a religious or political nature', or which are 'directed towards any religious or political end or [have] any relation to any industrial dispute'. There is to be no advertising designed to affect public opinion about pending legislation. A political party may not insert any sort of advertisement, even for staff or housing accommodations. A religious group may not urge attendance 'next Sunday at the church of your choice'.[57]

(c) Advertising Code

The IBA Code of Advertising Standards and Practices, first issued in July 1955, and revised several times since then, most recently December 1977 (with additional changes in September 1978), is a 20-page brochure covering almost all conceivable situations with the force of law. The American broadcasters too set standards for themselves in their radio and television codes, first adopted on 1 March 1952. By 1976, the Radio Code was in its 20th edition, and the Television Code in its 19th edition. But the American Codes are not legally binding, whereas the Television Act and the regulations promulgated under it must be observed by the IBA and all of its programme contractors.[58]

Initially, the IBA Code lays down general guidelines: broadcast advertising 'should be legal, decent, honest and truthful', and 'Advertisements must comply in every respect with the law, common or statute.' Furthermore, 'the detailed rules . . . are intended to be applied in the spirit as well as the letter and should be taken as laying down the minimum standards to be observed'.[59]

There are many prohibitions, including subliminal advertising, and a long list of things that may not be advertised at all: 'Breath testing devices and products which purport to mask the effects of alcohol'; matrimonial agencies; betting tips; cigarettes and cigarette tobacco (this ban became effective in 1965); and, private detective agencies.[60] It further stipulates: 'An advertisement for an acceptable product or service may be unacceptable should it seem to the Authority that its main purpose would be to publicise indirectly, the unacceptable product.'[61]

The IBA progressed by stages from limitations on cigarette advertising to a complete ban in 1965. (American law forbade all cigarette advertising effective in 1972.) In 1962, following a British government report on 'Smoking and Health', the Authority curtailed certain types of appeals as 'unacceptable'.[62] The manufacturers at that point agreed not to advertise any tobacco products before 9 p.m. because of children's viewing. When the United States Surgeon-General's report on Smoking and Health was published in January 1964, the ITA ruled that 'without valid evidence' the advertisements should not claim 'that it is safer to smoke one brand or type of cigarette than another'.[63] But it was not until 2 March 1965 that the Postmaster-General, using powers given him under Section 7 (5) of the Television Act of 1964, announced a complete ban on cigarette advertising in television, effective 1 August of that year.[64]

Comparison advertising is regulated: advertisements may not 'unfairly attack or discredit other products, advertisers, or advertisements directly or by implication'.[65] In both countries the amount of comparison advertising is increasing, although there is much less of it in the United Kingdom than in the United States. Misleading descriptions or claims are prohibited, nor shall there be references 'to lead the public to assume that the product advertised . . . has some special property or quality which is incapable of being established'.[66] Scientific terms and statistics may not be employed so as to confuse the viewer or listener, and advertisers must be prepared to produce evidence to substantiate any descriptions, claims or illustrations.[67] Related is the requirement that if words like 'guarantee' or 'warranty' are used, supporting data must be 'available for inspection by the Authority'. The term 'free' may be applied only to situations where goods or samples actually are supplied without cost 'other than actual postage or carriage'. Promises of employment must not accompany advertisements for courses of instruction, and normally only officially accredited correspondence schools may advertise.[68]

As the result of an agreement between the Authority and the principal distillers, there never has been much advertising of hard liquor on either radio or television, and recent code revisions have tightened the regulations. When such advertisements are accepted, they 'may not be addressed particularly to the young and no one associated with drinking in the advertisment should seem to be younger than about 25'.[69] They may not 'feature any personality who commands the loyalty of the young', and should not imply 'that drinking is essential to social success . . . or that refusal is a sign of weakness'. They 'must not feature or foster immoderate drinking', make any references to the 'buying of rounds of drinks', claim that alcohol has therapeutic qualities, or 'offer it expressly as a stimulant, sedative or tranquillizer'. While advertisements may 'refer to refreshment after physical performance, they must not give any impression that performance can be improved by drink', nor should they 'link drinking with driving or with the use of potentially dangerous machinery'. Liquor advertisements may not publicize competitions, claim or suggest 'that any drink can contribute toward sexual success', associate drinking with masculinity, or 'suggest that regular solitary drinking is acceptable'.*

(d) Advertising for Children

The Code contains three appendices, dealing respectively with advertising and children, financial advertising, and the advertising of medicines. The effects of television on children have been a subject of concern in every country with a television service, and during the great debate over commercial television the possibly bad influence of advertiser-controlled children's programmes was often brought up. The very strict rules for advertising on such programmes are a direct result of this concern, as well as of the reports received about children's programme excesses in the United States.[70]

The section of the IBA Code devoted to such advertising begins with a general proposition: 'No product or service may be advertised and no method of advertising may be used, in association with a programme intended for children or which large numbers of children are likely to see or hear, which might result in harm to them physically, mentally or morally. . . .'

The regulations lay down a code of conduct which many critics of American broadcasting would heartily endorse, because of its pertinence to advertising practices prevalent in the United States.[71] 'Advertisments must not directly urge children to purchase or ask their parents or others to make inquiries or purchases.' Furthermore:

No advertisement for a commercial product or service is allowed if it contains any appeal to children which suggests in any way that unless the children themselves buy or encourage other people to buy the product or service they will be failing in some duty or lacking in loyalty towards some person or organisation whether that person or organisation is the one making the appeal or not.

* The American Code (p. 5) states: 'The use of liquor and smoking in program content shall be de-emphasized. When shown, they should be consistent with thought and character development.' It also stipulates (p. 22) that 'Commercials involving beer and wine [should] avoid any representation of on-camera drinking'.

No advertisement is allowed which leads children to believe that if they do not own the product advertised, they will be inferior in some way to other children or that they are liable to be held in contempt or ridicule for not owning it.

Such products as alcoholic drinks, tobacco, and matches may not be advertised immediately before, during or after children's programmes. Advertisements featuring 'personalities associated with either ITV or BBC children's programmes and which promote products or services of special interest to children', and advertisements for children's medicines, must not be transmitted before 9 p.m.[72]

Advertisements for children's toys and games must give accurate price data, including the costs of batteries or other necessary accessories, and costs must not be minimized by the use of such words as 'only' or 'just'.[73] In accordance with good dental hygiene practice, 'Advertisements shall not encourage persistent sweet eating throughout the day nor the eating of sweet, sticky foods at bed-time'. Furthermore, advertisements for snack foods must not suggest that they 'may be substituted for proper meals'.

In the interests of safety, advertisements are never to show small children doing such things as playing in the street or crossing streets without due care; leaning dangerously out of windows or climbing cliffs; climbing to high shelves or reaching to get things from tables over their heads; or using matches, fire or electrical appliances in a way that might lead to their being burned or otherwise injured.[74] If an advertisement shows an open fire during a domestic scene, there always must be 'a fireguard clearly visible if a child is included in the scene'. Finally, children in advertisements must always be 'reasonably well-mannered and well-behaved'; must not be used to 'present or comment' on products about which they could not reasonably be expected to have 'direct interest or knowledge'; and must not 'be used to give formalised personal testimony', although they might make 'spontaneous comments on matters in which they have an obvious natural interest'.

(e) Financial Advertising

Appendix 2, dealing with financial advertising, specifies the 'kinds of investments and savings facilities [which] may be advertised'. It permits insurance, and credit and loan advertising, but excludes advertisments for commodity investments. The 1977 revision of the Code for the first time permitted stock exchange members to advertise, provided they did not recommend investments or comment on individual securities. Interesting is the requirement that actors 'may not purport to be chairmen, directors, officers or other employees of an advertiser', and that no one at all may 'give independent professional advice on any investment offer'. Furthermore, 'celebrated entertainers, writers or sportsmen may not present, endorse or recommend any investment or savings offer'. The Code also stipulates that advertisements for life insurance annuity plans must 'contain clear and unambiguous reference to the fact that the value of assets can move both up and down'.

(f) Medical Advertising

Second only to the space given to advertising and children is the attention to medical advertising.[75] All such advertising must comply with the Medicines Act 1968 which regulates medicine advertising generally. One rule laid down elsewhere in the Code has an obvious application here:

> Scientific terms, statistics, quotations from technical literature and the like must be used with a proper sense of responsibility to the ordinary viewer or listener. Irrelevant data and jargon must not be used to make claims appear to have a scientific basis they do not possess. Statistics of limited validity should not be presented in such a way as to make it appear they are universally true.[76]

'Unacceptable products or services' include, smoking cures, treatments for alcoholism, contact lenses, hair and scalp clinics, haemorrhoid treatments, pregnancy tests and 'hypnosis, hypnotherapy, psychology, psychoanalysis or psychiatry'.[77] The revision of 1977 permitted advertisements by reducing clinics, provided they offer 'treatments . . . based on dietary control'. Doctors, dentists, veterinarians and other health professionals may not make presentations 'which give the impression of professional advice or recommendations', nor are there to be 'reference to approval of, or preference for [a product] by the medical or veterinary professions'.

The rules for family planning and contraceptive advertising were changed during the year 1978–9. Originally, all advertisements for contraceptives were prohibited, although this did not 'preclude advertising of official or officially sponsored family planning services'. The new 'guidelines' permit such advertisements, but only if accepted through 'official or officially sponsored family planning centres', and if it is 'made clear that advice in alternative methods is available and should be sought. Advertisements may be addressed to the unmarried as well as to the married, but pre-marital sex may not be explicitly condoned. Great care will be needed to avoid giving undue offence.'

(g) Amount and Length of Advertising

In addition to specifications about content, there also is regulation of the amount and length of advertising.[78] The law expressly prohibits any advertising during religious services: (though not during all religious programmes), and rules drawn up jointly by the Authority and the Minister prohibit advertising in broadcasts of royal ceremonies or state occasions and in programmes for schools. Two-minute insulation periods without advertising are required before and after all such programmes, although for school broadcasts the separation requirement is 2 minutes before and 1 minute afterwards.

The Authority boasts that there is no internal advertising in over half of its television programmes, including—in addition to the examples mentioned above—all devotional programmes; some half-hour plays; some children's programmes; and Parliamentary programmes. ITN's 30-minute evening newscast includes one 2-minute advertising break at about the midpoint. Occasionally a programme which under the rules could include at least one middle break, runs for 55 or 56 minutes without interruption, if its total impact is thereby enhanced. While viewing ITV in the early summer of 1976, I encountered an example of this on one of the *World at War* programmes, a documentary series dealing with World War II. The programme was a moving exposition of Nazi Germany's treatment of minority races, and the uninterrupted presentation heightened the total dramatic impact.

The Second Schedule of the Act lays down some general and specific 'Rules as to Advertisements'.[79] Advertisements 'must be clearly distinguishable . . . and recognisably separate'; 'audible matter in advertisements must not be excessively noisy or strident'; and the amount of advertising time 'shall not be so great as to detract from the value of the programmes as a medium of information, education, entertainment'.

Introduced for the first time in the legislation of 1963 were clauses enabling the IBA to instruct programme companies as to the actual times when advertisements may be broadcast, the total amount of time to be assigned to them, the intervals which may elapse between them, as well as the exclusion of advertisements from specified broadcasts.[80] At the outset the Authority specified a maximum of 6 minutes of advertising during each hour of television, averaged over the day's programmes, with a normal maximum during any single clock hour (6 to 7 p.m., 7 to 8 p.m., etc.) of 7 minutes. In a programme between 20 and 40 minutes in length, the Authority now allows one advertising break of up to 2½ minutes; in programmes between 40 and 70 minutes long, one break of up to 3 minutes and two of up to 2½ minutes. But these must occur at 'natural breaks' in the programme.

One of the most widely discussed provisions of the legislation has been the requirement of the Second Schedule that advertisements be placed only 'at the beginning or the end of the programme or in natural breaks therein'—and Britain has argued over 'natural breaks' even more than the United States has discussed 'middle commercials'.[81] It is not difficult to find places for commercials at certain points in athletic contests, or between the acts of plays. But what about plays written for television, when the writer is told beforehand to include a given number of 'natural breaks'? How are the places for advertisements during telecasts of theatrical films determined? Some critics have claimed that the problem is not one of 'natural' but of 'manufactured breaks', while the Authority defends itself by saying that 'a break is not unnatural because it has been contemplated and foreseen; it must be judged, when it comes, for what it is'.[82]

(h) Radio Advertising

There is a separate set of rules for radio advertising, though in the main they parallel those for television.[83] However, radio advertising may take up to '9 minutes in a full clock hour'. Although there is no limit on the length of commercial radio breaks, it is recommended that they be held to 3 minutes. A series of advertisement spots lasting 5 minutes is 'permissible provided that the advertising nature of the material is closely established', although the maximum of 9 minutes per hour would still apply. The rules for radio advertising warn that 'undue repetition' may arouse 'irritation and annoyance', with the result that 'the programme companies and the advertiser [can lose] the good will of potential customers'.[84] For that reason it is recommended that 'advertisers planning an intensive campaign should be encouraged to produce more than one commercial and companies should ensure that a product or service is not advertised more than four times in any one clock-hour'.

Since the programme companies are legally obligated to enforce the Authority's advertising rules, they too have drawn up brochures which both repeat and extend the Authority's regulations. In 1962 they began publishing a series of 'notes of Guidance on Television Advertising', dealing with such subjects as the technical standards for film, slides, and video tape, and the procedures to be followed in getting copy and advertisements approved. To some extent these consist of direct quotations from the law and the Authority's Code; in other instances, they stipulate additional requirements imposed by the companies themselves. For example, preliminary consultation is advised in the preparation of advertisements for toilet paper, feminine hygiene, and foundation garments.[85] Sex is not to be treated so as to 'cause offence or be regarded as coarse or carrying any undesirable innuendo.'

PROGRAMME CONTRACTORS

Parliament did not want the ITA to produce programmes as does the BBC, and accordingly legislated that, for the most part, 'the programmes broadcast by the Authority shall ... be provided ... by "programme contractors" '. Under the British system, these contractors are somewhat the counterparts of America's broadcasting stations, and their contracts with the Authority are roughly equivalent to the licences received by American stations from the FCC. But the rules in Britain are much stricter and enforcement is both quicker and more certain.

In 1971 the IBA described its programme companies—legally 'programme contractors'—as

'profit-making bodies ... obtaining their capital from shareholders to whom the boards of directors are responsible and financing their ... operations from the sale of advertising in the programmes. They are the private enterprise element in the dual system of which the Authority is the representative of the public interest.[86]

The law requires that the programme companies be British-owned and controlled, and that they have no connections with advertising agencies, phonograph record manufacturers, music publishers, or theatrical employment agencies. Once constituted, they may not change ownership or corporate nature without the Authority's approval.[87]

There are various regulations pertaining to media cross-ownership, particularly in regard to newspapers. Effective with the legislation of 1963, either the Authority or the Minister—after consultation with the other, and with the approval of both Houses of Parliament—may suspend the contracts of programme companies if it appears to them that the participation of newspaper shareholders 'led or is leading to results which are contrary to the public interest'.[88] The law devotes almost two pages to the conditions under which newspapers may be shareholders in local radio programme companies.[89] No television programme company may have a controlling interest in a radio station serving the area of its television franchise.[90]

The 1954 Act did not limit the length of the contracts to be signed with the programme companies, and so the first ones were set to run for 10 years or until the expiration of the law in 1964, whichever came first. But because of dissatisfaction with the performance of some contractors, a 6-year limitation was added in 1963, only to be extended to 8 years by the 1980 law.[91] All contracts are renewable, although in the future the Authority may follow the procedure with television introduced for radio contracts, that is, awarding contracts for an initial period of 3 years, with a 1-year 'roll'—an annual extension on a yearly basis if the company is performing satisfactorily.[92] Recognizing the importance of news broadcasting, the 1963 and subsequent acts specified that there should be at least one organization to provide network news service for all television programme companies.[93] Actually, however, Independent Television News (ITN) was organized at the very beginning, and the legislation merely confirmed a practice already in effect.

The original and all subsequent legislation have required 'adequate competition to supply programmes between a number of programme contractors independent of each other both as to finance and as to control'.[94] Because the companies are expected to exchange programmes on a network basis, the 1963 law empowered the Authority to instruct them to do so, as well as to resolve whatever financial differences might arise during such exchanges.[95]

All contracts must provide for two types of payments from the companies: what are commonly known as 'rentals', set by the Authority to cover its own capital and operating costs; and 'additional payments', usually referred to as 'the levy', first authorized by the 1963 law to divert to the national treasury, via the IBA, a share of the profits received during years of very high returns. Foresightedly, the 1973 legislation—later reinforced by a clause in the 1980 law—provides for a similar procedure in the event of 'excessive profits' accruing to radio programme contractors.[96]

The Authority complained to the Pilkington Committee that its control over the programme companies was limited by the fact that, in case of infractions of the rules, it could impose only very minor or extreme penalties.[97] Accordingly, although the current law does not specifically empower the IBA to dissolve erring programme companies, all contracts must include a provision reserving to the Authority 'an absolute right' to suspend 'the Authority's obligations to transmit the programmes provided by the programme contractor' in case 'of any breaches' of the contract.[98] However, this severe penalty is to be applied only if the company 'has broken the contract on at least three occasions', and each time has been notified in writing by the Authority. Differences of opinion between the Authority and programme companies about the enforcement of this provision are to be arbitrated.

Among the most important and difficult responsibilities of the Authority is the selection of programme contractors. The Authority has often been charged with favouring applications from big business, and then of not holding the companies to their promises of performance, thus enabling them to make excessive profits. In any case, with the law and the accompanying Parliamentary debates as guides, the ITA in 1954 had to determine basic policies and select contractors.

One thing it had to decide was how to treat applications from companies with newspaper affiliations, in view of the theoretical desirability of diversified ownership of mass communications media. This question was widely discussed when it was learned that Conservative newspapers were associated with two of the first four companies chosen. But the Authority reasoned that if Parliament had intended to exclude newspapers, it would have said so, and that there was no reason to assume that a newspaper was any less likely than any other organization to develop good television programmes. Furthermore, after 30 years of BBC monopoly, no one else had broadcasting experience, so it was natural to look to the other media for contractors. As things turned out, newspapers from the start have been among the major shareholders in both television and radio, although the Authority's policy in regard to press holdings has varied from case to case, much as with the American FCC.[99]

Decisions also had to be made about financial requirements for contractors. Selection solely or largely on the basis of capacity to pay would have violated the Television Act both in letter and spirit, since the law did not charge the ITA to earn money for itself or the Treasury. But it did insist on programmes of 'high quality', and commercial television was expected to be—and indeed was—a money-loser at the outset. Anticipating this, major companies had to be prepared to lose a good deal of money initially; during its first 7 months on the air, for example, Associated Television in London lost £602,750, while the other London contractor, Associated Rediffusion, lost some £2,880,350 in its first 2 years. When the contracts were originally let, of course, no one expected programme company returns to be excessive. Wide concern over profits developed only after several years of operation showed how successful a commercial television monopoly could be.

Another problem for the Authority was its relationship with the programme companies. Should it be their leader, supervisor, or public relations spokesman? The law left no doubt as to the Authority's ultimate responsibility, or as to its legal obligation to enforce programme standards; but the Authority declared that it would rather work in partnership with the companies than sit in constant judgement over them. Later this attitude was severely criticized by observers who complained that, although the ITA was supposed to interpret and apply the rules, the programme companies in fact dominated the operation, with the Authority serving as their front and apologist.[100]

Under the law, the Authority could have run Independent Television centrally, much as the BBC does its services, but it chose instead to establish programme companies on a regional basis. In fact, the Annan Committee recommended that the name of the Authority be changed to Regional Television Authority, pointing out that the companies had 'stressed their regional role'.[101] In view of the legal requirement for competition between companies, the Authority decided to break up the country into regions; choose contractors on a competitive basis; encourage them to compete through exchanging programmes by network; and divide the time in each of the three major population areas between two different contractors.

On 24 August 1954, the Authority advertised for contractors and received twenty-five applications. After interviews, four contractors were selected for the first three stations. Stated as the main criterion for choice was the ability 'to produce as a long-term and continued operation balanced programmes of high quality'. Since the outlook was for months or even years of deficit operations, it was announced that only groups with large capital resources should apply, even though this requirement greatly narrowed the field. 'The Authority chose, therefore, from among the applicants who appeared to it to be adequately provided with finance, those it judged the most likely to put on well-balanced and high quality programmes.'[102] Accordingly, two companies served the London area, one Monday to Friday and the other on Saturday and Sunday; one of these and a third company shared the Midlands area, while the second Midlands company divided time with a fourth company in northern England. By 1964, the rest of the United Kingdom was divided among ten other contractors, each operating on a 7-day basis.

ITV's programme companies in the main have been, and are, owned and operated by big business, and often by such related media as newspapers, cinemas, and theatres. The important individual stockholders are mainly executives in companies with major interests in commercial broadcasting, but the principal executives are drawn from such non-broadcasting fields as finance, theatre, publishing, and the cinema.[103]

Among themselves the original companies organised what is in effect another programme company, Independent Television News (ITN), to previde network news and features for all ITV stations. ITN is owned and operated jointly by all the other programme companies, although the IBA must approve the appointment of its head (editor), and the IBA Director-General attends all ITN Board of Directors meetings. Independent Television Publications, Ltd, which has a subsidiary book publisher, ITV Books, Ltd, is another corporation owned jointly by all the companies in Great Britain and Northern Ireland (excluding, therefore, Channel Television), whose principal publication is *TV Times*, issued in fifteen different editions, one for each part of the country.[104]

In order to ensure close liaison between the Authority and the programme companies, all of the contracts provide for participation in a Standing Consultative Committee and a Programme Policy Committee, made up of several representatives from the Authority and one from each company. So that they may speak with one voice in relations with outside groups, the companies in May 1958 formed the Independent Television Companies Association (ITCA), with a governing board composed of programme company personnel.[105] The ITCA deals with company engineering, network programming, advertisement acceptance, overseas relations, performance rights, and labour relations. In 1968 the ITCA, acting jointly with the Incorporated Society of British Advertisers and the Institute of Practitioners in Advertising, set up the Joint Industry Committee for Television Advertising Research (JICTAR) to measure the British television audiences (see below, pp. 345–6).

In September 1963, as the contracts approached their expiration date in the following year, the Authority invited applications for new contracts, and received

22 applications for the 14 franchises, the applicants including all of the 14 existing contractors. Some groups, in fact, applied for more than one contract.[106] However, because of uncertainties about the outlook for a second ITV channel, and of the complications expected to coincide with the change from the 405-line VHF to the proposed 625-line UHF system, the Authority decided to extend until 1967 the contracts of all the existing companies.[107]

In 1966, as the time approached for re-application, the Authority announced that, beginning in 1968, when the new contracts would take effect, the geographical configuration of some of the service areas would be changed, and that except for London, which as the country's major metropolitan centre would still be divided between two companies, the remaining thirteen regions would have one contractor apiece. In February 1967, applications were invited, and thirty five were received from sixteen new and fourteen existing programme companies.[108] Many of these companies combined strong financial backing with support from some of the country's best-known newspapers, academic foundations, publishers, magazines, pension funds, banks and insurance companies, and cited the names of men and women prominent in politics, publishing, acting and broadcasting.

There followed what one observer described as a 'frenzied scramble . . . a genteel British version of such other financial stampedes as the gold rush in Alaska, the uranium panic in Canada and the nickel dash in Australia.'[109] According to this account, 'the competing consortia jostled and conspired like medieval barons as they tried to shape themselves into images that might appeal to Lord Hill and his twelve ITA Governors.'

The Authority's choices were announced on a Sunday, 11 June 1967, in order to minimize the effects of the decisions on the stock market values of the applicant companies. Contracts were given to eleven existing companies, three entirely new ones, and one which was an amalgamation of two existing companies. In announcing the allocations, ITA chairman Hill said that 'quality . . . programme service' was regarded as the main criterion in choosing companies. But he went on to ask: 'Must the doors of Independent Television remain forever closed to new applicants, however good they are? If the answer is "yes" then those companies already appointed are there for all time. But the Authority's answer must of course be "no".'[110]

Associated Television and Rediffusion, which previously had divided the London contract, were combined into Thames Television, to programme for the London area from Monday until 7 p.m. Friday. The original London company, Associated Television, although given the whole week in the Midlands, was replaced in London by a new group, London Weekend Television; this group, however, underwent some major financial, personnel and programme policy changes before finally settling into its new task.

In 1980 there were fifteen companies (plus ITN), which could be categorized as five large companies serving the major metropolitan and population areas, five large regional companies, and five small regional companies.[111] The rentals charged depended upon the financial potentials of the areas served, and not at all upon the Authority's costs in building and operating transmitters to cover the population (see below pp. 113–15).

IBA plans announced in February 1979 for new contracts to take effect in January 1982 were replaced by a subsequent set of proposals published in January 1980.[112] The deadline for the receipt of applications—both from new groups and existing contractors, for 6 year franchises—was set as 9 May 1980, with applicants to supply information about themselves and their programme plans much like that required by the American FCC of applicants for station licences. (It was specified, however, that the announcement was to be regarded as provisional until the Broadcasting Act 1980, then before Parliament, was finally enacted.) Public meetings were to be held throughout the country from June through October for discussion of the competing applicants and their proposals. IBA decisions on contract awards were scheduled for the end of 1980, giving the franchise-winners a year to complete their plans before beginning operations on 1 January 1982.

The Authority intended to continue the fifteen franchise areas much as before, although with provision for more regional programming in two new 'dual regions' in the East and West Midlands and in South and South-East England. The only innovative feature was for 'a nationwide breakfast-time service'. Despite the financial failure of the one experiment in such programming held several years before, the Authority invited applications for a 7 day service between 6 and 9.15 a.m. The announcement also referred to the anticipated ITV 2 service: 'The contract particulars provide for subscriptions from the contractors . . . for the financing of the Fourth Channel which it is hoped will be broadcasting, under separate IBA arrangements, at about the end of [1982].' Successful applicants will be expected to sell commercial time on the ITV 2 transmitters in their areas, and to cover the deficits—expected for the first few years, at least—from their first channel profits.

Contractual relations between the IBA and its radio programme companies follow the television pattern. The Authority appoints the companies, supervises their programming, controls their advertising, and operates their transmitters.[113] Although there was press participation in a number of the initial nineteen companies, and three newspaper chains had holdings in more than one company, the IBA has stated that 'in no company does even the aggregate of all newspapers' holdings approach a controlling interest'. Of the first thirteen companies, 10 per cent or less of the shares of eight were held by television programme companies, while five had no such relationship at all. Rentals are proportionate to potential income, although the London news and information station pays less, in view of its higher programme costs. All contracts provide for a 'secondary rental', which was 'conceived as a method of securing additional funds from the system, as and when a certain level of profit is achieved, to promote certain general purposes to the greater advantage of this new broadcasting service and its listeners'.[114] In addition, under the terms of the Sound Broadcasting Act, reinforced by the Broadcasting Act 1980, the government, if it believes the radio contractors are earning too high profits, may direct that 'additional payments'—a radio 'levy'—be made to the national treasury.

Over fifty applications were received for the first dozen stations. The first nineteen contracts approved were set for 3 years with a 1 year 'roll'; that is, annual yearly extension if 'towards the end of each year on the air, the company is considered to be making satisfactory progress'.[115]

THE ITA AND THE COMMITTEES

Chapter 2 on the BBC Constitution (pp. 7–13) reviewed the reports of the several government committees whose investigations contributed to the evolution of the Corporation. The IBA too has been subjected to committee scrutiny, and its structure and operations also underwent changes in consequence. Perhaps the fact that most of its original officers lacked expertise in broadcasting as well as in business administration explains in part the shortcomings of the ITA during its first decade. At any rate, the experience of its first 25 years, and the strengthening of its staff through the addition of experienced broadcasting executives, have led to a different situation now than existed in earlier days.

The Television Act of 1954 set up the Authority for 10 years, with the expectation that, as 1964 approached, a high-level government committee would investigate and report on all aspects of British broadcasting, after which Parliament would determine future policy. Before this happened, however, an inquiry and report in 1959 by the House of Commons Committee of Public Accounts documented some of the criticisms then being made of the programme companies' very high profits. Then came the appointment of the Pilkington Committee in 1960, whose 1962 report also was very severe, as was a 1972 report from the House of Commons Select Committee on Nationalized Industries. The most recent inquiry was that of the Annan Committee.

The position to be taken later by the Pilkington Committee was presaged by the Committee of Public Accounts of the House of Commons in 1959, at a time when high programme company profits were a subject of wide public discussion.[116]

In its report the committee said it was 'unfortunate' that rental rates were not reviewed more frequently, in view of the obvious capacity of the programme contractors to pay more, and suggested that future rentals, 'representing the contractors' capacity to pay, should be arrived at by competition, provided that the Authority judge the highest bidder to be of standing and technically and financially competent to provide the service'.[117]

The Pilkington Committee made the first comprehensive analysis of British broadcasting after the advent of ITV. Although its basic suggestions for restructuring Independent Television were not accepted by the government, its report nevertheless provided much ammunition for the critics of the commercial system, focused attention on ITA shortcomings, and led to the passage of the Television Act 1963 which corrected many of them.

While praising the BBC, the report was highly critical of the Authority, which, it believed, held 'too negative a conception of the purposes of broadcasting. And discounting the influence of the medium, they scaled down their responsibilities.'[118] Therefore, it was easy for the Authority to assume that its role was 'primarily and necessarily passive', a situation which 'disturbed' the committee. It found that the Authority was 'not in effective control of Independent Television', because it was serving more as 'advocate' than as controller. 'The initiative is held by the programme contractors, and for most practical purposes, by the four major companies', whose only concern is greater revenues.[119] The report spoke of too many stereotyped and violent programmes, poor advertising control, too many newspaper stockholders, and failure to control the power of the large contractors, who grew rich while the smaller companies lacked sufficient resources to make good programmes.

The committee recommended that the BBC be authorized to provide a second television service, with the ITA not to do so until it proved itself worthy.[120] 'The following major changes', concluded the committee, should be made in the Constitution and organization of Independent Television: 'the Authority to plan the programming' and 'to sell advertising time'; 'Programme companies to produce and sell to the Authority programme items for inclusion in the programme planned by the Authority'; and 'the Authority, after making provision for reserves, to pay any surplus revenue to the Exchequer'.[121] Even though many of the 500 organizations and individuals giving evidence were very critical of the Authority, it may be that the Committee's severe judgements did not accurately reflect public opinion, since a survey conducted by *The Sunday Times* indicated that only 18 per cent of a sample polled agreed with the Committee's judgements.[122] The Conservative Government then in power passed over the Committee's proposals for restructuring the Authority, but did enact legislation providing for tighter control along with a levy on profits.

Formal reactions came in White Papers issued in July and December 1962. The first of these, written before the government was able to digest the entire report, delayed reactions to most of its recommendations, although it did accept the recommendation that advertising magazines be abolished and subliminal advertising prohibited, even though the IBA had never done the latter.[123] The second White Paper firmly rejected the Pilkington Committee's proposals for changes in relationships between the Authority and the programme companies, but did instruct 'the Authority . . . [to] take a commanding position in the affairs of IT', and to review all contracts 'at least every three years'.[124] There also was a veiled threat that if programme company output 'failed to measure up to promise then the renewal of contracts would be in peril'.

Although the White Paper disagreed with the Committee's proposals that maximum percentages of press shares in programme companies be set by law, the 1963 legislation did direct the Authority to 'take power in its contracts to suspend or cancel the contract of a company should newspaper holdings give rise to abuse'.[125] In response to the criticisms of advertising, the government said that the Authority's advertising advisory committee should be strengthened; that more attention should be paid to the effects of advertising on children; and, that the Authority was to 'assume a more formal and direct control of the executive decisions relating to advertisements'. Although it did not devote much space to programme standards, the White Paper indicated that the government was seriously concerned about violence and trivality, and that it would discuss the subject with both the BBC and the ITA.

The Television Act 1963, in addition to extending the life of the Authority to 31

July 1976, strengthened the control of the ITA over its programme companies. One of its most important clauses was a provision for 'additional payments'—commonly known as 'the levy'—to siphon into the national treasury programme company excess profits, although this was not achieved without an extended Parliamentary battle. Despite an intensive lobbying campaign by the larger programme companies to get another channel for ITV, and to defeat the proposed levy, the bill passed.[126]

Retrospectively, the programme companies told the Annan Committee over a decade later:

> Shocked by the abrasive criticisms of the Pilkington Report and confronted with a new and more inclusive television Act, the companies and the ITA took stock of their position. The Authority began to exercise firmer control in the balance of programming. The companies were required to do more current affairs and other serious programmes. Axes fell on quiz games. An admonitory finger was pointed at weaker areas such as programmes for children. . . . In 1966 a half-hour *News at Ten* was urged on the companies, an act for which they since have had cause to be grateful.[127]

The Authority also was taken to task by the Select Committee on Nationalized Industries in 1972. Although its investigation was not as extensive as those of the Beveridge and Pilkington Committees, its published report, which ran to some 400 pages, again rendered severe judgements about ITA programmes, finances, advertising, and public accountability. Among other things, the committee looked with disfavour upon the circumstances surrounding the creation of London Weekend Television in 1968, the new organization chosen to provide programmes in London on Saturdays and Sundays, which soon after beginning operations faced financial disaster.

Perhaps for that reason, the company soon forgot the adventuresome programme plans which had been a major factor in winning its contract, and instituted an old favourites pattern, a change justified—in unfortunate terms—by the company's Programme Controller as follows: 'The first duty of a commercial television station is to survive. What do you think the public regards television as—a teaching medium?'[128] Thereafter, London Weekend was reconstituted; but the Committee commented that 'the claims which . . . gave L.W.T. the London week-end contract have never been published, a matter of some importance in view of the subsequent changes in management and shareholdings of the . . . company'.[129]

As to other items, the Committee thought that 'the Authority's reluctance to take a positive and initiating role' in programme supervision might be the result of its small staff, and believed that the regional companies had too much trouble getting programmes of merit into the network.[130] The Committee indicated a need for 'the provisions of the Act concerning natural breaks [to] be more strictly observed', and recommended that the Authority consider bunching advertisements up to a half an hour at a time, 'at the start of the evening's viewing', as was done in Switzerland, Italy and Holland.[131] Although 'its research and the letters it received' indicated few complaints about either specific advertisements or advertisements in general, the committee 'wondered whether the Authority should not adopt the practice of the [American] Fairness Doctrine . . . enabling consumer associations . . . to be given time on the air to answer the claims of advertisers'.[132]

In spite of whatever improvements resulted from the Pilkington inquiry, the Select Committee complained that ITV still was concerned more with audience size than significant programming, and that in comparison with the BBC, it 'produced a far smaller percentage of documentaries, hobbies, science, travel programmes and plays, and instead a far higher percentage of feature films during prime time'.[133] Finally, the committee recommended that no decision be taken on the fourth channel except as part of a general review of United Kingdom broadcasting.[134]

By the time the Annan Committee reported in March 1977, IBA services had improved greatly over what they had been at the time of the Pilkington report 15 years earlier, and its verdict therefore was much more favourable, although the Authority failed to get what it most wanted—a recommendation to receive the fourth television channel.[135] The committee also recommended that the Authority's radio services be combined with the local radio services of the BBC and assigned to a new Local Broadcasting Authority. Thereafter, the IBA would be renamed the Regional Television Authority.

Observing that the general public 'made hardly any suggestions for the use of the fourth channel', the committee proposed that it be given to a new Open Broadcasting Authority (OBA), in order to extend the range and type of programming, rather than continuing 'the present duopoly of BBC and IBA'.[136] OBA programmes, said the committee, would be provided by educational agencies, individual ITV companies, and a variety of other independent producers. The service would be financed through a combination of advertising and grants, something like the Public Broadcasting Service in the United States. But recognizing that there might not be sufficient funds to start up a fourth channel in the near future, the committee recommended delaying 'until the nation's economy will permit the kind of service which we have outlined. This may not be until the 1980s'.

After noting that its recommendations probably would 'not be welcomed in some quarters', the committee went on to say that in its opinion:

an ITV 2 will engage in a self-destructive battle for the ratings. We believe that to perpetuate the duopoly would be to stultify new initiatives in the formation of independent small production groups, which could bring new life and variety to television . . . . We think that our scheme is integral for the philosophy of our Report—namely to help broadcasting to evolve rather than ossify. If adopted in the 1980s, it would lead to better programmes, more diverse programmes, more socially useful programmes, and more enjoyable programmes for hundreds of thousands of people.

Nevertheless, the committee also praised ITV, noting that its proportion of serious programmes had increased, 'and that Independent Television, while remaining popular, has improved in quality'. All the educators who gave testimony 'said they considered both BBC and ITV provided programmes of the highest quality'; and the committee also remarked that ITN news was better than that of the BBC. Still, much of the Independent Television output was 'settled in well-worn grooves, safe, stereotyped and routine in its production', while some of the American films were 'deplorable'. The committee also recommended stricter control over advertising, and a reduction of press holdings in the programme companies. The 522 pages of the report contain many other comments on ITV programmes, some of which will be cited later in the course of this book.

In July 1978, the Labour Government issued a White Paper announcing its intention to establish an Open Broadcasting Authority 'to supervise a new service on the fourth television channel', and to extend the IBA's 'supervisory responsibilities . . . to embrace cable services'.[137] In view of its long campaign to acquire a second channel, the IBA was greatly disappointed by this announcement.

But the victory of the Conservatives in the May 1979 election changed all this, and led to a mention in the Queen's Speech of 15 May 1979, giving the Authority responsibility for the fourth channel, subject to 'strict safeguards' ensuring programmes of high quality, with opportunities for independent producers to contribute to the output.[138] This time it was the IBA's turn to rejoice. In a public address on 14 September of the same year, William Whitelaw, the Home Secretary, spelled out some of these 'strict safeguards'. Although the new channel would be supervised by the IBA and supported by advertising, the IBA 'will be expected not to allow rivalry for ratings between the two channels . . . nor to allow scheduling designed to obtain for each the largest possible audiences over the week'. Rather, its overall objective would be to offer a new and distinctive service, with special programmes for minorities not currently served. Initially, it would be a single nationally networked channel, although regional variations might be introduced later on. Its programmes for Wales would be scheduled cooperatively with those of the BBC so that viewers could have programmes in Welsh on one channel and in English on the other three.

Hoping to allay concerns that the big programme companies would dominate the fourth channel, Whitelaw said that its programmes should come from the regional ITV companies and independent producers as well as the major ITV companies, and that the IBA 'will be expected to make arrangements for the largest practicable proportion of programmes . . . to be supplied by organisations and persons other than the companies contracted to provide programmes on ITV-1'. But news would all come from ITN, in view of the high costs of setting up another news company. The starting date for all of this was set as the autumn of 1982.

Parliamentary consideration of the new Broadcasting Bill was delayed for various reasons, one being cabinet concern over losing revenues from the levy on ITV 1 profits because of the need to draw on them to support ITV 2—at least—during its early years. When the bill was finally introduced in February 1980, it followed closely the forecast given by Home Secretary Whitelaw in his September 1979 address, and most of its main features survived final passage.

The Authority is to create a new subsidiary to operate the fourth channel— referred to as Service 2—nationwide, although its programmes are to come from many sources, including ITV 1 contractors and independent producers, with the latter providing 'a substantial proportion'. In any case, ITV 2 is not to be a replica of ITV 1, since the Authority is to ensure that the programmes contain 'a suitable proportion of matter calculated to appeal to tastes and interests not generally catered to by Service 1; . . . to ensure that a suitable proportion of the programmes are of an educational nature; . . . [and] to encourage innovation and experiment in the form and content of programmes'. There is to be 'a proper balance' of subject-matter within each and between the two services. Special consideration is to be given to programmes for Wales, which are to contain 'a suitable proportion of matter in Welsh'.

Although programming for ITV 2 will be the responsibility of a subsidiary created especially for that purpose, and not of the ITV 1 contractors, the latter may receive payments for advertisements inserted in ITV 2 programmes in their respective areas; but taken together with other government and IBA pronouncements, it is clear that since ITV 2 receipts are expected to fall considerably short of needs, the ITV 1 contractors will be required to draw upon their ITV 1 profits to cover the deficit.

Other sections of the Broadcasting Act 1980 extend the life of the IBA through 1996; create a Broadcasting Complaints Commission to consider complaints of 'unjust or unfair treatment' or of 'infringement of privacy' by either IBA or BBC programmes; legalize a levy on ILR profits like that previously laid on ITV contractors; extend contractors' possible franchise life from 6 to 8 years; authorize the IBA to franchise either existing or new contractors to operate telex services commercially; add to the existing provisions relative to the exclusion from programmes of the opinions of the Authority and its contractors; and require the IBA to appoint advisory committees for Scotland, Wales and Northern Ireland (which it already had, even though not so required by law).

It is said by all concerned that the second service will go on the air towards the end of 1982, but it is always possible that national financial or material shortages may delay this date. In any case, only after ITV 2 has broadcast for a while can judgements be made about its supervision or programming, or about its relationships to and effects on Britain's other three television networks.

6 The Technical Facilities of British Broadcasting

Engineering is basic to broadcasting. Without transmitters, there can be no broadcasts. Without studios and other originating facilities, there can be no programmes. Unless there is an orderly allocation of radio frequencies and television channels, the best broadcasts would be meaningless jumbles of interfering sounds and pictures. Students of broadcast regulation and programming sometimes mistakenly assume that the electronic problems of broadcasting concern only engineers, whereas, in fact, some knowledge of the technical aspects is essential to an understanding of the social role of radio and television.

THE INTERNATIONAL ALLOCATION OF RADIO FREQUENCIES AND TELEVISION CHANNELS*

Since broadcast signals do not stop at national boundaries, there must be international agreements on spectrum use and frequency assignments. First, global agreements must allocate the various parts of the broadcast spectrum for optimum use. Thereafter, regional conferences, dealing with large geographical areas like Europe, North America, and Asia, must assign channels so as to minimize

---

* As defined in the International Telecommunication Convention of 1965, the word 'radio' includes, among other things, sound transmissions—usually called 'radio' in the United States, but sometimes referred to as 'sound radio' or 'sound broadcasting' in the United Kingdom—and television (International Telecommunication Union, *International Telecommunication Convention . . .*, Montreux, 1965, Annex 2, #417). 'Broadcasting', according to the Convention, is 'a radiocommunication service in which the transmissions are intended for direct reception by the general public. This . . . may include sound transmissions, television transmissions, or other types of transmissions.' (Similar definitions are given in the American *Communications Act of 1934*, #3 (a,b,c).) The word 'broadcasting', therefore, refers only to radio and television programmes intended for reception by the general public, and not to such point-to-point radio services as ship-to-shore, amateur, or police communications.

Certain common broadcasting terms have different meanings in the United Kingdom and the United States. When used at all in Britain, the word 'station' usually means a transmitter, rather than a single studio centre–single transmitter combination as in the United States. However, each BBC and IBA local radio 'station' has two transmitters, one AM and one FM. Seldom is a single transmitter programmed independently: normally two or more are joined to cover an area or region. 'Channel' may refer to a single television transmitter, just as Americans say 'Channel 2' or 'Channel 10' to identify a specific station, or to an entire national network—'the Fourth Channel', for example.

interference among transmitters in different countries operating on the same or adjacent frequencies. Finally, each country must make its own domestic assignments.

There have been frequent international conferences on broadcasting allocations since the early years of the twentieth century. At present such meetings are coordinated by the International Tele-communication Union, which in 1947 became the specialized agency of the UN dealing with telecommunications.[1] One of the ITU's fundamental tasks is to divide the spectrum among the many services seeking to use it. Although the world is most familiar with radio and television broadcasting for the general public, the ITU recognizes some twenty different services.[2] Competition among these for spectrum space is just as keen as among applicants for individual broadcast facilities. Since the number of requests always exceeds the amount of space available in a ratio of about five to one, no allocation can be made that will satisfy all groups.

Whereas in 1906 it was sufficient to assign only a few radio bands, leaving users to choose the frequencies they wanted, by the time of the Washington Conference in 1927, the allocation table ranged from 19 kilohertz (kHz) to 60 megahertz (MHz).[3] At the 1947 Atlantic City Conference, it extended from 10 KHz to 10 gigahertz (GHz); it subsequently was pushed up to 40 GHz at the 1959 Geneva Conference; and at the World Administrative Conference on Space Telecommunications in Geneva in 1971, there were allocations up to 12 GHz for satellite and terrestrial services, and in the regions of 42 and 86 GHz for broadcast satellite service.

In allocating bands, the 1959 Geneva Radio Conference divided the world into three regions, with reference to the propagation characteristics and spectrum needs of the several continents: Europe, USSR, Asia (excluding China), and Africa; North and South America and the Northeast Pacific; and Asia (excluding the USSR), Australia, New Zealand, and part of the Pacific. In Europe, but not the Americas, AM radio broadcasting is allocated to the band between 160 and 255 kHz (long-wave), and in both Europe and the Americas the band between 525 and 1605 kHz (medium-wave or standard broadcast.) Television allocations extend from 41 to 68 MHz (Band I—channels 1 to 5), and 174 to 216 MHz (to 223 in some countries) (Band III—channels 6 to 13) in Europe; and from 54 to 88 MHz (channels 2 to 6) and 174 to 216 MHz (channels 7 to 13) (the Very High Frequency band) in the Americas. Television also uses the band between 470 and 854 MHz (Bands IV and V—channels 21 to 68) in Europe, and between 470 and 890 MHz (channels 14 to 83) (the Ultra High Frequency band) in the United States. FM radio has allocations in the Very High Frequency band: between 66 and 73 MHz in Eastern Europe; between 87.5 and 104 MHz in Western Europe (Band II); and between 87.5 and 108 MHz in the Americas. In addition, a number of bands are assigned to short-wave broadcasting, these being much higher frequencies—or shorter wave—than the domestic service bands mentioned above.[4]

Once the spectrum is divided among the different types of services on a global basis, it is necessary to assign definite frequencies and channels to the countries in each area.[5] In Europe this has been done according to various plans, named after the cities in which they were drawn up Geneva (in 1926), Prague (1929), Lucerne

(1933), Montreux (1939), Copenhagen (1948) and Stockholm (in 1952 and 1961). The most recent of these, and the one under which radio allocations in the United Kingdom currently are made, was drawn up in Geneva in 1975 and came into effect on 23 November 1978.

Although these various plans have marked successive advances in the systematic assignment of channels, none of them has been entirely successful. In the first place, not all countries adhere to the conventions. Thus eighteen countries, wholly or partly within the European Broadcasting Area, were not parties to the 1948 Copenhagen convention. The USSR and other countries boycotted some meetings. The United States contributed to Europe's problems by operating high-power stations for the American forces and for international propaganda services in Germany after World War II.[6]

ALLOCATION PROBLEMS IN THE UNITED KINGDOM

Broadcast allocations in the United Kingdom are complicated by several factors: the proximity of the European continent, with many countries seeking spectrum space; the elongated shape of the United Kingdom itself; and the demands of the country's minority groups and geographical regions for special programme services.

The BBC and the IBA, it should be noted, have no control over the allocation of radio frequencies or television channels within the United Kingdom, nor have they any international status in arranging the assignment of facilities. The allocation problems dealt with in the United States by the FCC are in the United Kingdom the responsibility of the Home Secretary, along with all other technical matters pertaining to telephone, telegraph and broadcasting. In international negotiations, the United Kingdom is represented by official Home Office delegates, assisted by engineers from the BBC and IBA whenever broadcasting is involved.

The United Kingdom of Great Britain and Northern Ireland, which covers 94,209 square miles, is about equal in size to the two American states of New York and Pennsylvania, which together total 94,908 square miles. But the United Kingdom is far more populous than these two American states, having some 56,000,000 people to their 30,370,000.[7] Because of its configuration, however, the United Kingdom is more difficult to cover with radio and television signals than are New York and Pennsylvania. Great Britain is long from north to south and narrow from east to west, whereas New York and Pennsylvania are more compactly proportioned. Furthermore, the United Kingdom must provide a broadcasting service in Northern Ireland and the Isle of Man as well as to the Hebrides, Orkney, Shetland and Channel Islands, all of which are somewhat removed from the mainland.

Table 1 shows how the broadcasting frequencies allocated to the United Kingdom are assigned to BBC and IBA radio and television services.

TABLE 1   *Wavebands allotted to broadcasting in the United Kingdom*

Band	Frequencies	Use in United Kingdom
Long wave	160–255 kHz (1,875–1,176 m)	One frequency (200 kHz) assigned to BBC Radio 4.
Medium wave	525–1605 kHz (571–187 m)	Twenty-nine frequencies are assigned to the United Kingdom: Three (1053, 1089, and 1485 kHz) to BBC Radio 1; two (693 and 909 kHz) to Radio 2; two (1215 and 1197 kHz—the latter in the Cambridge area only)—to Radio 3. The transmitter on 200 kHz for Radio 4 is supplemented in some areas by transmitters on 603, 720, 1449, and 1485 kHz. There also are frequencies for BBC External Broadcasting to Europe, and for both BBC and ILR local radio.
Short wave	3,950–4,000 kHz (75 m band) 5,950–6,200 kHz (49 m band) 7,100–7,300 kHz (41 m band) 9,500–9,775 kHz (31 m band) 11,700–11,975 kHz (25 m band) 15,100–15,450 kHz (19 m band) 17,700–17,900 kHz (16 m band) 21,450–21,750 kHz (13 m band) 25,600–100 kHz (11 m band)	These frequencies are used as required by the BBC's External Services for broadcasting to European and overseas audiences. The frequencies chosen depend upon season and time of day.
Band I (very high frequency)	41–68 MHz	Five channels (1–5), 5 MHz wide, 405-line monochrome television for BBC 1.
Band II (very high frequency)	87.5–100 MHz (In certain European countries the band extends to 104 MHz, but in the UK it is limited as shown above.)	FM radio broadcasting: BBC and IBA.
Band III (very high frequency)	174–216 MHz	Eight channels (6–13), 5 MHz wide, 405-line monochrome television; BBC 1 and IBA.
Band IV (ultra high frequency)	470–582 MHz	Fourteen channels (21–34), 8 MHz wide, 625-line colour television: BBC 1, BBC 2, IBA, and 4th (programme when activated).

TABLE 1 *(Contd.)*

Band	Frequencies	Use in United Kingdom
Band V (ultra high frequency)	614–854 MHz	Thirty channels (39–68), 8 MHz wide, 625-line colour television: BBC 1, BBC 2 IBA, and 4th programme (when activated).
Band VI (super high frequency)	11,700–12,500 MHz	Terrestrial and satellite broadcasting.
Band VII (extremely high frequency)	41–43 GHz	Satellite broadcasting.
Band VIII (extremely high frequency)	84–86 GHz	Satellite broadcasting.

(Adapted from *BBC Handbook 1980*, p. 199.)

RADIO ASSIGNMENTS

Britain's problem always has been to get enough radio frequencies to provide an interference-free home service as well as some programmes for listeners in Europe.[8] Since 23 November 1978, long- and medium-wave assignments have been made under the plan drawn up in Geneva in 1975. The purpose of the new arrangement was to reduce night-time interference among European stations, but since the new plan assigns frequencies to some 2700 transmitters compared to 1450 under the old arrangement, it is by no means certain that things will improve; in fact, they may deteriorate. The United Kingdom situation is further complicated by the fact that in 1967 the BBC, and in 1973 the IBA, began operating local radio services, which placed still greater demands on the limited frequencies available.

The BBC reports that the 1978 frequency changes led to both improvements and deterioration in AM service, as Table 2 shows.[9] Radios 1 and 4 gained by the change, Radio 2 lost some night-time coverage, while Radio 3 lost both by day and night. But the Corporation states that, 'if Radio 3 had retained its original [AM] frequency, the night-time loss could eventually have been greater, for other

TABLE 2

Service	Radio 1		Radio 2		Radio 3		Radio 4	
Before/after frequency changes	Before	After	Before	After	Before	After	Before	After
Estimated percentage coverage of UK population (daytime)	87	96	98	98	92	87	87	98
Estimated percentage coverage of UK population (night-time)	38	55	85	65	71	38	64	91

countries are entitled to install high-power transmitters operating on this frequency'. When possible, auxiliary transmitters are being installed to improve reception.

With FM too, the United Kingdom has difficulty making assignments, although FM signals from all four services reach almost the entire population, provided that good aerials are installed where necessary. The United States does FM broadcasting between 87.5 and 108 MHZ, and in some European countries the band extends from 87.5 and 104 MHz; but in the United Kingdom it is limited to 87.5 to 100 MHz, the remainder being allocated to fire, ambulance, police and other mobile users.* The BBC began VHF radio broadcasting in 1965. Regular stereophonic broadcasting began in 1966, using the Pilot Tone System. Initially, it was used only for the Third Programme the British equivalent of a 'good music' service, but it now is on all services.[10] Both the BBC and the IBA have experimented with quadraphonic sound, although their systems are not entirely compatible, so that their broadcasts have been experimental in nature.[11] Almost all of the Independent Local Radio (ILR) services are carried by one low-power medium-wave AM and one VHF FM transmitter, the latter with stereo.[12] The AM transmitters range in power from 0.3 to 2 kilowatts (kW), except in London where they operate with 5.5 and 27.5 kW of power, respectively. The Effective Radiated Power of the IBA's FM transmitters varies from 0.05 to 5 kW.

TELEVISION ASSIGNMENTS

When the British went on the air in 1936 with the world's first regular television service, its 405-line system represented very high definition. The subsequent adoption of 525 lines by the United States, and then 625 lines by most of Europe, however, meant that Britain soon had the world's lowest definition. Therefore, when British UHF telecasting began in 1964, it was with the standard European 625-line system. (Table 1 shows the bands used by British television.)

By the late 1950s, it was clear that the United Kingdom would be limited to two—or at the most three—nationwide networks as long as it used only Bands I and III. In order to operate four or more services, therefore, it was necessary to move up into Bands IV and V, the approximate equivalent of America's UHF channels 14–83. If any change in line standards was to be made in the near future, it obviously should accompany a move to the higher frequencies, so it was decided to convert to the 625-line system.[13]

The advantages of change were obvious: picture quality would improve; scanning lines would be slightly less evident; the line-scan 'whistle' at 10 kc/s which had annoyed many viewers would be eliminated; and the international

* The United Kingdom also has some very low-power unauthorized 'pirate' stations operated by amateurs, whose total outlay may include only a transmitter worth £50 and studio equipment to match. They broadcast sporadically, for a few hours a day, programmes of recorded music, talk, interviews, and opinion, always subject, of course, to being taken off the air for operating illegally without a licence. Early in 1979 it was estimated that there were about thirty-two such units, including ten AM stations eight FM stations, and fourteen short-wave stations (*Time Out*, 23–29 March 1979).

exchange of programmes would be facilitated. Furthermore, if colour were added to the existing 405-line VHF transmissions, there would be more interference from continental stations than if Britain used 625-line UHF transmissions for its colour.[14] The only questions were: what colour system to adopt, and when to introduce it. As things turned out, Britain chose the PAL system because it appeared to be the best of the several systems available, because of its anticipated widespread use in that part of the world (France was the only western country not adopting it), and also in the hope of increasing the export of British-manufactured receivers.[15]

UHF broadcasting in Britain began with BBC 2 Monochrome transmissions in 1964, colour being added in 1967. BBC 1 and ITV began broadcasting on 625 lines in colour in 1969, thus making Britain the first country in the world to use UHF for its basic television transmissions. But 405-line monochrome broadcasts on VHF Bands I and III will continue into the 1980s, by which time all owners of VHF-only sets will have had time to replace them with newer model receivers. At some point in the future, it is likely that the VHF band will be reassigned to possibly two or more 625-line services for national coverage, although those plans are not yet completed.

At present, the BBC's 405-line monochrome programmes are broadcast by stations operating mainly on the five channels of Band I, although a few of its channels are in Band III. Approximately 99.5 per cent of the population is covered by these signals.[16] The IBA's stations, assigned to Channels 6–13 of Band III, reach approximately 98.7 per cent of the population. A total of forty-four frequencies are allocated for the two BBC and 1 IBA UHF services now being broadcast, and for ITV 2, expected to be activated in 1982. BBC 1, BBC 2, and ITV reach approximately 98 per cent of the population. The objective is to serve 99 per cent or more of the population with all three networks—or all four, when there is a fourth service—for which channel allocations have already been made.

Both BBC and IBA now originate programmes in colour on the 625-line standard, after which feeds to VHF transmitters are electronically converted to monochrome on the 405-line standard. Both organizations also can convert, with little or no loss of picture quality, from the American 525- to the British 625-line standard, and vice-versa, or from the old French 819-line standard to the British 625-line standard, and vice-versa.[17]

Both BBC and IBA operate all their own transmitters. This may seem self-evident to American broadcasters, but in many European countries the Post Office runs the transmitters, with the broadcasting organizations retaining technical responsibility only for studios. In the United Kingdom all long-distance lines for sound broadcasting, and radio relays and coaxial cables for television, are rented from the Post Office authorities, although both BBC and IBA have their own short-range relays for remote pickups plus some microwave links to transmitters. With minor exceptions, American practice is similar.

If two or more UHF stations are to be received at one point, it is important that their signals come from the same direction, even more so, in fact, than with VHF stations. Therefore, it was decided to co-site all BBC and IBA UHF transmitters serving the same areas.[18] Although initially facilities for only three networks were installed, space was reserved for four transmitters and aerials at all locations and legislation that became effective on 4 April 1979 authorized the Authority to start building a new network of UHF stations for ITV 2.

STUDIOS

The BBC operates a complete broadcasting service from programme planning and production through transmission. It is responsible for two nationwide television networks, four nationwide radio networks, a number of local radio stations, and an extensive foreign broadcasting service. The IBA, on the other hand, now has only one national television network plus some local radio stations; and all production is done by programme companies rather than by the IBA itself, although the Authority retains legal responsibility for the output. BBC facilities are much more extensive, therefore, even if the offices and studios of the programme companies are added to the headquarters and transmitter facilities of the IBA.

The magnitude of the BBC's establishment is related to the extent of its output. During a typical year, the Corporation broadcasts 134,000 hours of domestic radio programmes, 12,000 hours of television and 37,000 hours of external broadcasts.[19] Its 2500 engineering employees do research, architectural planning, and civil engineering, as well as being involved in studio and transmitter planning, construction, operation and maintenance.

The gleaming white façade of Broadcasting House has remained a world-wide symbol of the BBC, although 'BH', as it is affectionately known, has long since ceased to house the major portion of the Corporation's activities.[20] In the 1920s the BBC's London studios and offices were concentrated around one building at Savoy Hill on the Thames River embankment, in the vicinity of the Strand and Waterloo Bridge, while provincial studios gradually came into service in most of the outlying cities now serving as regional centres. In May 1932, headquarters were moved to Broadcasting House near Oxford Circus in central London, the only large building in the United Kingdom to be constructed especially for broadcasting until the new Television Centre was completed.

Broadcasting House, almost doubled in size by an addition completed in 1961, is still administrative headquarters for the Corporation. The offices of the Director-General, other key staff members, and the principal offices and studios for domestic radio are located there.[21] But even the enlarged Broadcasting House cannot hold all of the Corporation's domestic radio activities, and so it has overflowed into a number of nearby new and old hotels, apartment houses, and office buildings, as well as into some that are not near by. The Maida Vale skating rink is headquarters for the BBC symphony orchestra; a Catholic convent was converted to house the Corporation's transcription service; and an office building is used for the Corporation's publication division. The offices and studios for External Broadcasting are located in Bush House on the Strand. BBC Enterprises, which runs a highly profitable business distributing BBC programmes worldwide, is located some 10 miles west in Ealing.

The BBC maintains about 250 radio studios, of which about half are in the greater London area. They range in size and elaborateness from large concert studios to small ones for talks and interviews. Many of the latter are 'unattended', that is, they can be operated by the programme staff without engineering personnel. Sound treatment, microphones, control rooms, recording equipment and all the rest are typical of those found in well-equipped broadcasting installations all over the world. The extensive mobile equipment needed for broadcasts originating outside regular studios—called 'Outside Broadcasts' or 'OBs' in the United Kingdom, 'remotes' in the United States—is supplemented by permanent installations in London's three principal concert halls—the Royal Albert Hall, the Royal Festival Hall and the Queen Elizabeth Hall.

There are also centres with offices plus radio and television studios in the national regions—Northern Ireland, Scotland, and Wales, and in the English regions—including Manchester, Birmingham, and Bristol. The new broadcasting house in Manchester, for example, is a splendid six-storey building. Its largest television studio has 4500 square feet of floor space, and it also has accommodations for the BBC local radio station serving that area. Under construction is an extension to provide additional space for music, drama, and light entertainment programmes.

BBC television headquarters are in the new Television Centre in West London. Opened in June 1960, the Centre was, according to the BBC, 'the first building of its kind anywhere to be designed entirely as a television production complex'.[22] Ten locations were considered before the Corporation finally decided on a 13½ acre site in western London, the largest single undeveloped spot in London available for the purpose. Originally it was hoped to locate there all those BBC activities that could not be concentrated around Broadcasting House, but the space available proved adequate only for the Television Centre.

The building's main section, seven stories high, 'covers an area nearly twice the size of that occupied by St Paul's Cathedral', says the Corporation, and employs some 5500 people. It contains nine production studios plus a television theatre, of which the largest has 10,800 (108 by 100 feet) and the smallest two 3500 (70 by 50 feet) square feet of floor space. Audience seating space ranges from 100 to 480, depending upon studio size. In addition, there are small studios for announcements, weather forecasts, interviews, and other limited productions. Accompanying these are elaborate control rooms, with extensive facilities and all the other necessary paraphernalia, including forty colour video tape machines, thirty colour teleciné machines, and much editing equipment. Anticipating future technological changes, the BBC is experimenting with digital systems for transmitting and recording television pictures and sound.[23]

BBC television news headquarters are set apart in a spur off the main building. Its two studios, each with 1200 square feet of floor space, are surrounded by offices and technical areas. Studio cameras are operated entirely by remote control from the adjacent control rooms. 'Up to 20 shots per camera', says the BBC, 'can be preset, stored in a memory system and selected for instant recall on transmissions.' A news room with 3500 square feet of space houses the entire editorial operation for both BBC 1 and BBC 2. It also has its own film laboratory, film cutting rooms, a large teleciné area, and video tape machines.

Other Centre statistics are equally impressive. To cite only a few: there are 200 offices, 120 dressing rooms with accommodations for 500 people, and a restaurant that can serve 700 at a sitting, along with smaller snack bars and several executive dining rooms. There are music, record and script libraries, and a medical unit. All television sets and properties are constructed in a scenery block covering almost an acre of ground. The design group—'the largest in the world', says the BBC—has a staff of some 400 working on sets, costumes, make-up, graphics and visual effects of all kinds. Supplementing these facilities are colour studios elsewhere in London: two at Lime Grove, the Television Theatre at Shepherds Bush, used for programmes with studio audiences, and the Alexandra Palace installation, where some Open University programs are produced. Television film operations are housed in Ealing, in West London.[24]

The IBA headquarters building, in the Knightsbridge area of London, is modest in size, since it needs to house only the top officials and related staff activities of the Authority itself. IBA engineering headquarters are at Crawley Court near Winchester. Each programme company has its own offices and studios, and all thirteen regionally based companies have some office space in London as well. In London are facilities for the two London companies and for Independent Television News.

Together, the 15 programme companies and ITN in 1975 had 50 television studios, 24 outside broadcast units, 240 colour cameras, 96 colour telecinés, 88 colour video tape recorders (VTRs) and 16 cassette video recorders.[25] Most of this is owned by the five major companies: ATV in the midlands (Birmingham and Borehamwood); Granada in Lancashire (Manchester); Yorkshire in Yorkshire (Leeds); and Thames and London Weekend in London. In the London area, Thames Television has two studio centres, one in central London and one at Teddington on the River Thames. The latter includes three studios, the largest with 7500 square feet of floor space. Thames Television also has 5 outside broadcast units, 33 cameras, 10 colour telecines, and 13 VTRs. London Weekend Television describes its South Bank and Television Centre as 'one of the most comprehensive and technically sophisticated television studios in Europe', including 5 studios, 3 outside broadcast units, 27 colour cameras, 3 colour telecinés, 7 colour VTRs and two cassette video recorders.[26]

The largest ITV installation outside London is that of ATV in the Midlands, with 7 studios, 4 outside broadcast units, 36 colour cameras, 11 colour telecinés, 14 VTRs, and 2 cassette video recorders.[27] Not to be outdone by the BBC, IBA engineers, early in 1978, 'publicly demonstrated the world's first digital video tape recording system capable of producing high-quality colour television pictures on one-inch magnetic tape at a tape speed of under 10 inches per second.'[28] All of the independent radio stations have their own modest studios, associated equipment, and outside broadcasting facilities.

OTHER TECHNICAL DEVELOPMENTS

Both BBC and IBA have developed 'teletext' equipment, which utilizes unused and unseen blank lines at the top of the picture to place written information on video screens without interfering with normal transmissions. The BBC system, first announced in 1972, and made operational two years later, is called CEEFAX (it 'allows the viewer to *see facts* on his home television screen'); the corresponding IBA system is named ORACLE (Optional Reception of Announcements by Coded Line Electronics.)[29] (Other countries with similar systems include West Germany, France, Finland, and Sweden.)

All that is required to receive the signals is a small decoder box and a key pad looking something like a pocket calculator, which is attached to a conventional television set. Both systems provide information in words, numbers or diagrams in six colours plus white, in upper and lower case letters. The information can be superimposed on the television pictures or seen on a blank screen, depending on the viewer's preference.[30] Individual words can be flashed on and off for emphasis. Anyone with the necessary equipment can dial up news headlines, sports results, television programme details, weather forecasts, financial data, or whatever other types of information are available in the system. Editorial teams, working separately in the news headquarters of BBC and at Thames Television and ITN, gather information which is revised every hour or so, and made available for 18 hours each day on both BBC and IBA television. Another British system, formerly called Viewdata but now known as Prestel, has been developed by the Post Office. It permits a viewer to dial on his home telephone for information or messages, which then are flashed on his television screen. None of these systems has yet been widely used, with teletext delayed, in effect, by the high cost and not always satisfactory performances of the decoders. By the end of 1978, some 10,000 decoders were in use.

The distribution of radio programme to homes by wire began in Britain in 1925.[31] For some years there was considerable discussion as to whether this should be done privately or by the BBC, and to what extent relay companies should be required to carry BBC programmes along with those from other foreign stations, which originally were the staple of their service. In the event, however, radio relays continued under private auspices, but with requirements for giving first priority to domestic broadcasts.

The relay companies began distributing television in the early 1950s, first offering sound only, although later they were required to provide pictures too. In 1978, about 14 per cent of all homes with television received service from the approximately 2000 cable systems then in use, most of which had between six and nine channels of programmes.

The basic motivation for the development of wired radio and television was the same in Britain as in the United States: to improve reception or to make reception possible, in areas with poor signals. Cable distribution also eliminates unsightly forests of aerials from the roofs of multiple dwelling units. In some 'new towns' large housing developments have television signals fed from a central source along with such other public services as water and electricity. Most relay customers are served by one of four large private companies, although the Post Office does some television programme distribution too. One of the largest is Rediffusion, which also has close relationships with some television programme companies.

For the most part, the government has required relay companies to limit themselves to distributing BBC and IBA programmes, but in 1972, experiments in local community television production were authorized in London, Bristol, Sheffield, Swindon, Wellingborough, and Milton Keynes, the number of homes served in each case ranging from 5000 to 30,000. In those cities very modest production units provided short programmes of local news and activities. Since the services could not be adequately supported by normal subscription payments, some advertising was allowed; but in spite of this, financial problems caused several of the projects to close down. Nevertheless, the experiments attracted much attention, and were the subject of several Council of Europe publications.

Cable services undoubtedly will continue, but their exact future remains to be determined. Currently, the cable companies are losing customers as UHF broadcast coverage improves.[32] The Government White Paper responding to the Annan Report took an equivocal position: 'the option for a nationwide wideband cable system . . . must be kept open'; pay-television and community cable services should 'develop side by side', so that their future can be considered 'separately'; and finally, responsibility for 'supervising cable services' will be placed with the IBA.

ITV and the BBC regularly receive satellite transmissions of news, sports and other events from the United States, South Africa, Japan, the Middle East and other distant points, although feeds from the European continent almost always employ terrestrial links. Such uses surely will continue, and there are plans for a Eurovision satellite distribution system.

The future of satellites in British domestic broadcasting is, however, uncertain. The size of the United Kingdom is one factor: the Soviet Union was the first country to distribute programmes directly to transmitters by satellites, because it is so large, and because it lacked extensive terrestrial distribution facilities; but Britain is a small country, and it already has a well-developed cable and microwave relay interconnection system.

Technology is basic to the development of direct broadcasting to United Kingdom homes.[33] The BBC estimated in 1975 that it might be technically possible to have direct television transmissions from satellites to homes, beginning in 1980; although this clearly is not taking place. But while considering it 'important for the U.K. to seek [the necessary] frequency assignments', the Corporation did not think that direct transmissions would 'prove of great value for Britain at this stage'. Even though four extra television channels and twelve radio channels might be available by satellite, their domestic use would be complicated by the requirement for regional and local services, and furthermore would be expensive.

In 1972, the Television Advisory Committee thought it more practical to serve communities through wired networks than by direct satellite broadcasting, although that too would be expensive. A satellite service receivable on individual sets would cost at least £100 million to construct, while a comparable service for community receivers would cost £70 million. The committee therefore concluded that, although direct broadcasting from satellites to homes 'would become technically feasible on an experimental basis in the nineteen-eighties', its future was uncertain.[34]

7 Finances in British Broadcasting*

Independent Television's programme companies put the facts very succinctly to the Annan Committee in 1975: 'The ultimate relation between money and programmes is simple: No money, no television service.'[1] More than that, long-range programme policies often are predetermined by the methods of finance employed. Here the United Kingdom provides an interesting case study, since the BBC is supported by annual receiver licence fees, while IBA funds come from advertising.

THE SOURCES OF BBC SUPPORT

The BBC's current Charter and Licence, repeating essentially the provisions of earlier documents, contain several stipulations about finance.[2] The Corporation is authorized to receive funds from the government which it then must administer 'in accordance with the terms and conditions which may be attached' to them. The 1964 Licence did not specify any exact amount, instead leaving the matter to negotiation. It stated only that the government should provide the Corporation with 'the whole of the net licence revenue' after deduction of Post Office costs, 'or of such percentage or percentages thereof as the Treasury may from time to time determine'.[3] The BBC may receive or earn other money too, if used 'exclusively in furtherance of the purposes' of the Charter. Unless specifically identified as capital funds, such money may be applied either to current expenses or capital development, but it may not be 'divided by way of profit or otherwise' among the Corporation's governors. The BBC may borrow up to £100 million, of which £75 million can be used at the Board of Governors' discretion, although for the last £25 million the Home Secretary has to give his approval.

Other sections of the Charter authorize the Corporation to engage in a wide range of broadcast-related business activities, including the purchase and sale of property; the publication and sale of printed material; the acquisition of copyrights, trademarks and trade names along with the right to license their use; the production, manufacture and sale of films, video tapes and records; the acquisition of stocks, shares and securities; and the investment of its funds. Some of these activities require the prior approval of the Minister, who has authority to examine

* This chapter deals with the operational aspects of BBC and IBA income and expenses. The rationale for financing the BBC from licence fees is discussed in Chapter 2, pp. 23–6, and for IBA finances in Chapter 5, p. 65.

the accounts of the Corporation at any time. Annually, the Corporation is to be audited, and it is to publish a report on its financial and programme activities.

Most BBC income is from licence fees.[4] Anyone operating a television set, or obtaining programmes from a relay exchange, must purchase an annual licence. The purchase of radio licences became obligatory in November 1922. A combined radio – television licence was introduced in June 1946. Until 1971, there were radio-only licences and combined radio – television licences, but no television-only licences. In 1971, radio-only licences were abolished, leaving just television-only licences.* In November 1979, the cost of a television-only licence was increased to £12, and the colour television supplementary charge raised to £24, so that the maximum charge for a licence-holder became £34.

Table 3 lists licence charges from 1922 to 1979. British charges have consistently been much below those of the major continental countries, whose charges are listed in most BBC handbooks for comparison.

TABLE 3   *Broadcast receiving licence fees in the United Kingdom 1922–79*

	Radio	TV monochrome (combined with radio)	TV colour (combined with radio)	Note
1 November 1922	10s	—	—	
1 June 1946	£1.00s	£2.00	—	
1 June 1954	£1.00s	£3.00	—	
1 August 1957	£1.00s	£4.00	—	Excise duty of £1 imposed, not receivable by BBC
1 October 1963	£1.00s	£4.00	—	Excise duty abolished, BBC given full amount
1 August 1965	£1.5s	£5.00	—	
1 January 1968	£1.5s	£5.00	£10.00	Colour television supplementary of £5 introduced
1 January 1969	£1.5s	£6.00	£11.00	
1 February 1971	—	—		The radio-only licence fee was abolished
1 July 1971	—	£7.00	£12.00	
1 April 1975	—	£8.00	£18.00	Colour television supplementary increased to £10
29 July 1977	—	£9.00	£21.00	Colour television supplementary increased to £12
25 November 1978	—	£10.00	£25.00	Colour television supplementary increased to £15
24 November 1979	—	£12.00	£34.00	Colour television supplementary increased to £22

SOURCE: *BBC Handbook 1980*, p. 228.

* Blind persons formerly received radio-only licences free and after radio licences were discontinued their television licence fees were reduced by the amount of the radio licence. Since 1969, retirees of pensionable age living in old persons' homes have received television licences for the very nominal rate of 5 pence per year. The Annan Committee opposed such practices however, saying that it 'did not consider that the BBC should be expected to finance social benefits from the licence revenue . . . . We felt that such benefits were more properly a charge on general taxation' (*Annan*, #10.37).

In the early days of ITV, some people argued that because they viewed mainly Authority programmes, they should not be required to purchase licences to support the Corporation. The government ruled, however, that all viewers must have licences, regardless of how much they watched the BBC. One reason the Corporation is anxious to maintain good audience ratings is to avoid having too many IBA-only listeners and viewers press their representatives in Parliament to exempt them from licence liability, with a consequent loss in BBC income.

In Britain, as in all countries with receiver licences, there is the constant problem of set-users not purchasing licences, even though there is a fine for evasion. Beginning in 1967, the maximum fine for a first offence ranged from £10 to £50, although the average fine imposed has been around £5, which is less than the cost of the licence.[5] There was some improvement when new legislation in 1967 required dealers to report all sales, resales, and rentals to the postal authorities, but there still were 1¼ million unlicensed sets, costing the Corporation some £7.5 million per year, which the Director-General pointed out was, at the time, enough money to 'solve most of our problems'. In areas of high evasion, detector vans, which electronically pinpoint the location of receivers by measuring their radiation, are used to detect evaders. In fact, the mere appearance of such vans motivates many people to buy licences. Appeals over the air and in the press to purchase licences also are effective. However, no system is foolproof, and the BBC always loses some potential licence income.

Along with dependence on receiver fees goes the question of how much to charge for licences. Through the years the Corporation often has pressed the government to raise the rate—which, it should be noted, is set not by the Corporation but by the government. Faced with the need for additonal funds since World War II, the BBC has been chronically short of money, and recently, for the first time in its history, had several deficit years. But the government is reluctant to increase the charge, being concerned about overall public expenditures, inflation, and public reaction to price increases. Requests from the BBC, or proposals from the government, for increased license charges invariably become front-page news. The relatively few pounds assessed directly against listeners and viewers to support the BBC often pose a much greater psychological hazard for both public and government than do slight increases in the costs of many articles resulting from their being advertised on the IBA.

Licence income is supplemented by returns from publications and programme sales—big business by any standards—which usually are profitable. Even in 1927, its first year, the *Radio Times*, which gives detailed listings of all BBC domestic radio and television programs, sold an average of 851,657 copies each week, and by 1954, with a circulation of 8,223,612, it was the largest-circulated weekly magazine in the world. However, since the ITA began publishing its *TV Times* in 1955, the *Radio Times* has done less well; and in 1977, its net weekly sales were down to 3,748,903. The circulation of the *TV Times* then was 3,573,874.[6]

Both the *Radio Times* and *The Listener* carry advertising, and the former usually accounts for most of the profits from the Corporation's extensive publishing activities. The total profits from publications between 1947 and 1954, for example, constituted about 9 per cent of the Corporation's entire income,* a sum approximately equal to the BBC's allotments for capital expenditure during some of those years.[7] During the year ending 31 March 1979, Publications made a profit of £2,857,000, an increase of 6 per cent over the previous year. (Of this amount, £2,400,000 was earned by the *Radio times*.)

Another income-producing activity is BBC Enterprises, the department responsible for the worldwide sale of BBC television taped and filmed programmes, and some other materials.[8] In 1978–9, gross income reached £11 million, a 5 per cent increase over the previous year, which was itself a record, and profits before taxes were £4,004,000. BBC Enterprises now operates as a limited company with its own board of directors, although it still is wholly owned by the BBC. This change was made in the expectation that in its new form, Enterprises could compete more vigorously in the world market of television programme materials. Income also includes receipts from exhibitions, the sale of phonograph records and tapes, and the royalties from licences to use BBC titles and characters in connection with the manufacture and sales of commercial records.

The BBC has one other source of funds: It may borrow up to £100 million.[9] For the BBC, borrowing is more expensive than financing capital requirements from reserves. Expanding industrial companies may borrow money or issue new shares of capital stock anticipating that greater earning capacity will lead to higher profits, but the BBC must pay interest on its loans, cannot claim a tax advantage, since it pays taxes only on its few profit-making activities, and thereafter must seek additional funds to support any enlarged operation.

In the years ahead, the BBC will face some major financial problems. In 1977, for example, the BBC's top weekly public affairs programme, *Panorama*, exclusive of overhead, cost £11,000, compared to £11,650 for Thames Television's *This Week*, and £14,000 for Granada's *World in Action*; and costs have escalated greatly since then. BBC staff members at all levels have left to work at higher salaries for the IBA and its companies.[10] Licence-fee receipts will not continue to cover the Corporation's costs unless charges are regularly increased, since there is a decline in the number of new sets along with public opposition to higher fees, even though British charges are lower than those imposed in most Continental countries. Shortly after he became Director-General, Ian Trethowan, in October 1977, speculated about the possibility of direct treasury grants to supplement other income, even though fearing that such support might threaten the Corporation's programme independence.[11] He also has talked about a licence indexed to the cost of living, as in West Germany. Advertising as an additional revenue source probably would be ruled out by all concerned—by the IBA as competition, and by the BBC as forcing a change in programme objectives. One only can wait, watch, and wonder about the financial future of the BBC.

* It is interesting—and also surprising—to learn that in 1969, when it was proposed that the *Radio Times* discontinue cigarette advertisements, the Director-General and the Board of Management opposed the suggestion on the grounds that it would cost the magazine a quarter of a million pounds a year on revenue. Nevertheless, the Board of Governors voted 5 to 4 in favour of the ban (Hill, p. 121). However, the IBA's *TV Times* still carries cigarette advertisements, although the broadcasting of such commercials was ended in 1965.

GOVERNMENT CHARGES AGAINST LICENCE REVENUE

Not all of the licence revenue collected reaches the BBC, however. Some is retained by the Post Office to cover its costs of administration and collection, the elimination of interference, and the search for evaders. In earlier years a good deal was held back for general government expenses in no way related to broadcasting; a practice which ended, however, in 1961. In some cases, BBC surpluses above costs and allocations for reserves have been confiscated by the government. For a few years in the 1950s, when ITV was starting up, portions of the licence money not assigned to the BBC were earmarked—but never used—for some ITA programme costs. Finally, the Corporation is required to pay corporation taxes on profits derived from such non-broadcasting activities as publications.

During the year ending 31 March 1979, gross licence fee collections totalled £337,437,000.[12] After subtracting £25,158,000 for the costs of collection, administering the licence system, and interference investigations, £312,279,000 remained for the BBC. Deductions to cover such costs are defensible, but up to 1961, the government retained a portion of the licence income for its general expenses, and also up to that year and through 1964—if the Corporation either did not spend its entire income each year, or allocated some of it for reserves—it was required to pay an income tax on the amount saved, just as private companies must pay taxes on their profits. Fortunately, such charges and taxes no longer are assessed.[13]

EXPENDITURES FOR DOMESTIC BROADCASTING

The BBC—like all enterprises—faces the problem of operating within its income. Immediately after World War II, it had to make up its wartime material losses, modernize its technically outmoded equipment, and re-open its television service, all the while providing for normal expansion and meeting operating expenses. Television had to be extended to the entire country, and work had to be begun on a nationwide FM network. In the late 1950s, London's new Television Centre was constructed; BBC 2 began transmitting on 625 lines in the UHF band in 1964, with colour added in 1967; and 2 years later, BBC 1 started colour broadcasting in the same band. There also was local radio—for which no additional government funds were allocated, the first station going on the air in 1967 and the twentieth in 1973. The lifting of government limitations on the hours of television broadcasting in 1972 increased BBC programme costs by extending programme time. (Additional time gave ITV an opportunity to sell more commercials and thus increase its income, but for the BBC it meant only more programmes to develop, without additional funds.) Meanwhile, costs were increasing as a result of competition with the IBA for personnel and programmes, as well as because of the worldwide inflation, which was particularly severe in the United Kingdom.

After major income and expenditure projections are made by the Board of Management, they are submitted for approval to the Board of Governors.[14] Once policies have been approved, the managing heads of television, radio and external broadcasting have considerable autonomy in working out details. This is also true of the national broadcasting regions—Wales and Scotland. Although finances for Northern Ireland and the English regions still are supervised from London, the trend is towards more regional autonomy. But in 1970, the Controller of Finance pointed out two major weaknesses in the administration of BBC finances: the determination of short-term arrangements on the basis of political convenience, and the reluctance of the government to allow the Corporation to build up reserves for future capital expansion.

Expenditures for the BBC's domestic services for the year ending on 31 March 1979, as shown in Table 4, are summarized below. (Tables 5 and 6 following, provide more details about television and radio operating costs for the same year.) Of the total of £324,360,000, £288,887,000 went for operating costs, and £35,473,000 for capital outlay. Between the programme services, the division of operating costs was: television £207,696,000 (72 per cent); radio £81,191,000 (28 per cent). The division of capital expenditures was: television £24,094,000 (68 per cent); radio £11,379,000 (32 per cent). The year's deficit was £8,883,000. In recent years, the Corporation has spent more than it received, and between the general escalation of costs and continuing competition with the IBA, the outlook is for more years of deficit financing in the future—unless there are drastic cuts in expenditures. (Open University costs are not included in this analysis, since they are covered by a direct government grant made exclusively for that purpose.)

Tables 5 and 6 show the breakdown of expenditures among the several domestic broadcasting services. Taken together, the three tables indicate, among other things, that the relative operating expenditures on radio (28 per cent) and television (72 per cent) are not proportionate to the amount of radio and television use, and that costs for the four network radio services, as shown in Table 6, are not at all proportionate to their relative audience sizes and costs: Radio 1 (average of 35 per cent of all radio listening in the United Kingdom in 1979, as shown in Table 25, 9 per cent of costs); Radio 2 (24 per cent of listening, 19 per cent of costs); Radio 3 (1 per cent of listening, 18 per cent of costs); Radio 4 (11 per cent of listening, 22 per cent of costs).

In November 1979, when the government approved an increase in television licence fees from £10 to £12 for monochrome and from £25 to £34 for colour sets, instead of the £41 or £42 for colour receivers requested by the BBC, the Corporation was required to drastically reduce its expenditures, in order to bring income and expenses into line. Accordingly, at the end of February 1980, the Director-General, with Board of Governors approval, circulated a five-page single-spaced memorandum to 'All Staff' detailing the proposed cuts.

Over the next two years, said the statement, spending would have to be reduced by over £130 million—almost exactly the amount that would be represented by an additional £6 yearly licence fee increase. The largest part of this £130 million—some £90 million—will be achieved through the deferral of various capital development plans, with the remaining £40 million to come from the domestic television and radio services. Among other things, this will involve the elimination of about 1500 permanent and temporary positions, although with a yearly turnover of about 3000, it is expected that this can be done with few forced lay offs.

TABLE 4   *Home services: income and expenditure account for the year ended 31 March 1979*

Year ended 31 March 1978			Year ended 31 March 1979	
£000	£000		£000	£000
		Television and Radio Broadcasting		
		Income		
	261,826	Receivable from the Home Office		312,279
		Other Income		
		Trading Profits		
2,344		Publications—Radio Times	2,400	
356		—Others	457	
2,700			2,857	
3,096		Enterprises	4,004	
5,796			6,861	
49		Grant for Civil Defence expenditure	42	
452		Sales of assets taken out of service	420	
16		Interest receivable	151	
15		Other income	24	
6,328			7,498	
545		*Less:* Interest payable	855	
3,216		Corporation Tax	3,445	
3,761			4,300	
	2,567			3,198
	264,393			315,477
		Expenditure		
172,076		Operating Expenditure—Television	207,696	
66,637		—Radio	81,191	
18,789		Capital Expenditure —Television	24,094	
8,554		—Radio	11,379	
	266,056			324,360
	1,663	**Deficit for the year**		−8,883
		Open University		
		Income		
4,331		Receivable from the Open University	5,058	
		Expenditure		
4,201		Operating Expenditure	4,806	
130		Capital Expenditure	252	
4,331			5,058	
	3,459	**Deficit at 31 March 1978**		−5,122
	5,122	**Deficit at 31 March 1979**		14,005

SOURCE: *BBC Handbook 1980*, p. 89.

TABLE 5 *Statement of operating expenditure for the year ended 31 March 1979: Television*

Year ended 31 March 1978			Year ended 31 March 1979	
Amount £000	*Percentage of total %*		*Amount £000*	*Percentage of total %*
96,704	56.2	Production and other staff costs	118,572	57.1
		Artists, speakers, facility and		
		copyright fees, film recording		
51,638	30.0	and design materials, etc.	60,803	29.3
2,404	1.4	Intercommunication circuits	2,718	1.3
4,443	2.6	Power, lighting and heating	4,872	2.3
4,381	2.6	Building and plant maintenance	5,408	2.6
3,343	1.9	Rent and rates	4,273	2.0
1,929	1.1	Telephones	2,049	1.0
2,783	1.6	Transport	3,236	1.6
4,451	2.6	Other expenses	5,765	2.8
172,076	100.0		207,696	100.0
£m	*%*	*Whereof:*	*£m*	*%*
97	57	BBC 1	116	56
50	29	BBC 2	60	29
19	11	Regional services	25	12
6	3	Transmission and distribution	7	3
172	100		208	100
Hours	*%*	*Hours of output*	*Hours*	*%*
4,869	45	BBC 1	4,797	44
2,861	27	BBC 2	3,110	29
3,006	28	Regional services	2,993	27
10,736	100		10,900	100

SOURCE: *BBC Handbook 1980*, p. 94.

About £12 million will be taken from London television centre operations, and another £1¼ million from the three English television network centres. Radio's share will include a cut of £4 million in network operations, £500,000 from the remaining English regional radio centres, and £2 million from existing local stations. Radio 3 will sign off at 11.15 p.m. instead of midnight; a Radio 2 serial will be dropped; educational programmes will be reduced by ten per cent; and five radio orchestras will be eliminated (see pp. 148, 330–1).

As in the past when the BBC has proposed cuts in its services, for financial or other reasons, there were outcries from supporters of the services involved—especially music, Radio 3, and educational programmes. Discussion and pressures may alter the amounts of some of the cuts proposed, but there is no doubt that future BBC balance sheets will have smaller bottom line totals than those given in Tables 4, 5 and 6.

TABLE 6   *Statement of operating expenditure for the year ended 31 March 1979: Radio*

Year ended 31 March 1978			**Year ended 31 March 1979**	
Amount *£000*	*Percentage* *of total %*		*Amount* *£000*	*Percentage* *of total %*
36,649	55.0	Production and other staff costs Artists, speakers, performing rights, news royalties,	45,958	56.6
15,567	23.4	facility and copyright fees, etc.	18,157	22.4
3,556	5.3	House orchestras	4,050	5.0
691	1.0	Intercommunication circuits	786	1.0
1,589	2.4	Power, lighting and heating	1,849	2.3
1,924	2.9	Building and plant maintenance	2,511	3.1
3,124	4.7	Rent and rates	3,212	3.9
1,052	1.5	Telephones	1,181	1.4
574	0.9	Transport	594	0.7
1,911	2.9	Other expenses	2,893	3.6
66,637	100.0		81,191	100.0
£m	*%*	*Whereof:*	*£m*	*%*
7	10	Radio 1	7	9
12	18	Radio 2	15	19
13	19	Radio 3	15	18
15	22	Radio 4	18	22
10	15	Regional services	13	16
7	11	Local radio	9	11
3	5	Transmission and distribution	4	5
67	100		81	100
Hours	*%*	*Hours of output*	*Hours*	*%*
4,798	4	Radio 1	5,260	4
6,282	5	Radio 2	7,792	6
6,246	5	Radio 3	6,396	5
6,789	6	Radio 4	7,351	5
9,902	9	Regional services	13,097	10
34,017	29		39,896	30
82,958	71	Local radio	92,759	70
116,975	100		132,655	100

SOURCE: *BBC Handbook 1980*, p. 95.

FINANCING THE EXTERNAL SERVICES

External broadcasting—services for audiences outside the United Kingdom—is supported by a direct grant-in-aid from the British Treasury, although prior to World War II it was maintained by the BBC from its licence income. (For information about the programming of external broadcasting, see Chapter 21.) In spite of this, the BBC enjoys a high degree of independence in operating the External Services, even though the license states that such programming is to be done 'in accordance with any terms and conditions which may be attached to the grant thereof by Parliament or by the Treasury'.* In Britain, although it always has been considered proper to require the users of radio and television receivers to support the domestic services, general tax funds are now used for the External Services, since the projection of Britain abroad is regarded as a responsibility of all citizens.

The financial independence which the licence-fee system is supposed to provide for the domestic services is less important for the External Services, which are expected to be more responsive to the government (even though they are more independent than Radio Free Europe, Radio Liberty, and the Voice of America). Yet, External Services personnel often claim that the independence of the home services, assured in part by its licence-fee base, results in more credibility abroad for External Services output.[15]

When the BBC began an experimental Empire Service on its own initiative in 1927, it had to support the project out of licence revenue, and continued to do so until World War II, although its percentage of licence revenue was increased in 1937 to pay for the External Services and for television. During the war all BBC operations were supported by direct parliamentary grants. When the usual procedure was resumed for the domestic services in January 1947, direct subsidies were continued for External Broadcasting.

Plans for the nature and extent of the External Services are developed jointly by the BBC, the Foreign and Commonwealth Office, the Ministry of Defence and the Board of Trade. The first mentioned is most involved; the Ministry of Defence is concerned almost exclusively with the monitoring services; and the Board of Trade considers External Broadcasting as a way of promoting exports.[16] When agreement has been reached on such matters as how much broadcasting should be done, and how many and what languages should be used, the Corporation indicates its financial requirements for performing these services, after which the government decides how much money to allocate, and, in general, how it should be spent. Once this is done, however, the BBC has a high degree of freedom in working out programme details.

BBC FINANCES AND GOVERNMENT CONTROL

It is a maxim of government that control of the purse permits control of everything else. Clearly, the dependence of the BBC upon a government allocation makes it less free financially from government than are American commercial stations and networks. The licence-fee system was intended to free the BBC's domestic services from government influence. Yet, there are many theoretical and practical financial limitations on its independence.

* *1969 Licence*, #18. In most countries services for foreign audiences are financed directly by the government, rather than being charged against licence or commercial revenues. In the United States, the Voice of America, Radio Liberty, Radio Free Europe, and other foreign information activities are supported by direct congressional appropriations.

Both the Charter and Licence impose a number of financial controls.[17] Some of these are inevitable and eminently reasonable, others are questionable; but taken together they do limit the Corporation's freedom of action. For example, the BBC is required to use its money 'exclusively in furtherance of the purposes' of its Charter. Borrowing is limited, and the conditions for repayment, as well as for meeting depreciation, are prescribed. Otherwise, the BBC may use its revenues freely for capital outlay or current expenses, although its annual report to Parliament must include 'such information relating to . . . finance, administration and its work generally' as the Minister may specify. Furthermore, the Corporation must 'upon demand' give the Minister or his representatives 'full liberty to examine the accounts of the Corporation and furnish him and them with all forecasts, estimates, information and documents which he or they may require with regard to the financial transactions and engagements of the Corporation.'

A number of very important decisions affecting the Corporation's income are made by the government. Since almost all money for the domestic services comes from licence revenues, the government, by determining the cost of the licence, sets a top limit on the total amount available. It also decides how much of the gross receipts to withhold for Post Office administrative costs, and determines the percentage of net license income to go to the BBC. If the government should consider the licence fee annually, instead of setting it for a longer term, in accordance with long-range BBC development plans, that might carry with it a threat of indirect programme control. It is true that the Corporation is consulted when these various matters are discussed, but one or another department of the government makes the final decisions.

Once the BBC's percentage of net revenue has been set, the House of Commons must appropriate that sum. It has always done so, and probably always will; nevertheless this process gives the Cabinet, if not Parliament itself, a final veto. The Charter provides that licence revenue paid to the BBC is to be 'applied and administered' in accordance with the 'terms and conditions' which may be attached to the grant thereof; and while no written 'terms and conditions' have ever been attached, there always is the possibility that some might be. The Broadcasting Vote was made a separate budget item especially to facilitate parliamentary discussion of the BBC (although at the same time it was decided not to require the Corporation to submit to Parliament its plans for capital expenditures). On such occasions, very careful investigations are carried out by the Select Committee on Estimates, which has the right to examine the estimates for the Broadcasting vote. It has done so, however, only twice—in 1946 and in 1969.

Theoretically, the Corporation is free to spend its money as it wishes, but government approval is a prerequisite to long-range capital plans. In day-to-day expenditures, the Corporation is clearly independent, although it still must submit a final audit and report, which are presented to Parliament by the Home Secretary as a Command Paper. At that time, the House of Commons may discuss BBC affairs, and the Public Accounts Committee of the House of Commons may examine the Corporation's domestic service accounts. On several occasions it has done so, but it may not inquire into the Corporation's day-to-day business. (There is, of course, no restraint on Parliament's examining the External Services, where more frequent financial reports are required, and where government programme supervision is closer.)

The question of government control through finance has occasioned both official and unofficial comment. The Estimates Committee in 1969 wrote: 'The determination of the licence fee has come to be regarded as a political decision in the widest sense, equivalent to decisions on levels of taxation or charges in the National Health Service.'[18] The Standing Conference on Broadcasting, an independent group concerned with broadcasting, submitted a paper to the Annan Committee in January 1976 in which it observed that the licence fee 'is not, as is commonly assumed, free from government control. It is paid to the Treasury. In the early days of broadcasting only a percentage, decided by the government, was paid to the BBC.'[19]

Gerald Beadle, shortly after retiring from a long career in the Corporation, wrote that while government

> control over day-to-day management and over editorial matters is nil, I have to admit that the Government does exercise a broad financial control, which in turn governs the pace of the BBC's development and the scope of its activities, and this control could be very irksome and frustrating.[20]

Since 'the controlling hand is there . . . the question arises as to whether it is used wisely'. It was used, he said,

> in the decade after the war to hold the BBC's development back, and at the time of the debates about commercial television the BBC was unfairly accused of going slow in a number of respects. It is not for me to say whether the 'go slow' was necessary in the national interest, but I do know that it put the BBC in a weak position at a time when it needed all its strength.

More recently the Annan Committee reviewed the Corporation's financial base.[21] 'We do not deny [it concluded] that there is an element of Treasury control in the present system.' But on balance, the Committee thought there was no real problem.

The fact that powers of control exist does not, of course, prove that they are used; nor under the British system does the absence of a written prohibition necessarily indicate the absence of control. But it is only reasonable to assume that, in setting policies, in matters ranging from capital expenditures to programme emphasis, the Corporation is aware of the trend of opinion in Parliament. This is the case, for example, with those American institutions of higher learning supported by legislative appropriations, and one would expect the same to be true of the BBC. At the least, therefore, the BBC must be somewhat responsive to government influence; at the worst, it could be government-controlled. Which turn is taken will depend largely upon the traditions and policies of Parliament on the one hand, and of the BBC on the other.

There is no evidence, however, nor has it ever been charged, that the government has actually used its financial prerogatives to influence or control the

BBC's programme policies or output. It should be pointed out in this content that, just as the BBC has to wrangle with the government over how much licence revenue it will get, or what its tax situation will be, so must the IBA argue about what percentage of its surpluses the government should confiscate, or how the levy should be set.

FINANCES OF THE INDEPENDENT BROADCASTING AUTHORITY

Nowhere else in the world is there a system to finance broadcasting like that used for the Independent Broadcasting Authority. It involves two quite separate and distinct operations: that of the Authority itself; and those of the contractors providing the programmes. The IBA is a public corporation; the contractors are private companies.

The Authority gets most of its income from payments made by the programme companies for the privilege of broadcasting over its transmitters. The companies receive income by selling advertising. The government benefits financially from the arrangement, since it taxes both groups, has the right to confiscate some of the Authority's net income, and imposes levies on those programme company profits judged to be excessive.

The Television Act instructs the Authority to finance its radio and television activities separately; but in both cases it must ensure that revenues are 'at least sufficient' to meet ongoing expenses, amortize plants and equipment, and provide capital funds for expansion.[22] However the Authority is not entirely free to spend as it wishes. In the Authority's own words, the Minister may, with the approval of the Treasury, give the Authority 'such directions as he thinks fit relating to the establishment or management of the Reserve Fund', and also may control the disposition of any excess of revenues over the 'expenditure properly chargeable to revenue account', including the power of confiscating such funds for the national Treasury.[23]

When Independent Television was first debated in Parliament, some critics deplored its complete dependence on commercial revenue. Accordingly, the government introduced an amendment authorizing the Postmaster-General to give the Authority outright as much as £750,000 per year, if the programme companies were unwilling or unable to develop a sufficient number of educational and cultural balance programmes, but this was never done.[24] In 1972, the Authority was authorized to borrow from the Treasury up to £2 million to provide initial capital for the radio stations it then was authorized to develop.[25] This was continued by the 1973 law which consolidated the Television and Sound Acts of 1964 and 1972. Through the fiscal year ending 31 March 1978, £1.65 million had been borrowed.

Payments to the Authority by the television programme companies fall into two categories: rentals, to cover the Authority's current and capital expenditures; and 'additional payments', required by the law of 1963 to drain off excessive company profits.[26] The additional payments, commonly referred to as the 'levy', are not retained by the Authority, but are passed on to the national treasury of the United Kingdom or Northern Ireland, depending upon the locale of their source.

Under the law, the Authority's contracts with its television programme companies are to provide rentals insuring the 'appropriate contributions of the respective programme contractors' towards meeting the IBA's financial obligations.[27] In the early years, there was some debate about the criteria to be used in setting programme company rentals. The Authority took the position that it was required to charge only enough to provide a surplus above operating costs adequate to repay its loans to the Treasury, amortize its capital equipment, and create a reserve fund sufficient to finance such future developments as a second television network, the introduction of UHF, a change in line standards, and colour broadcasting. In 1959, the Authority told the Committee of Public Accounts that it could do this if annual rentals were set at about three times the actual costs of the administrative and engineering services it provided to the contractors.[28]

At the outset of each contract period, the IBA estimates its financial needs, and then sets the rentals, trying to leave all companies reasonable returns on their investments.[29] But the rates depend on the financial potentials of the individual companies, and not on the Authority's costs in building and operating transmitters in each area, so that, in fact, the larger companies subsidize the smaller ones.[30] The working of the system may be illustrated by reference to the rentals set in 1968 at the beginning of the new contract period, when the intitial charges were subject to three possible changes: if the retail price index went up or down by more than 5 per cent, rentals could be varied accordingly (this led to an increase of nearly 30 per cent between 1968 and 1971); the Authority could raise the rates if its income were insufficient to meet expenditures during any one year (the rates were raised in August 1971 to finance the introduction of the 625-line UHF colour service); and, without indicating any reason, the Authority could change the rates during the contract period, upon giving 6 months notice.

Table 7 indicates the basis for rentals payable from 1 October 1976. These depended upon net advertising revenue, and net advertising revenue share, as computed during the year ending 31 July 1976. (NARAL share: a company's share of the Net Advertising Revenue After Levy, earned by all the companies combined.) The actual rental charges are indicated in the second column from the right. The two London companies paid respectively £3,042,000 and £1,921,000 per year; Grampian Television paid £80,000; while Border Television paid £1000. But whereas one VHF and fourteen UHF transmitters were sufficient to serve the greater London area with its concentrated population area, Grampian Television required five VHF plus twenty-three UHF transmitters, while Border Television required four VHF and twenty-three UHF.[31]

A look at future ITV finances is provided by Table 7 B, based on a release from the IBA inviting applications for the period beginning 1 January 1982. The 'Current rental' column indicates charges as of January 1980, which were raised from the 1977 figures given in Table 7 A. The 'New rental' column gives the rates—plus or minus 10 per cent—expected when the new contracts become effective in January 1982. The 'Subscription' column indicates the amounts the new contractors are expected to contribute toward the operation of the second ITV channel when it goes on the air, probably at the end of 1982. The contractors will be able to offset portions of the subscription charges with ITV 2 commercial sales receipts, but

TABLE 7A   *Structure of the industry*

Area	Company	At 1 January 1977			Year Ended 31 July 1976			
		Total homes (000's)	ITV homes (000's)	Percentage share of ITV homes	Net Adv. Revenue (£000)	NAR share as percentage of total NAR	Rental from 1 October 1976 (£000)	Rental as percentage of total Rental
London	Thames	5,070	4,400	23.5	36,209	17.3	3,042	17.2
	LWT				23,572	11.3	1,921	10.9
Midlands	ATV	3,550	3,080	16.4	31,186	14.9	2,402	13.6
Lancashire	Granada	2,910	2,570	13.7	27,329	13.0	2,402	13.6
Yorkshire	Yorkshire	2,540	2,050	10.9	21,398	10.2	1,948	11.0
Southern England	Southern	2,090	1,615	8.6	16,549	7.9	2,055	11.6
Wales and West	HTV	1,695	1,430	7.6	13,386	6.4	961	5.4
Central Scotland	Scottish	1,405	1,235	6.6	10,620	5.1	961	5.4
Northeast England	Tyne Tees	965	895	4.8	8,771	4.2	907	5.1
East of England	Anglia	1,545	1,205	6.4	8,938	4.3	534	3.0
Southwest England	Westward	646	543	2.9	4,023	1.9	267	1.5
Northern Ireland	Ulster	446	409	2.2	3,047	1.5	213	1.2
Northeast Scotland	Grampian	432	358	1.9	2,331	1.1	80	0.5
Borders	Border	213	194	1.0	1,557	0.7	1	–
Channel Islands	Channel	N/A	–	–	350	0.2	–	–
TOTAL		19,420*	18,760*	106.5*	209,266	100.0	17,694	100.0

* These totals are smaller than the sum of company totals because of 'overlapping' areas in which homes are able to receive more than one contractor's programmes. The total of the percentage shares adds up to more than 100 per cent for the same reason.

SOURCE: Independent Broadcasting Authority.

TABLE 7B *Provisional rentals and subscriptions from 1 January 1982*

Region	Current rental (£)	New rental (£)	Percentage increase (or decrease) in rental (to nearest %)	Sub-scriptions for fourth channel (£)
London Weekday	(3,966,060)	6,200,000	+ 56%	11,100,000
London Weekend	(2,153,004)	3,600,000	+ 67%	8,700,000
Midlands	(3,059,532)	4,800,00	+ 57%	9,000,000
North West	(3,399,480)	5,200,000	+ 53%	10,800,000
Yorkshire	(2,492,952)	4,000,000	+ 60%	8,400,000
South of England	(2,492,952)	3,900,000	+ 56%	6,600,000
Central Scotland	(1,019,844)	1,650,000	+ 62%	3,300,000
Wales and West	(566,580)	500,000	− 12%	3,300,000
East of England	(1,019,844)	1,650,000	+ 62%	3,600,000
North East	(1,019,844)	1,600,000	+ 57%	3,300,000
South West	(339,948)	500,000	+ 47%	1,250,000
North Scotland	(56,658)	50,000	− 12%	200,000
Northern Ireland	(226,632)	300,000	+ 32%	250,000
Borders	(33,995)	40,000	+ 18%	150,000
Channel Isles	(5,666)	10,000	+ 76%	50,000
?National Breakfast-TV	—	500,000		? nil

NOTES
1. The basic annual rental which the contractor will be required to pay to the Authority will be not more than 10 per cent below or 10 per cent above the New Rental figure given above from 1 January 1982, the initial starting figure being determined by the Authority before the completion of contracts with successful applicants.
2. The Authority can only give at this stage a general indication of the likely total requirement for the first contract year of the fourth channel and a similarly broad indication of the subscription likely to be required of each company. At this point the total requirement is seen as lying within the £60m to 80m range (at 1979 prices) and for the purposes of calculating the individual amounts included for guidance for the individual contracts the mid-point of this scale, £/0m, has been used.
3. All the above figures are based on current prices and are subject to increase between now and the start of the new contracts in accordance with the changes in the Index of Retail Prices.
SOURCE: *Broadcast*, 4 February 1980, p. 9. Based on material accompanying IBA press release of 24 January 1980, 'IBA Invites Applications for Future Television Franchises'.

these are not expected to equal the subscription costs for at least several years.

Programme company profits were so high in the late 1950s as to invite some kind of special tax. A Television Advertisement Duty of 10—later raised to 11—per cent, payable by the advertisers, was assessed in 1961, but it had no important effects, and so it was replaced by the levy in the new law of 1963.[32]

It is interesting to review the things said from time to time by the Authority and its programme companies about these profits. In 1959 a high ITA official remarked to me that the ITA actually was embarrassed by its 'appalling profits'. The next year the Authority frankly told the Pilkington Committee that it 'could not defend' ITV's high profit levels, although its proposed solution was introducing a second commercial television network to compete with the first one.[33] It went on to comment that these profits were 'quite without parallel in present times'. £100 invested in the non-voting stock of one of the four original companies in 1959 was worth £11,200 in 1960. Some dividends ran as high as 450 per cent before taxes, and dividends of '100 per cent or greater have been common'. In 1961, in another memorandum to the Committee, the ITA, in order to reduce 'to a reasonable level the existing profits which [it] . . . cannot defend', listed six ways of limiting profitability, favouring a 'royalty calculated by reference to profits'.[34]

The second White Paper on the Pilkington Report stated that the government was 'including in the Television Bill a specific provision to ensure that adequate rentals are paid by the companies, which will include a substantial payment calculated by reference to the profits of the companies before tax'.[35] But the programme companies took a very dim view of this procedure, and lobbied actively against it.[36] Norman Collins, deputy chairman of ATV, went so far as to say that if the levy were imposed his company would go out of business and would not apply for a renewal of its franchise. Nevertheless, the bill was passed on 29 July 1963—and ATV is still among the Authority's major programme companies.

By the 1970s, the excitement had died down, and the remaining protests pertained more to the basis for determining the tax than to the tax itself. In 1970, the National Board for Prices and Incomes opened a 56-page report on the *Costs and Revenues of Independent Companies* with the sentence: 'The Television Act of 1964 made provision for the payment by commercial television contractors to the Exchequer of a "levy"—designed to reflect the fact that the state had conferred upon them the sole right to operate a commercial television service within a given area.'[37] In 1971, the Minister of Posts and Telecommunications told the Select Committee on Nationalised Industries that the levy ensured 'that part of the income from the exploitation of public property (in this case, the frequency channels) should accrue to public funds'.[38] In much the same vein, the Authority informed the Committee: 'The object of the levy is to secure for the Government a participation in the commercial value of the concessions in return for the use of the frequency spectrum.' Finally, in 1975, the programme companies, in their statement to the Annan Committee, showed a change of position from the line they had taken during the Parliamentary debates a dozen years before, observing that 'the Exchequer levy was introduced for the express purpose of returning to the public a proportion of the companies' profits in recognition of their privileged use of a scarce national commodity'.[39]

The levy is a progressive tax on what the Act of 1963 described as 'advertising receipts'.[40] Both the Authority and the programme companies urged that it be placed on net rather than gross income, since the original procedure made no allowance for programme costs. A spokesman for Scottish Television told the Select Committee on Nationalised Industries in March 1972 that even though they were operating on a deficit basis in 1969 and 1970, they had to pay a levy of over £750,000 because charges were made against gross rather than net income.[41] In the same hearing the Authority requested that the levy be assessed either on programme company profits, or on revenues less programme expenditures; and that of the two, it favoured the former.[42] This was the procedure laid down by the 1974 law, which based the levy on net profits.[43] In any case, although the rates were written into the law, the Minister, with the approval of the Treasury and after consultation with the Authority, may raise or lower them, although such changes do not take effect until approved by both Houses of Parliament.

During the first decade the levy was in effect, the rates did undergo changes as is shown in Table 8A.[44]

TABLE 8A   *Levy rates*

Effective dates	*Net advertising revenue (£ million)*	*Rate of levy (%)*	*Effective dates*	*Net advertising revenue (£ million)*	*Rate of levy (%)*
1 1964 to 1 July 1969	0 – 1½	Nil	**4** 26 February 1971 to	0– 2	Nil
	1½– 7½	25	23 June 1974	2– 6	10
	Over 7½	45		6– 9	17½
2 1 July 1969 to	0 – ½	Nil		9–12	20
April 1970	½– 1½	7		12–16	22½
	1½– 4	25		Over 16	25
	4 –10	35	**5** 23 June 1974 Profits		
	Over 10	47½	basis introduced:		
3 April 1970 to	0 – 2	Nil	The greater of		
26 February 1971	2 – 6	20	(i) 2 per cent of		
	6 – 9	35	net advertising		
	9 –12	40	revenue or		Nil
	12 – 16	45	(ii) £250,000		
	Over 16	50	Balance of profits		66.7

SOURCE: *ITCA to Annan*, p. 156.

IBA radio finances are handled in essentially the same way as those for television, and radio rentals follow the television pattern.[45] Initial radio profits were not expected to be large, but the law took the precaution of providing the Minister with power to require supplementary payments to assure 'that excessive profits do not accrue to [radio] programme contractors'. By the year ending 30 September 1978, seventeen of the nineteen ILR stations then on the air were profitable, and the following year all were, seven paying dividends to their stockholders.

The charges in effect from 1 October 1979 can be used to illustrate the rental pattern. On that date basic charges were increased, and secondary rentals were to be assessed on stations with outstandingly good financial returns. (Prior to 1 October 1978, four stations paid secondary rentals; effective that date the number was raised to seven). The most profitable of the group, Capital Radio in London, paid £525,320 primary rental, £1,236,000 secondary rental, £874,000 in taxes, £500,000 in dividends, and retained £491,000 in profits.

Like other British public corporations, the Authority secures government approval before incurring long-range capital expenditures, in addition to which its investment programme is reviewed annually by the Home secretary.[46] On occasion the government has requested the Authority to cut back its plans. Early in 1956, expenditures planned for the following year were reduced by 20 per cent; in 1965, because of the country's poor economic position, most major capital expenditures

TABLE 8B   *Rental pattern*

Station and location	Primary rental 1978–9 (£)	Primary rental 1979–80 (£)
LBC (London Broadcasting Company)	180,000	210,000
Capital (London)	525,320	925,000
Clyde (Glasgow)	144,593	230,000
BRMB (Birmingham)	130,145	195,000
Piccadilly (Piccadilly)	183,140	250,000
Metro (Tyne/Wear)	120,960	130,000
Swansea (Swansea)	24,097	25,000
Hallam (Sheffield and Rotherham)	49,400	60,000
City (Liverpool)	151,814	180,000
Forth (Edinburgh)	71,000	70,000
Plymouth (Plymouth)	21,446	15,000
Tees (Teesside)	51,471	60,000
Trent (Nottingham)	43,375	50,000
Pennine (Bradford)	28,917	25,000
Victory (Portsmouth)	33,298	30,000
Orwell (Ipswich)	15,181	15,000
210 (Reading)	19,527	20,000
Downtown (Belfast)	71,111	70,000
Beacon (Wolverhampton/Black Country	89,171	90,000
TOTAL	1,954,077	265,000,000

were deferred; following devaluation of the pound in 1967, both the BBC and the IBA were required to reduce capital expenditures, the Authority by about £1 million and the BBC by £3 million; and in 1970, the Authority was required to reduce by 6 per cent expenditures planned for the period 1972–3 to 1974–5.

The law requires the Authority to establish and maintain a reserve fund, and empowers the Minister, with Treasury approval, to direct the management and use of this fund. However, television and radio surpluses are not interchangeable.[47] If, after payments into the fund, surpluses remain, the Minister, with Treasury approval and after consultation with the Authority's chairman, may indicate how they should be disposed of—including surrender to the government. Like the BBC, the Authority is subject to a corporation tax, at the rate of 52 per cent, on its operating surpluses. Obviously, therefore, the IBA, as well as the BBC, is not entirely a free agent in managing its finances. Table 9 indicates the Authority's income and expenditure from 1955 to 1979. Table 10 provides the same figures with more detail for the year ending 31 March 1979.

The Authority itself, of course, is not intended to be a money-making activity, and it is not charged with earning a profit, which is the reason for its frequent payments to the Exchequer.[48] The Authority points out that up to 1979, Independent Television had

contributed about £726 million to the Exchequer. . . . Since the introduction of the Television Levy in 1964, the ITV companies have paid to the Consolidated Fund (the Exchequer) about £440 million. Normal taxation since 1954 has

TABLE 9 *Independent broadcasting authority income and expenditure, 1955–79 (£000)*

	1955	1956	1957	1958	1959	1960	1961	1962	1963
INCOME	—	424	1,710	2,306	2,917	3,832	4,311	4,879	5,649
EXPENDITURE									
Operating expenditure	31	194	421	579	864	1,104	1,307	1,819	2,178
Capital expenditure	29	706	784	448	467	641	749	1,198	990
Taxation	—	180	520	715	847	1,133	1,267	1,331	1,525
Payments to the Exchequer	—	—	—	—	—	—	450	531	—
Reserve fund	—	—	—	250	250	970	450	—	900

	1964	1965	1966	1967	1968	1969	1970	1971	1972
INCOME	6,218	7,508	8,905	9,439	9,480	8,232	7,722	8,588	11,932
EXPENDITURE									
Operating expenditure	2,334	2,978	2,836	2,960	3,242	3,890	4,534	5,552	6,161
Capital expenditure	671	1,111	1,186	608	2,378	2,578	2,742	3,019	4,000
Taxation	1,500	2,400	2,162	2,223	2,728	1,785	1,150	540	1,802
Payments to the Exchequer	400	750	2,700	1,800	—	—	—	—	—
Reserve fund	1,300	250	—	1,830	1,130	—	(700)	(500)	(30)

TABLE 9 (Contd.)

	1973		1974		1975		1976	
	TV	Radio	TV	Radio	TV	Radio	TV	Radio
INCOME	14,075	—	13,937	265	16,104	950	16,279	1,053
EXPENDITURE								
Operating expenditure	7,244	359	7,517	464	9,365	812	11,713	1,080
Interest	—	7	—	87	—	132	—	167
Capital expenditure	4,874	—	2,844	—	4,391	—	3,361	—
Taxation	1,996	(146)	3,856	(155)	2,269	17	1,269	(94)
Payments to the Exchequer	—	—	—	—	—	—	—	—
Reserve fund	(40)	—	(280)	—	—	—	—	—
Revenue account balance	225	(220)	225	(351)	304	(362)	240	(462)

	1977		1978		1979	
	TV	Radio	TV	Radio	TV	Radio
INCOME	18,245	1,440	20,460	2,177	20,851	3,211
EXPENDITURE						
Operating expenditure	13,519	1,024	14,903	1,314	16,529	1,510
Interest	—	184	—	181	—	181
Capital expenditure	2,900	125	3,849	362	3,642	1,762
Taxation	1,255	—	1,708	—	618	677
Payments to the Exchequer	571	—	—	—	—	—
Reserve fund	—	—	—	—	302	(954)
Revenue account balance	240	(355)	240	(35)	—	—

SOURCE: Independent Broadcasting Authority.

TABLE 10   *Independent Broadcasting Authority income and expenditure for year ending 31 March 1979*

	Television (£000)	Radio (£000)	Total (£000)
INCOME			
Programme Contractors'			
Rentals	19,185	3,132	22,317
Other Income	1,666	79	1,745
	20,851	3,211	24,062
EXPENDITURE			
Revenue Expenditure			
Maintenance and operation transmission network	10,914	435	11,349
Planning for construction of additions and modifications to the network	3,979	403	4,382
Programme and advertising control	1,636	672	2,308
Loan interest	–	181	181
	16,529	1,691	18,220
Taxation	618	677	1,295
	17,147	2,368	19,515
Capital Expenditure	3,642	373	4,015
	20,789	2,741	23,530
Surplus	62	470	532
	20,851	3,211	24,062

SOURCE: *IBA Television and Radio 1980*, p. 217.

amounted to not less than £247 million; and the Authority itself has during its life had to provide over £32 million for taxation as well as making direct contributions to the Exchequer of £7 million. In aggregate these payments to the public purse make up the total of around £726 million.

PROGRAMME COMPANY FINANCES

During their first years on the air, the programme companies lost a great deal of money, and some investors began to think that the future of commercial television would be marked by deficit financing rather than by bonanza earnings. Things soon changed, however, and in 1958 the average yearly profit before taxes of the contractors as a group was 130 per cent on their investments.

Programme company income depends upon a variety of factors. Basic is audience size. The companies serving the London area, with some 5 million, or 23.5 per cent, of all united Kingdom homes capable of receiving ITV programmes, obviously can reach more people than can Border Television on the Scottish-

English border, which covers only 213,000 homes (see Table 7 above). In the 1950s, the number of receivers equipped to tune in ITV signals was an important factor: people who bought their sets during the BBC-only period often could not receive ITV signals in Band III; but that is no longer a problem, since few sets now in use were manufactured before ITV came on the air in 1955. A change in advertising policies also may affect revenues. For example, effective August 1965 there was a prohibition on broadcast cigarette advertising, which lost the programme companies £8 million a year.[49]

Also important is average audience size for the entire network. During its first years on the air, ITV's single service was often watched by 70 per cent of the viewing public, with the BBC reaching only 30 per cent; but more recently, as a consequence of better programme planning and the operation of two networks by the Corporation, the average is more nearly 50–50: 50 per cent for the single ITV service, and 50 per cent for the two BBC services combined (see below, pp. 356–61).

Then there is the matter of individual programme appeal. Although advertisers cannot have their names associated with programmes as 'sponsors', as often is done in the United States, they may choose the time of day when their advertisements are run; and if their spots are placed next to popular programmes during peak viewing hours, they obviously will reach a greater part of the public than if they are aired at less good times, adjacent to programmes of lower audience appeal. Time charges, therefore, are higher, and income greater, for a spot adjacent to popular programmes broadcast during peak viewing hours.

Also related to profitability are competition from other media (newspapers, magazines, billboards, and cinema screens); programming costs; and such fixed charges as rental payments to the IBA, the levy and the corporation tax. Prospective advertisers must not only believe in broadcast advertising, but also must find it profitable, since advertising is vulnerable when business is poor.

IBA advertising must consist entirely of spot commercials, each usually 60 seconds or less in duration (30 seconds being most common), quite similar to those broadcast by American stations, except that they may in no way relate the product advertised to the programmes being broadcast.[50] (For information about other regulations pertaining to advertising, see above, pp. 69–76.)

Schedule 2 of the 1973 law lays down the 'Rules for Advertisements' in much the same terms as did the first Television Act in 1954. Among other things the law states: 'The charges made by any programme contractor for advertisements shall be in accordance with tariffs fixed by him from time to time, . . . drawn up in such detail and published in such form and manner as the Authority may determine.'[51] All companies must keep to their published rate cards, which must be approved by the Authority before they are issued. If companies wish to alter their charges for any reason, approval must be first be obtained from the Authority. The law also prohibits 'off-the-rate card' deals between the programme companies and their clients. There is no objection, however, to discounts for quantity sales, provided the rates are published and are available to all advertisers. The rates charged are not controlled by the Authority, although they are subject to government price restraints and policies relating to prices and incomes.[52]

Rates charged by Thames Television for time in the London area as of January 1980 illustrate how the system works. The basic cost for 30 seconds of air-time varied from £400 prior to 4 p.m., to £5900 between 6.45 and 10.15 p.m.[53] (The top charge for a 30-second spot advertisement on Capital Radio in London in October 1979 was £340, without quantity discount.) Production costs for the average 30-second commercial vary greatly, but the average cost ranges from £25,000 to £30,000.

Table 11 provides information as to the origin of Independent Television's

TABLE 11   *Origin of ITV contractors' advertising revenues 1976 (percentages)*

	ITV	Press
Food, drink and tobacco	40	16
Household equipment and supplies	15	10
Financial, charity and educational	2	10
Pharmaceutical toiletries and cosmetics	13	6
Clothing stores and mail order	10	26
Leisure	7	12
Government, office equipment agriculture, horticulture and motoring	6	13
Local advertisers	2	
Publishing institutional and industrial	5	7

SOURCE: Independent Broadcasting Authority.

advertising revenues in 1976, along with comparative data for the press. Table 12 shows the origin of radio programme company advertising revenues during February 1977.

In view of the importance of network exchanges to the programme and financial success of Independent Broadcasting, contracts with programme companies contain the requirement that, with only a few exceptions, all programmes originated by any company must be available to all the rest on terms mutually agreeable to the companies and the Authority. If the contractors cannot agree on

TABLE 12   *Origin of radio contractors' advertising revenues February 1977 (averaged percentages)*

Automotive	4.4
Cosmetic	7.7
Drinks	4.2
Entertainment	29.1
Food	11.4
Household stores	1.2
Medical	6.7
Publishing	19.4
Retail/fashion	11.2
Travel	4.1
Others	0.6

SOURCE: Independent Broadcasting Authority.

financial arrangements, the Authority may determine them unilaterally.[54] The five central companies exchange programmes among themselves on a no-profit, no-loss basis, following the Net Advertising Revenue After Levy (NARAL) formula (see Table 7). The regional companies pay for the programmes they receive from the central companies according to their NARAL income share. Independent Television News costs are shared by all fifteen companies according to the same formula.

There has been much debate about whether or not the television programme companies receive excessive profits. In the words of the Annan Committee:

> Since the companies have no capital investment in their main asset—the right to use the airwaves—their profits, expressed in the normal terms of profits on assets employed, appear extremely high. They were, according to the Authority, 24.8% in 1969, 14.6% in 1970, 40.5% in 1971, 59% in 1972, 78.5% in 1973 and 48.3% in 1974, before tax.[55]

Although the programme companies have been highly profitable since 1958, they were expected to lose money during their first years of operation—and they did. This was not remarkable: American television too, lost money in its early years. CBS, for example, invested $53,100,000 in television from 1934 to 1952 without a single year of profits.[56] The programme contractors as a group lost £10 million during their first two years of operation.[57] But they began to show profits in 1957, and by the end of 1958 had paid off their initial losses and accumulated a profit of approximately £30 million, a rate of earnings so high as to delight their investors, appall their critics, and embarrass their defenders. At that time, in fact, the average annual profit before taxes of the programme companies as a group was 130 per cent of their capital investment. Until the levy was created by the Television Act of 1963, there was no way of curtailing these profits before the contracts expired in 1964. Accordingly, the money rolled in and the criticisms mounted, with the result that the new contracts provided more freedom to the Authority to change rental rates after franchises had been given, and the levy was introduced.

The Committee also examined the question of diversification: to what extent should companies be allowed to 'diversify their interests with their profits'?[58] The committee decided 'that the acid test was whether a company had retained enough of its profits to provide the capital needed to finance new investment in equipment and programmes at all times'. In any case, the committee recommended unanimously that the companies be required to distinguish in their public accounts between their domestic television operations and all other profit-making activity. (The Authority has vetoed some diversification proposals by programme companies.)

Any review of ITV finances also should mention the revenue received from overseas sales by the programme companies. Like BBC Television, ITV's companies sell many programmes to broadcasters in foreign countries, from whom they receive considerable revenue. Thames Television, which programmes London on weekdays, for example, was placing its shows in 106 international markets in 1978, with gross receipts of $6,000,000.[59]

An approximate idea of programme company expenditures is provided by some averaging figures published by the Authority.[60] Using mid-1979 data, the IBA reported that ITV's total yearly income was about £385 million, 'of which about 97 per cent came from advertising sales and the remainder from other sources: sales of programmes overseas, publications, interest, etc. Each pound of this total was spent as shown in Table 13'. Comparable figures for Independent Local Radio were as shown in Table 14.

TABLE 13   *How the ITV companies spend their income*

Programmes	58p
Other services	4p
Depreciation on assets	3p
Rentals paid to the Authority	5p
The Levy (paid to the Government *via* the Authority)	18p
Corporation Tax (paid to the Government)	7p
Profit, after tax, to provide reserves, new equipment and dividends to shareholders	5p
	£1.00

SOURCE: IBA, *Television and Radio 1980*, p. 215.

Also part of overall IBA operations are Independent Television News (ITN) and Independent Television Publications (ITP). ITN was constituted in its present form in 1968, the year the new franchises came into operation. It is controlled by the fifteen television programme contractors, who provide its capital and operating costs in proportion to their net advertising income, and then retain the income from advertisements shown during news periods.[61] In 1978/9, it was budgeted at approximately £10 million. ITN's assignment is to prepare nationwide network news for ITV stations.

Independent Television Publications (ITP) was created in 1968 to publish the IBA programme journals and some other material. Like ITN, it is owned jointly by the television programme companies, excluding Channel Television. Stockholdings are proportionate to the incomes of the contractors, as computed on the NARAL formula.[62] It has two subsidiaries, Independent Television Books, Ltd, which publishes books and other materials related to ITV programmes, and Radio Guide, Ltd, which publishes *Tune In*, the programme journal of Independent Local

TABLE 14   *How the ILR companies spend their income*

Programmes	40p
Other services	24p
Depreciation or equipment leasing	3p
Rentals paid to the Authority (including secondary rentals)	15p
Corporation Tax, recovery of initial losses, provisions for new equipment and dividends to shareholders	18p
	£1.00

SOURCE: IBA, *Television and Radio 1980*, p. 214.

Radio. *TV Times*, issued in fifteen editions to cover all sections of the country, had an average weekly circulation in 1977 of 3,573,874. (that of the BBC's *Radio Times*, which covers both radio and television, was 3,748,903).[63] ITP paid no dividends between 1957 and 1965, but did become profitable the following year, profits before copyright fees and taxation ranging from £200,000 to £3,120,000, the latter—in 1976—being the high point up to that time.[64]

In view of the several financial controls that the British government has over the IBA, it should be noted that the IBA, like the BBC, is potentially subject to government influence through financial channels. Licence fees are not an issue, of course, but there are other government decisions that affect its welfare. Thus, the government was in a position to decide whether or not to provide start-up funds for both television and radio; it has certain controls over the Authority's capital expenditures; it can confiscate Authority surpluses; and, by legislating a levy, it can cut tremendously into company profits. Despite its use of the word 'independent in its title, therefore, the Independent Broadcasting Authority is by no means entirely free from potential government control as to finance, and as was pointed out above (pp. 66–8), in theory, at any rate, IBA programming, like that of the BBC, is subject to both law and regulation.

ADVERTISING AGENCIES

The Television Act of 1954 and its successors did their best to isolate both the Authority and the programme companies from advertiser influence and control. Yet, the very clause of the law which prohibits them from serving as advertising agents makes the agencies that much more indispensable, since someone must provide liaison between the companies and the advertisers. Current law stipulates: 'Orders for the insertion of . . . advertisements may be received either through advertising or other agents or direct from the advertiser, but neither the Authority nor any programme contractor shall act as an advertising agent.'[65] Programme contractors may sell advertising directly to advertisers, therefore, although most national advertising is placed by advertising agencies. However, neither television nor radio contractors may serve as advertising agents.

Although programme companies do not compete for the same audiences, except in the few instances where they have overlapping coverage, they do compete for advertising revenue. This obviously is the case in London, where two companies serve the same market—although they do not broadcast simultaneously, since one serves the weekly and the other the weekend audience. But there also is competition for sales among areas, with each salesman arguing the advantages of the area he represents.

Most programme contractors have sales departments operating in their respective regions, although the two Scottish companies work together, since Scotland is in effect one marketing area; Trident Television handles sales for its subsidiaries, Yorkshire and Tyne Tees Television; and national advertising for Channel Television (which must economize because of its size) is handled by Westward Television.[66] All companies have sales offices in London, where most agencies are located, and where most advertising is bought and sold. Broadcast time salesmen, the programme companies told the Annan Committee, engage in highly 'sophisticated selling. . . . Media selling in television is no job for the old-style door-to-door salesmen.'

Most buying and selling is done by advertising agencies working in all the media. Normally, an agency assumes responsibility for all aspects of its clients' advertising, coordinating work in the several media according to agreements reached with clients. The agencies buy time from programme companies, draw up plans for commercials, and write the scripts. They provide their own producers, directors, and performers (mostly engaged on a freelance basis), when the commercials are filmed, usually in the studios of companies specializing in such work. If the commercials are done live in programme company studios, the agencies are responsible for talent and supervision. Advertising agencies derive revenue both from programme companies and clients. They hold back from payments to the companies 15 per cent of the charges for the air-time purchased, and in addition bill the clients for all production costs.[67]

8 British Broadcasting Personnel

The BBC has many more employees than does Independent Broadcasting. But whereas the Corporation's entire staff is part of one organization, the people who contribute to IBA productions are divided among the IBA itself, fifteen television programme companies, Independent Television News, a number of radio stations, participating advertising agencies, and the peripheral groups which contribute to the Authority's output and yet are not a part of it.

The BBC has more full-time employees than any other broadcasting organization in the world, excepting that of the much larger USSR. As of 31 March 1979, the Corporation had 26,633 employees (17,048 men and 9585 women), of whom 25,283 (16,983 men and 8300 women) were full-time, and 1350 (65 men and 1285 women) part-time.[1] Classifying them another way, 15,890 were managerial, programme, technical, and executive staff; 5283 were secretarial and clerical; 4626 were weekly staff (including custodial employees); 694 catering and hostel workers; and 140 locally recruited overseas staff.* But serious financial shortages forced the Corporation to announce early in 1980 that it would eliminate about 1500 permanent and temporary posts in its domestic services, although it hoped to achieve much of this reduction through early retirement and natural wastage.

In 1979, the staff of the IBA itself included approximately 1300 people, of whom some 210 were in the London headquarters, 40 were involved elsewhere with regional programming, and about 550 were engineers operating the ITV and Independent Radio transmitters.[2] The various television companies employed some 12,400 people, of whom 70% worked for the five major companies. The largest companies averaged between 1200 and 2200 employees each, and the

---

* Short of conducting an extensive inquiry, it is impossible to determine whether the BBC—or Independent Broadcasting either—is overstaffed. Many American broadcasters, observing procedures around BBC studios, come away with the impression that the Corporation has more employees than it needs; but since many London productions are for national networks—whereas most American programmes, except those coming out of New York or Los Angeles, are locally distributed—comparisons are difficult to make. The McKinsey group told the Annan Committee 'that the BBC were by far and away the most efficient users of studios that they had come across anywhere in the world', and that ITV was comparable; in fact BBC crews, for the most part, were smaller than those used by some ITV companies (Annan, ##10.51, 10.54). The Annan Committee also observed that the staffing levels of the Corporation, 'on the studio floor and elsewhere, are notably lower than in some ITV companies', and then went on to say, 'Where the BBC is overmanned is at the top. The BBC suffers, so some of us guess, from a disease which affects all bureaucracies: bifurcation.'

smallest ones had about 250 employees. Independent Local Radio had 100 employees, and ITN 575. There were no exact data as to the number of employees in advertising agencies or independent film production units who were involved principally with broadcast sales or the production of advertisements, but the total number of full-time employees contributing to the IBA output in 1978 must have on the order of 15,575.

THE GOVERNING BOARDS

Heading the two hierarchies are their respective boards: the BBC Board of Governors and the Independent Broadcasting Authority. Individual members of the BBC Board are referred to as Governors, but the IBA's 'governors' are known as Members of the Authority. Nevertheless, Parliament undoubtedly had the BBC Board of Governors in mind when it constituted the ITA in 1954.

In 1926, the Crawford Committee, laying plans for the Corporation, which came into being the following year, rejected proposals that its board 'be composed of persons representing various interests, such as music, science, drama, education, finance, manufacturing and so forth.'[3] The Beveridge and Pilkington Committees spoke in the same vein. The former wrote in 1950: 'It will be necessary to appoint Governors of first-rate quality. The work of the BBC should be regarded as among the most important of the national services.'[4] The Pilkington Report in 1962 observed 'that the Governors of the BBC and the Members of the ITA should be remarkable men and women: remarkable in their understanding of their responsibilities, and able to defend that independence against the challenges it is bound to meet.' Furthermore, the Governors and Members must 'judge what the public interest is, and it is for this that they are answerable'. Above all, 'they must be ready to resist direct or indirect intervention by the Government in programming. Less obviously, but as important, they must be ready to convince Ministers that broadcasting must obtain or retain the resources it needs.'

The Crawford Committee recommended that BBC Governors not represent special interests, but rather 'be men and women of business acumen and experienced in affairs'. However, in its submission to the Annan Committee in 1975, the Corporation expressed approval of 'the unwritten convention which provides for a Trade Unionist, a diplomatist (to take a particular interest in External Broadcasting), a financial expert and an educationist to be members of the Board'.[5] Not until Sir Hugh Greene, formerly BBC Director-General, was appointed to the Board in 1969 had there been a governor with a background in broadcasting; but Greene is no longer on the Board, so that generalization applies again to both the BBC Board and the Authority.

The Annan recommendations were in line with those cited above. Governors and Members, the Committee said, should continue to be appointed by the government 'as persons and not as representatives', but more of them should be 'rooted in the working class'.[6] The 1978 White Paper endorsed the Committee's proposals, although, to the consternation of the BBC, it proposed supplementing the Corporation's Board of Governors with 'separate Management Boards for each of the three services'—Television, Radio, and External Broadcasting. But the Conservative Government that took office in 1979 dropped this proposal, to the great relief of both the BBC and the IBA.

The two chairmen play prominent and influential roles, because they usually are outstanding people, because of the positions they hold, and because they are the only members who are expected to make broadcasting their main interest. The Pilkington Committee observed: 'The choice of chairman [in either organization] is of special significance: his standing must be such as to command the respect and attention of Cabinet Ministers.'[7] The Annan Committee also regarded 'the appointment of the Chairman of each Authority . . . [as] a matter of considerable importance. Obviously the Chairman should be of high personal integrity, wide experience and of sufficient standing to command the respect of Cabinet Ministers.'[8] After Lord Simon of Wythenshawe left the chairmanship of the BBC in 1952, he wrote that future chairmen should be drawn from persons who had been governors for at least two years, since only then would they 'have the knowledge to know when and how to intervene effectively with a tough and experienced Director-General.'[9]

When Lord Hill became ITA Chairman in 1963—he later occupied the same position at the BBC—he was the first politician to head either organization.[10] After some years as the BBC's 'radio doctor', he became an MP and then a Conservative Cabinet Minister. Surprisingly enough, although appointed to the IBA by a Conservative Government in 1969, he was moved from there to the BBC by a Labour Government. Commenting on Lord Hill's political background, Wedell observed that perhaps these chairmanships are 'so important that only someone with the standing of a former Cabinet Minister can do justice to them. It can be further argued in matters of securing political impartiality, there is a good deal to be said for setting a thief to catch a thief.'[11] But Wedell concluded that it would 'be regrettable if the chairmanship of the broadcasting organisations were to be regarded as the exclusive preserve of politicians. Politics is only a part of broadcasting and not the most important.' No BBC chairman since Lord Hill has had mainly a political background, although Lord Aylestone, who succeeded Lord Hill at the ITA, had been in political life.

The BBC Charter provides that Governors should be appointed by the Queen in Council; and since this is done upon the recommendation of the Prime Minister, the appointment is in effect by the government of the day.[12] The Governors, therefore, are the choices of the party in power; but since their actions as Governors are not supposed to reflect party considerations, there is no requirement for maintaining a balance between parties in their appointments, as there is with the American FCC.[13] The Annan Committee received proposals that Governors be selected as representatives of a particular group, but the committee—agreeing with the Crawford Committee's 1926 judgement mentioned above—recommended that they 'should continue to be appointed as persons and not as representatives'.[14] Currently, there are twelve members on the BBC's Board of Governors, although their number has varied from time to time in the past. They are appointed for 5 years, usually with staggered terms.[15]

The 'inside story' of how someone becomes a BBC Governor or IBA Member has yet to be published, although such appointments usually are preceded by discussions between representatives of the BBC or IBA and senior government officials.[16] Presumably, these usually involve the prospective appointees too, although Lord Hill first learned that he was being considered for the ITA chairmanship by reading the newspapers, and four years later a reporter told him he was being proposed as the BBC's Chairman, before Hill met with Prime Minister Harold Wilson to discuss the matter.

One BBC Governor is nominated as Chairman, another as Vice-Chairman and three others as National Governors for Scotland, Wales and Northern Ireland, respectively.[17] The latter three are to be selected for their 'knowledge of the culture, characteristics and affairs' of the areas they serve. The government may remove a Governor at any time without cause, or for such reasons as having interests in conflict with those of the Corporation, for having 'become of unsound mind or bankrupt', or if repeatedly absent from meetings without consent. But no BBC Governor—or IBA Member—has ever been removed, although a number have resigned before their terms were completed.

Governors and Members are expected to devote only a portion of their time to broadcasting, although the chairmen of the two Boards usually work full-time. In theory the Governors and Members are part-time so that they can judge broadcasting from the outside, instead of viewing the rest of the world from the vantage point of the Corporation or the Authority. Thus constituted—so goes the rationale—the Boards can better bridge the gap between broadcasters and public. On the other hand, part-time members, being less informed than the full-time— and often strong-willed—professional staff, are apt to accept guidance too readily, thus taking the inside 'party line' uncritically.

Corresponding to the BBC's Governors are the IBA's Members. Strictly speaking, Members are appointed by the Home Secretary rather than by the Crown-in-Council, although in both cases the government of the day really makes the choices. The Authority's Deputy Chairman corresponds to the Corporation's Vice-Chairman, and the Authority too has Members who make the interests of Scotland, Wales and Northern Ireland their special concern.[18] The 'emoluments'—to use the British term—of IBA Members are the same as those of BBC Governors.

A great point is made of Authority Members not having financial interests in companies manufacturing broadcasting equipment.[19] The law states that before anyone can be appointed to the Authority, the Minister must 'satisfy himself' that the nominee 'will have no such financial or other interest . . . as is likely to affect prejudicially the discharge by him of his functions as a member of the Authority'. What is more, if the IBA has a contractual agreement in which a Member 'is in any way directly or indirectly interested' he must 'disclose the nature of his interest'.

The law disqualifies a BBC Governor from simultaneously serving as a Member of the Authority, although there is no similar reverse requirement; but it is reasonable to assume that the same principle would exclude Authority Members from serving as BBC Governors.[20] The appointment of any Member may be terminated at will by the government; and since the law does not specify the conditions, the government presumably is free to act as it wishes. But if the

Minister does dismiss a Member, he must provide both Houses of Parliament with notice to this effect, although there is no parallel requirement in the BBC Charter. In practice, of course, the dismissal of any Governor or Member would receive wide publicity, with or without notification to Parliament.

Legally, the Governors and the Members as corporate groups *are* the organizations which they govern: they hold title to all property; and they determine policies and procedures, subject only to the Charter and Licence on the one hand, and the IBA Act on the other, as well as to periodic government pronouncements. They have two basic functions: to govern their respective organizations, and to provide liaison with Parliament and the public. But they do not 'report' to a member of the Cabinet as do the boards of nationalized industries.

Lord Normanbrook, a former BBC Chairman, has described the Board's duties.[21] 'Constitutionally', he said, 'the Board of Governors *is* the BBC. . . . It takes the final decisions on all major questions of management and all matters of controversy (political, religious, or cultural) which may arouse strong feeling in Parliament or among large sections of public opinion.' The Board must approve all major proposals for expenditure, both capital and current, and it has 'an unfettered discretion in the appointment of the senior officials of the Corporation'. The Board also is responsible, it told the Annan Committee, 'to put the BBC's case to Government and society, and in certain situations to protect the BBC from undue or unfair criticisms or pressure. In addition to a broadly administrative role, the Board has, therefore, to be both a critic and a guardian of broadcasting.'[22]

Effective 1 January 1979, the Board's previous practice of a long meeting every 2 weeks was replaced by a committee approach. The Board as a whole still meets to consider major areas of the Corporation's work, but smaller groups of governors make up specialist committees. In addition, Governors often meet individually or in groups with staff members. The heads of radio and television programming appear at many meetings, reviewing previous plans and outlining plans for future broadcasts. 'Only occasionally', said Sir Michael Swann, who was Board Chairman in 1974, do these discussions 'lead to a clear-cut Board request not to repeat this, not to make any more in the same idiom as that, or to encourage the other.' But nevertheless, they give 'senior management . . . some idea of the Board's thinking.' In context, however, the implication of his statement was that the Board did have some effect on programme policies.[23]

Although the model of the BBC confronted the ITA when it was organized in 1954, the many differences between the two organizations gave their governing boards somewhat different assignments. At the very outset, the Members of the Authority were involved in structuring the system which they were to administer. One of their basic decisions, for example, was to decentralize production by having each programme contractor serve a different section of the country, rather than building a major production centre in London with substations in outlying areas. The IBA had to select and supervise the programme companies, something that was to prove very difficult. The Authority, therefore, does not serve as the head of a single monolithic organization, but rather as a governing board charged with supervising and coordinating the output of a number of legally distinct television and radio units.

Originally, the Authority's Members met monthly, and later every third week, but after Lord Hill became Chairman in 1963, they met every 2 weeks, in addition to attendance at other Authority affairs.[24] Like the BBC's Governors, the Members select major IBA department heads, some of whom appear at the Authority's meetings. Although the Authority is legally responsible for the output of its programme contractors, it has no direct control over the personnel of those companies, as the BBC Board of Governors has over Corporation staff.

The governing boards of the two organizations always have been involved in a certain amount of controversy. When there is public criticism of Corporation programmes, the Board has to decide how much to become involved.[25]

Public reaction to the Authority too has sometimes been very severe. The Authority's Members and Director-General have been accused of ignoring their obligations and serving as public relations spokesmen for the companies, while the contractors grew fabulously wealthy. In fact, what happened was, that after several bad years, the companies found they could hardly help earning handsome profits. But following drubbings from the Pilkington and Nationalized Industries Committees, Parliament, the press, and the public, attitudes were changed, laws strengthened, additional supervisory personnel employed, and procedures tightened up in the later 1960s.

Through the years there have been consistent complaints that most members of the BBC's Board of Governors—and in recent years, Members of the Authority too—were too old, too concervative, and too upper-class in outlook. As long ago as 1935, the Ullswater Committee remarked: 'In the appointment of governors we trust that full attention will be paid to width and variety of outlook . . . we think it important that any undue homogeneity of age or opinion should be avoided . . . the Board should be as ready to entertain new ideas as it is to be guided by mature judgement.'[26] Clement Attlee, a member of the Ullswater Committee, in a reservation to the Committee's report, proposed having more younger Governors, thought that the majority of them should be 'persons in the prime of life', and believed that they should retire at age 60.[27]

How well have these criteria been met? Not very well, it would seem.[28] An analysis of the membership of the Board of Governors between 1927 and 1955 indicates that during this period forty-one people served on the Board. They included some very eminent persons; their median age upon appointment was fifty-nine years; and they tended to be people who had attended such schools as Rugby, Eton, and Harrow, and then had gone on to Oxford and Cambridge. Professionally, they were mainly industrialists, businessmen, teachers, or writers, and politically they were of Conservative leaning. An examination of the BBC Governors serving between 1955 and 1976 provides much the same story. Of the forty-three persons on the Board during that period, the median starting age was 58 years, and two-thirds of the twenty-seven who went to a university attended either Oxford or Cambridge. However, there was more frequent representation of labour than before: four trade union leaders had been appointed since 1955.

The Members of the Authority have been remarkably similar to those serving the BBC, despite the anticipation that they would tend to be younger, and less representative of the Establishment. Between 1954 and 1976, the Authority had fifty-six Members, whose median age on appointment was 60 years, the youngest being 33 and the oldest 70. There were four Etonians, one Harrovian, and at least forty others who attended either a public school or grammar school. Thirty-four had university educations; twenty-five of them either at Oxford or Cambridge. Fourteen industrialists and other businessmen and fourteen professors and teachers served on the Authority, as did four politicians, five people in government service, and three journalists. Seven trade union leaders served, which corresponds to the amount of labour representation among the Governors of the BBC. But proportionally fewer lords and ladies have been on the Authority than on the Board: eleven in the Authority, thirteen on the Board.

But why should Authority Members be expected to be less upper class and less Establishment than BBC Governors? They are appointed by the government in the same manner. The directors and chief administrators of the programme companies naturally would be industrialists, oriented toward business ethics and conservative politics. Furthermore, throughout its history, the ITA/IBA has been the creation of the Conservative rather than Labour party.

The Establishment, a collection of essays on that subject first published in London in 1959, contained an analysis of the BBC which began:

> Of all the voices of the Establishment, the British Broadcasting Corporation's is the most powerful. . . . When a rival organization, the Independent Television Authority, was created [its members included men and women who, in another year or so] might have been appointed a governor of the B.B.C. itself; not one that did not represent the 'British mentality at its best', as Reith had insisted that the B.B.C. should do.[29]

THE DIRECTORS-GENERAL

With all due credit to the talents and contributions of the hard-working men and women who have served as heads and members of the two governing boards, the public at large probably knows the names of the Directors-General better than of the chairmen or board members, although in recent years the balance of power has shifted somewhat towards the Governors and Authority Members. Howard Thomas, who held a responsible position with the BBC prior to becoming managing director of one of the major television programme companies, wrote in 1962: 'The whole fascinating history of the BBC could be chaptered around the Directors-General and their respective terms of office. The relationship between Chairmen and Director-General provides the real key to the running of the BBC. . . . '[30]

The Directors-General are in both cases appointed by the governing boards, and are not the choices of the British government. As Sir Hugh Greene, BBC Director-General from 1960 to 1969, said in a speech given in New York in 1961:

> I know from my own personal experience that there was no consultation whatever with the British Government before I was appointed. . . . The

Government was told in a very informal way a couple of days before the public announcement. . . . Even if they had viewed my appointment with the utmost distaste, there was nothing whatever they could have done about it.[31]

The biggest name of course, was John Reith, the Managing Director of the British Broadcasting Company from 1922 to 1926, and Director-General of the Corporation from 1927 to 1938. John C. W. Reith (1889–1971), the son of a Scots Presbyterian minister, was educated as an engineer. After leaving the Corporation he was Chairman of Imperial Airways, held several high government posts during World War II, and in 1950 was made chairman of the Colonial Development Corporation. He became Sir John Reith in 1927, and Lord Reith in 1940.

Reith did more than any other person to set the pattern for BBC development, determine the nature of its relationship to the government, and instill high standards of performance in its programming. He had much to do with the adoption in 1926 of the non-commercial, licence-fee-supported monopoly which endured until the Television Act of 1954 set up the competing ITA. He helped define the public service objectives followed to this day by the BBC, against which the performance of the ITA and the IBA have been measured, and which to a degree serves as a world standard.

John Reith's serious-minded and religious outlook on life was reflected in such features as the austere Sabbath Day programme, which came to be called the 'Reith Sunday', and the many serious talks and educational programmes broadcast every day. Because of his great self-confidence and his autocratic personality, he was sure he knew what was good for both the public and the BBC staff. His opinion that British radio became the best in the world because of 'the brute force of Monopoly' has already been quoted (see pp. 16–17). Audience research was not introduced into the BBC until late in his term, because the idea of programme policies closely related to audience reaction was quite foreign to him and his lieutenants. Strict controls over employees' outside professional activities and some aspects of their private lives were largely the reflection of his opinions. He served the BBC well in its formative years, but his would not be the talents to head a broadcasting system today, when staff and public must be taken into account.

Unfortunately, Reith's halo was darkened by the publication in 1975 of certain excerpts from his diary, which confirmed the charges of authoritarianism often levelled against him when he was Director-General.[32] On 9 March 1933, he wrote: 'I am pretty certain . . . that the Nazis will clean things up and put Germany on the way to being a real power in Europe again. They are being ruthless and most determined.' In July 1934, about the infamous 'night of long knives', he thought: 'I really admire the way Hitler has cleaned up what looked like an incipient revolt against him by the Brown Shirt leaders. I really admire the drastic actions taken, which were obviously badly needed.' In August 1936 it was: 'I have a great admiration for the German way of doing things.' Even though he began to see things somewhat differently after Hitler occupied the Rhineland, as late as March 1939, after Prague had been occupied, Reith commented: 'Hitler continues his magnificent efficiency.

Reith took somewhat the same view of Mussolini. In November 1935, during the Abyssinian War, he told Marconi, then visiting England: 'I had always admired Mussolini immensely and I had constantly hailed him as the outstanding example of accomplishing high democratic purpose by means which, though not democratic, were the only possible ones.' Lord Clarendon, who as first chairman of the Board of Governors, often crossed swords with Reith, remarked at one point: 'Reith is a Mussolini. The staff are afraid of him because he is a hard man.'[33]

In his middle 70s, looking back on his term as Director-General, he told the wife of then Director-General, Hugh Greene, during a luncheon in January 1964: 'I made my point of view absolutely clear—that Hugh and I were fundamentally in complete opposition of outlook and attitude. I lead; he follows the crowd in all the digusting manifestations of the age.' In May 1964, he wrote to Sir Arthur Fforde, who had retired as chairman of the Board of Governors earlier that year:

> The BBC has lost dignity and repute; in the upper reaches of intellectual and ethical and social leadership it has abdicated its responsibility and its privilege. Its influence is disruptive and subversive; it is no longer the 'Lord's side'. I am sorry I ever had anything to do with it.

Another influential Director-General was Sir William Haley, who served from 1941 to 1952. Born in 1901, Haley stands as an example of a man without private school or Oxford–Cambridge background who rose to the top through sheer merit. He was educated at Victoria College in Jersey, served at sea during World War I, and then joined the *Manchester Evening News* as a reporter in 1922. Assisted by an intensive programme of self-education, he worked his way up to become Managing Editor of the *Manchester Guardian* and *Evening News* by 1939, and later became director of the Reuter News Agency and of the Press Association. He joined the BBC in 1942 as Editor-in-Chief, an executive position only slightly subordinate to that of the Director-General, and became Director-General the following year. He was knighted in 1946. He left the BBC in 1952 to become editor of *The Times*.

Haley helped crystallize BBC philosophies through his various speeches and writings, at the same time that he contributed to their execution by his direction of the post-war reorganization of the Corporation's staff structure and programme offerings. One of Haley's contributions was the structuring of BBC radio in 1946 into three differentiated programmes, including the famous Third Programme, a concept which followed from his experience that, given the opportunity, an ambitious and able person could improve his status in life through hard work and study.[34]

Sir Ian Jacob was born in 1899, the son of a professional British army officer who later became a field marshal. He was educated in several military schools and at Cambridge. A long military career brought him from second lieutenant up to lieutenant-general. From 1939 to 1946 he was Military Assistant Secretary to the War Cabinet. He was knighted in 1946, becoming Controller of BBC European Services the following year, and Director-General in 1952. He resigned from the Corporation in 1960. Sir Ian was the first Director-General to recognize the importance of television (see above, p. 56).

Sir Hugh Greene, Director-General from 1960 to 1969, shared some of the writing talents of his brother, novelist Graham Greene. Born in 1910, Greene attended one of the British public schools Berkhamsted, thereafter graduating from Merton College, Oxford. On the Berlin staff of *The Daily Telegraph* from 1934 to 1939, he was expelled from Germany in May of the latter year. Thereafter, he was a newspaper correspondent in Warsaw and other European countries during the first years of World War II. He became head of the BBC's German service in 1940, and served as Controller of Broadcasting in Germany from 1946 to 1948. From then until becoming Director-General in 1960, Greene held various BBC positions, mainly with the news and overseas services. Following his term as Director-General, he was on the Board of Governors from 1969 to 1971. He was the only BBC or IBA Director-General to have served on either governing board.

Greene was knighted in 1964. His business interests have included connections with a brewery (Chairman of Greene, King and Sons, a family enterprise), while among his publications are several anthologies of Victorian detective stories; *The Third Floor Front: A View of Broadcasting in the Sixties*; and *The Future of Broadcasting in Britain*. Greene was an energetic and aggressive Director-General. He insisted on the BBC's competing strongly with the IBA, and remaining free from government influence. During his regime, BBC programmes became very experimental and in some cases avant garde, which fact led many observers to conclude that he deliberately set out to erase the old image of the BBC as 'Auntie.'

Sir Charles Curran, Director-General from 1969 to 1977, was born in Dublin in 1921 and died in London in 1980. A graduate of Cambridge, he served with the Indian Army during World War II. He joined the Corporation as a talks producer in 1947, and served thereafter in a series of posts, including representative in Canada, Secretary of the BBC, and Director of External Broadcasting. After resigning from the Corporation in 1977, he became Managing Director of Visnews, the London-based television newsfilm agency, of which the BBC holds one-third of the shares. The late Sir Charles was president of the European Broadcasting Union from 1973 to 1978.

Ian Trethowan, who became the BBC's Director-General in October 1977, came to his new post with a good background both in the print and broadcast media. Before going into broadcasting, he had been a political correspondent for several newspapers, and in 1958 joined ITN, where he rose from newscaster and diplomatic correspondent to deputy editor and political editor. He went to the BBC in 1963 as a political commentator, became Managing Director of BBC radio in 1970, and Managing Director of television in 1976. One newspaper remarked of him that he had been through the mill, with distinction'.[35]

The first ITA Director-General was Sir Robert Fraser, who was chosen from 332 applicants for the post. Fraser's application, incidentally, resulted from his reading a newspaper advertisement, which was the same way John Reith first learned of the Managing Director opening in the British Broadcasting Company.[36] An Australian by birth, Fraser joined the Ministry of Information in 1939, and became head of the Central Office of Information in 1946. During his student days at the London

School of Economics, he was a protege of Harold Laski, who saw him as a potential Socialist cabinet minister. In 1930 he became an editorial writer on the staff of the Labour Party newspaper, *The Daily Herald*, and in 1935 he stood for Parliament as a Labour candidate. Such a background inevitably led to comments about his changed status as a central figure in the commercial television organization, whose very creation was strongly opposed by the Labour Party.

Fraser had the formidable assignment of serving as Director-General at the beginning, when ITV's financial survival was in doubt, and later when it became embarrassingly wealthy. He and his colleagues are to be commended for developing a new type of broadcasting organization, which not only survived but succeeded, and which won acceptance as a permanent aspect of British broadcasting. But there is much evidence to support the views of his critics that under him the Authority served more as public relations apologist for the programme companies than as their regulator. They pointed out that the Chairman during the period when the biggest profits were made, Sir Ivone Kirkpatrick, made his mark as a diplomat, while the Director-General had headed an information office.[37]

The IBA's second Director-General, Sir Brian Young, who took office in 1970, was originally an educator. Born in 1922, he went to Eton and then graduated from Kings College, Cambridge. He served as assistant master of Eton from 1947 to 1952, and as headmaster of Charterhouse, one of the country's most prestigious public schools, from 1952 to 1964. Thereafter, he was Director of the Nuffield Foundation from 1964 to 1970, Britain's largest foundation, which among other things supported a great many educational ventures. Prior to joining the IBA, however, he had no background in broadcasting.

In any large organization, long-term executive officers tend to dominate short-term board members, and in the BBC the strong personality of the first Director-General made this inevitable. When the first chairman of the British Broadcasting Company's Board told Reith in 1923 that 'we're leaving it all to you', Reith was pleased: 'I have always functioned best when responsibility for decision rested wholly and solely on me', he observed in retrospect.[38]

In 1931 Reith and Board Chairman J. H. Whitley drafted the so-called Whitley Document, which subordinated the role of the Governors to that of the Director-General. This was sent to all new Governors until 1952. But reflecting growing dissatisfaction with the limitation of the Whitley Document, the 1952 White Paper on broadcasting policy reversed the emphasis, declaring:

> Within the framework of the charter the Governors collectively will have unrestricted authority and power of decision, though the Chairman should have the recognized rights of making emergency decisions, subject to report to the Board.[39]

Lord Hill extended the influence of the Authority, which he headed from 1963 to 1967, and of the Corporation's Board of Governors, of which he was chairman from 1967 until 1972. He later wrote that he tried during his period at the IBA to 'Strengthen the role of the Authority', and many observers believed that he was moved to the BBC to tighten up certain aspects of Board control there, and to curb the liberalizing programme theories of Sir Hugh Greene.[40]

When Greene heard that Hill was to become the new Board Chairman, he nearly resigned in anger, and although he delayed his departure until July 1968, there was strife between him and Hill during much of that period, the basic problem being differences over the roles of the Board and of top management.[41] That the Board won was discretely indicated in what it told the Annan Committee: 'Since the Governors, including the chairman have always held part-time appointments, a detailed executive role is virtually precluded, but it would seem that, over the years, the Board has increased its influence.'[42] The Committee approved this trend: 'It is for the Governors, not the senior staff, to make the final judgment in the public interest. It would do worlds for the reputation of the BBC with the public if the Governors were seen to govern.'[43] The government reacted to this comment by suggesting 'certain changes in the internal structure of the BBC' which it believed would 're-emphasize the regulatory and supervisory role of the Governors . . . and to enable them to be more accountable for their trusteeship of the public interest'.[44]

ADVISORY COUNCILS AND COMMITTEES

From its earliest days—except during World War II when its committee structure was largely suspended—the BBC has drawn upon the advice of councils and committees made up of people from outside its ranks, and the IBA now does likewise.

Under the provisions of the 1964 Charter, the BBC's fifty-seven Advisory councils and committees are of four types: the General Advisory Council; the National Broadcasting Councils for Scotland and Wales (a council is to be set up for Northern Ireland if so requested by its government); the Regional Advisory Councils for Northern Ireland (in the absence of a National Broadcasting Council) and each of the English regions; and a number of advisory committees on special subject areas. Most of these groups are appointed by the BBC, although the advisory bodies in Scotland and Wales are chosen by their respective National Broadcasting Councils, and report to them.[45]

The Charter requires the BBC to appoint a General Advisory Council to advise it 'on all matters which may be of concern to the Corporation, or to bodies or persons interested in the broadcasting services of the Corporation'.[46] This now consists of some fifty-five members representing a wide range of interests, such as literature, philosophy, music, visual arts, theatre, film, science, medicine, economics, law, sports, journalism, religion, international affairs, politics, trade unions, industry, finance, social services, education at several levels, and agriculture. The Council meets four times a year to discuss the problems referred to it by the BBC or anything else it cares to take up. Since its meetings are attended by the Chairman of the Board of Governors, the Director-General, members of the Board of Management and other senior staff, Council members have opportunities to raise questions pertaining to all aspects of BBC activity. Subjects discussed have included general programme policy, BBC publications, violence in broadcasting, election broadcasts, medical programmes, sports coverage, public relations problems, industrial coverage, audience research, BBC organization, and news broadcasting. Periodically the Council requests the Corporation to prepare papers on subjects in which it is interested, and sometimes arranges for these to be published.[47]

The General Advisory Council is expected to bring prestige to the BBC, relate it to the main currents of British life, and offer advice on matters of policy. It is difficult to appraise its actual influence on the Corporation, but since its members are important people, and because statements are made to the press following each meeting, it surely can focus public attention on the BBC, even though it lacks authority to enforce its recommendations. The Annan Committee wrote that it was 'the function of the advisory bodies . . . to tell the Broadcasting Authorities their own personal reactions to programmes as people who keep in touch with what others think'. The current chairman of the General Advisory Council, who the report said had 'made that body considerably more lively', told the Committee that the 'point of the GAC was that—unlike the results of audience research—it could listen and speak back. It could express a whole range of opinions and was not continually seeking a consensus'.*

Recent Charters have required the appointment of National Broadcasting Councils for Wales and Scotland, and specify that a similar group be set up for Northern Ireland, if the government of Northern Ireland so requests.[48] The members—not less than eight nor more than twelve in each case—are selected, not directly by the BBC, as are all other council and committee members, but by a panel nominated by the General Advisory Council from its own membership. The National Councils must be truly representative of their 'countries', and their members are to be 'selected [only] after consultation with . . . representative cultural, religious and other bodies in Scotland and Wales, as the case may be'. The National Governors for Scotland and Wales serve as chairmen of their respective Councils. Northern Ireland has retained the purely advisory character of its Council ever since the 1952 Charter set it up, but the Scottish and Welsh National Councils now have almost complete control of their regional program-mes.[49]

The Advisory Councils for Northern Ireland and the eight English regions, which have only advisory functions, are appointed directly by the BBC. The Charter specifies that their members—usually from fifteen to twenty in

---

* Annan, #6.4. Stuart Hood, who worked for both the BBC and ITV, took a critical view of committees. Most of them, he said, consisted of people who had

> attained some eminence. . . . What they bring to their respective organisations is not a reflection of public taste so much as a constant stream of pressures—generally from some section or some sub-section of the Establishment. [Members] cheerfully castigate programmes they will then admit to not having seen. Like all amateurs they are prolific in advice to professional programme makers, who require a high degree of patience when listening to and then rejecting programme ideas any trainee director would know to be boring or impossible. . . . The best that can be said for them is that they are lightning conductors—opportunities for sectional interests and prejudices to be aired. . . . The fact is that committees are uncreative. (Hood, pp. 47–9.)

number—must 'be persons chosen for their individual qualities who are broadly representative of the general public . . . of the Region from which the Councils are appointed'. Real power in the regions, therefore, is vested in the local Controller, who reports to the Director-General in London.[50] These councils normally meet three or four times a year, although they may hold extra sessions if they wish. Senior members of the BBC's Board of Management usually are present.

Then there are the specialist committees. The 1964 Charter continued the previous practice of authorizing (but not requiring) the appointment of 'persons or committees [in addition to the General Advisory Council and the National and Regional Councils] for the purpose of advising the Corporation'.* These committees, made up of well-known experts in their fields, have both public relations and advisory functions. They usually meet three or four times a year with the heads of the programme areas concerned. In some instances, they deal with very difficult and thorny problems. For example, the Central Religious Advisory Committee, including both lay and church people from the main Christian denominations, helped the Corporation determine basic policy on such matters as whether or not religious programmes should actively proselytize for the Christian faith, and which religious groups should be invited to broadcast. The agenda of the Music Advisory Committee has ranged from the repertoire of the Promenade Concerts to disputes with the Musicians' Union. Most active of all, however, are the several school Broadcasting Councils, which have a very important role in the development and appraisal of BBC school broadcasts (see below, pp. 253–5).

From its beginning the Authority too was directed to seek advice about both its programmes and its advertising.[51] Initially, it was to appoint committees on religious programmes, children's programmes, and advertising, and was required to comply with their advice. But, acting upon recommendations from the Pilkington Committee, the government lightened the requirements effective with the law of 1963. Current legislation requires the appointment of committees on religious programmes, school programmes, advertising generally, medical advertising, and for each local radio station operated by the Authority. In addition, the IBA is authorized—but not required—to appoint a General Advisory Council as well as other committees 'to give advice to the Authority and programme contractors on such matters as the Authority may determine'. But the Authority is no longer required to follow their advice.

There are few specific requirements for committee members. They must be

---

* *1964 Charter*, #9. Standing committees appointed under this authority now include: a Central Religious Advisory Committee (which since 1954 has also served the IBA); four regional religious advisory committees; one central and three regional committees to determine policy in broadcasting appeals for contributions; a School Broadcasting Council for the United Kingdom, and separate councils for Wales and Scotland; a Further Education Advisory Council; one central and three regional Agricultural Advisory Committees; central and Scottish Music Advisory Music Committees; an Engineering Advisory Committee; a Science Consultative Group; an Asian Programme Advisory Committee; an Advisory Council on the Social Effects of Television; an Archives Advisory Committee; a Consultative Group on Industrial and Business Affairs; advisory committees on Gaelic, the Orkneys, and the Shetlands; and one local radio council for each area for which the BBC provides local radio service.

related to, representative of, and/or knowledgeable about the subjects about which they are to advise. The head of the advertising committee must have no 'financial or other interests in advertising ... likely to prejudice his independence as chairman'. The local radio committees, whose membership should reflect, 'so far as is reasonably practicable, the range of tastes and interests of persons residing in the area' served by each station, are to be chosen in part from people nominated by 'appropriate local authorities', and no committee member is to have any advertising connection that might 'prejudice his independence as a member of that committee'. The 1954 law required that the Authority itself have members representing Scotland, Northern Ireland and Wales, but there was no requirement for advisory committees for those areas, as there was with the BBC, even though the Authority voluntarily set up such committees.[52] But the 1980 law specified that there should be committees for those areas.

The IBA's General Advisory Council was first appointed in 1964, following a recommendation from the Pilkington Committee. The Council meets four times each year, and after each session its proceedings are reported to the full membership of the Authority.[53] The IBA described the purposes of the Council as being:

To keep under review the programmes of Independent [Radio and] Television and to make comments to the Authority thereon; to advise the Authority on the general pattern and content of programmes; and to consider such other matters affecting the Independent Broadcasting service as may from time to time be referred to it by the Authority.[54]

The Council normally meets five or six times each year, and takes up the same types of items as does the corresponding group of the BBC.

The IBA has fewer and smaller advisory committees than does the BBC, although it claims wider representation for them. In 1978, they included separate national committees for Scotland, Wales and Northern Ireland; Central Religious Advisory Committee (shared with the BBC); Panel of Religious Advisors; Advertising Advisory Committee; Medical Advisory Panel; Educational Advisory Council; Schools Committee; Adult Education Committee; central Appeals Advisory Committee (shared with the BBC); Scottish Appeals Advisory Committee (shared with the BBC); and advisory committees for local radio stations.

From its earliest years, British broadcasting's committees and councils have been criticized as being too limited in membership range. In 1972, the Select Committee on Nationalized Industries observed that in a number of European countries, 'representation on national or regional broadcasting councils is far more broadly based than it is on the councils of the B.B.C. or the Authority'.[55]

The Annan Committee had several comments on the broadcasting committees.[56] 'Few of those who gave evidence', it wrote, 'love these [advisory] bodies. Most thought them ineffective as a way of keeping in touch with public opinion.' Advice as to what to do with them ranged from suggestions for their elimination to their being given more independence and being democratically elected. But the Report concluded that 'these committees were performing a useful function and helped to keep the broadcasters in touch with developments in specialist fields. . . . All in all, we considered the specialist committees made a positive contribution to the quality of the output.' The *1978 White Paper* remarked that both the Board of Governors and the Authority consider, 'and the Government agrees, that these committees have worked well and that they should continue as an integral part of . . . broadcasting in this country'.[57]

STAFF PROCEDURES

In both the BBC and the IBA, the Directors-General and their principal staff members have weekly meetings. The Corporation's Director-General meets with his Board of Management, which includes the Managing Directors for television, radio and external broadcasting; the directors of engineering, public affairs, news and current affairs, personnel and finance; his special advisor and chief assistant; and the chief secretary.[58]

The three managing directors, whose posts were created in 1969 in accordance with the recommendations of a management consultant, have considerable independence. The Managing Director, Television, housed in the BBC Television Centre in Western London, is in charge of all aspects of television, including not only programming, but also finance, personnel, engineering, and public relations. The Managing Director, Radio, in Broadcasting House, supervises the manifold activities of the BBC's four national networks and its local radio stations. The Managing Director, External Broadcasting, is responsible for all broadcasts whose target audiences are outside the United Kingdom. Directors of Engineering, Personnel, and Finance work in the areas indicated by their titles. In recognition of their importance and sensitivity, all broadcasts of news and current affairs for domestic audiences on both radio and television are the responsibility of the Director of News and Current Affairs, who reports directly to the Director-General.

The complete separation of the BBC staff from the British government's civil service was deliberately arranged to provide one more assurance of the Corporation's freedom from government control. Therefore, the BBC, in effect, has set up its own civil service system, headed by a Director of Personnel who is assisted by the Controller, Personnel Services.[59] There are heads of personnel and personnel officers in each division of the Corporation.

BBC codified personnel practices read much like those of many American corporations, universities, and government units. By and large, staff regulations are reasonable by American standards.[60] Staff openings are announced on readily accessible BBC bulletin boards, are listed in such BBC publications as the *Listener* and the *Radio Times*, and often are advertised in the newspapers. Once on the staff, each employee is the subject of an annual report by his superior. This must be favourable if he is to receive his annual increment; if adverse, however, it always must be communicated to and discussed with the employee.

Staff members are guaranteed the right to see their Personnel Officer 'at any time to discuss or seek advice on any aspect of their employment', and there also are provisions for appeals against 'the termination of their employment', 'against downgrading involving a reduction in substantive salary', and other major sanctions.[61] The staff also may appeal 'on other matters substantially affecting their employment'. Dismissed employees, 'who are unsuccessful on internal appeal', often carry their cases to an Industrial Tribunal.[62] No staff member may 'be directly or indirectly in authority over a relative; if staff have to be removed from post as a result of this principle, the BBC will give them an opportunity to seek another suitable post under the normal resettlement machinery'. Otherwise, there is no objection to husbands, wives, parents and children working in the same department.[63]

Women staff members are entitled to grants for maternity leave. Men's and women's pay scales are identical, although due to higher living costs, London salaries are augmented. There are four weeks of paid vacation annually. BBC clubs, which provide recreational facilities near or on most BBC posts, arrange special charter trips in the United Kingdom and abroad. Some medical facilities are available to employees at work, and a personal accident plan provides payment in the event of permanent disability resulting from accidents occurring either on or off duty. Sixty is the normal retirement age. There are several pension plans, the one chosen depending upon the circumstances and the time the employee joined the staff.

In earlier decades, the Corporation had rules which severely limited employees' outside activities, but now the regulations have been relaxed, partly because of pressures from employees, and partly because of changing working relationships everywhere.[64] But there still are regulations, although the BBC 'wishes to allow staff as much freedom as possible to undertake [outside] activities so long as its legitimate interests are safeguarded'.[65] In this respect, staff are divided into two categories: restricted ('those who because of their position in the Corporation must exercise special care in regard to political or controversial activities', including some senior staff, those with 'an important degree of responsibility for news and current affairs programmes'; well-known performers; and 'those whose prime responsibility is to represent the Corporation in its contact with the public'); and unrestricted (all the rest). No staff members may 'engage in any business activity of their own or undertake any continuing work for any other employer unless the Corporation's written permission is obtained'. Unrestricted staff are free to do a certain amount of writing or lecturing, though they may not use Corporation material obtained during their work for the BBC without permission. For restricted staff, the rule is the same, 'with the additional proviso that permission is necessary if the subject matter is political or in the realm of public controversy'.

Permission normally is not given for BBC staff to work for other broadcasting or broadcast-related organizations, although they may be interviewed on Independent Television News 'If their outside activities form a genuine part of the news', and they may appear on Independent Television 'literary or magazine programmes' in connection with books, plays or other artistic works which they produced on their own. In all this, the BBC does not act differently from most American stations and networks, since broadcasters everywhere do not willingly share their staffs or stars with competitors.

As to political activities, the Corporation stated in the early 1950s that it was 'anxious to allow as much freedom as possible . . . and permission will not be unreasonably withheld so long as the Corporation's legitimate interests are safeguarded'.[66] The Corporation pointed out to the Annan Committee in 1974 that every member of its staff shared 'a responsibility for safeguarding the BBC's reputation for impartiality', and that its regulations governing 'outside activities are designed to safeguard public confidence in the BBC and to protect its legitimate interests as a broadcasting service, while at the same time allowing staff to undertake reasonable outside activities, including various forms of public service'.[67]

If a staff member in the 'restricted' category wishes to run (the British term is 'stand') for Parliament, he may receive 'up to six weeks' unpaid leave' during the campaign period, and he 'will be given a fair indication of whether or not he can expect to return to his former post should he not be elected, and, if not, an estimate of his chances for resettlement in some other suitable post so far as they can be foreseen'.[68] If a staff member is elected he must resign from the BBC.

The rules for an unrestricted staff member running for Parliament are about the same, except that, if not elected, he may return to his former post at the expiration of his period of unpaid leave. All staff members must get permission before running for local government offices, as must restricted staff before taking part in 'minor political activities'.

The Annan Committee said it was 'disturbed at the extent of the restrictions which the BBC in particular found it necessary to impose upon their staff'. They noticed particularly the requirement that staff not 'publish anything or speak in public about broadcasting generally, without seeking the Corporation's permission. We consider this an unnecessary restriction which in law would most likely be held against public policy.' Some restrictions on political activities, the committee thought, were 'essential if the broadcasters are to be accepted by the public as observing due impartiality in their programmes'. The committee concluded 'that the restrictions on staff duties, both in the BBC and in other broadcasting organisations, should be limited to the minimum essential for safeguarding public confidence in any broadcasting service. We recommend accordingly.'[69]

IBA staff procedures are less elaborate and less formalized than those of the BBC. The IBA is a newer and smaller organization; furthermore, much of the work done for the BBC by its employees is carried out by programme contractors, each of which is an independent corporation. At the IBA headquarters, the Director-General is assisted by a Deputy Director-General (aided by eight senior staff); a Director of Television (twelve senior staff); a Director of Finance (nine assistants); a Director of Radio (two senior staff); Head of Advertising Control (three senior staff); Head of Information (four assistants); and a Director of Engineering.[70] There are regional officers and several assistants in each of the ten IBA regional offices.

At the outset, the meetings of the Director-General and his senior staff were relatively informal, but as the staff grew, a more structured approach was necessary. Authority officers meet with representatives of the companies, sometimes in formal committee sessions and sometimes informally. In addition,

Authority representatives attend the meetings of the network programme planning committee and subcommittees.[71]

An important part of IBA liaison with the programme companies is carried out by its Standing Consultative Committee and Programme Policy Committee. The former group includes the Director-General and senior staff, along with the managing directors or chief executives of the fifteen television programme companies. At its monthly meetings, the committee reviews the entire gamut of Independent Broadcasting's problems. Typical agenda items have included: taxes on cinema films shown on television; cable television; ORACLE; the Exchequer Levy; diversification; the Fourth Channel; film policy; and future plans.[72]

> As an industry, Independent Television is relatively small [the companies told the Annan Committee; but at these monthly meetings] the twenty or so people who control it ... reach, by consensus and compromise, decisions which may not always be immediately advantageous to individual companies or a group of companies—or to the Authority for that matter—but which all accept as correct for ITV, its viewers and society.

The quarterly meetings of the Programme Policy Committee are 'attended by senior officers of the Authority's programme division, managing directors or chief executives of all fifteen companies, programme controllers of the five central companies, and the Editor of ITN. The chairman of the Authority takes the chair.' Agenda items range from plans to broadcast the debates of the House of Commons to sex, violence, and bad language in programmes.

Inevitably, the coming of ITV had the effect of raising broadcasters' salaries all round. In fact, one reason many BBC employees favoured the creation of ITV was that it would remove their dependence on a single employer and give them a larger market in which to sell their services.[73] Nevertheless, British broadcasters still are paid less than their American counterparts: Almost all salaries are lower in Britain than in the US; and neither British broadcasting organization has as much money to spend as do the American networks and large stations, although the IBA and its programme companies pay higher salaries than does the BBC. In part this resulted from a strict government pay ruling imposed on the BBC shortly after the IBA, by chance, had raised certain of its salaries, and also from the competition for staff, with the better financed programme companies able to outbid the BBC for talent.

BBC employees surely do not receive handsome salaries. The annual handbooks now list the number of employees receiving £10,000 or more during the previous year.[74] In 1978–9, only 964 of 26,633 staff members were in this category, and of those, 737 had salaries between £10,000 and £12,500. Only one—the Director-General—was in the £30,001–£32,500 range. (Prominent performers, writers and others sometimes resign from the staff and then are re-hired on a freelance basis at higher salaries. In other cases, a staff member may assume additional assignments on a contract basis, thus increasing his salary.) The situation at the Authority was much the same.[75] During the 1977–8 fiscal year, only thirty-one of its employees earned more than £10,000, and only one—the Director-General—was in the £22,501–£25,000 range. These figures apply only to the Authority itself; if the salaries of programme company executives were included, the ranges would be much higher than those paid for similar posts at the BBC. Therefore the IBA and its programme companies often hire away top BBC staff members and performers, much to the despair of the Corporation.

As was noted above, payments for musicians and actors are set after negotiating with the appropriate unions. Name stars, of course, command much more, although they do not do as well as their counterparts in the United States. Furthermore, American cinema, theatre, and entertainment luminaries perform in Britain for less than in the United States—which is not surprising, since the total audiences are smaller and the amount of money, therefore, less. They do so in order to receive such side benefits as increased attendance at their theatre or cinema performances, or greater sales for their recordings.[75]

UNION RELATIONS

Article 13 of the BBC Charter, and Section 32 of the Broadcasting Act 1973, in virtually identical language, require the two broadcasting organizations to consult with 'appropriate' organizations as to wages and conditions of work, and to provide for arbitration in those cases which cannot be settled by negotiation.[76] Up to the mid-1930s, the BBC maintained that no union representation was necessary, and that informal consultations could take care of any problems that might arise. Many other employers made similar claims in those years, so that the BBC's position was not exceptional. But inevitably the BBC had to change its position. In 1936, the Ullswater Committee rejected the BBC's argument that there was no need for union participation. Such representation, it wrote, could consist of 'the intervention of external Trade Unions or . . . the constitution of one or more internal associations'.[77] This recommendation received government approval, and the ensuing White Paper noted that 'The B.B.C. has agreed to adopt its recommendation.'[78] Implementation was delayed by the war, but nevertheless, two organizations were formed and recognized for bargaining purposes: a Staff Association of non-technical workers was formed in 1940; and the Association of BBC Engineers was set up in 1941. In 1945 the two merged into the BBC Staff Association.

It is interesting to review the justifications given by the Corporation to the Beveridge Committee in 1949 for its long refusal to recognize outside unions. Only in this way, said the BBC, could it live up to its

responsibility for impartiality. It is not beyond the bounds of possibility that some great national issue [like the General Strike in 1926] may again rise in which the trade unions and the rest of the nation do not see eye to eye. . . . The Corporation should be sure of its ability to discharge that duty in any circumstances. It seems most doubtful, however, if that could be possible if the trade unions were given the power they increasingly seek, and particularly so if they were to succeed in making a number of fields of activity in the BBC 'closed shops'.[79]

Despite such arguments, however, the Beveridge Report made recommendations which led to important changes. Among other things, the committee suggested that the BBC recognize 'any organisation able to prove that it had a membership of not less than, say, 40 percent of the total of that class in the Corporation's employ'.[80] Accordingly, the National Union of Journalists was accepted as a negotiating body for news and editorial staffs and foreign broadcast monitors on 1 January 1955—the first trade union in the United Kingdom ever recognized by the BBC besides the Staff Association. The Electrical Trades Union was subsequently recognized on 4 May 1955. These unions also drew up working agreements with the Association of Broadcasting Staff for joint representation

In Britain, as in the United States, the performers' unions have provided broadcasters with some difficult problems.[81] The Musicians' Union has often given trouble to the BBC; and the union, on its side, has written that it has 'greater difficulty in making agreements with the BBC than with other employers.'[82] The Corporation is Britain's largest employer of musicians, having had on its staff at the beginning of 1980, 551 full-time musicians, although the number was later reduced for financial reasons (see pp. 330–1). In addition, through studio broadcasts and public concerts, it provides many engagements for symphony orchestras, light orchestras, and dance bands outside its staff. Nevertheless the union is always asking it to do more.

It is the avowed purpose of the union eventually to eliminate the use of all phonograph records, forcing the Corporation to broadcast live music exclusively. Accordingly, as far back as 1933, taking advantage of the control which British copyright law gives record manufacturers over public performances—including the broadcasting—of their records, the union began to limit the airing of commercial records. As recently as 1974, it told the Annan Committee that it wanted obligations for the broadcasting of live music incorporated into the country's legislation.[83]

The British Actors' Equity Association, the Variety Federation, and the Musicians Union all hesitated over the pre-recording of programmes, although their objections have gradually been eroded, and recorded repeats now are usual.

In 1956 the BBC Staff Association changed its name to the Association of Broadcasting Staff, since many of its members were working for the ITA, which had gone on the air the previous year. This later evolved into the Association of Broadcasting and Allied Staffs, which includes staff members doing work at all grades and of all types, excepting performers and some top-level administrators. In addition the Corporation recognizes a number of other unions covering the entire range of work done by its employees. Although the BBC's annual reports tend to minimize whatever interruptions in service may have resulted from 'industrial action', the frequent newspaper reports of BBC (and also IBA) work stoppages give a somewhat different impression.[84]

Under the law, BBC, IBA, and programme company staff members, like all British citizens, are free to join or not join trade unions, and about half the BBC staff now are members. In fact, the Corporation told the Annan Committee that, since it is clearly in the interest of staff and of the BBC that the joint consultative and negotiating machinery which has been built up between the Unions and BBC be as effective and as generally representative as possible, the BBC encourages its staff to be members of an appropriate recognised Trade Union and to play an active part in the affairs of that Union. . . .[85]

IBA staff negotiations involve the programme companies much more than the Authority itself, since most IBA staff are engineering personnel. As was pointed out above, the Authority is required by law to negotiate with employees' unions, and to go to arbitration under the same conditions as the BBC. The law also states that wages paid by programme contractors, though it does not mention the Authority itself, should be comparable to those received by government employees doing similar work, and that any related disputes should be referred to the Industrial Arbitration Board.[86]

So that they may speak with one voice, the programme companies have set up a Labour Relations Committee, assisted by an advisor and staff.[87] Strikes causing interruptions of service are potentially more damaging to the Authority than to the BBC. The services of both organizations can be interrupted by strikes, but the commercial system suffers more severely, since its income is directly related to its broadcasting hours, whereas the BBC's income continues whether or not programmes are on the air. The companies told the Annan Committee in 1975, however, that in spite of their vulnerability, except for a few wildcat strikes, there have been few national strikes since they began operations in 1955. The reallocation of franchises in 1967 caused major problems, since one-third of the programme companies' 3000 employees were displaced, but the companies and the unions worked out a resettlement plan resulting in the re-employment of practically all of the displaced staff.

The Annan Committee received much evidence from many points of view on which to base its chapter on 'Industrial Relations'.[88] Its 'general impression was that, compared with some other industries, industrial relations in broadcasting were overall fairly good'. Union spokesmen gave the 'general impression . . . that the BBC management had failed to adapt sufficiently to changes in the social climate, particularly those changes which affected its relations with its staff'. Those ITV companies that 'do not have regular consultations with their unions on long term company policy should open negotiations with the unions forthwith', the committee wrote. Otherwise, the group thought the BBC had too much 'overmanning . . . particularly at the top', there being 'far too many executives'. Summarizing, the Committee remarked that 'these problems are not unique to broadcasting'. But it offered a warning: in earlier days the combination of newspaper revenues and low cost newsprint had 'led to . . . overmanning and restrictive [labour] practices'. Now it was 'important that buoyant advertising revenue in commercial broadcasting should not lead to similar practices'. The solution of such problems, it concluded, 'will depend on the wisdom and imagination of both sides'.

The biggest and longest strike against British television occurred in the autumn of 1979, when two unions—the National Association of Television, Theatrical and

Kine Employees, and the Association of Cinematograph Television and Allied Technicians—put ITV off the air for 11 weeks, from 10 August to 24 October. Initially, wages were the problem, but later work conditions and the introduction of the new and efficient ENG—electronic newsgathering—cameras entered into the negotiations. Union spokesmen claimed that the high profit levels of the programme companies automatically entitled them to high pay scales, a concept the companies refused to accept. Finally, broadcasting was resumed after a settlement that gave the workers 45 per cent pay raises over a 2-year period. But another round of difficult negotiations was predicted when the new IBA contracts take effect in 1982.

STAFF PERFORMANCE

Britain's broadcasters maintain high levels of competence and performance. The BBC, during its monopoly years, set standards, not only for itself, but also for the competing ITA when it came on the air in 1955.

The members of the two governing boards and the principal executives of both BBC and IBA are highly qualified. Governors and Authority Members are comparable to the members of university Boards of Regents and Trustees in the United States. Important BBC and IBA executive positions usually are held by well-rounded people, whose extensive professional accomplishments are complemented by the social graces for which the British are noted. Most of them have been well-educated, either in school or informally through their own efforts, and many also are eminent in other fields. The leaders often have come up through the ranks, working for years in various branches of broadcasting before reaching the top echelons.

As to programme and production staff, one might draw a continuum with BBC radio personnel at one end and IBA programme contractor staff at the other. In earlier days, although the absence of competition often made BBC radio programmes more content- than audience-oriented, it had the good effect of attracting staff whose primary interest was in service rather than sales. Even now, the Corporation's radio staff tends to be older—or at least older-minded, less competitive, more philosophical and less pragmatic—than workers in television. If there is smugness and superiority among British broadcasters, this is the place to find it. Until the mid-1970s, BBC radio faced no domestic competition at all, and in the foreseeable future expects to compete only on the local station level.

The BBC television staff occupies a position between BBC radio and the programme company groups. Like television broadcasters everywhere—the same generalization could be made about America's public television staffs—they are younger and younger-minded, more competitive, and more aggressive than their radio colleagues. Paradoxically, the heads of BBC publishing and enterprises, both of which departments must sell to survive, are much more profit-and-loss-minded than are most BBC divisions, whose primary interests are in programme production. In fact, in many ways, they talk and sound like Independent Broadcasting sales staff.

Next come the IBA leaders and headquarters staff who in many respects resemble their BBC analogues. Yet, presiding and controlling—or attempting to control—television programme companies and radio stations which must sell advertising to succeed, they are tougher-minded than the BBC heads. Programme company boards of directors include businessmen, political leaders and performers, plus public figures assembled partly for window-dressing and partly for expertise. Yet, because the British system is one of controlled—if vigorous— competition, the independent broadcasters must hold some of their commercialism in check, whether or not they want to.

The differences among programme producers working in the two organizations are not marked. People doing the same kind of work often have similar attitudes. Thus, the producers of educational programmes in both BBC and IBA resemble each other more than either resemble workers in light entertainment. Likewise, specialists in serious programmes—news, public affairs, talks, drama and concert music—have different backgrounds, personalities and attitudes than those in entertainment and sports.

In considering differences between the BBC and the IBA staffs, however, it must be noted that there is a good deal of interchange at all levels. Lord Hill was appointed by the government successively as chairman of the Independent Broadcasting Authority and then of the BBC Board of Governors. Top-level executives have switched back and forth between BBC and IBA. For example, Colin D. Shaw, formerly a high-level employee in the office of the BBC Director-General, is now Director of Television for IBA, while Ian Trethowan was with ITN in 1958, joined the BBC in 1963 to work in both radio and later television, and became Director-General of the Corporation in 1977. Programme heads have shifted back and forth among the BBC, the IBA and the programme companies; producers, directors and other staff members have frequently gone from one organization to another; even news anchor staff—'newsreaders' in British parlance—have changed allegiance; while freelance writers, artists, actors, and musicians sell their services to whoever needs them at the moment. This flow of staff back and forth is a good thing: each group can benefit from sharing the experiences and attitudes of the other.

For the most part, in both broadcasting organizations, morale is of a high order, although the increasing differential between BBC and IBA pay scales has led to a loss of personnel—especially in engineering—that has seriously handicapped the BBC and affected the work attitudes of many of its employees. Nevertheless, both young and old at the BBC extol the merits of non-commercial license-fee-supported broadcasting, while questioning the possibility of the commercially supported IBA to consistently perform well. Meanwhile, Authority employees hold forth enthusiastically on the number of awards their programme have received, the tremendous growth the organization has had in its relatively short life, the way in which they have stimulated the BBC to better efforts, the level of public esteem they have won, and the higher degree of identification shown by regional viewers to local ITV as compared to BBC programme services.

But despite competition between the two organizations, spokesmen for both readily agree that the British system—with the licence-fee-supported BBC and the commercially supported IBA competing under strict ground rules—is capable of maintaining a higher and more consistent level of national service than is the broadcasting system of any other country in the world, and that is a judgement with which I concur.

9 Programmes: Introduction

The BBC is chartered to 'provide ... broadcasting services ... for general reception' because of the 'great value of such services as means of disseminating information, education and entertainment'.[1] Its Licence requires it to 'send efficiently programmes in the Home Radio Services, the Television Services, and the External Services', and specifically to 'broadcast an impartial account day by day ... of the proceedings in both Houses of the United Kingdom Parliament'.[2] This is the extent of the exact programme requirements imposed upon the Corporation by either Charter or Licence, although there are other sections in those documents which pertain to programming and they are qualified by the 'prescriptions' issued from time to time (see above, pp. 29, 31).

In contrast to these very general instructions for the BBC, the laws for the IBA are much more explicit. Clearly, Parliament has much greater doubts about the performance of the commercial IBA than of the licence-fee supported by the BBC. Yet, the procedures detailed for the IBA are much like the few legal requirements and the many traditions governing BBC programming.

The function of the Authority is 'to provide in accordance with the provisions of this Act ... television and local sound broadcasting services, additional in each case to those of the BBC and of high quality, both as to the transmission and as to the matter transmitted'.[3] The law uses a phrase from the BBC's Charter in specifying that these services have the purpose of 'disseminating information, education and entertainment'. It goes on to say that they are to 'maintain a high general standard in all respects, and in particular with respect of their content and quality'. There also must be 'a proper balance and wide range in their subject matter, having regard both to the programmes as a whole and also to the days of the week on which, and the times of the day at which, the programmes are broadcast'. There are detailed instructions about how programme contractors are to be selected, and as to the control the Authority is to maintain over both programmes and advertisements.

The Annan Committee, after noting that broadcasting's role 'is to provide entertainment, information and education for large audiences', went on to remark:

It is hard to conceive of a programme which would not be held in some way to inform, educate or entertain at least some section of the population. We would add to the list a further objective ... namely enrichment. To enlarge people's interest, to convey to them new choices and possibilities in life, this is what broadcasting should try to achieve. Sir Hugh Wheldon, with remarkable brevity, has said that programmes should create delight and insight. This sums up our views.[4]

PROGRAMME OBJECTIVES

Clearly, the BBC was the prototype for the IBA, since the objectives and procedures established by the Corporation during its quarter century of monopoly service laid the foundation for programme concepts in the United Kingdom.

Broadcasting in the United Kingdom began in the early 1920s, was consolidated under the British Broadcasting Company in 1922, and established as a monopoly of the British Broadcasting Corporation in 1927. Under the leadership of John Reith, it assumed its basic structure during this period. At that time the Corporation stated that its policy was: 'Give the public something slightly better than it now thinks it likes.'[5] Twenty years later Lord Reith looked back and wrote:

So the responsibility as at the outset conceived, and despite all discouragements pursued, was to carry into the greatest number of homes everything that was best in every department of human knowledge, endeavour and achievement; and to avoid whatever was or might be hurtful. In earliest years accused of setting out to give the public not what it wanted but what the BBC thought it should have, the answer was that few knew what they wanted, fewer what they needed. In any event, it was better to over-estimate than to underestimate. If another policy had been adopted—that of the lowest common denominator—what then? Probably nobody would have protested; it would have been quite natural.*

A high conception of public service responsibility has always guided the BBC.[6] Summarizing what had been its policy for many years, the BBC told the Beveridge Committee in 1949 that its purpose was to provide 'information, education, and entertainment for the community at large . . . while playing its part in bringing about an informed democracy and in enriching the quality of public enjoyment'. The Corporation's 'policy with regard to programme structure' was 'founded upon two basic conceptions': a balanced programme service to meet the needs of all segments of the public, with regard for minority as well as to majority tastes; and the broadcasting 'at regular intervals of . . . the major musical and dramatic repertoire'. Furthermore, broadcasting should be used constructively in the general social interest and the 'educational impulse' maintained.

Hugh Greene, BBC Director-General when the Pilkington Committee investi-

---

* Reith, *Into the Wind*, p. 101. There is an interesting similarity between this statement from Reith and one from Sylvester I. Weaver in 1956, when the latter was president of the National Broadcasting Company.

From the beginning, we have been against the know nothings, the primitives because we do not believe that television should be run to give the people what they want. We believe that every NBC show should serve a purpose beyond diversion, and every time we can increase information, contacts, facts, knowledge, and we deliver a fact somewhere to a mind somewhere in the country, we have added one more tool, one more weapon in the fight against bigotry, stupidity, intolerance, and prejudice, and we have taken one more step forward toward sanity, maturity and adulthood. . . . And the people of the jungle who will fight this, who want everybody to do really what they are doing, they are wrong; and they are discredited already, and they know it, and that is probably why they become so often so very bitter.(*Variety*, 4 January 1956, p. 147).

gated British broadcasting in the early 1960s, told the committee that television was 'one of the main factors influencing the values and moral attitudes of our society'.[7] Its range of services, therefore, should be comprehensive. At times the Corporation 'regularly and deliberately put on programmes which would appeal immediately to a comparatively small audience, but tried so to present them as to attract and hold audiences'. The BBC also tried to provide leadership in the fields of literature and the arts. But whatever it broadcast, said Greene, 'we should try always to do the best we possibly can in every type of broadcast, without thinking that it is more important to put our best into information and education. It is just as important to put the best skills one can into entertainment.'

While approving BBC programme objectives and performance, the committee took a dim view of the ITA's inclination 'to regard as exaggerated the commonly held view that television exerted a high degree of influence'.[8] The Committee reported that the ITA

> rated the responsibility of the broadcaster lower than did others who gave us their views. In fact, the Authority told us that, though there was a duty to widen tastes and affirm standards, the broadcaster's task was essentially to mirror society and its tastes as they are. This was what independent television had done, the Authority agreed, and it was difficult to see how it could have done more.

The Committee was 'disturbed by these views', and concluded: 'Our general appraisal is that the Authority have too negative a conception of the purposes of broadcasting. In discounting the influence of the medium, they [therefore] scaled down their responsibilities.' But a dozen years later the IBA's Deputy Director for Programme Services spoke quite differently. In January 1975, Bernard Sendall reviewed the ITA's support of research into the effects of television violence, and stated 'that few of us today are content . . . with seeing the role of broadcasting as merely to mirror society as it is'.[9]

The Pilkington Report included some paragraphs on the perennial question of whether broadcasters should give the 'public what it wants', hoping thereby to attract 'the largest possible audience', or if they should 'give the public what someone thinks is good for it'.[10] To the Committee, these expressions, as commonly used, were misleading, since they seemed to appeal to democratic principles without really doing so: 'The choice is not between *either* ''giving the public what it wants'', *or* ''giving the public what someone thinks is good for it'', and nothing else. There is an area of possibility between the two; and it is within this area that the choice lies.' In 1977, the Annan Committee listed four requisites for good broadcasting: (1) Flexibility; (2) Diversity; (3) Editorial Independence; and (4) Accountability.[11]

To some extent programme policies in British broadcasting have reflected the personalities and attitudes of its leaders. When Reith was in charge between 1922 and 1938 (Managing Director of the Company from 1922 to 1926, and Director-General from 1927 to 1938), the BBC was noted for its dedication to intellectual excellence, as well as for such austerities as the Reith Sunday. But when Hugh Greene occupied the position from 1960 to 1969, a different approach was evident. As Greene himself put it: 'There was such an impression of arrogance when I began. I wanted to open windows and let the winds blow. I hope I succeeded.'[12]

The BBC told the Annan Committee in 1974 that, whereas in the 1920s and early 1930s, its 'programme policy was imperial, patrician, and Christian', it now 'is neither of the first two things and a good deal less of the third'.[13] It also told the Committee that it always had 'taken very seriously the coverage and reflection of those activities in the national life which, whether serious or entertaining, constitute an aspect of national unity varying from the State Opening of Parliament to the Derby and the Cup Final.' Charles Curran, while Director-General, stated in a public lecture in 1973: 'We are trying . . . to reduce the extent of incomprehension of the basic facts about our society.'[14]

In 1976, Sir Michael Swann, then Chairman of the BBC's Board of Governors, told an audience at Cambridge University:[15]

> For its first 30 years, set clearly on a path chosen by Reith, the BBC was firmly on the side of the Establishment, a high-minded one to be sure, but quite certainly the Establishment. But by the 1950s and in reality a good deal earlier, the BBC was getting out of step with a changing society. . . . By the 1960s, partly because of competition, partly as a reaction from the old-style image, partly because of a deliberate policy by the then Director-General, Hugh Greene, and partly because of a huge influx of young producers the BBC's social stance had altered all out of recognition, at least in television. As Malcolm Muggeridge, characteristically, and exaggeratedly wrote at the time: 'Auntie as we all know, has taken to drink, never goes to divine worship any more, gives noisy parties for disreputable friends and hangers-on, and endlessly uses four letter words. . . .' And, he might have added, frequently upsets respectable conservatives with progressive, permissive left-wing programmes.

In 1975, the ITCA gave the Annan Committee its comparison of the programme philosophies of the two organizations:

> The concept of ITV as the people's television and the BBC as establishment television is still current. If there is truth in it today, the reason . . . is that ITV has a more popular touch. For the two services place much the same emphasis on their three stated purposes: to inform, to educate, and to entertain; and their special respect for the 'family viewer' is shared.[16]

Two years later, in reacting to the Committee's report, the Companies, writing under the heading, 'A public service for whom?' elaborated: 'The difference between BBC and ITV is not one of "public service", which both provide. The difference is one of background, belief and attitude. If the BBC is seen as the Establishment of broadcasting, ITV represents the broader appeal of populism. . . .'[17]

Brian Groombridge, a former ITA Education Officer, offered (unofficially) in 1972, a statement of programme principles for both organizations:

It shall be the duty of the BBC and of the ITA to provide public services of education, information and entertainment, and to contribute, through their programmes and in other ways deemed appropriate, to the extension and invigoration of the nation's democratic life, and to understanding between the different segments of society.[18]

Writing in 1961, I had occasion to note. 'The BBC's more serious approach to broadcasting is reflected in the columns of its [programme] journal, which emphasizes the serious rather than the trivial, as so often does the *TV Times*'. The covers of the two magazines for the week of 30 August 1959, for example, bore this out. On 31 August President Eisenhower and Prime Minister Macmillan broadcast over both networks from 10 Downing Street. 'But whereas the *Radio Times* cover carried a picture of the two men, the *TV Times* cover showed five bathing girls who were appearing on a programme called ''Holiday Town Parade''.'*

THE RADIO SERVICES

As of 1 January 1980, the BBC had four national networks plus twenty local stations, while the IBA operated nineteen local services. In the near future, however, each organization expected to add additional local stations. For nearly 20 years—from 1927 to 1946—the BBC was able to offer its listeners a choice of only two networks, mainly because of a shortage of broadcasting frequencies. From 1930 to the outbreak of World War II, there were the National Service, uniform throughout the country, consisting mainly of London programmes of national appeal, and the Regional Service, made up of a London key station feeding six regional networks, which often cut away for local programmes.

In 1938, the BBC was on the air Sundays from 9.30 a.m. to 11 p.m., and weekdays from 10.15 a.m. until midnight. Up through the late 1930s, the BBC observed the famous 'Reith Sunday'; did not sign on until 12.30 p.m. (except for a 15-minute weather forecast at 10.30 a.m.; and then limited its offerings mainly to religious talks and serious music. Its programme schedule was much less diversified than in the post-war period; the basic National and Regional fares were not markedly differentiated; and both networks offered more straight music (both live and recorded) and fewer produced shows (drama, features, and outside broadcasts) than now. Furthermore, no news was broadcast before 6 p.m. until the

* In fairness it should be noted that the *TV Times* does have some very fine features. For example, the issue for the programme week of 22–28 May 1976, devoted the better part of six pages to pictures, charts and text relative to Thames Television's excellent series, *Destination America*. Yet, the *TV Times* for 29 April 1976 contained an article which said in part (p. 21): 'For many years actress, Victoria Anoux simply grinned and bared it when casting directors reckoned she looked better without any clothes on.' Said she: 'I didn't complain because work was steady.' After remarking that she would soon appear on a programme fully clothed, the magazine commented: 'Physically she looks stunning whatever her degree of clothing.' Adjacent was a large photograph of actress Anoux obviously chosen to document the text.

1938 Munich crisis (see below, pp. 190–1). Although the Corporation never entirely ignored popular taste, programme policies in those days were relatively inflexible. Too little attention was paid to listener interests, with the result that such foreign commercial stations as Radio Luxembourg and Radio Normandy made heavy inroads into the BBC's home audience.

World War II revolutionized British broadcasting.[19] On 1 September 1939, television broadcasting was suspended for the duration, and radio consolidated into one network, which assumed the name Home Service. In February 1940, a network for the British armed forces was introduced, again giving the United Kingdom a choice of two national services; this General Forces Programme also was beamed to British servicemen all over the world. During the war years British broadcasting was enriched through extensive contacts with broadcasters from other countries, including many from the United States. The General Forces Programme carried some American and Canadian features; the low-powered stations of the American Forces and the Canadian army, located at military camps throughout the United Kingdom, although established to serve the soldiers of those two countries, incidentally brought American and Canadian programmes to at least a few Britishers; and the BBC's Overseas Service accepted the concepts of competition for audiences and of close timing. These factors, taken together with the new social and political attitudes that emerged after the war, ensured a different approach to peacetime broadcasting.

In 1945, the General Forces Programme, which naturally had included much entertainment, was succeeded by the Light Programme, while the War-time Home Service became the permanent Home Service, with the six regional variants that had existed prior to the war. The opening of the Third Programme in September 1946 completed the post-war pattern for British radio broadcasting. The resulting BBC was much better and more realistic than the organization that had existed before 1939. The Light Programme was available to keep British listeners from Radio Luxembourg, the Home Service for the complete man, and the Third Programme for the intellectual. In fact, this pattern enlarged provided the basis for BBC's radio networks today.

The theory of the three programmes was that they should be complementary and cooperative rather than competitive.[20] Between the Home Service and the Light Programme, the differences were more of emphasis than of programme type, and they often repeated each other's programmes. The Third Programme stood apart from the other two, both in content and treatment; yet it too regularly exchanged items with the Home Service, just as Radio 3 now exchanges programmes with Radio 4. Overall scheduling was done cooperatively, so that the listener normally had a choice of three dissimilar programmes at any one moment, and access to a balanced range of items in the course of a day or evening.

The intended relation between the three services was stated by Sir William Haley, who as Director-General led in the post-war realignment of British broadcasting.[21] Drawing upon earlier statements by John Reith, although expressing them more eloquently, he described

the community as a broadly based cultural pyramid slowly aspiring upwards.

This pyramid is served by three main Programmes, differentiated but broadly over-lapping in levels and interest, each Programme leading on to the other, the listener being induced through the years increasingly to discriminate in favour of the things that are more worthwhile. Each Programme at any given moment must be ahead of its public, but not so much as to lose their confidence. The listener must be led from good to better by curiosity, liking, and a growth of understanding. As the standards of the education and culture of the community rise so should the programme pyramid rise as a whole.

Unfortunately, though, it did not work that way. There were good reasons for offering programmes for listeners with different levels of sophistication, but Sir William was wrong: 'the programme pyramid [did not] rise as a whole'. (For audience data on this and related matters, see Chapter 20 below.)

The advent of the ITA in the mid-1950s introduced competition into British broadcasting at the same time that BBC radio, like radio everywhere, began to lose much of its audience to television. Some adjustments were made in consequence. The former Third Programme, with specialized offerings for minority audiences, was limited to weekday evenings and from mid-afternoon afterwards on weekends. For a period, Network 3, using the remainder of the time on the former Third Programme transmitters, presented special programmes on such things as Further Education, music appreciation, and hobbies. In 1964, Network 3 became the Music Programme, with serious music during the daytime hours, although there still were no drastic changes, partly because a loss of audience did not affect BBC radio income as it did in countries with commercial systems. But when in 1964 the radio pirates began broadcasting popular music from sea-based stations outside of British territorial waters, something had to be done. (For more information about the 'pirates' see above, p. 22.) In 1967, the Marine &c. Broadcasting (Offences) Act authorized the government to shut down the pirates, thereby creating a void in popular music broadcasting. At the end of 1966, the government had authorized the BBC to set up a popular music programme and this was done in September 1967. Accordingly, the four BBC networks were renamed Radios 1, 2, 3 and 4.[22]

Then and more recently, much time and thought have gone into the restructuring of BBC radio, in recognition of the fact that both sociology and technology have created a new world for radio to serve. In July 1969, long-range radio plans were announced in a brochure, *Broadcasting in the Seventies: The BBC's plan for Network Radio and Non-metropolitan Broadcasting*, which created an uproar. Almost all the principal national and provincial newspapers editorialized against it. There were many letters to the editor, heated Parliamentary discussions, and much debate within the BBC itself. The whole situation was reminiscent of the furore over commercial television 15 years earlier.

Broadcasting in the Seventies proposed setting up four nationwide networks; expanding the Corporation's regional broadcasting activities; speeding the development of 'local radio as a major element in the BBC service'; and securing funds for the new services by stringent economies, one of which was a reduction in the number of musicians employed.

Each of the four networks was to specialize in one type of programming.[23] Radio 1 would concentrate on popular music; Radio 2 would be a light programme with mainly middle-of-the-road music; Radio 3 would serve the intellectual; and Radio 4 would be a general-purpose programme emphasizing news and current affairs. These changes were justified on several grounds. Much of the radio audience had gone to television, so that radio's peak hours were at breakfast and lunch time. Listening now was done 'on the run', so to speak, and often on portable transistors and automobile radios. At a time when 'centrifugal forces are apparent in society as a whole', the BBC's local experiment was proving sufficiently successful to justify more regional and local programmes. The public was losing interest in mixed programming, and now favoured specialized stations. Finally, in order to partially alleviate the BBC's financial problems, the Third Programme, at once the most expensive radio service and the one with the smallest audience, would be somewhat curtailed.

Most of the objections came from people who believed that the proposed changes would lower the BBC's standards. The idea of specialist networks evoked the criticism that a mixture of programme types would improve public taste by exposing the public by chance to new material. Many complaints related to the reduction in the number of serious talk programmes and to changes in the Third Programme. Third Programme devotees organized themselves into a highly effective pressure group, the effect of which still is evident today in the Corporation's operation of Radio 3, heard by only 1 per cent of the public, while accounting for 18 per cent of radio expenditures. Some Corporation employees became concerned about redundancy, since among other things the brochure proposed reducing the Corporation's house orchestras from 500 to 400 players—although this was not done. (see below, pp. 330–1). But otherwise, the BBC began operating according to its new plans in the spring of 1970, although ten years later financial stringencies forced it to make cuts in instrumentalists similar to those originally proposed in 1969.

In 1974 the Corporation commented with both insight and resignation to the Annan Committee:

> The row, for there is no other word for it, grew even more intense. It was, of course, a row among a minority of people about a set of programmes of minority interests, but it went to the heart of one of the principal justifications for the BBC's establishment and continued existence.[24]

As now constituted, Radio 1 is essentially a popular music service, the prime function of which 'is to provide the pop music—and the distinctive style of presentation—which appeals particularly to younger listeners'.[25] Yet, recognizing that many young people do little serious listening or newspaper reading, the service includes regular news summaries, a twice-daily news and current affairs programme, and occasional other features of serious nature.

Radio 2, the successor to the Light Programme, features what Americans would call 'middle-of-the-road music', plus some country and western, folk, and brass band music. It also broadcasts light entertainment and much sports. Radio 2 has 3-minute news summaries throughout much of the day, plus extensive coverage of such special occasions as national elections and budget messages. For financial reasons, Radios 1 and 2 formerly did much simulcasting, although they now do so only from midnight to 6 a.m.

The most bitter criticism of *Broadcasting in the Seventies* came from Third Programme adherents, who feared that its high artistic and intellectual standards would be sacrificed. In the daytime Radio 3 is mainly a good music service, while in the evening it continues the Third Programme traditions, with serious drama, poetry, documentaries, discussions, talks and music.

Radio 4 is the most diverse of the four, combining news, talks and discussions, general information, in-school broadcasting, and some entertainment. It devotes about 5 hours a day to news and current affairs, and when schools are in session, its FM transmitters carry several hours each of in-school material. Although Radios 1, 2 and 3 are uniform throughout the country, the transmitters carrying Radio 4 may opt out—to use the BBC term—and substitute programmes of particular interest to the areas they serve.

All four networks are available on both AM and FM, although there are changes in transmitter patterns from time to time.[26] In order to further diversify its offerings, the Corporation sometimes assigns specialized programmes, such as those for in-school use and for the Open University, to Radio 3 and 4 FM, while continuing general programming on the AM transmitters. A similar procedure is followed to provide regional and local programmes to Scotland and Wales. (In July 1978, the new director of BBC radio proposed that school and Open University programmes be broadcast in the middle of the night for tape recording by interested schools, thus releasing more stations for the day-time transmission of programmes of wider interest.)[27]

An analysis of BBC Radio network programmes for 1978–79 is provided in Table 15. Much in the lead are musical programmes, which take up 58.4 per cent of the schedule. The second largest category is current affairs, features and documentaries (15.2 per cent); and if the time devoted to news (6.2 per cent) were added in, 21.7 per cent of the radio output would consist of news and current affairs programmes.

There is considerable variation among the networks. Thus, Radio 1 devotes 92.2 per cent of its time to music, Radio 2 devotes 78.4 per cent, Radio 3 devotes 67.1 per cent, and Radio 4 only 6.6 per cent. But Radio 1 emphasizes pop music, Radio 2 middle-of-the-road, and Radio 3 the classical repertoire. The table also shows that Radios 1, 2 and 3 broadcast little news and current affairs, whereas Radio 4 devotes 57.3 per cent of its time to such material. (All Open University programmes are on Radio 3 and 4. In the table they are listed apart from the other categories, since the BBC produces them for the Open University, rather than as a part of its own programme service.)

The relationship between the BBC's network and regional radio activities is shown in Table 16 which supplements Table 15. Table 16 shows that 17.6 per cent of the entire programme schedule was produced in London, while 12.2 per cent came from the regions. In addition, the 20 local stations turned out 92,759 hours (60.4 per cent of the total) for broadcast on their transmitters only. Altogether,

TABLE 15 *Programme analysis 1978–9, Radio networks*

	Radio 1		Radio 2		Radio 3		Radio 4		Total	
	Hours	*%*	*Hours*	*%*	*Hours*	*%*	*Hours*	*%*	*Hours*	*%*
BBC productions										
Music	4,850	92.2	6,111	78.4	4,837	67.1	504	6.6	16,302	58.4
Current affairs, features and documentaries	137	2.6	49	0.6	648	9.0	3,391	44.5	4,225	15.2
News	92	1.8	446	5.7	198	2.7	980	12.8	1,716	6.2
Drama			125	1.6	149	2.1	826	10.8	1,100	3.9
Sport			591	7.6	257	3.6	91	1.2	939	3.4
Light entertainment			273	3.5	1		342	4.5	616	2.2
Religion	5	0.1	104	1.3	17	0.2	293	3.8	419	1.5
Schools					3		471	6.2	474	1.7
Further education			3	0.1	132	1.8	197	2.6	332	1.2
Children's programmes	174	3.3	90	1.2	6	0.1	67	0.9	247	0.9
Continuity	2				148	2.1	189	2.5	429	1.5
	5,260	100.0	7,792	100.0	6,396	88.7	7,351	96.4	26,799	96.1
Open University					816	11.3	274	3.6	1,090	3.9
	5,260	100.0	7,792	100.0	7,212	100.0	7,625	100.0	27,889	100.0
Simultaneous broadcasts (in addition to above) were:	2,529		1,179		8		90		3,806	

SOURCE: *BBC Handbook 1980*, p. 107.

TABLE 16 *Hours of output 1978–9, Radio*

	Network programmes (hours)					Regional Services Only (hours)	Local Radio (hours)	Total (hours)	Percentage
	Radio 1	Radio 2	Radio 3	Radio 4	Total				
Programmes produced in London	5,212	7,290	5,099	5,908	23,509			23,509	17.6
Programmes produced in regions:									
England South East						74		74	
Birmingham		205	178	516	899	104		1,003	
Manchester	47	190	401	340	978	104		1,082	
Bristol		35	275	447	757	104		861	
Norwich						520		520	
Newcastle						104		104	
Leeds									
Southampton						21		21	
Plymouth						487		487	
	47	430	854	1,303	2,634	1,518		4,152	
Scotland	1	50	203	59	313	4,449		4,762	
Wales*		2	147	53	202	4,123		4,325	
Northern Ireland		20	93	28	141	3,007		3,148	
Total programmes produced in regions:	48	502	1,297	1,443	3,290	13,097		16,387	12.2
	5,260	7,792	6,396	7,351	26,799	13,097		39,896	
Local radio							92,759	92,759	69.4
	5,260	7,792	6,396	7,351	26,799	13,097	92,759	132,655	
Open University			816	274	1,090			1,090	0.8
Total hours of broadcasting	5,260	7,792	7,212	7,625	27,889	13,097	92,759	133,745	100.0

* The output of Wales included 1,983 hours of programmes in the Welsh language

SOURCE: *BBC Handbook 1980*, p. 106.

therefore, the BBC produced 133,745 hours of domestic radio programmes during 1978–9.

Since the autumn of 1978, Radios 1 and 2 have been on the air 24 hours a day, simulcasting from midnight to 6 a.m., while Radio 3 has broadcast from 7 a.m. and Radio 4 from 6 a.m. to midnight. Before that their schedules seldom exceeded 17 hours a day each, and these were extensions of earlier and shorter schedules. The British government always has had legal authority to prescribe broadcasting hours, and did so because of concern over the social effects and the costs of broadcasting, and for a long time the BBC approved this policy.[28] But beginning in 1955 the ITA pressed for more time in order to sell more advertising, and in 1961 the BBC came to see the advantages of longer hours in terms of public service, so that it joined the ITA in asking the Pilkington Committee to recommend longer hours. Since 1964, British radio has been free to set its own hours, and there have been no restrictions on television since 1972. But the need to reduce spending by at least £130 million in 1980 and 1981 led to proposals to cut about £4 million from network radio costs, £500,000 in English radio station operations, and £2 million from the existing local radio station budgets, although it was expected to go ahead with the building of fifteen more local stations, bring their total up to thirty-five by the mid-1980s. Among other things, savings would be achieved by closing down Radio 3 at 11.15 p.m. instead of midnight, and by reducing educational radio programmes by 10 per cent.

The BBC wanted to develop local radio stations some years before it was authorized to put the first of them on the air in 1967. It felt that the decline in radio listening was slowing, at the same time that some people were becoming dissatisfied with television. It also believed that the future lay with highly flexible local rather than with network radio. The Corporation told the Pilkington Committee in 1960 that 'within 8 or 9 months after approval had been given', it was prepared to go on the air with 'a service of local news and other programmes reflecting the interests of smaller self-contained communities'.[29]

Although the Committee favoured local stations—run by the BBC rather than the ITA, however, which also was interested in radio—the government in July 1962, mentioning 'little evidence of any general public demand' for local radio, instructed the BBC to concentrate its resources 'on national requirements'.[30] But 4 years later, at the same time that it approved Radio 1, the government authorized the Corporation to experiment with 'a full scale local service', evaluation of the project to be made after several years of operation. Before the stations were put on the air, however, there were extensive consultations with local leaders and much closed-circuit experimentation.

In 1967, eight such stations were inaugurated, and in 1969, when the experiment was judged a success, the government authorized twelve additional stations and soon spoke of twenty more to come.[31] These twenty stations, all with both AM and FM transmitters, now reach about 75 per cent of the population by day, but appreciably less by night. Thus far, however, there are no BBC local stations in Scotland, Wales or Northern Ireland, although the fifteen more being planned may include some to serve those areas.

These BBC stations provide a full and comprehensive news and information service geared to local needs and interests.[32] In addition to majority interest programmes, they have services for such minority groups as the blind, the elderly, gardeners, anglers and motorists. Immigrants are invited to broadcast, sometimes in their native languages. Many educational programmes are developed for both adults and children, to supplement those from London. Although free to take programmes from any of the BBC's four networks, the station managers, with staffs ranging from twenty-five to sixty employees, enjoy a high degree of autonomy in programme development.

In March 1971, the government recommended to Parliament a commercially supported radio service, eventually to encompass sixty stations, to be assigned not to a new organization as had been advocated by some, but to the Independent Television Authority, whose name then would be changed to the Independent Broadcasting Authority.[33] The White Paper stated that each company would be appointed for an initial term of 3 years, subject to extension or renewal. Although one company might programme for two or more areas, no company 'will be allowed an excessive aggregate interest. The Authority will be expected to aim at a wide diversity of ownership.' This led to the Sound Broadcasting Act of 1972, the principal features of which were incorporated into the revised Independent Broadcasting Authority Act 1973 (see above, pp. 64–6).

The IBA radio structure (known as Independent Local Radio or ILR) parallels that of Independent Television. Programmes are provided by programme contractors and income by spot advertising, sponsorship being prohibited. Although deficit financing appeared likely for the early years, the law foresightedly permitted the raising of rentals and the confiscation of profits, should they prove excessive. (As things turned out, ILR was self-supporting and showed profits by 1978.) Since commercially supported stations might reduce the income of some publishers, local newspapers originally were guaranteed the right to own stock in the radio companies, although they were not to control them, but this prerogative was cancelled by the Broadcasting Act of 1980. No television company may control a radio station broadcasting in its own service area, although it may hold stock in, or operate companies serving, other areas. However, no such situations have yet developed.

Of the sixty ILR stations envisaged, nineteen were on the air on 1 January 1980, and twenty-four more had been approved by the government but were not yet operational.[34] Together they were expected to reach over 80 per cent of the country's population with their medium wave AM signals. The IBA's goal is to serve at least 90 per cent of the public with its radio stations. Sixty-four applications were received for the first nineteen franchises, and the first two stations went on the air in London in 1973. Over 300 interests hold 1 per cent or more of the shares in these companies, and local ownership usually runs to at least 80 per cent. Television companies do have small shares of stock, but only in nine of the first nineteen companies. Many, but not all, of the local newspapers entitled to purchase shares in radio companies have done so. With IBA, as with BBC, public meetings in the communities to be served by the new stations were held before programme plans were drawn up, and there are local advisory committees in all cases.

About half of the ILR stations broadcast 24 hours a day, and some 50 per cent of their programming consists of music, the rest being local news and information; such listener services as advice on finances and municipal facilities; and some drama, religion and education. Always reminding stations that it was the intention of Parliament that they be local rather than national is the phrase in the law requiring the Authority to provide 'local sound broadcasting services'.[35] However, a central news company, Independent Radio News, associated with one of the two London stations—London Broadcasting Company or LBC, supplies them with national and international news as does ITN for the Authority's television stations.

THE TELEVISION SERVICES

British television has several demarcation points: experimental beginnings (1936–9); wartime interruption (1939– 46); BBC post-war expansion to the status of a national service (1944– 55); the coming of the ITA (September 1955); the Pilkington Committee Report (1962) and the Television Act of 1964; the inauguration of BBC 2 (1964); the introduction of colour, the move to UHF and the new ITV franchises (1967–9); and the aftermath of the Annan Committee Report (1977 and following). (For a review of early television developments in the United Kingdom, see Chapter 4 above, pp. 46–56).

The United Kingdom now is served by three television networks, two operated by the BBC and one by the IBA, all three reaching over 98 per cent of the population. BBC 1 broadcasts in black and white using a 405-line system in the VHF band, and in colour with 625 lines in the UHF band (see above, p. 94). BBC 2 transmits colour programmes only, and on UHF. ITV, like BBC 1, offers black and white 405-line transmissions on VHF and 625-line colour transmissions on UHF. When the fourth channel is activated probably in late 1982, it will present colour programmes on UHF, using frequencies already reserved for its use. In the near future all monochrome transmissions will be discontinued, after which there will be the possibility of developing several new 625-line colour services in the VHF spectrum.

Except for a very few events of national importance or wide interest, such as major political programmes or outstanding sports contests, BBC and ITV never broadcast the same programme simultaneously. BBC 1 and BBC 2 are planned together, and frequently repeat each other's offerings, but ITV operates separately. However, the BBC and ITV do some cooperative planning to avoid duplication in such programme areas as education, some sports, and certain Welsh-language services.

The BBC regards its two networks as complementary rather than competitive. BBC 1 being the older began and has continued as a general service, while BBC 2, which came on the air in April 1964, emphasizes minority programming.[36] But it is by no means like Radio 3, since it also carries some light entertainment and sports. There are certain disadvantages to BBC 2's being a minority audience network, since that lessens the chance that its special interest programmes may be 'accidentally' viewed by a general audience tuned in for the preceding or following broadcast. BBC 2 is the more experimental of the two, although some of its offerings reach a larger public when they are repeated by BBC 1.[37] The audience division averages 42 per cent BBC 1, 8 per cent BBC 2 and 50 per cent ITV, although the ratings vary from time to time, with wide variations from programme to programme. (See Chapter 20, 'Audience Research', below.)

The controllers for BBC 1 and BBC 2 report to the Managing and Deputy Directors of Television. When BBC 2 began, the idea of having a separate production staff for the two networks was considered, but was rejected in favour of sharing programme and production personnel. Accordingly, there are departments dealing with news, current affairs, drama, light entertainment, outside broadcasts, music and art, documentary programmes, children's programmes, religious programmes, school broadcasting, further education, and Open University productions, along with support groups responsible for scenic design, lighting, costuming, and all the other things necessary for the operation of a large network.

The current emphasis on regional and local broadcasting, one aspect of the devolution manifested throughout the United Kingdom, was accelerated by the federal system introduced by Independent Television and extended by Independent Local Radio.[38] For many years the BBC had supplemented its national television networks with six regional services: the three 'countries' of Scotland, Wales, and northern Ireland; and the three English regions—the North of England, the West of England, and the Midlands. The national regions obviously were historical and cultural in basis, but the geographical outlines of the English regions were set arbitrarily by the coverage of the radio transmitters used in the 1920s for the Corporation's regional programmes.[39] Consequently the serving of the English regions was complicated because they included listeners and viewers of widely different interests. Each of these areas had first radio and then television origination facilities of its own, used to provide programmes based on local resources for national as well as local distribution.

The two national regions of Scotland and Wales now enjoy a high degree of autonomy. Most of their Programme decisions are made by their own Advisory Councils, and the annual reports of their broadcasting councils are separately indentified in the *BBC Handbook*. Many programmes in Wales are in the Welsh language, and some broadcasts in Scotland are in Gaelic. The Crawford Committee, appointed in 1973 to examine the coverage of radio and television in Scotland, Wales, Northern Ireland, and rural England, recommended that as soon as possible a fourth television channel be activated in Wales specializing in Welsh-language broadcasts and programmed jointly by the BBC and ITV. Although this proposal was accepted by both organizations, it had not gone into effect before the Broadcasting Act 1980, dealing with fourth channel operation and programming, required that programmes on that channel for reception in Wales must 'contain a suitable proportion of matter in Welsh.'[40]

The Corporation has set up Network Production Centres in Bristol, Birmingham, and Manchester, each with radio and television origination facilities which draw upon local resources to produce programmes for network distribution. The BBC's Natural History unit is located in Bristol, and its Agricultural and Asian programme units in Birmingham, although Manchester has no field of specialization. There also are regional production facilities at the three network centres as well as in Newcastle, Southampton, Norwich, Plymouth, and Leeds. All of them provide programmes for local audiences, including news, sports, and general interest material broadcast by BBC 1 regional transmitters during opt-out periods.[41]

Whereas the BBC is centralized, the IBA by choice is a federated organization. In its submission to the Annan Committee the Authority referred to its 'plural and regional service', while the BBC, describing its own expanding regional activities, referred to 'the developing challenge of federalised commercial television, both regionally and nationally '.[42] When I visited Granada Television headquarters in Manchester in 1976, the phrase 'federal system' was frequently used by my hosts to describe the nature of their operation. It will be recalled that the Annan Committee recommended that all radio be taken away from the IBA, and that it be renamed the Regional Television Authority.[43] However, the government decided against this change of name, since it continued the Authority's control over local commercial radio, and added responsibility for cable television and radio, pay-television, and some other services.

When it went on the air in 1955, the ITA, like the BBC a decade earlier, had to develop as rapidly as possible a net work of transmitters to cover the country.[44] By 1957, two-thirds of the population were served, by 1959 almost 90 per cent; and in 1962, with the addition of Channel Islands Television, national coverage was virtually complete.

Although ITV is a network in the sense that the programmes produced by its companies and by ITN often are transmitted simultaneously by all its stations, production is decentralized. Most of it comes from the five major companies— ATV, Granada, London Weekend, Thames and Yorkshire—which, because they serve the larger population centres, receive higher revenues, have access to the greatest range of talent, and maintain more elaborate production facilities. But all companies do some production, not only for their own areas but also for the network.

In recent years, the Authority's supervision of programmes has been much closer and firmer than at the outset. The Pilkington Committee in 1962 emphasized the need for this, and when Lord Hill became the chairman the following year, and the law was changed to give the ITA additional powers of control, the Authority became much more involved in programming. Among other things, it reduced the number of soap operas and quizzes, increased the amount of British material, coordinated sports coverage, insisted on more serious programmes during peak viewing hours, and solicited more network contributions from the regional companies. The process was further accelerated by the report of the Select Committee on Nationalized Industries in 1972, which recommended that the Authority strengthen its staff to 'deal with programme output'.[45] Headquarters staff now includes a Director of Television, a Deputy Director of Television, and several other programme officers, in addition to ten regional officers to provide direct liaison with the companies in their respective areas.[46]

Also involved are a Standing Consultative Committee, a Programme Policy Committee, and a Network Programme Committee, with high-level representation from the programme companies and the Authority. Although the five major companies still exert great influence, one of the results of the Pilkington inquiry was that the Authority now plays a much more important role. There is also a Programme Controllers Group made up of representatives from the five major companies and the IBA's Director of Television. Outside of these structured channels, there is much informal consultation between the Authority and the programme contractors. To improve long-range planning, the Authority instituted a series of programme consultations of two or three days' duration at which producers for all the companies and Authority representatives meet with subject-matter experts to exchange ideas on such topics as religious television, regional programmes, science and technology programmes, family viewing, school television, and news and current affairs.[47]

All companies must present their quarterly schedule proposals to the Authority well in advance of the dates when they are to take effect. These are carefully scrutinized, and the companies often are requested to alter them. In addition to the requirements imposed by law, there are many other things the Authority insists the companies do.[48] As it told the Annan Committee: 'One-third of all material will be 'serious non-fiction' and this must be 'sensibly distributed over the week as a whole in appropriate times'. The 'family viewing' policy requires that 'programmes shown before 9 p.m. should not be unsuitable for audiences which include children'. Each company must provide 'a suitable proportion of programmes calculated to appeal specially to the tastes and outlook of viewers in its area'.

Not more than 14 per cent of any company's programmes, averaged over the quarter, may be foreign import items, defined as programmes from countries other than Commonwealth countries. (Even though the Authority limits the amount of foreign material, 6 hours of it may be aired between 7.30 and 11 p.m., so that most of it is seen during peak viewing hours.) Although details vary from time to time, the programme companies told the Annan Committee in 1975 that not more than seven cinema films, foreign or British, could be broadcast during any week, and not more than five of these between 7 and 11 p.m. At least one must begin not earlier than 10.30 p.m. Furthermore, at least 2 hours must elapse between the end of one and the beginning of another film. Other 'mandated' programmes included one weekday and one weekend play, other than serials; two half-hour current affairs programmes weekly; special documentary programmes at least thirty-nine times a year, of which at least thirteen must be aired before 10.30 p.m.; a 'week-end special' at least twenty-six times a year; and the 'World of Sport' on Saturday afternoons. Companies may 'opt out' from some of these to substitute acceptable local programmes, provided they are of similar nature and quality.

On weekdays there must be an hour of children's programmes before 6 p.m., plus 15 minutes of lunchtime educational programmes for pre-school children. When schools are in session, all companies must carry at least 9 hours per week of material for in-school use, and at all times at least 3 hours of adult education programs. There must be between 2½ and 3 hours of religious programmes each week, some of which must be aired between 6.15 and 7.25 p.m. on Sundays.

All companies must take the ITN programmes Monday – Friday from 1 to 1.20, 5.45 to 6 and 10 to 10.30 p.m. Finally, companies are expected to carry six or so 'special events' each year, consisting of major operatic, dramatic, and similar presentations, each lasting 2 hours or more. IBA contracts with all regional companies include minimum requirements for local originations, which in the case of the large companies range from 7½ to 12 hours a week, and the small ones from 4 to 6 hours, although in practice these requirements usually are exceeded.

THE PATTERN OF BRITISH TELEVISION

Americans are always surprised at the short daily schedules of Europe's television services, and also at the way they sometimes leave the air for periods during the day. This, however, is typical of television everywhere outside of North America, which is the only place where stations stay on the air from early morning till late night, or broadcast 24 hours a day. Another point of difference is that, whereas American programmes almost always begin on the hour, or at 15, 30, or 45 minutes thereafter, British programmes often begin and end at odd minutes. The BBC—more prone to this than ITV—points out when it takes American programmes, it loses 10 minutes or so during each hour by having no commercial periods (ITV presumably, can fill in the gaps with its own commercials, which, however, take less time than in America). This may be true, but odd starting and ending times have long been, and still are, the rule with BBC radio, although it never did use a great many, and now uses almost no, American productions. Yet another difference is that in British television—both BBC and ITV, though especially the former—a programme series of presumed merit is not taken off the air after a few weeks if its audience is building slowly. British programmers will wait 13 weeks or more, especially if they think the series is important, and that it has a good likelihood of attracting more viewers.

In 1946, BBC television re-opened with an average schedule of 28 hours per week; by 1954 this had been increased to 41 hours; and effective with the ITA debut date of 22 September 1955, the maximum number of broadcasting hours for both was set by the government at 50 hours per week. As was pointed out above, until 1972 both broadcasting organizations were limited by government regulations as to the number of hours they could be on the air. But even in the absence of such regulations, there still were—and are—reasons for limited schedules.

Shortage of funds, space, and personnel all are factors, as formerly was the absence of competition, related to which is the consideration that for licence-fee-supported services, longer broadcasting schedules do not mean additional income, although they do involve higher operating expenses. Also important has been concern over the lack of sufficient talent to fill more hours, plus the fear that too much television is bad for the public.[49] European broadcasters generally believe that American stations greatly exceed their resources, a judgement with which many Americans concur.

An impression of a typical week of British television may be obtained from the listings in the BBC's *Radio Times* and the IBA's *TV Times*—although it should be noted that broadcast schedules always change, so that even the broadest generalizations may be out of date shortly after being printed, if not before. The

Radio Times, now published in twenty-five regional editions, lists the programmes on BBC network radio and television as well on local radio, while the *TV Times*, with fifteen regional editions, limits itself to television, since Independent Radio has its own programme publication. The reason for the regional editions, of course, is that since both BBC and ITV do regional and local programming, it is necessary to tell each part of the country about the programmes available only in its area.

As an example of current television scheduling, we may take the London schedule during the week from 2 to 8 June 1979. (Both programme journals go on sale on Thursday of each week, and listings run from Saturday to Friday.) All of the main network features probably were seen simultaneously or at other hours everywhere in the country, but each region had local programmes listed in its own programme journals, which replaced some London offerings. Although programmes on ITV transmitters succeed each other as on any American network, they in fact are originated by all fifteen programme companies, sometimes coming from the network live, and sometimes played locally from video-tape recordings. The screen always shows the company responsible, as do listings in the *TV Times*.

On Saturday 2 June, BBC 1 signed on at 9 a.m. with programmes for young viewers.* Its usual extensive Saturday sports coverage ran from 1 until after 5 p.m. The typical Saturday evening output consisted mainly of light entertainment: an American movie at 6.20; a live music programme; a feature film; 10 minutes of news at 10.35; and entertainment until 12.25.

On the same day BBC 2 offered Open University programmes—designed not for general viewing but as supplements to the studies of Open University students—from 7.40 a.m. to 1.30 p.m., after which it signed off. BBC 2 returned to the air at 2.20 with an American film; at 4 p.m. came the repeat of a science programme broadcast the previous week by BBC 1; at 4.30 a programme about handicapped people; at 5.30 a news analysis show; at 6 p.m. a review of the Rugby League year; at 7.05 a press conference; from 7.35 to 9 p.m. programmes about robots and word-use; and from 9 p.m. until 1.20 a.m. sign-off, The Hollywood Greats, jazz, a sports programme, and another American film.

A typical ITV Saturday schedule parallels that of BBC 1 more than of BBC 2. On Saturday, 2 June, it signed on with children's programmes at 8.35 a.m and devoted most of the afternoon to competitive sports. Late afternoon and evening provided light entertainment including the American teleseries, *Laverne and Shirley* at 5.15, a British-produced serial based on Robert Louis Stevenson's *Kidnapped* at 6.30, an ITV version of *Celebrity Squares* at 8 p.m., news at 10 p.m. a play at 10.15, and a 'lively interview programme' at 11.30, which ran until the 12.30 sign-off.

The next day, Sunday, 3 June, BBC 1 signed on at 9 a.m. and until noon

---

* For a time beginning in April 1977, two of Independent Television's regional companies, Tyne Tees in Northeast England and Yorkshire Television, programmed their 8.30–9.30 a.m. periods with a mixture of news, cartoons, and other miscellaneous material. At the end of 9 weeks, the experiment was discontinued, because of small audiences, since the 7 million television households in the two areas served by the two companies provided an average of only 150,000 viewers per morning (*Variety*, 6 July 1977, p. 46).

broadcast a mixture of special interest, hobby, and religious programmes. During the afternoon there were programmes about child care, farming, a Bing Crosby film, a documentary about Earl Mountbatten, the American series *Bonanza*, and a 50-minute period for young people. A 10-minute newscast at 6 p.m. was followed by a literary serial, *Songs of Praise* from a Roman Catholic church, another serial, a 90-minute cinema film, news, a 35-minute news-in-depth programme, and a 35-minute book programme. Five minutes of news at Midnight preceded sign-off.

BBC 2 devoted itself entirely to Open University programmes from its sign-on at 7.40 Sunday morning until 1.30 p.m. Then followed a long afternoon of cricket, and a news review from 6.45 to 7.15. The evening fare was somewhat heavier than that presented earlier in the day. At 7.15 *The World About Us* dealt with the Mojave Desert; 8.05 brought a light music show, followed by a 5-minute news review; at 9 p.m. there was a 75-minute episode from Dostoevsky's *Crime and Punishment*; swimming was the topic at 10.15; and from 11.15 to 12.55 a.m. there was a repeat of a dramatization of an F. Scott Fitzgerald story, *The Last of the Belles*.

On Sunday, 3 June, ITV opened at 8.40 with a science programme followed by a historical review of British shore defences against invasion and a feature about house purchasing and selling. *Morning Worship* at 10 a.m. brought together a mixture of faiths to celebrate the International Year of the Child, followed at 11 a.m. by a programme for disabled people. *Weekend World* from 12 noon to 1 p.m. a long-running series, was a review of world events. Programmes from then to 6 p.m. alternated between the serious and the light. Following a 10-minute news period at 6 p.m. was an elaborate recorded performance of Edward Elgar's oratorio, *The Dream of Gerontius*. At 7.25 ITV broadcast a 'star-studded' series of highlights from a programme celebrating the European Community with such artists as Yehudi Menuhin, the London Symphony Chorus, and The Circus of Europe. *The Stone Killer*, a 1973 film based on a John Gardner novel, came at 9.10; a literary film at 10.55; and the entertaining *Executive Suite* from 11.55 to 12.55 close.

In Britain as in the United States, television fare Monday to Friday follows much the same pattern day after day. During the week 2–8 June 1979, BBC 1 used its UHF transmitters to broadcast Open University programmes from 6.40 to 7.55 a.m., after which it signed off, returning to the air at times between 9.30 and 10 a.m. with programmes for schools and colleges which ran until 11.30, when the service signed off until the *Midday News* at 1.15, followed by a quarter-hour broadcast for young children. Mid-afternoon brought more school and college programmes, and late afternoon material for children's after-school viewing.

Adult services begin with a newscast at 5.40 p.m., followed by *Nationwide* from 5.55 to 6.55, which treats area and local news in a lighter vein. Except for 9 p.m., when BBC 1 offers its principal newscast of the day and BBC 2 starts a new programme, few programmes on BBC 1 and 2 begin at the same time. (This makes it difficult for viewers to tune from one network to the other, without missing portions of programmes. It also complicates tuning back and forth between either BBC service and ITV. Although BBC 1 and 2 cross-announce each other's offerings several times each evening, neither has a similar arrangement with ITV.)

BBC 1's weekday-evening schedule brings films, both light and serious; news analyses and discussion; some sports; and a mixture of other features, including, for example, serialized novels, programmes on *Multi-Racial Britain*, sports, and some American television programmes.

Except for the Open University programmes it carries each morning between 6.40 and 7.55, BBC 2 does little regular broadcasting—other than some short children's and other educational features—until it returns with more Open University programmes in the late afternoon. Between then and midnight, it offers a choice of serious and light programmes, emphasizing, however, the former. Typical programmes during the week in review included: several news analyses, averaging 30 minutes in length; *Crime and Punishment* (repeated the following Sunday); a live presentation of Verdi's opera, *Luisa Miller*, from the Royal Opera House; *Verse, Worse and Baby Grand*, 'A series of six programmes . . . (to) tickle your late-evening sensibilities with words and music, designed to undermine your gravity'; a rebroadcast of a German-language newscast from Germany (at times East German programmes are shown); *The Money Programme*, (a long-running feature, this one about preparing the nation's annual budget) and some serious plays.

With ITV as BBC, the Monday – Friday daytime schedule in London follows a regular pattern. School programmes take up the period from sign-on at 9.30 until noon, and programmes from 12 noon to 12.30 are for the 5 year old group. Mixed programes for adults—some serious, some light—fill the period until the first newscast of the day at 1 p.m., which brings 20 minutes of national and international news from ITN, plus 10 minutes of regional news produced by Thames Television for London, while the other regions carry their own local newscasts. A serial is broadcast at 1.30 and a women's programme at 2 p.m. The period until 4.15 is filled locally by the individual companies, with sports, feature films, or regional programmes. Children's programmes are mandated between 4.15 and 5.15, and more material not unsuitable for young viewers usually fills the time until the second ITN newscast at 5.45, which is followed by local news and features. From 7 until 10 p.m. there are films along with both British and American-produced entertainment shows. But there are some serious features as well, including news-oriented programmes from 8.30 to 9 p.m. on Monday and Thursday. All stations must carry the ITN news each evening, Monday to Friday, from 10 to 10.30.

After 10.30 p.m. during the week in review, the London transmitters broadcast a 30-minute programme on *Early Photography*, the first in a series of thirteen; an American film; *Inside Business*, a half-hour 'look at the world of international business'; *What The Papers Say*, a long-running examination of British newspapers of the week; and *The London Programme*, which this week examined the oil crisis.

ITV faces a problem in providing enough 'balance' programmes with only a single network. That difficulty, in fact, is one—although by no means the only—reason it so long requested a second channel. When its second channel is activated—in 1982 or later—it could programme as does the BBC, with predominantly—but not exclusively—serious material on that channel.

Whichever organization offers more serious programmes, there is no question that the BBC has always scheduled more of them in prime viewing time. For years the Corporation's official policy has been

to present many such programmes at times when the majority of people are at home and free to view them—the 'peak hours' between 7.00 and 10.30 p.m. These programmes would not serve their purpose fully if they were offered only at hours when relatively few are able to see them.[50]

On the ITV side, however, there have been divided councils, with the Authority sometimes saying one thing and the programme companies another. In the late 1950s—before the Pilkington Committee conducted its inquiry—an ITA report said that the Authority wished 'serious programmes to be spread as evenly as possible and the introduction during the year of regular monthly hour-long documentaries in the middle of the evening was a welcome step to this end'.[51] But the general manager of Associated Rediffusion argued that 'a majority programme should be transmitted when the majority are viewing. Enthusiastic minorities must give way to the majority and adjust their viewing hours accordingly.'[52]

This issue came up before the Pilkington Committee. The Director-General of the ITA stated that the timing and scheduling of balance programmes outside peak viewing hours 'is deliberate and sensible: the proof of the pudding is in the eating', and submitted tables showing that Independent Television programmes scheduled out of peak hours had more viewers than BBC programmes broadcast during peak periods. The complementary argument was offered by Roy Thomson, the publisher, then the major stockholder in Scottish Television, who said that since ITV's advertisers in effect were paying for viewers, 'it is inevitable in the system that you should be reaching generally for a maximum'.[53] But, as was noted above, as a consequence of the Pilkington and other government inquiries, ITV scheduling is now closely supervised by the Authority, so that it now contains a much greater proportion of serious programmes during peak viewing hours than formerly. The 1979 handbook pointed out: 'Informative programmes are expected to occupy at least one-third of the total output; in 1977–78 the average was in fact 38 per cent', with 30 per cent of the transmission time between 6 and 10.30 p.m. given over to such programmes.[54]

A comparative analysis of BBC and ITV output provides information about their respective practices to date, although it is impossible to make exact comparisons because the two organizations use different categories in classifying programmes. Furthermore, it is unfair to compare their output in recent years, unless consideration is given to the fact that the BBC has had a two-network service since 1964 whereas ITV has had only one.

In 1955–6, the average ITV company's transmissions included a much lower percentage of serious programmes than did BBC 1, but in recent years the differences have been slight. As is shown by Table 17, the figures for ITV and BBC 1 alone for 1978–9 are quite similar, but if both BBC networks are counted (see Tables 18 and 19), they are different.

Programme analyses for the two BBC television networks during 1978–9 and for the average ITV company during the same period are given in Tables 18 and 19.

TABLE 17 *Serious programming on television*

Year	ITV	BBC 1
1955–6	19	36.3
1965–6	36	33.8
1970–1	33	37
1971–2	34	35.8
1972–3	33	39.6
1973–4	34	40
1974–5	35	37.8
1975–6	39	36.4
1976–7	37.5	36
1977–8	38	35.8
1978–9	38.75	38

SOURCE: IBA, *Television and Radio 1977*, p. 11; Christopher Rowley, 'ITV's Programme Balance 1970–75, *Independent Broadcasting* (November 1975), pp. 2–4; IBA, *Television and Radio 1976*, p. 11; IBA, *Television and Radio 1979*, p. 12; *BBC Handbook 1972*, p. 44; *BBC Handbook 1973*, p. 47; *BBC Handbook 1974*, p. 128; *BBC Handbook 1975*, p. 126; *BBC Handbook 1976*, p. 118; *BBC Handbook 1977*, p. 117; *BBC Handbook 1979*, p. 105; IBA, *Annual Report and Accounts 1978–79*, p. 33; *BBC Handbook 1980*, p. 105.

TABLE 18 *Programme analysis 1978–9, television networks*

	BBC 1		BBC 2		Total	
	Hours	%	Hours	%	Hours	%
BBC Productions						
Current affairs, features and documentaries	798	15.9	816	19.9	1614	17.6
Sport	720	14.3	531	12.9	1251	13.7
Children's programmes	636	12.6	117	2.8	753	8.2
Light entertainment	357	7.1	229	5.6	586	6.4
Drama	261	5.2	214	5.2	475	5.2
Further education	234	4.6	190	4.6	424	4.6
News	252	5.0	136	3.3	388	4.2
Schools	368	7.3			368	4.0
Music	30	0.6	105	2.6	135	1.5
Religion	116	2.3	18	0.4	134	1.5
Programmes in Welsh	36	0.7			36	0.4
Continuity	272	5.4	201	4.9	473	5.2
	4080	81.0	2557	62.2	6637	72.5
British and foreign feature films and series	717	14.2	553	13.5	1270	13.9
	4797	95.2	3110	75.7	7907	86.4
Open University	241	4.8	1001	24.3	1242	13.6
	5038	100.0	4111	100.0	9149	100.0

SOURCE: *BBC Handbook 1980*, p. 105.

TABLE 19   *Weekly transmission hours of the average ITV company*

	1976–77 (hr. min.)		1977–78 (hr. min.)		1978–79 (hr. min.)	
News and news magazines	10.11	10%	10.23	10%	10.27	10½%
Current affairs, documentaries, arts	11.55	12%	12.20	12%	13.17	13%
Religion	2.36	2½%	2.50	3%	2.24	2½%
Adult education	3.28	3½%	3.08	3%	3.07	3%
School programmes	6.26	6½%	6.29	6½%	6.11	6¼%
Pre-school education	1.26	1½%	1.27	1½%	1.27	1½%
Children's informative	1.58	2%	2.06	2%	2.10	2%
'Informative'	38.00	38%	38.43	38%	39.03	38¾%
Plays, drama, TV movies	24.34	25%	24.12	24%	22.54	22¾%
Feature films	8.42	9%	8.27	8%	8.00	8%
'Narrative'	33.16	34%	32.39	32%	30.54	30¾%
Children's entertainment	7.24	7½%	8.17	8%	7.57	8%
Entertainment and music	11.39	11½%	13.19	13%	12.13	12%
'Entertainment'	19.03	19%	21.36	21%	20.10	20%
'Sport'	9.15	9%	9.27	9%	10.34	10½%
Total all all programmes	99.34	100%	102.25	100%	100.41	100%

SOURCE: ITA, *Television and Radio 1980*, p. 12

Even though the claim of the ITV's chief programming officer that the Authority's programmes have been better balanced than those of any other commercially supported service in the world is justified, my impression is that BBC 1 has scheduled more such programming during peak viewing hours than has ITV; and furthermore, that totally, the BBC—utilizing its two networks—offered greater variety than did Independent Television.[55] What the effect will be on British television scheduling when the IBA begins to operate its second channel remains to be seen.

10 Programme Standards and Codes

Questions of programme standards are forever encountered in the communicative arts. Such problems faced the Greeks, the Puritans in the sixteenth and seventeenth centuries, the film-makers in the twentieth century, radio broadcasters in the United States since about 1930, and now the world's telecasters. Well-organized campaigns have been mounted in the United Kingdom and elsewhere charging television with poor taste, bad language, the exploitation of sex and violence, and the undermining of public morality.

The major theme of this criticism is that the 'success' customarily attending aggressive behaviour in mass media fiction (without apparent social disapproval) must surely encourage the use of such tactics in real life. The waves of violence that have swept the United States and other western countries in recent years have given added emphasis to this conjecture.[1]

PROBLEMS OF CONTROL

With broadcasting, all the questions previously raised about the printed page, the cinema, and the stage are intensified because of the general assumption that radio and television should be more strictly regulated than the other media, despite vigorous claims by many broadcasters that the same standards should be applied to all. One argument for the closer regulation of radio and television relates to the shortage of broadcasting facilities. The Supreme Court of the United States in 1969 upheld the constitutionality of the FCC's action in the Red Lion Case by reasoning that the Commission could require broadcasting stations to observe the Fairness Doctrine, which requires stations to give air time to the major points of view in a discussion of controversial nature, without violating the freedom of speech guarantees of the First Amendment.[2] With the proliferation of broadcasting stations, this argument now is often questioned, although it remains valid in the United Kingdom, which has a much greater frequency-shortage problem than does the United States. Relating to this is the reasoning that, since the broadcasters have free access to the airwaves, they should be required to give something in return, including the maintenance of certain programme standards.

The laws of almost every country require its broadcasters to maintain at least a minimum quality of programme service. In the United Kingdom, both the BBC and the IBA must provide information and education, as well as entertainment. In the United States, Congress decreed that stations should be licensed only when the FCC finds that 'public convenience, interest or necessity will be served thereby'.[3] Many people believe that because broadcasts are received in family groups at home without benefit of preview, they must meet certain standards in regard to taste, sex and violence, not imposed on book shops, theatres or cinemas. The fact that children do much viewing is another justification for minimum programme standards.*

The Annan Committee took a pragmatic view of these problems: 'Public opinion cannot be totally disregarded in the pursuit of liberty.'[4] Of the 6000 letters it received—although it must be recognized that letter-writing is an addiction of the higher rather than lower socio-economic classes—'sexual innuendo and bad language came respectively first and second and violence third in terms of intensity of aversion'. There must be a distinction, it observed, 'between private and public offence'. Many people are 'fairly robust about . . . something that they and they alone witness. It is when they witness it in the company of others that their own private response is overlaid by social sensitivity and they begin to voice their disquiet. Whatever is published is presumed to be in some way approved or at best condoned, by the society which permits its publication'. Broadcasters, therefore, must avoid violating 'the current state of taste'.

The potential effects of broadcasts on law and order also are a factor. The most famous example, of course, was the CBS *War of the Worlds* scare in 1938, when Orson Welles' drama convinced thousands of people that hostile Martians were landing in various parts of the country. But that was not the first or the last case of its sort. Back in 1926 an imaginary BBC news bulletin reported a fictitious riot of the unemployed, during which a crowd wrecked the BBC studios and were looting the government offices in Whitehall.[5] Despite the fact that the programme—in Briggs' words—'included such unlikely details as the roasting alive of a well-known philanthropist in Trafalgar Square', consternation followed, and people all over the country called their friends, the BBC, and the newspapers to make frenzied inquiries.

On Monday, 10 September 1945, during a flashback in a BBC radio dramatic programme, a well-known BBC voice reread the announcement of the previous May that Tuesday, 8 May and Wednesday, 9 May would be VE Day holidays. This led to such widespread assumptions that Tuesday and Wednesday of the week of

* The question of whether broadcasting should have the same freedom as the print media was faced again by the United States Supreme Court in the Pacifica case in 1978. A New York radio station broadcast a monologue entitled 'Filthy Words', which repeated in various context seven words normally excluded from the airwaves, and also from general-circulation newspapers. The court decided:

'Of all forms of communication, broadcasting has the most limited First Amendment protection. Among the reasons for specially treating indecent broadcasting is the uniquely pervasive presence that medium of expression occupies in the lives of our people. Broadcasts extend into the privacy of the home and it is impossible completely to avoid those that are patently offensive. Broadcasting, moreover, is uniquely accessible to children'. (*United States Law Week*, 27 June 1978, 46LW5018).

the programme also would be holidays, that explanations had to be made over the air and in the newspapers.

In September 1957, a half-hour television programme in Hartford, Connecticut, opening Civil Defense Week, showed so realistically what might happen if Connecticut experienced an enemy attack, that many people were frightened into believing the country was actually being invaded. The programme was only on one local station, but before it was over, more than 100 telephone calls had been received by the town's newspapers and the police.[6]

The old story was re-enacted again on 20 February 1959, when Associated Rediffusion's presentation of Wesbrook Fuller's play, *Before the Sun Goes Down*, gave British viewers their first television *War of the Worlds* experience. The play began as an actor, impersonating a newscaster, interrupted the programme 'for an urgent announcement' that a new and 'terrifying space ship . . . hangs stationary over London'. Many people took this to be a real news announcement and were terrified. There followed calls to the stations carrying the programme, the police, and the newspapers, as well as to the BBC, to see if they too had news of the 'invasion'.

In due course there were letters to newspapers, questions in Parliament and an explanation from the ITA that there had been an error of judgement which would not be repeated. The play by itself created little or no comment, the reviewer for *The Times* dismissing it as 'beneath critical attention'. However, the lesson was learned, and a simulated news broadcast scheduled to introduce Thorton Wilder's *The Skin of Our Teeth* a month later was eliminated at ITA intructions.[7] Incidentally, the IBA programme code now provides: 'No simulation of a television news bulletin or news flash should be included in any programme . . . without the Authority having given its express previous approval in each case'.[8]

In 1967, an hour-long April Fool's Day broadcast over the German-language radio network in Switzerland, which was a simulated actuality report, convinced thousands that American spacemen had landed on the moon, and led many people to the hills to watch for the return of the spaceship. In 1973, a student radio station in the little community of Barseback, Sweden, dramatized a debate over a nuclear power station being constructed, and broadcast a fake news programme reporting a nuclear disaster. Thousands panicked, running to fall-out shelters, and it took several hours to restore calm.[9]*

---

* On 20 June 1977, IBA's Anglia Television broadcast a programme originally intended for April Fool's Day, but held over. Done in mock documentary style, it claimed to show the United States and the Soviet Union secretly colonizing Mars, as the earth slowly died in a haze of pollution. But the science-fiction fantasy was taken for real by many viewers, and switchboards at broadcasting stations, newspapers, and police stations were jammed by worried callers (*London Evening News*, 21 June 1977; *Daily Mirror*, 21 June 1977; *Daily Express*, 22 June 1977).

Another variation on the pattern was provided on 27 November 1977, when a group of student electronic enthusiasts used a home-made transmitter to inject a 6 minute taped message into the audio portion of a newscast being watched by television viewers in a 75-mile diameter area southwest of London. The message purported to come from 'Vrillon . . . of Ashtar Galactic Command', and said: 'I have a message for the planet Earth. . . . All your weapons of evil must be destroyed. You have only a short time to learn

Despite considerable research on both sides of the Atlantic as to the effects of programmes emphasizing sex, violence and bad language, there are conflicting data as to the influence of such programmes.[10] After reviewing the evidence, the Annan Committee summarized the matter succinctly—and pragmatically. Observing that the results were in doubt, although the intensity and nature of public reaction was clear, it concluded: 'What . . . is beyond conjecture is that programme standards [do] matter to the public; and therefore it is our unanimous view that the broadcasters have a case to answer.'[11] In 1970 Home Secretary James Callaghan, who became Prime Minister in 1976, told the BBC and the IBA that, although they had excellent codes on broadcast violence, they were not properly enforced.

While there is general agreement that some regulation is necessary, most informed observers oppose control if it goes so far as to eliminate all expression of moral opinion, or if it seriously curtails the creative talents of writers and producers. Again, the Annan Committee provided guidance, saying that there is 'a perennial debate . . . concerning what should, or should not, be said, done, or shown in public', the greatest alarm usually being shown about the influence of what is the most popular, and hence in their view potentially the most subversive medium for art in their times: in the eighteenth century the theatre, in the nineteenth the novel, in the post-World War I years the cinema, and today television.[12] But there must be programme standards. Consequently, 'the fact that something is "life-like" is not in itself a sufficient justification for showing it on the screen'. The expression of ideas, and especially of new ideas, is to be encouraged, but it must be kept within bounds. Conflicts and debates over programme substance will surely continue. However, 'The right corrective is not censorship but the self-discipline which springs from understanding the true nature of the debate about programme standards.'

In judging British material, Americans must realize that, by and large, the British allow language and scenes which would be edited out of telecasts in the United States. Along with this is a willingness to report and show frightening and sordid facts which the American media would either play down or avoid. Thus, a

---

to live together in peace . . . or leave the galaxy.' Thereafter, hundreds of viewers phoned the police and the television station (*The New York Times*, 28 November 1977, p. 3 c; *Broadcasting*, 19 December 1977, p. 56).

Under the headline, 'Fools rush in to save April', the London *Daily Star* reported on 2 April 1979: 'April 5 and 12 will not be cancelled after all. Jokers at London's Capital Radio restored the status quo last night after thousands of April fools jammed their switchboard in protest. Broadcaster John Irving started the stampede by announcing that putting the clocks back and forward every year had thrown the calendar out. The next two Thursdays, he revealed, would be cancelled to compensate'. 'People really were taken in', said spokesman Jan Reid. 'A young woman expecting twins on the 12th even phoned to ask what their new birthday would be.'

And again from London, in 1980, after the BBC's External Services had transmitted an April Fool's Day programme reporting that Big Ben was going digital, some listeners sent letters and telegrams complaining about such violence being done to the world's most famous clock. 'Surprisingly, few people thought it was funny,' said a BBC spokesman. 'We even offered to give the hands away to the first listeners who contacted us,' he said. (*The New York Times*, 7 April 1980, p. D 11).

Variety story at the end of 1975 reported that, 'compared with the U.S. and many other video markets, the British tend to impose fewer taboos on television drama themes. Like tonight's . . . decidedly down beat BBC Television yarn about a young woman who discovers a lump in her breast.' The play followed 'the woman through hospital surgery that confirms the worst', after which she demonstrated strength and courage when she received a straightforward account of the seriousness of her condition.[13] The fact that a thing really happened is taken as justification for showing it, as in the case of the BBC television documentary about an American nudist colony which I saw in the summer of 1976.

Both BBC and ITV precede certain programmes with verbal and visual warnings about their possible upsetting or disturbing nature. In addition, in the Midlands and Southern areas, some IBA programmes containing potentially disturbing material have displayed continuously in the lower left-hand corner of the screen, a small white rectangle warning symbol.[14] This has not been used during news or current affairs programmes, although when such programmes contain particularly distressing or harrowing sequences, viewers are warned in advance. But the Authority has instructed its producers that the symbol should never be employed merely 'to justify the production or acquisition of programme material that would otherwise not be acceptable.'

CODES AND COMPLAINTS: INDEPENDENT BROADCASTING AUTHORITY

Although both the BBC and IBA have long had their own guidelines about violence, sex and bad language, public concern over these subjects was greatly intensified in the 1960s, and consequently the broadcasters' action was increased. In Britain, leadership was provided by the group originally known as 'Clean up TV Campaign', later renamed 'National Listeners' and Viewers' Association'.[15]

Later the National Conferation of PTAs and others joined the movement. The leader of the groups, Mrs Mary Whitehouse, presented Parliament in June 1965 with a manifesto bearing 365,355 signatures complaining about BBC programmes. Among other things it said: 'In particular we object to the propaganda of disbelief, doubt and dirt that the BBC projects into millions of homes through the television screen.'[16] In spite of vigorous BBC denial that this group represented anything like a majority of the public, such pressures did have effects, especially when abetted by church groups. The extensive Surgeon-General's report on television violence in the United States was cited in support of their case.[17]

The Pilkington Committee in 1962 rejected the position of Independent Television that there was no need for a written violence code, and recommended that the Authority itself set policies about the portrayal of violence, rather than leaving the matter to the individual programme companies, and also that it require all programmes broadcast before 9 p.m. to be suitable for children.[18] Both of the ensuing White Papers took notice of the recommendation for a code, although neither suggested that one be legally required. In fact, the Second White Paper stated: 'In the last resort these are matters which must depend on the vigilance of the broadcasting authorities. Prescription by legislation of detailed programme standards would be ineffective.'[19] Nevertheless, the current law, using much the same phrases as earlier Television Acts, instructs the IBA to exclude from its programming anything 'which offends against good taste or decency or is likely to encourage or incite to crime or to lead to disorder or to be offensive to public feeling'.[20] In addition, the Authority must

> draw up, and from time to time review, a code giving guidance . . . as to the rules observed in regard to the showing of violence and in regard to the inclusion in local sound broadcasts of sounds suggestive of violence, particularly when large numbers of children and young persons may be expected to be watching or listening,

and it must require the provisions of the code to be observed by the programme companies.

The Annan Report cited research data indicating that on all three television channels, 'violence is frequent', especially on programmes imported from the United States. The report observed that whereas many American programmes contain too much violence, American stations 'reject some British material because it is too salacious, contains too many nude scenes, and includes too many unacceptable expletives.'[21] But the committee rejected outright proposals for a Tribunal of Taste to adjudicate complaints. Such responsibilities, it said, 'must lie with the Authority in charge of each broadcasting outlet'. The ensuing government White Paper stated that the 'broadcasting authorities [should] . . . assume undersirable effects unless convincing evidence to the contrary emerges, and that both agencies should regularly review and publish their operating codes.

There has been an ITV Code on Violence since 1964. In 1970, the Authority set up a Working Party on Violence, which published a revised Code in 1971. Reconstituted in 1977, the Working Party recommended a few changes in its report of the following year.[22] The Code's introduction answers 'yes' to the question of whether there need be any violence in television.

> First, [it says] conflict is of the essence of drama, and conflict often leads to violence. Second, the real world contains much violence in many forms, and when television seeks to reflect the world—in fact or in fiction—it would be unrealistic and untrue to ignore its violent aspects.

Violence can be physical, verbal, psychological, or even metaphysical or supernatural. But it must be realized that 'people seldom view just one programme. An acceptable minimum of violence in each individual programme may add up to an intolerable level over a period'.

In its *Annual Report* for 1978–9, the Authority further spelled out some of the problems it faces in applying codes to its output :

> It is not surprising that some plays [wrote the Authority] particularly those

attempting to examine aspects of contemporary life, should give rise to complaint. What is interesting is that they give rise to so little complaint. Such complaints as arise derive from the familiar trio of bad language, what is considered too explicit sex, or to a somewhat lesser extent what is regarded as gratuitous violence. There is a dilemma. On the one hand a comprehensive television service should provide opportunities for freedom of expression for writers; on the other hand television is seen by all sorts of and conditions of people in their homes. What might be acceptable in the theatre or the cinema, to which people have chosen to go, can be less acceptable in the living room. And so writers, drama producers, programme controllers, and the IBA are continually and conscientiously trying to determine what can or cannot be included in plays. A line has to be drawn about what is or is not acceptable or necessary and it is by no means easy to draw it. With so many people watching Independent Television's drama, some will inevitably think the line to have been wrongly drawn; allowing too much or allowing too little.

Examples of the kinds of complaints received by Britain's broadcasters were provided by a list of 'Interventions with Regard to Programme Content' supplied by the Authority in December 1971 to the Select Committee on Nationalized Industries.[23] Following a protest that a part of one ATV programme was 'dirty', investigation revealed what the Authority described as 'too much cheap and lavatorial humour for one programme', particularly since it was broadcast in family viewing time. The company expressed 'regret', and said it would direct scriptwriters and producers to eliminate such material in the future. In another case, Authority representatives previewed a London Weekend Television play which reviewed events 'between the death of a staunch trade-unionist and his burial'. Because of 'bad language', the Authority requested two cuts, one of a scene in a pub 'with a very considerable concentration of bad language; the second, of a conversation at the funeral party about a workman who had suffered sexual injuries'. It was cleared for broadcast, at a late evening hour, subject to these two cuts. (The American NAB Code says: 'Obscene, indecent or profane matter, as prescribed by law, is unacceptable.')[24]

When the Authority was invited by Thames Television to preview a 60-minute documentary set in a rehabilitation centre for drug addicts, it observed that one portion of the programme 'contained a group therapy sequence in which a considerable amount of swearing, including the usual four-letter sexual expletives, takes place'. The Authority ruled that the documentary could be broadcast at a later hour, if 'preceded by an announcement indicating the nature of the language that would be heard'.

A Granada programme about the proposed establishment of a 'sex boutique' was allowed to proceed, provided the broadcast time was changed from 8 to 9.30 p.m., and two cuts were made. Following the broadcast of a Thames Television programme about classroom hooliganism and vandalism, which contained 'damaging allegations' about one school, the Authority agreed that the criticisms were inaccurate, and so public apologies were made.

There always is a risk that a live programme may include some unintended offensive material. On 1 December 1976, a Thames television interviewer, during a 6 p.m. programme, had as guests the Sex Pistols rock group, noted for their crude manners and offensive language. During the broadcast several four-letter words were uttered—some viewers charged at the provocation of the interviewer. The reaction in telephone calls and press reports was strongly critical, the interviewer was given a short suspension, and the programme company offered public apology.[25]

Although sex vulgarity is disapproved, serious presentations of sex information fall into another category.[26] In July 1977, Yorkshire Television produced seven programmes, *Man and Woman*, described in one news story as including 'detailed diagrams of the bodily processes during lovemaking'. Sex education was the objective of this series, and reaction was generally favourable. Some critics noted that with an 11.15 p.m. air-time, the programme was too late to provide much help to those who most needed it, since younger childern would be asleep, and sexually active teenagers out on the town, leaving only those who already know about sex as the audience. Be that as it may, *The Times* review read: 'For this is a tale which has long been in the telling: others, bolder and rasher, have perished in the attempt.' The *Yorkshire Evening Post* published a basically favourable review stating that the programme 'has dealt with many aspects of sex from menopause to venereal disease and from contraception to sexual hang-ups in an explicit but unsensational way, [and it] could well be the forerunner to more series of this kind.' The newspaper stated that many people had written for the notes provided with the programme, and that the Family Planning Association, whose telephone number was given at the end of the broadcast, was 'inundated with inquiries—many, to the Association's surprise, from men'.

The Authority's Television Programme Guidelines cover other types of problems too, ranging from accuracy in news to the right of privacy. For example, 'reconstructions' in 'dramatised documentary' programmes must 'not distort reality', and must be 'labelled so that the viewer is not misled'.[27] A Granada programme dealing with certain events in the life of Soviet Marshal Grigorenko was based on the diary he kept while confined to a Russian mental hospital as punishment for criticizing the regime. The Authority approved the broadcast, but insisted 'that it should be absolutely clear to viewers that the programme was based on one man's diary and that it was a dramatised reconstruction not a piece of actuality of the events described'.

Also prohibited is 'the portrayal of dangerous behaviour easily imitated by children', in programmes aired before 9 p.m., along with hanging scenes prior to 9.30 p.m.[28] The Authority found an example of this in the London Weekend Television series entitled *The Odd Job*, which included 'some dangerous comedy with electricity, including a very simple device for rigging up an electric chair. Our inquiries to the company coincided with the producer's own realisation that what he was proposing was very dangerous indeed. The script was therefore being amended'.

CODES AND COMPLAINTS: BRITISH BROADCASTING CORPORATION

The BBC also has had problems in controlling its output to everyone's satisfaction. In 1960 its Controller of Programmes submitted a Code of Practice to the Pilkington Committee covering both adult and children's programmes, the last paragraph of which advised staff members, in case of doubt, to 'refer' upward for advice.[29] Continuing concern was indicated in a nine-page review in the *BBC Handbook* for 1966, which summarized reactions from various sections of the public to a variety of BBC programmes.[30]

In 1972, the Corporation published an extensive report by its own research department on television violence based on the monitoring of both BBC and IBA television between November 1970 and May 1971.[31] The published report, which ran to 220 pages with appendices, noted that criticisms of violence usually are based on the assumption 'that the "success" customarily attending aggressive behaviour . . . (without apparent social disapproval) must surely encourage the use of such tactics in real life'. In any case, half of the 1558 programmes monitored contained no major violence, while at the other extreme, one-eighth of them contained four or more such acts, the amount being about the same on all three networks, with only a slight increase after 9 p.m., when the protected 'family viewing time' ended. Programmes imported from America had over twice as much violence as those produced at home.

According to a survey of both ITV and BBC conducted in Bristol at the end of 1976, ITV viewers heard more blasphemies and saw more violence and extramarital sex activity per hour than did those watching the BBC. The report claimed that 'a person watching an average selection of output from three channels . . . for a whole average evening, will have observed five acts or results of injurious violence per hour, and between two and three sexual seductions outside of marriage per evening'.[32] But when it was announced that the American producer of the *Starsky and Hutch* show, carried by the BBC, stated during a BBC interview that because of 'enormous pressure' in the United States there would be less violence on that series in the future, many regular viewers of the series called to complain, saying that they found newscasts showing the killing of seal pups much more upsetting than the violence on the *Starsky and Hutch* show.

The BBC's code on *The Use of Violence in Television Programmes*, which came into operation in 1960, was expanded in 1972 to become, *The Portrayal of Violence in Television Programmes: A Note of Guidance*.[33] In 1973, the Corporation produced a study on *Taste and Standards in BBC Programmes* at the request of its General Advisory Committee, which provided a good review of Corporation practices and standards in news, current affairs, dramatic, and entertainment programmes. In 1979 the 1972 report was issued in revised form.[34]

In many respects these parallel the ITV Violence Code cited above. Thus, they point out that, since most people 'rarely encounter direct violence of a physical kind', television must be truthful in presenting violence. 'It must neither stir up unnecessary anxieties nor lead people to believe that physical violence is a readily acceptable solution to the problems and conflicts. Nor, however, must it disguise the fact that violence is a part of our nature and a part of life', which has been present in drama from the earliest times. Despite the absence of conclusive evidence as to the effects of television violence on viewers, programmers must 'pay regard to tradition, experience, a sense of responsibility, and a general public feeling that physical violence is a bad thing'.

They also deal with the effects of violence on children and young people, covering most of the points cited above from the IBA code, including an admonition to 'avoid setting examples which can be easily copied', as well as to choose carefully the risks 'to which characters are exposed, so that children are not encouraged to seek out the same hazards for themselves'. Generalizing about violence and adult audiences, the brochures warn. 'Excessive violence may rob the audience of its capacity to concentrate on anything else in the programme either at the time of its use or latter.' Violence should not be used merely 'to bolster a flagging plot, but must arise naturally from the story'. Details of violence should be avoided, and it should be remembered that 'violence towards defenceless objects [such as children, animals, and sometimes women] is more disturbing than violence towards . . . the man who can defend himself'. Violence should not be presented so as to 'glorify it or portray it as a proper solution to inter-personal conflicts'. But, nevertheless, 'there are occasions when authors and directors must use violence to make a substantial point about society and human relations'.

In April 1977, following the announcement of the findings of several research projects into the effects of violence on viewers, the publication of a brochure on *Social Research on Broadcasting: Proposals for Further Development*, by Elihu Katz (see below, p. 369), and a talk in which Shirley Williams, the British Minister of Education, publicly criticized violence in news and dramatic programmes, the BBC announced plans to fund an Independent Broadcasting Research Trust to examine the social effects of broadcasting.[35]

The Corporation's 1977 *Handbook* included a six-page report from the Board of Governors which observed, among other things, that it had become aware of public concern

> that bad language can cause a degree of offence to some people which wholly removes their pleasure from listening or viewing. It is, therefore, important that such offence should not be provoked needlessly, despite the greater acceptance by large numbers of people especially many of the young, of bad language as an element in everyday speech.[36]

Back in December 1954, the BBC broadcast a very vivid dramatization of George Orwell's *1984*, which aroused widespread criticism for its alleged 'brutality' and 'horror'; brought strong appeals from the public and some members of Parliament for the cancellation of its scheduled repeat; and made 'Big Brother' an everyday phrase in Britain. The telephone calls received during the broadcast, and the newspaper coverage and Parliamentary discussion afterwards, made this play the centre of one of the most heated controversies in the history of BBC television. Nevertheless, the repeat programme went on as scheduled, a decision applauded by the programme's defenders as a fearless presentation of the facts of life in totalitarian countries. In retrospect, it appears that this incident was taken as reaffirming the principle of BBC independence from government.[37]

When it was on the air, from 1964 to 1970, the Wednesday Play evoked some of the strongest reactions ever received by the BBC. This was an avant-garde series of contemporary plays, following in the tradition of John Osborne's *Look Back in Anger*, produced in 1956.[38]

> [The] distinctive mark of the series [wrote the Corporation, is that it] offers a regular outlet for contemporary playwrights both established and new; it offers them a weekly place on BBC Television to explore, sometimes directly, sometimes obliquely, our changing times. Its main targets are the turning points in a society which is changing too quickly for some, too slowly for others. [Its aim is] to provide one of those growing points [in the words of the Pilkington Report], at which . . . 'the challenges to existing assumptions and beliefs are made, where the claims to new knowledge and new awareness are stated.' It is one of these key series in which 'broadcasting must be most willing to make mistakes; for if it does not, it will make no discoveries.' Mistakes draw criticism, discoveries are uncomfortable. Both compel controversy. So on occasion does the *Wednesday Play*. It would be surprising—and disappointing—if it did not.

Reminiscing about his years as BBC chairman, Lord Hill wrote that while he approved Hugh Greene's 'opening of the windows' to new ideas, 'this new freedom was occasionally abused, with lapses of taste and language'.[39] Hill recalled a discussion by the full Board of Directors in May 1968 of a Wednesday Play in which the word 'bloody' was used several times, and another which had 'an over-explicit bedroom scene'.* The bedroom scene, as Lord Hill put it, 'had been full of sods, bastards and other swear words and contained a scene in which a young man had undressed a girl before having intercourse with her and had been shown in bed with her discussing the sexual act which they had just performed'. What is more, the play was broadcast at 8 p.m. well within 'family viewing time'.

One staff member defended the 'bloodies' as well as the bedroom scene not as lapses, but as justified in their context, although another commented that the problem was 'a lapse of vigilance on the part of those responsible', and that the matter had already been taken care of—presumably by reprimanding the producer and instructing him not to do such a thing again. The head of BBC Television observed—as Hill put it—that even though the Wednesday Play constituted only 5 per cent of the total television output, most offences were in that programme, probably because it is impossible to present contemporary plays without offending somebody.

On another occasion Lord Hill questioned a Wednesday Play, *On the Eve of Publication*, which he found 'most powerful and absorbing', even though it

* As an expletive 'bloody' is virtually meaningless to Americans although it is regarded as profane in the United Kingdom. The *Shorter Oxford English Dictionary* (third edition, 1973) gives its derivation as 'Probably [from] blood, 'sblood'. Under 'blood', '''sblood'' appears as an antiquated intensive equivalent to ''God's blood and Christ's blood'''.

included such scenes as 'a man relieving himself, and certain coarse words, for which I could not see justification on grounds of dramatic necessity'. He would be willing to defend such scenes, he said, if they were 'essential to the play', but he did not think these were.[40] As a former Chairman of the Board put it, since the moral values of young writers differ from those of their elders, this fact becomes evident when they have a platform. Should an older generation impose its standards of judgement on the output of contemporary writers?

The problem of public reaction to violence, sex, and profanity in broadcasting will always be with us. Standards and tastes may change, so that what is edited out one year may become quite acceptable a decade—or less—later, but there always will be some prohibited material. In the chapters ahead, these issues will be examined again, as different types of programmes are considered in turn.

11 News Programmes

Programmes involving news and news interpretation, current affairs, controversial issues, and politics are important for their content, and also because they are excellent indications of a country's attitude towards broadcasting. If any programmes are to be government-controlled, these will be among the first.

Both the BBC and the IBA assign great importance to news and current affairs.[1] The Corporation gives editorial responsibility for these areas to the Director of News and Current Affairs, since October 1977 a member of the Board of Management, who reports to the Director-General. The Director is responsible for the News Division, which provides radio and television news through its two wings, radio news and television news. Organizationally and managerially the current affairs departments are part of the radio and television directorate.

It might be noted that several BBC Directors-General had news backgrounds: Sir William Haley, Director-General from 1944 to 1952, came to the Corporation from the *Manchester Guardian* and *Evening News*, and left it to become editor of *The Times* of London; Sir Hugh Greene, Director-General from 1960 to 1969, became a broadcaster after having been a newspaper foreign correspondent and Director of News and Current Affairs for the Corporation from 1958 to 1959; and both Sir Ian Jacob, Director-General from 1952 to 1960, and Sir Charles Curran, Director-General from 1969 to 1977, were involved in the Corporation's External Broadcasting activities in Bush House prior to assuming the post of Director-General. Ian Trethowan, who became Director-General in 1977, had been a political correspondent for several newspapers, later held several ITN positions, and joined the BBC in 1963 as a political commentator.

The ITA indicated its regard for news by creating at the outset in 1955 a separate company to provide network news for all its programme contractors. All Authority television programme companies must carry the major ITN newscasts as well as maintaining their own regional and local news operations. (For material on ITN, see below, pp. 200–2.) A similar procedure is followed with Independent Local Radio stations, all of which must carry national and international news programmes from Independent Radio News (IRN).

The BBC's Charter and Licence make several references to news programmes. The Charter indicates the importance of broadcasting as a 'means of disseminating information, education and entertainment', and news certainly falls into the first if not the second of these categories. So that it may properly discharge its news broadcasting assignments, the Corporation is specifically authorized 'To collect news and information in any part of the world and in any manner it may be thought fit to establish and subscribe to news agencies.'[2] There also is the clause in the Licence—the only positive programme requirement legally imposed on the BBC:

'The Corporation shall broadcast impartial accounts day by day prepared by professional reporters of the proceedings in both Houses of the United Kingdom's Parliament.'[3] Although neither Charter nor Licence specify objectivity in news reporting, the directives against editorializing, and the admonition to be fair and impartial in treating controversial issues, have always been understood to apply to newscasts as well.

Here, as in so many other respects, the law for the IBA followed the pattern set by the BBC. Broadcasting is to be 'a public service for disseminating information, education and entertainment'.[4] The Authority must ensure 'that a sufficient amount of time . . . is given to news and news features and that all news given in the programmes (in whatever form) is presented with due accuracy and impartiality'. As a consequence of concern over press-broadcasting cross-media relationships, the law instructs the Authority to prevent newspaper and other press interests from controlling the programme contractors, at the same time that it guarantees local newspapers stock ownership in local radio companies in order to minimize their possible financial losses from radio competition.

BRITAIN'S EARLY NEWSCASTS

Despite the reputation built by BBC for its news coverage during World War II, and the emphasis now placed on news programmes, news broadcasting was slow to develop in the United Kingdom. It took 15 years of effort plus a world war to put day-round news bulletins on the BBC; and it required competition from the ITA to hasten the Corporation's transition from television radio news to effective television newscasting.

In Britain, as in the United States, the press feared radio competition, and therefore tried to limit the growth of radio news. It also tried unsuccessfully to hinder the Corporation's plans to publish the *Radio Times* and the *Listener*.[5] In the United States, too, the press tried to restrict news broadcasting, but with considerably less success. Ever since 1934, there has been at least one full-time news service available to American stations. In the United States, as in Britain, it was the crisis of World War II that overcame the last effective opposition to radio newscasts.

In 1922, press interests succeeded in getting into the British Broadcasting Company's original Licence a provision preventing it from broadcasting news unless purchased from Reuters, the Press Association, Central News, Exchange Telegraph, or other news agencies.[6] By thus prohibiting the Company from collecting news, the press group made it dependent on the news agencies, which they controlled. Reflecting the influence of the press, the Postmaster-General insisted throughout the negotiations which led to the chartering of the British Broadcasting Company, 'that broadcasting should in no way alienate the press interest'.[7]

On 11 November 1922 an agreement was drawn up for the news agencies to supply the Company with a daily news summary for broadcasting within the British Isles, with the stipulation, however, that 'the Parties to this Agreement enter into it in the full spirit and endeavour not to prejudice the newspapers'.[8] One presentation to the Sykes Committee in 1923 requested that transmitter power be held down so that British broadcasts could not be heard on the continent, lest sales of newspapers there be effected 'to the serious detriment of news agencies and newspapers'.

Since the company was young and inexperienced, short on funds with which to set up its news service, and lacking powerful friends to plead its case, it had to agree to broadcast news only between 7 p.m. and 1 a.m—that is, after the evening newspapers had been distributed and before the morning editions appeared. In addition, the Company agreed not to broadcast sports contests, including the famous Derby at Epsom Downs.[9] Beginning in 1924, although the 7 p.m.– 1 a.m. limits were retained, the Company was 'at liberty to broadcast ceremonies, speeches or other functions by microphone at any hour', provided that no 'description or comment' were given.[10]

In 1925, the Newspaper Proprietors' Association told the Crawford Committee that because news broadcasting could have disastrous results on newspaper circulation, it strongly opposed an increase in such programmes. But the Committee was sceptical, and wrote that in

the long run art will not be injured by science, and . . . the printed page will not be displaced by the spoken word . . . . Broadcasting is not only an institution, but has become a necessity throughout the civilised world. This country cannot withhold privileges so widely enjoyed without restriction elsewhere.[11]

These press-enforced limitations had to be lifted in 1926 during the General Strike, so that the BBC, the only source of news for the entire country, could broadcast bulletins throughout the day. In 1927, with the coming of the British Broadcasting Corporation, Reith got permission for the Corporation to broadcast news bulletins at 6.30 instead of 7 p.m., and to transmit a few eye-witness descriptions, although it still had to take its news exclusively from the press news agencies. Not until February 1930 did the BBC broadcast a complete news bulletin entirely edited by itself, and beginning at 6 p.m. instead of 6.30. In 1930, three teletype machines were installed in BBC headquarters for the first time, and in 1934 a news department was set up.

Thereafter, the restrictions were gradually relaxed, although even in 1938 news broadcasting was limited to the hours between 6 p.m. and 2 a.m., with exceptions 'in the case of events of urgent national importance or of exceptional public interest'. This opened the way for the BBC to initiate frequent news broadcasts during the Munich crisis in 1938 and after the outbreak of World War II in 1939, although even in December of the latter year, the Newspaper Proprietors' Association and the Newspaper Society requested a return to the former arrangement under which no news was broadcast before 6 p.m. But the Corporation refused, and the matter has never been raised again. As recently as 1949, however, the Newspaper Society told the Beveridge Committee that it viewed with great concern any further extension of news broadcasting, but the committee was unsympathetic.[12]

BBC NEWS CONCEPTS

With 30 years head-start, the BBC has had more time to do and to write about news broadcasting than has its younger rival. In 1936, the Ullswater Committee regarded the broadcasting of news as one of the Corporation's most important functions, and stated that it was 'of the utmost importance' that BBC newscasts 'should be a fair selection of items impartially presented'.[13]

In April 1938, the Home Service News editor, anticipating World War II, wrote about the way news should be reported in wartime: 'It seems to me the only way to strengthen the morale of the people . . . is to tell them the truth, and nothing but the truth, even if the truth is horrible.'[14] In 1951, 13 years later, the Beveridge Committee said much the same thing: 'The instant supply of News is the most vital of all the broadcasting services', and it went on to approve the BBC's objective

> to state the news of the day accurately, fairly, soberly, and impersonally. It is no part of the aim to induce either optimism or pessimism or to attract listeners by colourful or sensational reports. The listener has the right to hear from the BBC all the important news good or bad; it could only be wrong on a long-term view to suppress unpalatable facts. Moreover, the legitimate urge to be 'first with the news' must invariably be subjugated to the prior claims of accuracy. . . . In making its selection the BBC applies the sole test of news value . . . . The BBC does not make news; it reports the news.[15]

In 1960, the BBC told the Pilkington Committee that its news values were close to those of the *Daily Telegraph*, one of the British 'quality' newspapers, while the ITN editor said he was trying to produce a 'popular' news service which would observe the news values of the 'quality' press. The Committee observed, however, that 'only rarely did an important item of news appear in the BBC national television news and not in the ITN, or vice-versa'.[16]

Charles Curran, when Director-General in 1971, wrote: 'We have the responsibility . . . to provide a rationally based and balanced service of news which will enable adult people to make basic judgements about public policy in their capacity as voting citizens of a democracy.'[17] Two years later he said that he believed it possible

> for a body like the BBC, engaged in the business of journalism about public affairs, to present a view of the world—or rather a series of views—which, in their totality, will be regarded by most people for most of the time as reasonably balanced . . . . It is emphatically not our job to persuade our audiences about the truth of particular propositions which may be put forward by one party or another. [Broadcasting has] an over-whelming obligation, as the most omnipresent of the communications media, to satisfy the demand for true information which alone will make it possible for an increasingly urbanised, and a tolerant and understanding society to allow government to work.

Although news and current affairs are closely related, the Corporation organizes them separately, and their outputs are identified as one or the other by presentation or by placement in the schedules.[18] The distinction between the two is maintained even when both elements form part of the same sequence, as in the *Today* or *World at One* programmes on radio. In practice, however, these distinctions are often blurred, and the juxtaposition of news bulletins and reports from 'our special correspondent' often makes the division hard to grasp. Anthony Smith, in an insightful essay on 'Television and Political Life', forecasts that in the 1980s we may begin to see the re-unification of these branches of factual broadcasting. Nevertheless, a study made for the BBC General Advisory Council stated: 'News seeks above all to answer the questions *who, what, where, when* and *how*. It is primarily concerned with new facts and the factual background to them'. The function of the news department is to organize and present the news, or to use the British term, 'news bulletins'. Explanations as to *why*, on the other hand, are provided not in news bulletins, but in current affairs programmes. 'This division of responsibility is the BBC's way of observing the traditional boundary between fact and comment. Whenever the disciplines are practised too close together there is a risk that the boundary will become merged'.[19]

There have, of course, been many changes in attitude and policies in British news broadcasting since the days when BBC radio was alone in the field. Integrity and accuracy remain constant goals, but the formal and often stuffy approach of the 1930s has been left behind. Obviously, British news reflects British interests and values, just as American newscasts reflect those of the United States; but the good and the bad about everyone and everything from the Prime Minister and the Royal Family down to the lowliest person and the most hated national enemy still are reported fairly and objectively, if considered newsworthy.

Although criticisms of undue sex and violence on television bring to mind fictional programmes, some of the same problems are faced by newscasters too. A survey of violence in news, documentary and current affairs programmes on British television during one week in 1972 found that in the course of fifty-six news, documentary and current affairs programmes broadcast by BBC 1 and ITV, thirty-nine, or 69.7 per cent, contained some violence, mostly in news programmes, averaging two incidents per national telecast.[20]

Both BBC and ITV have laid out guidelines for their news editors. The BBC told its news staff to ask itself 'what purpose is served by the use of the [violent] material? Secondly, is that purpose sufficiently important to outweigh the objections which the use of the material may evoke from some of the audience?' Admonitions also were made about violence in early-evening news bulletins apt to be seen by many children.[21] In addition to repeating pretty much what the BBC wrote, the IBA pointed out:

Scenes of human suffering and distress are often an integral part of any report of the effects of natural disaster, accident or human violence, and may be a proper subject for direct portrayal rather than indirect reporting. But before presenting such scenes, a producer needs to balance the wish to serve the needs of truth and the desire for compassion against the risk of sensationalism and the possibility of an unwarranted invasion of privacy.

Somewhat related to all this are the policies of both BBC and ITN, at the discretion of their respective editors, to withhold certain information in order to facilitate the work of the police when lives are at stake. In its 1977 *Handbook* the Corporation noted that in one case armed men had held hostages while listening 'continuously to the radio in the hope of hearing news of police counter-moves from news bulletins'.[22] In another case, when a girl was kidnapped in London, the BBC, ITA and the press 'kept totally silent until the girl was found unharmed more than a week later, thus vindicating the voluntary embargo'.

BBC RADIO NEWS

All BBC news and current affairs programmes are the responsibility of the Director of News and Current Affairs, who reports to the Director-General.[23] The radio news staff has two functional divisions. The first of these includes those people who compile news bulletins and put them on the air (the newsroom staff) of some ninety journalists of varying grades, including two senior Editors of the Day, who alternate in their responsibilities. The other group is made up of those who gather the news, including eighteen overseas-based correspondents, a dozen specialist correspondents in such fields as economics, industrial affairs, and science; a political unit of several correspondents, serving both radio and television; and some twenty general reporters working mostly within the United Kingdom, but who are sent abroad as occasion demands. There also is a special unit of four journalists dealing with financial affairs. A portion of the editorial team devotes its full time to the radio broadcasting of Parliament, which began in April 1978 (see below, pp. 233–6). There also are a number of supporting groups consisting of non-journalists. Engineering services are provided by central staff employees who work closely with the news department, but are not organizationally a part of it.

For its television and radio news departments, the Corporation subscribes to the major domestic and foreign news services, including UPI, AP, Exchange Telegraph, Press Association, and Reuters. Since 1934, it has had its own reporters at home and abroad, although it was not until World War II that it sent full-time newsmen overseas, and not until 1945 that one of its correspondents was admitted to the Parliamentary press gallery. When necessary, roving correspondents cover such events as the Korean War, the Vietnam War, the Soviet invasion of Afghanistan, and foreign tours by members of the Royal Family. All BBC regional and local installations have news collection facilities, which are used to develop programmes for their own areas as well as for network distribution. Operating 24 hours a day, a general news service desk at Broadcasting House collates wire reports from all over the world and distributes them on a private teleprinter network to BBC news staffs in London and elsewhere.

News also is received from the monitoring unit in Caversham, which monitors all foreign broadcasts received in the United Kingdom , and exchanges material with similar services in the United States. Its total daily output of some 250,000 words in fifty languages from 200 countries is reduced to 15,000 words for distribution.[24]

Broadcasting schedules vary from year to year, but the year 1978–9 may be taken as fairly typical of the percentages of time allocated to news and current affairs programmes. As is shown in Table 15, in that year the four BBC radio networks devoted 6.2 per cent of their time to news. By far the greater part of this was on Radio 4, which allocated 980 hours, or 12.8 per cent of its time, to such programmes. When the 3391 hours or 44.5 per cent of Radio 4's time devoted to current affairs, features and documentaries, is added to this figure, it is seen that Radio 4 heavily emphasized programmes of that nature.

For some years after 1938 many Britons planned their evenings around BBC Radio's 9 o'clock news. Americans living in the United Kingdom during World War II will recall how—in the words of Sir Hugh Greene:

> that bulletin was the great moment of the day's broadcasting. Everyone listened to it and to all nine strokes of Big Ben. People associated it with the splendours and miseries of the war and with the Churchillian speechs of long ago. . . .[But, Greene continued] by 1959 the nine o'clock news was a shadow of its former self. The bulk of its audience was elsewhere. So we placed the main radio bulletin of the evening at ten p.m. and followed it with discussion and comment on the day's events. The uproar from those who detested change was really quite remarkable. I had betrayed a sacret trust. I was like a Beefeater tampering with the Crown Jewels. But in a few months all was quiet—at any rate on that front.[25]

At present, Radios 1, 2 and 3 have periodic news bulletins up to 15 minutes in length, but by far the greater proportion of BBC radio network news is aired by Radio 4, which on an average weekday broadcasts a dozen hourly news bulletins, some of which are followed by current affairs broadcasts ranging in length from 30 to 60 minutes. Sunday schedules depart somewhat from this pattern. Regional and local radio newscasts, produced with local resources, are regularly available in all parts of the country on BBC 4 and local radio services.

A typical BBC radio news bulletin usually opens with a few headlines followed by details, and longer newscasts frequently have a summary at the end. In addition to political and economic news, the BBC regularly covers significant developments in literature, the arts, science, and other fields of learning. Natural disasters, crimes and accidents also are reported—more so now than in earlier years—but the gruesome aspects usually are omitted. Britain being a sports-minded country, much attention is given to sports, although details are left to the sports roundups which follow certain news bulletins. Most programmes include weather forecasts, but since the range and intensity of United Kingdom weather is less than that of the United States, American listeners would find most BBC weather forecasts rather sketchy. For many years news broadcasting was considered too serious to include much levity, but recently some humour has appeared, frequently in wind-up stories, as on American programmes.

Objectivity and accuracy are stressed above all. One way the BBC tries to maintain objectivity is by never adding 'colour' to a story that is not intrinisically colourful.[26] It also avoids the use of adjectives and verbs which might imply editorial judgement. For example, a participant in a Parliamentary or Congressional debate is never reported to have 'asserted' or 'retorted' something, although the atmosphere of the debate would be factually described; he merely 'stated' or 'said' the words in question. The 1975 edition of the BBC's news guide lists the following as the 'standards' for BBC news: responsibility, impartiality, fairness, independence, sobriety, accuracy, and good taste.[27] Underlined on one page of the guide is the sentence: 'We do not take sides.'

News is read by announcers carefully chosen for that purpose. Incidentally, the Corporation has used both men and women news readers on its domestic and foreign services for many years. (In British radio and television, the term 'news reader' is employed rather than 'anchor man' or 'anchor person'.) Before World War II, all news readers were anonymous, but beginning in 1940, when the German Blitzkrieg brought the Wehrmacht to the coast of France and there was concern about a possible invasion, announcers began introducing themselves by name, in order to familiarize the British public with their voices as a safeguard against misleading enemy broadcasts on BBC wavelengths.[28] Although news readers lapsed into anonymity again in 1945, they now are regularly named on both radio and television.

BBC news is read in a straightforward, impersonal and unemotional style, in order to safeguard against the injection of editorial feeling. The combination of such editing and reading makes the programmes even in tenor and rather unexciting—though not dull. But the years have brought changes, and news reading is now livelier than it used to be. Also noticeable is a greater range of voices and accents. Some BBC announcers still speak conventional Oxford, southern or 'BBC' English, but the Corporation also uses regional voices. Americans may get an idea of BBC radio news by sampling some of the bulletins in the world services, easily tuned in on most short-wave receivers in the United States. Materials for these overseas audiences are selected somewhat differently than for domestic listeners, but the basic style is much the same.

BBC TELEVISION NEWSCASTS

The Corporation encountered difficulties in developing television newscasting, because of a lack of enthusiasm for television in general by its top leadership, and because, in earlier days, the radio news division succeeded in controlling television news according to radio standards. Grace Wyndham Goldie, who was involved with BBC Television Talks and Current Affairs for many years, writing retrospectively, said:

> From the beginning of broadcasting there had been special anxieties about broadcast news. These sprang from two sources: the jealous fears of the Press that broadcast news would affect the sale of newspapers, and the very proper fear which had been felt by the early Committees that it would be all too easy to broadcast irresponsible or slanted news.[29]

In 1946, Sir William Haley, then Director-General, said that while he had 'no objections to the development of news reels', the time had not yet come to present 'a completely visual news bulletin'. Accordingly, the best that BBC television could come up with in the years following the war was its own newsreel beginning in 1948.

Writing in 1953, Lord Simon of Wythenshawe, Chairman of BBC's Board of Governors from 1947 to 1952, probably reflected Corporation opinion when he said:

The News is the most important sound radio service, listened to every day by a majority of the population and giving instantaneous world coverage. A great majority of the items are of such a nature that they cannot either now or ever be shown visually; of those that could be shown on television the majority occur overseas, often from distant countries, and it will be a long time before television films can be flown from all over the world to London on the day on which things happen. Television newsreels will, of course, continue to develop and be of the greatest interest and attention, but there is surely not the least possibility that they will ever replace the news on sound.[30]

By the end of 1950 there were three editions of the Television Newsreel each week, and in 1953 the Director-General stipulated that the Radio News Division would henceforth be responsible both for news and newsreels. Finally, on 5 July 1954, shortly after BBC television news had taken over the old Alexandra Palace facilities (the rest of television had moved to the (then) new Shepherd's Bush facilities in West London), the News and Newsreel programme began. It was introduced by Richard Baker, still a regular BBC television news reader, with the words: 'Here is an illustrated summary of the news. It will be followed by the latest film of events and happenings at home and abroad.'[31] For some time thereafter, news readers were kept off the screen, although some corerespondents appeared in view.

In more recent years, BBC television news has become a very strong department, although it took both the support of television-minded executives in the Corporation and competition from the ITA to achieve this. Sir Hugh Greene wrote that before he became Director of News and Current Affairs, in 1958, news had been the 'Kremlin of the BBC'.[32] Up to then, for example, BBC correspondents 'had not been allowed to achieve a scoop'. They had to share stories with their press colleagues before they could be broadcast by the BBC. But Greene changed all that. In August 1978, responding to a letter to *The Times* from a former news editor criticizing current news output, Sir Hugh wrote that the old policies had 'led to dullness and obscurity, and to unacceptable restraints on the development of television news, without ensuring any greater degree of accuracy'.[33]

BBC television news now is located in the Television Centre in West London, where it has elaborate and well-equipped space. The sources available for radio also are used by television, in addition to which the Corporation receives much television material from Visnews, of which it is a 30 per cent shareholder, other owners being Reuters and the Broadcasting Corporations of Australia, Canada, and New Zealand. The BBC exchanges news film with NBC through a reciprocal arrangement, and with CBS as a member of Eurovision. Both BBC and ITN, in fact, are active participants in Eurovision, which, among other things, provides for the exchange of news pictures and sound among twenty-five West European countries three times daily. Eurovision in turn exchanges with East Europe, Asia, and North and South America. (For more on Eurovision, see below, pp. 204–6.) BBC—often cooperatively with ITN and other broadcasters—hires time on satellites to provide quick access to overseas material of timely significance. In 1978–9, 4.2 per cent of BBC television's output consisted of news. As Table 18 indicates, approximately the same percentage of time is given to news on both networks (BBC 1, 5 per cent; BBC 2, 3.3 per cent). On weekdays, BBC 1 schedules 15-minute bulletins at 12.45 and 5.40 p.m., and its principal newscast from 9.00 to 9.25 p.m. BBC 2 newscasts, usually of 5 minutes duration but sometimes as long as 15 minutes, are interspersed among evening programmes. The regional services have their own local and regional newscasts.

Currently, the BBC and IBA newscasts are quite similar. One reason for this may be their periodic exchange of personnel. Even the current BBC Director-General, Ian Trethowen, once worked for ITN. The principal BBC television newscast, on the air Monday to Friday from 9 to 9.25 p.m., opens very simply, as the announcer on duty says: 'Here is the news, read by . . .'. This is followed by the news signature tune, and some combination of filmed titles, visual headlines, and the reading of the headlines by the news reader. ITN, following the American pattern, put its newscasters on camera from the very outset of programming in September 1955. The BBC, perhaps anticipating this, began showing its news readers on 4 September of the same year, a few weeks before ITN took to the air.

The BBC uses a single announcer on each programme, although it has experimented with two. In the 1950s, the Corporation used women news readers for a time, and now uses them on both network and regional newscasts. The head of BBC news told me that their news readers are 'trained to be news readers and just that', although some of them have backgrounds as reporters. They are instructed to be impersonal, while the ITN readers, usually more vivid and colourful to begin with, are encouraged to 'come into the living room', to quote an ITN spokesman. ITN places more emphasis on having journalists as news readers, and on some broadcasts they interview guests, either on tape or live, while the programme is in progress.

People used to American television news will find BBC news readers—and those on ITN, too, though to a less degree—much quieter than those normally seen in the United States. The contrasting terms applied to them—'news readers' as opposed to 'anchor persons'—clearly indicates the differences in their roles. They assume much less importance than do their opposite numbers in American, and, incidentally, their salaries are pathetically small compared to those paid network anchor people in the United States, even though they are nationally known and often are written about in the press. While in principle the idea of substance coming before presentation cannot be faulted, it is my feeling, after watching many British newscasts, that BBC television news would improve if more emphasis were placed on the news readers' role. Perhaps the ideal would be a middle ground—more personality from the British news readers, and more subordination of anchor persons to substance in the United States. But it any case, presentation and reading are smooth, and the production and reading team work together well, as one would expect from experienced veterans.

British, like American newspapers, take great delight in gossiping about television newscasters. Thus, the BBC's Angela Rippon, the senior woman news reader in the United Kingdom (although she is only in her early thirties), has been reported as earning a basic salary of £8000 (approximately $16,000) per year, an astonishingly low figure for a person who talks to much of the nation several times each week. The popular press may devote more space to her hairdo or jewelry than to some of the serious international items she reports. If anyone doubts that the British can be as silly as the Americans, let him review the report that when Miss Rippon was scheduled to take part in a dance sequence on a Christmas Day entertainment show in 1976, so that the public could see her legs—she normally sits behind a desk while reading news—a staff member was dismissed for selling 'pirated' pictures of her taken off the screen during rehearsals. Yet this is not to Miss Rippon's liking: she told me at some length how difficult it is for her and the other women news readers to gain acceptance as serious journalists in the face of such press treatment, although she stated that it is the national rather than the regional or local press which most offends.

The items covered on British television news are the British equivalents of those on American telecasts. A comparison of BBC television news and the London *Times'* front pages for October 1975 indicated a very high correlation between broadcast and newspaper items. Lacking from the BBC are some of the juicy and scandalous stories so often found in Britain's 'popular press', but the serious coverage is about the same as for *The Times*.[34]

A visiting American is apt to feel that coverage of the United States is inadequate; but since broadcast time is limited, and the United States is not the country being served by the programmes, coverage is reasonably fair. Nevertheless, American items, such as political conventions and developments affecting Britain and Europe are almost always covered, often directly by the Corporation's American correspondents.

Much use is made of such specialists as our 'Parliamentary Correspondent' or our 'Financial Correspondent'. Immediately following those news bulletins which need backgrounding, the special correspondent often will add material and indicate the significance of the items in review. However, such presentations definitely are analyses rather than editorials, and therefore do not violate the Corporation's commitment to impartiality. At the end, there usually is a run-down of sports scores. As in American television, the BBC and ITV allow each other to use on newscasts fragments from sport actualities originated by the other service.

Although weather forecasts are not included as a part of newscasts, most newscasts are followed by brief weather forecasts, presented by staff from the meteorological office. Despite maps and symbols, these forecasts, usually done by people lacking presentation skill and charisma, are as feeble as American forecasts are flamboyant. Here is another case where a middle ground might be sought. Surely the BBC or ITN, before too long, will break away from this limitation—just as the BBC has been doing in regard to news generally throughout the years—to present livelier and more attractive forecasts.

The BBC has an excellent and unique news programme for children, named after its presenter, *John Craven's Newsround*. Scheduled several afternoons a week at around 5 p.m., following other children's programmes, but somewhat before the 5.45 news for adults, it draws upon the resources of BBC television news to cover events of interest to children. Although it deals with many serious and often potentially disturbing stories, it attempts to treat them so that children will not be upset. In the words of the creator, 'our only criteria are: Is it news? and will it interest children without distressing them?'[35]

NEWS ON IBA

Network news for ITV is prepared in London by Independent Television News (ITN), while network news for Independent Local Radio is based upon the output of LBC (London Broadcasting Company), Independent Local Radio's news and information service in London. In both cases, however, there are local news-originating facilities in each section of the country.

ITN is jointly owned and controlled by the fifteen ITV programme companies. Although originally involved with current affairs as well as news, since 1967 it has concentrated on news, all current affairs programming now being done by the programme companies.[36] ITN's total staff of 575 includes, among others, 110 journalists, 290 engineers and technicians, and ninety administrative personnel. Its annual budget is over £10 million, funds being provided by the programme companies in proportion to their net incomes. In turn, the companies retain the income received from whatever advertisements they schedule during the commercial breaks on, or adjacent to, news (as all other) programmes.

ITN is London-based, its only two full-time outside correspondents being stationed in the north of England and in Washington, DC. However, it maintains three or four reporters and camera crews for quick dispatch to other parts of the world, and in the United Kingdom gets material from ITV regional news staffs. Like the BBC, ITN subscribes to the principal wire services as well as to the UPITN video news service, of which it is a joint owner with UPI and Paramount Pictures. Through UPITN, ITN exchanges news pictures with all parts of the world, and in the United States, there is a complete news exchange between ITN and ABC. Since ITN, like BBC, participates in Eurovision, it therefore receives about the same range of television news material as does the Corporation.

ITN House, to which ITN moved in 1969, was rebuilt for that purpose. In addition to office space, in 1978 it contained two studios with seven colour cameras, elaborate control rooms, three colour telecinés and eleven video-tape recorders.[37] It has digital converters to convert programmes from the European to the American standard and vice-versa, with no loss of quality; time-code editing facilities; sound recording equipment; a film laboratory; an outside broadcast unit; and a network of freelance contributors throughout the British Isles and overseas.

ITN began in 1955 with short news bulletins which gradually evolved into longer and more elaborate programmes. At the outset, news transmissions totalled 20 minutes a day, with the main bulletins at approximately 6 and 9 p.m., although there now is an average of over an hour of ITN news per day. In 1955–6, the average ITV company devoted 7 per cent of its time (3 hours 15 minutes a week) to news and news magazines, while by 1978–9, this had grown to 10.5 per cent (10 hours 27 minutes). (The number of hours increased more than the percentages because ITV air schedules were extended following the removal of limitations on broadcasting hours in 1972.) During 1955–6, 8 per cent of transmission time (3 hours 56 minutes a week) was devoted to current affairs and documentaries, while the figure in 1978–9 was 13 per cent (13 hours 17 minutes.) Combining the two categories, in 1955–6 15 per cent of the average programme company's time (7 hours 11 minutes) was devoted to such programmes, while in 1978–9 the figure was 23.5 per cent (23 hours 44 minutes).

On weekdays, ITN's *News at One* is aired from 1 to 1.20 p.m., while its late afternoon newscast runs from 5.45 to 6 p.m. Programme companies follow these two network presentations—which they are required to carry—with local news or news magazines of their own.

ITN's main news programme has been broadcast from 10 to 10.30 p.m. Monday to Friday since July 1967. An Authority handbook described the setting of the programme at that hour 'as one of the most significant moves in television news broadcasting', since it provided time for 'full coverage of all the outstanding news events at home and overseas, . . . [and also for] sufficient explanatory background and interviews to reveal much of their broader significance'.[38] But this was not achieved easily, and many of the programme companies still oppose the change. As Lord Hill of Luton, chairman of the IBA from 1963 to 1967, put it: 'The nightly half-hour news bulletin, *News at Ten*, was one of the biggest steps forward during my years as chairman of IBA. [But] To achieve it required a battle with the programme companies.'[39]

As the former chairman described it, ITN's problem had always been getting enough air-time to cover the news adequately. In 1964, ITN had only 23 minutes and 40 seconds for its two daily news bulletins. The staff wanted more air-time, but the Board of Directors, consisting of representatives of the programme companies, disagreed. Two matters were at issue: when should the programme be broadcast, and for how long?

The news staff wanted to delay ITN's 8.55 p.m. programme until 10 p.m. in order to include in it more American and other foreign items, as well as later reports from Parliament, which often sits late into the evening. The argument for a longer programme was the obvious one that an extended period would allow more complete coverage. But the programme companies wanted an earlier and shorter programme that would not interfere with their entertainment features. Certain types of programmes cannot be broadcast prior to 9 p.m. because of family viewing requirements, and a 10 p.m. newscast would shorten the time available for such entertainment programmes. But after discussion, the Director-General and the Deputy Director-General informed the companies—in Lord Hill's words—that 'if they did not act the Authority would. They acted. The new programme, *News at*

Ten, which began in July 1967, was a resounding succeess from the outset, becoming an equal competitor for news with the BBC.'

The official position now is that *News at Ten* is ideally scheduled. The programme companies told the Annan Committee in 1975 that the move to 10 p.m. resulted from the need for

> a regular and extended news programme to cover important issues at adequate length and accommodate the growing volume of news made available in pictures through technical developments. The recognition was the IBA's. The views of the companies were mixed, with some in vigorous dissent, but all now agree that the decision was a correct one.[40]

But the argument still goes on. ITN spokesmen told me that the programme companies still want to move the time back to 9 p.m., and the former managing director of Thames Television, who also is a member of the ITN Board of Directors, said: 'The ten o'clock news need not be sacrosanct.'

ITN presentation procedures are basically similar to those of the BBC, the differences being mainly of emphasis. *News at Ten* opens with a slide of Westminster Clock Tower as we hear the recorded 'bongs' of Big Ben. During the programme, the two news readers alternate, although they indulge in little or none of the small talk so prevalent on many American newscasts. Effective 9 March 1978 ITN added to its staff a woman news reader, Anna Ford, who previously had appeared on some BBC current affairs programmes. As was observed above, ITN news readers have stronger personalities than those on the BBC, and they are encouraged to project themselves more. Anthony Smith, commenting on the demarcation between news and current affairs on British radio and television, remarked of this programme that it 'has evolved a great deal of the way towards a fusion of the styles [of news and current affairs]. At the end of the 1970s it has become clear that the two are to merge one day or at least to reallocate their functions . . .'.

ILR news has a short history, since the first IBA radio station did not go on the air until 1973.[41] The counterpart of ITN for the radio service is Independent Radio News (IRN) a 'sister company' to LBC—London Broadcasting Company—in London. Drawing upon the usual wire services, and with reporter teams of its own, IRN feeds twenty-four on-the-hour news bulletins to all independent local radio stations. Some carry the feeds live, while others record them for delayed presentation. In all cases, Independent Radio stations develop their own local stories. One of the two ILR stations in London, LBC, offers a 24-hour all-news service which uses most of the IRN material plus a wide range of news and information of its own.

COMMENT AND APPRAISAL

In Britain as in America, television news is often discussed and written about. The 'popular press', as it is known in the United Kingdom, such quality national newspapers as the *Daily Telegraph* and *The Times*, and the regional press cover television news substance and personalities. Inevitably, the *Annan Report* devoted considerable space to news programmes, and its chapter on 'News and Current Affairs' is a good essay on that topic.[42] Among its observations: because of the scarcity of channels, impartiality and fairness are essential; covering Northern Ireland is difficult, although both BBC and TV 'struggle to report fairly a situation in which the difficulties are gargantuan'; 'the broadcasters were not guilty of deliberate and calculated bias' in their coverage of industrial affairs, even though it is 'in some respects inadequate and unsatisfactory'; 'We agree [with some critics that] the choice of [foreign] news items is often parochial.'

In its over-all survey of ITV, the Committee stated: 'There is one department in which the commercial sector has by common consent surpassed the BBC. That is in the presentation of news.'[43] Later in its report, the Committee wrote that both services, but particularly that of the BBC, 'could be improved. News is presented in too stereotyped a fashion: there is too little variety, too little punch and there are too few attempts to give explanatory comments.' The report went on to say:

British broadcasting should extend its coverage. Who would feel from watching BBC news that the BBC had a mission to show world events each day to the nation? There is too much coverage of minor home news and pseudo-events, and too little of foreign issues which can intimately affect the lives of all of us. News is particularly singled out by many experienced foreign observers as the one weak spot in an output for which otherwise they have the highest praise. The broadcasting organisations should concentrate more on strengthening and varying their television news programmes.

Appendix F to the Annan Report, a review of 'Research Findings on Broadcasting' by J. D. Halloran and P. Croll, which devotes a number of pages to news and current affairs, contains this summary statement:[44]

It is interesting . . . to note that far from being struck by the differences in news coverage around the world in the course of our research, we were far more impressed by the universal similarity of news. Whether it be New York, London, Lagos, Stockholm, Dublin, or Belfast, news values too are shared, often of course because they have been exported along with the news.

There also have been articles and books appraising—and often severely criticising—broadcast news. In January 1975, John Birt, Head of Current Affairs, London Weekend Television, and Peter Jay, also with London Weekend Television, and Economic Editor of *The Times*, circulated privately a paper on *TV News and Current Affairs*, with the subtitle, *Some Thoughts on the BBC*. These were subsequently published by *The Times* on 28 February, 30 September and 1 October, of the same year. This rather extensive criticism of television journalism, which among other things claimed that both the BBC and ITN television news services failed to provide sufficient background material, generated much debate, caused considerable soul-searching among newscasters in both services, and led among other things to the study for the BBC General Advisory Council, *The Task of Broadcasting News*, mentioned above.[45]

Another much-discussed publication was *Bad News*, by the Glasgow University Media Group, which used various statistical methods to analyse BBC and ITN coverage of industrial news, and concluded that the media showed anti-trade-union bias.[46] The broadcasters again reacted strenuously, and Sir Geoffrey Cox, who was head of ITN news from 1955 to 1968, in a review of the book stated: 'For this book is indeed Bad News; not, however, for television, but for scholarship.'

Short of making an intensive content analysis, it would be impossible to decide which of the two television services provides the most comprehensive news coverage, but a good deal of viewing has left me with the impression that there is little choice so far as substance goes. BBC editing, presentation, and reading still reflect the conservative background of radio, although the difference is not marked. A somewhat breezy review of the development of television news in Britain, written from the ITN point of view, generalized: 'Gradually the two news organisations moved towards middle ground, the BBC becoming more human and ITN less brash.'[47] I have talked at considerable length with news editors, directors and news readers in both organizations, and found them to be capable and well-informed people, dedicated to the objective of presenting the news as fully and as clearly as time and resources permit. But my total impression is that ITN has more fully adapted to television. Its writing is tighter and better, the reading more forceful, and the use of video-tape and other visual material more effective. However, both are very good services, and I would not care to recommend one or the other as a superior news source. So far as the British public has voted preference by amounts of viewing, the two stand about even.

INTERNATIONAL EXCHANGE PROGRAMMES

Much news, special events, and outside broadcast material is exchanged among Europe's broadcasters via Eurovision, the world's foremost international television programme exchange project, which was initiated by the BBC and developed under the aegis of the European Broadcasting Union. Through Eurovision, all the countries of Western Europe share some of their best programmes. Eurovision's scope is further extended through exchanges with Eastern Europe's Intervision, as well as by satellite exchanges with the rest of the world. The BBC became a charter member of Eurovision in 1954, and the ITV joined in 1957, the IBA and the Independent Television Companies Association now holding a joint membership.[48]

Eurovision—the name was supplied by George Campey, a public relations staff member of the BBC—began officially on 6 June 1954, with experimental transmissions over a temporary network linking Belgium, Denmark, France, West Germany, Italy, the Netherlands, Switzerland, and the United Kingdom. A temporary technical centre at Lille, France, supervised the experiment, and converted signals to 405-, 625- and 819-line standards, as required. Enthusiastic public and press response led to the establishment of a permanent coordination centre in Brussels the following year.

Eurovision's technical statistics now are very impressive. According to the European Broadcasting Union, as of 1 January 1979, forty-seven television services in twenty-five countries of Western Europe and North America participated regularly. The total length of the available vision circuits was some 187500 miles. The entire network included over 15000 transmitters serving a potential audience of 400 million people who had more than 105 million receivers at their disposal.

In addition to its programme headquarters in Geneva and its technical centre in Brussels, Eurovision has a New York office which obtains programmes from the United States and other parts of the globe through satellite relay.[49] Since Europe and North America were first linked for live television by Telstar I on 21 July 1962, progressively more sophisticated satellites have been available at the same time that rates have been reduced, so that Eurovision now has access to news and actualities from all over the globe. The EBU cooperates very closely with the three American networks, obtaining from them such materials as the United States space missions and presidential election campaigns. In return, the American networks receive programmes from Eurovision. There also are exchanges with Latin American through Spanish television, with the Arab States' Broadcasting Union, and—daily—with East Europe's Intervision.

Although Eurovision grew out of the international exchange of state events and ceremonies, sports programmes were its staple in earlier years. Little news was transmitted before 1961, but since then there have been more news than sports items.[50] Naturals for international exchange were events like the European Common Market negotiations; President Kennedy's trip to Europe (June 1953), and later his assassination and funeral (November 1963); the deaths of Popes John XXIII (1963), Paul VI and John Paul I (1978); the installation of John Paul II (1978); and the United States Presidential elections (1964, 1968, 1972, 1976, 1980.)

The BBC has always been among the most active participants in Eurovision exchanges. In 1978, it originated fifty-one programmes with a duration of 110 hours 18 minutes and received 165 programmes with a duration of 342 hours 45 minutes.[51] During the same year, ITV originated fifteen programmes with a duration of 27 hours 19 minutes, and received 115 programmes lasting 229 hours 44 minutes. In 1978, the BBC contributed 1450 news items to Eurovision and received 2087, while ITN originated 728 items and received 2558.

Both BBC and ITN participate in EBU news exchanges. This extensive service, which began on a trial basis in October 1958 involving twenty-five countries with five broadcasting organizations taking part, is now an elaborate project for the exchange of film and video-taped items by international closed-circuit television three times each day, at noon, 5 p.m., and 6.55 p.m.[52] Each of these is preceded by an international telephone editorial conference during which representatives of each broadcasting service indicate what material they have to share, and what they would like to receive. During the actual transmissions, each receiving service makes its own video-tape copies, later inserting commentary in its own language.

Intervision, which began experimental news exchanges in 1965, and has done so on a daily basis since 1971, now both contributes to and receives Eurovision news, the two services exchanging daily through the intermediary of Austrian television.[53]

In addition to making it possible for countries to share each other's programmes, Eurovision organizes some events itself. A good example is the annual Eurovision Song Contest, the first programme produced jointly by Eurovision members, which was inaugurated in 1956 and now is carried by radio and television to all parts of Europe. The purpose of the contest is to stimulate the composition and performance of popular music. I have seen a number of these broadcasts, all of which follow the same basic pattern, even though they originate in a different country each year. Against elaborate sets, vocalists and instrumentalists compete before a panel representing all the participants, although the balloting is conducted so that no one votes on a performance by his own country. Although the Eurovision Song Contest has slight artistic merit, it attracts so much popular interest that it is carried continent-wide.[54]

Although the programme advantages of Eurovision are obvious, its exact achievements are difficult to measure. Clearly, Eurovision has enriched television schedules by facilitating the exchange of interesting and significant programmes, and it is reasonable to assume that such exchanges may also lead to better international understanding. Eurovision makes it possible for all of Europe to see certain events at the moment they occur. Some programmes—concerts, operas and plays, for example—do not lose by being recorded for delayed presentation. In fact, until Eurovision circuits carry stereophonic sound, recordings may be superior in many cases. But many news and actuality items require immediacy, or only slight delay, if they are to achieve maximum effect, and this Eurovision provides.

12 Current Affairs, Opinions, and Controversy

Programmes of opinion and controversy provide excellent examples of how the scope of British broadcasting has expanded since the days of the British Broadcasting Company in the 1920s. For years the government and the political parties were reluctant to let radio and television deal freely with controversial subjects. There were a number of reasons for this. Fear that the Company—when it was the country's only broadcasting organization—might be biased was one, although not the major, concern. Some people believed—or at least said they believed—that controversy by radio would be unacceptable in the home.

The Fourteen-Day Rule (see pp. 208–10) grew out of fears that broadcasting might unsurp the role of Parliament as the place for discussing and determining national issues. The party leaders wanted to control political broadcasting in order to give themselves more, and the backbenchers less, public exposure.[1] The press also played a role: too much participation by broadcasters in the electoral process might undermine newspaper influence. When it was Britain's only broadcasting organization—and particularly in the years before World War II—the BBC was reluctant to press hard for its right and obligation to schedule controversial programmes. Finally, at the operational level, there was a slowness on all sides to agree on rules for political broadcasting.

Controls were strictest in the 1920s during the regime of the British Broadcasting Company. In 1922 and 1923 there were occasional programmes on such topics as tariff reform and communism, along with some sporadic political broadcasts, but the Postmaster-General turned down proposals for the party leaders to broadcast during the general election of 1923, although some political speeches were aired the following year.[2] Then and later, John Reith argued strongly for more freedom. The Sykes Committee in 1923 did not 'think it necessary to exclude everything that was controversial', but was willing to leave the decision to the Postmaster-General, while the Crawford Committee recommended in 1925 that a 'moderate amount of controversial material should be broadcast, provided the material is of high quality and distributed with scrupulous fairness'.[3]

Using its power under the Licence to prohibit the broadcasting of any class of material, the government, on 15 November 1926, forbade the BBC to express its own editorial opinions, or to 'broadcast by speech or lecture . . . matter on topics of political, religious or industrial controversy'.[4] John Reith wrote in his autobiography that despite the Crawford Committee's recommendation, and 'the obvious desirability of controversial broadcasting', it was necessary to argue against 'Post Office apprehensions and timidities throughout 1927'. The ban finally was lifted 'experimentally' on 15 March 1928, and never reimposed, although the prohibition against editorializing remained, and was applied in 1954 by the Television Act to the ITA as well.

Most controversial broadcasting was suspended during World War II, although it never ceased entirely.[5] The post-war governments did not even consider reimposing the ban on controversial broadcasting, although some limitations on political broadcasting were continued. Sir Charles Curran, in a public address in 1968 when he was Director-General, said that the most 'decisive advances' in the treatment of controversial matter were made during the regime of Sir Hugh Greene, and that there is 'now no subject of which it could be said that the BBC cannot, in any circumstances, allow to be discussed on the air'.[6]

Had Sir Charles cared to elaborate, however, he might have gone on to list several legal barriers to free discussion. The Official Secrets Act, which is strictly enforced, prohibits the revelation of anything the government deems vital to national security, while both Parliament and the courts may use their powers of contempt to punish anyone who publishes unauthorized information, including Parliamentary reports not yet approved for release. Court news must be limited to the factual reporting of proceedings. Therefore, anything approaching America's newspaper inquiries into Watergate would have been ruled out, since current court proceedings did impinge on the issues. Despite strong objections from both the printed and electronic press, however, these limitations continue.

THE FOURTEEN-DAY RULE

An example of a severe limitation on the coverage of public affairs was the Fourteen-Day—or Fortnight—Rule, in effect between 1944 and 1957, which forbade the broadcasting of any talks, discussions or debates on topics currently being discussed in Parliament, or for 2 weeks before such debates were scheduled. Furthermore, it prohibited broadcasts by Members of Parliament on all matters currently 'subjects of legislation'. Consequently, whenever Parliamentary discussions of any topic were scheduled on short notice, the BBC—and after 1955 the ITA also—had to immediately cancel any programmes previously arranged on the subject.

The Rule also is a good case-study of the problems faced by Britain's broadcasters in overcoming government resistance to certain types of controversial programming.[7] Fortunately, it did not preclude the reporting of Parliamentary proceedings on news programmes; in fact, after 1946 the BBC's Licence expressly required it to broadcast a summary of Parliamentary proceedings each day Parliament was in session. But it did seriously curtail broadcasts on important controversial issues at the very time the public most needed enlightenment about them. The rule did not apply, however, to programmes for overseas listeners produced by the BBC's External Broadcasting services.

The Fourteen-Day Rule was introduced voluntarily by the BBC in 1944, in order to avoid pressure from ministers wishing to broadcast on matters of current legislation, especially as reconstruction issues began to strain the war-time coalition, and as the post-war election grew closer. It was formalized on 6 February 1947, with additional qualifications added in July 1948, by the BBC, the government, and the opposition in an 'Aide-Mémoire', although the BBC soon realized that what at first appeared an ingenious way to ration air-time to ministers anxious to broadcast was becoming a troublesome boomerang.[8]

The BBC's subsequent dissatisfaction with the agreement was reflected in a strong recommendation against it by the Beveridge Committee in 1951. The Committee, though dismissing as probably 'harmful' direct broadcasts from Parliament, advocated abolishing the Fortnight Rule on the grounds that the ensuing debates would 'both increase popular interest in Parliament and popular capacity to judge the wisdom of Parliament. Both these things are gains from the point of view of good democratic government.'[9] In 1953, the Corporation asked to have the rule revoked, promising to adhere to its spirit, and to avoid scheduling talks or discussions on important controversial subjects during the fortnight period.

In the words of Asa Briggs: 'In effect, the BBC was claiming the right for the first time in its history to decide how to present current issues to the public without external constraint, for as the Governors then put it, "the matter was the responsibility of the BBC, which had a duty to be impartial, and not of the Parties".' When the party leaders—Winston Churchill and Clement Attlee—refused to lift the rule, the BBC requested a directive defining it, which was given by the Postmaster-General—Charles Hill, later chairman (in succession) of the ITA and of the BBC—with the full support of the Labour opposition, but in spite of protests of the Liberal MPs, on 27 July 1955. Although the ITA was still in the programme-planning stage in July 1955—it went on the air in September of that year—its Director-General joined his BBC opposite number in meeting with representatives of the political parties to oppose the Fourteen-Day Rule on 14 September of that year, the day before ITV began broadcasting.

The pertinent portions of the directive, which applied equally to the ITA when it came on the air, read as follows:

> the Corporation shall not, on any issue, arrange discussions or *ex-parte* statements which are to be broadcast during a period of a fortnight before the issue is debated in either House or while it is being so debated; ... when legislation is introduced in Parliament on any subject, the Corporation shall not, on such subject, arrange broadcasts by any Member of Parliament which are to be made during the period between the introduction of the legislation and the time when it either receives the Royal Assent or is previously withdrawn or dropped.[10]

The Fourteen-Day Rule was opposed by groups and people with such varied points of view as the BBC, the ITA, the Liberal party, *The Times*, the *Observer*, and many individual members of Parliament. Objections were based on the grounds that the rule was a limitation on freedom of speech, a gag rule on individual Members of Parliament, and a deprivation of the public's right to hear discussions of legislation while it was under consideration in Parliament.

The reason given for the limitation was that it presumably would safeguard the position of Parliament as the national political forum. Many people in Britain believed that American radio and television had usurped some congressional prerogatives, and they wanted to avoid such developments in the United Kingdom. Winston Churchill told the House of Commons on 23 February 1955:

> I am quite sure that the bringing on of exciting debates in these vast new robot organizations of television and BBC broadcasting, to take place before a debate in this House, might have very deleterious effects upon our general interests, and that hon. Members should be considering the interests of the House of Commons, to whom we all owe a lot.[11]

The basic principle of the Fourteen-Day Rule was upheld by a free (non-party) vote of 271 to 126 after debate in the House on 31 November 1955.[12] Leaders of both parties favoured the rule, the main government spokesman outlining the arguments in its favour. What opposition there was came from backbenchers on both sides, a circumstance that supports the hypothesis that one reason for the rule was to enforce party discipline by removing the opportunity for nonconformists to appeal directly to the country by radio or television. As *The Times* put it:

> This is a case of the Parliamentary party wishing to have a closed shop for debate. They cannot enforce it on the ordinary citizen. They cannot enforce it on the press. They cannot talk convincingly about wanting any form of democracy while they behave in such a fashion.[13]

On 9 February 1956 the House of Commons appointed a select committee to review the Fortnight Rule.[14] Both the BBC and the IBA testified in favour of abolishing it. Although the committee was authorized only to consider a change in the rule's application, rather than the principle of the limitation itself, it recommended a 7-day—rather than a 14-day—rule, with restrictions reduced as much as possible. It also questioned the justification for more limitations on broadcasting than on other media.

On 18 December 1956 the Prime Minister announced in the House of Commons that the government had decided to suspend the Fourteen-Day Rule for an experimental period of 6 months, and stated that he hoped the broadcasting organizations would do nothing to 'derogate from the primacy of Parliament as the forum for debating the affairs of the nation'. On 25 July 1957 this was extended for an indefinite period, thereby ending an unfortunate limitation on the freedom of radio and television to serve their public.[15]

CURRENT AFFAIRS CONCEPTS

What are the differences between news and current affairs? What is the distinction between editorial opinion and analysis?

The foreign editor of the BBC remarked in 1965:

Any journalist knows that he must add relevant information, background and interpretation to the bare news if it is to become understandable. The foreign correspondent must nearly always add more than the man who is reporting on the home scene, simply because the background of foreign countries is less familiar than our own.

Jeremy Isaacs, Controller of Current Affairs and later Director of Programmes for Thames Television, told an ITA Consultation on News and Current Affairs Programmes in Bristol in January 1972:[16]

If the job of a news service was to tell us what was happening at any given moment, then the job of current affairs was to try to help us understand what was happening. They had to try to do that by reporting on situations which persisted over weeks, months, and years, and which lay behind and gave rise to the events that daily made the headlines; current affairs had the duty to explain the background for what was going on.

The BBC told the Annan Committee in 1974 that, in the interests of impartiality and fairness,

the principle has been evolved of making a clear distinction between reporting of news and the presentation of Current Affairs. In the former, the BBC's practice was to seek to limit itself to the reporting of ascertainable facts or the deductions which can properly be made from those facts. [But the Corporation realized that, in addition to] giving a complete picture of public affairs . . . [it is not enough] to report the events of the day, but [it also is necessary] to offer the public the range of opinions which were being expressed about those events. It is necessary, in order to achieve this, to offer programmes concerned explicitly with the presentation of opinions. These became the responsibility of the Current Affairs Departments in radio and television.[17]

Both broadcasting organizations always have been instructed not to editorialize, and both have endeavoured to be consistently impartial. The old British Broadcasting Company initiated a policy of impartiality 'as an indispensable condition [for] the freedom of the broadcasting service to deal independently with news, events and opinion. . . . The BBC has regarded this policy as a trust ever since and has never wished to alter it.'[18] In 1927 the Corporation was 'directed [by the Government] not to broadcast its own opinion on current affairs or on matters of public policy', a rule that remains in effect.[19]

In 1964, a letter from the BBC Chairman to the Postmaster-General formalized a long-standing Corporation practice that it 'must ensure that, so far as possible, due impartiality is preserved in news programmes and programmes dealing with matters of public policy, and also in the treatment of controversial subjects generally'.

In one of its submissions to the Annan Committee, the BBC observed: 'It would be wrong for a public body financed by public money . . . to commit itself to the promotion of particular views sponsored by individual sections of the community.'[20] But every society has its basic assumptions, and these are accepted by its media. Thus, in a public address in 1965, midway through his term as Director-General, Hugh Greene reminded his listeners that the BBC tried to 'treat with due impartiality' all controversial subjects.[21] But, he went on,

> there are some respects in which it is not neutral, unbiased or impartial. That is, where there are clashes for and against the basic moral values—truthfulness, justice, freedom, compassion, tolerance, for example. Nor do I believe that we should be impartial about certain things like racialism or extreme forms of political belief. . . . But the case must be clear, and the potential effects immediate and damaging. before we can claim the right to exclude.

The Annan Committee summarized the ITN's comments on this point as being 'more cautious' than those of the BBC. 'They told us that their duty was to reflect all the differences within Parliament, but that it was not for them "to go outside and, as it were, bring in ideas which we like better than those ideas that have been produced by Parliament". '[22]

What is impartiality? Sir William Haley, when Director-General, wrote in 1945: 'Impartiality does not mean so artifically "balancing" the speakers that the listeners can never come to a conclusion on the basis of the argument. '[23] Sir Hugh Greene said:

> We have to balance different points of view in our programmes but not necessarily within each individual programme. Nothing is more stultifying than the current affairs programme in which all the opposing opinions cancel each other out. Sometimes one has to use that method but in general it makes for greater liveliness and impact if the balance can be achieved over a period, perhaps within a series of related programmes.

The BBC now follows the precept: 'Balance within the single programme is not sought after religiously in every occasion but only where the circumstances, and the nature of the issue being discussed, are deemed to call for it.'

In this context, as in so many others, the laws relative to the IBA have applied to it the same standards followed by the Corporation, either because of specific requirements or as a result of traditional practice. In its enabling legislation, the IBA was instructed 'to secure the exclusion' from its programmes 'of all expressions' of its own opinions, as well as those of its employees and programme contractors.[24] The law also requires the Authority to ensure 'that due impartiality is preserved . . . as respects matters of political or industrial controversy or relating to current public policy'. (Notice that *all* editorial opinion is to be eliminated, but there need only be *'due* accuracy and impartiality'.) The law states that, in applying the requirement for impartiality, 'a series of programmes may be considered as a whole'.

The Authority's definition of 'impartiality' accords with that of the Corporation. It told the Annan Committee:

In its simplest terms 'due' impartiality means that the Authority is not required to secure impartiality on matters about which society, even today, is virtually unanimous; but discussions which form the subject for television programmes on current affairs inevitably tend to centre on the grey areas where there is no public consensus on what is black and what is white.[25]

Acceptance of the BBC and IBA interpretations was given by a government spokesman in a House of Lords debate:

The BBC and the IBA are obliged to preserve due impartiality in their programmes. The word 'due' is important. It means they are free to lend their weight to civilised moral standards. . . . Nor does the duty mean that all programmes must be bland or void of any strong expression of opinion: it means a balance of objective presentation taking one programme with another.[26]

CURRENT AFFAIRS PROGRAMMES

BBC radio current affairs programmes originate in studios in Broadcasting House in central London adjacent to those used for news programmes, while television current affairs is separated physically from television news, being located not in the Television Centre in west London, but rather some distance away at the Lime Grove studios in Shepherds Bush. This, however, is the result of a shortage of space rather than of a desire to emphasize administrative separation. IBA current affairs programmes are originated by the various programme companies, although not by the same personnel who do regional and local newscasts.

British radio and television offer a wide range of current affairs programmes (see Tables 15 and 18 and 19 for the percentages of BBC and IBA programmes in these categories). During 1978–9, BBC radio devoted 15.2 per cent of its time (4225 hours) to 'Current Affairs, Features and Documentaries'. Most of this (3391 hours) was on Radio 4, which turned over 44.5 per cent of its schedule to such programmes. BBC television allocated 17.6 per cent (1614 hours) of its time to current affairs, Features and Doumentaries—14.3 per cent (720 hours) of BBC 1 air-time and 12.9 per cent (531 hours) of BBC 2 air-time. During the same period, the average ITV company devoted 13 per cent of its air-time (13 hours 17 minutes) to current affairs and documentaries). The 10.5 per cent of the average company's time spent on 'News and news magazines', may have included some of the 'Features' counted in the BBC figures cited above. It should be noted, during the following review of BBC and IBA network programmes that all of the regional and local services have their own programmes, supplementing the national output. In fact, about half of the total output is regional or local.[27]

Titles and schedules vary from year to year, but the week of 2–8 June 1979 may be taken as reasonably typical. During the Monday to Friday period, BBC Radio 4 broadcast *Today* from 6.30 to 8.45 a.m.; *The World at One*, from 1 to 1.40; *PM*, from 5 to 5.50; *The Six O'Clock News*, from 6 to 6.30; and *The World Tonight* from 10 to 10.40 p.m. In addition there were *The Financial World Tonight* at 11.20 p.m., and when Parliament is in session, *Today in Parliament* at 11.30 p.m., repeated the following morning as *Yesterday in Parliament*. Although the BBC notes differences among these programmes, they all are news reports plus probing analyses and discussions of a wide range of international, national and local events. News bulletins and news analyses often occupy adjacent time-periods, particularly during longer programmes, but they are clearly demarked, so that the listener—or viewer—knows when one ends and the other begins. On both BBC and IBA political leaders contribute; and there are commentaries and explanations from experts. BBC local radio deals in much the same fashion with local issues, and also presents local reactions to national and international developments, as does ILR, while the Authority's all-news station in London reports, analyses and interprets world, national and local news 24 hours a day.

Members of Parliament do a great deal of broadcasting, appearing frequently on newscasts and discussion programmes, as well as in formally arranged political programmes.[28] During the Parliamentary year 1 October 1977 to 30 September 1978, there were 1950 appearances by MPs on BBC network radio and 470 on BBC network television programmes, and it is reasonable to assume that approximately the same number appeared on ITV as on BBC television.[29]

As with any group of politicians, Members of Parliament vary greatly in their performances, even though the main parties maintain studio facilities in which to coach their members. Despite the close relationship between Parliament and both broadcasting organizations, and the, at least theoretical, controls the government maintains over both, the interviewers on news and discussion programmes are very probing, and the politican with something to conceal will not do so very long when confronted by a typical BBC or IBA interviewer. I have heard and seen some excellent programmes, conducted with great skill by interviewers who were well informed about politics and highly competent in their mastery of the broadcast media.

The Annan Committee wrote that the weakest part of the BBC's output 'seemed to us to be the current affairs programmes, and to a lesser extent the news. By and large, we subscribe to the generally held view that ITN has the edge over BBC news and that ITV current affairs is more adventurous and interesting'. Furthermore, some of the Committee's members 'thought that the BBC was too disinclined to go in for investigative journalism'.[30] The committee probably based its generalizations on more evidence than I was able to collect, but such viewing as I did in the spring and summer of 1976 and the autumn of 1978, did not leave the impression that ITV outdid the BBC in current affairs programming. From time to time, I have heard and seen current affairs presentations that were too long for their material, slow-moving, dull and tedious—although such programmes were in a minority. But on the whole, my impressions of this part of the British output are very good; almost every evening brings one or more such programmes, most of them at least good, and many are outstanding.

On its first television network, BBC has *Nationwide* from 5.55 to 6.50 p.m., following the 5.40 network newscast. *Nationwide* opens in London, after which the regions break away for about 25 minutes of local news and current affairs, London meanwhile having its own programme after which London feeds the network again. The Editor of News and Current Affairs for the BBC states that such programmes aim at 'capturing the attention of the people we are talking to and then increasing their understanding'.[31] They are intended not only for the readers of quality newspapers like *The Times* and *Guardian*, but also for people who do not read newspapers.

Britain's longest-running current affairs feature is *Panorama*, which the Corporation describes as 'a weekly 50-minute [mid evening] programme on major international and domestic issues'.[32] Initiated in 1955, *Panorama* includes interviews, discussions, and short documentary films on political, social and economic events. Typical programmes that I have seen included stories of British mercenaries in the Angola War (tough SS elite-type parachutists and soldiers of fortune); a very well-handled and thorough interview with Jack Jones, Transport and General Workers Union; a review of the current struggle for leadership in the Liberal Party; and an interview with Presidential aspirant, Jimmy Carter. These were well done: The questioning was thorough, film and video-tape cuttings were well integrated, and a high level of interest was maintained. In May 1977 *Panorama* carried an interview with President Carter, taped at the White House prior to his departure for an economic summit meeting in London, for which the interviewers included BBC, German, and French television representatives.*[33]

The Conservative and Labour Party conferences and the strike against the Ford Motor Company dominated many current affairs programmes on both services, when I viewed in October 1978. *Panorama* courageously examined the government's practice of blacklisting companies not abiding by its pay policies without giving the firms full hearings. Another programme dealt with a rocket-test range in Zaire run by German engineers apparently trying surreptitiously to develop a spy satellite. Between the BBC and IBA, both radio and television thoroughly explored the conferences and the wage disputes, while the rocket programme was as absorbing as a fictional spy story.

For several years, on Tuesdays, Wednesdays and Thursdays at approximately 11 p.m., BBC 1 presented *Tonight*, a series varying from 30 to 45 minutes in length, described by the Corporation as 'programmes of topical talks and discussion'. Subjects covered by its predecessor series during 1975–6 included alcoholism, the National Health Service, and the life of the late Viscount Montgomery. One programme interviewed John Pardoe and other candidates for the leadership of the Liberal Party.

---

* The BBC's ongoing audience research reported in 1976 on *Panorama*. One of its best-received editions was its examination of Rhodesia ten years after UDI [Unilateral Declaration of Independence—1965]. Most of its viewers found it balanced and comprehensive, and thought that it had presented the conflicting viewpoints extremely well. . . . There was praise for the reporter, Richard Lindley, whose approach to the subject, viewers felt, had been both fair and searching, and who had obviously won the confidence of both sides. (BBC, *Annual Review of BBC Audience Research Findings*, No. 3, 1975/6, p. 19.)

Nationwide, broadcast Monday–Friday between 5.55 and 6.55 p.m. by BBC 1, is 'an early-evening domestic magazine . . . produced in association with BBC News centres outside London and regional studios'. This basically non-political series ranges from reports from a consumers' unit group to programmes on giving up smoking. During 1976–7 it originated entire programmes from BBC regional centres in Bristol, Norwich, Southampton, Glasgow and Belfast. The 2000 programme items treated that year 'covered all the major issues facing the nation', including the heroin trade, secrecy in government, bogus university degrees, questionable charities, and cruelty to horses.[34] *Nationwide* always contained something of interest for me, even though it is more British in focus than the preceding newscast. I was intrigued by one programme at the end of the September 1978 when an official of the (nationalized) gas and electric authority replied to questions and criticisms put to him live by customers in various parts of the country. *Nationwide* probably would not stand up to tough competition, but it does bring informational programmes from the various regions to the entire country.

Typical of programmes of its type was *Newsday*, formerly on BBC 2 weekday evenings from 7.30 to 8 p.m. with 'longer news bulletins, interviews, profiles and debates'. Politicians, trade unionists and other important figures from Britain and abroad participated. I saw a member of the British Cabinet interviewed about the Turkish invasion of Cyprus; a talk with the president of the Amalgamated Union of Electrical Workers about high labour turnover and unemployment; a small-scale documentary on Czechoslovakia; an interview with a distinguished 80-year-old iconoclast peeress; a conversation with two writers who predicted that democracy would last only 10 years more in the United Kingdom; and a very sharp and revealing quiz of Shirley Williams, a member of the British Cabinet regarded as having considerable political promise.

Another outstanding series is *The Money Programme*, an intellectually demanding weekly 'series on economic, industrial and other aspects of money'. One programme, described as 'uncensored', dealt with Bulgaria, which Nikita Khrushchev had called 'the shop window' of communism. Another, *All People's Houses*, debated whether it is more economical to be an apartment renter or owner. Not overlooking the media themselves, BBC 2 also had a series on television in Canada, Czechoslovakia, France, Brazil, Cuba, Mexico and India, done by long-time BBC broadcaster and executive, Frank Gillard. The one on American television which I saw was interesting, but seemed to go out of its way in emphasizing the shortcomings of the system, to the exclusion of its many strong points.

Although the BBC with its two networks has had more time for current affairs than ITV, the IBA offerings are fully as good. Its main network current affairs weekend programme is *Weekend World*, networked to the entire country from noon to 1 p.m. since October 1972, and broadcast 30 weeks each year.[35] On one programme I heard then Secretary of State Henry Kissinger talk about Africa, after which there was a feature on the current drought in the United Kingdom. On another broadcast some labour leaders presented their point of view on the current pay negotiations between their union and the government.

Thames News, which runs opposite *Nationwide*, has recently undergone some changes of emphasis, and now—all live—offers news along with current affairs. On a typical evening it might present interviews with people in the news, an item about wasted government funds, a discussion of medical developments, an interview with a new author, and some Hedda Hopper-type items clearly put on for laughs. The programme's producer told me that '*Thames News* is trying hard to blur the distinctions between news and current affairs', a trend which he believes 'will increase in British Television'.

Thames *TV Eye* (formerly *This Week*) is broadcast 46 weeks each year on Thursdays from 8.30 to 9 p.m., and has a fairly large staff as such programmes go—four reporters, four film directors and crews, one studio director, and five researchers.[36] The broadcasts I saw included a well-done study of the Greek–Turkish conflict in Cyprus; a good treatment of energy-saving by the construction industries; a review of Irish history from 1916 to date; and a short documentary about a small British Nazi party.

Granada Television, working out of Manchester, provides the network on Monday evenings from 8.30 to 9 p.m. with *World in Action*, which covers

events or subjects . . . not always immediately topical, relying on film to illuminate vividly, often aggressively, the story it sets out to put to the viewer. It is tabloid in style, investigative in approach and controversial by intent, tackling subjects like corruption in local government at home and torture in totalitarian governments overseas.[37]

Put together by a team of two dozen producers and researchers, the series deals with such subjects as physically handicapped children, health hazards, and industrial dangers. In addition to forty ½-hour programmes per year, there also may be five or six 1-hour specials. Approximately 35 per cent of the subject-matter is foreign and the remainder domestic.

Three programmes—two seen in 1976 and one in 1978—impressed me very much. *Out of Line*, filmed on location, reported that at least 3000 of the 154 000 patients in British mental hospitals should not be there at all. One man had been hospitalized for over 50 years for a petty theft committed as a youth, while a retarded woman was incarcerated because she had borne an illegitimate child many years before. The audience was invited to offer home stays for some of these people, and there were a good many takers.

Another programme, filmed in Moscow in April 1976 and smuggled out, included interviews with a Russian dissident, and reports of Germans and Jews being mistreated in the USSR. Despite poor technical quality, the programme was gripping, including not only interviews but also pictures taken from a car cruising along the Moscow streets. One producer told me that after they had done a similar programme in Yugoslavia a year or so before, the person they interviewed was sentenced to jail, along with the lawyer who defended him. The third *World in Action* programme, broadcast in October 1978, dealt with transexuals in Britain. People with various points of view on the subject were interviewed, and one scene showed how after surgical treatment of male transexuals, training was offered on acquiring feminine mannerisms and deportment.

A good many *World in Action* programmes are sold abroad: for example three of them dealing with the American CIA were sold to a number of foreign broadcasting organizations. On 22 November 1976, at 8.30 p.m., *World in Action* dealt with The National Party, an ultra-right-wing political group with strong racist convictions. One of the producers reported that the programme 'was totally misunderstood by some of the very people we expected to applaud it'. Its showing to a group of schoolchildren demonstrated 'that television coverage of racial hatred is even more hazardous than we thought'. But the National Party virtually collapsed in portions of the country as a result of the programme.[38]

Granada Television's *The State of the Nation* has demonstrated since 1972 'that television can penetrate the previously secret places of politics, can indeed reveal to millions knowledge about the way Britain is governed that had previously not been available even to experts'.[39] In 1976–7, it included three programmes on Parliament, the exact topics chosen after a series of dinners with twenty Members of Parliament at which all conversations were recorded. One of these programmes—in which seven Members of Parliament took part—simulated a Parliamentary debate about whether or not the House of Commons needed certain reforms.

When Britain held its first national referendum on 5 June 1975, on whether or not to join the European Economic Community, the BBC and the IBA worked together with the three main political parties and the two principal organizations campaigning for and against the proposal, in scheduling a number of special broadcasts. (The Common Market Referendum was unprecedented in British constitutional history. Prior to the election victory which brought it to power in February 1974, the Labour Party had committed itself to a referendum, it being understood that membership in the EEC would depend upon the popular vote.) It was decided to assign equal amounts of time to both sides, rather than basing allotments on the balance of parties in Parliament, as is done with political broadcasts, partly because the parties themselves were divided on the issue. Accordingly, each of the two pressure groups received four 30-minute periods on the three television networks, three of the programmes being transmitted simultaneously by all three services.[40]

When these formal programmes were not deemed sufficient by either organization, BBC 1 broadcast thirty additional programmes on the subject, occupying over 20 hours, as well as televising an Oxford Union Debate. BBC Radio 4 scheduled ten live 55-minute telephone call-in programmes, and Radio 3 had a debate series. There also were local BBC programmes on how it would affect local areas. After it was all over, Radio 4 provided 7 hours coverage of the outcome, including interviews with world statesmen. On its own, ITV covered the campaign somewhat as it does General Elections, and gave extra time to it on ITN reports, and on *This Week* and *Weekend World*. There also was regional ITV coverage of 'matters of local and regional concern'.[41] ILR stations produced their own debates and discussions, pro and con.

British broadcasters have done much to provide air access to minority interest groups and individuals.[42] One device much used by both BBC and ILR is the call-in programme, of which there are both national and local examples. From their very beginning, the commercial radio stations adopted the American call-in pattern and the BBC followed. In fact, during the two 1974 general elections, the BBC scheduled call-ins to leading politicians every morning, thus introducing a new procedure to British political broadcasting. Prominent people and authoritative subject-matter experts now participate in these programmes, and the questions asked are often very probing.

I heard a BBC broadcast on which the American Ambassador to Britain, Anne Armstrong, answered questions about the United States. In the autumn of 1978, the BBC's local London station broadcast a programme for Black Londoners, covering news, play reviews, and discussions of interest to that audience which included a call-in. By coincidence, one of the ILR stations in London ran a call-in at the same time, although for a different audience. Other programmes have ranged over such subjects as alcoholism, cancer, care of the aged, local government, family planning, budgeting, home decoration, and the care of pets.

BBC 2's late evening *Open Doors* series, which began in April 1973, is operated by a Community Programme Unit which provides advice, facilities, budget and other assistance, but regards itself as 'a publisher working for a group which wants to bring out their own newspaper or magazine'.[43] *Open Doors* owed something to a programme on WGBH in Boston, as well as to a New York City cable television project. Tyne Tees Television had a somewhat similar project entitled *Access*. Among them, these broadcasts cover a wide range of subjects: black teachers, sex liberation, contemporary poets, private investigators, academic freedom, the problems of night cleaners, battered wives, trade unions, old age pensioners, gypsy education, abortion, and one-parent families.

AUDIENCE AND GOVERNMENT PRESSURES

When there are news programmes there are sure to be complaints about news selection, placement, and treatment; and when there are current affairs programmes, there always are critical listeners and viewers. The more thorough and outspoken the programmes, the more complaints. As the Annan Report put it: 'As news and current affairs programmes are at the interface between broadcasting and politics, they are at the centre of controversy.'[44] There is considerable documentation as to pressure on both the BBC and the IBA by the government, Members of Parliament, and the public, but little or no evidence that it has turned the broadcasters aside from their purpose of reporting and analysing the news. But pressure from all sides is a constant pressure factor in the lives of broadcasters.

As Wyndham Goldie put it:

[A]lthough the freedom of the broadcasting organisations from political interference in their day-to-day running is agreed in principle by all concerned, successive governments have in practice brought pressures to bear, indirect as well as in more subtle ways, on broadcasting organisations in an attempt to increase their own share of broadcasting opportunities and to deny equal opportunities to the Opposition.[45]

The examples that follow are typical, but by no means inclusive, of all such complaints.

When Lord Hill was the BBC's chairman, a comedian on a Corporation programme applied to then Prime Minister Harold Wilson a phrase which Hill said had earlier been used in connection with Lyndon Johnson: 'If his lips are moving, he's lying.'[46] Several days later the same remark was repeated on another programme. Although the Corporation expressed its regrets, the Prime Minister asked for a more formal apology. Himself a former politician, Hill replied that all politicians 'have to take a good deal of abuse', and that to publicize an apology would merely give the insulting remark additional circulation. Accordingly, he called on the Prime Minister, and in the course of a 1¼ hour visit, during which the two 'consumed two decent-sized Scotches', talked him out of his request.

In 1969, David Dimbleby, covering the arrival at Heathrow Airport of President Richard M. Nixon for a one-day visit with Prime Minister Wilson, remarked that both Wilson and Nixon had 'expensively hired press secretaries whose job is to disguise the truth', and that Nixon was 'wearing his face for all seasons'.[47] The same commentator reported Nixon's departure with the words, 'Well, the road show is on the way', and went on to describe the accompanying press contingent as 'These dancing girls of the president who go strewing words before him and behind him. . . .' Both Hill and the Director-General formally apologized for these gratuitous remarks to the Prime Minister and to the American Ambassador. 'There followed a minor storm in the press and inside the BBC, not because of Dimbleby's words but because of our decision to apologize.'

Another programme which caused considerable flurry was *Yesterday's Men*, a documentary study of the effects of defeat on the senior members of the Labour government that went out of office in June 1970.* The title itself raised some objections. Even though it was a phrase previously applied by the Labour Party to their Conservative opponents, its use on the broadcast of 17 June 1971 clearly characterized the Labour Party leaders—out of power since 1970—as 'Yesterday's Men'.

While the programme was being recorded, Prime Minister Wilson was asked by interviewer David Dimblely how much he had been paid for his recently published memoirs. Wilson, considering the question to be irrelevant to the programme,

---

* Hill, pp. 178–92; Davis, p. 124; Munro, pp. 130–3. For an extended review of the programme and of Labour's reactions, see 'Yesterday's Men', in Tracey, *The Production of Political Television*, pp. 183–201. In his book Hill remarked:

'Incidentally, during my five-and-a-half years of chairmanship, two programmes were previewed by the governors—*Yesterday's Men* and *A Man Alive* on housing and the Rent Act. One programme, *The Question of Ulster*, was discussed by the governors in advance of transmission. All three were transmitted' (Hill, p. 189).

Anthony Smith (*The Shadow in the Cave*, pp. 145–6) states that as a consequence of the 'pressures and protests which blew up in wake of "Yesterday's Men" ', the BBC set up the Complaints Commission (see pp. 369–72, below). Smith later referred to the latter programme as the 'classic row'; said it 'could never be made again'; and commented that 'Politicians are not for mockery' (Smith, *Television and Political Life*, p. 11).

objected, asked that the recording be stopped, and immediately called the Director-General on the telephone, requesting that section of the interview to be deleted. Headline stories in the national press later reported the incident. Subsequently, Wilson requested still other changes. Nevertheless, after the Board of Governors previewed the programme, it was broadcast, although without the question on royalties. But press discussion continued. Whatever the merits of the case, the incident did leave a residue of bad feeling, probably led to the setting up of the BBC Complaints Commission in October of the same year, and may have had something to do with the appointment of some members to the Annan Committee expected to be severe with the Corporation.

Another cause célèbre was *The Question of Ulster—An Enquiry into the Future*, broadcast in 1972, which presented eight proposed solutions for the problems of Northern Ireland. The production of news and current affairs programmes about Northern Ireland has been a continuing problem for both broadcasting organizations, and everyone concerned has sought to report and discuss fully and responsibly without inciting additional violence. The Home Secretary objected to *The Question of Ulster*, fearing that it might provoke violence, and also questioned its format: a chairman and three others were to hear eight Irish speakers and then render their 'decision'.[48] Some British newspapers opposed the programme as irresponsible, and a letter from the government said that the broadcast, 'in the form in which it has been devised would do no good and could do some harm'.

Nevertheless, the Corporation put it on the air, saying that the BBC 'could not be diverted from the public service of presenting all points of view by a campaign of pressure by a newspaper or by anyone else'. After the programme was broadcast (in Eire as well as in Britain), Lord Hill commented: 'One fringe benefit of the programme was that with so many people watching, Northern Ireland had one of its quietest nights for weeks'. The reaction of many viewers was that the programme was dull rather than inflammatory.

Until the basic problems of Northern Ireland are resolved, it is unlikely that the broadcasters can escape criticism from one side or the other for programmes that deal in the forthright manner with the troubles of that unhappy political division of the United Kingdom. Early in 1977, for example, the Secretary of State for Northern Ireland said, at a private dinner in Belfast given for BBC and Ulster officials, that the BBC's treatment of Northern Ireland news sometimes was ill-advised to the point of being disloyal, and that the IRA would long since have been defeated had the Northern Ireland Office directed BBC policy. He also recommended three months' ban on the news coverage of all terrorist activities.[49]

The National Union of Journalists strongly opposed such censorship, however, and neither the BBC nor the IBA acceded to the request for a blackout. In August of the same year, one of the IBA programme companies, Thames Television, cancelled a report on the Queen's recent visit to Ulster after the IBA rules that the programme contained a direct incitement to violence. In November there were complaints about a Thames production dealing with the alleged ill-treatment of suspects, it being charged that the programme subjected members of the Royal Ulster Constabulary to great risks.

With its many hard-hitting programmes, the IBA has had its share of brickbats in other respects, too. Milton Shulman, formerly a current affairs producer for Rediffusion Television and later a television critic, has related his experiences when producer of the political series *Decision* in 1963.[50] Prime Minister Wilson objected to the speakers chosen for one broadcast as weighted against him. Thereafter, some changes were made, but otherwise the programme was broadcast as originally planned. Although Shulman was unhappy with the willingness of Rediffusion Television to make even minor changes in the participants, the nevertheless observed that

> the independence of British broadcasting has become an almost inviolate constitutional principle. As we have seen, in matters of crisis like the General Strike and Suez, this principle has sometimes been subject to severe strain and buffeting. But with the determination of men like Reith . . . the BBC had managed to resist such pressures and kept the politicians firmly in their place.

Later he again praised the BBC:

> After almost three years of Wilson's government there were still some satire shows on the BBC tilting irreverently at political figures including the Prime Minister himself . . . . There was not a title of evidence that Sir Hugh Greene, the BBC's Director General, had been in any way overawed or affected by government pressure; the BBC's coverage of contemporary events showed no compromise of its usual standards of objective and forthright comment.

Another IBA programme, Granada's *World in Action*, of 17 March 1975, which dealt with British-owned tea plantations in Sri Lanka and Southern India, drew criticism from industry rather than government.[51] The aggrieved party was the Cooperative Wholesale Society, some of whose tea estates were filmed for the programme. The Authority reviewed these complaints with Granada, and commented:

> These programmes . . . did not live up in every respect to the requirements of due impartiality expected by the Authority in the field of current affairs. The Authority believes that it was a wholly justified undertaking by Granada to seek to bring to the attention of the British viewing public the poor working and living conditions of the people on British-owned tea estates. However, it sees some substance in the criticism that more care should have been taken to relate the conditions on the tea estates to the wider context of living conditions amongst agricultural workers in Sri Lanka and southern India generally.

This incident was widely reported in the British press, under such headlines as 'IBA Rebuke', 'Granada Documentary Criticized by IBA', and 'Granada TV Reprimanded'.

In December 1977 Associated Television scheduled a three-part documentary entitled *The South African Experience*. Tate and Lyle, the producer of sugar and sugar products, objected to the third programme, which it said 'grossly distorted' its operations in South Africa. When the IBA refused to cancel the broadcast, Tate and Lyle obtained a court injunction against its showing, which, however, was subsequently withdrawn. When the programme was telecast, the sugar firm took newspaper advertisements in which it questioned 'the professional ethics and responsibility of ATV in screening the programme'. Following the broadcast, ATV scheduled an hour-long live debate in which pro and con views on the film were presented—with considerable heat.

The decision of the IBA to delay a Thames Television *This Week* current affairs programme on Northern Ireland, originally scheduled for 8 June 1978, initiated a chain reaction, involving not only the IBA and Thames Television but also the BBC.[52] An investigation conducted by a group called Amnesty International supported allegations of police brutality in Ireland. Although the report had been leaked to the press and had received a fair amount of publicity, the Authority refused to permit *This Week* to cover it until it was formally published, 'thereby giving those involved and the general public a chance to study it in detail'. Thames then offered the programme to the BBC, which screened portions of it, while IBA technicians put their network off the air during the half hour in which the cancelled programme had been originally scheduled, so that the substitute programme could not be aired.

The IBA justified its decision, in part, on the ground that the law requires it to be impartial 'as respects matters of political or industrial controversy or relating to current public policy'. But a spokesman for the team that produced the programme called the ban 'an outrageous act of political censorship'. *The Sunday Times* editorialized that the IBA was 'one of the biggest menaces to free communication now at work in this country', and said that the Authority chairman, Lady Plowden, and Director-General, Sir Brian Young, preferred the natural habits of the British establishment, favouring caution over boldness, silence over publicity and bureaucratic control rather than the unpredictable disturbances implicit in the best journalism.

Benefits from previous victories determined the course of events in 1980 when ITV scheduled *Death of a Princess*, a programme co-produced by ATV in the United Kingdom; WGBH, one of American public television's most creative stations; and the Telepicture Corporation in New York. This telecast turned the basic facts about an adulterous love affair between a Saudi Arabian princess and her commoner lover into a two-hour 'docu-drama'. The technique used was that of taking actuality films of the researcher's interviewing as he visited Saudi Arabia and other countries in quest of the facts, and cutting to dramatic reconstructions of his findings. At both the beginning and the end of the programme, viewers saw the shooting of the princess and the beheading of her lover as punishment for their misdeeds.

Saudi Arabia attempted to prevent the showing of the film in the United Kingdom and later in other countries, including the United States. Preceding the American broadcast, the Saudi Ambassador to Washington wrote to the acting Secretary of State about his country's objections:

The documentary style of the picture is so convincingly done that I fear the casual viewer could consider it a collection of factual and historical events when in reality it is just the opposite. The film shows a completely false picture of the life, religion, customs and traditions of Saudi Arabia. It also, in many ways, is disparaging to the Moslem religion. The film is therefore offensive, not only to Saudi Arabia but to the entire Islamic world.

When the film was first announced for presentation on ITV, Saudi Arabia, it was reported, offered to buy it up for $11 million. After ATV refused to cancel the showing, Saudi Arabia protested to the British government, and later 'reviewed Saudi–British economic relations, particularly the position of the British companies operating in Saudi Arabia'. But the British government refused to intervene, citing the country's free press traditions, although it offered 'profound regret'. After the programme was shown on 9 April, the Saudi royal family denounced it as anti-Islamic, and cancelled a scheduled visit to London by King Khaled; the British Ambassador to Saudi Arabia was temporarily withdrawn at Saudi request; and the Saudis threatened to withdraw economic aid bank deposits from any other countries broadcasting the film.

The film's airing by America's PBS on 12 May evoked a tremendous amount of discussion. Again Saudi Arabia protested to the government, but to no avail, although there was reference to the matter in Congress and a great deal of discussion in the press, both of the factual accuracy of the programme and of the possible effects of its showing on American oil supplies. As usually happens in widely publicized censorship cases, the wide discussion of the programme brought it a very much larger audience than it otherwise would have had.

These selected examples by no means exhaust the list of programmes which have attracted strong responses from the government, powerful industrial groups, and the public, but they do show that hard-hitting programmes are presented, that objections from high places are received, and that the broadcasters normally react responsibly, usually holding their ground against their critics.

PARTY POLITICAL, MINISTERIAL, AND BUDGET BROADCASTS

British political parties are directly involved in four types of programmes: party political broadcasts (broadcasts by party spokesmen between elections); ministerial broadcasts (reports to the nation by government spokesmen); budget broadcasts (talks on the government's budget proposals by the Chancellor of the Exchequer and the Shadow Chancellor); and party election broadcasts during general election campaigns.

Party political broadcasts are scheduled at intervals between general elections so that the three principal parties may present their points of view on current issues.[53] When it was agreed that political broadcasting should be resumed following World War II, the government and the major parties drafted an Aide Mémoire in 1947, which, among other things, laid the basis for party political and ministerial broadcasts. Subsequently revised in 1948, 1955, and 1969, and now accepted by the IBA as well, it said in part:

A limited number of controversial party political broadcasts shall be allocated to the various parties in accordance with their polls at the last General Election. The allocation shall be calculated on a yearly basis and the total number of such broadcasts shall be a matter for discussion between the parties and the BBC.

The Television Act of 1954 forbade the ITA to originate programmes 'designed to serve the interests of any political party', but did give ITV permission to carry 'relays of the whole (but not of some only) of a series of the BBC's party political broadcasts'. Later revisions of the Television Act for some reason omitted this provision, although ITV continues to take all party political broadcasts.

The Aide Mémoire also said: 'The BBC reserve the right, after consultation with the party leaders, to invite to the microphone a member of either House of outstanding national eminence who may have become detached from any party'. This sentence resulted from an unfortunate situation in the 1930s when the parties were able to keep Winston Churchill off the air. Significant in itself, the affair was important also because it turned Churchill against the BBC, predisposing him to remain aloof during the important early stages of the commercial television controversy, when he might easily have killed the movement.

In the 1930s Churchill was a dissenting member of the Conservative Party. He felt deeply, and was very anxious to express his views about British rearmament and India policy. He did make a number of broadcasts—ten or twelve—between 1928 and 1938, but he wanted to make more, and pressed the BBC for air-time. However, the Conservatives did not want Churchill to broadcast his (to them) unorthodox views; Labour did not intend to nominate a Conservative as one of its speakers; and the BBC was not willing to invite Churchill to broadcast in the face of obvious objections from his party. Accordingly, he was kept off the air, although his views were frequently reported on BBC newscasts.

In another case, in 1931, the government itself—as distinct from the parties—brought pressure on the BBC to cancel a projected series on India in which Churchill wished to participate. In the words of the then Director-General, after Churchill asked 'to be allowed to broadcast his views', the chairman of the Board of Governors and Reith

went to see the Secretary of State [for India]. He was most apprehensive of the effect of such a series of talks at that time; it would do immense harm in India. The board [of Governors] decided to accede to the request so emphatically made by the minister responsible for dealing with a particularly delicate and critical situation. One does not need to endorse his attitude and apprehensions to understand the board's decision.[54]

The first party political broadcasts took place in 1933, but there were only a few of them, and they did not assume much importance until after World War II, although they now are a yearly fixture. The first party political broadcast on television was in 1953.[55] In practice, arrangements are worked out by the Committee on Party Political Broadcasting, made up of representatives from the two broadcasting organizations and of the main political parties. During the first two years after a general election, the number of broadcasts is proportionate to the number of votes each party received at the previous election; thereafter, time is based two-thirds on the results of the general election and one-third on subsequent by-elections.[56] Speakers and subject matter are chosen by the parties, which also are free to determine production techniques. During the calendar year 1978, for example, the Labour Party had six television broadcasts, each of 10 minutes duration; the Conservative Party six 10-minute telecasts; and the Liberal Party three 10 minute telecasts. On BBC Radio 4, Labour had six broadcasts of 5 minutes each plus two of 5 minutes on Radios 1 and 2, and one of 5 minutes on Radio 2; the Conservative Party had six 5-minute broadcasts on Radio 4, plus three 5-minute periods on Radios 1 and 2; while the Liberal Party had three 5-minute periods on Radio 4 and one 5-minute period on Radios 1 and 2.*

These broadcasts are much more important to the parties than to the average listener or viewer. Until recently the telecasts were carried simultaneously by all three channels, although now either the BBC or ITV sometimes repeats them at a later hour, because the political party concerned (usually the Conservatives) is willing to try it, or because, in view of the scheduling of other programmes, the party involved agrees to non-simultaneity. Noting public criticism of the cancellation of entertainment programmes for simultaneous telecasts of party political broadcasts, the Annan Committee recommended that in the future these programmes 'not be transmitted simultaneously on all television channels except during General Election campaigns'.[57] The government accepted this recommendation to the extent of stating that it would 'initiate through the usual channels discussions with the . . . political parties' on this issue.

The party political and ministerial programmes provide both good and bad examples of broadcasting. At times they are done live, but more often they are pre-recorded. Considerable use is made of film and other video materials. I have seen some excellent and some poor presentations, one of the former being by a professional broadcaster and producer turned politician, who displayed all the skills one associates with a carefully filmed television presentation. But many of these programmes, if not poorly done, at least are very dull.

'Ministerial broadcasts' are another type of programme involving the parties. In the United Kingdom, as in the United States, the government uses television and radio to address the public.[58] Although ministerial broadcasts were subject of the 1947 Aide Mémoire mentioned above, television never carried them until 1956, when Anthony Eden reported to the nation on the recent visit of Khrushchev and Bulganin. Now, of course, television is by all odds the favoured medium of British politicians.

The first category of ministerial broadcasts consists of situations when a Minister of the Crown or one of his senior colleagues seeks public cooperation 'in

---

* Since 1965, in response to extended complaints, the Scottish and Welsh national parties have been given time in Scotland and Wales respectively. During 1978, for example, the Scottish National Party received three 10-minute telecasts in Scotland, and the Welsh National Party one 10-minute telecast in Wales. The Scottish National Party also received five 5-minute radio periods in Scotland, and the Welsh Party one 10-minute programme in Wales.

matters where there is a general consensus of opinion'. Independent Television originally was barred from relaying such broadcasts, but at the time of the Suez crisis in 1956, Eden wanted ITV also to carry his statements, and so his first broadcast immediately after Nasser nationalized the Canal was delayed 24 hours so that a common transmission time could be arranged. The second category of ministerial broadcasts includes those sufficiently controversial to justify a reply. It was Eden's broadcasts at the time of the Suez crisis (see above, pp. 38–9) that led to the setting up of this category of ministerial broadcasts. Currently, there seldom are more than two ministerial broadcasts a year, and the trend has been towards fewer rather than more of them.[59]

The Annan Committee had 'serious doubts about the need for ministerial statements on non-controversial issues to be encapsulated in separate ministerial broadcasts,' recommending that these should be broadcast 'within the normal news and public affairs services of the broadcasters'. On the other hand, 'Ministerial statements are nationally important, but controversial issues are another matter. On such issues it should be possible for a Minister directly to address the nation and the Opposition should have a right of reply.' But the government's *1978 White Paper* rejected the committee's recommendation about statements on non-controversial issues, and ruled that 'The obligation on the BBC to broadcast such statements will therefore be retained.'[60]

Obviously, there often are questions as to whether a Minister speaking under category one really has been impartial, or if he has justified his party's position in a controversial matter. If the opposition—or any other party—feels that a reply is in order, but cannot persuade the party in power that the original programme was indeed controversial, then it may appeal to the BBC, which is responsible for judging the validity of the request. When a reply is scheduled,—to a statement made under category one or two—it usually comes within 3 days of the original broadcast. In that case, there is a third programme too, with participants from the government, the opposition, and the Liberal Party, nominated by the BBC. Since 1971, ITV has carried all ministerial broadcasts involving a right of reply.

A major political event is the presentation of the budget to Parliament. Since the budget usually is voted much as proposed by the Cabinet, its details are of greater interest in Britain than are comparable proposals to the American Congress by the President of the United States. But Britain was slow to accept the concept of broadcasting budget debates. Expressing what seems to have been the opinion of many, the secretary to Neville Chamberlain, Chancellor of the Exchequer in the early 1930s, wrote:

> It would be very undesirable, especially in difficult and critical times like these, to make the budget the subject of a controversial debate on the wireless before an audience which is uninstructed in all the complexities and problems of the financial position at home and abroad.[61]

Nevertheless, there was some radio debate on the budget in 1934, and the practice became more or less standardized by the end of the decade, although not many people were prepared to accept the judgement of the *Manchester Guardian* that broadcasting was going to cause 'a profound change' in 'the whole technique of elections'. Nevertheless, there were sporadic budget broadcasts after 1928, which usually involved opposition replies too. Regular budget broadcasts were begun in 1934, and by 1939 the practice had become well established. The first budget broadcast on television was in 1953.

This, of course, is long since, and broadcasts now are always scheduled at budget time, of which those given in March 1977 may serve as an example.[62] The budget presentation to the House of Commons was made on Tuesday 29 March by the (Labour) Chancellor of the Exchequer, Denis Healey. BBC 1 scheduled *Budget 77* from 3.15 to 5.40 that afternoon, with budget summaries at 4.30, 5 and 5.80, plus reports and analyses by government and private tax experts, labour and industry spokesmen, and BBC specialist commentators. That evening at 9.25, the Chancellor of the Exchequer gave a 10-minute broadcast on BBC 1, which was repeated at 10.20 on BBC 2. The next evening Sir Geoffrey Howe, the (Conservative) 'Shadow Chancellor', appeared for the opposition on both services. All of this, of course, was in addition to reports and comments on regular newscasts.

Radio 4 had a Budget Special from 4 to 6 p.m. on Tuesday afternoon, 29 March, and at 10 p.m. a 45-minute programme including a 10-minute presentation by the Chancellor himself, followed by reactions from around the world. (The evening presentation by Mr Healey was the sound track from the earlier BBC 1 presentation.) The following evening, Sir Geoffrey Howe spoke for the opposition at the same hour, again followed by analysis and comment.

The IBA devoted a little less time to the event, but nevertheless covered it quite thoroughly. ITV scheduled its Tuesday afternoon programme from 1.25 to 5.45, proceeding much as did the BBC, and the *TV Times* devoted two-thirds of a page to charts intended to help viewers determine the likely effects of any proposed changes on their own financial situations. That evening at 10.30 the Chancellor of the Exchequer made a 10-minute presentation following *News at Ten*, and the opposition spokesman was scheduled at the same time the next evening, these being recorded repeats of the BBC Television presentations.

The Conservative Party's budget of June 1979 was treated in basically the same way, with the added feature that on the afternoon of 12 June 1979 BBC Radio 4 broadcast the presentation live from the House of Commons, including the presentation by the Chancellor of the Exchequer, and the response of the Labour Party head, after which several 'leading figures' spoke from the studio 'to help you understand what the Chancellor proposed'.

PARTY ELECTION BROADCASTS

There is no better way to appreciate the development of British broadcasting in recent years than by reviewing the history of party election broadcasts—that is, of broadcasts by the political parties during the campaign periods preceding the periodic nationwide elections for the House of Commons. Stringent regulations by leading politicians, who ran broadcast electioneering from the front benches of

Parliament—which the BBC was quite willing to accept—gave way in 1959 to a much wider and more democratic use of the media. As the BBC's historian summarizes the situation:

> It is clear . . . that it was the BBC and not the political parties which sterilized political broadcasting at the end of the war, doubtless fearing that if it were to seek to become a more active influence there would be so many pitfalls ahead that the independence of the BBC, secured with difficulty during the war, would be in danger. Prudential motives—which critics of the BBC described more simply as 'timidity'—prevailed. The idea that the Corporation should refrain from trespassing on the powers of Parliament was nowhere held more strongly than in Broadcasting House. 'Parliament', [Director-General Sir William] Haley always maintained, 'is the only grand forum of the nation'.[63]

Although general election broadcasting developed slowly in Britain, the first such programmes took place as long ago as 1924, when Ramsay MacDonald (Labour), and Herbert Asquith (Liberal) broadcast from public meetings, and Stanley Baldwin (Conservative) talked from the studio. Although John Reith argued persistently for a wider use of radio, the general attitude was one of doubt and timidity, despite sporadic broadcasting in 1928 and 1931.

The basic principles now followed in assigning air-time were quite well established by 1939. As each election approached, the BBC met with the three main parties to allocate broadcast periods between the dissolution of Parliament and election day. (Since 1955, of course, the IBA also has been involved in these negotiations.) Allocations are proportionate to party strength in the House of Commons, now computed as follows: for the three major United Kingdom parties (Labour, Conservative, Liberal), one 10-minute television broadcast for each 2 million votes received by the party at the previous general election. For the 1979 election this would have given a proportion of Labour six 10-minute programmes, Conservative five, and Liberals three, but the Labour Party agreed to drop one of their periods, making the final allocation 5 : 5 : 3. (Were air-time based on national votes for the three major parties, or were there proportionate representation in Parliament, the Liberal Party almost always would have more than its present broadcast allocations.) Since 1950, minor parties also have received time if they have fifty or more candidates in the field by nomination day—and this included time for the Communist Party in 1945, 1950, 1966, and 1970, and for the National Front in the February and October 1974 elections. Currently, parties meeting the qualifications have 5-minute television and 5-minute radio periods.

During the 1979 General Election period, the various political parties had the following broadcast times: Television: Labour and Conservative, five of 10 minutes each; Liberals, three of 10 minutes; Scottish Nationalists, three of 10 minutes (in Scotland only); Plaid Cymru, one of 10 minutes (in Wales only); National Front and Ecology Party, one of 5 minutes each. Radio: Labour and Conservative, four of 10 minutes each on Radio 4, plus three of 5 minutes each on Radio 2; Liberals, three of 10 minutes on Radio 4, plus two of 5 minutes on Radio

2; Scottish Nationalists, three of 10 minutes on Radio Scotland; Plaid Cymru, one of 10 minutes on Radio Wales and Radio Cymru; National Front and Ecology Party, one of 5 minutes each on Radio 4. Some of these programmes were also carried by IBA stations.

All time is free, since the BBC is entirely non-commercial, and the IBA Act expressly precludes the sale of time for political broadcasting.[64]* Both radio and television broadcasts are scheduled during peak evening hours, the government appearing first and last, although there is no political broadcasting on the day before or on polling day, in order to minimize the advantage of the government's having the last say. The parties, not the broadcasters, select the topics and speakers, although assistance is offered in programme preparation and rehearsal. Most of the broadcasts are pre-recorded, either by the BBC or elsewhere. The radio programmes also are broadcast worldwide by short wave to British seamen and citizens abroad, and the texts of the talks are printed in the *Listener*. Since both BBC and IBA news bulletins, as well as the national press, cover the things said on general election broadcasts, the material presented during these programmes is very widely available.

The rules laid down by the IBA for non-political broadcasts during campaign periods by candidates for office parallel those of the BBC.[65]

> It can plausibly be argued that any television appearance (however non-political in character) by a politician may give him, or his party, some advantage over his opponents by virtue of the increased familiarity, prestige and popularity that television can sometimes bring.

Thereafter, the regulations state that candidates may never appear during campaigns as newscasters or interviewers on current affairs programmes.

It is difficult to believe how many limitations were imposed on election and other political broadcasts prior to 1959. After 1939, during all general election periods, the BBC—and the ITA too when it came on the air in 1955—cancelled all broadcasts which any way referred to or might conceivably influence voter opinion. This ban applied to all talks, discussions, plays, documentaries—and

---

* Political broadcasting in the United States is governed by Section 315 of the Communications Act of 1934, which specifies: 'If any licensee shall permit any person who is a legally qualified candidate for any public office to use a broadcasting station, he shall afford equal opportunities to all other such candidates for that office in the use of such broadcasting station.' But exceptions are made for appearances by candidates on newscasts, news interviews, and news documentaries, although in the latter cases stations still must treat all candidates equally.

Congress amended the Communications Act on 24 August 1960, suspending the equal opportunity provision during the 1960 presidential and vice-presidential campaigns, thus enabling American stations to carry the Nixon–Kennedy debates without having to offer equal time to other candidates for the office of President. The debates between Carter and Ford in 1976 were authorized under an interpretation of the law resting on the assumption that the confrontations between the Presidential and Vice Presidential candidates constituted 'on-the-spot coverage of bona fide news events', again relieving stations from the obligation of offering equal time to other candidates for those two offices.

even newscasts—on both radio and television.[66] The purpose of this policy was to preserve absolute neutrality by the broadcasters during the campaign.

In 1969, Hugh Greene, who had been the BBC Director-General from 1960 to 1969, had this to say about BBC election practices in earlier years:

It is almost impossible now to believe that the General Election of 1959 was the first reported by the BBC in its news bulletins and the first in which there was questioning of representatives of the parties and some discussion of the issues in current affairs programmes. Before that the official Election series in which time was given to political parties was the sum total of all that was done about the General Election in broadcasting. This had always seemed to me to be an abdication by the BBC of its responsibilities. The theory was that the BBC must be completely impartial and not risk saying or reporting anything that might affect the way in which any member exercised his vote. The BBC and ITV showed in 1959 and showed again in 1964 and 1966 that responsible and impartial coverage of a General Election campaign is perfectly possible.[67]

These limitations on the use of broadcasting to inform the electorate about the issues and the candidates resulted from several factors. Basic was the vulnerable position of the BBC, the only broadcasting organization during most of these years. Its status as a public corporation over which the government held certain reserve powers of control required it to be careful in references to government policies and practices, lest its broadcasts be taken as official statements.[68] The Corporation was—and still is—legally obliged to be politically neutral, and until the late 1950s, it was very timid in defining its role.

Then there were the parties. The procedure long in effect gave the leaders a good deal of control over what was said over the air, and focused attention on the front benches. In addition, each of the two major parties was concerned lest something happen that would accrue to the advantage of the other one, and neither wanted a strong third party to emerge. The woman who headed BBC Television Talks and Current Affairs for many years has pointed out that 'there was no attempt by the political parties to use television to make a direct appeal to the electorate until the autumn of 1951', at which time they accepted the invitation of the Corporation to participate in three experiments in Party Election broadcasting.[69]

Once the ITA was in the field, however, the situation improved. From the beginning, the ITA had certain advantages over the BBC, even though it was subject to exactly the same government controls. When created in the 1950s, it benefited from the victories the BBC had won through the years for freedom of broadcasting; it was imbued with the spirit of competition; and its financial resources were largely independent of the government.[70]

While most restrictions on broadcasting during general elections have now been eliminated, a clause in the Representation of the People Act 1969 makes it illegal for a candidate to take part in a broadcast to his constituency unless all other candidates in that constituency either take part or consent to the broadcast without their participation.[71] Consequently, a candidate who for any reason wishes to keep an opponent off the air, has only to refuse to take part in such a programme, or to withhold consent to its proceeding in his absence, and it must be cancelled. (Such a situation could not occur in the United States, since a broadcasting station needs only to provide equal broadcast opportunities to all candidates, whether or not they take advantage of the offer.)

The Representation of the People Act 1949 made it illegal, in connection with Parliamentary elections, for candidates to make use of foreign broadcasting stations, as, for example, Radio Luxembourg. Because some candidates used the 'Pirate' stations during local elections, when the law was revised in 1969 the words 'Parliamentary election' were replaced by 'Parliamentary or local government election', and a reference to 'wireless transmitting stations outside the United Kingdom' was amended to apply to television stations as well.[72]

There now are few valid bases for complaints about general election broadcast procedures in Britain, except for the above-cited provision of the law which permits a candidate to keep his rivals off the air, either by refusing to broadcast with them, or by not allowing them to go on the air in his absence. The fact that British general elections seldom last more than 3 or 4 weeks while American national campaigns run on for months is in many ways an advantage for the candidates, the parties, the public, and whoever has to pay the bills. However, one might criticize the limited amount of time assigned—in 1979, for example, each of the two major parties received only five 10-minute telecasts. Surely there must be enough material to fill 5 hours rather than only 50 minutes. This shortcoming is somewhat alleviated, however, by the time given to election issues and candidates on current affairs programmes. Both BBC and IBA cover election news fully, while their current affairs programmes bring to the air national and local candidates in discussions of all aspects of the campaign. Finally, it should be noted that Britain's broadcasters go all out in covering the election itself, following basically the same pattern as their American colleagues.

One also might criticize the practice of allotting air-time according to representation in the old Parliament, since this makes it difficult for minorities to use the broadcast media in order to become majority parties. But since most people probably do not care to view or listen to programmes presenting the views of small minority groups, it may be that little is lost. Several British friends have pointed out to me that, whereas the allocation of political broadcast time in the United States depends partly upon the size of the party treasuries, the major parties in the United Kingdom are treated equally—and, more fairly—whatever their financial status. In fact, to ensure that parties and candidates with more money will not purchase time from the IBA, the law specifies that the Authority may carry no political advertisements.

My feeling, after having studied and observed the subject off and on for some years, is that British broadcasting is fair to all concerned in its treatment of national and local elections. The United Kingdom has no national nominating conventions like those which play such an important role in the United States, so the problem of broadcasting them does not arise. However, the annual party conferences are put on the air, either live or recorded; excerpts are used on most radio and television newscasts; and the current affairs programmes analyse them thoroughly, as I noticed while listening and viewing in the autumn of 1978.

BROADCASTS OF PARLIAMENT*

Radio and television newscasts have covered Parliament for many years, but there were no live broadcasts of Parliamentary proceedings until 1975, and no regular broadcasts until 1978.[73] The BBC began broadcasting weekly summaries in 1929, and these became daily in October 1945. Saturday mornings on Radio 4, when Parliament is in session, the *Week in Westminster* brings together members from both Houses to review the events of the week, while on Saturday nights BBC 2 may offer *Westminister*, described in the *Radio Times* as a 'closer look at the politicians, the tactics and progress of Parliament'. In addition, the Radio 4 services in Scotland and Wales review Parliament from their points of view.

Like some other legislative bodies, the United Kingdom's Parliament periodically considered broadcasting its proceedings, but for many years all such suggestions were turned down.[74] The first request—to broadcast the King's speech at the opening of Parliament in 1923—was denied. In 1926, Reith's application to carry live a speech of Chancellor of the Exchequer, Winston Churchill, was likewise rejected, and in the same year Prime Minister Baldwin told the House of Commons that, after reviewing the matter with the several party leaders, he had decided that 'there was a greatly preponderating body of opinion against broadcasting proceedings of the House'. At this point, one member interjected, 'May I thank the Prime Minister on behalf of a long-suffering public'.[75] In 1935, the Ullswater Report, while stating 'that broadcasting should look toward Parliament as a focal point of political thought', decided that broadcasts from Parliament were 'impractical', although approving the idea of having reporters cover Parliamentary debates.[76]

During World War II a proposal to record some of Winston Churchill's speeches for delayed broadcasting was rejected because some members feared establishing a bad precedent, and in 1944 a member's request for regular radio coverage was denied, although this did lead to the regular presentation of *Today in Parliament* after 1945. In 1951, the Beveridge Committee reviewed the possibility of Parliamentary broadcasts, but decided not to 'advocate' them, since 'simultaneous broadcasting of the Parliamentary debates themselves could hardly fail to influence the character of the Debates in a way in which most people in Britain would think harmful'.[77] Four years later Winston Churchill, in effect, told the House of Commons the same thing during a debate on the Fourteen-Day Rule. Parliament, he said, must not surrender to the media its traditional role as the centre of the country's political life (see p. 210 above).

A long-time worker in BBC political television has summarized the arguments against televising Parliament—and they are almost exactly the same as those advanced in the United States against broadcasting American legislatures and Congress.[78] Members of Parliament would play to the cameras rather than talking to each other; exhibitionists would seek attention; the public would not know that much of Parliament's work is done in committees rather than on the floor of the

---

* Strictly speaking, broadcasts of Parliament are 'outside' rather than 'political' broadcasts, but they are considered here because of their political ramifications.

House; the rules of procedure would be meaningless to many viewers; and, if the cameras showed only a few members in attendance during a debate, the public might think its representatives were neglecting their work, whereas in fact they might be attending meetings or talking to their constituents. Who could be trusted to edit down the proceedings for broadcasting? Finally, 'Would not the intrusion of television destroy the intangible atmosphere which shaped the deliberations of an assembly so rooted in British history?'

But despite all the objections, on 28 October 1958, the state opening of Parliament was broadcast on radio and television for the first time.[79] The practice has been continued ever since, although initially some Members of Parliament thought that the Queen's reading of the speech—prepared of course by the government of the day—would give the impression that she had put aside her political impartiality to espouse the point of view of the party in power, while others feared that this might lead to the regular broadcasting of Parliament.[80] The following year MP Aneurin Bevan suggested an investigation into televising parliamentary proceedings, arguing that MPs should reestablish 'intelligent communications between the House of Commons and the electorate as a whole. That surely is a democratic process.' But nothing came of Bevan's proposal.

In the latter 1960s, and early 1970s, some members joined the BBC and IBA in urging at least experimental closed-circuit television coverage, pointing out that there was live or delayed broadcasting in France, Italy, the Netherlands, the German Federal Republic, Denmark, Norway, Sweden, Finland, Hungary, Australia, New Zealand, and some other commonwealth countries.[81]

One or the other House of Parliament considered radio or television broadcasting in 1966, 1968, 1971, 1972, 1974 and 1975.[82] The great increase in the number of receivers was one factor which aroused interest. In addition, Labour members supported the proposal in the hope that broadcasting might counter the influence of the press, which they believed generally favoured the Conservative Party. Therefore, when Labour formed a new government after the general election of 1964, the outlook for televising Parliament improved.[83] But in 1966 a free vote of 131–130 in the Commons turned down a proposal for a closed-circuit television and radio experiment.

In 1968 the House of Lords authorised a 3-day closed-circuit experiment, and there was a 4-week closed-circuit radio experiment in the House of Commons. In July 1971 a House Committee considered live radio broadcasts of the debates on Britain's entry into the Common Market, but voted against it, 6–4. The next year a House of Commons proposal for experimental radio and television broadcasts lost by 165–191 on a free vote. In 1974 a bill to establish a broadcasting unit to prepare experimental radio and television broadcasts failed to reach a second reading. In 1975 a government motion to authorize experimental radio and television broadcasts was introduced in the House. Television was rejected 275–263, but radio was approved 354–182, and the experiment took place from 9 June to 4 July of that year, with both the BBC and the IBA taking part.

Since the broadcasters were very anxious for the experiment to succeed, they put much effort into it.[84] Much attention was attracted by the opening live broadcast, on 9 June 1975, of Question Time, when the Prime Minister reported the results of the recently held national referendum on Britain's joining the Common Market. During the 4 weeks of the experiment, BBC radio devoted almost 22 hours to live broadcasts from Parliament, and used over 1000 recorded excerpts in its regional and local newscasts. *Today in Parliament*, extended from 15 to 30 minutes during the experiment in order to include recorded excerpts from the proceedings, reported an average of 300 000 listeners above normal. Excerpts also were used in the External Services and were supplied to foreign services all over the world. BBC television used radio sound on 16 of the 20 days of the experiment. The Corporation was delighted with the outcome, and was prepared to continue such broadcasts on a regular basis. A BBC survey showed general public approval of such broadcasts: 76 per cent of a sample questioned wanted the service to continue; 84 per cent approved the Corporation's handling of the project; and 66 per cent said the broadcasts increased their information of parliamentary affairs.

The IBA, equally enthusiastic, supplied live and recorded excerpts to all its radio stations as well as to ITN. The London all-news station frequently broadcast Question Time live, in addition to carrying other live and recorded excerpts. All told, Independent Radio News used 12½ hours of programmes, turning out nineteen live relays, fifteen live reports, and 500 recorded excerpts for local newscasts.[85]

After the experiment was finished, a House of Commons debate led to the adoption, by the overwhelming vote of 299–124, of the following motion on 16 March 1976: 'That this House supports the proposal that public sound broadcasting of its proceedings should be arranged on a permanent basis.'[86] Regular live broadcasts began on 3 April 1978. In addition to the occasional live broadcasts of sessions expected to be of special interest, every word spoken both in the Commons and the Lords now is recorded. The BBC uses excerpts in its radio and television news and current affairs programmes, while IRN provides several daily packages for its stations. ITN also has access to the recordings, as do the BBC's overseas services and foreign broadcasters.

Many listeners, never having attended parliamentary debates, were surprised and dismayed at how apparently disorderly many of them are. One newspaper political writer observed that certain exchanges between the Prime Minister and the Leader of the Opposition 'sounded like a title fight for a heavyweight crown', and one radio critic wrote 'The Westminster follies has opened to lousy reviews, all round and, if this were a normal radio show, it is doubtful if it would last beyond the current series.' But even this was less severe than the statement from one of the MPs who helped arrange the broadcasts:

We have on our hands a public relations disaster. We are in real danger of making a monumental laughing stock of ourself. The great majority of listeners have been appalled at the noise—the bellowing, the abuse, the hee-hawing and the rest. People simply do not understand that the House of Commons is an excitable, emotional and noisy place.*

* Once arrangements were completed to provide short excerpts from United States House of Representatives sessions to the broadcast media, Speaker Thomas O'Neill cautioned his colleagues about properly decorous conduct. The Speaker's warning came on

Looking back on its first year of live broadcasts from Parliament, the BBC observed:

> The new service was not welcomed in its entirety. We found that the live broadcast of Prime Minister's Questions when Members were at their most vociferous . . . upset some people . . . and irritated others . . . . After a period of experimentation the BBC came to the conclusion that live broadcasting was at its best when the event had special significance and the excitement of the occasion was felt by the audience as well as by Members. A Budget Speech was such an event; a routine session of Questions to Ministers was probably not. Existing news coverage, including that provided by the programmes called *Yesterday in Parliament* and *Today in Parliament*, gained much from the use of excerpts from speeches recorded in the House.

The final verdict is clearly in favour of the continued radio broadcasting of a combination of live and recorded excerpts from the British Parliament. The next step undoubtedly will be television, but various hurdles remain to be taken in London, just as in the campaign to televise Congress in Washington much has to be done before there will be regular television coverage of regular sessions in both houses.

---

the day following statements by one representative during an emotional late-night debate in which he said: 'We're laughing, joking and playing games. We're tearing this legislation apart. Some members are sleepy, some are slightly intoxicated.' Subsequently, the representative withdrew his statement about some members being drunk, but not until the recorded excerpt had been broadcast across the country (AP Radio Wire report, 16 August 1978).

13 Talks, Features, and Documentaries

Talks, features, and documentaries are somewhat related types of programmes. As the terms are used by the BBC, a 'talk' is a short talk or interview; a 'feature' is a programme based on facts which includes some fictional dramatization; and a 'documentary' is based entirely on actuality recordings, with no fictional additions of any sort. These three types of programmes are significant parts of British broadcasting.

RADIO TALKS

Although talks are not as important in British radio today as they were in earlier years, they still are broadcast regularly, especially by Radios 2, 3, and 4. Their subject range is as broad as life itself. As a recent *BBC Handbook* expressed it: 'The Talks and Documentaries Department provides [radio] programmes on the arts and sciences, world affairs, environment, and poetry'.[1] But it is not responsible for current affairs, which are produced by the Current Affairs Group.

To plan and produce radio talks, the BBC in London has a department of over twenty-five people (exclusive of secretarial employees), including producers with special interests in such major subject fields as history, literature, music, and politics. Great emphasis is placed on getting speakers who are experts; in fact, presentational skill is sometimes subordinated to subject-matter expertise. All speakers are paid. The current rate is £5 per minute, with extra remuneration for recorded repeats or publication in the *Listener*. The final script for a programme is worked out very carefully in conferences between the speaker and the producer. Nowadays, however, much material which formerly was presented as talks is broadcast in interview form.

An important adjunct to the work of the radio talks department, as well as to television programmes which emphasize the spoken word, is the *Listener*, which prints the texts of some of the main talks and interviews, occasional articles written especially for it, and reviews of books, BBC and IBA broadcasts, art exhibits, films, concerts, and plays. Begun in 1929, with opposition from the press which reached as high as the Prime Minister himself, the *Listener* had worked up its weekly sales to almost 150,000 copies per week by the middle 1950s, North American sales alone averaging 6000 per week. But readership has since declined, and total circulation now hovers around 36,000.[2] The *Listener*, like the *Radio Times*, carriers advertisements. Although at one time it was self-supporting, it now regularly runs a deficit, having to justify itself on a prestige rather than a profit basis. Nevertheless, the *Listener* provides a real service in giving listeners and viewers an opportunity to read about broadcasts they have missed, or to review their substance again. In any case, it is an excellent publication, read by many people in the United States and elsewhere, purely for its merits as a magazine.

Although 25 years ago approximately 10 per cent of the BBC domestic radio output consisted of talks and discussions, the percentage now has dropped drastically. At present, there are hardly any talks on Radio 1, which specializes in popular music, or on Radio 2. Evenings on Radio 3, however, bring demanding talks of the kind formerly found on the Third Programme. Thus, during the week of 26 March – 1 April 1977, titles and subjects included: 'Decomposition or Rebirth?' four talks on 'Recent Directions in Roman Catholic Theology'; the pros and cons of having a constitutional convention to amend the United States constitution; 'The Fantasy of Marxism'; 'The Character of Ireland'; 'The Arts Worldwide'; 'Paisiello and Politics'; and a report on Finnish opera and ballet.[3]

In the 1950s, I complained that Third Programme talks often used 'a written rather than spoken style', and that little effort was made to attract or hold listeners by selecting colourful speakers or rewriting their scripts. On the whole, things have improved over the years, and yet an issue of the *Listener* for May 1978 devoted some eight columns to a talk by an Oxford Professor in a series 'Fictional Fact and France', on Radio 3, which began with the unbelievable sentence:

> In the very apocalyptic, endlessly and rather fussily moralising Demo-Christian prospect offered by the French novelist of Belgian origin (his family originally came from Flemish-speaking Bruges), Maxence van der Meersch (and what a typically northern Christian name to have), an implacably urban geography— brick, woollen mills, tram-lines, estaminets, canals, locks, and the dark and rather oily cobbles of the north, the terrible pavé du nord which is the terror of Belgian, Dutch and French professional cyclists as they tackle the most frightful of all the long-distance cycle races, Paris to Roubaix—is exploited really only as a constant background to the blind and brutal Saturday-night weekend violence of alcoholism and of gin-drinking.

Radio 4's spoken word programmes usually concern news and public affairs, but it also carries *Woman's Hour*, talks on agriculture for rural audiences, and discussions of such general topics as developments in medicine. Radio 3 talks usually run from 20 to 30 minutes, usually being both shorter and brighter than those which used to be on the Third Programme. Radio 4 talks are shorter than those on Radio 3. Supplementing BBC radio's network talks are regional and local productions treating area problems and interests.[4]

One general characteristic of BBC radio is that it continues many programme types now discontinued by most American stations. For example, the BBC *Woman's Hour*, on the air since 1947, formerly broadcast in mid-afternoon on the Light Programme, now occupies an hour of early afternoon time on Radio 4. Intended to help women do their work better, its subject-matter ranges from home mangement to books, film and theatre reviews, politics, fashions, and serial book readings. *Woman's Hour* is much like the programmes of that name which used to be on American stations, except that it is more purposefully arranged, more educational, and considerably more sophisticated.

The best-known BBC talks are the Reith Lectures, named after the first Director-General, and broadcast annually since 1948. On these programmes, distinguished authorities in various fields present from four to eight 30-minute lectures intended for non-specialist audiences. As the list in Table 20 below shows, some of the guests have been Americans, including Daniel J. Boorstin, the American historian and Librarian of Congress, who discussed *The Exploring Spirit: America and the World Experience*, during the year of the American Bicentennial. All of the Reith Lectures are available on discs and tapes for use by radio stations overseas, many have been carried by America's public stations, and most have been published.[5]

The Talks Department also is responsible for poetry programmes and for serial book readings. One *BBC Handbook* referred to the 'quiet popularity of Radio 4's book readings', with the adaptations made with great care, and the reading done either by professional readers or by the authors themselves. For example, on a series entitled *With Great Pleasure*, Lord Hailsham, J. B. Priestley, and Hermione Gingold read some of their favourite poetry and prose.[6] *A Book at Bedtime* on Radio 4 at 11 p.m. brings serial readings from George Eliot, Evelyn Waugh, Hugh Walpole, O. Henry, Marghanita Laski, and the like.

BBC TELEVISION DOCUMENTARIES

In its earlier years, BBC television applied the term 'talks' to certain of its programmes, but as more television production techniques were used, the name was dropped. A recent example of a 'talk' was *World Wide*, a monthly series on television in foreign countries, on which veteran BBC radio and television reporter and administrator Frank Gillard discussed television in Canada, Czechoslovkia, France, Brazil, Mexico, the United States, and India. The one I saw, dealing with the United States, included excerpts from a number of American programmes, so that it was in effect a talk illustrated with films and video-tapes.[7] Another somewhat similar production is *The Money Programme*, which reviews the economic, industrial, and other uses of money. Authoritatively presented, but still meaningful to non-experts, this series uses an anchor person plus explanations and commentaries by knowledgeable correspondents.

The television counterpart of the Reith Lectures are the Richard Dimbleby Lectures, founded in 1973, named after a well-known radio and television actuality reporter. The first three were given, respectively, by Lord Annan—later chairman of the committee bearing his name, Sir Robert Mark, and Lord Goodman. I saw the fourth one, an excellent talk entitled *The British Experience in Television*, given by Sir Hugh Wheldon, a BBC programmer, broadcaster, and administrator.[8] Subsequent speakers included Lord Hailsham, labour leader Jack Jones, and Lord Rotheschild.

A brochure by several BBC producers sought to define a television documen-

TABLE 20   *Reith Lectures, 1948–79*
The Reith Lectures, inaugurated in 1947 and named after the BBC's first Director-General are broadcast annually. Each year the BBC invites a person of authority to undertake a study of original research and to give the results of his work in a series of broadcasts. A list follows with publication details.

1948 Bertrand Russell, *Authority and the individual* (Allen & Unwin, 1949. n.e. paperback 1977. £1.25)

1949 Robert Birley, *Britain in Europe: reflections on the development of a European society* (unpublished)

1950 John Zachary Young, *Doubt and certainty in science* (OUP, 1950, o.p.; Galaxy Books 1960. 75p)

1951 Cyril John Radcliffe, *The problem of power* (Secker & Warburg, 1952. o.p.)

1952 Arnold Toynbee, *The world and the west* (OUP, 1953, o.p.)

1953 J. Robert Oppenheimer, *Science and the common understanding* (OUP, 1954, o.p.)

1954 Oliver Franks, *Britain and the tide of world affairs* (OUP, 1955, o.p.)

1955 Nikolaus Pevsner, *The Englishness of English art* (Architectural Press, 1956, o.p.; Penguin Books 1961. £2.50)

1956 Edward Appleton, *Science and the nation* (Edinburgh UP, 1957, o.p.)

1957 George F. Kennan, *Russia, the atom and the West* (OUP, 1958, o.p.)

1958 A. C. Bernard Lovell, *The individual and the universe* (OUP, 1959, o.p.; paperback 1961, 25p)

1959 Peter Medawar, *The future of man* (Methuen, 1960, o.p.)

1960 Edgar Wind, *Art and anarchy* (Faber, 1963. o.p.; Vintage Books, n.e. 1974, 90p)

1961 Margery Perham, *The colonial reckoning* (Collins, 1962, o.p.; Greenwood Press, US, 1977, £12.25)

1962 George M. Carstairs, *This island now* (Hogarth Press, 1963, o.p.)

1963 Albert E. Sloman, *A university in the making* (BBC, 1964, o.p.)

1964 Leon Bagrit, *The age of automation* (Weidenfeld and Nicolson, 1965, o.p.)

1965 Robert Gardiner, *A world of peoples* (BBC, 1966 o.p.)

1966 John Kenneth Galbraith, *The new industrial state* (Hamish Hamilton, 1967, o.p.; Deutsch, 1972, £4.25; Penguin Books, 1968, £1.25; includes the 1966 lectures)

1967 Edmund Leach, *A runaway world?* (BBC, 1968. o.p.; OUP, 1968, o.p.)

1968 Lester Pearson, *Peace in the family of man* (BBC, 1969, o.p.)

1969 Frank Fraser Darling, *Wilderness and plenty* (BBC, 1970, o.p.; Ballantine, 1971, o.p.)

1970 Donald Schon, *Beyond the stable state* (Temple Smith, 1971. £3.25; includes material from 1970 lectures)

1971 Richard Hoggart, *Only connect* (Chatto & Windus, 1972, £1.50)

1972 Andrew Shonfield, *Europe: journey to an unknown destination* (Allen Lane, 1973, £1.50; Penguin Books, 1973, o.p.)

1973 Alastair Buchan, *Change without war: the shifting structures of world power* (Chatto & Windus, 1974, £2.25)

1974 Ralf Dahrendorf, *The new liberty: survival and justice in a changing world* (Routledge and Kegan Paul, 1975, £3.50; paperback £1.60)

1975 Daniel J. Boorstin, *The exploring spirit: America and the world experience* (BBC, 1976, £3.50)

1976 Colin Blakemore, *Mechanics of the mind* (CUP, 1977, £10.50; paperback £3.95)

1977 A. H. Halsey, *Change in British society* (OUP, 1978, £4.50; paperback £1.95)

1978 Edward Norman, *Christianity and the world order* (OUP, 1979, £3.50; paperback £1.50)

1979 Ali Mazrui, *The African condition.*

SOURCE: *BBC Handbook 1980*, p. 254.
n.e. = new edition.
o.p. = out of print.

tary. In its widest sense, they wrote, 'the term ''documentary'' is used to mean the entire non-fiction output of television, including news and current affairs and some OBs' [Outside Broadcasts, or in American Parlance, 'remotes'].[9] A documentary is a programme that 'explores a factual subject in depth'; 'usually presents its subject at first hand', as by location filming; is creative; takes a long time to produce; and varies in length from a few minutes to several hours. But the key sentence in the description was: 'A documentary may confine itself to undisputed facts, or it may be concerned—partly or totally—with opinion. It does not, however, normally make use of fiction.' BBC television documentaries are produced by almost a dozen departments, including the Documentary Programmes Department; the Features Group (Art Features and General Features); the Children's Programmes Department; the Music Programmes Department; Outside Broadcasts Group; Religious Broadcasting; Schools Broadcasting; and Further Education.

Some of the Corporation's biggest and best-known documentary and dramatic productions have been produced jointly with one or another foreign service or funding source, thus providing the Corporation with additional resources. But the BBC insists that, however financed, such productions must be 'unmistakably a BBC programme or series of programmes'.[10] The Corporation told the Annan Committee: 'Because the BBC believes that its programmes cannot be directed other than towards the interests of audiences in Britain, some opportunities for partnership have accordingly had to be declined.'

Co-productions—BBC distinguishes between them and 'underwriting'—were first done in the 1950s with French television.[11] There were few co-productions until the 1970s, when BBC television began to feel the effects of inflation on programming costs. But the BBC 'was only prepared to see money invested in its own productions as long as it kept the majority share of the costs and retained firm production and editorial control'. In Europe the BBC has cooperated with almost every broadcasting organization; it has worked jointly with French-speaking production groups in both Europe and Canada; it has done work with Iranian Television and Australia; and it has developed a number of programmes with the United States, France, and West Germany. The sums of money involved are considerable, exceeding £2,200,000 between 1971 and 1974. Among the documentaries produced as a result of such arrangements have been Alistair Cooke's *America*, Jacob Bronowski's *Ascent of Man*, and Christopher Ralling's productions *The Search for the Nile* and *The Fight Against Slavery*.[12]

Along with co-production and co-finance has come underwriting, examples being the BBC's relationships with America's Public Broadcasting Service. The BBC itself covered all domestic production costs for (then) Sir Kenneth Clark's *Civilisation* series, but Xerox underwrote the expenses for its American showing by the Public Broadcasting Service. Incidentally, few co-productions have been controversial in nature, since the Corporation feels that such programmes 'are best left for purely national production and tramsmission in an overall context of balance.... [Therefore] the BBC will normally expect to produce controversial programmes with its own resources.'

Among the best-known BBC documentaries in the United States are several which have been broadcast and re-broadcast by America's Public Broadcasting Service. In addition to Kenneth Clark's *Civilisation*, they include Jacob Bronowski's *The Ascent of Man*, Alistair Cooke's *America*, and John Kenneth Galbraith's *The Age of Uncertainty*. First of this distinguished quartet was *Civilisation*. It is interesting to note that Clark, long known as an art student and critic in Britain, served as chairman of the ITA from 1954 to 1957. *Civilisation*, broadcast originally in the spring of 1969, dealt with the development of civilization in Western Europe. Tongue in cheek, in the introduction to the book which grew out of the broadcasts, Clark said that a more descriptive title would have been 'Speculations on the Nature of Civilisation as Illustrated by the Changing Faces of Civilised Life in Western Europe from the Dark Ages to the Present Day'.[13]

This splendid series, developed over a period of two years, utilized a great deal of location filming as well as already-available still pictures of many major art works in Europe. Looking back on his broadcast experience, Lord Clark wrote that he was

> convinced that a combination of words and music, colour and movement can extend human experience in a way that words alone cannot do. For this reason, I believe in television as a medium, and was prepared to give up two years' writing to see what could be done with it. Thanks to skilful and imaginative directors and an expert camera crew, I believe that certain moments in the film were genuinely moving and enlightening. They are lost in a book.

Nevertheless, the book was published.

The Ascent of Man was, according to Jacob Bronowski, intended to 'present the development of science in a series of television programmes to match those of Lord Clark on *Civilisation*'.[14] Bronowski had been a regular broadcaster in Britain since the radio days. He also was a prolific writer about both literature and science, generally adopting a philosophical rather than merely descriptive approach. The series was a major undertaking from its first outline in July 1969 to the final film shot December 1972. Again to quote Bronowski:

> There has been a deep change in the temper of science in the last twenty years: the focus of attention has shifted from the physical to the life sciences. As a result, science is drawn more and more to the study of individuality . . . . I owe a debt for the good fortune that carried me into two seminal fields of science [mathematics and physics] in one lifetime; and though I do not know to whom the debt is due, I conceived *The Ascent of Man* in gratitude to repay it.*

* Audience research studies accompanied the first broadcast of this series on BBC television. Audiences were small in percentages, but large in absolute numbers: between 4 and 7 per cent of the population saw the broadcasts, the middle-aged and elderly being more apt to view than the under-45 group. Of 2000 viewers approached, only eighty-one proved to have been fairly regular viewers, but, said the report: 'Viewers' reactions to the . . . programmes . . . were generally very favourable, despite minority opinion that it was 'all above my head'. (BBC, *Annual Review of BBC Audience Research Findings, Number 1, 1973/4*, pp. 44–50.)

Alistair Cooke, born in Britain, but now a naturalized American citizen, has been a regular contributor to British broadcasting for many years, during most of which he worked to explain and interpret the United States to the United Kingdom. In addition to serving as American correspondent, first for *The Times* and then for what was the *Manchester Guardian*, he has prepared a weekly *Letter from America* for BBC radio since 1946, and also has appeared on ITV, as for example in an ATV production about George III with Prince Charles on Easter Monday, 19 April 1977.

Alistair Cooke's *America* was first shown on BBC 2 in the autumn of 1972. Its awards include four Emmys and one Peabody. In addition, Cooke personally received the Benjamin Franklin Medal of the Royal Society of Arts, made annually for contributions to Anglo-American relations. *America* is, in essence, a well-illustrated, although necessarily superficial, history of the United States from Columbus to the date of broadcast. The combination of Cooke's skill as writer and narrator, the well-chosen still pictures, and the skilfully executed location films, added up to a very attractive series which had a considerable audience. So did the subsequent book, which in the United States was a Book-of-the-Month Club best-seller.[15]

The last of these four major projects featured the American economist, John Kenneth Galbraith, in a 13-week series, *The Age of Uncertainty*. Galbraith has had academic appointments at Princeton and Harvard; government service culminating as United States Ambassador to India from 1961 to 1963; and political activity which included service as chairman of Americans for Democratic Action from 1967 to 1969. His best-known publication, prior to the book related to this series, was *The Affluent Society*, first published in 1958 and issued in a new edition in 1970, although he has written other books and articles on economic topics.

Galbraith explained that, in preparing the broadcasts, he first 'wrote careful essays on each of the subjects to be covered'. The television scripts were drawn from these essays and the book combined material from both essays and scripts. In his foreword to the book, the author wrote that *The Age of Uncertainty* was chosen as the title because 'It sounded well; it did not confine thought; and it suggested the basic scene: we would contrast the great certainties in economic thought in the last century with the great uncertainty with which problems are faced in our time.'[16] Titles for the individual Galbraith broadcasts refer to such concepts and people as classical capitalism, Karl Marx, Lenin, 'The Rise of Money', 'The Big Corporation', and, finally, 'Democracy, Leadership, Commitment'. *The Age of Uncertainty*, with its highly controversial concepts of economics, evoked some very strong reactions. In Britain, a critic for the *Daily Telegraph* referred to it as 'A

In the autumn of 1975, when *The Ascent of Man* was being screened by America's Public Broadcasting Service, 200 institutions of higher learning used it as the basis for a course of study and over 2000 students enrolled nationwide. During a repeat of the series, the number of schools increased to 500 and the number of students to 25,000. An accompanying study showed generally high enthusiasm over the series, and especially over Bronowski as teacher, and ended with recommendations for the development of more such television study projects in the future. (Marjorie E. Hoachlander, *A Case Study Volume 1. Summary. The Ascent of Man: A Multiple of Uses?*)

Hymn of Hate', while *Spectator* magazine brushed it off as 'more banality'. But *The Financial Times* dubbed it 'superb', and the television critic for the *Daily Mail* wrote, 'I'll go all the way with J.K.G.'.

The book was reviewed in *The New York Times* under the headline 'Galbraith on the Loose', and the reviewer had both good and bad things to say. The book, he wrote, 'is a splendid opportunity for Mr. Galbraith to roam around and show off'. After noting the wide range of subject-matter covered, the reviewer characterized the project as 'outrageous, but . . . also enormously entertaining', and concluded by saying: 'We indulge Mr. Galbraith because he is such excellent company and we like him almost as much as he likes himself.'[17]

Although BBC documentary productions are always adequate, and sometimes outstanding, the day-to-day documentaries cannot be expected to be—and are not—on a level with the major series described above. Subject-matter is almost always interesting if not significant, but production excellence varies considerably. On 25 May 1976 BBC 1 broadcast a documentary about the spread of rabies by foxes, a pertinent subject in view of a well-justified rabies scare. *Pioneer Photography*, broadcast by BBC 2 on 26 April 1976, was a well-done and interesting review of some motion picture experiments in the late nineteenth century. *Shell the Giant*, developed jointly with the Netherlands Broadcasting Foundation and broadcast by BBC 2 on 26 April 1976, was a study of Shell Oil as a typical multinational company. Additional viewing in the autumn of 1978 did not significantly add to the range of examples that could be cited in this chapter.

Quite different was the *Great British Art Show* on BBC 2, on 24 April 1976, which reviewed the British painting and sculpture in a recent show in Milan, Italy. Critics discussed the pictures and talked with some of the artists. For viewers this was a demanding programme, although not unduly technical. On seven Sunday afternoons in April and May 1976, BBC 1 had *The Yugoslav Way*, a series of half-hour episodes on life in Yugoslavia. Very remarkable was *Inside Story: Liz Thomas*, presented on 6 May 1976 by BBC 2, which told the story of a young English nurse who, despite overwhelming odds, chose to work in the Saigon slums helping children, prostitutes, and street people. The films, made mainly in Saigon, included graphic presentations of Liz Thomas's life and work. This was one of the most moving programmes I saw during 3 months of British television viewing in 1976.

Observing America's bicentennial, BBC 1 broadcast in May 1976 three programmes on *The Spirit of 76*. I saw one which allegedly dealt with the deterioration of family life in America, although most of it had been made in nudist camps. With the frankness typical of British television, many 'topless women' were shown; and had any critics objected, truth would have been cited as the justification. The programme may have been an accurate representation of a nudist camp, but it didn't deal with the American family life I have come to know!

Very unique was an experiment on living in the past which provided the basis for a BBC documentary produced in 1978.[18] Given front-page space by *The New York Times*, *Living in the Past* was based on the experiences of ten young people, recruited from over 1000 volunteers, who lived for a year in an isolated British country lane, using the tools and relying on the resources that would have been available during the Iron Age, 200 years before the birth of Christ. Once each week they were visited by a camera crew, and the resulting film was edited into a series of twelve documentaries.

A variation on the documentary form was the award-winning series of ten programmes entitled *Explorers*—co-financed by the West Deutscher Rundfund—which were fictionalized dramatizations of the experiences of such men as Christopher Columbus; Captain James Cook, the famous navigator and explorer of the early eighteenth century; and Roald Amundsen, the discoverer of the South Pole. These were convincing recreations, demonstrating once again that while the ships were made of wood, the men certainly were of iron.* Another interesting BBC project was the film *If Britain Had Fallen*, first shown on 12 September 1972. The book, though based on the television show, went somewhat beyond it to describe what might have happened had Britain been occupied by an invading German army.[19]

Although there is no reason why the IBA programme companies should not deal with Britain's Royal family and national occasions just as the BBC does, the Corporation usually takes the lead in such productions. To observe the 25th anniversary of Queen Elizabeth II's coronation in 1977, the BBC produced nine 60-minute documentaries spanning 900 years of history. The first programme was broadcast in April 1977 so that the final one would come during the jubilee week.

The series reviewed the British monarchy from mediaeval days to the twentieth century. Prince Charles discussed the role of the Prince of Wales; his father, Prince Philip, talked about Royal carriages; and Queen Elizabeth displayed the 900-year-old coronation crown, which, incidentally, may be handled by only two people—the Queen herself and the Keeper of the Crown Jewels. In parts of this programme, incidentally, she put aside her prepared script and ad-libbed directly to the camera.[20]

On 2 November 1977, the BBC observed the first anniversary of the election of Jimmy Carter as President of the United States with a 60-minute documentary.[21] A film crew and a news staff of eight people spent a month in Plains, Georgia, filming the documentary, which included interviews with the President, his brother Billy Carter, and his mother, 'Miss Lillian'. This programme was described in *Variety* as 'one of the most costly documentaries ever shot in the United States. Seldom has a television unit spent an entire month on such a project'. Two previous specials, made at intervals of 6 months, dealt with the changing life-styles of Plains citizens since the election of Jimmy Carter.

ITV DOCUMENTARIES

During a normal week, the ITV network devotes an hour or more to documentary

---

* The BBC's Department of Audience Research found that the favourite programme in this series was the one dealing with James Cook, a programme 'which intrigued its viewers with its picture of eighteenth-century sea-going life. They commended the ''restrained and life-like'' performances, and rhapsodised over the beautiful location filming'. (BBC, *Annual Review of BBC Audience Research Findings*, Number 3 (1975/6), p. 25.)

programmes, produced by both the central and the regional companies. A conspicuous example was *The World at War*, from Thames Television in London, on which production began in 1971, with the initial transmissions from October 1973 to March 1974.[22] Originally estimated to cost £500,000, it finally came in at double that amount. This was such a large project that it took over 3½ years to plan, prepare for and produce the twenty-six hour-long programmes in the series. The production team of over fifty people included: nine producers and directors, ten writers, three researchers, five film editors, two dubbing editors, a dubbing-mixing specialist, five graphic designers, an associate producer, and a team of historical and technical advisors. Camera teams visited fourteen countries to interview World War II survivors and eye-witnesses, and after talking with 1250 people, filmed interviews with 250 of them. Film researchers examined 4 million feet of film in the archives of fourteen countries, scrutinized 1 million feet, and finally selected 40,000 feet for the programmes. Special music was composed and recorded, and the famous British actor, Laurence Olivier, served as principal narrator. The programme has been broadcast and repeated in Britain, and has been sold to foreign countries, including the United States, where it has been purchased by individual stations rather than by networks, however.[23]

Subsequently, Thames Television underwrote a 340-page book 'to accompany the television series', although 'it is not the book of the film', being instead a 'general account of the war for everyone, and especially for those whose interest in it may have been sharpened or awakened by watching the television programmes'.[24]

To mark the American bicentennial in 1976, Thames Television produced *Destination America*, an eight-part documentary on immigration to the United States.[25] In addition to many contemporary posters and pictures, the series used many interviews made in various parts of the United States and Europe with immigrants and their descendants. Such national groups as the Irish, Italians, Poles, Germans, Jews, and British were represented. Among other things the series showed how newly arrived immigrants were exploited by their employers. But after each wave established itself and improved its occupations and housing, it was succeeded by another wave which underwent the same experiences, often being looked down upon by the earlier arrivals. Much work and £400,000 went into the series. One picture researcher spent 6 months in New York and Washington collecting thousands of photographs, although only several hundred were used. A real find was some film made in 1896 showing dirt roads in Washington and New York.

This honest, carefully done series was widely praised by television critics on both sides of the Atlantic, although to me it was less exciting than the same company's *World At War*, since the imigration story, based on still pictures, posters and interviews, could not compete for dramatic interest with films made on battlefields.[26] Nevertheless, after being broadcast, *Destination America* will provide some important source material for schools and colleges.

Related to the series was a 256-page book by Maldwyn A. Jones, Professor of American history at the University of London, which contained many contemporary pictures, cartoons, and posters.[27] In his introduction the author stated that, although the book covered 'ground similar to that of the television programmes, it does not follow them rigidly. I have tried to amplify the themes of these programmes, and also to add complementary material with a view to providing a general introductory account of the Atlantic migration.'

In May 1976 ITV broadcast nine 15-minute documentaries following the ITN evening news, which reviewed the events of the 1926 General Strike on their exact 50th anniversary dates. Although produced by Yorkshire Television, a number of other companies supplied material relative to events taking place in their regions. The organizer and writer of the series, Robert Kee, stated:

> In this day-by-day report of the nine days of the Strike as it happened, we did not pretend at any time that we were really in any other year but 1976—However, by the use of the techniques of a modern news programme—film, still photographs, regional reporters, interviews with experts, and particularly by taking advantage of the 'historic present tense' we hoped to convey the vividness and actuality of the events so that viewers could, if they chose, often imagine that they were watching a contemporary television news report.

I watched most of these programmes, and found them interesting. Obviously, despite some remarkable films of the events of 1926, many gaps had to be filled in by description, so that interest was not always sustained. Nevertheless, it was a worthwhile series.

One of the most sensational programmes of its type was Yorkshire Television's *The Case of Yoland McShane*, broadcast in August 1977. In March 1976, the police, on a tip received from the operators of a nursing home in the county of Sussex, surreptitiously made a sound-film recording of a conversation between an 86-year-old woman and her daughter.[28] When it was broadcast, viewers heard the daughter say: 'It isn't cowardly, Mum, for goodness sake. If you had a dog in this state you would take it to the vet, wouldn't you?' The mother replied: 'A dog hasn't got a soul. I'm so afraid of being punished after.' Then the daughter replied: 'Oh, Mummy, for this you wouldn't be punished for this. . . . Don't be having any doubts. . . . Don't bungle it, Mummy, don't make a mess of it.' Then the daughter gave her mother some barbituate tablets and urged her to take them with a 'big drink of whiskey, that's always fatal, Mummy', and then walked out. But the police moved in immediately, confiscated the drugs and arrested the daughter, who subsequently was sent to prison for 2 years for aiding and abetting an attempted suicide. Her conviction, which took place in January 1977, resulted largely from the recording made by the hidden police video-tape machine, which was the first time a British court had accepted such evidence.

When the video-tape was made available to Yorkshire Television, the resulting broadcast—made after the Authority had previewed and approved the programme—set off a furor. The head of Yorkshire Documentaries said: 'I have no doubt that . . . this programme represents the most important single event of the decade for television. We've stepped through a mirror onto ground that is totally new and there can be no going back.' The Chief Constable of Sussex, defending the actions of his detective in making the video-tape available, said: 'My prime task was saving and protecting a life. We are no longer in the 1890s.' But one Member of Parliament declared: 'This programme should frighten every thinking person. The techniques used by the police are those we deplore in the Soviet Union or Chile.' Most newspapers supported his position.

In addition to blockbusters, ITV like BBC has many documentaries seldom seen outside of the British Isles. Outstanding was the 1975 production by Yorkshire Television of *Johnny Go Home*, a prize-winning dramatization of the unfortunate experiences of young people who leave their rural homes for the bright lights of London, only to be caught up in lives of crime and vice.[29] Some 25,000 children arrive in London every year, and any night of the year 300 of them sleep in the streets, in boxes, or other inadequate shelters. The fact that some of the films made for this programme unintentionally recorded the background to a subsequent murder gave the programme additional exposure. A special showing, in fact, was arranged for members of the House of Commons, and it was discussed on the floor of the House. The debate was about the government's funding and inspection of facilities for runaways, and the coordination of government departments which dealt with runaways and their problems. Each participant referred to the television programme, and some of them commended Yorkshire Television for producing the programme.

Southern Television's long-running *Farm Progress* deals with the politics, economics, and technology of farming in the South of England.[30] Somewhat related is another Southern Television production, *Out of Town*, which tells city people about life in the country. There also have been HTV programmes about *West Country Farming* and the life of a Yorkshire farmer.

In 1976, designated as Age Action Year, Anglia Television's *Ripe Old Age* dealt with the problems facing old people.[31] Railroads also have attracted ITV documentary producers. I saw one programme from the series, *The Great Little Trains of Wales*, developed by Wynford Vaughan-Thomas, a long-time BBC contributor, which quietly and nostalgically showed us somewhat the Welsh equivalent of America's Toonerville Trolley.[32]

Many of the smaller regional companies develop programmes for their own areas.[33] During the first 3 years that Southern Television operated a documentary unit, it produced 150 half-hour features, including: *Do Not Exceed the Stated Dose* (teenagers addicted to over-the-counter medicine); *A Suitable Case for Treatment* (a union jurisdictional dispute at a hospital); *The Nightmare That Never Ends* (a family whose two children were dying of muscular dystrophy); and three programmes on Britain's contribution to NATO.

One of the endearing traits of the British is their ability to laugh at themselves, and this ATV did in its thirteen-part series, *In Search of the Great English Eccentric*, for which the producers travelled the length and breadth of the country filming 115 separate items.[34] When finally assembled, the programmes included demonstrations by several champion (women) 'shouters'; a programme about a woman with fourteen Pomeranian dogs named after Queen Victoria's daughters and granddaughters, who lived in their own large dolls-house equipped with furniture to scale; and a programme showing some knights wearing home-made armour as they re-created pages from the tournaments of the past.

Documentaries are among British broadcasting's outstanding achievements. As was observed above, not all are as brilliant as *Alistair Cooke's America*, Jacob Bronowski's *Ascent of Man*, or Thames Television's *The World at War*. To say that average British productions do not consistently match those standards is not to condemn them, but merely to recognize that no broadcasting network has the resources to produce prize-winners every time. American networks also turn out some fine documentaries—and they steadily improve, and no comparison should suggest that those produced in the United States lack merit. But, on balance, I would give higher marks to the British. There are more of them—almost every week brings one or two such programmes on BBC 1, BBC 2 or ITV. But above all, as with drama, the British build on a long radio and—later—television background and tradition; they plan and prepare carefully and well; and above all—their first objective is to turn out outstanding programmes, with audience size a second consideration, something our system makes it very hard for American networks to do.

14 Educational Broadcasting*

All programmes provide some combination of information and education, although the term 'educational broadcasting' is never applied to the total output. The BBC has observed that for 'many people . . . broadcasting in one form or another may be the main educative influence in their lives'.† It told the Annan Committee that 'educational' broadcasting is 'far richer' than either 'instructional' or 'educative' broadcasting—the latter including drama, current affairs, documentary programmes and news. The chief aim of 'educational broadcasting', stated the Corporation, is to 'stimulate the listener to further activity and participation'. However this may be, both BBC and IBA apply the adjective 'educational' to programmes which, in a formal and organized manner, attempt to 'educate' the public.

Both organizations accept a public obligation to present such programmes. All of the BBC's Charters have referred to the 'great value' of broadcasting 'as means of disseminating information, education and entertainment', while the Parliamentary acts setting up the IBA have mandated it to provide 'television and local sound broadcasting services as a public service for disseminating information, education and entertainment'.[1]

The Corporation groups its educational programmes in three categories: those for pre- and in-school use; those intended primarily for adults at home (Further Education); and those produced for the Open University.[2] Also 'educational' are programmes on English as a second language and certain broadcasts for professional groups. In order to coordinate all of these programmes effectively, one person—the Controller, of Educational Broadcasting—is in charge of both the radio and television output, although the five production departments are separately organized. (Religious programmes, music programmes, and news and current affairs also follow this procedure, although the Editor, News and Current Affairs reports directly to the Director-General, while the Controller, Educational

---

* Since this book deals only with broadcast—as opposed to closed-circuit, cable, or other non-broadcast uses of radio and television—there is no discussion here of any of the interesting closed-circuit educational experiments that have taken place in the United Kingdom.

† BBC Memorandum, *Education and Broadcasting*, #2. Webster's *Third New International Dictionary of the English Language* states that the word 'educate' means to 'provide or assist in providing with knowledge or wisdom, moral balance, or good physical condition esp. by means of formal education'. One of its definitions of 'educational' is, 'of, relating to, or concerned with education, i.e. 'educational television'. To many people, a programme offering formal instruction is 'instructional', although others would call it 'educational'. 'Educative' is defined as 'having to do with education'.

Broadcasting, the Controller, Music, and the Head of Religious Broadcasting report to the Managing Director, Radio.) The Corporation has policy-making and advisory groups to assist in planning its educational programmes, and prepares much printed and recorded material to accompany them. During a typical school year, the BBC spends over £6 million of its licence revenue on educational programmes, plus £5 million on the Open University—the latter of which, however, is reimbursed by the government's Department of Education and Science.

The IBA also emphasizes education, for both strategic and substantive reasons. During the Parliamentary debates which culminated in the Television Act of 1954, and on all occasions when the Authority has been under attack, questions have been raised about its serious programming, so there are good reasons for the Authority to outdo itself in education. Although the IBA observed to the Annan Committee that 'its obligation to educate as well as inform and entertain has to be discharged chiefly through the general output, and only additionally through the expressly educational programmes', it nevertheless makes an honest and success-ful attempt to develop such material.[3]

But the Annan Committee characterized as a 'dangerously broad definition' the IBA's statement that ILR educational broadcasting included 'all output which tends to help members of the audience become better informed about local affairs and matters which touch on their daily lives'. (One IBA official pointed out to me that the statement quoted by the Committee had been made when ILR had been on the air only a short time, without having had adequate opportunity to develop either its programmes or its programme philosophy.) The report went on to observe that it was difficult 'to obtain meaningful overall figures of the amount of educational material' offered by ILR because of their listing programmes from 60 seconds to an hour in length as being educational.

Under the current rules, all television contractors must carry not less than 9 hours a week of in-school programmes while schools are in session, and must broadcast on a 'regular pattern educational programmes for adults'. The latter average about 3 hours a week.[4] Approximately £5 million is spent by the programme companies each year in producing educational material for ITV.

The Annan Committee compared the amount of educational broadcasting done by both services during 1974–5 and found that the BBC's output was much greater than that of ITV. However, in making such comparisons, one must bear in mind that the Authority's radio services are limited, so that it cannot compete equally with the BBC in that medium, and that the Corporation than had two television networks to the Authority's one, which clearly gave the BBC an opportunity to do more educational telecasting.[5]

BROADCASTS FOR SCHOOLS

The BBC operates one of the oldest, surely the largest, and probably the best school broadcasting service in the world. In the 1950s it was joined by the ITA which, although later in the field and with less extensive services, also presents some excellent programmes.

Broadcasting to schools was begun in 1924, 2 years after the British Broadcasting Company was formed.[6] In 1927 the newly chartered British Broadcasting Corporation and the Kent Education Authority, with funds from the Carnegie Trust, made an extensive investigation of the subject. The resulting report upheld the principles of school broadcasting, and pointed the way to its further development, among other things stressing the need for close cooperation between broadcasters and educators. Consequently in 1929 there was established the Central Council for School Broadcasting, which in 1947 became the School Broadcasting Council. School broadcasting continued uninterrupted and actually expanded during World War II, and underwent further expansion and change thereafter.

School broadcasting inevitably is conditioned by the educational system it serves. At present such programmes in the United States are for regional or local schools, but in most countries, including the United Kingdom, a national audience usually is the target—although Britain's new local radio stations serve their immediate localities. This broad aim complicates the task in the United Kingdom just as it did for America's national networks when they broadcast to schools in the 1930s and 1940s. Although the United Kingdom is about the size of Pennsylvania and New York combined—but with twice their population—its schools are administratively decentralized. There are active National Ministries of Education for England and Wales, Scotland, and Northern Ireland, but they are neither empowered to, nor do they try to, dictate uniform curricula. Furthermore, there is intense regional feeling in many parts of England, and strong national consciousness in Scotland, Wales, and Northern Ireland. In Britain, as in the United States, therefore, elementary and secondary education is largely a local affair.*

There are approximately 38,290 schools in the United Kingdom,[7] almost all of which are equipped to receive radio and television programmes; most have audio-tape recorders. 'School radio is used mainly in recorded form in secondary schools, and both recorded and off-air in primary schools. School television is still used mainly off-air in primary schools', only 10 percent of which have video-tape recorders, while in secondary schools, 75 per cent of which are equipped with recorders, it is increasingly used in recorded form.[8] In Britain, as in the United States, the lower grades make the greatest use of school programmes. According to BBC figures, in 1978–9, about 92 per cent of all primary schools used BBC and/or IBA television, compared to 83 per cent of the secondary schools.

---

* To the outsider such British private schools—'public' in British terminology—as Eton, Rugby, Charterhouse, and Harrow are much better known than the tax-supported ones attended by most children. But since the vast majority of schools are state schools, reference here is limited to them. Children from 5 to 10 years of age, and of all levels of ability, attend 'primary' schools. From age 11 to 16 more than 80 per cent of them now attend non-selective comprehensive secondary schools; the remainder either still attend selective grammar schools or other secondary schools, depending upon the rate of progress towards comprehensive secondary education in different areas of the United Kingdom. About half of all the 16-year-olds remain in school for 1 or 2 more years.

Almost all European countries and American states with Schools of the Air, agree on the objectives of such programmes.[9] The British, like the Americans, believe that school broadcasting should provide something that the teacher alone cannot give, and especially that it should supplement the work of the school on the imaginative side.[10] In order to accomplish this objective, all the resources of broadcasting are utilized to bring to the classroom the faces and voices of outstanding men and women who are worth hearing for what they have to say; provide first-class performances in music, drama and poetry reading; extend children's awareness and understanding of the present and the past, at home and abroad, by dramatizations, and eye-witness descriptions; by the same or similar means, sometimes combined with commentaries or readings, enrich children's enjoyment and awareness of the world of literature; provide examples of radio and television forms in their own right, and give training in selective and critical listening and viewing; provide specially written commentaries on topical events; and provide the help and offer the example of specialist teachers in subjects in which the listening teachers are not specialists. These principles apply equally to BBC and ITV School Broadcasting.

It also is generally agreed that in-school programmes need not be self-sufficient. In 1974, the BBC told the Annan Committee:

It is not the BBC's purpose that programmes should be self-sufficient. They are intended to be developed by the teacher in accordance with the needs of his or her invididual classes. [Therefore] Assistance to the teacher in the work of development is provided through a wide range of notes and pamphlets published by the BBC.[11]

The Independent Companies, which take basically the same position, told the Annan Committee:

Schools broadcasts have never been intended to replace the teacher, still less the book. Today they are increasingly being seen as resource material to be stored on video-tape or film and used by teacher or children as and when appropriate.[12]

THE SCHOOL BROADCASTING COUNCILS

Educational broadcasters always face the problem of maintaining liaison with educators. Broadcasting staffs include many experts on programme planning and production, but generally fewer on educational policy or school needs. Consequently, the world over, subject-matter experts and educators have been asked to work with broadcasters in preparing educational programmes. In Britain, this is done at all age levels by both broadcasting organizations.

The BBC set up the School Broadcasting Councils to represent the schools and its own School Broadcasting Departments to do the actual broadcasting.[13] At present, there are councils for the entire United Kingdom, plus separate ones for Wales, Scotland, and Northern Ireland, although the latter three areas also are represented on the United Kingdom Council. The United Kingdom Council has three programme subcommittees, each dealing with students of different age groups. The Council meets twice a year, and the subcommittees three times a year. The Councils in Scotland, Wales and Northern Ireland follow similar procedures.

Considering the jealousy with which the BBC guards its prerogatives, it is remarkable that it willingly surrendered a considerable degree of control over school broadcasting to an independent Council. As it hold the Annan Committee:

> The BBC does not seek to set itself up as an educational institution. In a strictly formal sense it has no educational policy of its own. . . . The BBC has recognized from the start that in the area of School broadcasting it needs advice and guidance. For this it turns principally to the school Broadcasting Council of the United Kingdom. . . . The BBC will not broadcast or publish any material for schools which does not have the support of the Council and its Committees. Again, however, the BBC retains the final responsibility for what is transmitted.*

The School Broadcasting Council for the United Kingdom has some forty members nominated and/or appointed, as the case may be, by educational organizations and groups in all parts of the country, as well as by the BBC. Members are chosen because of their positions, their subject-matter competence, and their broadcasting expertise.[14] The Council has a permanent staff of some sixty members, including fifteen education officers, with appropriate administrative support, chosen by the Council but paid by the BBC, and housed in space provided by the Corporation in London. The Councils in Edinburgh with fifteen members, Belfast with twenty-one, and Cardiff with twenty-five, have their own smaller headquarters facilities.

The constitution of the School Broadcasting Council states that it is to study educational practices and trends to determine how broadcasts can best assist the schools; formulate general policy; determine the general aims and scope of the several series and the associated materials; survey and assess the results; facilitate 'the development of school broadcasting and be the official link between the Corporation and the educational world in the respect of the duties of the Council'.[15]

---

* BBC, *Education and Broadcasting*, #11–12. The long-time head of the BBC School Television Department, Kenneth Fawdry, in *Everything But Alf Garnett: A Personal View of BBC School Broadcasting* (p. 107) wrote:

> The creation of this council [for school broadcasting], involving the abrogation by the BBC of a small piece of its cherished independence was judicious. It has helped to protect the BBC from public controversy in an area where this would doubtfully have had any constructive effects. It has put the Council in turn under an obligation to use with great discretion its power to impose guidelines and, in the last resort, to withhold sponsorship. It was an action designed to last; and so it has, in all its essentials, to this day.

One BBC official suggested to me that concern about Nazi Germany's example of media control by government was at least an incidental factor in giving the School Broadcasting Council an absolute veto over school programme substance.

The Council also assists in developing courses on school broadcasting for teacher training institutions.

When it began developing broadcasts for schools in the mid-1950s, the ITA followed the same pattern. Several senior Authority staff members in London devote their time to educational programme services, and the programme companies too have staff members with such responsibilities. The IBA has an Educational Advisory Council, with Schools and Adult Education Committees which have some overlapping membership. Those programme companies doing radio or television school broadcasting have their own advisory groups.

Programme planning and production is a year-round affair at both BBC and ITA. Some months before a series takes to the air, the related programme subcommittees describe the aim and scope of the series they wish to have broadcast. Formal statements, indicating the subject, educational purpose, matter of treatment, age and ability levels of the audience, and whatever else is necessary, are submitted to the production departments. If they find the assignment feasible, they then produce the programmes for broadcast during the ensuing year.

BBC SCHOOL PROGRAMMES

The BBC's radio and television School Broadcasting Departments, both of which report to the Controller, Educational Broadcasting, are highly independent of other Corporation activities. School Radio, which dates from 1924, occupies a four-storey building just across a broad avenue from Broadcasting House in Central London.[16] It has a full-time staff of about seventy people, including four administrators, thirty-one producers, and thirty-five clerical employees. However, it draws upon the resources of other departments as required, and employs freelance writers, actors, and directors when necessary. It uses the BBC's range of radio studios, including several especially equipped for its needs. Because teaching experience is regarded as more important than radio skill, most of its producers are recruited from teachers and educators rather than from broadcasters.

As long ago as 1947, in response to suggestions from the School Broadcasting Council, and with the encouragement of the Beveridge Committee, the BBC announced plans to experiment with school television.[17] Accordingly, a pilot closed-circuit experiment was conducted in six schools in Middlesex in 1952, after which the Council recommended further programming. Due to national economic problems there was a hiatus of several years, but the Corporation did commence regular school television in the autumn of 1957. Although the ITA had begun regional programming in May 1957, the BBC maintains that in September of that year it inaugurated the world's first permanent nationwide school television service. But the coming of television has not reduced the number of radio programmes; in fact, school radio is doing better than ever. The Corporation regards the two as complementary rather than competitive, each being used to its best advantage.

School Television is located in Ealing, a West London suburb. Its staff, comparable in size to that for School Radio, includes four administrators, eighteen producers, and twenty-one producers' assistants. Programmes are produced in the main studios at the BBC Television Centre.

To support school broadcasting, the BBC spends over £3.2 million of its licence revenue each year, and in addition allocates £450,000 to the School Broadcasting Council.[18] School broadcasting salaries compare favourably with those paid elsewhere in the Corporation, except for some 'name' performers and writers appearing in dramatic and entertainment shows. The BBC told the Annan Committee that 'educational broadcasting in general, whether for young people or for adults, should be a charge on licence fee income', since that way it can be 'editorially independent'.[19] However, the Corporation would 'welcome a reciprocal investment by educational authorities to . . . make possible a more vigorous policy in installing television and radio sets, recorders for both, and adequate supplies of tapes and reliable back-up technical resources'. But the Corporation does not want government funds to directly support programmes.

Teachers' notes, pupils' handbooks, and other supplementary material, prepared jointly by the School Broadcasting Council and the School Broadcasting Departments, are an important accompaniment to school broadcasting.[20] Each term, all listening schools receive free copies of a 30×20 inch bulletin board chart listing all the broadcasts for that term. There also is a free teachers' brochure of some eighty pages outlining the series for the coming year. In 1978–9 the Corporation produced and sold some 375 publications in connection with school radio and television, the total output approximating 6,350,000, including pupils' pamphlets, teachers' notes, and various audio-visual and other aids. These materials were purchased by about 34,500 of the nation's 37,000 schools.[21]

During a typical year, London School Radio produces approximately 1000 and regional radio puts out 500 programmes, for a total of 1500 new programmes annually. In the course of a year BBC radio does approximately 1934 original transmissions and 112 repeats, totaling 2046 transmissions. These programmes are carried nationally by the FM transmitters of Radio 4 during the 28 weeks of the year when schools are in session; that is between the latter part of September and the middle of July. They are on the air Monday to Friday during various periods between 9 a.m. and noon and between 2 and 3 p.m. Most radio programmes are 20 minutes long. In 1978–9, school programmes occupied 471 hours or 6.2 per cent of Radio 4's airtime, or 1.7 per cent of the output for all four services. A London newspaper report of 17 July 1978 stated that the new Managing Director of BBC Radio, Aubrey Singer, had proposed that all secondary school and Open University radio programmes be broadcast at 2 a.m. for tape-recording by interested schools or individuals, thus freeing the broadcast transmitters for general-interest programming during daytime hours.[22] Sooner or later, some such proceedure seems inevitable with television as well as radio programmes. An experiment to this end was conducted during early morning hours in February and March 1979, using radio recording equipment with time switches provided by the BBC.

In addition to these network and regional programmes, the BBC's local radio stations broadcast (on both AM and FM) about 360 school series each year. Each of these stations has a specialist education producer who works with local authorities and teachers in developing programmes and also trains teachers in effective programme utilization.

London School Television turns out 220 and Regional Television does 95 productions annually, for a total of 315.[23] Television normally presents about 700 original transmissions and 690 repeats each year, for a total of some 1390 transmissions. (The reason for the greater number of television than radio repeats is that more schools have audio-than video-tape facilities.) These are aired by BBC 1 between 9 a.m. and noon. Like the radio programmes, they too average 20 minutes in length, although some are as short as 7 and others as long as 30 minutes. In 1978–9, BBC 1 assigned 368 hours to school programmes, which constituted 7.3 per cent of its air-time, or 4 per cent of the time of the two services together.

In view of the large number of schools equipped to make off-the-air recordings, both the BBC and the IBA have encouraged them to do so.[24] For the most part, schools can legally make off-the-air recordings of BBC and IBA School and Further Education (but not Open University) broadcasts, provided they are made at the school site or at a designated resource centre, are used for instructional purposes only, and are destroyed within 3 years of being recorded. Teacher training institutions have approximately the same recording prerogatives, although legally, general-output programmes—that is, those not intended for school or Further Education use—may be recorded only with the prior consent of the broadcasting organizations, the copyright holders, and the performers.

BBC school services are of such extent that only a suggestion can be given as to the range of subjects covered.[25] Programmes for 1978–9 were described in an 88-page octavo-sized brochure, which gave a precis for each series, provided information about radiovision (film strips with accompanying sound tapes), listed related Further Education programmes, offered suggestions for good reception, reviewed the rules for off-the-air recording, and outlined the conditions for purchasing or renting programmes. Programmes were listed in a number of subject categories, of which a few were: art, counselling, drama, English, geography, health, history, humanities, home economics, mathematics, French, German, Italian, European studies, Spanish, music, social studies, religion, and science. There were also programmes for small children and for students with learning disabilities, plus special series for Northern Ireland, Scotland (including Gaelic), and Wales (four in English and fifteen in Welsh.)

In 1977–8, on Mondays from 11 to 11.20 a.m. and Thursdays from 2.14 to 2.35 p.m., the BBC broadcast the American series, *The Electric Company*, produced by the Children's Television Workshop in New York, which it said 'may help children discouraged by reading failure to associate the practice of basic reading skills with pleasure'. * But this was not offered again in 1978–9.

---

* *Radio and Television Annual Programme for Schools and Colleges*, 1977–8, p. 25. Kenneth Fawdry, formerly head of Schools Television, wrote about the companion American program, *Sesame Street*:

We all enjoyed and admired *Sesame Street*; but direct transfer . . . [of it to the BBC] was never on the map. First, the programmes' background and idiom were of course American, and one might surely question without being accused of chauvinism whether

The television series *Watch!* broadcast on Tuesdays from 11 to 11.15 a.m., and repeated on Wednesdays from 2.01 to 2.16 p.m. tried to 'widen the experience of young children by arousing their curiosity and stimulating their imagination'.[26] Normally, the programmes explored a single theme each week through documentary films, stories, and music. Subjects included snails, water power, David and Goliath, and the moon. The radio series, *Listening and Reading*, in two levels for children age 6 and 8, broadcast on Mondays from 2.20 to 2.30 during the autumn and spring terms, was 'an attempt to supply material children will want to read: writing of such power and closeness to their inner and outer concerns that it may show them what reading is for'. The handbook recommended that each programme be recorded off the air 'so that small groups of children can listen to it again and again over a period of time, with the booklets that contain the texts open in front of them'.

Several rather unusual programmes also should be mentioned. On Fridays from 11.30 a.m. to noon, and from 2.35 to 3 p.m., during the summer months, *Preview for Teachers* on television gave teachers a chance to sample programmes for several new series scheduled for the coming year.[27] Beginning in 1969–70, the Corporation introduced sex education programmes for primary schools, consisting initially of a combination of radio vision (film strips with accompanying sound tapes) and television, which grew into a regular television series for several succeeding years.[28] More recently these have constituted three television programmes which 'set out to answer the kind of questions that children of this age might ask: Where do babies come from? How do they get out? What makes them start to grow?'

For slow learners, it was recommended that teachers use programmes for younger children along with *Television Club* for ages 11–14, broadcast on Tuesdays from 2.40 to 3 p.m. with a repeat on Wednesdays from 10 to 10.20 a.m. These programmes 'aim to awaken new interests, to build and develop existing ones and to inspire a wide range of practical and imaginative activities including speech and writing'. Some were dramatized stories about an inner city youth club.[29] Both BBC and IBA have programmes for retarded children, described in a magazine article co-authored by staff members from both organizations.[30] The authors identified retarded children as handicapped slow learners or immigrant

---

this alone did not rule it out as an educational contribution to British children of so tender an age. There were doubts, too, about its educational approach.

One of the Corporation's consultants said that *Sesame Street*

would present a serious challenge to the professional judgement of our teachers, basically because it raises the issue of the permissible or desirable degree of structured conditioning as an educational method, contrasted with methods more concerned with provoking thought and appreciation.

(Kenneth Fawdry, *Everything But Alf Garnett: A Personal View of BBC School Broadcasting*, p. 99.) (For the reaction of the Director of Children's Programmes to *Sesame Street*, see below, p. 309.)

children facing the dual problem of having to learn a new language or of having little education before coming to Britain.

IBA SCHOOL PROGRAMMES

Inevitably, the school services of the IBA are overshadowed by those of the BBC. The Corporation was there first; it had some 30 years during which to establish a well-deserved reputation before the ITA came on to the scene; and it has never ceased to expand and improve its offerings. Nevertheless, the ITA got off to a good start, and by now has earned an excellent record for itself.

IBA school programming is decentralized, like all its productions, and therefore is more difficult to describe than that of the BBC. The Authority's senior staff includes several people involved full-time with school and other educational programmes. There is an Educational Advisory Council of some fifteen members representing various educational groups, and there also are school and adult education committees with some over-lapping membership.

An example of the type of advice received—and acted upon—is provided by one sentence in a recent Authority handbook, which reported that in 1979, certain programmes would 'reflect the advisors' concern that ITV should respond to current national needs, such as help to young people facing the problems of a transition from school to adult life, including employment or the lack of it'.

The Authority, relying on its controls over the contractors, requires all ITV companies to carry *For Schools*, a solid block of school material broadcast Monday to Friday from 9.30 a.m. to 12 noon, produced mainly by the five major companies—ATV, Granada, Thames, London Weekend, and Yorkshire. The various companies specialize in different kinds of programmes: ATV in foreign languages, mathematics and integrated studies; Granada in science programmes, history and health education; Thames continuing the tradition of its antecedent, Rediffusion, in drama, French, and dramatized documentary programmes for school-leavers; and Yorkshire in programmes for very young students.[31] No advertising is allowed during IBA school broadcasts, and there must be a 2-minute insulation period without commercials before, and a 1-minute period after, all such programmes. However, the time devoted to school services may be counted in computing the total amount of advertising time which may be sold (see above, p. 75).

The output of these companies is coordinated by the Network Educational Sub-committee of the ITCA Network Programme Committee, which meets once each month.[32] This subcommittee is also responsible for publishing and distributing programme information and for educational liaison with the EBU and the BBC. Education is one area in which the BBC and the IBA work together closely in order to coordinate planning, avoid scheduling conflicts, and study programme utilization and results.

Strictly speaking, the ITA broadcast school television programmes before the BBC did, although the Corporation conducted a closed-circuit experiment in 1952 and began regular programming in 1957. As it was, programmes produced by

Associated Rediffusion beginning on 13 May 1957 were carried simultaneously in the Midlands by Associated Television.[33] In the same year, Scottish Television began school programmes in central Scotland, and the next year began carrying Associated-Rediffusion programmes. Granada came on the scene in 1959, and Associated Television in 1961.

The companies publish and distribute a wide range of accompanying material. There are bulletin board charts listing current programmes; teachers' handbooks for each series; and for approximately 50 per cent of the programmes, material for students too. Cassette, tapes, and films also are available. The rules for recording ITV programmes off the air parallel those of the BBC. The programme companies observed to the Annan Committee, however, that it will be some time before such recordings can replace live transmissions: 'Unless a national source of free tapes or cassettes becomes available, or funds are provided for their purchase, schools will remain dependent on transmissions, even if equipped for recording.'[34]

During 1975–6, the television programme companies produced more than 750 school programmes in approximately fifty-five network and local series.[35] During 1974–5, ITV reported 276 first transmissions of school broadcasts, taking 75 hours of air-time, and 738 repeat transmissions taking 194.5 hours.[36] In addition to these network programmes, 170 hours were transmitted locally. All told, in 1976–7, ITV companies spent about £2 million on programmes for schools. In 1978–9 the average ITV company transmitted 6 hours 11 minutes of school programmes each week, which approximated 6.25 per cent of its total broadcast hours.[37]

Although ITV's output of school programmes is less than that of the BBC, the service is approached no less seriously, and its quality measures up well to the Corporation's standards. Some of the offerings for 1976–7 illustrate the range of its programmes. For example, the chemistry series, *Experiment*, broadcast Tuesdays from 10.09 to 10.24 a.m. and Fridays from 11.43 to 11.58 a.m., was tied to the 'A' level chemistry syllabus. A combined teachers' and pupils' booklet costing 40p provided a theoretical background for the series. It was recommended that teachers use only those programmes best suited to their needs. Among the topics covered were microanalysis, mass spectrometry, bomb calorimetry, and magnetochemistry. Film recordings of these productions could be rented or purchased from the producer, Granada Television.[38]

Facts for Life, a health education programme for ages 15–18, broadcast alternate weeks on Tuesdays from 9.47 to 10.07 a.m., and Thursdays from 9.42 to 10.02 a.m., dealt with such practical topics as drug-dependency, drinking and smoking, the skin, bone injuries, the heart and lungs, infections, and different methods of contraception. The latter programme, described in the accompanying brochure as making a particular contribution to education for parenthood', covered contraception, growth in the womb, birth, and the early development of a child.

Writers Gallery, for ages 14–18, broadcast Mondays from 10.40 to 11 a.m., presented current writers discussing their own works. *The Land* explored the physical landscape of Britain and man's interaction with it. *Music Scene*, for older pupils, designed for non-music classes and for classes without music specialist teachers, dealt with all kinds of music, popular and serious, old and contemporary. *Looking at Television* told how television is organized, discussed programme theories, reviewed audience measurement methods, and speculated about 'the impact of American television on the rest of the world'. *Exploration Man*, for ages 10 and above, broadcast alternate weeks on Mondays from 10.20 to 10.35 a.m., and Fridays from 10.01 to 10.25 a.m., aimed 'to introduce children to different ways of finding out about man'.[39] For it, the producing company provided a brochure selling for 35p. Subjects included Bar Mitzvah; a comparison of life in the city and the country; archaeology; and the study of an athlete's performance. A teacher's manual available at 35p suggested how teachers might use the series. The four pages about the programme on archeology, *Digging Up Man*, contained a half-page summary of the broadcast, offered general comments about the programme, gave suggestions as to how it might be used, and provided a list of follow-up discussions and activities.

Although most IBA educational programmes are prepared for network distribution by the five major companies, there are other programmes from these, as well as the smaller companies, for their respective regions.[40] Yorkshire Television produced *Leaving School* 'to take the sting out of prospective unemployment for hundreds of Yorkshire school-leavers'; Ulster Television turned out *Let's Look at Ulster*, reviewing some local industries; Scottish Television's *Time to Think* was intended to help English teachers prepare students for advanced examinations; HTV in Wales and West England developed programmes for schools in Welsh as well as in English; and Grampian, a small company in northwest Scotland, did Britain's first sex education series for junior high-school pupils.

Considerable research has accompanied both the BBC and IBA school services, one example being a study completed in 1976 of a French-language series, *Le Nouvel Arrivé*, produced by Thames Television.[41] This series used the device of having an English schoolboy spend 3 weeks with a French family. Not surprisingly, the author of the study, after finding the series generally helpful, emphasied that it was 'not the programmes themselves but the role played by the teacher in exploiting them which is the determining factor in the amount of benefit which pupils derive from them'.

The general verdict of all concerned is that school broadcasting in the United Kingdom is a great success. The fact that 95 per cent of all schools use radio and 92 per cent television, and that the 34,500 schools buying publications and related material purchase 8,9000,000 copies from the BBC alone in the course of a year, surely indicates wide acceptance.[42] The Annan Committee, however, wanted more definite proof of school broadcasting's value. It noted that 'broadcasters and leading educational bodies told us that they were convinced of . . . [the] effectiveness' of such broadcasting, but went on to observe that 'there was little research material to substantiate this act of faith', and accordingly suggested further inquiries to determine whether or not broadcasting really was 'an effective educational medium'.[43]

FURTHER EDUCATION ON THE BBC

Although the BBC has been broadcasting adult education programmes for many years, the term 'Further Education' was adopted only in the late 1950s, and then in reflection of national terminology rather than of any change in programme philosophy. The Pilkington Committee in 1962 reported that various groups had urged it to recommend an increased number of such programmes. It judged the Corporation's radio output in this category to be 'very good', and noted that a start—'but only a start'—had been made in television adult education by BBC and ITV. Thereafter, the committee regretted that the Postmaster-General 'would not agree that adult educational broadcasts should not count towards the permitted total of hours of broadcasting' and urged that the rules be changed accordingly.[44]

Thereafter, the first of the two White Papers on the Pilkington Report said that because the government favoured more adult education programming, it was 'prepared to authorize at once additional hours for the . . . television services, provided these are used . . . for programmes for the education of adults', and developed by the BBC and the ITA according to a formula arrived at 'in consultation with the educational authorities'.[45]

Five months later, in a second White Paper, the government accepted the criteria drawn up by the two broadcasting groups, which it quoted as follows:

> Educational television programmes for adults are programmes (other than school broadcasts) arranged in series and planned in consultation with appropriate educational bodies to help viewers towards a progressive mastery or understanding of some skill or body of knowledge.

Therefore, the White Paper continued, since the government had accepted this formula, it would 'consider applications [from both the BBC and the ITA] for additional hours of television which are consistent with the formula'. But 'they should cooperate as fully as possible in preparing their proposals so that the greatest benefit may be obtained from the new opportunities'.

A decade later, a working party representing the IBA, some of its advisors, and its television programme companies, submitted another definition of 'adult education', as the Authority prefers to call it, based upon a definition developed by the EBU. However, this did not differ fundamentally from the White Paper definition.[46]

> Adult education programmes are programmes aimed at leading adults to a progressive comprehension of a body of knowledge or acquisition of a skill in a defined field, which will contribute to the development of the individual and his understanding of a changing society, or equip him better for participation in community life. The attainment of this aim can normally best be achieved:
>
> (a) when the programmes are organised in series
> (b) when during or after transmission the viewer is encouraged to adopt a 'participating' attitude towards the subject matter of the programme

(c) when the programmes are reinforced by other learning opportunities
     (booklets, inquiry service, written documents, correspondence courses,
     study or discussion groups, and other organised local opportunities).

These programmes should always be planned and devised in consultation with
appropriately qualified advisers.

Early adult education broadcasts in the United Kingdom involved elaborately
organized group listening activities.[47] Complex arrangements were made to
organize these groups, for which the BBC presented talks on current and often
controversial subjects at peak evening listening hours. But the number of listeners
remained small in proportion to radio's potential, the total group listening audience
at any one time never exceeding 20,000, even though over-all, radio audiences in
the 1930s reached into the millions. In spite of enthusiastic support from adult
educators, therefore, the group listening movement was judged to have failed.

The BBC began its most recent phase of Further Education programming in
October 1963 on BBC 1—then its only television service, expanding these
offerings in April of the following year coincident with the opening of BBC 2.[48] In
1964, Further Education broadcasts were scheduled for 1 hour each weekday
evening on Radio 3, with weekend repeats on Radio 4. In 1965 the Corporation set
up Further Education departments in both television and radio, and replaced its
Adult Education Liaison Committee and Higher Education Working Party with a
Further Education Advisory Council, corresponding to the Council for School
Broadcasting. In 1967, when the first BBC local radio stations were opened, they
began adult education programming for their respective localities. During an
average year, the Corporation spends approximately £2.1 million on its Further
Education output.[49]

The structure and organization of Further Education resemble those for school
broadcasting.[50] The heads of the separate radio and television production
departments report to the Controller, Educational Broadcasting. Further Education, Radio, is housed near Broadcasting House in central London, while Further
Education, Television, is in Villiers House in Ealing in West London. Although
there are no Further Education production departments in Scotland, Wales, or
Northern Ireland, these areas have programmes of that type, which are the
responsibility of their respective Regional Broadcasting Councils, rather than of
the Further Education Advisory Council in London. The Further Education
production staff, exclusive of producers' assistants and secretaries, consists of
fourteen radio and fourty-six television employees.[51] Six Education Officers
attached to the Further Education Advisory Council are charged with encouraging
the use of the broadcasts by both individuals and collegiate institutions.

Basic procedures resemble those described above for school broadcasting.
Long-range planning is done jointly by the Advisory Council and the production
departments. Programmes are publicized through brochures and study guides; and
quarterly inserts in the *Radio Times* ('Look Listen Learn') list the main
programmes for the ensuing 3 months.

In 1978–9, the BBC provided over 100 television and radio Further Education
series.[52] In addition, Scotland had one and Wales two series. In that year, the

Corporation offered 132 hours of Further Education on Radio 3 (1.8 per cent of its air-time), and 197 hours on Radio 4 (2.6 per cent of its air-time), for a total of 332 hours, constituting 0.9 per cent of all radio network time. (Further Education uses Radio 3's medium-wave transmitters.) BBC 1 devoted 234 hours (4.6 per cent of its air-time) to Further Education, BBC 2 190 hours (4.6 per cent of its air-time), for a total of 424 hours (4.6 per cent of all BBC television time).

Further Education series announced for 1977–8 were grouped in ten categories: day-time series for college and group use, work and training, languages, literacy, arts, music, science and environment, community and public affairs, home and family, and leisure time.[53] Most Further Education programmes are intended primarily for reception by individuals at home rather than in institutions of higher learning, although a few are planned for use that way In 1977–8, three series were designed especially for colleges of further education: *Engineering Craft Studies*, *Focus* (general education), and *The Caterers*. The Work and Training group, comprising thirteen series, covered business education; nursing; *Work Talk*, for workers who speak little English; *A Woman's Place*, examining the role and status of women in society today; and *Teaching Music*, for instrumental teachers. Grouped as Community and Public Affairs were programmes on economics, the sociology of the city, disadvantaged groups in society, the problems of South Africa, and *Morals Today*. The language group had one series to help Asian women learn English; programmes on German, Russian, French, Spanish and Welsh; and a unique series consisting of the retransmission of television newscasts from French and German stations.

In addition to formal programmes in series, there were informal television presentations on such varied subjects as toymaking, minor sports, dressmaking, programmes for the over-60s, vegetable and flower gardening, health and vocational training.[54] Other subjects included history and contemporary affairs, communications media and anthropology. Radio topics included: home and family (*Family Matters, Families Crisis* and the *One-Parent Family*); work and training (*Why Work? Who Manages?* and *Organising the Organisation*); languages; the *Police in Britain*; and *The Parliamentary Process*.[55]

The BBC offers such a wealth of Further Education material that it is difficult to describe adequately its range and nature. One programme which impressed me was an interview on BBC 2 with Lord Avon (Anthony Eden). Although based on a book he had just written about his first years in politics, the broadcast contained few references to the publication, it being in the main an interesting conversation with a famous man, which will have considerable archival value.

The weekly film series, *Horizon*, which observed its 12th year in 1975–6, dealt with the entire field of science. One evening from 9.50 to 10.40 p.m. on BBC 2, I saw *Why Did Stuart Die?* which dealt with crib deaths. The mother of a deceased child was interviewed, and there was a summary of post-mortem findings, all to produce a well-done programme on an important subject. Quite different was *What's Wrong with the Sun?* broadcast from 9.50 to 10.40 p.m. The subject of the programme—the *Radio Times* gave it a quarter page that week—was the sun and how it is changing. One Monday from 9.50 to 10.40 p.m., *A Lesson for Teachers* summarized recent research on contrasting styles of teaching in Britain. The first part of the programme was filmed in a progressive school and the second in a more conventional school, with parents' comments after each section. Then the results of the research were cited, which favoured the conservative school's approach. This programme, among other things, was very timely, since the research on which it was based had been released very shortly before the broadcast.[56]

The Corporation has always had medical programmes.[57] Radio programmes on medicine are produced by the Science Unit of Documentary Programmes, while those for television are the responsibility of the Science and Features Department. Radio averages more than one programme per week, subjects varying from the common cold and tooth decay to 'pulling the plug' on terminally ill patients.

Some television programmes deal entirely with medical problems, while others are included in general series like *In Tomorrow's World* (transplantation, backache, pregnancy tests); *Tonight* (alcoholism, childless couples, psychopaths); and *Nationwide* (birth by induction, smoking, heart transplants). One evening from 9.50 to 10.20 I saw *Inside Medicine*, one in a series investigating the way in which medicine plays an increasingly important role in our lives. Each week the programme dealt with a different aspect of medicine, on this occasion with the female menopause. Several physicians, including a young woman, took part, and good questions were asked and answered.

Among the refresher courses for professionals have been some for medical doctors. In January 1965, in response to suggestions from the Association for the Study of Medical Education, the BBC began a series of monthly programmes for physicians.[58] By the end of 1968, forty-one half-hour programme had been transmitted. Research showed that, among other things, between 25 and 40 per cent of those physicians with sets capable of receiving the series (it was on BBC 2 in the London area only) watched the programme.

At the request of the BBC's General Advisory Council, the Audience Research Department surveyed public reactions to *The Changing Face of Medicine*, three 50-minute documentaries broadcast by BBC 1 on successive Thursdays in November.[59] It was found that those who were squeamish about medical matters, and particularly upset when seeing surgical operations on television, were considerably less likely to watch the series than were less squeamish people; 70 per cent of the general practitioners surveyed favoured medical programmes on television; the middle class were more apt to watch than were working-class viewers; most viewers were between the ages of 30 and 49; and viewers of the entire series acquired some desirable concepts as a result of watching.

IBA ADULT EDUCATION PROGRAMMES

Like the BBC, ITV in 1962 took advantage of the change in the regulations about broadcasting hours to develop a number of Further Education programmes— although the Authority refers to them as Adult Education. Despite some good work, however, the Authority approaches Adult Education somewhat more gingerly than does the BBC—an understandable position, in view of its commercial support basis—and writes about Adult Education in terms designed to disarm those viewers who dislike—or think they dislike—such programmes.

Under the title *Learning Through Television*, the Authority in its 1976 handbook said:

> The mention of educational programmes may provoke a shiver of discomfort and a 'not for me, thank you' type of response from some viewers. Yet despite any aversion to the more formal and structured approach to learning, the general output of television makes significant contributions to the education of a large part of the audience.[60]

In its 1977 handbook, the Authority stated that while the title, Adult Education,

> sounds formal, it is hoped the programmes are not. They are designed to be as entertaining as possible to a wide range of people, including those who cannot get to classes. They are intended, though, to be more than entertainment; and it is hoped people will be motivated into taking part, into doing something, into following up.

In their presentation to the Annan Committee, the programme companies, under the subhead 'Dilemmas', raised questions which could indicate a lack of enthusiasm.[61] After asking—and not answering—the question, 'What is an adult education programme?' they continued: 'Another permanent dilemma is the audience. Should its apparent interests be met or should it be persuaded that it has interests of which it is unaware?' The companies went on to observe: 'Adult education is not only an area of minority interest but an area of minority interests within that minority. Since 1963, there has been a decline in the number of ITV series designed to assist small groups of students achieve specific educational objectives', in favour of programmes for larger minorities. 'The final dilemma', said the companies, 'is this: if the term "adult education" is interpreted in its broadest sense, to what extent should the viewer be conscious of it as a concept?' And the question was answered: 'ITV's educational broadcasters believe that the best placing for these programmes is on the network of general output with no distinguishing label'. Yet, whether or not it has doubts about such programmes, the Authority is taking an affirmative approach to developing them.

Comments from the BBC, too, have shown concern about frightening away these audiences most needing education. It already has been pointed out that the Corporation changed the name of its adult education periods on Radio 3 from *Study on Three* to *Lifelines* (Which is no longer broadcast, however), in the hope of attracting more listeners with low motivation. The former Director-General, Charles Curran, in a speech given in 1972, explained that in addition to educational broadcasts of a formal nature, the Corporation tried 'to provide a service of information and education of a much less formal kind by means of its general broadcasting services'.[62]

Curran went on to quote some lines written by the first Director-General, John Reith, in 1923:

A closer inspection of the word 'entertainment' is sufficient to show how incomplete is the ordinarily accepted meaning. To entertain means to occupy agreeably.... Enjoyment may be sought not with a view to returning refreshed to the day's work, but as a mere means of passing the time, and therefore of wasting it, or of relieving the tedium of life which is induced by deficiency, mental or physical. On the other hand, it may be part of a systematic and sustained endeavour to recreate, to build up knowledge, experience and character, perhaps even in the face of obstacles. Broadcasting enjoys the cooperation of the leaders of that section of the community whose duty and pleasure it is to give relaxation to the rest, but it also is aided by the discoverers of the intellectual forces which are moulding humanity, who are striving to show how time may be occupied not only agreeably but well.

The airing of a good many adult education programmes by Independent Television is assured by the requirement written into the contracts of all the companies that they must 'broadcast on a regular pattern educational programmes for adults planned in consultation with the Authority and its education advisors, and designed to help viewers towards a progressive mastery or understanding of some skill or body of knowledge'.[63]

In their presentation to the Annan Committee, the companies stated that following the de-restriction of broadcasting hours in 1972, they all 'gave an undertaking to the IBA that adult education programmes would not be swept aside by the expanded output of general programming. This committed all regions to continue to transmit at least three hours of formally validated adult education each week. Most companies have been screening more than the minimum.'[64] The companies indicated that the target audience for such programmes consisted of 'those who, whether from choice or force of circumstance, had given up full-time education at the earliest opportunity'. While the BBC 'with an appropriate subsidy', developed programmes for the Open University, ITV concentrated 'on the complementary activity of broadening the general education of early school-leavers and the enhancement of their aptitude to enjoy life and leisure. Recent research by both IBA and BBC has shown that a large majority of the target audience, those who left school at fourteen or fifteen, regard ITV as "their channel".'

The IBA senior staff involved with school programmes have similar responsibilities for adult education broadcasts. They are assisted by an Adult Education Advisory Committee, subsidiary to the Educational Advisory Council and consisting of representative adult educators. In addition, the programme companies have their own adult education staffs and advisory groups. The Network Educational Subcommittee coordinates proposals to avoid omission and duplication, and also has coordination meetings with representatives of the BBC. During 1978–9, the average ITV company devoted 3 hours 7 minutes, or 3 per cent of its weekly time, to adult education programmes.[65] Between September 1974 and August 1975, ITV had 253 first transmissions (118.25 hours), and 85 repeat transmissions (36.75 hours). These were scheduled throughout the day, including peak evening hours. In 1974–5, ITV spent about £690,000 on these programmes.

The ITA began regular adult education programming with *Midnight Oil* in the summer of 1962.[66] In January of the following year the morning *Sunday Session* was added. More recently London Weekend Television has broadcast literacy classes to assist people with reading difficulties to pass their driving tests.[67] In *Don't Ask Me*, botanist David Bellamy dealt with down-to-earth scientific topics, answering such questions as 'Why is my reflection upside down on one side of the spoon but right way up on the other?' Other questions were, 'Why is yawning catching?', 'Why do cats purr?' and 'Why do wheels on stage coaches seem to go backwards in films and on television?'

Bellamy has continued to be a regular ITV contributor. In 1979 the IBA referred to his series, *Botanic Man*, as the 'major [adult education] success of the year'.[68] Dealing with evolution and ecology, the Thames Television series explained such subjects as mitosis, zygotes and the nitrogen cycle, and was accompanied by a National Extension College Correspondence Course that brought 3500 inquiries. Over 30,000 copies of a hardback book for the series were sold. Reporting the audience response to such a series—it ranked among the top twenty programmes during its 10-week run—the Authority wrote: 'This is an unprecedented achievement for adult education and one that confirms the belief that when this sector of programming is given talent, resources and attractive scheduling it can achieve large and appreciative audiences comparable to those attracted to less demanding ''shows''.'

A Matter of Life broadcast in 1977, was a medical documentary trilogy. The first one, *It's a Bit Frightening*, dealt with a surgical operation that destroyed a part of a woman's brain through electric shocks in order to curb her violent behaviour. The programme raised the question of whether it is ethical to change someone's personality by neurosurgery. The second documentary, *The Boy in the Bubble*, described the life of a child in Houston, Texas, who lived in a large plastic bubble because a shortage of white blood cells left him without resistence to disease. The final programme surveyed the current status of medical practice in general.

Other programmes, certainly 'informational' if not 'educational', have included *Disappearing World*, about science, and *Survival* on Wildlife. In *Being a Child* a psychiatrist discussed points of view on adolescence. I watched with interest programmes in a long-running Yorkshire Television series on science. One was about sheepdogs, based on animal behaviour studies by a Nobel prizewinner, which concluded that dogs' skill in sheep-herding derived not from training but from inherited wolf-pack behaviour. A programme on microsurgery showed how British surgeons have transplanted toes and restored sight and hearing. My comment was: 'A fascinating programme. Operation done with a microscope'.

More recently ITV has been emphasizing programmes to assist young people make the transition from school to work, reflecting the recommendations of a study group including both BBC and IBA broadcasters, a foundation, and a government agency. There is the *London Weekend Show*, described in the 1979 handbook as a 'features/current affairs magazine programme [which] covers a range of topics, from . . . the recruitment policies of the youth wing of the National Front . . . to the activities of the latest punk rock bands . . .'. More specialised were *It's Your*

Future (Thames Television) and *Making a Living* (Yorkshire), the latter 'intended to help young people to understand industrial and political life'.

THE OPEN UNIVERSITY

The United Kingdom's Open University is the most elaborate educational project anywhere in the world utilizing radio and television as instructional tools. Originally known as the University of the Air, it was renamed the Open University, partly to emphasize that it is open to all adult students, and partly because broadcasting—originally its core—was later integrated with independent study to the point where broadcasting assumed a smaller—though still important—role.

The Open University is an entirely new, different, and autonomous university. It is not an amalgam of other institutions, although it works closely with many of them.[69] It was created to enable working adults, aged 21 years and over, to work towards baccaleaureate and postgraduate degrees, or to achieve short-term educational objectives. It is not primarily a system of teaching by radio and television, but rather a new approach to higher education, which utilizes independent study, radio listening, television viewing, and occasional courses in residence. In 1980 there were over 70,000 Open University students in Britain, and some 21,000 had graduated from its courses.

Walter Perry, the Open University's first Vice-Chancellor, has written:

The concept of the Open University evolved from the convergence of three major postwar educational trends. The first of these concerns developments in the provision for adult education, the second the growth of educational broadcasting and the third the political objective of promoting the spread of egalitarianism in education.[70]

This new project was first mentioned with the title University of the Air in a campaign speech by Labour leader Harold Wilson 8 September 1963. After he became Prime Minister the following year, a government committee headed by Jenny Lee, MP, later Secretary for Education and Science, and now Baroness Lee of Asheridge, which included several educators and one broadcaster, made an inquiry, and in February 1966 issued a White Paper, *A University of the Air*.[71] Among other things this said: 'From the outset it must be made clear that there can be no question of offering to students a make-shift project inferior in quality to other universities. That would defeat its whole purpose, as its status will be determined by the quality of its teaching.' In September 1967 a committee, including some distinguished educators and a few broadcasters, was appointed to draw up plans for an Open University. Its report was published early in 1969.

The committee summarized its objectives as being 'to provide opportunities, at both undergraduate and postgraduate level, of higher education to all those, who for any reason, have been or are being precluded from achieving their aims through an existing institution of higher education'. The intention, continued the report, was not to compete with existing institutions, but rather to supplement their efforts.[72]

The University is interested mainly in students over 21 years of age, since other opportunities are available for young people between 16 and 21. In addition to serving adults who did not complete their educations, the Open University provides refresher courses for workers in industry, along with non-technical and cultural information for the general public. Another of its objectives is to facilitate movement among and within occupations, thus breaking the rigid structure which often results from curtailed educational opportunities during a person's early years.

The charter of the Open University, awarded 1 April 1969, created it as a new institution set up exclusively to administer this one project. Since the initial announcement of the Open University was met with severe criticism, the administrative officers and staff were chosen in the hope of winning both public and educator support.[73]

The first Vice-Chancellor (equivalent to a president or chancellor in the United States) was Professor Walter Perry, previously vice-principal of the University of Edinburgh, a prestigious member of the national academic community. The principal members of the academic staff are engaged full-time, and receive salaries comparable to those in other national universities, rather than being drawn from various institutions for part-time contributions. The University has its own publication department, since a great deal of printed study material is distributed. Headquarters are in Milton Keynes, 50 miles from London, in order to provide close contact with BBC production facilities, and to facilitate transportation to all parts of the country. Thirteen regional offices are located in various parts of Britain. When Open University broadcasts began, they were produced in Alexandra Palace (see above, p. 97), but in 1979 work was completed on an Open University production centre at Milton Keynes, capable of turning out 400 radio and 400 television programmes each year.[74]

Student applications were received beginning in January 1970, and teaching began 1 year later. Approximately 250 instructors are permanently attached to the University, along with some 4000 part-time tutors and counsellors, most of them teachers in other institutions of higher learning.

A typical one-credit Open University course consists of 34 weekly units of work, each requiring from 10 to 15 hours of study, attendance at a 1-week residential summer school, and a 3-hour final examination.[75] The completion of six undergraduate credits qualifies a student for a BA degree; of eight such credits for a BA honours degree. At the normal rate of progress, it takes an average student 6 years to earn a BA, and eight to receive an honours degree.

The courses fall into what the British call 'faculties'—Arts, Mathematics, Science, Social Sciences, Technology, and Educational Studies. Students are expected to spend approximately 65 per cent of their time studying textbooks and recommended readings; 10 per cent listening to and watching radio and television programmes; 15 per cent in counselling sessions, either at study centres or in summer schools; and 10 per cent doing written assignments and taking final examinations. Broadcasting, obviously, represents a small part of the total project, although that does not mean that the programmes are carelessly developed or lack merit, and, indeed, the programmes take up 20 per cent of the total costs of the Open University.*

There are about 70,000 Open University students—the maximum number that can be efficiently served—and some 21,000 have graduated.[76] Men outnumber women by a ratio of about three to two. One-third of the registrants are teachers, 13 per cent housewives, 10 per cent technical personnel, 11 per cent from the professions and the arts, 9 per cent clerical and office workers, and the remainder from a variety of occupations. Thus far, the Open University has not attained its objective of attracting a high proportion of early school-leavers and low-income workers as students, although progress is being made in that direction. As the BBC put it: 'The movement from the more affluent and better qualified occupations to tne less affluent and less qualified is certainly slow; but it is discernable.'

Open University costs are considerably less than those of traditional instruction, since the overall expense for an Open University student is about half of that incurred by a student attending a conventional residential university. It costs an average of £400 for an Open University student to complete the work for a BA degree. The government's Department of Education and Science covers most of the costs, with BBC costs amounting to about one-sixth of the total. All of the Open University's radio and television production and transmission is done by the BBC, for which the Corporation received £5,058,000 in 1978–9.[77] (The entire budget for the Open University is about £33 million per year.)

Under the agreement between the University and the Corporation, the University has ultimate responsibility for substantive matters and the BBC for production, although it is understood that there must be close coordination at all stages between teachers and producers if successful broadcasting is to result.[78] Accordingly, academicians and producers work as teams, their size varying from a few to as many as twenty members, depending upon the nature of the project. The production staff attends preliminary planning sessions, which may run from 6 months to a year before production is begun, and thus are involved from the very beginning, rather than only after substantive matters have been determined. Thereafter, a small working group, consisting typically of one academician, one BBC producer, and one educational technologist, sees the series through recording. In theory, final control over the programme content is held by the Open University, though, of course, in an extreme case, the BBC could refuse to carry certain programmes if, in its opinion, they failed to meet minimum technical and programme standards.

The broadcasting staff, including some 370 people plus assistants and secretaries, are all BBC employees.[79] Departing from the usual procedure, these people may work in radio, television, and film, instead of concentrating on just one medium. Since many of them were chosen for their teaching backgrounds, they

* Perry, p. 268. Inevitably, with television accounting for 20 per cent of the expenditures but only 5 per cent of student study time, the question has come up 'Is it worth it?' Vice-Chancellor Perry believes 'that the answer must be "Yes" ', but the question surely will be periodically reviewed in the future.

include scientists, mathematicians, social scientists, and educators. Most of them have college degrees, and many are experienced in adult education.

For the Open University the BBC normally produces some 300 new radio and 300 new television programmes each year, and transmits 2500 radio and 2500 television programmes, including repeats, during 34 weeks of each year. This adds up to approximately 36 hours of television and 30 hours of radio time every week. Finding air-time for Open University programmes is not easy for the BBC, partly because its own Further Education offerings seek additional time. From the very beginning, Jennie Lee hoped that ultimately the fourth television channel would be available solely or partially for Open University programmes, and this was envisaged by the Annan Committee in its recommendation for a new authority to administer the fourth channel; but the assignment of that channel to the IBA has left open the likelihood of its carrying many Open University broadcasts. In the spring of 1980, the radio programmes were broadcast by the FM transmitters of Radio 3, Monday to Friday from 6 to 7 a.m.; on Saturday from 6 to 8 a.m.; and on Sunday from 6 to 8 a.m. and from midnight to 1 a.m. The FM transmitters of Radio 4 were pressed into service weekdays from 11.30 p.m. to 12.10 a.m.; Saturday from 9.05 to 10.30 a.m., from 11.20 a.m. to noon, and from 2 to 6 p.m., and Sunday from 7.15 to 10.15 a.m. In 1978–9, Radio 3 devoted 816 hours or 11.3 per cent of its air time to Open University programmes, and Radio 4 274 hours or 3.6 per cent of its time, the total being 1090 hours or 3.9 per cent of all radio network time.[80]

In the spring of 1980 BBC 1 carried Open University material (on the UHF band only) Monday to Friday from 6.40 to 7.55 a.m., and on Saturday and Sunday from 7.40 to 8.30 a.m. BBC 2 had Open University programmes Monday to Friday from 6.40 to 7.55 a.m. and from 4.50 to 5.40 p.m.; on Saturday from 7.40 a.m. to 1.5 p.m. and 1.30 to 3.10 p.m. and on Sunday from 7.40 a.m. to 5.15 p.m. In 1978–9, these programmes took up 241 hours (4.8 per cent) on BBC 1 and 1001 hours (24.3 per cent) on BBC 2, for a total of 1242 hours (13.6 per cent) of BBC television network time.

Not surprisingly, BBC television officials object strongly to the assignment of that much good viewing time to programmes that, despite unquestioned education merit, are of very limited audience appeal, and their feelings have been intensified by the financial cutbacks forced on the Corporation in 1980, as well as by the advent of ITV 2. How can they compete—with a reduced programme budget—if they must devote 36 hours a week to Open University programmes? A partial solution, of course, would be for ITV 2 to carry some of these programmes. The next few years surely will see much earnest discussion of that point.

It should be emphasized again, however, that other learning aides besides broadcasting are employed. Thus, for a history course on *War and Society*, the Open University recommended a dozen books, ranging from a specially written textbook to collections of documents. There also were fifteen films, lasting about 25 minutes each, and fifteen audio-tape cassettes. A foundation course in science had twenty-five suggested readings, about as many films, and some fifteen audio-tapes, along with a Home Experiment Kit containing over 100 pieces of apparatus, including glassware, a chemical balance, a microscope, and a colorimeter. About two-thirds of the students watch the television and one-third hear the radio programmes.

While in London in the spring of 1976, I watched a number of Open University telecasts. A 25-minute film on *Democracy in India* dealt with population, classes, poverty, and life. Like most Open University programmes, it was quiet but well done. Another effective programme filmed on location in West Berlin was about architecture. Interesting was a programme on solving equations, which instead of being technical, reviewed the life of a famous mathematican in the Middle Ages. It told how great mathematicians often vied with each other in public contests. Another programme, about Parliamentary elections in the 1830s, was based on contemporary prints by Hogarth and others.

Personality and Learning was a short drama about an altercation between a student and a teacher. The incident was shown, in turn, through the eyes of the teacher, the student, and an onlooker, after which it was pointed out that each emphasized those aspects of the conflict which supported his contention. There also was a film about land use in the city of Chicago. Filmed in Chicago, it carefully reviewed different features of the city, which, it said, was located on Lake 'Mitchigan', a surprising mispronunciation, in view of the BBC's usual meticulous accuracy.

Some Open University courses have been offered experimentally in various parts of the United States using the same books and audio-visual materials prepared for students in Britain.[81] Among the institutions involved have been the Universities of Maryland, Houston, Southern Illinois, and California, and Rutgers University in New Jersey. Although general reaction has been favourable, the Open University has been less successful in the United States than in the United Kingdom, because of the countries' quite different educational systems, and because of problems encountered in coordinating the many aspects of Open University instruction—readings, broadcasts, and contacts with advisors—for which the Open University maintains elaborate machinery in Britain. Open University materials also are used in Canada, Australia, New Zealand, and South East Africa; a few of its more elaborate television productions have been broadcast as general documentaries in some European Countries and in Australia; and a Centre for International Cooperation and Services has been set up to coordinate some of its international activities.

Britain's educational broadcasts rank among its best productions. The British Broadcasting Company and the successor Corporation enthusiastically accepted their obligation to educate both in school and at home, thus establishing a precedent and developing basic skills on which later generations could build. What began as a fine radio service led to an equally excellent television output by both the BBC and ITV, while radio educational programming was maintained at almost its pre-television level. Once again Britain has shown how the right combination of basic objectives, good leadership, and adequate funding, operating under a system that stresses programme service rather than profits, can develop broadcasting as a public service with a high level of attainment.

15 Religious Broadcasting

In Britain, religious broadcasting is almost as old as radio itself. The British Broadcasting company made its first religious broadcast on Christmas Eve 1922, 6 weeks after beginning regular daily operations, and several weeks before receiving its first Licence on 18 January 1923,[1] and a short religious service has been broadcast by the Corporation every day since January 1928. The fact that the first director, John Reith, was the son of a Scottish minister undoubtedly contributed to the emphasis placed first by the Company and then by the Corporation on religion.

Religious broadcasting—along with other religious activities—continues, despite periodic reiterations of despair over a presumed lack of public interest. A 1919 report concluded that 'there is [now] little or no life in the Church. . . . It is an antiquated institution, standing by dogmas, expressed in archaic language, and clearly out of touch with modern thought and living experience'.[2] In 1924, John Reith wrote that in many circles the observance of the Sabbath has 'come in large measure to be regarded as an archaic absurdity . . . and [as an] unwarranted interference with the liberties of the people'.[3]

In 1977, the Annan Committee noted that despite widespread discouragement over declining church attendance, more people went to church on Sunday than to football matches on Saturday afternoon.[4] It continued:

> We do not belong to a country where all the springs of religious life have dried up. The evangelical movement in the Church of England and the free churches is by no means moribund: of all the witnesses who gave evidence to us the fiercest in commitment was a practising Christian. . . . The eternal questions which religions answer each in its own way are not only being asked by those who practise some form of religion: numbers of disbelievers have been exploring them and are seen and heard doing so in television and radio programmes.

LEGISLATIVE REQUIREMENTS

The BBC is not legally obliged to do religious broadcasting, nor is there any reference to its having a religious advisory committee. But there never have been many formal rules for the Corporation, and in any case, its early dedication to religion made such requirements unnecessary.

As usual, the regulations for the IBA are much more detailed. Taken together, the debates on the Television Act of 1954 and several clauses in the law clearly indicated Parliament's fear of the possibility of sponsored religious broadcasting and of denominational competition. Although the Authority is not legally required to broadcast religious material, the stipulation that its schedules must 'maintain . . . a proper balance and a wide range in their subject matter', taken together with the fact that one of its original contracting companies (Associated Television) was anxious to produce religious programmes, resulted in regular religious programming from the very beginning.[5]

The original 1954 and all succeeding legislation has required the Authority to appoint or arrange for the assistance of . . . a committee representative of the main streams of religious thought . . . to give advice' about any religious programmes or 'publications issued by the Authority'.[6]

But religious material is not to be the subject of any advertisements: 'No advertisement shall be . . . inserted by or on behalf of any body the objects whereof are wholly or mainly of a religious . . . nature, and no advertisement shall be permitted which is directed towards any religious . . . end. . . .'[7] Finally, the Authority is to draw up regulations 'as to the classes of broadcasts . . . in which advertisements may not be inserted', of which the only one specified is 'any religious service'. Accordingly, the Authority forbids middle commercials in religious broadcasts (and in some others—see pp. 74–5) and requires an insulation period with no advertising, 2 minutes before and 1 minute after such programmes.[8]

It obviously was Parliament's expectation, therefore, that the IBA would broadcast religious programmes. Some critics had feared that a commercial broadcasting system would place emphasis first on profits and second on service, for which reason most of the major church groups opposed the creation of the ITA. Consequently, once the law was passed, the Authority saw the importance of serving religion well, if it was to survive future legislative tests.

ADVISORY COMMITTEES

Religious broadcasting is one—the Central Appeals Advisory Committee is the other—example of a single committee—the Central Religious Advisory Committee (CRAC)—serving both the BBC and the IBA. The Sunday Committee, formed in 1923, was the first of the BBC's national advisory committees.[9] Its name was changed to CRAC in 1927, and it has continued ever since to advise the Corporation. During the Parliamentary debate on the Television Bill in 1953, it was strongly urged that the new ITA, rather than setting up its own committee, should use the BBC's CRAC, thus ensuring uniformity of programme policy.[10] This was done, with the BBC continuing to appoint the committee, although after informal consultation with the Authority. Since 1972, the appointments have been formally joint. The BBC provides the secretariat, although at joint sessions the secretariat is shared.

But sharing has not always worked smoothly. In February 1962, the BBC told the Pilkington Committee that the time had come to end the dual arrangement, because the committee was devoting so much attention to televison that radio broadcasting had 'come to be regarded as only of secondary interest, whereas in fact the Corporation's religious output in its sound services is much greater than in television and no less important'.[11] Although the Pilkington Committee recommended that each organization have its own advisory group, and that the Authority no longer be obliged to appoint such a committee, subsequent legislation required the Authority to continue its religious advisory committee, although leaving it up to the two broadcasting agencies as to whether there should be a joint or separate committees.[12]

Both the BBC and the IBA concurred with CRAC on this point, although the Annan Committee was not convinced, and recommended separate panels for each.[13] But CRAC disagreed: 'CRAC does not regard itself as an immutable or unavoidable part of religious broadcasting, but it seems right to its members that ... it or a similar body with an advisory function, should have oversight of religious broadcasting as a whole'.

The BBC now supplements CRAC with separate committees of its own for Northern Ireland, Scotland, and Wales, while the IBA has a six-member panel of advisors, representing the Church of England, the Free Churches, the Roman Catholic Church and the churches in Northern Ireland, Scotland, and Wales.[14] In addition, each programme company has religious advisors from its own area, and there is a Network Religious Subcommittee to provide liaison among companies, which also allocates Sunday Morning Worship air-time.

At present CRAC has about thirty members, of whom twenty-four represent the mainstream churches—the Church of England, the Church of Scotland, the Church in Wales, the Roman Catholic Church, the Baptist, Methodist, and the United Reformed Churches.[15] Once consisting entirely of clerics from the mainstream churches, under the chairmanship of a Church of England Bishop, the membership of CRAC has grown steadily more mixed, ever since the Pilkington Report in 1962 recommended the injection of a lay element. In recent years, its members have included a Quaker, a Pentecostalist, the President of the Independent Free Churches, a West Indian Anglican priest, a former Buddhist from Ceylon, and a Jewish Reform Rabbi.

Religion is one of the three areas in which BBC radio and television programmers report to a single head, the other two being news and current affairs, and school broadcasting.[16] Of the more than 100 employees in religious broadcasting, about half are producers. Most key members of the department are ordained ministers, representing a number of denominations.* Corporation employees involved in the religious output include over twenty in the national and English regions. The Corporation's annual budget of £2 million for religious programming is largely spent on television, although this is because of the higher

---

* The Roman Catholic Church pointed out to the Beveridge Committee in 1959 that its adherents in the United Kingdom were numerically 'far ahead of all the Free Churches together, and our practising members are few short of the Anglican figure'. ('Memorandum of Evidence by the Roman Catholic Church in the United Kingdom', *Beveridge II*, pp. 420–1). Yet it went on: 'This state of affairs is not reflected either in the structure of the Religious Department [of the BBC] or in its programmes', since none of its key members were Catholics. Whatever effect this recommendation may have had, there now is a Roman Catholic assistant to the Head of Religious Broadcasting.

costs of television: the radio output is much greater, and has been so for at least the last 20 years.

The IBA headquarters staff includes a Religious Broadcasting Officer and a small staff. Depending on their size, the programme companies have specialist production units, which often double for educational programming too. Overall budgets are difficult to assess for ITV, although the 'exchange rate' charged among companies for Sunday evening religious programmes is around £5000 a week.

The programme companies pointed out to the Annan Committee that from their very first days on the air, ITV 'programme-makers and religious advisors in companies have challenged, with a fundamentally different approach, the output of a BBC department staffed and controlled largely by clerics'.[17] But a report prepared by the Broadcasting Commission of the General Synod of the Church of England explained that few programme producers are chosen specifically for work on religious programmes, with the result that 'it is not uncommon for atheists, humanists, agnostics and other non-Christians to produce them'. It remarked further that 'the task of making meaningful programmes on Christian themes is enormously complicated when the producer lacks fundamental sympathy with the Christian faith'.[18]

POLICY PROBLEMS

Several policy problems have had to be settled through the years. Who should be allowed to broadcast? What should be the objectives of religious broadcasting? What limitations should be placed on what is said?

In 1924, John Reith wrote that from the outset British broadcasting had 'a definite, though restrained, association with religion in general, and with the Christian religion in particular'.[19] Christianity, he noted, 'happens to be the stated and official religion of this country; it is recognised by the Crown. This is a fact which those who have criticised our right to broadcast the Christian religion would do well to bear in mind.' But he also said: 'The Christianity which is broadcast is unassociated with any particular creed or denomination. . . . It is a thorough-going, optimistic and manly religion. It does not put a stained glass window between the observer and the facts.'

Originally, the policy was established of permitting broadcasts only by churches in what came to be called 'the mainstream of historic Christianity', that is, the Church of England, Church of Scotland, Roman Catholic, and the main Free Churches—Methodist, Presbyterian, Congregational, and Baptist. In 1928 the BBC was advised by CRAC that nothing should be broadcast 'likely to provoke or offend large numbers of their Christian audience. . . . This policy excludes sectarian propaganda or contentious arguments.'[20]

In 1947 the Governors decided that 'controversial [religious] broadcasting' should be undertaken, meaning in this context, broadcasting by non-Christian groups.[21] But as Sir William Haley, then Director-General, told the British Council of Churches the next year, this did not mean that British broadcasting is neutral where Christian values are concerned.[22] 'We are citizens of a Christian country, and the BBC—an institution set up by the State—bases its policy upon a positive attitude towards the Christian values. It seeks to safeguard those values and to foster acceptance of them. The whole preponderant weitht of its programme is directed to this end.' This policy, he went on, does not prevent the broadcasting of anti-Christian plays of literary value; it no longer keeps entertainment off the air on Sundays; nor was it an inherent duty of all BBC broadcasters to make people embrace the Christian faith. But, he concluded, the BBC should 'never fail to put the Christian point of view wherever it is relevant'.

The Beveridge, Pilkington, and Annan Committees all received requests for air-time from religious groups not meeting the 'main stream' criterion, and in 1951 the Beveridge Committee recommended such a change.[23]

It appears to us clear . . . that the object of religious broadcasting should be conceived, not as that of seeking converts to one particular church but as that of maintaining the common element in all religious bodies as against those who deny spiritual values. From this point of view a body like the Unitarians, with a long tradition of spiritual service, has claims to consideration out of accord with its numbers. If we accept the view, on the one hand, that the object of religious broadcasting is not to obtain converts to any one church, and, on the other hand, that its object is to bring religious ideas and ideals home to people who are outside all churches, religious broadcasting should be administered on a broad view and not governed by fine differences of doctrine.

This proposal was truly revolutionary from the standpoint of the organized churches. As might be expected, the BBC's Central Religious Advisory Committee, composed of mainstream churchmen, rejected it, and so did the BBC Board of Governors after extended discussion. However, it was decided to give more time on the air to ethical talks, religious discussions, and minority religious groups.[24] This marked a definitive change in policy, since previously there had been little broadcasting by denominations not in the 'main stream'.

When the Pilkington Committee wrote its report in 1962, it said that, although the 'term religious broadcasting need not denote only Christian religious broadcasting', the concept of religious toleration has been so well established in the United Kingdom that any broadcasting organization charged with providing a comprehensive service 'might be regarded, in theory at any rate, as being responsible for providing religious broadcasting to satisfy the needs of any religious body with enough adherents'.[25]

The policy was progressively liberalized through the years, and there was increasing tolerance for churches not in the 'main stream'. Some of the credit—or blame, depending upon one's point of view—for this must be given to Sir Hugh Greene, Director-General from 1960 to 1969. In a talk in Rome to the International Catholic Association for Radio and Television in 1965, he came out strongly for 'the examination of views and opinions in an atmosphere of healthy scepticism'. To which the General Assembly of the Church of Scotland replied 3 months later with a resolution of disapproval, which, among other things, realising that democracy and society can be damaged as much by a decadent morality as by subversive politics and that the Christian conscience of Scotland has been outraged, call[ed] upon the Chairman and Governors of the BBC to reverse immediately the policy recently put forward by the Director-General, in order that the high moral standards of the BBC may be restored.[26]

But the Chairman and Governor did not repudiate the Director-General's statement.

In 1975, CRAC told the Annan Committee that 'over-emphasis on the "mainstream" concept' might imply that the broadcasters were 'primarily concerned in the field of religious broadcasting with the provision of propaganda, suitably rationed, from the major Churches in Britain. This in fact is not so.'[27] Because by 1975 there were more churches, as well as differing approaches within denominations, CRAC recommended that the 'range of religious broadcasting should continue to be extended', and also that its own membership 'should become more widely representative'.

Here, as elsewhere, the programme companies took a liberal view towards religious broadcasting, telling the Annan Committee:

While the companies have pressed for the most liberal interpretation [as to what is a religious programme], the churches have vacillated.[28] Sometimes they have acknowledged the rationale of the companies' position which aims at keeping alive the broad Christian ethic. At others they have developed an uneasy feeling that they are perhaps forgoing too readily the opportunity which this unique protection affords to propagate a hard-line, didactic message even at the cost of reducing the audience for the closed period still further. This uncertainty is seen by some churchmen to be a reflection of the churches' own central dilemma on their role in society today.

CRAC told the Annan Committee that, although the objectives the BBC had presented to the Pilkington Committee in 1960 were still 'valid as a rough working guide', they needed revision and re-interpretation, and accordingly supported new guidelines which had grown out of discussion with the BBC and the IBA.[29]

(i) to seek to reflect the worship, thought and action of the principal religious traditions represented in Britain, recognising that those traditions are mainly, though not exclusively, Christian;

(ii) to seek to present to viewers and listeners those beliefs, ideas, issues and experiences in the contemporary world which are evidently related to a religious interpretation or dimension of life;

(iii) to seek also to meet the religious interests, concerns and needs of those on the fringe of, or outside, the organized life of the Churches.

This statement, thought the Committee,

is important because it departs fundamentally from the previous definitions of objectives. It recognises that religion in this country is no longer synonymous with Christianity, and it no longer requires broadcasting to pretend that it is. It abandons the notion that broadcasting should reflect only the life of the churches in the main stream of Britain's Christian tradition. It wants to provide some programmes which would present a religious interpretation of the world rather than specifically a Christian interpretation. It asks broadcasting to cater for the religious needs of people outside the churches, but not to proselytise. This is an important change because it makes clear that even if their religion lays a duty upon believers to proselytise, they must not use broadcasting to fulfil that duty. In other words, religious broadcasting should not be the religious equivalent of party political broadcasts.[30]

Worthy of note in this context was an observation by the Broadcasting Commission of the Church of England that British commercial television, through its programmes and its effects on BBC programme policies,

has profoundly affected the relationship between society and broadcasting. . . . . It seems clear that commercial television must profoundly influence the behaviour of society. From the Christian standpoint it is therefore very unwise to regard its apparently trivial programme fare as of little consequence. Commercial television can too easily reflect and stimulate a grossly materialistic view of life. When it does this it implies that consumption is happiness and that the accumulation of material goods will inevitably lead to a fulfilled and satisfying life.

After pointing out that commercial broadcasting necessarily places great emphasis on building an audience for its advertisers, the report went on to say that:

the creation of inflated expectations among its recipients [audience] must be in danger of propagating a philosophy and life-style contrary to the teaching and example of Christ. Attempts to reconcile Christian truth with such a system's programming must always run the risk of falsifying it. This is not to say that it cannot be done but only that the opposing nature of the two philosophies must not be obscured by the use of ambiguous and hypocritical language, when the purposes of broadcasting are being considered.[31]

THE CLOSED PERIOD

The story of television's closed period on Sundays demonstrates clearly the influence of the churches, and the paternalistic attitude of the government towards broadcasting. In June 1925 the BBC agreed that no religious services would be broadcast during regular church hours, lest they provide an inducement for people to stay home from church, a commitment held by radio until World War II, and by television up to 1957.[32] Following the same reasoning, during the 1950s no children's programmes were broadcast between 2 and 4 p.m. on Sundays, when

British Sunday schools normally meet. Prior to July 1959, only religious programmes, broadcasts of outside events, or Welsh language programmes could be telecast before 2 p.m. on Sundays, and for some years, there was no telecasting at all between 6.15 and 7.25 p.m. on Sundays, lest it compete with evening church services.

When the ban was lifted in 1959, largely because of pressure from the then new ITA, the schedules of both BBC Television and ITV during those hours were limited to religious material, outside pick-ups of sporting or public events the duration of which the broadcasters could not control, programmes in the Welsh language, and programmes for the deaf.[33] Another evidence of church influence was that, as long as broadcasting hours were limited, religious programmes did not count in computing the maximum allowable time. Between 1957 and 1972, the period between 6.15 and 7.25 p.m. was identified officially as 'the closed period', although it was also known irreverently as the 'God Slot' and the 'Ghetto'.

Rather than objecting to such controls, both broadcasting groups welcomed them. In 1958 the programme companies joined CRAC in resisting moves to abolish the closed period.[34] In 1962 an Independent Television publication stated that the closed period had been 'Of much benefit to religious television' because it encouraged the companies 'to experiment with religious programmes at a really good viewing time'. In 1971, shortly before the government lifted all controls on broadcasting hours, the BBC stated that the closed period 'assists religious broadcasting' by assuring a good programme time along with adequate financial and personnel support.[35] However, in 1975 the programme companies questioned 'whether a protected period of 70 minutes is not overlong. Some doubt its relevance at all in the 1970s'.[36]

From the public's standpoint, these limitations on programme choice were like the simultaneous broadcasts of party political programmes on almost all the broadcast media, in the hope that larger audiences would result (see above, pp. 224–8). However, there is no evidence of complaints about this policy, nor did the Beveridge, Pilkington or Annan Committees report negative public re-actions. An IBA audience study, however, found that during the closed period there was a significant fall in total ratings, although as the years went on, they increased.[37]

Finally, in January 1972 the Minister of Posts and Telecommunications suspended all controls over television broadcasting hours, including those for the Sunday closed period.[38] Nevertheless, both the BBC and the IBA at once announced their intention to treat the closed period as before, and not to change anything until after joint consultation with CRAC.

With the concurrence of both organizations, CRAC in May 1976 recommended 'a measure of flexibility' in scheduling.[39] On Sundays there would be at least 70 minutes of religious television on both BBC 1 and ITV, of which 35 minutes would be broadcast simultaneously from 6.40 to 7.15 p.m. BBC 2 programming between 6.05 and 7.15 p.m. would be similar to that previously aired at that time—that is, not light entertainment with great audience appeal to compete with any religious offerings on the other two networks. It also was agreed to replace with family-type broadcasts any religious programmes moved out of the former closed period. The

Corporation announced that it would move some of its religious programmes to 10.15 p.m., while the IBA, though expecting to broadcast 70 minutes of programming in a block, stated that some such material would come between 4 and 6.15 p.m. A review of the schedules in effect in the summer of 1980 shows that these committments have been generally met.

Although religious broadcasting clearly is desirable, the British went too far in paternalistically protecting the churches against competition from television. Since other forms of public entertainment proceeded as usual during those hours, it is strange that this restriction persisted for so long. Perhaps it was a carry-over from the Reith Sunday; a consequence of the influence of organized religious groups; or a projection into religious broadcasting of the policy followed so long with party political broadcasts.

RELIGIOUS PROGRAMMES—BBC

The basic British experience in religious broadcasting, as in everything else, was provided by the BBC. The original priority was to bring worship programmes to Christian homes; therefore, the sick and the elderly constituted a large portion of the intended audience. But later it was discovered that most of the audience did not belong to any denomination and attended no services at all. Accordingly programmes were developed which, rather than transmitting or reproducing church services, employed new techniques to explore religious subjects.

The first religious programme was aired on Christmas Eve 1922. At the end of 1923, a weekly Sunday service was begun, although previously the Company had scheduled religious talks during the intermissions of Sunday orchestral concerts.[40] There followed broadcasts from churches, along with programmes of religious talks and hymns from the studios.

Short daily morning services were begun by the London station in 1928, becoming a network feature the following year. When Broadcasting House was completed in 1932, it included a religious studio, although the Corporation soon learned that broadcasts from churches were preferred over studio originations—by the churches, because it gave them publicity, and by the audiences because they felt they were taking part in real services.[41]

The Reith Sunday, introduced at the instigation of John Reith in January 1927, caused more controversy in the 1930s than did any other programme policy. Several years before, in 1924, Reith had written: 'The programmes which are broadcast on Sunday are . . . framed with the day itself in mind.' But that did not mean they had to be dull, because if they were, 'then something is wrong somewhere'.[42] When the Reith Sunday was in effect, there was no broadcasting at all before 3.30 in the afternoon; after that it consisted entirely of religious material, plus a few serious features like talks, discussions and symphony concerts.

Whatever effect such scheduling may have had on religious belief in Britain, there is no doubt that it drove over half the audience to powerful commercial stations like Radio Luxembourg and Radio Normandy, whose programmes of light music with advertising, easily receivable in most of the United Kingdom, achieved their largest audiences on Sundays. Nevertheless, the Corporation made only limited concessions on this point until the outbreak of World War II, when the policy was replaced by a more realistic one. Since 1945, Sunday radio and television, along with excellent religious broadcasts, have included a wide range of news, entertainment and sports.

During 1978–9, the BBC devoted 419 hours or 1.5 per cent of its radio time to religious programmes, most of them on Radios 2 and 4. [43] During the same period, BBC television assigned 134 hours or 1.5 per cent of its time to religion, mainly on BBC 1 (116 hours, 2.3 per cent.) Back in 1955–6, the average ITV company gave 1 hour 5 minutes (2 per cent) of its weekly time to religious programmes. With an expanded schedule, the figure in 1966 was 3 hours 15 minutes (5 per cent), although this dropped to 2 hours 24 minutes (2½ per cent) in 1978–9. [44] (Including local radio, there were about 4000 hours of religious programming in the United Kingdom in 1977, divided about evenly between the BBC and IBA, which together put out 500 hours on television and 1500 on radio.)

At present, these programmes fall into two categories: (1) worship and preaching programmes, broadcast almost entirely on Sunday mornings; and, (2) programmes about religion, of which there is a considerable variety, ranging from light music in religious vein to drama and films.

BBC radio now offers one or more religious programmes every day of the week. Sunday morning services, usually from churches, are broadcast on Radio 4. The Sunday half-hour, on Radio 2 from 8.30 to 9 p.m., consists of old favourite hymns. I enjoyed listening one evening as the congregation in a Welsh church sang with feeling and fervour.

On weekdays, *Prayer for the Day* is heard at 6.45 a.m. on Radio 4, and *Thought for the Day* an hour later. At 10.30 a.m., Radio 4 presents *The Daily Service*, on the air since 1928, and undoubtedly one of the oldest uninterrupted series in all of broadcasting. [45]

On Sunday morning BBC 1 broadcasts services from churches in various parts of the United Kingdom. When the closed period was still in effect, BBC 1 scheduled religious films, appropriate music and drama, hymn-singing and some additional pick-ups from churches. Beginning in the autumn of 1974 it initiated the religious magazine, *Anno Domini*—later renamed *Everyman*, though no longer on the air—covering subjects highly varied in nature, although all related to religion. [46] There were a tour of the Holy Land, a study of the religion of the American Indians, a series on popular religious music, and a programme about Canterbury Cathedral. In June 1976, I saw *A Report from South Korea*, filmed in Seoul, which dealt with human rights in that country, and among other things pointed out that the United States was supporting the South Korean regime.

The English regions, Scotland, Wales, and Northern Ireland often opt out of the radio and television feeds from London to present their own material. [47] A list of the religious features for Scottish listeners in 1979 took a half-column of *Handbook* space, and included programmes from the Church of Scotland, broadcasts for Roman Catholic listeners, and Sunday services in Gaelic.

Wales also has its own programmes, many in Welsh. In keeping with tradition, there is much hymn-singing, a high point being the New Year's Eve broadcast of mass community singing. Welsh television has presented films of village life in India, sermons filmed on location, and a series of Old Testament stories. Radio and television programmes from Northern Ireland have included Protestant and Catholic services, singing, and contributions to BBC 1's *Everyman*.

RELIGIOUS PROGRAMMES—IBA

IBA must be credited with some ingenious religious programming. When Parliament was debating the Television Act in the early 1950s, Anglican and other church leaders strongly opposed commercial television, which may be one reason ITV decided to go all out with its religious programming. In addition to developing a committee structure paralleling that of the BBC, the Authority also organized religious broadcasting workshops attended by representatives of various churches.[48] The Authority also set up a series of 'Consultations' on a variety of subjects, several dealing with religious broadcasting. Such Consultations were held at Oxford in 1961, Cambridge in 1963, Durham in 1965, Canterbury in 1968, Edinburgh in 1973, and Bath in 1978. The latter was attended by 145 people, including Authority members, ITV staff members, members of CRAC, company religious advisors, and others.

Ever since 1957—the ITA began operations in 1955—ITV has had Sunday morning broadcasts of church services from all parts of the country. I have seen several of these, all handled with skill and reverence. With ITV, as with BBC, production centres outside London have developed programmes for their own viewers. Thus, Scottish Television produced its first Jewish series in 1976, while the companies in Wales and Ulster have turned out many programmes.[49] On Sunday 26 April 1976 I watched a programme originated by London Weekend. Developed in cooperation with a liberal Jewish synagogue, according to the IBA this was 'television's first act of Jewish worship in a service specially devised for the studio'.[50] Formal, dignified, and very well done, the presentation utilized men and women speakers, a small mixed chorus, and a 'cello soloist, with cut-ins of relevant art and sculpture. On one of its school series, Tyne Tees Television had a rabbi explain the symbols associated with a Passover meal. Each evening's programming on Thames Television, which supplies London programmes Monday to Friday, ends with a minute or so of poetry or prayers, with appropriate visual material.

For the school series *Believe-It-Or-Not*, in the spring of 1976, ATV scheduled ten programmes with such titles as *Who Am I?*, *Are We Free?*, *Sin, Life and Death*, and *Does God Exist?*[51] The purpose of the series, said the accompanying 24-page brochure, was 'to reveal the importance of religious belief in the development of man and to examine the role of Christianity in this context'. The programme therefore sought 'to encourage young people of 13 and over to think purposefully about both the opportunities and the difficulties of being human in our complex world'. The brochure contained summaries of the programmes, suggestions for follow-up class work, and reading lists. (In 1977, 13 per cent of the nation's elementary schools watched these programmes.)

The IBA seeks to find room for broadcasts by churches outside of the 'main stream'. As it remarked in its 1977 handbook: 'Until now it would have been reasonable for the viewer to assume that religious television in this country meant Christian television. Certainly, with a few exceptions, programmes in the past have related more or less obviously to the Christian tradition.'[52] But now, continued the Authority, adherents of other faiths are moving to Britain in such substantial numbers that it 'would be arrogant for Christians to claim an exclusive right to religious broadcasting'. Therefore, ITV is developing programmes for these groups, at the same time explaining 'the rites and beliefs of other religions to the host community'. Thus, under the title *One Man's Faith*, London Weekend Television broadcast the views of an authority on Buddhism. The same company also broadcast an Eastern Orthodox service. The IBA's local radio stations average about 90 minutes of religious programming each week.

Generally speaking, the IBA has been more willing than the BBC to get away from traditional patterns in programming. This may be due to its commercial basis, and the resulting pressures for audience-building. Undoubtedly, though, it also stems from the fact that ITV's competing programme companies are highly motivated to develop new programme concepts.

CONTROVERSIAL DRAMATIC PROGRAMMES ON RELIGIOUS THEMES

If they depart too far from tradition, religious programmes often evoke very strong responses. Thus, there were strong reactions in 1941, 1969, and 1977 to dramatic presentations of the life of Christ. In 1941, BBC radio broadcast a children's cycle of religious plays, *The Man Born to be King*, written by Dorothy Sayers, better known for her detective stories, although she had done a Nativity Play for the Christmas season in 1938. About the 1941 series, she said she would write the scripts only if she could introduce Jesus as a real person.[53] When the project was announced, protests poured in—almost entirely from people who had not seen the scripts—to the BBC, the Archbishop of Canterbury, the Prime Minister, and the Minister of Information, who told the Director-General that 'he did not want religious controversy at this moment', and asked for a careful reconsideration of the project. Nevertheless, the cycle was broadcast, and although many abusive letters were received the series was regarded as generally successful, and was repeated in later years, subsequently being regarded as a broadcast classic.

The BBC commented some years later: 'Probably the biggest single row in the history of religious broadcasting in Britain [in fact, one of the biggest rows over a broadcast on any subject] . . . was over . . . *The Man Born to be King*. This was broadcast in 1941, and 'for a while the rigours of war-time Britain were forgotten as protest was matched by counter protest'. There were Parliamentary questions and letters to the newspapers 'complaining about the "blasphemy" of an actor playing the role of Christ on the radio'. But when, 15 years later, 'the BBC put on a television dramatization of the Life of Christ, *Jesus of Nazareth*, the protests were comparatively muted'.[54] The Sayers cycle was repeated on Sunday evenings in

1975 from a new recording, but by then it had 'lost its unintended capacity to shock but . . . not . . . its appeal to audiences'.

In April 1969 the corporation broadcast a play by Dennis Potter, *Son of Man*, 'the story of an entirely human Christ', by an author who 'did not conceal his disbelief in Christ's divinity'.[55] Charles Curran, Director-General of the BBC at the time, remarked in a talk to a religious press group the following year that many people objected to 'the portrayal of Christ as a rather tough, simple man'. Others 'objected to the brutality of the Crucifixion scene and the scourgings which led up to it. Finally, there were those who protested Dennis Potter's presentation of Christ as a man and not as a divine person.' Defending the programme, Curran said that Potter 'tried to embody in his play a non-believer's view of Christ. It is quite clear, both from the play itself and from what he wrote in *Radio Times*, that he did not write the play with any intention of showing contempt. Rather, he was trying to state his view of the importance of Christ's preaching about love.'

The broadcasts in both the United Kingdom and the United States of the 6-hour film, *Jesus of Nazareth*, on Palm Sunday and Easter Sunday 1977, provided an opportunity to compare reactions in the two countries. Co-produced by Lew Grade's ATV in London and RAI TV in Italy, *Jesus* was originally filmed in six 1-hour episodes on location in Morocco and Tunisia, with an all-star cast at a reported cost of some $18 million.[56] It was broadcast in two instalments in both countries—in Britain on ITV, and in the United States by NBC—and was repeated in the United Kingdom in 1979. Under new rules just adopted, the IBA permitted some advertisements during the broadcast, although only after very careful consideration of what commercials to allow and where to put them.

For the most part, British reaction was favourable. The churchmen from many denominations who previewed it almost unanimously give it high marks, and when broadcast on two successive Sunday evenings—beginning at 6.15 p.m., the time previously included in the closed period—it attracted large audiences as well as praise from most critics. That also was the case in the United States, although some of the initial reaction was highly negative.[57]

The American press reported director Franco Zeffirelli as saying: 'I see Jesus as an ordinary man, gentle, fragile, simple. Of course the public might be annoyed that I am destroying their myths'. But the president of a conservative religious college in South Carolina was more than annoyed, and replied: 'If the film is as director Zeffirelli says . . . then it is the most wicked thing to ever be shown on television. The blasphemy of humanizing Jesus and denying his deity will not help the image of General Motors [the prospective sponsor]. I am surprised that the company would be party to this kind of thing.' A minister in Baltimore, Maryland—who, like the college president had not seen the film—in a radio broadcast asked his listeners to protest to both NBC and General Motors about the film's 'misrepresentation of Jesus. We believe that if we're going to have the representation of Jesus at Easter, let's have the Christ of Scripture rather than the Christ of Zeffirelli'.

Although NBC reviewed the credentials of the production and screened the film for a number of clergymen, General Motors nevertheless gave up its sponsorship to Procter and Gamble, the soap manufacturers, who got it at a bargain price under the circumstances. In the event, things went well, and reactions from religious commentators and the general public—the audience was very large—were overwhelmingly favourable.

British broadcasting always has served religion very well. No doubt the members of the Establishment who made and enforced the rules of the 1930s and 1940s, which excluded from the air all except the mainstream churches, thought they were doing the right thing in terms of the national interest; fortunately more liberal attitudes now prevail, and today almost every faith has a chance to broadcast. The total amount of time assigned to religion is about right, and it is well distributed, with formal services on Sunday mornings and other types of programmes at varied hours on other days. The prohibition against the sale of time for religious broadcasting avoids the imbalance of conservative religious broadcasts that take up such a disproportionate share of American broadcasting time, especially on local stations. Finally, it must be noted that great skill is shown in producing these programmes, from the formal church services to religious discussions and drama.

16 Drama, Films, and Light Entertainment

One expects—and gets—good drama both from the BBC and the IBA. The basic reason for this far antedates broadcasting: a long tradition of excellent stage and radio drama underlies today's television drama successes.

DRAMATIC PROGRAMMES

The BBC is instructed by its charter to disseminate not only 'information' and 'education', but also 'entertainment', and drama might fall into any of these categories. The law for the IBA, in almost identical phrasing, states that the Authority is to disseminate 'information, education and entertainment', while maintaining 'a proper balance and wide range in subject-matter'.[1] The Corporation believes it has the

> duty . . . to see that performances are given at regular intervals of what may be called the major musical and dramatic repertoire. . . . There are many great works which might well escape public performance for long stretches of time; it is the duty of the BBC actively to ensure that this does not happen. The great masterpieces, however unfashionable or unhackneyed, should periodically be offered afresh to listeners for new appraisal and possibly increased understanding and appreciation.[2]

That part of the American audience which hears and views public radio and television has more first-hand contact with British broadcasting's drama than with any other aspect of its output. American listeners became aware of the excellence of BBC radio drama in the 1940s and 1950s when some of its finest productions were carried by educational stations in all parts of the country. During the past dozen years, BBC television and ITV dramatic series have built enthusiastic followings. On Public Broadcasting System screens there first were the classics, and then contemporary material, adapted from both novels and stage plays. American commercial television also carries some British-produced programmes.

Broadcast Drama in the Schedule
Dramatic programmes occupy a great deal of air-time, ranking, for example,

fourth among the BBC radio categories.[3] There is no drama on Radio 1, which consists mainly of popular music; but during 1978–9, 125 hours (1.6 per cent) of Radio 2's schedule was devoted to drama; 149 hours (2.1 per cent) of Radio 3; and 824 hours (10.8 per cent) of Radio 4. The total for all four networks was 1100 hours (3.9 per cent of all radio air-time).

These programmes are well-spaced throughout the day and week. Taking the week of 2 to 8 June 1979, as an example, Radio 4 offered various types of plays, varying in length from 30 to 60 minutes, most afternoons. Radio 4 also had a daily episode of *The Archers* (see below, pp. 291–2). A major carry-over from World War II days is *Saturday Night Theatre*, broadcast from 8.30 to 10 p.m. Radio 3 offered fewer but more demanding plays.

Drama ranked fifth among BBC television's programme categories. In 1978–9 it occupied 246 hours (5.2 per cent) of the BBC 1 schedule; 214 hours (5.2 per cent) of BBC 2 time; and 475 hours (5.2 per cent) of the total television time.[4] There are dramatic programmes almost every day of the week, on one if not both networks. (On those evenings when there is no play, there usually is recorded American television drama or a cinema film).

Drama also occupies much ITV time. In 1978–9, 22 hours and 54 minutes, or 22¾ per cent of the weekly transmission hours of the average programme company, were devoted to 'plays, drama TV movies'.[5] Although the proportion of such programmes dropped during the 1970s, the 1978–9 figure approximated that of the previous two years. During a normal week, ITV offers a British-produced play or series six nights out of seven, in addition to daytime series, repeats of some plays during afternoon periods, and the long-running *Coronation Street*, from 7.30 to 8 p.m. on Mondays and Wednesdays.

Most of this drama is produced by the participating organizations, although the domestic output is supplemented with foreign—largely American—television shows and cinema films. The casts include many highly competent performers who appear regularly in radio, television, film and stage presentations, supplemented as required by the best names of the London stage.

BBC television's Drama Group in London is organized in two divisions.[6] One produces single plays, such as *Play of the Month* and *Play for Today*, while the other does series and serials. There are approximately 400 full-time employees in the Drama Group, their work being supported by the departments which provide scenery, make-up, wardrobe, lighting, and other needed services. The regional studios also have drama production departments.

With drama, more than almost any other type of programme, it is unfair to lump together the entire ITV output without reference to the originating companies, since each proceeds in its own way. For obvious reasons, the big five companies, located in larger cities and with greater resources, turn out more pretentious programmes, and a greater number of dramatic programmes, than do the regional contractors. But in any case, the weekly output from the companies' own studios averages about 10 hours, including single plays, anthologies, serials, and series.[7] Some idea of the productions of the individual companies is given below in the discussion of repertoire, since the name of the producing company is given in each case.

The Repertoire—BBC Radio

There is drama for every taste and mood, with a repertoire that hardly could be surpassed. In contrast to the situation in the United States, where television has virtually eliminated radio drama, there actually has been an increase in the amount of dramatic material on British radio. Programme merit weighs more heavily than audience ratings; and since radio drama is recognized as having artistic and instrinsic value, it is continued, even though its audiences are much smaller than they were 25 years ago. Then, too, radio's fund base has not been eroded by the increased popularity of television. Although radio licences have not been required since February 1971, the television licence fee includes money for radio too, so that a reduction in the use of radio has not lowered its income.

During a typical year, BBC radio broadcasts over 1000 dramatic programmes, of which about half are adaptations of stage or television plays, 300 are new plays for radio, and 150 each are novels, adaptations or dramatic features.[8] Obviously, only a few of these can be mentioned here. The first BBC dramatic broadcast was a scene from Shakespeare's *Julius Caesar*, aired on 16 February 1923.[9] When West End theatre impressarios forbade the broadcasting of excerpts from their plays, the Corporation decided to write and produce its own, the very first being *Danger* by Richard Hughes, a play set in a coal mine, heard in January 1924. This was the world's first play written especially for radio.

Throughout the years, BBC radio has served drama very well. Many outstanding contemporary British playwrights—Robert Bolt, Giles Cooper and John Arden, for example—got their start that way. Harold Pinter, after the failure of *The Birthday Party* in the commercial theatre, was commissioned to write radio plays; the late Dylan Thomas produced *Under Milkwood* for the BBC; Samuel Beckett's *All That Fall* was written for the Third Programme; and William Golding's novel, *Lord of the Flies*, was adapted as a radio play before it became a film. Foreign dramatists introduced to Britain by BBC radio include Jean Anouilh, Ugo Betti, and Eugene Ionesco, whose *Rhinoceros* had its world premiere on the Third Programme in an English translation commissioned by the Corporation.

Most such programmes now are on Radios 3 and 4, which together offer dramatic material ranging from the very light to the very demanding, almost every day of the week.[10] In 1978–9, wrote the BBC, its 'Radio Drama Department . . . [was] the greatest single patron of creative writing in the country and greater by far, in that respect, than any other broadcasting organisation in the world. Last year the department introduced 60 new playwrights and produced 500 new and original plays for radio.' On *Afternoon Theatre*, Radio 4 offers such lighter material as serializations of long plays or novels by authors like Arnold Bennett, Walter Scott, Daphne DuMaurier, Jane Austen, and Thomas Hardy. The *Monday [Evening] Play* has included George Bernard Shaw's *Man and Superman* and *Caesar and Cleopatra*, Molière's *The Miser*, Noel Coward's *Present Laughter*, John Milton's *Samson Agonistes*, Shakespeare's *Julius Caesar*, Terrence Rattigan's *The Deep Blue Sea*, and adaptations of novels by Thomas Hardy, Henry James and Joseph Conrad.[11] To conclude the week, there is *Saturday Night Theatre*, a 90-minute series of programmes for relaxation, which is a carry-over from World War II days. Before 1939, few dramatic programmes lasted more than an hour, but the blackout, together with the closing of many entertainment facilities, kept the British public at home, accustoming them to hearing long programmes, a practice maintained since 1945. The Corporation is very competitive in seeking broadcast rights. In October 1975, after 9 months of negotiations, it secured the rights to half-hour radio dramatizations of *The Killers* and thirteen other short stories by Ernest Hemingway.[12] Up to then the author's estate, while permitting the reading of Hemingway stories, had not approved their dramatization.

Radio 3's plays, as would be expected, are more serious, and under such titles as *Classics*, *Contemporary British Plays*, they have included major works by George Bernard Shaw, Henrik Ibsen, Eugene O'Neill, Sophocles, William Shakespeare, Euripedes, and outstanding contemporary authors. In 1978, Radio 3 proudly reported

> several outstanding drama achievements [including] two plays by the imprisoned Czech playwright Vaclav Havel, a rumbustious production (in quadraphony) of John Gay's *The Beggar's Opera* and a memorable production of Eugene O'Neill's *A Moon for the Misbegotten*.... Another dramatic occasion ... was a production of the original version of *The Importance of Being Earnest* which included the 'missing' act and the 'new' role of Mr. Grigsby.

The English regions, as well as the national regions of Scotland, Wales, and Northern Ireland, have their own dramatic offerings, largely but not exclusively by their own writers, some for regional and some for network distribution.

The expression 'serial drama' has different connotations in Britain and the United States. During the radio-only days, most BBC serials were instalment treatments of standard literary works, broadcast in sections, because of their length. But there also were a few dramatic situation comedies, roughly comparable to America's daytime soap serials. The two most notable were *Mrs. Dale's Diary*, broadcast from January 1948 to 25 April 1969, and *The Archers*, begun in 1951 and still on the air each evening with repeats the following afternoon and an omnibus edition on Sunday mornings.[13] *The Archers* with a rural setting, deals to a considerable extent with agricultural problems, although it appeals as much to urban as to rural listeners. But the programmes never take on the maudlin sentimentality of the old American radio serials, instead using the continued story device to present entertainment with a touch of information and wholesome—if homely—philosophy.

Audience reaction to these serials resembles that to American daytime serials in their heyday. For one thing, they have many listeners, although *The Archers* does not attract the 25 per cent of the country's population it reached before television. Another point of similarity is that listeners often mistake the characters for real people. If Dan Archer advertises for a farm worker, he gets applications from all over the country, and if his cows develop mastitis, many people send in suggestions for treatment. The death of Grace Archer on 22 September 1955—the ITA's debut day—even took some headline space away from the new television service! As a result of the continued popularity of the series, BBC publications has put out several books about *The Archers*.

The Repertoire—BBC Television

In a 1969 lecture, the former head of BBC television drama said that there are 'two wide gaps between television theatre, and the theatre that built up to it for so many years'.[14] One is a 'sense of occasion'. Before television, in order to see a play, one had to travel—perhaps long distances, buy a ticket, and share with an audience 'the implicit excitements, tensions, and enjoyments of the group; to have the occasion, as it were, served up'. All this required some effort, which gave 'the occasion its identity and importance'. But now we watch at home 'in slippers and shirt sleeves; we are no longer present for the express purpose of enjoying a particular drama presentation. Indeed, some of our household seem intent on ensuring that we do not.' (This is true of all television, of course, not just drama.)

During a typical year, the BBC broadcasts some 500 hours of television drama—in the words of the former director—of

> every size, shape, style, and form ... be it play, series or serial .... It ranges from the humanities of 'Boy Meets Girl' to the up-to-date vigours of the Wednesday Play, from the twice-weekly social serials to lavish classic adaptations. It spans science fiction, the human villainies, and the professions in all their aspects. It revives the Greek theatre of the past, it seeks the theatre of the present; it considers children and coteries. This mass of drama is not all done to perfection, much of it is adequate, some is bad. What matters is that it is done at all. ... Some areas of drama will attract only a moderate audience, and this is known and accepted before ever they are produced. The criterion is this—if they are well made and sincerely made, they are a success.[15]

There is drama almost every day of the year. Without equal in its class is the *BBC World Theatre*, the name and idea for which were borrowed from BBC radio. This includes 90-minute adaptations of the familiar and unfamiliar plays of Shakespeare, Chekhov, Euripides, Shaw, Gogol, Ibsen, O'Neill, Gorky, and their equals. BBC 1's *Play for the Day* was a 'series of plays with contemporary themes'.[16] In 1975–6 the *Play of the Month*, a 'series of major plays, including adaptations of outstanding theatre plays and novels', included *The Skin Game* by John Galsworthy, *The Linden Tree* by J. B. Priestley, *Electra* by Sophocles, *The Wood Demon* by Anton Chekhov, *Robinson Crusoe* by Daniel Defoe, *School for Scandal* by Richard Brimsley Sheridan, and *King Lear* by William Shakespeare. There also was *Churchill's People*, a series of plays suggested by Winston Churchill's *A History of English-Speaking Peoples*.*

---

* The BBC's *Annual Review of Audience Research Findings* for 1974–5 had the following summary of audience reactions for the 23 March 1975 presentation of *King Lear*.

> Of the production ... there was criticism that 'austere' sets, dim lighting and unrelenting close-ups tended to accentuate the gloomy depressing nature of a play that some viewers said they had always found difficult, but others thought these factors successfully focused

In 1978 BBC 2 mounted an elaborate production of Tolstoy's *Anna Karenina*, and during the same year the Corporation began work on a 6-year project to record for television all thirty-six Shakespeare plays, which it described as 'the largest project [it had ever] undertaken,' and the first time anywhere in the world the 'Complete Works' had been recorded. The first of the series appeared on Public Broadcasting System screens in 1979. Budgeting, expected to average around $250,000 per play (ABC's popular *Charlies' Angels* costs more for an hour than the sums being allocated to each of these 2- and 3-hour productions!), is being aided by grants from several large American companies which will receive screen credits when the programmes are broadcast.

The Annan Report praised the concept of the single play as providing opportunities for new writers to explore ideas within one production.[17] Both the BBC and the commercial broadcasters, said the report, have an obligation to produce single plays, so long as good scripts are available, even though they are more expensive to mount than serial presentations. Through the years the Corporation has made a good many such programmes. One very successful example was Frederick Knott's *Dial M for Murder*, which, after premiering on BBC television in 1952, had long runs on both the London and Broadway stages, was made into a first-rate movie by Alfred Hitchcock, and still is broadcast by BBC television from time to time. Also notable was *The Wednesday Play* series, with experimental and avant-garde scripts including the controversial and prizewinning *Up the Junction* and *Cathy, Come Home*.

Serials include classic serials—which usually begin their run on BBC 2, family serials, children's serials, and thriller serials. The former have included adaptations of such classic plays and novels as Richard Llewellyn's *How Green Was My Valley*, Charles Dickens' *Our Mutual Friend*, and Anthony Trollope's *The Pallisers*. A very popular and long-running thriller, *Z Cars*, was broadcast from 1962 to 1978.*

The Repertoire—IBA Television
IBA directors also like to philosophize. In 1976 one of them observed that

attention on the 'human' aspect of the tragedy. There were many comments warmly welcoming the chance of seeing Shakespeare 'presented specifically for television rather than conceived as a stage production'. [The audience was about 2 million.] (BBC, *Annual Review of BBC Audience Research Findings*, Number 2, pp. 21–2.)

* The Corporation's summary of audience research for 1974–5 had the following comment about *The Pallisers*:

The twenty-six-instalment dramatisation of Trollope's 'political novels', *The Pallisers*, inevitably invited comparison with the well-remembered *Forsyte Saga*. Though delighting those who stayed with it, neither the size of the audiences nor the warmth of their response quite matched those of the earlier serial.... Audiences averaged 2½ million, or 5% of the population, for the Saturday originations, compared with 7% of those who could then get BBC-2 for the first showings of the *Forsyte Saga*, whilst Reaction Indices (summing up reaction to the programmes) varied between 67 and 84 for *The Pallisers*, as against 78 to 86 for the Forsytes. (BBC, *Annual Review of BBC Audience Research Findings* Number 2, p. 22.)

television drama offered its viewers 'something . . . about half way between reading a novel and seeing a stage play'. The novel allowed the reader to create for himself the scenes, the people, and the action. Although limited to a single stage, the theatre nevertheless had 'a compelling presence unique to a live performance'.[18] One reason for television's success was that it allowed the viewer to 'enjoy some of the best of both worlds'. A television performance, thanks to technology, could take him to more places than could any stage play. Those who prefer to read might complain that television imposes an inflexible schedule, while those dedicated to the theatre might say that television viewed in a living room, without an audience, lacks 'theatrical magnetism'. But, in spite of these drawbacks, the millions of people who watch dramatic telecasts, 'know that in terms of presentation they are deriving a great deal of enjoyment from their viewing'.

Each week ITV's companies produce twenty or more dramatic programmes. Their range of output approximates that of the BBC, although Authority programmes tend more towards light material, probably because thus far ITV has only one network to the BBC's two, and due to IBA's commercial financial basis.

Like the BBC, Independent Television also has done the classics, having serialized or adapted plays and novels by Shakespeare, Tolstoy, Trollope and Dickens. ATV took the Royal Shakespeare Company's stage version of *Antony and Cleopatra* and made it into a television production. The same actors spoke the same lines, but the sets and the costumes were changed.[19] For secondary-school students, ATV offered a six-part serialization of Shakespeare's *King Lear*, and supplemented it with six 1-hour plays about life in Shakespeare's London.[20]

The IBA is especially proud of ATV's 13-week series on the life of Edward VII, which also has been broadcast by some stations in the United States.[21] *Jenny, Lady Randolph Churchill*, produced by Thames Television, and shown in the United States by the Public Broadcasting System, received several awards, including an Emmy. Particularly successful was *Upstairs, Downstairs*, a London Weekend production. After having been turned down by all three American television networks, it was finally shown in the United States by the Public Broadcasting System, attracting a large and appreciative audience, winning much praise in the press, and receiving several prestigious awards, including an Emmy.[22] The original concept for the series, with the working title of *165 Eaton Place*, was taken up by London Weekend after having been rejected by other producers. Once on the air, it proved unexpectedly popular, and so was moved from a non-competitive late Sunday evening spot to peak time, first on Friday and then on Saturday evenings. All together five series under this title were produced during successive seasons, carrying its cast from their Edwardian beginnings to a dozen years beyond World War I. This series is often mistakenly credited to the BBC by American viewers, and BBC staff members visiting in the United States relate with amusement how they often have to decline credit for its production.

Granada Television contracted with Lord Olivier to produce and appear in a series of specials by outstanding British and European playwrights. Recorded in their Manchester studios, the productions included Tennessee Williams' *Cat on a Hot Tin Roof* and Harold Pinter's *The Collection*.[23] After having been networked by ITV, these were distributed to some European systems as well as to America's NBC. Douglas Livingstone adapted some novels by Arnold Bennett into the twenty-six episodes for *Clayhanger*.[24] Other serial presentations included an adaptation by Allan Plater for Granada of A. J. Cronin's *The Stars Look Down*. The well-known British writer, Wolf Mankowitz, wrote for Yorkshire Television a ten-part series of 1-hour dramas dealing with the life of Charles Dickens in London from the age of 11.[25] One of the smaller companies, Anglia Television, in addition to turning out a number of major plays, produced twenty-six short programmes based on the work of classic writers, introduced by Orson Welles.[26]

In 1978, London Weekend produced a drama series about Lillie Langtry, whose many claims to fame include a period as mistress to the Prince of Wales who later became Edward VII. Lillie was played by Francesca Annis, who previously had appeared in one episode of the series on Edward VII. 'Attention to Detail' was the subhead for the section of the IBA's 1979 handbook which devoted three pages to *Edward and Mrs. Simpson*, a seven-episode series produced by Thames Television.[27] Despite great claims to historical accuracy, the showing in Britain evoked some vigorous charges of factual errors, and its release in the United States was the occasion for a long article in *The New York Times Magazine*. Whatever the merits of these programmes, their showing—on both public and commercial television—in the United States continues to give British television large American audiences.

An outstanding example of the single play was Thames Television's *The Naked Civil Servant*, described by the Authority as a 'powerfully realistic dramatised documentary on the life of the homosexual Quentin Crisp. . . . Over three-quarters of the audience viewed with understanding, sympathy and pleasure'.[28] The programme won a number of awards in Britain and abroad, including a Prix Italia award in international competition, an International Emmy, as well as British awards from the Broadcasting Press Guild as the best single documentary, and from the Academy of Film and Television Arts for directing and acting. Reporting the success of the play, *Variety* magazine, after mentioning that it had been sold for use in Canada, Australia, New Zealand, Sweden, Denmark, and Holland, said that the awards the Programme had won 'may have sufficiently bolstered the "acceptability" of the drama to swing a U.S. sale. Even so, heavy cutting would be expected.' I was greatly impressed by this production: it had a fine script, good direction, and excellent acting. It deserves wide showing by American stations—without cuts.

In addition to commenting on the single play, the Annan Committee observed that 'the series and the serial can provide actors and both new and experienced writers with an opportunity to develop characterisations'.[29] However,

The serial can overstretch its material, and the series constrict its writers to produce the blandly predictable. In particular, we would suggest that long running serials, such as *The Archers* and *Coronation Street*, should consider ways of developing their style and content to provide more enjoyment and discrimination among their audiences.

From its first years on the air, ITV has successfully held audiences, if not won awards, with light drama comparable to that found on American afternoon television schedules. Notable was Associated Television's *Emergency-Ward 10*, broadcast during early evening hours from 1957 to 1967, a human-interest serial that re-created life in a typical British hospital. The programme was well received by the medical profession, and its acceptance by viewers was indicated by large audiences (it usually was among the top ten), as well as by frequent requests to its cast for medical advice. The programme achieved additional stature by being made into a motion picture in which most major roles were played by the actors appearing in the television version.[30] Roughly comparable was ITV's *Boyd, Q.C.*, a series of criminal trials in which the jury's verdict was delayed until after the last commercial; *Probation Officers*, with the probation service as its background; *Deadline Midnight*, based on the lives of newspaper men; and *No Hiding Place*, with Scotland Yard as inspiration. Both ITV and BBC offer many one-time 30-minute mysteries and crime programmes.

A characteristic of these light dramatic serials is that each programme tells a complete story, although the characters and locations are common to a number of programmes and some story lines may be carried through several episodes. Typical examples include London Weekend's *New Scotland Yard*, Yorkshire's *Hadleigh* and ATV's *Crossroads*.[31] The most successful of these is *Coronation Street*, produced by Granada Television since 1960 and now broadcast two evenings a week from 7.30 to 8 p.m. One or the other episode of *Coronation Street* turns up in almost every top ten list. The nature of the various episodes is indicated by such lines in the *TV Times* as: 'What will Rita Littlewood's final answer be to the marriage proposal?'

FILMS

Films and video-tapes are indispensable to television. 'Films' may be 'feature' or other films intended originally for cinema showings, many of which are seen on television too. In addition, many entertainment and documentary programmes produced primarily for television are recorded on film, and film also is shot on location for insertion into studio productions or for use on newscasts. As the terms are used here, however, 'cinema films' or 'feature films' are just that, even though used on television, while filmed entertainment shows—like the two series *Kojak* or *Starsky and Hutch*—are referred to as 'television movies' or 'television films'.[32]

Before cinema films can be telecast, several major barriers must be surmounted. Theatre-owners and motion-picture producers the world over have opposed the televising of cinema films lest that reduce their audiences, and accordingly film rental rates usually are very high. Various British labour groups, including the National Union of Journalists, the British Actors Equity Association, the Musicians Union, and the Association of Directors and Producers, while not flatly opposing the telecasting of all cinema films, favour limiting the televising of films in the hope of increasing employment for their members.[33] Both the Pilkington and Annan Committees were asked by these groups to recommend a fixed quota for the importation of cinema and television films.[34] But the Pilkington Committee in 1962 disagreed, remarking that, since the objective was to provide the best possible television for the country, the number, amount and type of foreign imports should depend upon overall considerations of balance and quality. The Annan Committee in 1977 concurred with this position. Other groups have opposed the televising of some American films on quality grounds, have argued that British viewers should not be excessively exposed to the values of a foreign society, and have maintained that these programmes contain far too much sex and violence.[35]

When the Television Act of 1954 was being debated in Parliament, representations from various interested individuals and groups led to a provision in the law which has been continued through its several revisions. 'It shall be the duty of the Authority to satisfy themselves that, so far as possible, . . . proper proportions of the recorded and other matter included in the programmes are of British origin and of British performance.'[36] Although the expressions, 'proper proportion', 'British origins', and 'British performance' are not defined in the Act, the IBA considers a film to be British 'only when all the constituent elements in it are British'. During the parliamentary debates, Labour spokesmen suggested that the allowable amount of foreign material be set at not more than 20 per cent, but the government rejected a specific figure as administratively unworkable, although in practice both ITV and BBC tried to maintain a 14 per cent figure.[37] In determining national origin, a number of factors are considered. 'If a studio is to be used in the production, this must be in British territory. If a film is made by a company, that company must be British and have a majority of British directors. Other relevant factors are the nationalities of producers, directors, writers, actors, composers, musicians, and technicians. '[38]

In consequence of this legal mandate, the IBA has laid down some very explicit rules.[39] No more than seven feature films may be carried by the ITV network in any one week. There is no stated limit on the number of television films which may be imported. However, up to 1979 the IBA required that not more than 14 per cent of the total output—including both television and cinema films—could be of foreign origin. But effective in the summer of that year, under new rules promulgated in July 1978, the Authority announced that the total amount of British produced material would be increased from its 1978 level of 84½ per cent to 86 per cent; that programmes from the Commonwealth would be included in the foreign quota; and that only 5½ hours of foreign programming could be telecast during prime time, which was redefined to be from 6.30 to 10.30 p.m., as opposed to the former definition of 7.30 to 11 p.m. It was expected that this new ruling would reduce the amount of foreign programming by 2 hours per week or more.

In addition, there may be no more than five feature films or television movies each week between 7 and 11 p.m., at least one of which must begin not earlier than 10.30 p.m.; and there shall be an average of not more than three British feature films per week over a year's time. In any case, 2 hours must elapse between the end of one feature film and the beginning of another one. The first company to transmit a feature film or television movie is responsible for classifying it in one of four categories: SAT (suitable any time); Post-7.30 p.m.; Post-9 p.m.; and—if the film contains a possibly disturbing incident, such as a hanging, which cannot be edited out—Post-9.30 p.m. But ITV has no regulations about live programmes from abroad, or live originations in the United Kingdom by foreign performers, although it recognizes its general responsibility for encouraging British writers and performers.

Film Scheduling

Feature and television films are an important part of the British television output.[40] During 1978–9, on BBC 1, 14.2 per cent (717 hours) of all programmes were films, on BBC 2, 13.5 per cent (553 hours), and on the two services together, 13.9 per cent (1270 hours.) In the same year, 8 per cent of the weekly transmissions of the average ITV company consisted of feature films.[41] (In 1977–8 the figure was 8 per cent; in 1976–7 it was 9 per cent; and in 1975–6 it was 10.5 per cent.)

The Annan Committee observed that the BBC showed more films from more countries than did ITV, probably because its two networks require more programmes; but in any case, American sources 'dominated' the film schedules of both organizations.[42] It also noted that the BBC uses more cinema films, while ITV relies more on television movies, of which many are 'crime stories'. The Committee said that one reason for this heavy use of American films was the common language, although it might have gone further to observe that most American television films are available at a good price, since their basic costs are written off during their original American presentations.

In addition to airing films made by others, the BBC and the companies maintain film units to produce complete programmes, make inserts for studio productions, and sometimes record actualities for news shows. BBC film operations are centred in Ealing, West London, in the building formerly used by the famous Ealing film studios. There are auxiliary facilities at the Lime Grove, Alexandra Palace, and some other London and regional BBC studios, and dubbing theatres at the Television Centre, Lime Grove, and the Ealing Studios, all of which operate on a two-shift basis, 7 days a week. The film and video-tape library located at Brentford, Middlesex, contains, among other things, over 350 million feet of film.

For the most part, films are broadcast in their entirety, although certain cuts are made, especially of scenes judged to be excessively violent. There also are some programmes about films, such as *Clapperboard*, a long-time Granada feature, the purpose of which is to stimulate young people to develop an interest in film, its art, history, and production techniques. The programme often visits studios to see films in production, and to talk to the 'people behind the cameras rather than the stars'.[43] By 1977, 240 programmes had been presented. Special effects, scenery, set design and construction, and music for films have been among the subjects treated.

Although some are of British origin, a good share of the cinema features and television movies broadcast come from the United States. Thus, the cinema films broadcast by BBC 1 during the spring of 1976 included such titles, actors, and producers as: *Bugs Bunny, Easter Parade*, Laurel and Hardy, *Here Come the Co-eds, Deputy Dawg, Boss Cat, The Wonderful World of Disney*, Charlie Chaplin, Walt Disney, *Guess Who's Coming to Dinner?*, *Huckleberry Hound*,

Hell Fighters, D-Day, The Quiet Man , and *Barefoot Executive*. Television movies included: *Cannon, The Olympiad, Starsky and Hutch, Kojak, The Shari Lewis Show*, and the *Invisible Man.**

BBC 2 schedules less film material since its air-time is shorter. Among the cinema films offered were: *The Women, A Double Life, Adam's Rib, Gunpoint, The Thin Man Goes Home, A Star is Born, High Sierra*, and *White Heat*. Television movies on BBC 2 included *The Waltons* and *Rhoda*.

During one quarter, ITV films included: *Guns of Navarone, The King and I, South Pacific, Looking Glass War, Reflections in a Golden Eye, From Russia with Love, our Mother's House, Murphy's War, Gentlemen Prefer Blondes, There's No Business like Show Business*, and *Two Mules for Sister Sarah*. Of the cinema films on ITV, the Annan Committee remarked: 'ITV's choice of films from the American market shown in peak viewing hours is at times deplorable', although that generalization surely could not be applied to all of the titles listed above.[44] Its television movies included: *Police Surgeon, Batman, 77 Sunset Strip, The Flintstones, The Hound of the Baskervilles, Born Free, Bionic Woman, Eleanor and Franklin, The Beachcombers, The Jetsons, Wild Women, Columbo, Policewomen, Six Million Dollar Man, Return to the Planet of the Apes, Fantastic Voyage, Run Joe Run, The Lone Ranger, Spiderman*, and *The Man From Uncle*.

The 1980 reports on film programming by both the BBC and the IBA contained some interesting similarities.[45] The Corporation wrote:

> Traditionally, the BBC's home-produced programmes have always been augmented by a strand of feature films or American-produced television series, like *Kojak*, which supplied a crop of well-made action/adventure stories. . . .This was the first year in which the shortage of feature films and the absence of any very good purchasable cops and robbers series on the American market made itself felt.

The IBA referred to 'the increasing difficulty of acquiring feature films suitable for showing to a domestic audience. This difficulty may diminish in time if the current trend in the cinema for explicitness in sex, violence and language in turn diminishes.'

---

* A BBC Audience Research Report had the following comments relative to *Kojak*:

Of the various American crime and detection series, *Kojak* made by far the greatest impact with Monday night audiences of some 13 millions. This was 'American cops-and-robbers with a difference'—unsmart, provocative, 'socially significant': 'a good portrayal of man at his best, at his worst, and at his most vulnerable'. It was noted that even some of the endings were 'true-to-life', and not improbably 'clear-cut' as the detective convention so often demands. Acting and production were said to be equally 'realistic', whilst the locations and sets—'none of those penthouse office-suites', but dark streets, drab tenements, a really 'awful' police station—apparently 'spoke volumes' about life in the poorer districts of New York.

(BBC, *Annual Review of BBC Audience Research Findings Number 2*, 1974–5, p. 20.)

LIGHT ENTERTAINMENT

Programmes of information, education, and entertainment are the mainstay of broadcasting. To the serious-minded person, informational, educational, and cultural programmes may be the most important—and indeed they are important. But the significance of entertainment features should not be overlooked. Because they attract the most—including many of the least sophisticated—listeners and viewers, they may have the greatest public impact. They unquestionably have the largest audiences, and therefore build audiences for serious programmes. Finally, it is their success that determines a commercial system's income level, for which reason many of the principal policy decisions in any commercial broadcasting organization concern its entertainment output.

John Reith, whose name suggests austerity, the 'Reith Sunday', and the high ideals of the BBC, had some interesting things to say about entertainment back in 1924.[46]

A closer inspection of the word 'entertainment' [he wrote] is sufficient to show how incomplete is the ordinarily accepted meaning. To entertain means to occupy agreeably. . . . Enjoyment may be sought . . . as a mere means of passing the time, and therefore of wasting it. . . . On the other hand, it may be a part of a systematic and sustained endeavour to re-create, to build up knowledge, experience and character, perhaps even in the face of obstacles.

Fifty years later Lady Plowden, when IBA Chairman, told the Royal Television Society:[47] 'Television's contribution to society is not made only in serious documentaries. Everybody needs occasions when they see or hear something which simply makes them feel good. The forgetting of sorrow, fear for the future, pain, old age and loneliness can relieve pressures and give courage.'

In 1975 the programme companies provided the Annan Committee with some ideas about light entertainment.[48]

Television is the natural medium for relaxation [they wrote, and then noted that although the] average family is not averse to a limited intrusion of unpleasant facts and uninvited politicians in its sitting room, . . . what most viewers want most of the time is to be made to smile and laugh. [However] success in comedy is not easily achieved. The qualities of characterization, dialogue and timing that distinguish the best of comedy remain elusive. Tribute should be paid to the BBC for reaching some high peaks. ITV has reached them less frequently, although more often in the last two years. This, even more than most, is an area which demands experiment and where the failure rate is high. A programme may be polished and re-polished to the complete satisfaction of its makers but exposure to the viewer is the only real test of whether or not it is funny.

Like broadcasting systems all over the world, those in Britain offer a good deal of light entertainment.[49] In 1978–9, Radio 2 devoted 3.5 per cent and Radio 4 4.5 per cent of their hours to variety. The figure for BBC 1 was 7.1 per cent, and for

BBC 2 it was 5.6 per cent, the two-network average being 6.4 per cent. Direct comparisons between BBC television and ITV are hard to make because of the different categories they use in classifying their programme output. During 1978– 9, the typical ITV company devoted 12 hours 13 minutes (12 per cent) of its weekly time to 'entertainment and music.' In 1956, the average was 14 hours 36 minutes (21 per cent). When the disproportionate amount of light entertainment on ITV was widely criticized (see above, pp. 82–6), the figures changed, and in 1966, only 7 hours 38 minutes (11 per cent) of the weekly time of the average company was devoted to such material. (In making these comparisons, however, it should be noted that the total number of ITV broadcasting hours has increased considerably over the last two decades: 1956—47 hours; 1966—66 hours 39 minutes; 1976—92 hours 55 minutes.) But despite the difficulty of making BBC–ITV comparisons, there clearly is more light entertainment on the commercial service than on either BBC network, an impression which is confirmed by even casual viewing. It is possible, of course, that with a second network at its disposal, ITV programme balances may change in future years.

The BBC Light Entertainment Department is responsible for 'radio entertainment shows of many kinds, including situation comedy, satire, quiz and panel games'.[50] Its head, like those of the other programme departments, reports to the Managing Director, Radio. BBC television divides its Light Entertainment Group into two departments, Variety and Comedy, the latter being responsible for situation comedy (*Porridge, Fawlty Towers*) as well as off-beat humour like *Monty Python's Flying Circus* and *The Goodies*. The head of the Television Light Entertainment Group reports to the Managing Director, Television.

Entertainment Programmes
Radio light entertainment programmes today could be classified as comedy, quiz and panel games, and music.[51] One successful long-running scripted series is *The Goon Show*, broadcast to American audiences by NPR during the last several years. Success also has been achieved with *Dad's Army*, a radio adaptation of a television series of the same name.

Among quiz and panel shows are *Top of the Form, Does the Team Think*? and *The Half Open University*, the latter appropriately placed on Radio 3, which normally stays away from comedy fare. Long enduring is the annual search for the *Brain of Britain*, in which contestants answer Information-Please-type questions, which become increasingly difficult as each year's series runs its course.* In 1979 Radio 2 brought back 'for the first time in a decade, hour-long variety bills, from *The Frankie Howerd Variety Show* and *Variety Club* . . . [with a combination of old and new] comics, instrumentalists and impressionists.'

Although the BBC's light entertainment and comedy programmes often

---

* I was a contestant on this programme several times in 1954, lasting into the semifinals before being eliminated by the eventual top 'brain'. What would the BBC have done if I—a Fulbright Scholar from America—by some good luck had emerged as 'The Brain of Britain'? Actually, there was very little chance of that happening, since the winner's encyclopaedic mind left me way behind. Incidentally, much more difficult questions are asked now than 25 years ago.

outdraw those of the IBA, the BBC handbooks devote much less space to them than do the yearly publications of the IBA, probably indicating thereby the different programme emphases of the two organizations.[52] BBC 2 carried a programme on 26 June 1976, from 8.35 to 10.15 p.m. called *The Sound of Laughter*, which as the *Radio Times* put it, 'takes an affectionate look at radio comedy from the earliest days of the British Broadcasting Company right up the present'. A number of famous radio comedians—some still on the air but most of them not—talked about the old days, and we saw film and kinescope recordings made during actual broadcasts. Although the programme was long and slow-moving, it offered older viewers a chance to relax on a Saturday evening, and to recall nostalgically some radio shows from the past.

Most British top-rated entertainment programmes now are situation comedies. One highly successful series was *Dad's Army*, a caricature of the Home Guard during World War II. Although it built its audience gradually, it eventually proved very popular both with the Home Guard generation and its children. Another popular BBC series was *Porridge*, set in a prison, which related the experiences of some prisoners who always outwitted their guards—somewhat as Hogan's Heroes hoodwinked their captors in the American series of that name. According to the BBC, the strength of the series 'lay not only in the comic writing but in the poignancy of many of the situations'.* The *Porridge* series has been replaced by *Going Straight*, in which the principal characters of the old series leave prison, and try 'to survive in an outside world that is sometimes bizarre, sometimes rather hostile'.

Comedy of the way-out variety is provided by *Monty Python's Flying Circus* and *The Goodies*, both of which have been aired by America's Public Broadcasting System.[53] The BBC also thinks highly of *The Good Life* and *Fawlty Towers*, which received prizes and attracted large audiences. ITV situation comedies have included the Thames series, *Man About the House* and *Rising Damp*. Miss Piggy, one of the characters in ATV's *The Muppet Show*, has won fame on both sides of the Atlantic, while *Charlies' Angels* now appear on ITV.

The IBA points with pride to Thames Television's *Love Thy Neighbour*, which encouraged viewers to 'laugh *with* coloured people not *at* them'.[54] As one of the scriptwriters described it: 'It appeared . . . that to take a white man who had all the bigoted, prejudiced attitudes towards black people and give him a black neighbour who in turn wasn't particularly fond of white people would provide an excellent platform for a comedy series.' Over a 5-year period there were eight series of *Love*

---

* *BBC Handbook, 1977*, p. 18; *BBC Handbook, 1979*, p. 8. In 1975 BBC Audience Research Department reported on this series as follows.

The outstanding success of the year on BBC television proved to be *Porridge* . . . . A prison setting was something new in comedy, it was noted after the first show, and with Ronnie Barker 'inside', promised a really amusing series. Most viewers felt this first episode certainly augured well, and an excellent script, combined with splendid acting, kept many laughing throughout as they had not laughed for some time. A minority had reservations, but the Reaction Index was 72, and the audience 14 millions.

(BBC, *Annual Review of BBC Audience Research Findings*, Number 2, 1974–75, p. 22.) The BBC has published several books of *Porridge* scripts for general reading.

Thy Neighbour, which always had high ratings, and sometimes placed among the top 20. It was supplemented by an American production, *The Fosters*, 'the first all-black show on TV in the United Kingdom', in which 'a perfectly normal family who happen to be black' had a normal series of family experiences. Then came London Weekend's *Mixed Blessings*, 'about Susan and Thomas, the young partners of a mixed marriage'. The episode I saw, in October 1978, was 'light' comedy, whatever the colour of the principals. Its very thin plot-line ended when the black bride's father took his (obviously unwelcome) white son-in-law to a black pub. The final scene showed everyone roaring drunk—and colour-blind. My query was: is drunkenness the preferred way to bridge the colour gap?

Both services have audience participation programmes. The BBC used to carry *What's My Line*, based on the American model, while ITV had *The 64,000 Question, 21, Spot the Tune, Double Your Money, Beat the Clock*, and *Dotto*. Other ITV programmes of this type have included the *Sweepstakes Game* (London Weekend) emceed by Bernard Braden, *Sale of the Century* (Anglia), and *Winner Takes All* (Yorkshire.)[55] Since 1962, Granada has had *University Challenge*, a general knowledge contest which brings together teams of university students from various parts of the United Kingdom. When hearing and seeing participants doing very well on audience participation shows, I am reminded of a conversation in the middle 1950s with a BBC programme executive who explained that the Corporation did not develop such programmes because the British people were naturally shy and would not like to compete, and that if they did, they would make poor performers.

The BBC brought *This Is Your Life* over from America in the autumn of 1955, with Eammon Andrews, a popular British emcee, in the role originally taken by Ralph Edwards. Discriminating British viewers agree with many American critics that the programme is in doubtful taste. Yet it still holds forth on Thames Television, with the same master of ceremonies who introduced it originally on the BBC. Among the longest-running television shows was ATV's *Sunday Night at the London Palladium* which, from its debut in September 1955 until 1968, was usually among the top audience shows. The series originated in the London Palladium, which called itself 'the world's most famous variety theatre', and whose director, Val Parnell, also was managing director of ATV. Each programme had a star of international reputation (often an American), a chorus line and orchestra, a short audience-participation game with prizes, and a few music-hall acts, the whole thing being tied together by a master of ceremonies, or to use the British term, 'a compere'. It was unsuccessfully revived for a short time in 1973. Remarking on its demise the ITCA said:

> Personality programmes no longer brew the same magic, . . . [and] many shows glittering with popular groups and international stars cannot now attract audiences as large as the amateur talent contests. . . . Professionally, today's trend favours the one off special with the single star: Julie Andrews, Benny Hill, Stanley Baxter.[56]

Although *Sunday Night at the Palladium* is no longer around, one of its contemporaries does survive, the BBC's *Black and White Minstrel Show*, which I saw—with just the same format—25 years ago. The men—all whites—have blackened faces and the women—also whites—white faces. They sing and dance, and there are several 1930 vaudeville-style comics. But the programme is not a minstrel show, and there is no attempt to approximate the speech or humour of black people. It would seem that the blacks in Britain might complain, but apparently they do not.[57]

In contrast is BBC 1's *Top of the Pops* for teenagers, which features rock groups performing with their standard gyrations.* Deplorable was an ITV light music programme broadcast during a later afternoon period one day in September 1978, *Get it Together*, on which a young man sang as two young women in abbreviated costumes did a hip-jiggling dance that never would have passed America's network censors. More imaginative—and much more sophisticated in approach—was Oscar Peterson's Piano Party, a series consisting mainly of performances by outstanding black jazz players. A special guest one evening was Edward Heath, Conservative Prime Minister from 1970 to 1974, with organ playing, orchestra conducting, and sailing among his avocations, who played a Bach Prelude on a clavichord. On the same programme a former cinema pianist improvised an accompaniment to some silent films she was seeing for the first time.

Other programmes are built around a single star. I saw Shirley Bassey sing in some very elaborate settings, as well as Vera Lynn, 'the forces' sweetheart' of World War II, with the late Bing Crosby as a guest. Lynn's performance may have delighted her former admirers, but it seemed flat and dull to me. BBC solo specials also have been built around Twiggy, Perry Como, and other singers from both sides of the Atlantic.

ITV too has musical entertainment.[58] Arthur Askey, a 79-year-old-star of yesterday, in Tyne Tees' *Songs that Topped the Shows*, took his audience on a 'trip down Memory Lane'. Hot violinist Stephane Grappelli took part in a folk series created by HTV and West, and Ann Margret—identified incidentally by her full name of Ann-Margret Olsson—appeared with Tina Turner. Danny Kaye and Mia Farrow joined in ATV's 2-hour production of *Peter Pan*.

Big bands are seen and heard on both BBC and ITV.[59] In 1975, BBC 2 did *Big Bands from the Dorchester* [Hotel], with Count Basie, Stan Kenton, Johnny Dankworth, Buddy Rich, Woody Herman, Ted Heath and Duke Ellington. Granada drew upon familiar classics, jazz, rock, and soul music for its *International Pop Proms*, presented before an audience of over 3000 in the Belle

---

* The BBC's Audience Research Department had a report on the 600th edition of *Top of the Pops*, broadcast on 9 October 1975, which

> attracted its usual large audience of about 11 millions, but was a little more coolly received than usual. Some of its viewers, for instance, thought that the occasion warranted a special programme (chart-toppers going back over the year, perhaps, as at Christmas time), others complaining that the format was dull and stale or the songs and artists this week rather poor. The majority, however, enjoyed it well enough.

(BBC, *Annual Review of BBC Audience Research Findings* Number 3, 1975/6, p. 24.)

Vue Auditorium in Manchester. The jacket of a long-playing record accompanying the series said it was developed on the assumption 'that some contemporary pop music had reached a maturity approaching the classical'. Although the jacket praised highly the performance of the 50-piece orchestra and the Les Humphrey Singers, the playing and the sound seemed to me much inferior to the standards set by André Kostelanetz, Morton Gould, and their American contemporaries.

In ATV's *Jack Parnell's Big Band Show*, a well-known British band leader led a sixteen-piece organization with instrumentation like that of the big bands of the 1930s and 1940s in popular music of various periods, assisted by such guests as Stephane Grappelli, Anne Shelton, Johnny Dankworth and others. London Weekend's *All You Need is Love*—which could be described as a light entertainment documentary—ranged from rhythmn and blues to swing. Guest stars, including Bing Crosby, Aretha Franklin, Paul McCartney, Benny Goodman, Richard Rogers, Roy Rogers, Dave Brubeck, and Dizzie Gillespie, were filmed on location in various parts of the world, and archival films showing actual performances by Charlie Parker and Scott Joplin were included.

17 Children's Programmes

The many critics of children's broadcasts in the United States would heartily endorse the way such programmes are produced in the United Kingdom. Back in 1949, the BBC wrote that its Children's Hour tried 'to entertain the children in a stimulating way, guiding their reading, encouraging their various interests and including Christian principles of love of God and of their neighbour'.[1] Although the radio Children's Hour was discontinued in 1964, when its audience left it for television, the BBC now offers the children responsible and well-produced television programmes. ITV's performance has wavered at times, but its current record is good.

It was assumed from the outset that the IBA would have children's programmes, but because of doubts as to the quality of such broadcasts from a commercially supported organization, special safeguards were written into the Television Act of 1954. The original law prescribed an advisory committee for all children's programmes, both in and out of school, although, in accordance with a recommendation from the Pilkington Committee in 1962, subsequent legislation required a committee for school programmes only. However, the Pilkington Report did specify that it should 'be part of the Authority's general duty to consider the nature of programmes for children, as well as to consider the effect of other programmes on children when large numbers may be expected to be viewing'.[2]

The current law requires the Authority to draw up a violence code for all programmes, and it makes special reference to times 'when large numbers of children and young persons may be expected to be watching or listening'.[3] The BBC violence code also refers to children's programmes, although it is not legally required to have such a code. The Authority writes into its contracts with the programme companies—in addition to the stipulation that they carry 9 hours of school programmes while schools are in session—the requirement that they 'broadcast, at a suitable early evening time, at least an hour from Monday to Friday of programmes specially designed for children, and at least half an hour at a suitable time each Saturday or Sunday'.

In BBC television the Children's Programmes Department, which is among the twenty or so reporting to the Managing Director, Television, produces most corporation programmes of this type, although some are made by the Drama Group, the Light Entertainment Group, and the Natural History Unit in Bristol.[4] In addition, some local and network programmes are produced in the national and regional broadcasting centres. The Annan Committee remarked that this was

> one area where the BBC is helped by its structure. . . . The Children's
> Programmes Department . . . has been able to exercise a good deal of autonomy

within the time periods and the overall departmental budgets allocated by the Channel Controllers. This has allowed the department to plan for variety in their programmes and to build up an expertise and confidence. They mix their own productions with bought-in material, drama with comedy, serious programmes with lighter material in a self-contained schedule.[5]

BBC radio for children began in 1922 with birthday greeting programmes like those broadcast by many American stations, and in 1923 various BBC staff members went on the air as Uncle Arthur, Uncle Caractus, Uncle Leslie, Uncle Jim, Uncle Rex, Uncle Humpty Dumpty, Uncle Jack Frost, Aunt Sophie, and Aunt Phyllis. One of the 'uncles' wrote in 1924 that 'there is no section of our programme work upon which more time and thought is spent than that termed The Children's Hour'.[6] It is a matter of record that one of the first plays written especially for radio was for *The Children's Hour*, and that the first orchestral piece broadcast by a BBC ensemble, Roger Quilter's *Children's Overture*, also was on *The Children's Hour*. Another high point in children's radio history was the cycle of religious plays by Dorothy Sayer, *The Man Born to be King*, first broadcast in 1941.[7] Because its scripts treated Jesus as a real person, the broadcasts created what the Corporation later described as probably 'the biggest single row in the history of religious broadcasting in Britain'.[8] Yet, the series was broadcast, and was so well received that it was repeated a number of times in later years.

The Children's Hour, which varied from 15 to 60 minutes in length, during later years occupied the period from 5 p.m. to 5.55 each weekday afternoon on the Home Service. *Listen With Mother*, produced by the School Broadcasting Department, and aired at 1.45 p.m. Monday to Friday, was introduced in 1950, and there was a Saturday programme at the same hour called *Listen on Saturday*, now discontinued, its place being taken for a time by television's *Watch With Mother*.

Many precedents established during the radio days carried over into television, including the concept that *The Children's Hour* should be a miniature BBC, offering its listeners in all age ranges much the same choice of material available to adults: stories; fairy tales; biographies; a few appropriate 'thrillers'; serial adaptations of classic children's books; short talks on subjects ranging from animals and music to travelling and hobbies; occasional round tables which gave children a chance to question experts; music; and quizzes. In 1961, when the Corporation became aware of a progressive decline in listeners, it was decided to phase out *The Children's Hour*, and it was discontinued entirely in 1964, though not without some strong protests.[9]

ITV programmes for children got off to a slow start, although their development was accelerated by a Programme Consultation held by the IBA and the companies in 1965.[10] Long-range planning now is done by a subcommittee of the Network Programming Committee, made up of representatives of the five central and two of the regional companies, with one person from the IBA present at all meetings. This subcommittee 'undertakes forward planning of programmes, co-ordinates the production resources of companies and considers the quality, balance, supply and performance of children's programmes'. Although all the central and most of the regional companies produce some children's programmes, the major network suppliers are Thames Television in London and Southern Television in Southampton, and increasingly for original drama, HTV in Bristol and Cardiff.

PROGRAMME PRINCIPLES AND OBJECTIVES

The head of BBC Children's Programmes outlined in 1966 certain principles that still are observed, and are accepted by ITV as well.[11]

1. The Corporation has 'a responsibility to use the experiences and powerful medium of television to enlarge and enrich the total experiences of the children who choose to watch its programmes'.
2. Because British television is competitive, and the Corporation therefore does not have a captive audience, programmes must be sufficiently attractive so that children will deliberately choose to watch them.
3. If this is to occur, the programmes must be entertaining. 'At the end . . . [the audience] should be left with a sense of enjoyment, wonder, and stimulation.'
4. Finally, 'at all times children must be treated with respect and without condescension'.[12]

Children's programmes encourage active rather than passive reactions.[13] Children are invited to write in; collect anything from money to spoons and forks to be melted down to finance holidays for needy children; make designs; write poems; and design new clothing. Some producers try to watch their programmes with children in order to better judge their effects.

But it is not all work and no play. As the head of BBC Children's Programmes once wrote:

> For some of the time available each day we try to provide relaxation and refreshment through laughter or excitement. We try to ensure that the escapist programmes are good of their kind, and however much some parents may deplore the two American cartoons included each week [this was written in 1971], their immense popularity with children shows that they satisfy a craving for 'easy' entertainment which is as appropriate for the eight-year-old as some sport or light entertainment is for their parents.

In Britain, as in America, there is the problem of violence. A BBC Note of Guidance warns against showing undesirable conduct that could easily be copied, such as using knives or broken bottles in fights, or locking up 'prisoners' in outhouses, empty rooms, or cellars.[14] Violence should not normally be presented as the 'inevitable solution' to problems, and when shown, should not be in contexts relating to the child's own life.

As one BBC spokesman put it:[15]

Children cannot grow up in a cosy unreal world and while television rightly provides escapist fantasies it must also accurately reflect real life. I think that the main danger of too much violence in television is not that it may lead to aggressive behaviour in certain individuals, although it can do this, but that it may become accepted as something ordinary and unremarkable. If children only see films in which the solution to any problem is a fight they will get a distorted view of life. We cannot pretend, however, that children do not enjoy watching violent actions. When we invited child viewers to tell us how they would like the plot of a drama serial to develop we had to abandon many of their ideas because they were too bloodthirsty and too frightening.*

The Corporation has decided that it will not present special programmes for deprived children. There are programmes for children of limited skills, but the children viewing such programmes are unlikely to realize that the programmes have been designed especially for them. In this connection, it is interesting to notice that the favourite television programme of many deaf children was a series of popular music programmes called *Top of the Pops*, which, when it was on the air, also was favoured by children with normal hearing.[16]

There has been discussion both in the United States and the United Kingdom about the BBC's reaction to *Sesame Street*. As the director of BBC Children's Programmes put it, the BBC's *Play School* differs in approach from

> the well-publicized didactic intention of the American 'Sesame Street'. Each programme has evolved out of the very different traditions of children's television in each country. 'Sesame Street' uses the techniques of commercials and cartoons to teach with humour and repetition the alphabet, numbers, and certain basic concepts while 'Play School' aims to provide an imaginative and intellectual stimulus and to encourage creative activity.[17]

Sesame Street, however, has been shown by ITV with good response. (For the reaction of the BBC School Broadcasting Department to *Sesame Street*, see pp. 257–8n.)

One of radio's special problems is what to do about popular records which are obscene, or contain undesirable references to drugs and sex.[18] For a time a committee of producers checked every new record, but this had to be discontinued because there were too many records, so responsibility now rests on the shoulders

---

* The NAB codes lay down general principles greatly in accord with those of the British broadcasters. The Television Code says, in part:

Broadcasters have a special responsibility to children. Programmes designed primarily for children should take into account the range of interests and needs of children from instructional and cultural material to a wide variety of entertainment material. In their totality, programmes should contribute to the sound, balanced development of children to help them achieve a sense of the world at large and informed adjustments to their society. (*NAB Television Code*, p. 3.)

The Code also states: 'Children should also be exposed, at the appropriate times, to a reasonable range of the realities which exist in the world sufficient to help them make the transition to adulthood.'

of individual producers. However, the BBC does not publicize its lists of banned records, lest it thereby win them additional publicity and circulation.

There also is concern about the possible long-term effects on youth of disc jockey speech. As the BBC itself admitted: 'In some quarters speech on Radio 1 has a bad name.'[19] Although there are differences of opinion on the subject, the Corporation found that 'the appeal of disc jockeys for many youngsters lies in the fact that they cannot be equated with the world of teachers, employers, officers and superiors. It is indeed the domination of Radio 1 by non-establishment figures which is a part of its attraction for young people.'

IBA guidelines approximate those of the BBC.[20] Its children's programmes are based on a formula developed jointly by the companies and the Authority. Air-time is divided between drama, information, and light entertainment programmes, and 'outside bought film' is used in limited quantities. The companies described their role with an interesting reference to the BBC: 'In the avuncular tradition of the BBC, producers stand in loco parentis. Children can be safely left with the set and will come to no harm from what they see. The programmes will aim at giving enjoyment and the thoughts expressed in them will be unexceptional.'

The following lines from an IBA publication could well have been written by the BBC.[21]

In broad terms, ITV aims to hold a balance in its children's provision between pure entertainment and factual information. The intention is that the material aimed at the child's intellect will be as entertaining as possible while the stories, cartoons and light entertainment shows which appeal primarily to his imagination will use simple enjoyment as a means of conveying information. What is essential is that each programme be produced to the highest possible standard and above all be stimulating as well as entertaining.

Accordingly, the IBA attempts to provide in its afternoon children's hour 'a whole service in miniature in which every kind of programme, including news, has its place'.

A commercial note was introduced by the executive producer of children's dramatic programmes at Southern Television: 'If there is any basic philosophy which links our dramatised programmes for children, it is to keep it moving. The younger audience resists lengthy dialogue scenes.'[22] The IBA agrees with the BBC as to the importance of children's listening actively rather than passively. 'Nearly every programme', states the Authority, 'has some suggestion for making or playing games with ordinary household articles, and some of the ideas are reinforced in published material. . . .'

The questions of family insecurity, marital infidelity, and sex are more difficult to resolve. Most programmes emphasizing these topics are scheduled after the Watershed hour of 9 p.m., but rules also have been drawn up for broadcasts before that hour. The IBA Violence Code contains several admonitions which approximate those laid down by the BBC.[23]

The portrayal of violence is one of the main considerations which determine whether or not a programme is suitable for transmission during 'family viewing time.' Programmes shown before 9 p.m. should not be unsuitable for an audience in which children are present. . . . Scenes which may unsettle young children need special care. Insecurity is less tolerable for a child—particularly an emotionally unstable child—than for a mature adult. Violence, menace and threats can take many forms—emotional, physical and verbal. Scenes of domestic friction, whether or not accompanied by physical violence, can easily cause fear and insecurity.

Children appear on the programmes of both broadcasting organizations, although under somewhat different circumstances. The head of BBC's Children's Television wrote in 1971:

Children do not . . . appear in programmes as show business performers because we do not wish to exploit or over-praise immature talent for the envy of other children, who have no hope of appearing in a programme, nor for the entertainment of adults. We prefer to use experienced and professional adult artists in light entertainment shows.[24]

However, children do appear on BBC programmes, taking part in general-knowledge quiz shows, in questioning celebrities, or discussing contemporary issues of the sort in which young people are interested.[25]

The IBA programme companies use children both as actors and participants, but under fairly detailed rules drawn up to protect them from exploitation.[26] The IBA handbook for 1976 devoted two pages to 'The Young Actor', remarking: 'Children often appear in the programmes especially made for their interest and enjoyment—as the audience, as participants in a variety of studio and outdoor activities and as performers.' Thereafter the handbook identified several young people who, after beginning in children's programmes, went on to successful careers on stage and screen. As to 'participation programs', *Anything You Can Do* drew upon all regions 'in organizing a knock-out competition of skills between children all over the country', and later arranged a programme involving English and Dutch children. Yorkshire's *Junior Showtime* has given 'hundreds of children the opportunity to perform on television'.[27]

THE PROGRAMMES

Considerable time is given to children's programmes on television, although there now are few such programmes on radio. During 1978–9, for example, the BBC's radio networks devoted 247 hours, or 0.9 per cent of their time, to children's programmes, most of which—174 hours—was on Radio 1.[28] Television did much better, with BBC 1 devoting 636 hours or 12.6 per cent of its time to children's programmes, and BBC 2 devoting 117 hours or 2.8 per cent, for a total of 753 hours or 8.2 per cent of the time on both networks. In addition to these radio and television network programmes for children, there also are regional and local broadcasts on both BBC and IBA stations.

The IBA divides its programmes into two categories. During 1978–9, 'Children's Informative' programmes occupied an average of 2 hours 10 minutes, or 2 per cent of the time of a typical ITV company each week, while 'Children's Entertainment' averaged 7 hours 57 minutes, or 8 per cent of the time.[29] Children's programmes therefore occupied 8.2 per cent of BBC-Television time and 10 per cent of ITV time, although direct comparisons are not possible, since the Corporation did not divide its programmes into separate 'information' and 'entertainment' categories.

Monday to Friday there is a programme for pre-school children on BBC 2 from 11 to 11.25 a.m., the programme being repeated the same afternoon by BBC 1 from 3.55 to 4.20 p.m. The children's programme 'slot' runs from 4.20 to 5.40 p.m., the block being broken into shorter sections varying in length from 5 to 20 minutes. Among them, they offer programmes for several age groups each afternoon, including films, stories, news, and some utilizing young performers.

ITV has programmes for pre-school children each weekday at noon. They follow immediately the morning series for schools which runs from 9.30 to 12 noon. The other children's period extends from 4.15 to 5.45, at about the same time as the BBC's offering, the scheduling being intentional in order to give children viewing at that hour a choice mainly of programmes intended for them. In addition, the whole of Saturday mornings is devoted to a children's package— special shows, feature films, and cartoons, while the Sunday afternoon schedule includes a drama series intended for children's viewing in a family group.

Both BBC and IBA adhere to the 'Watershed Policy' under which adult programmes unsuitable for an audience in which children are present are not scheduled before 9 p.m. But this is not to say that every programme broadcast during the early evening is suitable for every child since children, like adults are individuals, and what one 9-year-old could view with impunity might have an adverse effect on another one. Accordingly, the Corporation maintains, only someone who knows a child very well, like a parent or older sibling, can decide what he or she can assimilate, and a child's viewing should be planned accordingly.[30]

The IBA wrote that

> parents themselves should accept responsibility for what their children view and also that adult viewers have a right to expect adult material. By *TV Times* billings, press notices and broadcast trailers, Independent Television provides parents with sufficient advance information about programme content for prudent judgements to be formed.[31]

The BBC does likewise, although it spoke for both in saying that, even though the Watershed Policy offered 'only limited protection', it still was 'worth having. Whatever its weaknesses, it is the best practical solution that anyone has so far been able to devise.'[32]

In addition to programmes for children, aged approximately 5–7, 8–11, and

12–14, both broadcasting organizations serve pre-school children. The longest-running of these is *Play School*, a daily BBC feature since 1953, an outgrowth of radio's *Listen With Mother* and, like it, intended to be viewed by mother and child together. *Play School* now is broadcast by BBC 2 weekday mornings at 11 a.m., with a BBC 1 repeat at 3.55 p.m. During its 25 minutes, the programme uses music, poetry, stories, film, and simple experiments to suggest types of children's play. *Play School* has done programmes jointly with Israel, Canada, Switzerland, Austria, and Norway. Since many homes do not have an adult available to watch with children, the programme speaks to the child directly.[33]

There are so many programmes for children of school age on both BBC and ITV that only a few can be mentioned here.[34] Outstanding is the *Blue Peter* series. I remember the enthusiasm with which my children watched it in London in 1958 and 1959, and I personally found it intriguing then and in 1976 and 1978, when I viewed again. The programme now is on the air several days a week during the late afternoon children's period. To develop an understanding of other countries, *Blue Peter* goes exploring, and via films has visited such places as Mexico, Ceylon, Morocco, the West Indies, Africa, Europe, and the United States. Like most BBC children's programmes, *Blue Peter* encourages its viewers to both thought and action. In 1973, *Blue Peter* was instrumental in collecting and selling so many stamps that the proceeds were adequate to send some modern agricultural equipment to a drought-stricken area in Ethiopia. The next year a Labrador puppy, 'Buttons', was purchased with returns from a special appeal to select and train a guide dog for the blind to replace a previous *Blue Peter* guide dog, retired after 10 years of service.[35] On one occasion, after *Blue Peter* had mentioned a vintage car race from London to Brighton, the route was lined with children wearing *Blue Peter* badges. Another time half a million packages of scrap metal were collected for charity use. A competition for a 'Keep Britain Tidy' poster brought 150,000 entries. Several books have been published by the BBC based on the *Blue Peter* series.

When I viewed the programme on several occasions during the spring of 1976, *Blue Peter* did a live report from Washington on the first flight of the Concorde from London to the United States; took a trip to France on a Hovercraft; described the origin of the Garter Ceremony; offered an amusing demonstration of bathing live triplet babies, and showed some films of animal subjects. In the autumn of 1978, *Blue Peter* took its audience by film on a trip to Texas. *Blue Peter* is a delight to children and adults alike, and certainly is excellent by any standards.

Another interesting project was John Craven's *Newsround*, a newscast produced cooperatively with BBC-Television news, and transmitted from approximately 5 p.m. to 5.10, four days a week. Its aim was to provide children

with a news bulletin of special interest to them, carrying news of important world events with background information which sets them in context. It also included stories about people or animals which did not find a place in the evening bulletins. The compilers asked themselves: Is it news and will it interest children without distressing them?[36]

An attempt was made to cover important, but potentially distressing events, in a way that would reassure rather than upset children. For example, when a jet crashed on take-off in Nairobi, in contrast to a London evening newspaper headline, 'Jumbo Jet Crash Horror', *Newsround* began: 'A plane crashed on take-off—but 93 walk away from the wreck.'

Other BBC children's programmes include documentaries, serial dramas, single plays, and films purchased from such varied sources as Czechoslovakia, Japan, the USSR, the United States, France, Canada, and Spain. Subtitles are not used during broadcasts of foreign-language films, incidentally, because the child audience cannot read well enough, so the films either are dubbed into English or the original dialogue is faded down and an English-language narration added to explain the action.[37] Programmes also are produced in the various national and regional centres for network dissemination, as well as for local consumption, and Wales has programmes in the Welsh language.[38]

The IBA has been broadcasting programmes for pre-school children each weekday at noon since October 1972.[39] Four companies—Thames, Granada, Yorkshire, and ATV—produce these, with Thames accounting for about 40 per cent of the total. Recent examples have included *Rainbow, Stepping Stones*, and *Pipkins*. Although each of these was separate and distinct from the others, they shared several objectives. They all recognized the importance of language, and aimed 'to develop interest in stories, poems and song to be a starting point for children to explore and expand their language in play and in everyday life'.[40] *Rainbow*, which won the British Academy award for the best young children's programme in February 1975, tried 'to help children below school age to expand their experience of the world and the people around them'. The series was believed to be 'unique in the world, in that it began in 1974 making full length documentaries specially for the under fives'. One programme was a 'special' about the arrival of a new baby.[41] There often were suggestions for making and playing games with ordinary household articles. Some supplementary material was available to accompany these programmes.

Lighter in approach was Southern Television's *How*—'Ten series spread over as many years, more than a hundred programmes and over 2,000 experiments on what is probably the most famous table top in children's television'.[42] A 'blend of information and wit', according to the IBA handbook, this programme used a 'lively sense of humour' to explain such varied things as how Stonehenge was built and how a British rifleman can see at night.

Thames Television, which supplies over 140 hours of children's programmes to ITV each year, serves especially children up to the age of 12.[43] The long-running *Magpie*, broadcast twice a week, which includes *Newsdesk*, a short but serious newscast for children, is for children aged 8–12. *Magpie*, ITV's 'serious' answer to *Blue Peter*, has won a number of major international awards. Thames also had seven plays treating the theme of ghosts, entitled *Shadows*, which included one written specially for the series by J. B. Priestley. Another interesting Thames project was *You Must Be Joking*, entirely written and performed by a cast of London East End children aged 11–17. Commenting on it the Authority wrote: 'It has been both hailed as a new departure in "access" programming and condemned as giving children false ideas of their own importance.' Thames had *Sounds Exciting*, about the instruments of the orchestra and musical form. The ITCA companies pointed to the award-winning Thames surrealistic comedy *Do Not Adjust Your Set* as leading to the BBC's *Monty Python's Flying Circus*.[44]

A number of European services have adult programmes on which the police ask the public to assist in locating wanted criminals, and for 10 years London Weekend Television has broadcast the weekly 5-minute *Police Five*, an adult programme featuring Detective Shaw Taylor.[45] More recently Taylor developed a similar series for children—Junior Police Five—although the children are instructed to consult with their parents before bringing any clues to the attention of the police. The programme has been very successful. In a typical year, it deals with some sixty cases, mainly robberies, in about half of which useful information is provided by young viewers, who, among other things, have helped locate forty-eight stolen cars, assisted in the return of a valuable solar cell stolen from an exhibition, and helped find the mother of an abandoned child.

VIEWING PATTERNS

In Britain, as in America, there is concern over the amount of television viewing done by children. The Annan Committee remarked that children were 'the country's most diligent television viewers'.[46] The BBC told the Committee that in 1975 children between the ages of 5 and 14 averaged 24 hours per week of viewing. Even more important were the data that as many as 61 per cent of all children aged 12–14 were still watching at 9 p.m. weekday evenings, and as many as 18 per cent at 11 p.m. Even among the 8–11-year-old group, 13 per cent watched until 10.30 p.m.

A BBC study reported that children in general, and especially those between 12 and 14 years of age, watch more television than do adults.[47] Seldom does an adult programme reach 40 per cent of the public, but children's programmes often reach 40 per cent or more of their intended age groups. The BBC says that the most popular of its children's programmes—*Blue Peter, Cracker-Jack*, serial drama, and cartoons—are viewed by more than 60 per cent of all the children in the country between the ages of 5 and 14.[48] Furthermore, some adult programmes are viewed by more children than adults. But Britain's children listen very little to the radio, and when they do, it usually is to the popular music of Radio 1.

In their presentation to the Annan Committee, the television programme companies observed that in the late 1960s their children's programmes had more viewers than did the BBC's.[49] They lost the lead in 1972, however, after which 'fresh series were introduced and some of the long-runners abandoned'. In 1973–4, their average share of the children's audience was 59 per cent for the programmes broadcast at 4.25 and 52 per cent for those aired at 4.55 p.m. But audience data from different sources seldom agree, and the BBC's figures indicate, on the whole, larger audiences for their programmes than for the competition.[50]

In 1972, the IBA commissioned Britain's Opinion Research Centre to study children's viewing. When over 1300 children were asked to name everything they had done the previous day, they reported, on the average, eight activities, of which television was the most important.[51] Television was the most enjoyed leisure-time activity, playing with friends was second, sporting activities third, and reading a very poor fourth. When asked to name four or more programmes seen during the previous day, half of the children aged 5–7 listed a children's programme first, but one-third of them put an adult programme first; and as older children were polled, the preference for adult programmes increased. The overall favourite of all age groups was comedy.

It also was found that when parents attempted to influence their children's viewing, they favoured programmes different from those the children preferred. For the most part, parents recommended a programme for 'broadly educational reasons', whereas

what appeals to children is principally a short term mental arousal: they like programmes that are funny, or exciting; more long-term stimulus, reflected in reasons such as that a programme has a 'good story' or is 'informative' only accounted for 12 and 5 per cent respectively of children's reasons for liking programmes.

Twenty-eight per cent of the parents never tried to stop their children from viewing anything, although there were 'more permissive parents (34 per cent) among the lowest than among the highest social class group (21 per cent)'.

In 1978 the BBC published a report on the radio and television habits of adolescents and young adults.[52] Although it dealt with an older group than the programmes being considered in this chapter, some of its findings further illustrate various points made here. Young adults, defined as people between the ages of 15 and 25, watched television somewhat less than other age groups, because their active social lives took them away from home, but they listened to the radio more, greatly preferring Radio 1's popular music, with ILR second. Favourite television programmes included films, way-out comedy series like *Monty Python*, and drama series, although their ranking television programme was *Top of the Pops*, a popular music programme watched by 44 per cent of the 15–19 age group.

Disappointing was the low rank given to serious news and current affairs. Radio 4, specializing in such programmes, commands 'only a minute audience (less than one per cent) among this young age group'. These people were less critical of violence, bad language, and nudity than their elders, a finding on which the report commented:

Should the BBC conclude that its present safeguards (in regard to such programmes) are therefore adequate, or should it feel that the tolerance of the young derives from the fact that their opinions are unformed and that consequently there is some responsibility to offer young adults help or support in making their own value judgements?

APPRAISAL

Just how good are these programmes? Has their total quality improved or deteriorated as a result of competition?

The verdict as to programme quality is clearly favourable. The objectives of both BBC and IBA are beyond question—and they are sufficiently flexible to change in accord with the times. The programmes certainly are accepted by their audiences: many of them are viewed by 40 per cent or more of the age groups for which they are intended, a figure rarely achieved by adult programmes.

Observers have consistently praised the output. Initially there were doubts as to whether the ITV programmes would measure up to those of the BBC, but these questions have been resolved. The Pilkington Committee in 1962, despite its generally severe treatment of ITV, found no major fault in its children's output, and a Ministry of Education Memorandum submitted to the Committee in August 1961 stated that there was 'little difference in the type of programme put out for children on different channels and in general a high standard is reached'.[53]

The Annan Committee asked: 'But what of the programmes tailored to children's needs? Can parents rely on these programmes to be consistent and not be suitable one week and unsuitably violent the next? Most people think they can, and congratulate the broadcasters.'[54] This was the consensus of most of the evidence submitted to the Committee.

It is our verdict also [said the report] . . . Some of the best and most imaginative programme creators are working on children's programmes and the result has been that children have been offered an admirable menu of exciting, entertaining and edifying programmes which are a delight to children and parents and a credit to the broadcasting organisations. Both the BBC and ITV have made excellent programmes with the BBC in particular introducing several interesting new types of programmes.

Being as they are a microcosm of the output of both broadcasting organizations, children's programmes provide a good basis on which to judge the effects of competition on programme standards (see above, pp. 41–5). During the debates which preceded the passage of the Television Act in 1954, the backers of monopoly—the BBC and its most ardent supporters—argued that competition would cheapen programming, while advocates of competitive commercial television claimed the opposite. Generally speaking, however, there has been agreement in recent years that competition has been a good thing—but seldom has there been such unanimity as in the case of children's television.

The Director of BBC Children's Television Programmes in the 1960s referred favourably to the 'challenge of commercial television'.[55] In the United States, where there was no tradition of a strong public service corporation, she said, 'the children have been the target of competitive commercial networks seeking the largest audience for the least expenditure'. On the other hand, 'in [Continental] Europe lack of stimulation from competition has meant slower development'. But in the United Kingdom, 'with the advent of competition the challenge we had to meet in the BBC was to give the children worth-while programmes which would make demands on them to think and would stimulate their ideas but which they would want to watch as their first choice.' In their presentation to the Annan Committee in 1975, the programme companies very flatly stated: 'The BBC's high standards in catering for children are a continuing challenge to ITV.'[56]

Before leaving the subject, however, it should be noted that children's programming, like all broadcasting in the United Kingdom, is controlled competition. The BBC always provided good programmes for children and was expected to continue to do so. Because there were doubts as to the performance of the ITA, the original legislation setting up the Authority, and the rules promulgated under it, required that the companies present children's programmes of high quality during certain hours, and the IBA has voluntarily continued this requirement. So, the situation is one of 'controlled' rather than 'cut throat' competition. Without the law, the regulations, the BBC Board of Governors, and the IBA, it might be otherwise.

18 Outside Broadcasts and Sports

When the British refer to an outside broadcast—usually abbreviated 'OB'—they mean a programme originating outside a studio. Because the origination point is remote from—or away from a studio, such a programme is called a 'remote broadcast' or a 'remote' in the United States. Outside broadcasts can be divided into two categories: public events and sports.

BBC radio's Sport and Outside Broadcasts Department is responsible for all radio sports programmes, as well as for all other outside broadcasts, and the BBC television Outside Broadcasts Group assumes similar responsibilities.[1] These departments also provide technical facilities for outside broadcasts by the External Services and by foreign stations. The Corporation's regional and local centres have their own OB staffs and facilities, as does each IBA programme company. Independent Broadcasting's sports broadcasts are coordinated by a Network Sports Subcommittee, which works with the Network Programme Committee.[2] The full Network Sports Subcommittee makes recommendations about network sports policy, and allocates the various forthcoming events to producers and companies. There also are a chief sports negotiator, a racing advisor, and a network sports coordinator.

The yearly BBC and IBA programme analysis charts have categories for sports, but not for special events programmes[3] (see above, pp. 162, 175, 176). Radios 1 and 4 devote little time—around 90 hours a year, together—to sports, but in 1978–9, Radio 2 assigned 591 hours or 7.6 per cent of its time to sports, and Radio 3—suprisingly—257 hours or 3.6 per cent of its time. However, because of the almost complete absence of sports on Radios 1 and 4, the average for the four BBC radio networks combined was only 3.4 per cent.

All three television networks have OBs. To sports, in 1978–9, BBC 1 devoted 720 hours (14.3 per cent), and BBC 2 devoted 531 hours (12.9 per cent), for a total of 1251 hours or 13.7 per cent of their combined time. During the same year, the average ITV company assigned 10.5 per cent (10 hours 34 minutes) of its air-time to sports. (Whereas Americans use the plural 'sports' when referring to sporting events collectively, the British use the singular, 'sport'.)

PUBLIC EVENTS

In both the United Kingdom and the United States, public events have always been regarded as prestige features and audience-builders. American transcontinental television was inaugurated with President Harry S. Truman's address to the Japanese Peace Treaty Conference in San Francisco on 4 September 1951.

Ninety-four of the 107 television stations then on the air broadcast the programme to 40 million viewers.[4] More recently, the openings of Congressional sessions, Presidential inaugurations, the funeral of President John F. Kennedy, and similar occasions have been thoroughly covered by both radio and television.

Peter Dimmock, for many years head of OBs for the BBC, believes that 'the essence of the true OB is to report the real happenings, while they happen and from where they happen. ...'[5] At first the novelty of live programmes from St Peter's Basilica in Rome or from a submerged submarine may suffice to attract an audience, 'but even magic carpets wear thin and nowadays it's nearly always the intrinsic interest of the event that counts'. Keen editorial judgement is essential in deciding which OBs to carry, 'just as a newspaper decides on the allocation of space according to the known or anticipated interests of its readers'. The Miss World Contest or the Grand National will bring a television audience of between 20 and 30 million people.* But in the interests of a balanced schedule, the Corporation also picks up programmes from research laboratories and schools.

The British have a great television resource in their royal events and Parliament openings, and they have made the most of them. Since the coming of ITV, these events have been covered by both organizations. When there is insufficient room for installations by both, the BBC has priority, although it then must share its pictures and sound with the IBA, which thereupon assumes a portion of the costs (see above pp. 44, 166). The BBC also supplies feeds to foreign broadcasters when they request them. However, the ITV and the larger foreign groups often make their own pick-ups of the accompanying events, and usually supply their own announcers, who either describe the scenes live or off monitor screens.

The coronation of George VI on 12 May 1937, was one of the high points of early television history, even though cameras were not admitted to Westminster Abbey, and post-war British television set its re-opening for 7 June 1946, in order to broadcast the Victory in Europe parade on the following day. But the telecast of the coronation of Elizabeth II on 2 June 1953 stands pre-eminent, not only as one of the most elaborate and best of all outside broadcasts, but also as probably the most widely viewed, since the BBC's pictures appreared simultaneously, or later by recording, on most of the television screens of the world.[6]

Coverage of public events now includes such yearly occurrences as Trooping

---

* The appeal of the Miss World Contest was documented by a paragraph in the BBC's review of Audience Research Findings for 1974–5:

Miss World's audience even topped that for the Ali/Foreman contest [broadcast on 30 October 1974], this year's estimated 24 million people reversing a trend towards smaller audiences for Miss World over recent years. ... Contrary to some people's expectations, it is not men who are the mainstay of Miss World audiences, but women. ... This year, the figures were 44% [men] and 52% [women]. As in previous years, roughly equal proportions of viewers from all three socio-economic groups and from all 'adult' age groups watched. The highest proportion of any group to watch was that amongst the twelve- to fourteen-year-olds, of whom 67% saw the event! Despite being described as banal, over-long and practically the same as all the other years, it evidently continues to exert its own peculiar fascination, viewers finding themselves caught up—often almost against their will—in the business of trying to spot winners. (BBC, Annual Review of BBC Audience Research Findings, Number 2, 1974–5, pp. 23–4.)

the Colour, in which several thousand brilliantly uniformed guardsmen, ahorse and afoot, accompanied by five or six military bands, parade in elaborate formation before the Queen, who is mounted on horseback.[7] There also are the processions preceding the annual Opening of Parliament, and the Speech from the Throne. There are memorial services; visits by monarchs and heads of state; the Festival of Remembrance—the British equivalent of the American Armistice Day; Christmas broadcasts from King's College Chapel at Cambridge University; and the annual Christmas broadcast of the Queen, which originates in one of the royal residences. In 1978 there was extensive coverage of events related to the Silver Jubilee of Queen Elizabeth II. Less exalted, but probably of greater interest to the viewing public, are broadcasts of circuses, ice shows and similar events; of dog, flower, automobile and boat shows; and of the annual Miss World Contest. Since 1978, there have been regular radio broadcasts of Parliamentary proceedings, and television coverage cannot be far off (see above, pp. 233–6). The BBC and the ITV alternate in televising the annual Royal Variety Performance.*

SPORTS EVENTS

Although broadcasts of public events and athletic contests now are recognized universally as among broadcasting's main services, the same kind of reasoning that initially limited news broadcasting in Britain (see pp. 190–1) also delayed special events and sports broadcasting.[8] In 1924 and 1925, John Reith requested permission to broadcast public daytime ceremonies as well as descriptions of the Oxford/Cambridge boat race, the Derby, and the Cup Final. The answer was 'no'; however, in the case of the Derby, permission was given to broadcast crowd noises and the sounds of the horses' hoofs! It was not until 1927 that the Corporation was allowed to present eye-witness accounts of some events, although the Football League frequently banned all broadcasting. The BBC's historian wrote that

the detailed history of the BBC's approach to sport between 1945 and 1955 is a history not only of memorable sporting events, increased broadcasting activity over a wide range, and the evolution of new arts and techniques of production, but of institutional wrangles, almost always protracted, with occasional moments of dramatic confrontation, usually but not always behind the scenes.

In spite of all these obstacles, the Derby was telecast, using the Baird low-definition system, in 1931, and it was carried by the high-definition service in

---

* Up to the middle 1950s the BBC often made pick-ups of stage plays and musical comedies direct from theatres, and also broadcast ballroom dancing contests. In earlier years British audiences liked to 'be in the theatre' with the performers, partly because there was very little theatre attendance outside of the metropolitan centres. But nowadays, studio presentations are preferred, except for a few events like circuses, ice shows, symphony concerts, and operatic performances, in which economy and the desire of the audience to 'be there' dictate remote pick-ups.

1937 and 1938.[9] But because of objections from its sponsors, it was off television—though not radio—from 1946 until 1960.* Combined radio and television coverage of the Olympic Games in 1948 was declared by the BBC to be 'the biggest broadcasting operation . . . yet . . . carried out in any country'.

At present Britain's radio and television sports coverage is as complete as time, equipment, and finances permit. Few major events are omitted, and many minor sports go on the air. During a typical year, the BBC devotes almost 2000 hours to sports, including live or recorded coverage of all the major events 'for which contracts can be obtained.' On a normal Saturday afternoon, BBC 1 carries sports from 12.30 until approximately 5 p.m., the period being divided into 30- or 40-minute blocks for (say) football, snooker, horse racing, boxing, motorcycle racing, rugby, and other events scheduled throughout the country and abroad. Each issue of the *Radio Times* indicates the exact times for each section of programming, although the warning is given that 'timings may be changed by events'. The BBC 2 Saturday afternoon schedule is organized in the same way. But to avoid reducing attendance at some events, the *Radio Times* often states: 'Action highlights from two of today's crucial [unnamed] First Division matches' will be broadcast at a certain evening hour—say 10.10 p.m.[10] ITV proceeds in the same way.

ITV, the companies told the Annan Committee, puts its sports emphasis first on football and then on racing, 'both traditional British sports which enjoy outstanding popularity with viewers.'[11] During an average week, ITV devotes approximately 10 hours to sports programming, of which about half are in the *World of Sport* introduced in 1965 as a Saturday afternoon fixture. The format followed since 1969 goes on the assumption that few people want to watch continuously from 12.30 to 5 p.m., but that many are interested in selected items, so these are listed in advance in the *TV Times*. The several self-contained sections of about 30 minutes each deal in turn with such sports as association football (soccer), rugby football, and—on occasion—even baseball; many types of racing—motorcycle, automobile, horse and bobsleigh; and also with skiing, figure-skating, boxing, wrestling, and weightlifting. Like the BBC, ITV, on Sunday afternoons and on certain evenings following *News at Ten*, broadcasts recorded excerpts from football matches for which the participants were not previously announced. Just as the BBC reviews with great pride its coverage of the coronation of Elizabeth II in 1953 and the funeral of Winston Churchill in 1965, so the IBA reports how Scottish and Tyne Tees Television broadcast the 1976 European Cup Final to all of Europe from Glasgow.[12]

---

* The Derby is a good example of the opposition encountered by the broadcasters in obtaining television rights to major sporting events. In the words of the BBC:

In the Television News in 1955 on Derby Day itself the result was given over a still picture of the winning post, though by arrangement with a cinema newsreel company, film of the race was carried the next day. Again in 1956 and 1957 the result was reported only with still pictures, but in 1958 and 1959 Television News' own film cameras were able to take pictures from a moving car of the race which were included in the news the same day. The broadcast in 1960 was live.

THE EFFECTS OF BROADCASTING ON SPORTS

Sports broadcasts inevitably lead to debates about the effects of broadcasting—especially television—on attendance and on the events themselves. Sir Stanley Rous, formerly president of the International Football Federation, and widely known in Britain as businessman, public servant, and sports devotee, believes that broadcasting helps attendance at minor sports (show jumping, gymnastics, canoeing and skiing), and has no effect on sellout events (the Olympic Games, the Cricket Test Matches, and the Wimbledon Tennis Tournaments), but loses audiences for average football, cricket and athletic contests.[13] Usually, however, payments for broadcasting to the sponsors of events constitute a substantial part of their income.

There also have been discussions of the effects of broadcasting on the referees and the players. Sir Stanley wrote that instant replays in slow motion, if accompanied by highly critical analysis, are not 'conducive to good discipline on the field nor to the health of the game—in many cases it is positively harmful'.[14] As to violence on the field, he believes it unfair to draw attention to a player's lapse of behaviour when the player may almost immediately have regretted what he did. Furthermore, such lapses may give the wrong impression to 'younger, more impressionable players who are watching their particular heroes during their moments of lapse, and who then proceed to emulate them'. Finally, said Sir Stanley, television commentators at times exceed their authority, 'and I cannot think there is any occasion when this has happened which has been for the benefit of the sport'. Therefore, the media should assume 'a positive, educative role', in order 'to deepen and widen' the public's understanding of competitive athletics.

This indeed is what has happened, and there are adult education programmes on both services dealing with sports. ITV has presented information about angling, chess, soccer, cycling, yoga, and other minority sports, along with an informative series tracing the social history of sport.[15] The Corporation has produced series about rugby, gymnastics, swimming, and fencing. These programmes, in addition to 'helping the audience appreciate the finer points of a particular sport . . . also showed them how to do it themselves'.

DUPLICATE COVERAGE

The problem of duplication in sports coverage is especially important in a small country like Britain, which has only two broadcasting organizations and—until 1982 at least—three television networks. Fearing that the commercially supported—and presumably wealthier—ITV might make 'exclusive arrangements for the broadcasting of sporting or other events of national interest', the Television Act of 1954 and its successors gave the government authority to draw up regulations to prevent this, although such intervention has never been necessary.[16] In fact, the BBC has ably held its own in competing with ITV for broadcasting rights. In 1978, it took London Weekend Television and the Football League to court for allegedly breaching an agreement for joint rather than unilateral arrangements for televising League soccer matches.[17] The BBC and the IBA have agreed not to seek exclusive coverage of the six major national sporting events—the Derby, the Grand National Steeplechase, the Football Association Cup Final, the Cricket Test Matches, the Wimbledon Tennis Tournament, and the Oxford/Cambridge boat race—as well as of such irregular events as the Commonwealth Games or the Olympic Games when held in Britain. But ITV has never covered the Grand National or the boat race, has broadcast only one test match, and withdrew from the lawn tennis championships at Wimbledon in 1969 because of low audience ratings.

The question of whether both should simultaneously cover major events will probably never be settled to everyone's satisfaction. The BBC broadcasts them because it always has, because the public expects it to do so, and because— according to its figures—the audience prefers BBC to ITV sports coverage. Furthermore, 'since ITV was set up to compete with BBC, it would be strange if the BBC as the national and senior broadcasting organisation were in effect to withdraw from that competition in such an important area'.[18]

ITV also takes a firm position. It told the Annan Committee that, although the BBC long enjoyed a lead in athletic coverage, in recent years

ITV has provided competition, particularly in football and racing where it has either outstripped the BBC or at least achieved parity. Intense rivalry has raised the quality of sports programmes provided by both services, and in production terms British television coverage of sport is today the most advanced in the world.[19]

There is much public resentment, said the programme companies, when two channels transmit the same event. 'This . . ., the darker side of competition, . . . arises inevitably from the fact that the BBC was first in the field. [But] ITV, . . . cannot be expected to abandon the arena at the time of the greatest events in those sports which it covers regularly and for which it has won very large audiences.' The companies then pointed out: 'Duplication will continue until the two broadcasting organisations can agree upon a rational system of alternating the major events or in some cases sharing production facilities. This the ITV companies strongly advocated.' But to date, no such system has been devised, and the problem of duplication, therefore, remains.

In 1974, the IBA and its programme companies proposed to the BBC that the two alternate in television coverage of the World Cup matches.[20] Although the BBC rejected this suggestion, the Authority repeated it for the World Cup matches in Argentina scheduled for the summer of 1979, for the 1980 Olympic Games, and for the 1982 World Cup matches. The Corporation was agreeable to dividing some events, but not these, with the likely result, in the case of the Argentina contest, said the IBA, of 'the screening of at least six matches with identical pictures at the same times on ITV and BBC 1'. Next the IBA suggested that an independent arbitrator be named 'to make a judgement in the interests of the public', or that a coin be tossed to determine which should air the programmes. But the BBC's position was that, whereas it covers both majority- and minority-interest sports, the ITV is interested only in the former, so that any alternation puts the Corporation into a no-win situation. Disputes of this nature, whatever their outcome, illustrate the bitter competition between the two organizations for major sports coverage.

After reviewing the pros and cons, the Annan Committee thought it 'reasonable for the BBC to recognise ITV's wish to carry some major national sporting events without the audience having to pay the price of duplicated coverage'.[21] (The Annan Committee also noted that in order to secure exclusive coverage, the BBC sometimes paid three or four times as much for certain sporting events as did ITV, which, the Committee felt, was excessive.)[22] It also recommended 'that they should reduce other instances when they cover the same event at the same time to the barest minimum and, holding discussions on this matter, should make a public announcement of the agreement reached'. The ensuing government White Paper endorsed this suggestion, but made it clear that such problems should be solved by the broadcasters, rather than being arbitrated by the government. On the subject of competitive bidding, the Committee felt that it would be 'particularly hard to justify two organisations competing to spend money which will go abroad'. As to events at home, though concluding that at times the BBC has paid too much for exclusive rights, the committee said that in general 'we believe the BBC has used the security provided by a contract to build up its coverage and expertise. It may be no coincidence that public interest has increased in those events where the BBC has been able to negotiate exclusive contracts.'

But finally, in June 1979, agreements involving the BBC, ITV, and the Football League extended the principle of alternating coverage to the World Cup, the Olympics, and the European Football Championships.

For a long time the IBA talked of how it would improve its television sports coverage, once it was given another channel. In fact, more than any other single type of programming, unless it be Welsh-language programmes for Wales, the broadcasting of sporting events brought up the question of the Fourth Channel. In 1968 the head of BBC television OBs wrote that one 'important aspect of our sports coverage has been the availability of BBC 2 for covering sports events in depth'.[23] The ITA told the Minister of Posts and Telecommunications in December 1971 that with a second ITV channel,

Extended coverage would be possible for a number of sporting events of all kinds. The interests of those who like sport often conflict, on a single channel, with needs of schools or housewives or children or general viewers. . . . Clearly lovers of sport, and haters of sport, are much better served by two channels.[24]

ADVERTISING AND SPORTS BROADCASTING

All broadcasting organizations, licence-fee as well as commercially supported, face the problem of advertisements being intentionally placed so as to ensure their being picked up by cameras covering sporting events. There are billboards in football, hockey, and soccer stadiums; advertising messages on race cars; and trade names on clothing and sports equipment; along with the sponsorship of both sports and cultural events by business concerns.[25] Both the BBC and ITV have guidelines to cover such situations.

If the advertising is too blatant, the BBC will cancel its plans to broadcast. It refused to televise a boxing match until the seconds in one corner had removed smocks carrying a firm's name, and in another instance decided not to broadcast the Monaco Grand Prix automobile race because of advertisements on cars. Another race posed the unusual problem of contraceptive advertising on some cars. At the last minute, the Corporation decided not to broadcast the race, not because of the contraceptive advertising, *per se*—after all, the government supported family planning—but rather because it was considered improper and inconsistent to televise such ads while refusing to broadcast similarly displayed advertisements for clothing and home applicances. But both the BBC and the IBA now take the position that if an advertisement is not located in a certain place just because of the cameras, and if it does not interfere with the picture or unduly intrude into it, it may be transmitted 'as a normal part of the background'.

Problems also are posed by the commercial sponsorship of certain sporting and other events. Tobacco companies, now that cigarette advertisements are kept off the air, have tried to gain favourable public exposure by sponsoring athletic contests and other public events, including some which need subsidies. In such cases, the Corporation refers to the sponsor in its *Radio Times* listing, and provides two spoken credits during the broadcast, but does not pick up any related advertising from the field.

The IBA rules are very similar.[26] Since the law expressly prohibits sponsorship, cameras carefully avoid picking up anything which would give viewers the impression that the programme was 'suggested or provided by an advertiser'. Other rules limit the number of sponsors' signs which may be televised during broadcasts from race courses and sports arenas, as well as the number of verbal credits to the sponsor which may be given on a broadcast. Guidelines developed jointly in 1974 by the Race Course Association, ITV, and BBC govern procedures for horse racing. There also are special regulations about picking up advertisements for cigarettes, when tobacco manufacturers sponsor sporting events.[27]

The British are justified in claiming that their sports coverage is both extensive and very good. It also is technically excellent, even though fewer electronic gimmicks are used than on American broadcasts. Fortunately, most British commentators follow the advice laid down by the former General Manager for BBC OBs: 'O.B. commentary is an art in itself. Working from their monitor screens as well as from what they can see, commentators are to interpret the picture without annoying the viewer by describing the obvious.'[28] Taken as a group, the commentators on both services are highly competent and very knowledgeable about the events they describe. At times they, like American commentators, talk too much, but on the whole they are less guilty of that offence than are those in the United States.

The Annan Committee declared:

The coverage of sport on television and radio has been one of the success stories of broadcasting. The BBC, and in a more restricted way, the ITV companies, provide generally a superb service. They have succeeded in bringing to the public major sporting events.... They have kindled an interest in [some] sports ... which hitherto had been followed by a comparatively small number of afficionados.[29]

The Committee also observed that the broadcasters, in addition to entertaining, can 'increase people's understanding of a game's basic principles, refine the appreciation of the armchair experts, and inspire some to take an active part in sport themselves'.

19 Music

Britain's broadcasters deserve high marks for their musical programmes. In the pages that follow, the BBC will be mentioned more frequently than the IBA, because the Corporation's much more extensive radio facilities lend themselves so well to music transmissions, and because its having two television networks facilitated the televising of more music than did ITV's single network. But the IBA also broadcasts music on both television and radio, for which all due credit should be given.*

MUSIC POLICY

In its 1976 handbook the Corporation stated that its music policy

is based upon the aims of excellence of performance, enterprise in presentation and variety of content. The repertoire ranges from the contemporary and avant-garde back to the beginnings of western music, and also includes some programmes devoted to other, non-European traditions. Within this span of time and content, the emphasis goes first on the mainstream of western music, the accepted masterpieces which have the greatest appeal to the audience and which, more often than not, are the works which bring appreciation of music for the first time to new listeners.

The BBC also accepts responsibility to present new kinds of music, to make the unfamiliar more familiar and to help to develop more catholic tastes: for example, to push back the frontiers in time through first-class performances of pre-classical music, and on the other hand to encourage the work of composers of the present day.[1]

Although the IBA broadcasts much less music than does the BBC, it too has stated its policies. In its 1976 handbook the Authority wrote:[2]

Television's great contribution to what for the sake of brevity we will call The Arts is that it allows millions of non-adherents to dip into the vast treasure houses of drama, music, dancing, painting, poetry, sculpture, and the rest, in the convenient comfort of their own homes. Many no doubt will quickly dip out

---

* This section deals mainly with 'classical' or serious music. In the BBC, popular music is the responsibility of the Radio 1 and Radio 2 Music Departments, rather than of the Music Division, whose work is described here.

again, others will like what they see. But all are given a chance to find out, at the turn of a switch.

The electronic transmission of music in Britain predates broadcasting, since in the early 1890s, performances in London, Birmingham, Liverpool, and elsewhere were transmitted 'with entire success' by wire to the Crystal Palace in London.[3] Music was the principal staple of broadcasting in the early days, although the Company—as it was in the 1920s—always tried to do more than routine programming. Phonograph record concerts were begun in 1922; the BBC relayed a performance of Mozart's *The Magic Flute* from Convent Garden in January 1923—the first outside opera broadcast, and in the same year broadcast dance music from the Savoy Hotel as well as programmes by a studio orchestra consisting of nine musicians, each with his own microphone.

By 1923 all of the principal broadcasting centres had their own orchestras of about eighteen musicians each, frequently augmented for special occasions. Significant was the fact that, to avoid the abuse of the deputy system, under which musicians who had attended rehearsals could send deputies to the concerts if they themselves did not wish to play, all members of BBC orchestras were required to play at least six broadcasts each week. In 1924, the BBC military band was founded (although it was permanently disbanded in 1943, since there then were many good Army bands available), as was a permanent chorus. In the same year the Company began remote pick-ups of symphony concerts, and in 1925 produced the first studio opera broadcast—of Bizet's *Carmen*.[4]

From the very beginning, impresarios, theatre managers, and even music publishers feared that broadcasting might affect their audiences or their sales. The managing director of Queen's Hall, then London's principal concert hall, refused to let the BBC broadcast from the hall, or arrange broadcasts by artists under contract to him. There was much opposition to the founding of the BBC Symphony Orchestra in 1930, and in 1935 the famous conductor, Sir Thomas Beecham, who later did much broadcasting and recording, complained that broadcasts by that and other orchestras were retarding the development of live music, and that anyway, 'The performance of music through this or any other kindred contrivance cannot be other than a ludicrous caricature.'[5] In reply, the BBC stated that it had 'no desire to monopolize concert-giving, and recognizes that the concert-giving societies of the country had been and ought to remain the backbone of musical culture'. In time such opposition disappeared, and since World War II there have been few complaints from musicians that BBC Broadcasts hurt them. In fact, as is pointed out below, now they complain whenever the BBC wants to reduce the number of staff musicians.

STAFF

BBC radio music is the responsibility of the Controller of Music, who reports to the Managing Director of Radio. The Music Division of BBC radio includes several departments, the head of each reporting to the Controller of Music.[6] The separate

Music Departments of Radio 1 and Radio 2 programme music on their respective networks, drawing upon commercial records, BBC recordings, and some live performances. The Radio 2 Music Department also provides some light programmes for Radio 3. The Gramophone Programmes Unit serves Radios 3 and 4, and produces music and talk features utilizing recordings. Finally, though perhaps most important of all, the Music Programmes Department is in charge of serious music programmes not based on recordings, including studio originations, outside relays, and talks about music.

The BBC television Music Department was not organized until 1951, although the Corporation had employed television music producers before then.[7] The Music and Arts Department is now responsible for most programmes concerning the arts, including opera, ballet, and music.[8]

Among the BBC's many advisory groups are the Central Music Advisory Committee, and the Scottish Music Advisory Committee, made up of outstanding music personalities, including composers, performers, conductors, and scholars.[9] The former committee, known as the Music Advisory Committee, when originally constituted in 1925, was one of the first BBC advisory committees. Its membership normally ranges from fifteen to twenty people, and it has two day-long meetings each year, one at Broadcasting House—the centre for BBC radio—and the other at the Television Centre. Agendas include the financial problems of broadcasting music, music on television, radio and television simulcasts, and general music policy.

Since its earliest days, the Corporation has employed a large number of musicians.[10] At the beginning of 1980, it had on its staff 551 full-time orchestral musicians (about one-third of the permanently employed musicians in the country) and about 75 singers as follows: BBC Symphony Orchestra in London 101; BBC Northern Symphony 70; BBC Scottish Symphony 69; BBC Welsh Symphony 66; BBC Concert Orchestra 54; BBC Radio Orchestra 56; BBC Midland Radio Orchestra 32; BBC Northern Ireland Orchestra 30; BBC Scottish Radio Orchestra 32; BBC Northern Radio Orchestra 22; and London Studio Players 19. For choral music there were the 28 BBC Singers, a professional choir in London, and the BBC Northern Singers, a semi-professional body based in Manchester. There also was the BBC Symphony Chorus. Performances by staff musicians are supplemented by other orchestras, soloists, singers, and opera companies from all over Britain, as well as by many visiting orchestras and artists.

This is more musicians than the BBC actually needs. There can be no doubt of the important contributions of the BBC Symphony Orchestra, the Corporation's major musical group; and in certain areas of England as well as in Northern Ireland, Scotland and Wales, BBC instrumental organizations are the principal orchestras in their regions. But some other groups are maintained only because of pressures brought by the Musicians' Union and music lovers, rather than because of necessity.

In 1969, in outlining its plans for network radio broadcasting in the 1970s, the Corporation announced that it really needed only 279 orchestral players, and proposed terminating the Scottish Symphony, the Northern Dance Orchestra, and the London Studio players, with a total membership of 104, as well as the BBC

Chorus of 28 members.[11] The BBC was willing to continue the Concert Orchestra, the Welsh Orchestra and the Northern Ireland Orchestra with a total membership of 128, if the Arts Council of Great Britain, Wales, and Northern Ireland could share the costs. But the resulting furor forced a retreat, and all of these groups were continued.

Early in 1980, however, the Corporation was forced, by financial stringencies, to make cuts of over £130 million in its planned expenditures during the next two years, these to include the elimination of 1500 positions. A part of this involved cutting the number of orchestras from eleven to six, and the number of instrumentalists from 551 to 379, with an anticipated saving of about one-third of the funds previously allocated for their support. Actually, however, the net saving would be less than half of this, since the BBC planned to hire outside orchestras and freelance musicians to fill some of the resulting programme gaps. Although it is hard to forecast the effects of these cuts on the musical repertoire, it is reasonable to assume that they will not be extensive. But in any case, the data and figures cited below on programming may not be entirely typical in future years.

The Annan Committee distinguished between broadcasters as producers of programmes and as patrons of the arts, saying:

> In our view, broadcasters should see themselves primarily as impresarios, ensuring that the best talents are secured for current programmes, and recognising that they must pursue, encourage and bring along the talented but inexperienced.[12] [But it went on to express] strong doubts about whether the BBC's role ... [required] it to maintain its commitment to the continued employment of all the existing 13 musical bodies which it supports at the cost of some 3 million each year. ... The BBC must feel able to make cuts where it judges it will least affect its programmes, not simply in places where they cannot affect musicians.

RADIO MUSIC

During 1978–9, 58.4 per cent (16,302 hours) of the combined output of the four networks consisted of music, allocated as follows: Radio 1, 92.2 per cent (4850 hours); Radio 2, 78.2 per cent (6111 hours); Radio 3, 67.1 per cent (4837 hours); and Radio 4, 6.6 per cent (504 hours). Not included in these figures are the music programmes broadcast by the Corporation's local radio stations, which consist mainly of light and popular music.

A quick review of music scheduling during a typical week will illustrate the range of these services. Radio 1 is on the air 24 hours a day, although it simulcasts with Radio 2 from midnight to 6 a.m. Its programmes consist mainly of current popular hits introduced by 'name' disc jockeys, with occasional news and talk features. Radio 2, also on the air 24 hours a day, with a middle-of-the-road repertoire, has somewhat less music than Radio 1—78.4 per cent of its time as compared to 92.2 per cent of Radio 1. Radio 3 is the BBC's 'good music' service, since most of its daytime and some of its evening programmes consist of music.

Radio 4, basically a news and information service, devotes very little time to music, although at times it carries evening symphony concerts.

The BBC's four radio networks broadcast approximately 39 hours of music every day, ranging from the pre-baroque to contemporary avant garde, and from symphony, opera, and art songs to jazz and rock. The total repertoire is so great that only suggestions can be made as to its extent.[13] The Corporation also encourages the writing of music. The Annan Committee remarked:

> We particularly welcome the BBC's encouragement of new work, by its commissioning of plays and musical works. We consider it has been exercising the proper impresario functions of a broadcaster in organising, over the last 50 years, the Henry Wood Promenade Concerts, in promoting the Sir Robert Mayer Children's Concerts and in sponsoring serious music competitions for new musicians.[14]

Particularly outstanding are the many programmes of instrumental music, both live and recorded. During a typical season, the BBC Symphony Orchestra, in addition to studio broadcasts, gives twenty public concerts in London, plus some in the provinces and abroad, almost all of which are broadcast. Supplementing these are regular concerts by the Corporation's other musical organizations. Many British symphony orchestras and musical groups also are heard, in both studio and public concerts, and visiting orchestras from France, the Netherlands, Germany, Austria, and elsewhere frequently broadcast. Among programmes of chamber works are the weekly Monday lunchtime recitals from St John's Church in Smith Square, London. Tickets are available at low cost, and all the programmes are broadcast, live or delayed. Other series present young artists of promise.[15]

The Promenade Concerts have become a British institution.[16] Begun under the direction of Sir Henry Wood in 1895, they were taken over and financed by the BBC in 1927. Most of the Proms, as they are called, are played in the Royal Albert Hall during 8 weeks in July, August, and September, although a few are scheduled in such places as Westminster Cathedral and the Round House in North London. The series got its name from the fact that the seats in the middle of the hall are removed, thus providing standing—or strolling—room for promenaders. The Proms are not programmes of light classics, but rather full-scale concerts, with a wide range of repertoire. All are broadcast live in stereo by Radios 2, 3 or 4; many are relayed by short wave in the World Service; recordings of some are made available by BBC Enterprises for broadcasting by foreign stations; and some seven or eight—including the last one—are carried by BBC television with simultaneous sound on Radio 3. The closing concert of the season, lighter in vein than most, finds many of the young promenaders engaging in high jinks; and the conductor, if he is so inclined, reacts to their moods.

In 1975, the Promenades included fifty-seven concerts by thirty different orchestras and ensembles, fourteen choirs, ninety-two singers, forty-six solo instrumentalists, and forty conductors. There were visiting orchestras from Cleveland and New York, plus the International Youth Symphony. Some years continental orchestras also participate. Of the 228 compositions scheduled in

1975, 103 were played at the Proms for the first time. Pierre Boulez, Sir Michael Tippett, and Aaron Copland conducted their own music, and of the four premiered works by British composers, three had been commissioned especially for the Proms.[17]

Britain, with a long tradition for choral music, has many fine choruses. The BBC Symphony Chorus, described by the Corporation as 'the only amateur choir to broadcast regularly', performs 'a uniquely interesting repertoire', specializing in compositions not often presented by other choral groups.[18] It gives about twenty concerts per year, many with the BBC Symphony Orchestra, and usually appears at some Promenade Concerts. Supplementing programmes by the BBC Singers, an independent group under contract to the Corporation, are frequent broadcasts by fine amateur choruses from all parts of the country. During the main Christian religious festivals there are regular broadcasts of the Bach *Passions* and Handel's *Messiah*.

Opera is well covered in studio organizations and pick-ups from opera houses in various parts of the United Kingdom. All the major—and many smaller—British opera companies are heard, and there are relays from both British and foreign music festivals. The regional and national production centres also originate programmes.[19] Brass and military bands are popular in Britain, and the Corporation broadcasts some of their concerts, often from competitions held in London and Manchester. The BBC also promotes its own competition, 'Challenging Brass'.

Radio 1 has taken its programmes and announcers out on the road to meet the public. It also interviews artists like the Osmonds, The Beach Boys, the Who, and Simon and Garfunkel. On Radio 2 the fifty-four-piece BBC Concert Orchestra plays for the long-running series, *Friday Night is Music Night*.[20] The Corporation mounts, in association with the Greater London Council, an annual Festival of Light Music at the Royal Festival Hall. Like Radio 1, Radio 2 originates programmes from all parts of the country, including live presentations by light orchestral ensembles.

Radio 3, Britain's 'good music service', devotes approximately 90 hours per week to serious music. As mentioned above, major broadcasts of live music, whether orchestral, chamber, or opera usually are heard on Radio 3. Broadcasts of serious jazz also are assigned to Radio 3, although there are not enough of them to please the jazz enthusiasts. The Annan Committee reported: 'Jazz devotees told us that the broadcasters were treating jazz most shabbily; and the Musicians' Union blamed this on the broadcasters' obsession with large audiences. The Jazz Centre Society proposed that a fixed number of hours of broadcasting time should be set aside for jazz on all outlets'.[21]

The Corporation probably has the world's finest and largest collection of phonograph records, with over 1 million discs—its only possible rival being the Library of Congress in Washington, DC. Since most records are purchased in duplicate, however, the number of different items is about 500,000.[22] These are built into many types of programmes, including retrospective performances by great artists of the past like Emil Sauer, Felix Weingartner, Serge Koussevitzky and the Budapest String Quartet; cyclical presentations (Brahms chamber music,

Mozart piano trios, Mendelssohn's piano music, and the works of Gabriel Fauré); and celebrations of composers' birthdays and other anniversaries. At times there are talks on musical subjects. On the evening of Thursday 6 May 1976 I heard a discussion of the relationship between Anton Bruckner and Richard Wagner which, among other things, told of their famous meeting at Bayreuth in the 1870s. The talk was supplemented with recordings of the music of both composers. Another series discussed and illustrated 25 years of the long-playing record.[23]

Drawing upon the tremendous resources of the BBC sound archives are programmes based upon historical recordings.[24] Thus, Radios 1 and 2 have featured performances by Ray Conniff and other British popular artists; Radio 3 offered *Clarinet Virtuosos of the Past*; while Radio 4 had *Fascinatin' Rhythm*, based on the life and music of George Gershwin, along with four programmes, *Those Dancing Years*, recalling the great American dance bands of the 1940s and 1950s.

NEEDLE TIME

All broadcasting organzations must negotiate with a variety of associations and unions to obtain permission to use copyrighted material, and to draw up contracts with their unionized employees. For music programmes, this has been especially a problem because of the control which the British copyright act has for many years given record manufacturers over public performances—including the broadcasting—of their records, in addition to, and quite apart from, the rights of the composers or performers of the records in question. Under the former American Copyright Act of 1909, the manufacturer of a record had no control over its public use, although the 1978 law does contain the potential for such control, but British law has provided this for a long time. Since the British Musicians' Union has maintained that the broadcasting of commercial records reduces its members' employment, it has brought pressure on the record manufacturers to limit the amount of 'needle time' available to both BBC and IBA.[25]

By 1949, the Musicians' Union had succeeded in reducing the Corporation's use of commercial records on domestic broadcasts to the low point of 22 hours per week, and wanted to reduce it even more. Fortunately for the BBC, however, the External Services always have been allowed enough needle time.[26]

These limitations became especially onerous after the Government's 1962 White Paper authorized the Corporation to initiate Radio 1 and to introduce a 'good music' service on the Third Programme transmitters, because the new services could not begin without more needle time. But finally, in 1964, an agreement was reached for the Corporation—on payment of a substantial fee—to use up to 75 hours of records each week on its domestic service. Needle time has been less a problem for television than radio, since television plays much less recorded music. Currently, BBC television may use up to 5 hours per week of commercial records, and may add an extra hour in return for additional payments. There also have been difficulties about pre-recording television programmes, repeating programmes from recordings, relaying performances from theatres and concert halls, and television and radio simulcasts. The IBA radio and television programme companies, of course, encounter the same problems as does the BBC.

TELEVISION MUSIC

There are doubts in Britain as in America about telecasting instrumental music. Most people see the advantages of opera and ballet on television, but instrumental music usually is regarded as so basically aural as to belong to radio instead. Except for occasional programmes originated or relayed by its public stations, American television has left instrumental music to radio. But the BBC, along with the other television organizations of Europe, maintains a steady—though well-spaced—output of such programmes.

BBC television began experimenting with music in the pre-war days, and has broadcast all types of music since 1946. In 1978–9 BBC 2 devoted about 105 hours or 2.6 per cent of its time to music. BBC 1's 30 hours (0.6 per cent) lowered the average of the two services to 4 per cent, even though the combined total was 135 hours. (These figures do not include light and popular music, classified under Light Entertainment.)[27]

Any recent year could be taken to illustrate BBC television's output of serious instrumental music.[28] During 1975, BBC 1 had seven broadcasts of the summer Promenades. André Previn, who also has broadcast with the Pittsburgh Symphony Orchestra in the United States for PBS, appeared as conductor, interviewer, speaker, and pianist. BBC 2 broadcast profiles of several internationally known opera singers, who were interviewed before they sang; programmes on the music of Busoni, Elgar, Schoenberg and Bartok; and Beethoven's last five string quartets, transmitted on five consecutive evenings, preceded by *Workshop Programmes*.

Experiments with television opera date back to pre-war days. During recent years, BBC television has presented studio productions and remote relays of Mozart's *The Marriage of Figaro*, Menotti's *Amahl and the Night Visitors*, and Verdi's *La Traviata*.* The BBC reported that nearly 5 million people saw its relay of *Cavelleria Rusticana* and *I Pagliacci* from the Covent Garden Opera House at Easter 1976. An international success was scored with Johann Strauss's *Die Fledermaus*, at the beginning of 1978. When the Royal Opera at Covent Garden decided to re-establish a long-time tradition of staging *Die Fledermaus* New Year's Eve, arrangements were made by the BBC and America's Metromedia Broadcasting Corporation to have the performance transmitted by satellite for

---

* *Annan* #21. 9; *BBC Handbook, 1976*, p. 144. The BBC Audience Research Department reported that *La Traviata* was given

> an enthusiastic reception by an audience of about 1½ million . . ., which was generally thought to have been well adapted for the small screen. Verdi's beautiful music, the splendid singing and acting, and a visually-pleasing production made very satisfying entertainment for all but a minority and it seemed that enjoyment was enhanced by the fact that the opera was sung in English. (BBC, *Annual Review of BBC Audience Research Findings*, Number 1, 1973–4, p. 21.)

recording and presentation in the United States during an appropriate evening period. Metromedia co-financed the production with the BBC, and arranged to sell it to other American stations. Originally it was seen in New York, Los Angeles, Washington, Minneapolis, Kansas City, and Cincinnati. In Minneapolis, I watched the programme from start to finish, both when first presented and when repeated on 1 January 1979, found it delightful, and was pleased to note that Metromedia planned to continue its cooperation with European broadcasting organizations to present a series of cultural events on commercial television of a type hitherto limited to the PBS network. After the performance, *The New York Times* critic, on the basis of seeing the performance live in London, wrote: 'The production was handsome, the singing was of top international standards and everybody—especially the cast—had a wonderful time.'[29]

There have been broadcasts from the Royal Festival Hall and the Albert Hall by the principal British orchestras and some visiting groups, with conductors like Sir Georg Solti, Sir Charles Groves, Bernard Haitink, André Previn, and Neville Mariner, and soloists like Mstislav Rostropovich. The Corporation began experimenting with ballet even before commencing its regular television service in 1936, and regularly brings to the screen the best dancers and ballet companies of the age. In 1975—which may be taken as a typical year—ballets included John Cranko's *Romeo and Juliet*, danced by the Stuttgart Ballet Company, while there were concert recitals by Garrick Ohlsson, Henryk Szeryng, and others. The *Five Faces of the Guitar*, a studio production. illustrated different syles of guitar playing.

Although television music is a complicated process, the BBC's regional and national studios also produce such programmes, for their own audiences as well as for the entire country.[30] In 1975, Northern Ireland produced a programme on Victorian music, recorded before an audience in a museum; *Sounding Voices*, a series of band programmes with soloists and choirs; a musical documentary about an American folk group now living in Ireland; and excerpts from Handel's *Messiah*.

It is difficult to compare the BBC and ITV outputs because of the different ways they categorize their programmes. Twelve per cent of the 1978–9 output—an average of 12 hours 13 minutes per week—of the typical ITV company was devoted to entertainment and music, although most of this was in the lighter vein.[31] On its opening night in 1955, Associated-Rediffusion telecast music by the Hallé Orchestra of Manchester, and during the following years often brought the orchestra to its screen. But the problems of producing instrumental music on television, together with low audience ratings, led to fewer symphony broadcasts in later years, and then only during off-peak hours. However, ITV does have occasional concerts by local and visiting orchestras, from the Hallé orchestra, the Scottish National Orchestra, and the National Youth Orchestra of Britain to the Philadelphia and New York Philharmonic Orchestras from the United States. I was in the audience in the Albert Hall in the summer of 1976 when London Weekend Television taped a concert of American music by the New York Philharmonic Orchestra under the direction of Leonard Bernstein for broadcast on the evening of 4 July—which was aired by America's PBS on 4 July 1979.

Associated-Rediffusion takes credit for Britain's first full-length opera on television, Benjamin Britten's *The Turn of the Screw*, presented in two instalments on 25 and 28 December 1959. Major ITV presentations include yearly relays from the Glyndebourne Opera House by Southern Television, while other companies make occasional pick-ups from the Covent Garden Opera House.[32] But for the most part, ITV's treatment of serious music is more sporadic than that of the BBC. During 1966 Thames Television had a series, *Musical Triangles*, about 'the intriguing musical triangle of composer/instrument/performer', and along with it offered a supplementary long-playing record. The following year, Yorkshire's *Play Another Tune* presented basic information about playing the guitar and the recorder. Granada went back to the Renaissance with *What Did They All Sound Like?* which examined old families of instruments. Yorkshire also had six half-hour concerts in a country home, while HTV mounted a half-hour opera by Alun Hoddinott, *Murder the Magician*.

Both BBC and IBA have talk and discussion programmes dealing with the arts, which cover opera, concerts, and ballet. For some years the BBC had *Omnibus* and *Chronicle*, presented during peak viewing hours.[33] In 1976, *Omnibus* included a programme about Nijinsky, *God of the Dance*; *Here to Make Music*, featuring violinist Pinchas Zucherman; an interview with British conductor Colin Davis about Sibelius; and a programme with André Previn on the waltz. The cornerstone of ITV's art and music programme is London Weekend's *South Bank Show* (formerly *Aquarius*), which covers music, theatre, film, painting, and the other arts.[34] In 1976, it had two programmes in honour of the 90-year-old pianist, Arthur Rubinstein, as well as presentations about the Thirtieth Edinburgh Festival. In 1978, it won the Italia Prize for music with an adaptation of Covent Garden's ballet *Mayerling*.

Some of the BBC 2 programmes I saw in London in 1976 will illustrate the range of British television's output. On Sunday 6 June, from 9.05 to 10.10 p.m., *The Death of a Virtuoso* presented information about, and recordings of the music of Carl Maria von Weber. On Thursday 22 April, from 8 until 9.30 p.m., there was a programme in honor of the 60th birthday of Yehudi Menuhin, on which the violinist was interviewed, talked with members of his family, and played music with them. Unique was an examination of the Royal Festival Hall Organ—*A Thousand Instruments*—by Simon Preston, broadcast on Sunday 20 June, from 9.25 to 10.10 p.m. It was an interesting programme demonstrating the resources of a large modern concert organ.

Light in vein was *Strauss from Vienna*, Monday 19 April, from 10.15 p.m. to 12.05 a.m., on which the Vienna Philharmonic Orchestra and the Vienna State Opera Ballet conducted by Willi Boskovsky were seen in a Strauss concert recorded in Vienna on New Year's Day. Very impressive was the relay on Easter Sunday 18 April 1976, from 9.45 to 10.30 p.m., of a concert by a 1000-voice Welsh choir from the Metropolitan Cathedral in Liverpool. On Saturday 15 May 1976, from 8.35 to 9.25 p.m., BBC 2 (with stereo sound on Radio 3) broadcast Berlioz's *Te Deum*, in which an orchestra appeared with chorus and organ in a studio set suggesting a church. On Sunday 9 May, from 9.30 to 11.15 p.m., the BBC broadcast a video-tape recording of Berlioz's gigantic *Requiem* made in the

Church des Invalides in Paris, where the work received its first performance in 1837. The total effect was overwhelming, although the vastness of the resources, coupled with insufficient rehearsal, made the performance less perfect than impressive.

Quite different was the review on Sunday 2 May, from 9.45 to 10.30 p.m., of the first 25 years of the Royal Festival Hall on which BBC television news reader (anchorman) Richard Baker, himself a music-lover, who announces some light classical programmes for Radio 4, introduced film and video-tape recordings of performances by Maria Callas and Igor Stravinsky, and the Finale of the Beethoven *Ninth Symphony* conducted by Otto Klemperer. Although the latter work showed the aged conductor's infirmities, the total performance was moving and interesting. In connection with the centennial of the Richard Wagner Festival in Bayreuth, Bavaria, BBC 2 scheduled broadcasts on the evenings of 22 and 23 May 1976. Written and narrated by broadcast music expert, John Culshaw, they included interesting films—which, among other things, showed Hitler coming to some of the operas, and members of the Wagner family—along with recordings of excerpts from some performances. The second broadcast concluded with a performance of one scene from *Die Meistersinger*.

Outstanding was the tribute to contralto Kathleen Ferrier broadcast on 30 September 1978, to mark the twenty-fifth anniversary of her death at the age of 41. Films showing the late singer and recordings of her voice were skilfully combined with tributes from contemporary artist friends to provide a beautiful and moving tribute to one of the great voices of the century. BBC radio also broadcast programmes in memory of Kathleen Ferrier.

APPRAISAL

Great care goes into the planning and production of musical broadcasts.[35] The BBC's live broadcasts use the best high-fidelity stereo equipment. Although the lack of reverberation in the Royal Festival Hall led to criticism of its acoustical qualities, the reverberation time was extended through a combination of microphones and small speakers set in the ceiling. In any case, pick-ups benefit from a permanently installed control room, effective microphone placement, and, if necessary, reverberation chambers, so that broadcast sound is highly satisfactory. The large cavernous Royal Albert Hall, which resembles many American municipal auditoriums, does duty for everything from rock concerts and prize fights to the Promenade Concerts. But the erection of a large canopy over the orchestra, together with effective microphone placement, has brought very satisfactory results.

Microphone placement and volume control—even of phonograph records—are the responsibility of musically trained staff members who work from scores. Spoken continuity usually is confined to simple statements about the composer, selection and performer, with only a few explanatory remarks, although there are a few 'music appreciation' programmes on both radio and television. Incidentally the BBC, as it did during the war years, still schedules symphony intermission talks on subjects entirely unrelated to the programme.

Television instrumental programmes follow standard procedures. The head of BBC television music in the early 1950s put it well when he wrote that 'the more significant the music the less the producer should have to "fuss it about"'.[36] Camera shots are well planned, the important instruments televised when heard, and a good balance maintained between wide shots of the orchestra, tight shots of the instruments and conductor, and occasional relief shots of the audience. As was mentioned above, the audience provides the main show during the last Promenade Concert of each season.

Evidence of excellence was provided by the awards received by both BBC and ITV at the 1977 Prix Italia in Venice. The BBC won for a documentary study of guitar-player Julian Bream, *A Life in the Country* who, in addition to playing, was shown organizing and taking part in a cricket game, gardening, discussing the design and making of guitars, and appearing as all-round good fellow.[37] Thames Television was actually surprised when it received a first prize for a performance of Benjamin Britten's *St Nicholas Cantata* recorded as it was transmitted from St Alban's Cathedral in Hertfordshire.[38] Although a horseracing pick-up at Newmarket the following day seriously limited the time for both rehearsal and recording, the total result was very moving, showing as it did the choir, the organ, a symphony orchestra, and the church audience itself, all in the setting of a beautiful Gothic cathedral. While not begrudging ITV this and other deserved awards, the BBC does much more for music than does IBA: its four radio networks and various local stations provide excellent all-round music coverage; and its two television services offer both more and better music programmes than does ITV, even allowing for the Corporation's advantage in having had two outlets to ITV's one.

The Annan Committee wrote: 'The BBC is arguably the single most important cultural organisation in the nation.'[39] After noting that many of its correspondents 'expressed their deep appreciation of broadcasts of classical music', the committee observed: 'The BBC's output in particular is widely recognised to be of the highest order both for the range and the depth of its coverage: and for this they deserve unstinted praise.' The Committee quoted from a report by Lord Redcliffe-Maud on *Support for the Arts in England and Wales*, which, among other things said: 'Broadcasting . . . can claim to have done more for the artist in Britain than any other agency during the last half-century.' The Annan Report quoted some musicians, playwrights, actors, and poets to the effect 'that the BBC was in a position to exert too great a control over the careers and reputations of British musicians' and other performers. But the Committee put these concerns aside, pointing out that the Corporation, after all, had to make value-judgements in its programming, and that on the whole it discharged such responsibilities very adequately. The Committee agreed, and so do I.

Finally, it should be observed that public reactions to broadcasts of music are about the same in the United Kingdom as in the United States. Even though the level of music appreciation has risen greatly in recent years—and for this much credit must go to broadcasting in both countries—the audiences for serious music are not large. In Britain, from 1 to 2 per cent of the adult population tunes in to symphony programmes, and chamber-music concerts attract even fewer listeners, while most listening is to the popular music of Radio 1. Because of differences between the two countries, and the different methods used to measure audiences, exact comparisons cannot be made; but it does appear that the standards and tastes in both are about the same, despite the greater amount of serious music broadcast in the United Kingdom.

20 Audience Research

In April 1975 the British Broadcasting Corporation told the Annan Committee that to keep in touch with its public it conducted audience research; analysed programme mail; appointed advisory committees; maintained continuing contacts with Parliament and other national bodies; dispersed publicity; arranged public lectures; issued publications like the *Radio Times* and *The Listener*; and had a Programmes Complaints Commission.[1] Had the IBA submitted a comparable memorandum to the Annan Committee, it probably would have said about the same things.

Despite various attempts by the broadcasting organizations to keep informed about audience reactions, the Annan Committee began its chapter on 'Broadcasting and the Public' by saying:

> The most voluminous evidence we've received was from those who wanted more public scrutiny of broadcasting; and even if much of this came from organisations or individuals professionally concerned with broadcasting, the number of other submissions we received convinced us that there must be some change in the structure of broadcasting, so that the public and the interest groups are better able to put their views directly to the broadcasting organisations.[2]

All of the BBC Charters and IBA legislation have required the broadcasters to maintain contacts with their audiences, and as the years have gone by the instructions have become more specific. The Corporation must appoint a General Advisory Council, National Broadcasting Councils for Scotland and Wales, and Regional Advisory Councils for Northern Ireland and England; and it may set up additional committees if it wishes.[3] Following proposals from the Beveridge Committee, and in accordance with recommendations in the 1952 White Paper, the 1952 and 1964 Charters instructed the Corporation to bring its work 'under constant and effective review', and to relay to its staff 'criticisms and suggestions' received from the public.[4]

As a consequence of the report of the Pilkington Committee, the Television Acts of 1963, 1964, and 1973 required the IBA to keep its programmes 'under constant and effective review', to ascertain 'the state of public opinion concerning the programmes (including advertisements) broadcast by the Authority', and to make 'provisions for full consideration by the Authority of the facts, comments and suggestions so obtained'.[5] The law also requires the Authority to appoint advisory committees on religious broadcasts, advertising, and certain educational programmes; a medical advisory panel; and committees in the geographical areas where the Authority sets up local radio stations.[6]

Culminating a decade's pressure to conduct their audience studies jointly, the BBC and the IBA agreed in 1978 to merge their research activities, but so many obstacles were encountered that at the time this book went to press in 1980, no final agreement had been reached. Therefore, the two organizations' procedures and findings are reported separately.

BBC AUDIENCE RESEARCH

Despite good performance now, in the early days the BBC lagged far behind its American counterparts in developing systematic audience studies. The basic reason was that the Corporation's non-commercial monopoly status did not provide the motivation for audience research which came naturally to America's competitive networks, stations, sponsors, and advertising agencies. Furthermore, early BBC programme executives underestimated the importance and misunderstood the uses of audience research. They dismissed it as 'nose-counting', interesting only to commercial broadcasters. They failed to realize that comprehensive audience research could be an excellent source of qualitative information for the producers of verse dramas and serious talks as well as for the directors of variety shows.

Year after year the Corporation in its annual reports pointed with pride to the increase in the number of radio licences as evidence of public approval, while it depended on advisory councils and listeners' letters for detailed audience information. Beginning in May 1922, listeners' letters were read and answered by the Programme Correspondence Section.[7] Although in 1930 some staff members began to press the case for systematic audience studies, there were generally negative reactions to such proposals.

Yet in the late 1920s and in the 1930s, some information was gained from polls conducted by British newspapers and by the Institute of Incorporated Practitioners in Advertising. A survey made by the latter in 1935 showed that on Sundays—the Reith Sunday policy then was in effect—half of the British public listened regularly to Radio Luxembourg, although on weekdays—when the Corporation had a more balanced programme schedule—only 11 per cent did.[8]

Although Reith was opposed to systematic audience surveys, he wrote in his autobiography that in 1935 he told King Edward VIII 'that water engineers could provide a pretty clear indication of the popularity of broadcast items. When there was anything specially interesting, water consumption fell; immediately afterward there was a sudden, sometimes alarming, peak load.'*

---

* Briggs II, p. 266; Reith, *Into the Wind*, p. 244. See also Maurice Gorham, *Broadcasting and Television Since 1900*, p. 149, and *idem.*, *Sound and Fury*, p. 59. In 1936 Sir Stephen Tallents, Controller for Public Relations, wrote: 'There is a lot of information to be got indirectly from indirect sources such as gas and electric light companies—and even water companies, for the water engineer at Portsmouth has just sent us a graph showing how everyone ceased to use water for cooking, washing etc., while the broadcast of the King's funeral [28 January 1936] was on.' In May 1953, readers of America's *Business Week* were amused at a story linking water consumption to the popularity of television programmes:

Both logic and prejudice underlay these early objections to audience research. Some people feared that if there were intensive audience studies, programme policies might be determined mainly by programme popularity—a reasonable objection, heard today both in Britain and the United States. Prejudice was another factor. One staff member wrote: 'The real degradation of the BBC started with the invention of the hellish department which is called "Listener Research". That Abominable Statistic is supposed to show "what listeners *like*"—and, of course, what they like is the red-nosed comedian and the Wurlitzer Organ.'[9]

In 1948, Sir Harold Nicolson, author, critic, diplomat, and one of the BBC's governors when the Third Programme was launched in 1946, wrote of it: 'The whole intention and purpose of the experiment as originally conceived was to provide at least one programme . . . which should aim solely at qualitative values and which should utterly ignore, condemn and abjure all quantitative values.' But a decline took place after the first year, owing to the influence of 'an ingenious organization known as Listener Research'. He then complained of the application of quantitative research findings, apparently never realizing that qualitative data also could be compiled which would permit Third Programme standards to be maintained at the same time that its audiences were increased.[10]

But despite such doubts, systematic audience research had already begun. In October 1936, the Corporation set up a Department of Listener Research, headed by Robert J. E. Silvey, previously with the research staff of the London Press Exchange, who held the position until his retirement in 1968. Regular field work began in December 1939. During the war years, research techniques were developed into more of a science, and 1946 found the BBC with a fully-functioning audience research department.[11] The original name, Listener Research Department, was changed to Audience Research Department in 1950, when its work was enlarged to include television, but, for the sake of uniformity, the latter name is used throughout this book.

The BBC Audience Research Department is the largest department of its type maintained by any broadcasting organization in the world.[12] It measures audiences for all BBC and IBA domestic programmes; sets up listening and viewing panels to provide qualitative reactions to broadcasts; makes special studies of individual programmes and groups of programmes; conducts pre-broadcast inquiries to determine the needs and interests of audiences for programmes in their planning stages; inquires into the sociological effects of television and the impact of broadcasting on children; and experiments to improve its own research techniques.

From a modest beginning in 1936, with one professional and one secretarial employee, the department now has a full-time professional staff of forty, plus seventy secretarial and clerical employees. It maintains a pool of 1800 part-time paid field interviewers, supplemented by 5500 unpaid volunteers, in its nationwide listening and viewing panels. The department is concerned only with out-of-school

---

consumption was down during interesting telecasts, but when less attractive programmes or commercials came on, there was a great increase, indicating that there were fewer people before their sets. ('Why Water Charts ZigZag at Night', *Business Week*, 2 May 1953, pp. 44–6).

audiences in the United Kingdom. Studies of BBC—and also of IBA—school reception are made by the School Broadcasting Council, while External Broadcasting conducts its own surveys. Its total annual budget is about £1 million of which 75 per cent goes for the daily survey described below.

The first and most basic assignment of the Audience Research Department is its daily survey of listening and viewing, which reports the size of BBC and ITV radio and television audiences, along with some demographic data.[13] Some 2500 different people are interviewed each day—over 1,000,000 a year—selected to be representative of the entire population over the age of 5, as to geographical distribution, age, sex, employment status, and socioeconomic class. Interviewers take people through their listening and viewing of the previous day, and help them to remember what they heard or viewed, the results being recorded on 'log sheets' (sheets listing the previous day's programmes), with spaces in which to enter the subject's name, age, address, occupation, and social class, as well as to note whether he had television and radio sets, or received programmes from relay services. A person is reported as hearing or viewing a programme only if he has heard or seen over half of it.

To supplement these measurements of audience size, the BBC maintains panels of 4000 listeners and 2000 viewers to provide information about audience reactions.[14] Panellists, who serve for 12 months, are asked to continue their normal listening and viewing habits rather than commenting on programmes they would not have heard or seen, had they not been panel members. They receive questionnaires asking for information on a wide variety of topics, such as whether they regard a programme as important or trivial; about actors, direction, and scripts; and requesting opinions on each act of a variety show. There also is space for comments. In addition to these ongoing surveys, there are *ad hoc* investigations of audience reactions to certain types of programmes, such as sports, medical information broadcasts, and news. Studies also have been made of the understandability of talk programmes, reactions to proposed changes in the programme schedule, various documentaries, attitudes towards pirate broadcasting, and television violence.[15]

The purpose of this research, says the BBC, is 'to collect information . . . as a basis for evaluation or decision-making by those concerned with programmes and policy'.[16] Therefore, audience research reports are widely circulated among staff members, and are freely available to anyone in the Corporation who wishes to see them. The regular output includes Barometers of Listening and Viewing, comparisons and demographic analyses of BBC and ITV audiences, regional viewing summaries, and reactions to programmes selected for special study. Although in its earlier years the Corporation was very reluctant to make such information public, it now has some publications surveying research findings, and periodically releases reviews to the press. Since 1973–4 an *Annual Report of BBC Audience Research Findings* has been available to the public at nominal cost, and each issue of the handbook announces that the public may obtain information about audience research methods from the Audience Research Information Desk, Broadcasting House, London.[17]

The old policy of secrecy was justified on the grounds that individual programme ratings lack meaning unless interpreted with reference to certain information usually possessed only by professionals, such as which network carried the programme, the hour of the broadcast, the programmes which preceded and followed it, and the nature of the competing programmes. Critics replied, however, that the BBC withheld this information partly because of a generally conservative approach, and partly because it feared public disapproval of its policy of providing extensive—and expensive—services for small minorities. The entrance of the ITA into the field in the middle 1950s, with its touting of research findings, accelerated the decision of the BBC to 'go public' with some of its data, but increased the confidentiality of other material that might be of help to its new rival. However, the original objections to wide dissemination of research data still are recalled when public misinterpretation of results is claimed, although they are no longer advanced as reasons for withholding such information.

IBA AUDIENCE RESEARCH

Because of Independent Television's diversified structure, its research is dispersed. At headquarters the Authority has had a Research Department since 1966, with a head and deputy head, along with five other researchers.[18] Together, programme companies, their advertisers and clients, contract for measurements of audience size, while appreciation is measured separately by and for the Authority. Ad hoc studies, much like those of the BBC, are undertaken by the Authority and programme companies as needed.

As would be expected, even before the first ITA station went on the air in 1955, arrangements were made for audience measurements. During 1955 and 1956, Independent Television companies and advertising agencies purchased audience data from the BBC, but they soon engaged the services of Television Audience Measurement (TAM), which got its basic data from meters installed in 850 representative homes in all parts of the country equipped to receive both BBC and ITV programmes. Two-thirds of these homes also kept viewing diaries, which provided audience composition information. From these data, reports were compiled of the minute-to-minute audiences of both ITV and BBC. From 1955 to 1959, the A.C. Nielsen organization also ran a meter-based survey in competition with TAM, but in the latter year the two decided not to compete and joined forces to do audience research in Britain and Western Europe.[19] In those earlier years, Associated Rediffusion and Associated Television surveyed their own school audiences, but this was discontinued in 1967 when the School Broadcasting Council agreed to do research for both groups.

The Independent Television Companies Association, the Incorporated Society of British Advertisers, and the Institute of Practitioners in Advertising have contracted with Audits of Great Britain (AGB) to conduct general audience surveys. The resulting Joint Industry Committee for Television Advertising Research (JICTAR) measures set-use much as TAM did, through meters attached to receivers in a representative sample of 2655 homes which can receive ITV signals.[20] Participating households also are required to keep diaries indicating on a quarter-hour basis the age, sex, and some other characteristics of viewers. As incentives for working with JICTAR, AGB keeps the receiving sets of participating homes in good repair, and diary-keeping households are eligible to win substantial prizes.

Audience measurement for Independent Local Radio is the responsibility of the Joint Industry Committee for Radio Audience Research (JICRAR), which represents the Association of Independent Radio Contractors, the Institute of Practitioners in Advertising, the Institute of the Incorporated Society of British Advertisers, and the IBA. JICRAR surveying is done by Research Surveys of Great Britain, Ltd., keeping diaries of their listening. In addition to its on-going studies, beginning in 1977 JICRAR initiated an annual simultaneous survey of radio audiences in those areas served by ILR.[21] Over a 4-week period, listening to all stations is recorded in specially prepared diaries by a sample of over 12,000 adults aged 15 and above, and by a separate sample of 3000 children, aged between 5 and 14.

The JICTAR data are used to graph minute-to-minute fluctuations in television audience size, with the proportion of sets tuned to any given service constituting its 'rating'. Each week JICTAR publishes the names of the top twenty programmes, and each month issues a press release which, among other things, provides the often quoted BBC : ITV audience ratios. From the outset, the ITCA was more inclined than the BBC to publish its findings, and these often are the subject of press reports and comments.

The IBA research department arranges research into television audience appreciation, sometimes doing the work itself but often contracting it out to other agencies.[22] Diaries are sent every second week to 900 members of a representative panel in the London area, and on alternate weeks to about 900 people in other ITV regions. Each respondent is asked to rate each BBC or ITV programme watched on a six-point scale, ranging from 'extremely interesting and/or enjoyable' to 'not at all interesting/or enjoyable', and to comment on them and anything else pertaining to television. Each programme is given an Appreciation Index, which in theory could range from 0 to 100, although it seldom goes below 40 or over 90. These AIs, as they are called, tell the IBA, the programme companies, and any others concerned, which programmes are best and least liked, and—sometimes—why, without reference to audience size. They also provide some demographic data.

Various *ad hoc* studies by market research companies solicit opinions on such matters as the fairness of news and current affairs broadcasts, offensiveness in programming, the relative images of the BBC and ITV, reactions to the radio broadcasting of parliamentary proceedings, and public attitudes toward advertising (there are comparable studies for ILR). In addition, the Authority conducts an annual public opinion survey, asking 1000 people from all parts of the country for their opinions about television in general, and commissions in-depth research, 'the aim of which is to identify and analyse patterns and regularities in viewing behaviour, and so better to understand not only the structure of programme preferences of the viewers but also the probable consequences of changes in scheduling'.[23]

Inevitably, since different methods of measurement are used, the data collected by the BBC and IBA do not entirely agree, and, as in the United States, there are widely publicized arguments as to which figures are correct. The BBC counts individuals throughout the entire population, whether or not they have receiving sets, whereas JICTAR samples only those households with multi-channel sets which can receive both services.[24] Furthermore, the Corporation counts the number of *people* viewing, while until recently JICTAR has dealt only with *homes* viewing, although since the autumn of 1977 JICTAR also has reported network audience shifts based on data from individual diaries.

Summarizing its comparison of the two methods, the BBC wrote: 'Neither method is perfect. Both have inherent weaknesses.'[25] The Annan Committee observed that 'the most significant difference is that the BBC measures what the individual views, while ITV measures which sets are switched on to which channel', and went on to make what some of the researchers regarded as the offensively gratuitous remark that 'the method on which each system is based consistently produces the most favourable results for those who pay for it'.[26]

During July 1976, when the BBC was making the most of its exclusive coverage of the Montreal Olympics, it claimed that 63 per cent of the audience was tuned to its two services, while ITV reported that the true balance was ITV 50 per cent, BBC 1 41 per cent, and BBC 2 9 per cent.[27] For one top event, the BBC claimed 20.5 million viewers, although ITV insisted that only 13 million people were watching. Similar differences are reported periodically, although seldom with that much discrepancy. Reviewing these differences, the highly respected *Financial Times* remarked:

> Clearly, the differences between the two claims are so considerable as to make any comparisons worthless. There have been efforts recently to get the two sides to measure in the same way. Talks broke down. Unless the Annan Committee . . . suggests that the two sides get together for their research—and the government forces them to do so—the arguments are likely to continue whenever a major event comes along.[28]

The British trade magazine *Broadcast* commented: 'There comes a point when the playing around with meaningless figures becomes counter-productive.'[29] Another set of diverse claims prompted the correspondent for the American publication *Variety* to write: 'That's not just a gap—it's a chasm.'[30]

Despite indignant responses from the researchers that the over-all differences were much less than they were made out to be by the press, the Annan Committee recommended that the two organizations develop a common method of measurement.[31] In fact, Sir Hugh Greene, who had been Director-General of the BBC from 1960 to 1969, was among those who told the committee that all audience measurement should be done by a single independent organization. The Committee noted that both sides 'were worried that the cost of audience measurement was too high, and that the apparent discrepancies between the ratings . . . could result in both systems becoming discredited in the eyes of the press and the public'. Furthermore, the evidence received from those paying for audience measurement 'showed that they all recognised the advantages in devising a common system of audience measurement. . . . We recommend therefore that the BBC and ITCA at once devise a combined system for assessing audience ratings for all broadcast channels.' The 1968 government White Paper agreed, suggesting a combined system to survey all British radio and television audiences.[32]

In fact, the BBC and the IBA had long realized the advantages of combined audience measurement, and even had conducted a joint experiment in 1976, which, however, proved unsatisfactory. Finally, in April 1978, the Chairman of the BBC Board of Governors and the Chairman of the ITCA Council signed an agreement for jointly conducted and financed audience measurements.[33] The letter of agreement cited two 'significant advantages' to the new understanding. Emphasis henceforth would be moved 'from head-counting towards qualitative and audience appreciation studies, while . . . the danger would be remove[d] of our two organisations appearing to differ in public on matters which many say should not be open to more than one interpretation'. Because the new arrangements had not come into effect when this book went to press, no data from the combined system were available for this chapter.

RECEIVER OWNERSHIP

The British Post Office, which sells receiver licences, reported that in March 1979, 18,381,116 homes or dwelling units in the United Kingdom were licensed to operate television receivers, of which 6,249,716 were monochrome and 12,131,445 colour sets. (A licence-holder may operate more than one set; the number of sets, therefore, will always be greater than the number of licences.) These and other data relative to set ownership from 1927 to 1979 are given in Table 21.[34] Since there always are some evaders—at any one time there are at least a million homes with receivers but without licences—the actual number of homes with television receivers in 1979 was probably on the order of 20 million. Since radio-only and combined radio–television licences were eliminated in February 1971, the licence figures available since then pertain only to television.

Since the end of World War II, practically every British home has had one or more radio receivers. In 1978, as Table 22 shows, the BBC reported that there were 50,600,000 sets in the entire country. Other BBC data indicate that, although 62 per cent of the population in 1975 was able to receive FM, only 25 per cent regularly listened, and only 8 per cent of all sets could reproduce stereophonic transmissions. This disappointed the BBC, since its FM network was developed, not primarily to provide additional programme services, but because so much medium-wave reception in the United Kingdom was unsatisfactory. As the Corporation put it: 'Evidently, for many people first class reception of radio broadcasting is not a high priority.'[35]

It is difficult to get comparable data on set ownership and use for the United States and the United Kingdom, although Table 23 provides some basis for comparison. As of 1 January 1978, 74.6 million, or 98.6 per cent of all United States homes had one or more radios.[36] The total number of radios in working order was estimated at about 444 million, of which 328 million were home and personal

TABLE 21 *Broadcasting receiving licences, 1927–79*

| Licences at 31 March | | Total | Issued free for blind persons | Issued for payment | | |
| | | | | Radio only | Radio & television combined | |
					Monochrome	Colour
1927		2,269,644	5,750	2,263,894		
1930		3,092,324	16,496	3,075,828		
1935		7,011,753	41,868	6,969,885		
1940		8,951,045	53,427	8,897,618		
1945		9,710,230	46,861	9,663,369		
1946		10,395,551	47,720	10,347,831		
1947		10,777,704	49,846	10,713,298	14,560	
1948		11,179,676	52,135	11,081,977	45,564	
1949		11,747,448	53,654	11,567,227	126,567	
1950		12,219,448	56,376	11,819,190	343,882	
1951		12,369,027	58,161	11,546,925	763,941	
1952		12,753,506	60,105	11,244,141	1,449,260	
1953		12,892,231	61,095	10,688,684	2,142,452	
1954		13,436,793	62,389	10,125,512	3,248,892	
1955		13,980,496	62,506	9,414,224	4,503,766	
1956		14,261,551	62,745	8,459,213	5,739,593	
1957		14,525,099	62,453	7,496,390	6,966,256	
1958		14,646,350	61,387	6,494,960	8,090,003	
1959		14,736,413	57,784	5,423,207	9,255,422	
1960		15,005,011	54,958	4,480,300	10,469,753	
1961		15,176,725	50,852	3,858,132	11,267,741	
1962		15,372,219	46,782	3,491,725	11,833,712	
1963		15,698,991	43,371	3,212,814	12,442,806	
1964		15,884,679	40,337	2,959,011	12,885,331	
1965		16,046,603	34,355	2,759,203	13,253,045	
1966		16,178,156	31,499	2,579,567	13,567,090	
1967		16,773,205	29,662	2,476,272	14,267,271	
1968		17,645,821	27,564	2,529,750	15,068,079	20,428
1969		17,959,933	24,966	2,438,906	15,396,642	99,419
1970		18,183,719	22,174	2,279,017	15,609,131	273,397
1971	*(Note 1)*	15,943,190	—	—	15,333,221	609,969
1972		16,658,451	—	—	15,023,691	1,634,760
1973		17,124,619	—	—	13,792,623	3,331,996
1974		17,324,570	—	—	11,766,424	5,558,146
1975		17,700,815	—	—	10,120,493	7,580,322
1976		17,787,984	—	—	9,148,732	8,639,252
1977		18,056,058	—	—	8,098,386	9,957,672
1978		18,148,918	—	—	7,099,726	11,049,192
1979	*(Note 5)*	18,381,161	—	—	6,249,716	12,131,445

NOTES:
1. Owing to industrial action within the Post Office between January and March 1971 the licences in force at 31 March 1971 do not reflect the true licensing position at that date.
2. Radio-only licences were abolished on 1 February 1971.
3. Combined radio and television licences were also abolished on 1 February 1971. From that date television-only licences have been issued.
4. Dealer's demonstration fees and concessionary licences for residents of old people's homes have been excluded from the figures.
5. Owing to industrial action within the Post Office the licences in force at 31 March 1979 do not reflect the true licensing position at that date.

SOURCE: *BBC Handbook, 1980*, p. 103.

TABLE 22   *Radio receivers in the United Kingdom in 1978*

Type of radio set	Number	Percentage	Per household
Portables	26,700,000	54	1.35
Plug-in sets	17,000,000	32	0.82
Fixed car radios	6,900,000	14	0.36
	50,600,000	100	2.53

SOURCE: BBC.

TABLE 23   *Trend of radio and television ownership in the United States*

Year	Radio homes (millions)	TV homes (millions)	Year	Radio homes (millions)	TV homes (millions)
1949	40.8	1.6	1964	54.0	52.6
1950	42.1	5.9	1965	55.2	53.8
1951	43.6	12.4	1966	57.0	54.9
1952	44.8	17.3	1967	57.5	56.0
1953	45.0	23.4	1968	58.5	57.0
1954	45.4	28.2	1969	60.6	58.5
1955	46.2	32.3	1970	62.0	60.1
1956	47.2	36.7	1971	62.5	62.1
1957	48.2	40.3	1972	64.1	64.8
1958	48.9	43.0	1973	67.4	66.2
1959	49.5	44.5	1974	68.9	68.5
1960	49.5	45.2	1975	70.4	69.6
1961	49.5	46.9	1976	71.4	71.2
1962	51.1	49.0	1977	72.9	72.9
1963	52.3	51.3	1978	74.6	74.5

sets and 116 million out-of-home receivers. As of September 1978, 74.5 million or 98 per cent of all United States homes (excluding those in Alaska and Hawaii) had one or more television sets, and 60.29 million or 81 per cent of all television homes had colour receivers.

Table 24 indicates the proportion of the British population with radio and television receivers from 1952 to 1978. The right-hand column shows how the number of radio-only persons steadily declined as the number of television persons increased. (Until 1955, all television transmissions were from the BBC's 405-line monochrome stations in Band I, which approximates Unites States Channels 2–6. But in that year, when ITV went on the air with stations in Band III—approximately Channels 6–13 in the United States, and the BBC added a few Band III stations, the public began to buy sets covering both bands. BBC 2 began broadcasting monochrome signals on UHF in 1964 and added colour in 1967. BBC and ITV began duplicating their Bands I and III services in colour on UHF in 1969.)

Comparable data from the IBA include the following. At the beginning of 1962, of the 16.6 million homes in those sections of the United Kingdom receiving ITV

TABLE 24   *Trend of radio and television ownership in the United Kingdom (percentages)*

	With Band I* (BBC only)	With Band III* (BBC and ITV)	With UHF (BBC 1, BBC 2 and ITV)		With television	With radio but not television
			Monochrome	Colour		
1952	14.0	N/A†	N/A	N/A	14.0	
1953	21.8	N/A	N/A	N/A	21.8	73.9
1954	30.6	N/A	N/A	N/A	30.6	67.0
1955	35.1	4.5	N/A	N/A	39.6	57.7
1956	30.3	17.7	N/A	N/A	48.0	48.9
1957	31.0	25.3	N/A	N/A	56.3	41.0
1958	19.8	45.0	N/A	N/A	64.8	33.0
1959	13.7	60.7	N/A	N/A	74.4	23.5
1960	9.9	71.9	N/A	N/A	81:8	16.4
1961	4.8	80.2	N/A	N/A	87.4	13.3
1962	3.7	83.7	N/A	N/A	88.8	11.2
1963	2.3	86.5	N/A	N/A	90.8	10.0
1964		87.6	3.2	N/A	90.8	8.2
1965		83.9	7.9	N/A	91.8	7.2
1966		80.5	11.8	N/A	92.3	6.6
1967		70.3	22.5	N/A	92.8	6.1
1968		60.8	32.4	N/A	93.2	5.7
1969		52.0	41.8	N/A	93.7	5.4
1970		42.6	48.3	3.2	94.2	4.8
1971		30.8	55.7	8.1	94.6	4.6
1972		18.2	60.2	17.4	95.8	3.6
1973		10.7	54.4	30.9	96.0	3.5
1974		5.9	47.4	43.3	96.6	2.9
1975		3.8	42.1	51.2	97.1	2.5
1976		2.4	35.2	59.7	97.3	2.4
1977			32.3	65.1	97.4	
1978			26.7	71.0	97.7	

NOTE: From 1952 to 1959 the figures refer to the population aged 16 and over; from 1960 onwards to the population aged 5 and over.

SOURCE: B. P. Emmett, 'The Television and Radio Audience in Britain'. In Denis McQuail, ed., *Sociology of Mass Communications*, p. 197 (hereafter cited as Emmett), with updating from the BBC.

  * For an explanation of 'Band I' and 'Band III', see above, p. 350.

  † N/A = Not available.

services, 12.8 million had receivers, of which 11.3 million or 68 per cent were able to pick-up ITV. By January 1975, all but 0.6 million of the country's 19.2 million homes had acquired television sets, and of these 18.6 million television-equipped homes 18.4 million could pick-up ITV. By 1979, 97 per cent of all sets could receive UHF.[37]

In Britain, as elsewhere, the more affluent middle-class families were the first to buy television receivers, because they could better afford them, and the same was true of the acquisition of colour sets. However, relatively few British homes have more than one television set. In January 1975 one million, or 6 per cent, of all homes had two or more sets. Table 25 shows the spread of ownership of colour receivers from 1971 to 1978, by socio-economic classes: A (top 6 per cent); B

TABLE 25 *Ownership of color television sets by socio-economic class (percentages)*

| Year | Quarter | Socio-economic class | | | Total |
		A	B	C	
1971	1				4
	2				5
	3				6
	4	21	12	5	8
1972	1	24	15	·7	10
	2	27	17	9	12
	3	29	20	12	14
	4	32	24	14	18
1973	1	37	28	17	21
	2	40	30	20	24
	3	43	34	23	27
	4	49	38	27	31
1974	1	53	42	32	36
	2	53	43	34	37
	3	56	46	35	39
	4	58	51	39	43
1975	1	61	55	42	47
	2	61	56	45	49
	3	61	57	46	49
	4	62	58	47	51
1976	1	66	60	49	55
	2	65	62	52	55
	3	68	63	53	56
	4	72	66	56	60
1977	1	76	68	58	61
	2	76	67	58	62
	3	75	70	58	63
	4	77	72	66	66
1978	1				68
	2				69
	3				69
	4				71
1979	1				73

(next 26 per cent); C (bottom 68 per cent, with the 'C' group subdivided beginning with the last quarter of 1977.) (Information from the BBC.)

LISTENING AND VIEWING PATTERNS

'Tastes . . . seem to be essentially stable', the BBC told the Annan Committee in 1975, looking back on almost 40 years of audience studies. The Corporation might have added that programme tastes are basically similar in all countries, if allowances are made for local preferences, particularly in light entertainment. Almost everyone everywhere listens to or watches news; nearly everyone enjoys plays and light entertainment; generation after generation of young people tunes to popular music broadcasts; and most men—though fewer women—follow sports. But relatively few people are devotees of opera, chamber music, or poetry.*

TABLE 26   *Listening and Viewing per head of population per week (hours and minutes)*

October/ December	Listening 7 a.m.–6 p.m.	6 p.m.–11 p.m.	Total	Viewing	Transmissions (hours and minutes)
1952	7:50	7:05	14:55		17:30
1953	6:25	5:55	12:20		17:30
1954	6:25	5:15	11:40		22:50
1955	6:10	4:30	10:40	4:25	28:00
1956	6:05	4:20	10:25	6:00	30:00
1957	5:55	3:20	9:15	6:50	35:00
1958	5:45	3:05	8:50	8:25	35:00
1959	5:55	2:30	8:25	9:10	35:00
1960	6:05	1:40	7:45	13:35	47:00
1961	6:25	1:20	7:45	13:20	47:00
1962	7:20	1:15	8:35	13:55	47:00
1963	7:30	1:10	8:40	13:55	47:00
1964	7:05	0:55	8:00	14:05	47:00
1965	6:45	0:50	7:35	14:50	47:00
1966	6:45	0:50	7:35	14:50	47:00
1967	7:55	0:55	8:50	14:25	47:00
1968	7:30	0:55	8:25	14:25	47:00
1969	7:31	0:58	8:29	16:20	58:00
1970	7:16	1:11	8:27	16:27	58:00
	Before 5 p.m.	*After 5 p.m.*			
1971	7:50	1:26	9:16	17:10	
1972	7:26	1:16	8:40	16:43	
1973	7:29	1:10	8:39	18:31	
1974	7:27	1:12	8:39	19:05	
1975	7:01	0:58	7:59	19:33	
1976	7:39	1:05	8:44	19:40	
1977	7:41	1:57	8:38	18:38	
1978	7:32	1:05	8:37	18:33	

SOURCE: Emmett, p. 200, and additional information from the BBC. Includes Independent Local Radio beginning in 1976.

* BBC Memo, *The Radio and Television Audience*, ##34– 37. America's *TV Guide* for 9 July 1977 contained an article, 'The Awful Truth about British TV', which reported surprise at finding that the 'truth about British TV' was that the top ten shows were not the imports aired by America's Public Broadcasting System—*Upstairs, Downstairs; Civilisation; The Ascent of Man*; etc., but such things as *This Is Your Life* and *Coronation Street*. But anyone who has regularly compared British and American audience ratings would not find this similarity of taste surprising.

TABLE 27 Weekly listening by age, sex, and socio-economic group (hours and minutes)

	Average transmission per week	Age group 5–15	16–19	20–29	30–49	50–64	65+	Boys under 16 (at school)	Men employed and in full-time education	Men not employed (mainly retired)	Girls under 16 (at school)	Women employed and in full-time education	Women not employed (mainly house wives)	Social class of adults (16+) Upper middle class	Lower middle class	Working Class Skilled	Unskilled	Average hours and minutes	Percentage of Listening
1978*																			
Radio 1	92:25	1:35	7:13	6:16	3:23	1:25	0:23	1:15	3:25	1:16	2:02	4:24	2:39	1:57	2:40	3:57	2:52	3:00	33
Radio 2	125:03	0:28	0:53	1:43	3:29	3:54	2:56	0:28	2:29	2:40	0:29	2:43	4:01	2:45	3:12	2:58	2:50	2:34	28
Radio 3	114:38	–	0:03	0:07	0:14	0:16	0:12	0:02	0:12	0:19	–	0:09	0:12	0:36	0:24	0:08	0:03	0:10	2
Radio 4	119:08	0:06	0:08	0:50	1:25	1:55	2:43	0:02	1:01	1:44	0:05	1:19	2:21	3:37	2:33	1:04	0:49	1:17	14
BBC Local	§	0:07	0:10	0:23	0:34	1:08	1:30	0:11	0:30	1:36	0:04	0:30	1:08	0:26	0:37	0:47	1:03	0:41	7
Other BBC[1]	§	–	0:02	0:04	0:08	0:09	0:11	–	0:06	0:14	0:01	0:06	0:10	0:14	0:11	0:05	0:08	0:07	1
All BBC	§	2:16	8:29	9:23	9:13	8:47	7:55	1:58	7:43	7:49	2:41	9:11	10:31	9:35	9:37	8:59	7:45	7:49	85
Radio Lux, etc.	§	0:05	0:25	0:12	0:02	0:01	0:03	0:03	0:08	0:08	0:08	0:09	0:02	0:04	0:07	0:06	0:05	0:06	1
ILR	§	0:53	2:00	2:11	1:34	0:51	0:46	0:50	1:26	0:56	0:56	1:35	1:18	0:31	1:19	1:31	1:31	1:19	14
All non-BBC	§	0:58	2:25	2:23	1:36	0:52	0:49	0:53	1:34	1:04	1:04	1:44	1:20	0:35	1:26	1:37	1:36	1:25	15
Any radio	§	3:14	10:54	11:56	10:49	9:39	8:44	2:51	9:17	8:53	3:45	10:55	11:51	10:10	11:03	10:36	9:21	9:14	100
BBC : non-BBC	70:30	78:22	79:21	85:15	91:09	91:09		69:31	83:17	88:12	72:28	84:16	89:11	94:06	87:13	85:15	83:17	85:15	

1979†																		
Radio 1	123:00	1:44	9:09	7:55	3:46	1:18	0:17	1:31	4:23	1:19	1:56	4:38	3:00	2:18	3:10	4:19	3:50	3:25	35
Radio 2	168:00	0:32	0:45	1:41	3:34	4:14	2:50	0:40	2:35	3:17	0:24	2:51	3:52	2:57	3:32	3:06	2:31	2:35	26
Radio 3	122:23	–	0:03	0:06	0:10	0:11	0:11	–	0:10	0:15	–	0:06	0:09	0:36	0:18	0:04	0:03	0:07	1
Radio 4	127:00	0:03	0:13	0:41	1:18	1:43	2:11	0:04	0:56	1:34	0:02	1:08	2:00	3:07	2:13	0:56	0:47	1:06	11
BBC Local	135:15	0:05	0:10	0:25	0:50	1:19	1:35	0:04	0:39	1:30	0:06	0:50	1:15	0:49	0:46	1:00	1:01	0:47	8
Other BBC‡	168:00	–	0:02	0:06	0:12	0:14	0:23	0:01	0:08	0:18	–	0:09	0:18	0:17	0:14	0:10	0:14	0:10	2
All BBC	168:00	2:24	10:22	10:54	9:50	8:59	7:27	2:20	8:51	8:13	2:28	9:42	10:34	10:04	10:13	9:35	8:26	8:10	83
Radio Lux, etc.	168:00	0:02	0:16	0:05	0:02	0:01	–	0:03	0:04	0:03	0:01	0:13	0:01	0:03	0:02	0:03	0:04	0:03	–
ILR	168:00	0:41	2:53	2:26	1:50	1:15	0:45	0:31	1:48	0:48	0:46	0:02	1:35	1:10	1:32	1:51	1:48	1:31	16
All non-BBC	168:00	0:43	3:09	2:31	1:52	1:16	0:45	0:34	1:52	0:51	0:47	2:05	1:36	1:13	1:34	1:54	1:52	1:34	17
Any radio	168:00	3:07	13:31	13:25	11:42	10:15	8:12	2:54	10:43	9:04	3:15	11:47	12:10	1:17	11:47	11:29	10:18	9:44	100
BBC : non-BBC		77:23	77:23	81:19	84:16	88:12	91:09	80:20	83:17	91:09	76:24	82:18	87:13	89:11	87:13	83:17	82:18	84:16	100

1978* Increase in transmission hours on Radio 1 and Radio 2 (Sporting Fixtures)
1979† Radio 1 and 2 separate/24 hour service on Radio 2.
‡ Other BBC : National regions and world service.
§ Figures not available.

The worldwide experience of radio has been its loss of audience to television, and in this respect the British experience has been a repetition of the American one, as is shown in Table 27, which supplies data about listening and viewing per head of population per week from 1952 to 1978. Between 1952 and 1978, the average amount of listening dropped from 14 hours 55 minutes to 8 hours 37 minutes per week, while viewing increased from 4 hours 25 minutes in 1955, the year the BBC's single service was joined by ITV, to 18 hours 33 minutes in 1978. It will be noted that, despite television, listening remained about the same during the day throughout these years, the big drop-off occurring in the evening hours.

Table 27 categorizes listening by the whole population to those national services available in 1978 and 1979 by age, sex and socio-economic group.[38] People aged 5–15 listened 3 hours 7 minutes per week in 1979; those aged 16–19, 13 hours 31 minutes; those aged 20–29, 13 hours 25 minutes; those aged 30–49, 11 hours 42 minutes; those 50–64, 10 hours 15 minutes; and those 65 and older 8 hours 12 minutes per week. Young people liked Radio 1, and (to a less extent) ILR, while older listeners preferred Radios 2 and 4. The upper middle class showed a preference for Radio 4, the lower middle class for Radios 1 and 2, with 4 not far behind, while the working class had an obvious preference for Radio 1, with Radio 2 second, and ILR third. Radio 3 was hardly in the running, Nationwide, the order of preference was Radio 1, Radio 2, ILR, and Radio 4, with Radio 3 a poor fifth, garnering only 1 per cent of all listening.

This table should be supplemented with information provided by the JICRAR 1978 survey of radio audiences in the areas served by ILR.[39] According to its findings, ILR was the most-heard radio service in those areas reached by its signals. The study ranked the percentage of listening during the spring of 1978 as follows: ILR—32; BBC Radio 1—25; BBC Radio 2—20; BBC Radio 4—13; BBC local radio—5; BBC Radio 3—2; Radio Luxembourg—1; other—2. The report dealt with the age, sex, and social class of ILR's audiences. It should be noted that this survey covered only the nineteen areas which then had ILR stations. The BBC studies cited in this chapter average out all listening nationwide, thus putting the ILR at a disadvantage. The IBA's report concluded: 'The general findings of the 1978 JICRAR survey may be considered most encouraging for ILR.'

Table 28 shows the average amount of viewing by the entire United Kingdom, aged 5 and above, during 2 weeks in mid-February 1978, divided as to age, sex, and socio-economic status.[40] (Other BBC data show that during this year, the average person viewed television 17¾ hours per week, which was about the same as for the preceding 4 years.) As to age groups, the very young and the elderly did the most viewing; the 16–19 age group viewed least; women viewed more than men; and people of higher social status viewed less than those of lower status. These findings are generally compatible those for most other countries, including the United States.

These data are supplemented by Table 29, which shows the average amount of viewing by the entire country's population, aged 5 and above, during the first quarter of 1979, divided as to days and times. (Figures in parentheses are for the first quarter of 1978.) The average person watched television 19 hours 57 minutes

TABLE 28 *Viewing by age, sex, and socio-economic group during 2 weeks in mid-February 1978 (hours and minutes)*

	Age group						Boys under 16 (at school)	Men employed	Men not employed	Girls under 16 (at school)	Women employed	Women not employed	Social class of adults (16 +)			
													Upper Middle Class	Lower Middle Class	Working Class	
	5–15	16–19	20–29	30–49	50–64	65 +									Skilled	Unskilled
BBC 1	13.25	7.30	7.58	8.38	8.14	8.30	14.10	8.05	8.58	12.51	7.30	8.54	8.27	8.47	8.23	7.31
BBC 2	0.30	0.59	1.13	1.30	1.25	1.21	0.35	1.24	1.29	0.27	1.15	1.25	1.56	1.43	1.16	1.03
All BBC	13.55	8.29	9.11	10.08	9.39	9.51	14.45	9.29	10.27	13.18	8.45	10.19	10.23	10.30	9.39	8.34
ITV	9.44	9.02	9.04	8.40	9.55	12.15	10.17	7.23	11.18	9.26	9.38	12.25	5.21	6.56	10.19	12.12
Total	23.39	17.31	18.15	18.48	19.34	22.06	25.32	16.52	21.45	22.44	18.23	22.44	15.44	17.26	19.58	20.46

TABLE 29 Average amount of viewing in the first quarter of 1979 (hours and minutes per head per week by population of the United Kingdom aged 5 and above)

	Saturday and Sunday (before 5.45 p.m.)		Monday – Friday (before 5.45 p.m.)		All days (after 5.45 p.m.)		All hours	
BBC 1 (av. 95:03 per week)	1:05	(1:03)	1:06	(1:02)	6.44	(6.44)	8:55	(8:49)
BBC 2 (av. 66:56 per week)	0:08	(0:06)	0:03	(0:02)	1:43	(0:58)	1:54	(1:06)
All BBC	1:13	(1:09)	1:09	(1:04)	8:27	(7:42)	10:49	(9:55)
ITV (av. 110:0 per week)	0:58	(0:58)	1:10	(1:04)	7:00	(7:46)	9:08	(9:48)
Total	2:11	(2:07)	2:19	(2:08)	15:27	(15:28)	19:57	(19:43)
Share of viewing (ratio)								
BBC 1	50	(49)	48	(48)	44	(44)	44	(45)
BBC 2	6	(5)	2	(2)	11	(6)	10	(5)
All BBC	56	(54)	50	(50)	55	(50)	54	(50)
ITV	44	(46)	50	(50)	45	(50)	46	(50)
Total	100	(100)	100	(100)	100	(100)	100	(100)
Viewing in time-band as percentage of total	11%	(11%)	11%	(12%)	78%	(77%)	100%	(100%)

per week, as follows: BBC 1—44 per cent; BBC 2—10 per cent (for a total of 54 per cent for the BBC); and, ITV—46 per cent. (Although the data in Tables 26 and 27 may appear to conflict, it should be noted that the time-spans and dates vary too.)

Direct comparisons of the number of hours of viewing per person per home in the United Kingdom and the United States must be made with great care. Most American cities have one or more stations on the air at least 18 hours a day, with many broadcasting longer than that, and most of their programmes are designed for the general viewer. In Britain, on the other hand, there is hardly any general programming before noon on weekdays, the morning broadcasts being principally for school use or as supplements to Open University courses, and there is little programming after midnight. Nevertheless, total viewing per head of the population was very much the same in both countries.

A series of Roper surveys reported the median hours of viewing per person per week in the United States as follows: November 1961—15 hours 59 minutes; November 1963—17 hours 58 minutes; November 1964—18 hours 26 minutes; January 1967—18 hours 47 minutes; November 1968—19 hours 29 minutes; January 1971—19 hours 50 minutes; November 1972—19 hours 50 minutes; November 1974—21 hours 14 minutes; November 1976—20 hours 11 minutes.[41]

TABLE 30   *Association between amount of television viewing and educational level: 1958 and 1975 findings compared (percentages)*

Year	School-learning age	Light	Average	Heavy	Unclassified	Total
1975	15 and under	21	33	42	4	100
1958	14 and under	27	34	39	–	100
1975	16–19	37	38	18	7	100
1958	16–17	41	34	25	–	100
1975	20 and over	54	22	16	8	100
1958	18 and over	55	24	21	–	100

SOURCE: BBC.

Table 30 shows the effects of educational level on amounts of television viewing. People who attended school up to age 20 or older (they would be called 'college-educated' in an American survey), view television less, while those with less education view it more. Other BBC data, from 1971, show that the better-educated do more radio listening than do less well educated people, although there is much viewing and listening among all educational categories. (It should be noted that the lighter viewing and heavier listening of those people with college educations are outweighed by the data for the rest of the population.) Much the same information has been received from American surveys, as Table 31 below (1970 data) shows.[42]

In general, BBC 1 viewers tend to be of higher socio-economic and educational

TABLE 31   *Weekly average viewing time by adults in the United States*

Total average hours	21.5
Ages	
18–19	17.4
20–24	19.6
25–34	21.3
35–49	20.5
50–64	23.1
65+	24.5
Education	
Postgraduate	15.4
College graduate	17.3
Some college	18.5
High-School Graduates only	21.7
Some High School	23.8
No High School	23.5
Household income	
$25,000 and over	16.3
$15,000–$24,999	17.6
$10,000–$14,999	19.6
$ 8,000–$ 9,999	20.7
$ 5,000–$ 7,999	23.5
$ 3,000–$ 4,999	25.5
Under $ 3,000	23.8

status than do ITV viewers, although BBC 2 viewers rank highest of all.[43] The BBC reported in February 1975 that the 'numerically-small "A" socio-economic group spent 16 per cent of its viewing time watching BBC 2, whereas the "C" group gave only 7 per cent of its time to BBC 2. Conversely, ITV attracted most of the viewing of the C group, 58 per cent in fact, but only 34 per cent of the viewing of the A's.' IBA data agreed with the BBC on ths point, and the Authority told the Annan Committee that 'a higher proportion of lower class viewers than of higher class watch ITV'. But that is not necessarily to the Authority's financial disadvantage, since the C group is numerically larger, is apt to view television more, and is more likely to buy the things advertised.[44]

Table 32 reproduces figures supplied by the BBC as to the division of audiences among the three television services from 1962 to 1978. (Until 1968/9, there was no differentiation between BBC 1 and BBC 2. BBC 2 came on the air in 1964.) There always are differences between the BBC and the JICTAR estimates of share-of-viewing, mostly because of differences in the population sampled, and also because of different definitions of what constitutes viewing. JICTAR data for the first quarter of 1978 indicated that the average ITV share of audience was 50 per cent on weekends; 59 per cent on weekdays; 55 per cent for evenings (6 p.m. to 10.30); with an all-week average of 55 per cent.[45] The Authority reported that, during the year ending 31 March 1979, '53 per cent of the total time watching

TABLE 32 *Division of audiences, United Kingdom,*
1962–72 (percentages of viewing time)

	All BBC	BBC 1	BBC 2	ITV
1962/3	50			50
1963/4	48			52
1964/5	45			55
1965/6	45			55
1966/7	49			51
1967/8	50			50
1968/9	56			66
1969/70		46	4	50
1970/1		48	5	47
1971/2		44	7	49
1972/3		46	7	47
1973/4		43	8	49
1974/5		44	8	48
1975/6		47	8	45
1976/7		48	8	44
1977/8		46	8	46

television in homes able to view both BBC and ITV was spent watching Independent Television'.[46]

PROGRAMME PREFERENCES

Audience-size figures averaged over a week, month, or year do not reveal hour-to-hour variations, nor individual programme preferences. Each year the *BBC Handbook* names the Corporation programmes with the largest number of listeners and viewers. For 1979, the radio list was as follows:[47]

The *Top Twenty* still attracted by far the largest radio audience, with an average of 7 million. Also well in the forefront was *Junior Choice*, with 5 million on Saturday and 4 million on Sunday. Noel Edmonds' Sunday morning programme, together with *Family Favourities*, and *Terry Wogan's* daily morning spot regularly drew 3 million listeners, 2½ million tuning in to *Simon Bates*, *Dave Lee Travis, All There Is to Hear* and *Jimmy Saville's Old Record Club*.

With the start of live broadcasting from Parliament, coverage of the *Budget Speech* attracted Radio 4's highest audience of the year, rising to 2½ million. The 8 am *News* was heard by 2 million and the part of the *Today* programme which followed it, 1½ million. The audience for the One O'Clock *News* also averaged 1½ million, as did that the *The World at One*. On Saturdays, *Any Questions?* attracted 900,000 listeners, while *Woman's Hour* and the afternoon edition of *The Archers*, between 750,000 and 800,000.

Among radio programmes highly praised by the listening panel were, on Radio 3, *Donald Wolfit's King Lear* and *The Defect* (a talk by Ian Kennedy about society's response to defective children) and, on Radio 4, *Goodnight Children*

Everywhere and *A Voice is a Person* (Sir Peter Pears' tribute to Kathleen Ferrier).

Comparable information for BBC television during the same year was phrased as follows:[48]

As in previous years, the highest audiences of the year were recorded over the Christmas holiday, with 26½ million watching the Christmas Day presentation of *The Sound of Music* and 25 million the *Queen's Speech* earlier in the afternoon. The film *Oliver*, also in Christmas week, attracted 22½ million and *The Two Ronnies*, on Boxing Day, 20½ million. Apart from Christmas programmes, sport featured high on the list of the year's top audiences, with the BBC's coverage of the *World Cup Final* and the match between *England and Brazil* earlier in the year being seen by 19½ million and the *Grand National* by 19 million.

Light entertainment programmes were, as always, extremely popular. *The Two Ronnies* regularly drew audiences of 19 million and Frank Spencer's misadventures in *Some Mothers Do 'Ave 'Em* averaged 18 million. Larry Grayson's *Generation Game* and *That's Life*, with Esther Rantzen, achieved average audiences of 15½ million, while the audience for *The Good Life Special*, performed in the presence of the Queen, was 14½ million. *Dick Emery, Blankety Blank* and *The Liver Birds*, all topped 14 million and the *World Circus Championships* in February were seen by 13½ million, which was also the average for the repeat of *The Good Life*. Other popular series were *The Ronnie Corbett Thursday Special* and *Top of the Pops* (13 million), the repeat of *Butterflies* (12 million), *Mastermind, Citizen Smith, It's a Knockout* and *Are You Being Served?* (11½ million) and *Val Doonican* (11 million).

Moving from Sunday to its Saturday night placing, *All Creatures Great and Small* regularly attracted audiences of 15 million. The tough police series *Target* and the Sunday afternoon serialisation of *Pinocchio* both achieved audiences of 10 million – indeed, serials were generally popular, with between 9 and 9½ million viewers following *The Aphrodite Inheritance* and *Running Blind* and 7½ to 8 million *The Onedin Line, A Horseman Riding By* and *Telford's Change* on Sunday evenings. *Play for Today* had an average audience of five million, particularly favourable reception being accorded to *Waterloo Sunset* and *Donal and Sally*, while *The Voysey Inheritance* was the most highly praised Play of the Month presentation.

Among imported programmes most impact was made by *Holocaust*. Shown on four consecutive evenings on BBC 1, it attracted audiences ranging from 14½ to 19 million. There was almost universal agreement about the significance and importance of the subject-matter, although the response to the series itself was more diverse. Three-quarters of the viewers felt that the handling of the subject had been both appropriate and successful, and in general these viewers considered the series authentic and convincing in all respects. In contrast, the minority of one-quarter who disliked the treatment of the subject mainly condemned the series as unconvincing in dialogue, characters and story. It is perhaps also interesting to note that the majority of those people who did not watch *Holocaust* had made a positive decision not to see any of it. Thus, for viewers and non-viewers alike, *Holocaust* aroused a deeply emotional response.

Jim'll Fix It was easily the favourite children's programme, averaging 13 million viewers, followed by *Noel Edmond's Lucky Numbers* (8½ million), *Go with Noakes* and *Dr Who* (8 million), *Grange Hill* and *Basil Brush* (7½ million).

Turning to sport, *The Superstars* was seen by 14½ million, *Match of the Day* 9 million and *Sportsnight* 8 million. Documentary series on BBC 1 included *Hong Kong Beat* and *Wildlife on One*, both seen by 8½ million, and *The Undersea World of Jacques Cousteau* and *James Burke's Connections*, which drew 7 million. Eight million viewers watched the *Nine O'Clock News*, while the audiences for *Nationwide* and *Panorama* averaged 6½ and 3½ million respectively.

On BBC 2, the highest audiences of the year were achieved by *Fawlty Towers*, with an average of 11½ million. *Olivia*, repeated from BBC 1 and featuring Olivia Newton John, gained an audience of 10½ million, with another repeat series – *Roots* – attracting 9 million viewers. Outstanding in drama, the Play of the Week presentation of *On Giant's Shoulders* – the true story of the adoption of thalidomide victim Terry Wiles (played by himself) – achieved an audience of 8 million and was widely commended for its moving and sensitive handling of its subject. David Attenborough's major natural history series *Life On Earth* set new standards of excellence, with audiences averaging 6½ million (rising to 9 million) and the highest possible praise for both the photography and narration.

Shows by *Des O'Connor, Marti Caine* and *Lennie and Jerry* averaged between 6 and 6½ million. The serialisation of Daphne du Maurier's *Rebecca* achieved 6 million and *Tigris* – four programmes telling the story of Thor Heyerdahl's Sumerian Voyage – 5½ million. Five-and-a-half million people also stayed up late to watch the *World Professional Snooker Championships*, while darts, a sport new to television, gained an instant success, with audiences averaging 4½ million for the *World Championships* in February. Repeats of *Monty Python's Flying Circus* averaged 5 million, *The Voyage of Charles Darwin* 4 million, *Man Alive* 3 million (with particular praise for the edition dealing with brain surgery in Belfast) and *The World About Us* 2 million.

The BBC's six-year project covering the complete canon of Shakespeare's plays started well, with audiences for the first half-dozen plays averaging 1½ million and a generally appreciative response, especially for *Henry VIII, Measure for Measure,* and *Richard II.*

Britain's JICTAR rating service, like those in America, has its weekly 'Top 20' chart. After observing that audience size is influenced by such factors as the time of broadcast, the ratings of the preceding and following programmes, and the nature of the competition, the IBA told the Annan Committee that:

ITV programmes have tended to dominate the "Top Twenty" lists; in recent years, 80% of all entries in the weekly charts over the course of a year have been

ITV programmes. This indicates that, in peak viewing time, at least, ITV produces the majority of the most popular programmes, if popularity is measured by audience size.[49]

Always among the leaders is Granada's *Coronation Street*, plus other light entertainment programmes. The BBC's *Nine O'Clock News* and ITN's *News at Ten* often are included, although they never are at the very top. At times an outstanding dramatic series of high appeal will make the list, such as *The Forsyte Saga*, *Edward VII*, *Edward and Mrs. Simpson*, or *Upstairs, Downstairs*. National figures, given in approximate numbers of viewers, extend from about 18 million for the leaders down to 12 or 13 million for those in 19th and 20th places. The broadcasting trade publications publish JICTAR ratings regularly, while some of them are reported by the general press too.

The principal conclusion to be drawn from this survey of audience data is that British preferences are like those everywhere else. After World War II, Sir William Haley, Director-General from 1944 to 1952, thought that if radio were divided into three networks with varying levels of demand, the audience would gradually become more sophisticated, working up from the popular Light Programme to the intellectually demanding Third Programme. But that did not happen. A country's intellectual and cultural level is the result of a great many interacting factors, of which broadcasting is only one. Fundamental are historical, educational, racial, and cultural traditions. These are affected by the output of the schools, churches, newspapers, broadcasting, and other means of information, education, and communication, always operating within the current social, economic, and political setting. Therefore it is impossible to evaluate broadcasting by itself, nor is it reasonable to expect it alone to bring about a millennium.

PROGRAMME APPRAISALS AND APPRECIATION

Both broadcasting organizations collect programme appraisals to supplement their data on audience size. The BBC, for example, solicits audience reactions to over 5000 of its programmes each year, by means of the listener/viewer panels mentioned above.[50] As Reaction Profiles and special programme reports, these are circulated among programme executives and producers, and some of the findings are published in the *Annual Review of BBC Audience Research*, the first of which covered the year 1973–4. Although most of these reports will not be meaningful to people who have neither heard nor seen the broadcasts, a few nevertheless can be cited as examples.

On 12 November 1973 both BBC 1 and ITV broadcast an interview with Princess Anne and Captain Mark Phillips 2 days before their wedding.[51] (The programme was repeated twice by radio on 13 November.) This interview was not an unqualified success, mainly because of 'the curious mixture of deferential, impertinent and downright idiotic' questions put to the couple, who, nevertheless, 'responded with exceptional tolerance and good humour'. But the Corporation estimated that the average person in the United Kingdom spent 2½ hours watching the telecast of the wedding itself on 14 November.

A study was made of the response to *Till Death Do Us Part*, a situation comedy series aired periodically since 1966. The model of America's highly popular *All in the Family*, the British series, according to its script-writer, tried to amuse its audience while striking at prejudice and bigotry.[52] Britain, like America, asked whether such programmes reduce or increase prejudice and bigotry. In Britain it was found that most viewers regarded the key figure of the series, Alf Garnett, 'as a harmless buffoon and there is no evidence that viewing of the series has much (if any) *direct* effect on relevant attitudes and prejudices, in *either* direction—despite the conviction of about one person in five that it can do harm'.

Americans will be particularly interested in the British public's reaction to the Corporation's Watergate coverage in 1974.[53]

> Already at the beginning of the year, . . . [wrote the BBC] many British listeners and viewers felt that they had had enough of Watergate. To most people American politics seemed distant and irrelevant, and the story itself was long and extremely confusing—bugging, cover up, courts, Senate hearings, who lied and about what, were all parts of the story, but how they fitted together was a mystery. American politics had always been corrupt, they felt, and nobody, including the BBC, would ever get to the bottom of it. There were far more important and relevant issues here at home—The Common Market, North Sea Oil, The Economy. Let America clear up its own mess.

This also was the year the BBC broadcast a 26-instalment dramatization of Trollope's political novels, *The Pallisers*, which, the BBC reported 'inevitably invited comparison with the well-remembered *Forsyte Saga*'. But the *Forsyte Saga* 'won out', with Reaction Indices between 78 and 86 while those for *The Pallisers* were from 67 to 84.[54]

The presentation on 21 November 1977 of John Osborne's *Look Back in Anger* 'was not on the whole enjoyed. . . . In spite of "fine performances", many viewers complained of too many verbal fireworks making for tedious viewing, and found the play dated and depressing.'[55] But enthusiasm greeted *I, Claudius*, for which appreciation

> tended to show a steady increase as the story progressed, so that the last episode had an exceptionally good reception. It was commended for giving a 'full-blooded recreation of the grandeur and corruption of Imperial Rome' that had most of its viewers totally enthralled. The cast was unanimously praised, in particular Derek Jacob's 'beautifully paced' Claudius.

There also were reports on radio receiver distribution and use; studies of the day-to-day activities of a typical family; reaction to coverage of the 1974 World Cup match; and the 1974 Promenade Concerts.[56] Listening audiences for the Prom Concerts averaged about 200,000 persons, while the telecast of the closing night's concert was seen by 6 or 7 million people, 'a very large number by radio standards, though considerably smaller than is normal for BBC 1 at this time on a Saturday evening'.

The 1975– 6 *Annual Review of Audience Research Findings* surveyed 'Forty Years of Listening and Viewing in Britain'; reported on coverage of the EEC referendum campaign; reviewed listener reaction to the experiment in broadcasting Parliament; and analyzed public reaction to the television series, *Play for Today* and *The Changing Faces of Medicine*.[57]

In 1973 the Audience Research Department published a 220-page book, *Violence on Television: Programme Content and Viewer Perception*, based on an intensive inquiry during which some seventy programmes on both BBC and ITV were monitored.[58] It was found that the most violent actions, apart from those in newscasts or documentaries, occurred mainly in entertainment programmes imported from the United States. The Department also contributes to publications prepared for the General Advisory Council, providing data for such brochures as *Children as Viewers and Listeners*, *The Coverage of Sport on BBC Television*, *The Task of Broadcasting News*, and *The BBC's Medical Programmes and Their Effects on Lay Audiences*.

IBA Appreciation Reports are produced weekly, alternate weeks dealing with London and the other ITV areas.[59] Programmes are divided into eight categories on the basis of content: action (adventure), romance, sports, comedy/light entertainment, news, general interest/information, feature films/plays and children's programmes. The Authority points out that Appreciation Indices should be compared only on a week-to-week basis, and then only within the same programme classes. Thus, it would not be valid to compare Appreciation Indices for serious documentaries with those for light comedies, since different criteria are used in judging them. A few generalizations can be made, however. Women tend to evaluate all programmes higher then men, and give considerably higher evaluations to programmes in the 'romance' category; news programmes are better liked in London than elsewhere; countrywide, sports programmes are liked more by men than women, but in London women find them equally enjoyable; and except for general interest and informational programmes, viewers of lower socio-economic status are apt generally to evaluate programmes higher than do other classes.

The IBA presented the Annan Committee with a report on *Attitudes to Broadcasting: A Survey of Public Opinion*, based on a survey conducted 'to measure changes in public attitudes towards broadcasting and particular aspects of programmes'.[60] Among other things it was found that 'Television is the most important news source for people of all [socio-economic] groups. When asked to mention just one source, 62% said television, 22% said newspapers and 11% said radio.' 'More people said they watched news mostly on ITV (44%) than said they watched it mostly on BBC (35%).' 'In terms of general output, 36% of the sample said they enjoyed ITV most, 21% said BBC 1 and 9% said BBC 2', although 32 per cent were undecided. More people thought both ITV and BBC 1 programmes had 'got worse during the year than thought they had improved', although the reverse was true for BBC 2. 'Too many repeats' was the principal reason given for saying that a channel had 'got worse'.

Seventy-three per cent of the public said that ITV showed no political bias and 68 per cent said the same thing of the BBC. Those 'detecting' bias thought that ITV was Labour-oriented and the BBC Conservative-oriented, 'although the BBC's Conservative bias was more positively expressed than was ITV's Labour bias'. However, approximately the same number of people perceived the two services as fair in dealing with political, social, and industrial controversies.

Forty per cent said they saw or heard 'offensive things on television', for which they held both services equally responsible. 'Bad language, sex and violence... were the predominant causes of offensiveness on television', with references to violence showing an increase over the previous years.

Somewhat surprisingly, respondents said they would like to see more documentaries and light entertainment programmes and less sports. An over-whelming proportion of the sample—84 per cent—said they preferred to have ITV supported by advertising than by licence fees (the figure in a similar survey conducted in 1964 was 74 per cent). Fifty-seven per cent of the respondents found advertisements enjoyable, 18 per cent judged them to be 'generally in bad taste', while 46 per cent thought 'they are generally misleading'.

AUDIENCE STUDIES BY OUTSIDE GROUPS

The BBC, with a large audience study department of its own, assigns supplementary research projects to its own personnel more often than does the IBA, which, with a small research department, usually commissions such studies from the outside. Even then, however, the IBA has not supported supplementary research as well as has the BBC. In 1974, the BBC spent about £120,000 or 16 per cent of its audience research budget on such studies, while the IBA assigned approximately £30,000.[61] But the IBA and its companies have studied children's programmes, women's reactions to afternoon serials and the Thames Television series *The World at war*. A study financed jointly by London Weekend Television, ATV, and Grampian surveyed parents' and children's reactions to *Sesame Street*. The Annan Committee observed, however, that while the IBA's research was 'on a considerably smaller scale than that of the BBC, [it] was in someways better focused'.

The Advertising Association has periodically engaged the British Market Research Bureau to survey public attitudes toward advertising.[62] During field work carried out in April and May 1972, a sample of 1260 adults aged 15 years and older was interviewed. Among other things, it was found that most people are not interested in advertising as such, and that over 90 per cent of the population does not talk about it and sees no reason for changes in advertising procedures. The government and the trade unions were examples of topics 'which [do] arouse much more interest and much more opposition'. People of higher education and social class have considerably more interest in advertising than does the rest of the population. The brochure reporting on this inquiry pointed out that 'it is particularly noticeable that the people most interested in advertising in the abstract are those who are firm opponents rather than supporters'. This fact, therefore, 'helps to explain why the volume of discussion and criticism about advertising is greater than would be warranted by the amount of general public interest it arouses'. As to specific findings, whereas 79 per cent of a sample interviewed in 1969 had approved of advertising, only 67 per cent did in a 1972 survey. The main reasons given for disapproval were that advertising raises prices and is misleading.

The IBA provided funding for a study by J. G. Goodhardt, A. S. C. Ehrenberg and M. A. Collins, published in 1975, which was intended to go beyond audience measurement studies 'to more generalised findings about viewer behaviour'.[63] There were two main findings. Only about 55 per cent of the viewers of one episode in a series normally watch the next episode. The other finding was described by the authors as follows:

> The extent to which different programmes share the same viewers . . . is expressed by the duplication of viewing law. Thus for any two programmes the level of duplication in their audience depends on the *ratings* of the programmes and not on their *content*. One pair of programmes generally has the same degree of audience duplication as any other pair of programmes with the same ratings.

Although 25 years ago British universities did relatively little mass media research compared to their counterparts in the United States, the situation has changed, and their output now is extensive. There is research of one kind or another at universities in Leicester, Leeds, Birmingham, and Glasgow, among others, with such authors as Jay G. Blumler, David E. Butler, Brian Groombridge, James D. Halloran, Denis McQuail, Richard Rose, Anthony Smith, and E. G. Wedell, to mention only a few. Some of this is supported by funds from the broadcasting organizations. In 1961, for example, the ITA funded research into the effects of television on young people, which grew into a study of television's total role in society.[64]

A number of academicians have written about broadcasting in recent years, and all of the British general elections since 1945 have been the subject of book-length studies. Those dealing with the elections of 1950 and later have had chapters about broadcasting and in 1969 a book was published dealing entirely with television and politics.[65] Another interesting book drew upon two recent studies to review the effects of television-viewing on the British working class.[66] The authors concluded that when working-class families adopt middle-class values, their television-viewing changes accordingly, with the result that their new points of view are reinforced by being exposed to the middle-class values of these programmes.

Without question, the most elaborate study of British broadcasting to date is the BBC-subsidized *History of Broadcasting in the United Kingdom* by Asa Briggs. Thus far four volumes have been published, with a total of 2936 pages, and at least one more is to come. These have been frequently cited in this book, and it is hard to see how anyone can write extensively about British broadcasting for some years without having recourse to the Briggs volumes. Briggs also has a recent book on the BBC's governors: *Governing the BBC*.

The Annan Committee commissioned a paper on 'Research Findings on Broadcasting' which surveyed British broadcasting research.[67] The authors divided their report into three sections: 'An interpretation of research into the effects of television'; 'a content analysis of certain types of programmes'; and 'Public attitudes towards television'. A few of these findings have been mentioned above but most are too detailed to be reviewed here.

The Annan Committee wrote early in 1977 that much of the research done was not used effectively; that the BBC Research Department should get 'a good deal closer to individual production departments and individual producers'; and that the IBA should press the programme companies to do more research on their own. The Committee also recommended that the two research departments work more closely with academic institutions, in order to 'know the academic scene and follow the findings of academic research, so as to be able to interpret it to those within their own organisations. They need to exchange ideas and discuss problems at conferences with those less immersed in day-to-day operations.'*

In 1977 the BBC published a 116-page book by Elihu Katz, Director of the Communications Institute at the Hebrew University of Jerusalem, entitled *Social Research on Broadcasting: Proposals for Further Development*. This was the result of an assignment given to Professor Katz 'to prepare an ''agenda for new projects of social research in the field of broadcasting'' which would (1) take account of past and ongoing work in Britain and elsewhere, and (2) have policy/editorial implications for the BBC'.[68] After interviewing broadcasters and grouping their questions into six categories, Katz listed thirty-five possible areas of research, and suggested broadly the approaches that might be used in exploiting them. Thereafter, the Corporation directly commissioned several research projects by independent academics, and suggested creating an independent Broadcasting Research Trust to conduct such research for all broadcasters. One of the first published reactions to the Katz report was a 50-page symposium in the spring 1978 issue of the American quarterly, *Journal of Communication*, in which five researchers conducted a 'debate on the Katz Report, with an epilogue' by Katz himself. It is to be hoped that the end is not in sight, and that this and similar ventures will stimulate basic thought, research, and publication about the broadcasting media in society.

PROGRAMME COMPLAINT BOARDS

The Broadcasting Act 1980 created a Broadcasting Complaints Commission to receive and assess certain types of complaints against the BBC and the IBA. This is the successor to the BBC's Programme Complaints Commission and the IBA's Programme Review Board which were set up as a consequence of the furor created in June 1971 when the BBC broadcast, *Yesterday's Men*, which was highly critical of some of the ranking members of The Labour Party—then out of power, but

* *Annan*, # #29.14, 29.16. When I showed the above paragraph to the Director of Audience Research for the BBC he noted: 'BBC Audience Research replies that the implication that their staff do not maintain contacts with the academic world, do not attend conferences, etc. is wholly false. ''Working with'' academic institutions is always welcomed but has often proved difficult to achieve in practice.'

neverthless an influential factor in British politics. In a public address the following year, Sir Hugh Greene, former BBC Director-General, spoke scathingly of

> the disastrous decision to set up a Complaints Commission of three distinguished elderly gentlemen... [who show] a complete ignorance of the necessary processes of television journalism. But however ignorant their condemnation it remains a condemnation—overriding the considered views of the Board of Governors and the Director-General.[69] In the atmosphere of today [1972], that can lead to a throttling of enterprising and crusading journalism to the detriment of the public interest.... The very different internal machinery for dealing with complaints adopted by the IBA may not have been any more necessary but at least it showed much greater political wisdom, and did not involve automatic publication of the results.[70]

At any rate, in 1971, Lord Hill, then Chairman of the Corporation's Board of Governors, stressed the need for 'an external scrutinizing board, a so-called council for broadcasting', because 'some form of protection for individuals wronged by broadcasts was desirable'. He apparently had in mind such things as the improper use of edited extracts, inadequate reporting, and the unfair questioning of interviewees. After discussion by the Governors and some top staff members, it was decided to set up such a board, provided it 'would not weaken the BBC's independence'. The Programme Complaints Commission was created in October 1971, and consisted of three members from outside the Corporation's staff, appointed by the BBC and provided by the Corporation with office facilities (off BBC property), a small staff, and an operating budget.[71]

Under its Constitution, the Complaints Commission was to deal with written complaints received within 30 days of the alleged offence, 'from individuals or organizations claiming themselves to have been treated unjustly or unfairly in connection with a programme or a related series of programmes as broadcast. Unjust or unfair treatment shall include unwarranted invasion of privacy and misrepresentation.' However, the complainant must agree in advance 'not to have recourse to the courts of law in connection with his complaint'. After hearing a case, the Commission was to report its decision to the Corporation which was to undertake 'to publish each adjudication in one of its journals' (usually *The Listener*), or the Commission could 'require' the Corporation to broadcast the findings. But the BBC was not compelled to abide by the Commission's decisions or recommendations.

In the same year the IBA set up a Complaints Review Board with five members chosen from the Authority's Advisory Council and top management.[72] This Board had somewhat wider terms of reference than did the BBC's Complaints Commission, since it was to review all programme complaints received by the Authority and could, if it wished, select items for investigation on its own. As with the BBC, however, before the Commission would consider a complaint, the complainant had to agree not to take the matter to law. In the words of the ITCA, the IBA Complaints Review Board received complaints ranging from displeasure at the time change of a favourite programme to 'the allegation that television is introducing witches into the living room'.[73]

An example of the BBC Complaints Commission's action was the case of Mr D. Smithers, a former deputy director of Christian Aid, who claimed that three Radio 4 programmes broadcast in 1976 misrepresented his views, and furthermore that he had been denied an opportunity to participate in the programmes.[74] The BBC in reply claimed that its decisions about these programmes represented a proper exercise of its editorial responsibilities. The decision, which occupied a page and a half in *The Listener*, reviewed the arguments offered by both sides, concluded that the BBC's procedures were 'a proper exercise of their editorial judgement', and rejected all of Smithers' complaints.

Another case concerned an organization called Leisure Arts, Ltd., which claimed that a BBC programme broadcast on 22 February 1976 misrepresented the advertisements for a model sailing ship and a Black Forest clock it offered for sale.[75] During the broadcast in question, the Corporation cited an expert as saying there were sixty-four things wrong with the model. It also said that Leisure Arts had 'refused to talk' to the BBC about the charges. This time, the commission faulted the BBC for stating that Leisure Arts had refused to take part in the programme, but did not uphold the rest of the complaint. The annual reports of the two broadcasting agencies summarize the current work of their respective complaint commissions, most of the cases being substantially similar to those cited above.

Despite the existence of the BBC's Programme Complaints Commission and the IBA's Complaints Review Board, the Annan Committee said that neither arrangement commanded public confidence even though both were 'scrupulous, judicious and impartial'.[76] The BBC's procedures, it wrote, were described by some critics as 'cavalier . . . aggressive and arrogant'. Criticisms also had been received becasue both the Commission and the Board were set up by the broadcasting authorities themselves, that people bringing protests had to waive their rights to subsequent legal action, that the BBC was free to accept, reject, or act upon its Board's recommendations, and that the IBA board refused to consider complaints about advertising. Thereafter, the committee recommended that 'one body on the lines of the BBC's Programme Complaints Commission should be established to deal with complaints against all Broadcasting Authorities of misrepresentation or unjust or unfair treatment in broadcast programmes', the expenses to be shared by both broadcasting groups.

The BBC agreed with the recommendation for a single Complaints Commission, 'having proposed something similar to the IBA on more than one occasion'; the programme companies noted that perhaps 'an independent body . . . may be more acceptable to the public'; and the IBA had a similar reaction, though expressing certain reservations about the proposal for a 'legal waiver'. The government White Paper accepted the Annan proposal for an independent Broadcasting Complaint Commission.

The new law set up a Broadcasting Complaints Commission made up of three or more members, appointed by the Home Secretary, who are not to be connected in any way with either the BBC or the IBA.[77] It is empowered only 'to consider complaints of unjust or unfair treatment . . . [or] infringement of privacy' in either agencies' programmes. If the Commission feels that a complaint merits investigation, it may, at its option, hold hearings or otherwise consider the matter. The Commission may require the broadcasting agency charged, if found liable, to publish its findings, but it has no other powers of punishment. Unlike the BBC and IBA procedures which this provision replaced, complainants do not have to waive their rights to subsequent legal action.

21 External Broadcasting

The British Broadcasting Corporation's coat of arms is inscribed: 'Nation shall Speak Peace unto Nation'. This motto suggests a familiar Biblical quotation. Isaiah 2:4 reads: 'And he shall rebuke many people: and they shall beat their swords into plough shares, and their spears into pruning hooks: nation shall not lift up sword against nation, neither shall they learn war any more.' That phrase was adopted as its motto several years before the Corporation began regular broadcasts for overseas audiences, a decade before World War II brought international broadcasting to a high peak of development, and 20 years before the Cold War gave what promises to be permanent status to radio as an international political instrument.

In Britain, as in other countries, many people have been disappointed because international broadcasting has not been limited to messages of peace. But given the world of the twentieth century, the BBC has used the international airwaves very well: its Empire Service was the world's first regularly scheduled short-wave service; its wartime broadcasts were the most highly acclaimed of all World War II international broadcasts; and its extensive post-war External Broadcasting activities in every way have maintained its earlier reputation.

External Broadcasting is broadcasting for audiences outside the United Kingdom.* The External Broadcasting Division presents over 700 hours a week of programmes in some 40 languages for listeners all over the world. It operates a transcription service which distributes recordings to stations in many countries. It maintains a monitoring service to report on foreign broadcasts. It provides liaison in the United Kingdom between the Corporation and the external services of foreign broadcasting organizations.

All this is done, of course, to serve the United Kingdom: the programmes are 'propaganda' in the root sense of the term. As used here, the word 'propaganda' need not have a bad connotation. According to Funk and Wagnall's *New Standard Dictionary*, propaganda is 'any institution or systematic scheme for propagating a doctrine or system'. Webster's *New International Dictionary* defines it as 'a group or movement organized for spreading a particular doctrine or system of principles'. L. John Martin, in his *International Propaganda*, reviewed twenty-six different definitions, and found they all agreed that 'propaganda is the art of influencing, manipulating, controlling, promoting, changing, inducing, or secur-

---

* The term 'External Broadcasting' was applied to this aspect of the BBC's work beginning in 1948. From 1932 up to World War II, the term 'Empire Service' was used; during World War II there were 'Overseas Services' and 'European Services'; and since 1948 all such activities have been referred to as 'External Broadcasting'.

ing the acceptance of opinions, attitudes, actions or behavior'.[1] He then offered his own definition: 'propaganda is a systematic attempt through mass communications to influence the thinking and thereby the behavior of people in the interest of some in-group'. The BBC always has observed high standards of truth and honesty in its broadcasts, and thereby has established a great reputation. Many of its overseas listeners believe: 'It's true—if the BBC says so.'

THE EMPIRE SERVICE

The initiative for broadcasting to listeners outside the United Kingdom came from the BBC.[2] John Reith stressed its importance in the middle 1920s, but technical limitations and financial shortages delayed the development of Empire Broadcasting. Following discussions at Colonial and Imperial Conferences in 1929 and 1930, the government slowly began to understand the potentialities of short-wave broadcasting, but because of the world financial crisis in 1931 it had no money for the proposed service, so the BBC decided to support the operation from licence-fee revenue. On its own initiative, therefore, the Corporation began an Empire Service in 1932, the world's first regularly scheduled short-wave programme service.[3]

The Corporation justified the expenditure by looking at

the question of national interests ... broadly. Everywhere short-wave stations were springing up, which put the view-points of their respective countries before short-wave listeners ... all over the world, and it seemed contrary to the interests of the [domestic] listener, as a citizen, that Britain alone should be without a world-wide voice, seeing that it is both the focal point of a world-wide Empire and dependent upon world-wide exports and capital investments. [Furthermore, short-wave exchanges might provide] interesting programme matter ... from the Empire, the United States, or South America.[4]

The Empire Service opened officially on 19 December 1932, with programmes for Australasia. Initially it had very modest proportions, broadcasting five 2-hour periods daily. Fewer than ten full-time staff members were directly involved, and some twenty or thirty more were concerned indirectly, on the technical side. The programme budget was only £10 a week, and up to 1938 English was the only language. Until world events in 1938 and 1939 forced it to become a political instrument, the BBC's short-wave service was intended mainly to develop and maintain political, cultural, and economic links within the Empire.

But the BBC soon found that it also was reaching English-speaking audiences outside the Empire, British communities in foreign countries, and listeners in the United States, so it added a new programme objective. In 1935 it stated that the

Empire Service ... has the further mission of putting the British outlook [before the world]. France, Germany, Italy and the United States in the web of societies, [and] the Vatican and the League of Nations in the realm of ideas, all possess short-wave services, . . . and the British Commonwealth, both as community and as idea, cannot but take its turn on the platform.[5]

It is important to notice, in view of the relatively high degree of independence the External Services now possess, that the Empire Service enjoyed much autonomy from the very outset.[6] News bulletins were a regular feature, and after 1934 the Empire Service had its own news section. In contrast to the earlier reluctance of the British press to provide news for the domestic services, the Empire Press Union, Reuters, and the Newspaper Proprietors' Association agreed in December 1931 to supply copy for news bulletins in the forthcoming Empire Service.

Special talks were broadcast from London by dominion ministers and colonial high commissioners on dominion and colonial holidays, and the different sections of the Empire were encouraged to develop documentary reports on themselves for worldwide distribution. In 1932, some 5 years after Reith had first suggested it, the practice of an annual Christmas message to the Empire from the King was begun.[7] In order to conserve both talent and money, many programmes, then as now, were drawn from the BBC's domestic services. Shared programmes included entertainment shows, and sports and special events, with particular emphasis on sport classics of interest to the British Empire, such as inter-Empire cricket and football matches.

Hand in hand with the development of the Empire Service came the rebroadcasting of British programmes by foreign stations.[8] As far back as 1930, the American networks began relaying short-wave broadcasts of important addresses by King George V, the Prince of Wales, and leading government ministers. The next year a description of the Oxford/Cambridge boat race was carried in the United States, Germany, Austria, and Hungary; and a talk on his *Saint Joan* by George Bernard Shaw in the United States, Norway, Sweden, Denmark, and Finland. Symphony concerts were heard, as well as the Derby and the Wimbledon tennis championships. Millions of Americans rose before dawn on 29 November 1934 to hear relays of the marriage of the Duke of Kent and Princess Marina of Greece. In 1936 King Edward VIII's farewell talk was broadcast all over the globe, and on 12 May of the following year the world heard the coronation of George VI, just as it was to see—as well as to hear—his daughter's coronation 16 years later.

These broadcast links with the New World were deemed important enough for the BBC to set up a New York office in November 1935. In addition to expediting the distribution of BBC programmes in the United States, it arranged for many return broadcasts. Outstanding public occasions like the inauguration of President Roosevelt in 1933 had been relayed regularly by the BBC for several years, and special programmes were arranged for home listeners. Fifteen-minute weekly analyses of American events were begun by Raymond Gram Swing in 1934, to be continued by other journalists. In 1938, long before *Omnibus* or the Public Broadcasting Service made his face familiar in American homes, Alistair Cooke, American correspondent for the *Manchester Guardian*, began a series of short-wave reports on life in the United States—a series still on the air.

THE EXTERNAL SERVICES IN WORLD WAR II

Britain was driven inevitably by the force of events to engage in radio propaganda warfare beginning in 1938.[9] Germany was especially active. The German Republic carried on radio debates with the Eiffel Tower station during the Ruhr invasion of 1923, as well as with Poland in 1931. Although international agreements dating from the 1920s forbade international radio propaganda broadcasts, the Goebbels propaganda machine nevertheless stepped up its output. Medium-wave broadcasts were successfully used to influence public opinion in the Saar at the time of the 1935 plebiscite, and during the long campaign for Anschluss with Austria. To further its designs against Czechoslovakia, Germany again made extensive use of radio, with medium- and long-wave programmes to listeners in Czechoslovakia, France, and the United Kingdom, as well as short-wave broadcasts for overseas listeners. To all of this the Czech government replied with vigorous broadcasts of its own.

Nazi Germany also exploited the intercontinental possibilities of short-wave transmissions each day to all parts of the globe. German radio propaganda came to be more and more seconded by that of Italy, whose first radio campaign was in preparation for the Ethiopian War. By early 1937 Italy was broadcasting regularly in eight languages, her programmes being designed mainly for the Mediterranean and Middle Eastern areas. The United Kingdom, with which Italy had conflicting Mediterranean ambitions, was singled out as the target for many bitter and vituperative attacks.

The BBC was ahead of the British government in recognizing the need for foreign language broadcasts, just as it had assumed leadership with the Empire Service a half-dozen years earlier. In 1935, the Ullswater Committee, in addition to recommending that the Empire Service 'should be expressly authorised in the new Charter', and supported by an increased share of licence receipts, had said: 'In the interest of British prestige and influence in world affairs, we think that the appropriate use of languages other than English should be encouraged.'[10]

But the government remained hesitant to develop foreign language broadcasts, even though the Director-General, Sir John Reith, as he described it, 'tried periodically and urgently for three years to have this matter taken seriously'. But Reith was not so anxious to extend the range of the BBC's overseas output as to be willing to relinquish its control to the government: The Corporation, of course would remain 'in touch with the Foreign Office in matters which concerned them . . . but the BBC must be responsible'.[11] These arguments, plus the pressure of events, finally caused the Postmaster-General to announce in Parliament on 29 October 1937 that the BBC would begin broadcasting 'in foreign languages', and that when news was being broadcast, it would be 'straight' and not propaganda.[12] Several days later the Chancellor of the Exchequer said: 'I should like to make it clear that, in this new service, the Corporation will have the same full responsibilities and duties as are set forth in the Charter . . . in relation to their existing service.'

A service in Arabic directed to the Middle East went on the air on 3 January 1938 to answer the Italian Arabic broadcasts, although programmes in Spanish and

Portuguese for Latin America, begun on 5 March 1938, were announced at the same time 'to avoid giving unduly pointed offence to the Italian Dictator'.[13] From the very outset, the BBC insisted on strict adherence to the facts. When it was suggested that items in the Arabic service should be chosen for their impression on the audience, a BBC spokesman replied that 'the *omission* of unwelcome *facts* of News and consequent impression of truth runs counter to the Corporation's policy as laid down by appropriate authority'.[14] But a post-war director of External Broadcasting, who later became Director-General of the Corporation, looked back on these events as marking a new emphasis: 'We became for the first time an explicitly political service, and we have continued in that vein ever since, while still maintaining a certain tradition in the World Service of reflecting to overseas listeners the kind of broadcasting which we have here in Britain.'[15]

Beginning on 27 September 1938, the day of Chamberlain's domestic broadcast at the height of the Munich crisis, the BBC began to broadcast nightly news programmes for European reception in French, German, and Italian. Thereafter, the language services were rapidly expanded. On 4 June 1939 Spanish and Portuguese services for Europe were begun, and soon the BBC was broadcasting in most European languages.[16]

Once the war began, it was inevitable that the Allies should make the United Kingdom their European radio centre, just as it served their air forces as an unsinkable aircraft carrier, and their armies as the build-up point from which to launch the final invasion of Europe. Because of its nearness to the Continent, Great Britain was the natural studio and transmitter centre. Furthermore, it had a great concentration of political talent to plan and broadcast programmes, since most of the government-in-exile made their headquarters in London.

When broadcasting reached its peak at the time of D-day in mid-1944, the BBC was putting out some 125 programme hours each day for all parts of the globe, using short-, medium-, and long-wave transmitters for a daily aggregate of about 750 hours of operation. The number of short-wave transmitters rose from thirteen at the beginning of the war to forty by 1942.[17]

In developing programmes for this world audience the BBC, under the pressure of competition, showed an awareness of audience needs and a readiness to tailor broadcasts to listener's interests which the Home Services had not previously manifested. This was destined to continue as a feature of the External Services after the war, and was carried over into domestic programming too. Very important was the willingness to devise programmes that would appeal to local interests in both content and style. Foreign experts were employed to provide guidance, and personnel exchanges were made with the dominions and colonies. Authorities on the culture, history, and politics of all the target countries were pressed into service. Scheduling was done on a strict quarter-hour basis (something new to the BBC), in order to build audiences in countries like the United States where rebroadcasting by commercial stations was important, and to lessen the danger to listeners in enemy-controlled Europe, where it was essential that audiences hear the programmes intended for them without listening any longer than necessary.[18]

Programme objectives and content varied with intended audience. The North

American Service included much entertainment, both to build audiences and to project political concepts in a pleasant guise. London was toured by night and by day, even during air raids (*London after Dark, London Carries On*), broadcasts coming from canteens, anti-aircraft gun emplacements, and air-raid shelters. Children evacuated to America talked to their parents at home, while North America listened on one or another network. Many programmes were developed jointly by the BBC and American broadcasters: *Trans-Atlantic Quiz* with CBS; *Quiz* with the Blue Network; and *Trans-Atlantic Spotlight* with NBC. After 1942, soldier interview shows were exchanged to let the folks at home hear first-hand reports from their men abroad. There were farmer-to-farmer, housewife-to-housewife, and doctor-to-doctor programmes, as well as broadcasts in which people in similar communities, and sometimes in cities with the same names, talked to each other.[19]

The effectiveness of these programmes was tremendously enhanced through extensive rebroadcasting.[20] The Mutual Network carried BBC news broadcasts for several years, and during most of the war all four networks carried at least one BBC programme regularly. KELO in Sioux Falls, South Dakota, which between February 1944 and the end of the war relayed over 2000 shows, led all American stations in rebroadcasting BBC programmes. Many of Churchill's great speeches were taken by all the American networks. On D-day, 725 out of the 914 American stations then on the air rebroadcast BBC reports. British objectives were further advanced through broadcasts to America by sympathetic American correspondents stationed in the United Kingdom, of whom the late Edward R. Murrow was best known. Here the BBC was involved only in providing studios and some relay facilities, since these were American and not British programmes.

A wide range of news sources was necessary to maintain such a world schedule. To supplement the United Kingdom's news agencies, the BBC operated a radio monitoring service which covered all available programmes from Allied, neutral, and enemy sources.[21] Foreign-language broadcasting requires a detailed knowledge of internal conditions in the target countries, and it was realized that war would cut off normal news channels. Therefore, monitoring was begun during the tense days of 1938. More than a million words in thirty languages were monitored each day during 1944, of which 300,000 were transcribed and 100,000 printed in a daily digest. The BBC's own war reporters were another important news source. Their output was intended primarily for domestic programmes, but many of their dispatches were carried by the External Services too.

The British always made a great point of their accuracy and objectivity in reporting, even when the balance of battle was going against them. In theory, at least, only the needs of military security kept important news off the air.

One study indicated that, during the Battle of Britain, between 10 July and 31 October 1940, although the British overstated their case by 55 per cent, the Germans overstated theirs by 234 percent.[22] A comparison of broadcast reports of German and British air losses between 16 August and 6 September 1940 showed the British version to be more accurate than that of the Germans. Actual British losses of 343 planes were reported by the BBC as 292, and by Deutschland Sender as 1114. German losses of 527 planes were raised by the BBC to 855, but reduced by the Germans to 314.[23] Some 30 years later, Charles J. Curran, who had just been promoted from Director of External Broadcasting to Director-General, surveyed the situation in retrospect. The BBC was believed by its Continental listeners, he said, because: 'We reported defeats. We reported them accurately, and when the time came to report victories, we were believed, because people knew we had been honest about our failures.'[24]

The Corporation, of course, did broadcast programmes of comment and analysis, but unlike the Axis, separated news from opinion. *Flash Back* repeated the words of Hitler and Mussolini—often in their own voices from off-the-air recordings the BBC had foresightedly made since the early 1930s—matching them with subsequent inconsistent statements and developments. *Listening Post* made prompt exposures of the distortions of enemy propaganda. Introduced first on the North American Service in 1940, *Radio Newsreel*, a combination of actuality recordings and dramatizations, soon spread into other non-European services, and became a fixture on the post-war domestic Light Programme.

BRITISH–AMERICAN COOPERATION

These British developments were paralleled in the United States, where the approach of World War II spurred a great expansion of short-wave output. In 1938 the World Wide Broadcasting Foundation, NBC, and CBS greatly extended and improved their programming, and initiated European services. The decision of the FCC to allow the commercial sponsorship of short-wave programmes after May 1939 accelerated this trend, and by September of that year the United States was offering an improved radio reply to the Axis propaganda line, although its output was still inferior in both programmes and signal strength to that of the other major powers.

The United States government did not take over and operate the short-wave transmitters until 4 November 1942, although previously it had begun to work with the private licensees. The major government agency involved was the Office of War Information, established in June 1942. At its peak the OWI was broadcasting in twenty-five languages from New York, and in twenty-two from San Francisco. Between 1941 and 1945 the number of American short-wave transmitters grew from thirteen to thirty-six. In addition, the United States government installed twelve transmitters in the European area and two in the Pacific, and also became involved in the operation of captured facilities at Bari and Luxembourg.

The BBC supplied technical facilities for many United States broadcasts to Europe. Beginning in February 1942, it relayed—first by recording and then live—many American short-wave transmissions. By the end of 1943, 107 periods a week were devoted to *America Calling Europe*, and beginning in May 1944, these were increased to 200 periods a week in nineteen languages. This cooperation still continues, and some VOA programmes for Europe and Asia are relayed by BBC facilities in Woofferton in the West Midlands. On 30 April 1944, the American Broadcasting Station in Europe (ABSIE) went on the air over BBC transmitters from studios in a converted film building in London's Wardour Street.

Its programmes—equivalent to the BBC's European Service—continued until 4 July 1945. Beginning in December 1944, after the Germans evacuated Luxembourg, the powerful transmitter of Radio Luxembourg was operated by a SHAEF staff including American, British, and other Allied military and civilian personnel.[25]

The BBC also assisted in the development of the American Forces Network, a fifty-five-station network of very low-power transmitters located near the major American troop encampments, which opened on 4 July 1943 (see above pp. 15, 158). This carried a few BBC news and entertainment programmes, its own news reports, transcriptions of a great many American entertainment shows from which the commercials had been removed, disc-jockey programmes, and some local originations. Later AFN developed European outlets at Paris and in Germany. American Forces programming was entirely under United States military control, however. Beginning 7 June 1944, the day following the Normandy landings, the BBC provided the technical facilities for the Allied Expeditionary Forces Program which followed the Allied troops across Europe. This service received programme contributions from American, Canadian, and other sources, and its policies were jointly determined.[26]

WARTIME AUDIENCES

There was a good audience for wartime international broadcasts, particularly in enemy and enemy-occupied countries, where there was great demand for news of political and military events, and yet limited access to accurate information. The Germans forbade their own people, and all the foreign peoples under their domination, except the Danes, who had more freedom in this respect as in many others, from listening to any foreign broadcasts. In Poland the very possession of a radio was illegal. The Nazis even prohibited their own people from tuning in German programmes intended for reception abroad, lest the inconsistencies of their several programme services be discovered. They also jammed Allied broadcasts to make listening difficult if not impossible. But the people of Europe were living under very trying conditions, isolated physically and spiritually from the rest of the world. Public discussion of current affairs was impossible, communications were poor, and it was difficult to know what was happening even in one's own neighbourhood. Under such conditions, therefore, it is not surprising that many people risked their lives to get dependable and authentic news.

The major sources of information about the Continental reception of BBC programmes were the reports of the Allied interrogation and intelligence teams which went into Europe right after the war. All of these found that there was much listening to BBC programmes. There also were many informal observations to that effect by Allied military and civilian personnel, along with independent poll data.[27] In May 1946, a survey in the Netherlands showed much listening to London during the war. Seventy-eight per cent said they listened 'during the years of occupation to the transmissions from London of Radio Orange', 57 per cent to those of Radio Belgium, 50 per cent to the BBC European Service, and 23 per cent to the BBC Home Service. Then there were the letters. In May 1942, for example, one from a French village read: 'Out of 150 households there are 110 wireless sets. Out of the 110 owners of these sets, 105 at least listen to the BBC regularly.'[28]

The regularity with which the German and Italian press and radio attacked BBC broadcasters by name indicated concern about the effects of their programmes. There also were such humorous stories as the one about the German woman who arranged a memorial service for her soldier husband, after he had been officially reported dead. On the day preceding the service, she heard over the BBC that he was a prisoner of war, but decided it would not be safe to admit that she had been listening, and accordingly prepared to go through with the service. But upon arriving at the church she found no one there, not even the minister, he and her friends also having learned of her husband's capture, either from direct listening to the BBC or from relayed reports.

The 'V' campaign was one of the best examples of the BBC's successful impact. On 14 January 1941 Victor de Laveleye, the BBC's Belgian programme organizer, suggested in a French-language broadcast to Belgium that the initial 'V' from the French, Flemish and English words for 'Victory' be taken as a rallying symbol for the Allied cause, and be marked on walls and signboards all over Europe.[29] Soon afterwards Douglas Ritchie, as 'Colonel Britton', in one of his Friday evening English-language broadcasts to Europe, took up the campaign; and on 27 June of the same year the 'V' symbol was put into Morse code (. . . –) and its rhythmic similarity to the opening theme of the Beethoven *Fifth Symphony* noted. The idea caught on quickly, and before long the 'V' became the Allies' symbol, and was seen throughout the occupied countries.

There was, incidentally, considerable listening in the United Kingdom to broadcasts from the Continent, and some in the United States too. (The British and American governments, of course, never forbade such listening, nor did they ever jam Axis transmissions. But see below, p. 389, for a later example of British jamming.) One of the first assignments given the BBC Audience Research Department, which was set up in 1936, and began regular field work at the end of 1939, was to study the audience size and effects of the propaganda beamed to Britain from Hamburg, including those by Germany's best-known English-language propaganda broadcaster, William Joyce (Lord Haw-Haw.)[30]

In December 1939 about one person in four listened to news from Hamburg, the heaviest listeners, incidentally, being readers of *The Times* and the other quality newspapers, and the lightest the readers of the tabloids. Lord Haw-Haw was popular, said some of his listeners, because 'his version of the news was so fantastic that it is funny', because 'so many other people listen to him and talk about it', and because people were 'amused at his voice and manner'. Less important was a desire to hear the German point of view. However, there was little or no evidence that listening to Hamburg indicated distrust of British news sources or sympathy with Germany. But as soon as the 'phony' war (1939–April 1940) gave way to the Blitzkrieg of the low countries, the invasion of Scandinavia, and the Battle of Britain (July 1940), Hamburg's audience diminished to insignificance.

THE PERMANENT SERVICES

One fundamental fact underlies the development of international broadcasting: it is possible for radio waves to travel from transmitter to receiver over territory controlled by neither broadcaster nor listener. At present, radio is much better than television for this purpose, because land-based television transmitters have little more than line-of-sight coverage, whereas radio, especially short-wave radio, may reach out thousands of miles.[31] However, there are many examples of 'spillover audiences' in adjacent countries for television programmes, and friendly countries—and sometimes countries not so friendly—often rebroadcast each other's television programmes, as in the case of Britain's *English by Television*. Eventually there may be international telecasting by satellite directly to viewers. Although that is not yet a reality, when it does become technically feasible, there may be jamming of signals or the actual shooting down of satellites by countries trying to prevent the reception of unwanted television signals from abroad.

After World War II it was decided in Britain to continue international broadcasting on a permanent basis. Accordingly, the Overseas and European Services were combined as the External Services in 1948. The principle of support by Parliamentary grant-in-aid begun during the war was continued, so that the External Services have a closer financial tie with the government than do the domestic services. During the year ending 31 March 1979, £34,085,000 were spent on the External Services, of which about £31,000,000, or 91 per cent, were allocated to the External Broadcasting Services and £3,000,000, or 9 per cent, to monitoring.[32] In the autumn of 1979 the new Conservative Government announced some major cuts in external broadcasting funds as part of a general austerity budget, but these proposals were dropped following strong support for the BBC from the press and from MPs of both parties.*

* International broadcasting in the United States is the responsibility of two quite separate organizations: the International Communication Agency (ICA), whose activities include the Voice of America (VOA) and Radio in the American Sector of Berlin (RIAS); and, Radio Free Europe–Radio Liberty (RFI–RL), which continues the broadcasting formerly done separately by the two units whose names it bears.

The International Communication Agency, an agency of the Executive Branch of the United States government, with headquarters in Washington, DC, came into being 1 April 1978. Its director reports to the President and the Secretary of State. The new ICA is a consolidation of the former United States Information Agency and the former Bureau of Educational and Cultural Affairs of the Department of State. In December 1978 the VOA was broadcasting 804 hours of programmes per week in thirty-six languages (including English) to almost every country in the world (*BBC Handbook, 1979*, p. 57).

Radio Free Europe and Radio Liberty, founded in 1950 and 1951, respectively, were merged on 1 October 1976. Originally financed mainly by the CIA, they have been openly supported by the State Department since 1971, and by direct congressional appropriations after 1973. Legally, RFE–RL is a non-profit corporation, operated by the Board for International Broadcasting.

The Radio Free Europe Division broadcasts 554 hours per week to Bulgaria, Czechoslovakia, Hungary, Poland and Romania. (East Germany is the target for RIAS, controlled by the ICA, but the recipient of extensive funds from West Germany.) Radio Liberty broadcasts 455 hours per week, entirely to the Soviet Union. All RFE and RL programmes are in the languages of their target areas; neither service, therefore, broadcasts in English.

Like the Voice of America, Britain's post-war External Services have periodically been subject to government investigations—in fact, on eight occasions: 1952–4, 1958–9, 1961–2, 1964–5, 1967, 1968–9, 1974, and 1975–7.[33] Although these several inquiries provided uncomfortable moments for the External Services and their supporters, the operation has continued, though with reduced funds. One long-term outcome of these investigations has been the official determination of overseas broadcasting objectives. A Parliamentary committee appointed in 1952 to survey all British Government information services reported that post-war 'national propaganda overseas would still be required . . . (i) to support our foreign policy; (ii) to preserve and strengthen the Commonwealth and Empire; and, (iii) to increase our trade and protect our investments overseas'. Specifically, it appraised overseas broadcasting with reference to 'the extent to which it is likely to advance the political or commercial interests in this country either now or in the future'.[34]

A report published in 1978 stated that the Government believed that

the nation benefits from the unique reputation of the BBC's External Services as a well-informed and unbiased source of world news and comments, and from the attention which is therefore paid to the information they provide about Britain and British policies . . . . The BBC's External Services are a proven success and represent a national asset which we should be careful to preserve.[35]

The BBC on several occasions has restated these general principles in terms of its output. The 'projection of Britain' always is a function of the External Services. Sir Ian Jacob, formerly Controller of European Services and later Director General, wrote in 1948 that there always was to be a 'Clear and reasonable statement of the British point of view. No hedging on this statement, but at the same time, no abuse of opponents, and frank recognition of their point of view.'[36]

Sir Charles Curran, Director of External Broadcasting before becoming Director-General in 1966, spoke very precisely in 1968 about the political objectives of external broadcasting:[37]

We always insist, in the External Services, on our objectivity, our impartiality. And sometimes people may even think of us as being outside, or even above, politics. That would be a grave error. External Broadcasting is not something which can be divorced from the political course of the country. Broadcasting to overseas audiences is, primarily, about politics, and even when it isn't directly about politics, then it is about the background to politics, the life of the country, the way we think, the way we behave, the way we look at other peoples. And our external broadcasting must respond to changes in the political scene, here and overseas.

Sir Charles then reviewed the different phases of External Broadcasting. The Empire Service in 1932 was 'designed, primarily, to bring to expatriates the benefits which had been brought into British life by Lord Reith through the creation of the BBC.' Foreign-language services to counter Axis propaganda were introduced in 1938, when the BBC 'became for the first time an explicitly political service, and we have continued in that vein ever since . . .'. By the end of World War II, 'we had developed a massive weapon of information which was directed towards support of the war effort, and toward eventual victory'. The late 1940s brought the 'Cold War of the Air', following the introduction of a permanent BBC Russian service in 1946. Since then, the External Services have expanded and contracted, and changed in languages and emphasis, reacting among other things, to events in Eastern Europe. 'Our broadcasting has changed its content as the thaw within these countries has brought new subjects into prominence.'

The relation between the BBC and the British government in regard to policy control of the External Services is a typical British compromise, in which several apparent contradictions produce a smooth-running organization whose output is approved and accepted by all concerned. The 1964 Charter stated that the Corporation was to provide broadcasting services 'within the British Commonwealth of Nations and in other countries and places overseas'.[38] The Licence and Agreement of 1969, using essentially the same language as the several preceding Licences, said: 'The Corporation shall send programmes in the External Services to such countries, in such languages and at such times as, after consultation with the Corporation, may from time to time be prescribed. . . .' It is to 'obtain and accept' from the government such information 'as will enable the Corporation to plan and prepare its programmes in the External Services in the national interest'. There also is a requirement for the operation of a monitoring service.

Further to tighten the Government's theoretical control, there is the Licence provision, applying to the External as well as the domestic services, requiring the BBC, 'whenever so requested by any Minister of Her Majesty's Government . . . [to] send . . . any announcement, . . . which such Minister may request the Corporation to broadcast . . . .'[39] Finally there is the veto power, applicable to the External as well as the domestic services: 'The Postmaster-General may . . . require the Corporation to refrain at any specified time or at all times from sending any matter. . . .'

Yet another potential for control results from the method of financing the External Services. Before the war, costs were met from the BBC's licence revenue, and during the war both the domestic and foreign services were supported by direct parliamentary grants-in-aid. On the resumption in 1946 of the pre-war licence support system for the domestic services, the practice of maintaining the External Services by direct parliamentary appropriations was continued. In theory, at least, this provides a greater measure of government control than would a licence-fee system.

And yet a great point is made of the BBC's freedom in running the External Services, and the policy of the Labour Government, as expressed in a White Paper on Broadcasting Policy in 1946, has never been altered:

> The Government intend that the Corporation should remain independent in the preparation of programmes for overseas audiences, though it should obtain from the Government Departments concerned such information about conditions in

those countries and the policies of His Majesty's Government towards them as will permit it to plan its programmes in the national interest.[40]

In 1978 another Labour Government at once endorsed and justified this policy: 'Their [the External Services'] complete independence from the Government in matters of programme content means that they can be more effective and influential than the Government's own information service.'

In many ways the BBC—Government relationship in regard to the External Services is like that maintained for the domestic services, in spite of the theoretical differences between the two claimed by the Corporation. This sort of relationship seems to work very well in the United Kingdom, although it probably would break down in the United States. For example, a Parliamentary committee, commenting in 1978 on the Review of Overseas Representation conducted previously by a Central Policy Review Staff, quoted the director of the External Services as having 'catagorically denied' that, 'on certain past occasions, notably at the time of the Suez crisis, the BBC had come under Government pressure to modify its editorial output'. However,

he did instance two subsequent cases where strong representations were made by the Government of the day that to proceed with particular programmes or news items could be prejudicial to the national interest or to the safety of individuals. In both cases the BBC accommodated the Government's wishes, although no formal instruction was ever issued.

Commenting, the Committee noted

a considerable difference in principle between requests to withhold or defer items likely to harm British interests or individuals, and pressure aimed at suppressing programmes which are merely politically embarrassing to the Government of the day. . . . The BBC's independence was in no way vitiated, no formal instruction was issued in either case and the corporation could, had it wished, have ignored the Government's requests.[41]

What happens in practice is that, by a 'gentleman's agreement', the programmes of the External Services are planned and presented by the BBC, with due regard but not exclusive commitment to the framework of government foreign policy, without the public debates which at times have threatened to tear apart the Voice of America. In accordance with the Licence, the government determines the target countries, languages, and broadcast times. Thereafter, schedules are drawn up by the BBC for discussion with the departments concerned, and the Corporation keeps in close contact with them, so that serious differences usually are avoided. No occasion has ever arisen in which the government has formally vetoed any External Services programme, although it has at times strongly urged the BBC to modify particular broadcasts. Matters have always been settled by friendly arrangement rather than formal request.[42]

PEACETIME PROGRAMMES

The External Services are one of the five major divisions of the Corporation, and its head—Managing Director, External Services—is a member of the Director-General's Board of Management, together with the heads of television, radio, engineering, public affairs, personnel, and finance.[43] External broadcasting is divided into eleven sections, each with its own head. There are three programme groups: European Services, Overseas Services, and English Services. The others include administration, External Services News, Central Talks and Features, Central Current Affairs Talks, Monitoring Service, English by Radio and Television, and its own Audience Research division. Some of the Corporation's permanent overseas offices including those in Cairo, Singapore, Berlin, and Brussels, also are a part of External Broadcasting.

The External Services full-time staff totals some 1925 persons, of whom about 1135 are in administrative and programme work, 411 in monitoring, and the remainder in engineering. Its total output in 1978 averaged 711 hours per week, and programmes were transmitted in English and thirty-eight other languages. The total output of the External Services, therefore, is more than of the BBC's four radio networks and two television services combined.[44]

Most of the programmes originate in the fifty-two studios of Bush House, the London headquarters of External Services.[45] They are carried by seventy-nine high-powered transmitters (forty-seven in the United Kingdom, thirty-two overseas.) Most of these are short-wave transmitters, but some high-powered medium- and long-wave transmitters are used in broadcasting to the European Continent. Relay stations are located at various strategic positions to improve coverage: Berlin, East Mediterranean Station (Cyprus), Eastern Relay Station, Far Eastern Relay Station (Singapore), Atlantic Relay Station (Ascension Island), Caribbean Relay Station (Antigua—shared with Deutsche Welle, USA, Canada, and Lesotho (Africa).[46]

The Corporation divides its audiences according to geographical location and language. The European services are subdivided into the French-language Service (the Continent and Africa); the German-language Service (Continent); the East European Service (Russian, Bulgarian, Romanian, Serbo-Croat and Slovene); the Central European Service (Polish, Hungarian, Czech, Slovak, and Finnish); and the South European Service (Italian, Spanish, Portuguese, Greek, and Turkish.)

The World Service is a 24-hour a day English-language service described by the Corporation as:

unique amongst the world's external broadcasting services in providing not only news and every kind of talks programme, but also sport, drama, light entertainment and music in continuous transmission addressed to all parts of the world and to all who can understand English.[47]

The Overseas Services include the African Service (Hausa, Somali, and Swahili for Africa, plus some English-language broadcasts); the Arabic Service (the Middle East, the Gulf and North Africa); the Eastern Service (Persian, Urdu,

Hindi, Bengali, Burmese, Tamil, and Nepali); the Far Eastern Service (Chinese, Japanese, Indonesian, Malay, Thai, and Vietnamese); the Latin American Service (Spanish and Portuguese); and the Overseas Regional Service (English-language programmes for North America, the West Indies, Australia, New Zealand and the Pacific Isles.)[48]

News is the indispensable basis for all External Service operations. A million words a day reach the Bush House newsroom, to be made into 250 programmes broadcast each 24 hours in English and thirty-eight other languages. There are a number of 9-minute bulletins, and also a twice daily 30-minute sequence. These programmes, say the Corporation, 'are prepared all day by a newsroom, which, with an editorial staff of well over 100, is the biggest in the BBC and one of the largest in the world'.[49]

A former External Service head wrote that the External Service should always 'state the truth with as much exactitude and sincerity as it is given to human beings to achieve'.[50] But that does not keep the service from being politically oriented. In 1980, the World Service in addition to over fifty newscasts a day, had four daily editions of the current affairs programme, *Twenty-Four Hours*; *Outlook*, a topical magazine; *Europa*, a review of European developments; *People and Politics*, about leading British and international commerce; *Commentary*, a backgrounding of world events; and surveys of both weekly and daily newspapers. Thirty-minute documentaries covered such subjects as Southeast Asia after Vietnam, the General Strike of 1926, solar power, and Spain in transition. For promotion and as an aid to listeners, the Corporation publishes *London Calling*, a monthly magazine about programmes and wavelengths; other programme guides, including a thrice-yearly *African Schedule*; an *Arts Review* guide to drama, music, and documentaries to be heard on the World Service; and *Huna London*, a monthly journal about the BBC's Arabic Service.

Most programmes are especially produced for the External Services, although some are recorded repeats of domestic broadcasts. There are four plays each week, varying in length from 15 to 90 minutes; religious talks, live and recorded serious music (but little jazz); Home News from Britain; descriptions of sporting events and sports news roundups; broadcasts of special events; readings of short stories and poetry; and entertainment features.[51]

An important extension of the External Services is their extensive rebroadcasting by countries all over the world, thus bringing the British output directly to listeners through their own domestic services.[52] In 1978 there were 146 daily relays of the BBC World News by fifty stations in thirty-eight countries. Listeners to America's 200 National Public Radio stations regularly hear excerpts from BBC foreign correspondents mainly recorded off the air for use on NPR network and local programmes. There also are live feeds for domestic use in Australia, Canada, and some other countries.

The BBC transcription service in 1976 sold more than 40,000 hours of radio materials to 150 broadcasting and other organizations, the programmes ranging from popular music to classical concerts, and from drama to thirteen 60-minute programmes on the history of music in Britain. Available through the transcription service are programmes taken from the domestic services as well as some produced especially for export. Over 500 hours of such programmes were produced in 1976, and some income was realized from their sale, although the service is not entirely self-supporting. Some 350 sets of BBC Topical Tapes are distributed weekly to stations in nearly sixty-five countries all over the world, for regular broadcast by over 300 stations, including some in the United States and Canada. The sale and distribution of BBC television programmes abroad is a function of BBC Enterprises, rather than of the External Services.

To meet a general demand for adult-level lessons in the English language, and to build audiences for its broadcasts, the BBC began to teach *English by Radio* as far back as 1939 in its Arabic service. This proved so successful that in July 1943 a separate *English by Radio* unit was set up, and programmes to Europe begun. What started as an experimental 5-minute series to help Europeans brush up their English has since grown into a major project. In 1979 radio stations in 120 countries broadcast *English by Radio*, while almost as many countries used *English by Television*.[53]

The basic programmes consist of dramatized sections dealing with the language problems of, for example, a foreign couple visiting its English opposite numbers, or a foreign businessman taking a sales trip to England. Interspersed among short dialogues are explanations of language and grammar, given in the language of the audience for beginning courses, and in English for the more advanced programmes. External Services now broadcasts about 230 15-minute transmissions each week, constituting almost 10 per cent of its total output. Textbooks in many languages have been sold, and courses on records and tapes are available to radio stations throughout the world. Although *English by Radio and Television* is not entirely self-supporting, a good share of the costs is covered by income from the sales of accompanying materials, sold in some fifty countries by a network of BBC *English by Radio and Television* agents.[54]

English by Radio and Television constantly expand its services. In 1978, a new set of radio broadcasts for Latin America was inaugurated, including some programmes for workers in the oilfields, appropriately entitled 'The Petroleum Programme'. For migrant workers in Australia, there are *English by Radio* programmes with explanations in Arabic and Turkish. Recently the Soviet Union and China have purchased some *English by Television* series, although students using these in Canton were warned that 'the content of this teaching material serves to propagate the rotten capitalist class viewpoint and to prettify the mode of life of the capitalist class'. *English by Radio and Television* now has entered on a multi-media co-production project involving television in West Germany, Austria, and Switzerland, the Council of Europe, and the adult education authorities in West Germany, which will take students

> from absolute beginner level to a level of basic general competence . . . and will be transmitted on all German TV stations, on Austrian television and on television in Switzerland; radio stations in all three countries will carry the radio programmes in parallel with the television transmissions, whilst the published materials will be available to the individual student at home and to learners in adult evening institutes.

It is remarkable and astonishing that many East European countries broadcast *English by Television*, since the programmes expound British concepts while teaching language. In the late 1960s, on Warsaw television, I saw a programme in the *Walter and Connie* series (now replaced by *Walter and Connie Reporting*) in which the dramatization dealt with a court trial for a minor traffic offence. The script demonstrated the fairness of British justice, which Polish viewers might well have noted gave more rights to the accused than did their own legal system.

JAMMING

British and other foreign programmes beamed at Eastern Europe have encountered periodic jamming ever since the late 1940s.* This should not be surprising, since countries believing in controlling and censoring news may regard unwanted foreign broadcasts as a serious breach of the information barrier. In addition to counteracting them as best they can through their own media, such countries regularly resort to jamming.[55] This is not a new practice. It was begun in 1934, when the Dollfus government in Austria jammed radio attacks from Nazi Germany. The next year Germany began jamming Austria, and from then until the fall of Hitler there hardly was a time when jamming did not occur somewhere in the world. Jamming stopped for about a year after the end of the war, but soon began again, when programmes from the BBC, the Voice of America, Radio Liberty, Radio Free Europe, West Germany, and Vatican Radio were jammed by Moscow and some other East European countries.

Despite the fact that the United Nations General Assembly in December 1950 formally condemned jamming as a 'denial of the right of all persons to be fully informed concerning news, opinions and ideas regardless of frontiers',[56] the British government itself, on 5 March 1956, departed from its wartime policy of never interfering with radio transmissions from abroad when it began 'experimentally' to jam Greek broadcasts to Cyprus on the grounds that they were 'inciting violence'. This decision backfired, however. During most of 1955–6, the Athens radio had relayed the BBC's daily news bulletins and press review in Greek, thus

---

* Jamming consists of broadcasting noise or another programme on or near the frequency of the station whose programmes it is desired to exclude. This can be done to long-, medium-, or short-wave transmissions. Powerful sky-wave signals can be radiated into the ionosphere and reflected back to earth at distant points. In this way it is possible to jam over large areas, even in foreign countries, as the USSR has done in Poland and some other countries from time to time. Alternatively, several low-power transmitters can be used to disrupt local reception by using ground-wave signals originated in the immediate vicinity. This procedure is often used in large cities. Through a combination of sky- and ground-wave propagation, a government may attempt to blot out reception in an entire country (information paraphrased and quoted from Voice of America statement, *'Background on Radio "Jamming"'*). There are discussions of the legal aspects of jamming in John Martin, *International Propaganda*, pp. 85–7, and of both its legal and technical aspects in Delbert D. Smith, *International Telecommunication Control*, pp. 5–17. For a good explanation in layman's language of the technical procedures of jamming, see the *World Radio TV Handbook 1980*, pp. 38–41.

giving the British an opportunity to present their point of view over the Greek air. But when the Athens broadcasts to Cyprus were jammed, the Greek Premier ordered the immediate cancellation of the relay. Beginning 28 July 1956 the British government also jammed Greek-language broadcasts from the Cairo radio to Cyprus on the ground that they 'included objectionable and subversive material'—which, of course, is exactly what the East European countries often have said about some of the foreign broadcasts beamed into their territories.[57]

Jamming reflects the international climate, so that when relations become tense, and there are good reasons for the East European countries to exclude various foreign broadcasts, they resume jamming, and vice-versa.[58] But jamming is never entirely effective, and some items usually get through. Nevertheless, jamming does seriously interfere with reception, and therefore must be reckoned with in sending radio signals to countries which believe in the censorship and control of news media. Since jamming is a off-and-on practice, what is written one day may not be true when it is published. However, in recent years, the Soviet Union has consistently jammed Radio Liberty, and at times the Voice of America, the BBC, West Germany's Deutsche Welle, Radio Israel, and Radio Vatican. The other Eastern countries (except for Romania and Hungary) now jam Radio Free Europe. I occasionally have heard these jamming signals (faintly) in the United States, and in London (loud and clear), although they are not designed to interfere with short-wave reception in those parts of the world.

THE MONITORING SERVICE

The Monitoring Service, which works cooperatively with the Deutsche Welle and a similar United States government organization, the Foreign Broadcast Information Service of the Central Intelligence Agency, monitors foreign broadcasts, and reports their contents to BBC news and to some British government departments. In addition, it sells its findings to commercial news agencies—which is why so many Moscow news stories have a London dateline.

The Monitoring Service began as a very small operation in 1935, when English-language news bulletins from various foreign stations were monitored during the Italo-Abyssinian War.[59] The monitoring of Italian news broadcasts in Arabic was begun in the late summer of 1937. By 1940 the Monitoring Service was producing a *Daily Digest of World Broadcasts*, ranging from 100,000 to 150,000 words per issue, plus an abridgement of about 4000 words. It is now located in Caversham Park near Reading, an area relatively free of electrical interference. Its multilingual staff transcribes some 120,000 words during an average day in the course of covering broadcasts from more than forty countries in thirty-four languages. Urgent items are transmitted by teletype directly to the BBC's newsrooms, and printed reports are circulated daily and weekly.*

* Monitoring was done by both sides during World War II, while today Soviet monitoring services provide material for their media comparable to those distributed by the United States and the United Kingdom. In November 1939 the BBC's Monitoring Service reported: 'Two hours and fifteen minutes after Mr. Churchill's speech it was caricatured on

Information received from Caversham is supplemented by the output of a small unit in Nairobi which listens to broadcasts from Africa and by material from the Deutsche Welle in West Germany. Worldwide there is an ongoing arrangement between the Foreign Broadcast Information Service of the United States and the BBC, under which the BBC covers the USSR and Eastern Europe, while the FBIS listens to China and the Far East. All told, these several monitoring centres analyse the output of 120 countries in fifty languages, although this is still only a small part of the total amount broadcast.

The BBC's monitoring service served as an intermediary between the USSR and the United States at the time of the Cuban blockade at the end of October 1962.[60] While the world was waiting for Soviet reactions to the American blockade, the Moscow radio home service broadcast a message from Nikita Khrushchev, Chairman of the Council of Ministers, to President John F. Kennedy, which, among other things, said that the Soviet government had issued an order 'for the weapons which you [Kennedy] describe as "offensive" to be dismantled, packed up and returned to the Soviet Union'. Heard at Caversham, it was translated and dispatched post-haste to President Kennedy in the White House, who replied without waiting for an official copy of Khruschev's message, saying: 'I am replying at once to your broadcast message of October 28, even though the official text has not yet reached me, because of the great importance I attach to moving forward promptly to the settlement of the Cuban crisis. . . .'

PEACETIME AUDIENCES

Is there an audience for foreign broadcasts in peacetime? Americans are in an unusual position in this respect, and must not assume that world listening follows their pattern. They have the world's best access to information, the greatest number of domestic radio and television stations, the biggest and most varied range of newspapers and magazines, and the most books. Therefore, they have little reason to listen to radio programmes from abroad. Furthermore, unless they live near the Mexican or Canadian borders, they cannot regularly receive foreign programmes on the medium-waveband to which they tune for domestic broadcasts.

But people in many countries are differently situated. Some live under dictatorships which seriously limit their sources of information, or in countries with uncensored—but inadequate—news services. Others, like the French and Germans, can readily tune in to the domestic radio and often television programmes of their immediate neighbours. The East European countries are subject to a barrage of short- and medium-wave programmes beamed towards them, often via relays close to their borders, from the United Kingdom, the United

---

the German wireless. We admire the comprehensiveness of their monitoring services.' (BBC Monitoring Service, *Weekly Analysis*, 21 November 1939, quoted in Briggs III, p. 190n) While working in London in 1944 and 1945, I listened regularly to English-language newscasts from Germany at 9.30 p.m., which frequently commented upon BBC Home Service News bulletins broadcast half an hour earlier.

States, West Germany, and other countries. Furthermore, many Soviet citizens have short-wave receivers, since the USSR uses the short-waveband for some domestic services, because of the country's great size. To such people, therefore, foreign broadcasts offer much more, and are more readily available, than to people in the United States.

It is difficult to measure the audiences for foreign broadcasts, particularly in totalitarian countries which interfere as much as possible with listening, periodically jam unwanted signals, and prohibit polling activities on their territories. The BBC External Services does its own audience surveys, and also draws data from studies made for the United States International Communication Agency, Radio Free Europe and Radio Liberty. In 1978 the External Services received 335,000 letters and cards from listeners in all parts of the world, and postal questionnaires were sent to listeners' panels in some of the western countries from which a good deal of mail was received.[61] Reports also are received from diplomatic posts abroad, from visitors and travellors, and from conversations with the representatives of foreign countries, including even diplomats and broadcasters from the communist world.

Although the percentage of listeners at any one time is low, their actual numbers may be quite high. Surveys in 1976 showed that the BBC reached, at least once a week, 500,000 adults in Italy, 600,000 in Spain, 500,000 in Japan, 200,000 in Mexico, and 121,000 (for broadcasts in English) in Israel.[62] Comparisons of audiences for the British External Services with those for the Voice of America, Radio Liberty, Radio Free Europe and West Germany show relatively high ratings for the British output.

Measurements of listening in the Soviet Union must be based upon a combination of personal observations by westerners in the USSR, and on the incomplete surveys of Soviet visitors conducted in Western Europe by Radio Liberty.[63] In 1974–5, 42 per cent of a Radio Liberty sample reported listening to the Voice of America, while 29 per cent listened to the BBC, 23 per cent to Radio Liberty, and 16 per cent to West Germany. A Radio Liberty survey reported that Radio Liberty's estimated weekly audience for the two-year period ending in June 1979 stands at over 7 million listeners, of which about 39% also hear VOA in the course of a week, 29% BBC, and about 16% Deutsche Welle.' An Israeli study made in 1973 found that of recently arrived Russian-speaking Jewish emigrants from the USSR, 73 per cent had listened to BBC Russian-language broadcasts at least once a week during the year, although it must be noted that a group of people looking forward to emigrating would have high motivation for such listening.

Solzhenitsyn is reported to have been a regular BBC listener, and he and other prominent Russian expatriates have frequently talked of hearing western programmes. British travellers in the Soviet Union and Soviet travellers in the West have testified that the chief commentator of the BBC Russian service is, as the BBC puts it, 'a well-known personality in the USSR'. In the Soviet Union and other East European countries, I encountered much evidence of listening to Western programmes among broadcasting officials, Intourist guides, teachers, and others to whom I talked. In Moscow I once had a conversation with several teenage boys, who approached me with the standard request for gum, candy, or the like.

When I replied that I didn't have anything to give them, they identified me as an American, because they said, from listening to the BBC and the Voice of America they had learned to distinguish between British and American English.

Listeners to Western radio generally have higher than average education, and they include many writers, journalists, professional people, professors, and students. In comparison with other external services, the BBC seems to attract a larger proportion of the upper intellectual classes, and probably does so deliberately on the theory that such people are most important in determining policies in their own countries.

The BBC quotes Radio Liberty research as indicating

> that a greater percentage of respondents with higher education . . . listened to Western radio for information than viewed Soviet television for news. . . . Western radio's most faithful audience is drawn from respondents in their 30's with higher education, with 91 percent listening overall and 83 percent listening for information. . . . As educational levels increase, Western radio as a source of information rates higher than the domestic television news.[64]

In a comparative analysis of external programming, the BBC remarked that listeners often regard Radio Free Europe and Radio Liberty programmes as 'the voice of internal opposition. This makes them at the same time more attractive to a substantial part of the population, and somewhat suspect as an impartial sources of news'. The Corporation remarked that the Voice of America 'appears to suffer from the inhibitions of its editorial policy resulting from the organization being the official mouthpiece of the US government. This is often reflected in a loss of topicality and relevance in output.' About West Germany, the report indicated: 'In spite of painful memories of the last war and the unpopularity of everything German among large sections of the population, it appears to have attracted audiences—in Russia and Czechoslovakia probably large ones—partly because of the good signal produced by its new transmitters.'

About its own output, the BBC remarked that 'there can be little doubt that among those who listen to the BBC, its standing and "credibility" factor are the highest among all foreign broadcasters', something credited to honest reporting during World War II and ever since. During my travels in Eastern Europe, when I have asked my broadcaster hosts to rank Western broadcasters on the basis of credibility, the BBC is always put at the top, followed by the VOA and West Germany, with RL and RFE least favoured, the latter two usually being described as 'subversive'.

For worldwide short-wave listeners, the BBC's External Services offer, day in and day out, a dependable and objective summary of the important news of the world, edited by experts who skilfully select those items which are, or may soon become, of basic importance; a good range of opinions on the interpretation of that news; and a considerable range of drama, music, and other entertainment features for those with adequately good reception to make such listening enjoyable. For serious-minded people, therefore, in search of a significant radio service, the

BBC's external Services have a great deal to offer. Although the External Services were 'outside . . . [the] remit' of the Annan Committee, its report nevertheless stated that those of its members 'who talked to British men and women who work and live abroad, or to foreigners to listen to them, learnt in what high regard they are held. The editorial independence of the BBC in its relations with Government is nearly always praised. . . . '[65]

22 Commentary

British broadcasting is done by and for Britons, and cannot be judged properly except in its own context. Nevertheless, because I believe that the United Kingdom is better served by the BBC and the IBA than is the United States by its combined commercial and public systems, I shall conclude this examination of British broadcasting by drawing some comparisons between it and broadcasting in the United States.[1]

Obviously, British broadcasting is not perfect, and American broadcasting has its achievements. The latter provides much enjoyable entertainment, good sports coverage, and some excellent news and public affairs. For the most part, major programmes of all types are well—and often superbly—produced. But American broadcasting is weak on programme balance, and heavy on sex and violence. During peak viewing and listening hours, as networks and stations compete for large audiences, it offers a choice of basically similar entertainment most of the time, with relatively little for people with specialized interests or sophisticated tastes. Finally, its commercial support base, although not necessarily faulty in itself, has an unfortunate influence on programme policy, at the same time that it plagues its audiences with commercials which at the best are too frequent and too long, and at the worst objectionable.

Great credit must be given to America's public broadcasters, who, despite organizational growing pains and limited budgets, struggle valiantly to redress the balance. It is a matter of historical record that they originally grew up to counterbalance the deficiencies of the commercial system, and they do indeed produce many fine programmes. Given more experience and much more money, they will play an increasingly important role. But they alone have not been, and never will be, able to compensate for the deficiencies of their commercial colleagues, who will have to solve their own problems, alone if possible, or if necessary, with outside help and pressure.

Why is British better than American broadcasting? Fundamentally because of the differences in motivation. British broadcasting is regarded as a service, whereas American commercial broadcasting thinks of itself as a business, with profit-making as the major criterion of programme policy; in fact, it calls itself an 'industry'. At the outset the BBC was set up because of broadcasting's 'great value . . . as [a] means of disseminating information, education and entertainment', and through the years it has been operated that way. The same words are used in the laws constituting the IBA. The Authority's programme companies often have been tempted to adopt the American 'industry' concept—and surely they have enjoyed very high profit returns. But if they depart too far from the objectives laid down in the enabling legislation, there are the Authority itself, the probes of government investigating committees, the press, and enlightened public opinion to put them back on the right track.

How is British broadcasting better? Perhaps the most important reason is its balanced programme schedule. By law the IBA not only must provide 'a public service for disseminating information, education and entertainment', with 'a high general standard in all respects', but its programmes must 'maintain a proper balance and wide range in their subject matter, having regard both to the programmes as a whole and also to the days of the week on which, and the times of the day at which, the programmes are broadcast'. It always has been understood that the BBC, even in the absence of specific instructions, is to observe similar standards.

While there are occasional lapses from this ideal, on the whole the BBC and the IBA provide a wide range of choice. Almost every evening there are light entertainment, drama, documentaries, news, and discussions. Rare indeed is the evening without 'balance' programmes. When the Fourth Channel, under IBA auspices, goes on the air, it undoubtedly will widen the range of choice, since the Authority has been saying for several years that with a second channel of its own, it could do more balance programming. As to radio, among them the BBC's four networks and the local stations operated by the BBC and the IBA provide an almost constant range of choice.

From its first years, the BBC has provided educational and cultural leadership for the nation, something American broadcasting has done very poorly. The Corporation told the Beveridge Committee in 1949 that its programme structure was 'founded upon two basic conceptions': a balanced programme service to meet the needs of all segments of the public, with reference to minority as well as to majority tastes; and the broadcasting 'at regular intervals of . . . the major musical and dramatic repertoire'. Furthermore, broadcasting should be used constructively in the general social interest, and the 'educational impulse' maintained. From its earliest years, the BBC was greatly influenced by its strong-willed first Director-General, John Reith, whose ideas about the social responsibilities of broadcasting still are cited.

The Corporation regularly commissions writers, dramatists, composers and other workers in the arts to create material for broadcasting. It is the nation's largest employer of orchestral musicians, it engages many other musical performers, and it employs many actors. Although the IBA's record is less good, it surely outstrips that of America's networks. When the IBA has its second channel, it will be able to compete with the BBC on equal terms in the fields of education and culture.

There also is much educational material, extending from the excellent school services of both the BBC and the IBA to formal and informal instructional programmes for adults. The many documentaries also might fall into this category. The Open University should be mentioned here, too, although it is not basically a broadcasting project, but rather a complete university system which uses radio and television as one of its teaching resources.

All this is done, it should be noted, without slighting popular programming designed to meet all tastes. There are comedy, light drama, contemporary music, and sports. Like audiences everywhere, those in the United Kingdom want most of all to be diverted, and the BBC and the IBA compete with each other in providing top entertainment fare. Many of America's large-audience programmes are seen in Britain regularly, in addition to which both broadcasting agencies produce much entertainment of their own. Because Britain is a nation of sports-lovers, its broadcasters carry a wide range of sporting events, including rugby football, soccer, boxing, wrestling, horse-racing and jumping, tennis, and all the rest.

Most of these are 'good' programmes in their own way. Whether symphony or rock, light comedy or serious drama, public event or poetry-reading, newscast or sports, religious service or quiz show, production is of a high level. Writing (when writing is involved) is good; personnel (acting, reading, performing) expert; production (lighting, camera-work, picture quality, sound) up to world standards. When America's Public Broadcasting Service or commercial stations carry British dramas, documentaries, or public events, critical reaction is almost always very favourable.

The bugaboos of sex and violence plague broadcasters in the United Kingdom as well as in the United States, although the British controls are, on average, more effective. The 'Watershed' rule requires that all programmes aired before 9 p.m. —the presumed bedtime for children—do not contain anything unsuitable for immature viewers. Elaborate codes result in the elimination of many scenes freely screened in America, although on the other hand, some sex, nudity, and profanity accepted in Britain must be edited out in the United States. Only in the context of the two country's stage and cultural histories can this situation be understood. The factual reporting and representation of things found in real life—sex, nudity, homosexuality, disease, depravity, and bad language—regularly screened in Britain are cut out on the other side of the Atlantic.

In view of the natural scepticism with which we appraise broadcasting in a country with theoretically close relationships between broadcasters and government, it should be understood that in fact Britain's broadcasters are well insulated from government control of substantive matter. The daily newscasts are as objective and balanced as those anywhere, and the accompanying analyses and discussions definitely both fair and thorough. In earlier days the parties limited service in the political sphere, but this is no longer the case. Air-time is regularly provided without cost to the major and minor political parties, allocations being proportionate to voter support at the previous election. Supplementing formal political programmes, whose timing and frequency are planned jointly by the broadcasters and the parties, are the news and current affairs programmes, on which practically every politician or other proponent of a significant issue or idea gets a hearing, often accompanied by a grilling. Elections are covered from the Parliamentary dissolution date through the final vote counting.

There are pressures in British as in all broadcasting, and through the years there have been debates as to just how independent the broadcasters should be of government, but the broadcasters have won all of them. At times they have 'bent' to minimize conflict, but always with ultimate victory for the main principle at issue. The continuing attitude of the government towards the BBC (now applied as well to the IBA) was indicated by the Postmaster-General back in 1926 in the

House of Commons when he said: 'While I am prepared to take the responsibility for broad issues of policy, on minor issues and measures of domestic policy and measures of day-to-day control, I want to leave things to the free judgement of the Corporation.' In effect, therefore, the BBC and the IBA are public corporations which are independent of government.

Controls over IBA advertising are almost exemplary. There is strict regulation of the length, frequency, and nature of all commercials. While there is no question that the financial support base of the Authority influences its programme policies in the direction of popular audience-building shows, there also is no doubt that the relationship between advertising and programming is much less close than in the United States. Perfection is not achieved, but compared to America's many interrupting and frequently distressing commercials, the British system seems like a haven of refuge.

Highly commendable is the British practice of periodically appointing high-level *ad hoc* committees to review the performance and make proposals for the future of broadcasting. Such committees were appointed in 1923, 1925, 1934, 1935, 1949, 1969, and 1974. (In addition, Parliamentary standing committees often conduct their own inquiries at other times.) The most recent inquiry was by 'The Committee on the Future of Broadcasting', commonly referred to by the name of its chairman, Lord Annan, which was convened in 1974 and reported in March 1977. It received extensive memoranda from both the BBC and the IBA, oral and written evidence from some 750 other groups, and letters from 6000 individuals. The committee's report of 500 pages, like its predecessors, contained much information about broadcasting, and concluded with an elaborate set of recommendations—although the Annan Committee, like its predecessors—had no legislative powers.

America's broadcasters always have opposed such reviews, charging that they would interfere with their freedom of performance. Surely such reactions are motivated mainly by fears that extensive discussions of their shortcomings may lead to programme policy changes which would lower profitability, rather than only from First Amendment concerns. It is difficult to see how independent groups like the two Carnegie Commissions set up to study public broadcasting could seriously jeopardize media freedom. Whether or not their criticisms and recommendations were acted on, the whole investigative process would attract national attention, and might lead to changes in procedures or laws, if found necessary.

This is not to say that British broadcasting is perfect. Like ours, it has its shortcomings and abuses. The privately owned programme contractors are rich and powerful companies, many with far-reaching commercial and political ties, and they are just as aggressive in attempting to weaken the legislation or soften the application of the rules as are their American counterparts. The important difference is not that Britain's commerical broadcasters are faultless while ours have mercenary objectives, but rather that the IBA has a strong mandate, plus the will and the power to control such excesses, while our FCC does not.

Unfortunately, most if not all of the basic programme decisions in the United States relate to audience size—and thus to income. Week after week, survey results are cited so that all many know which network is 'winning' the rating war. Thereafter, programmes are dropped, added, or changed in the hope of gaining a few percentage points, and therefore millions of dollars in revenue. The virtual absence of serious programmes on commercial stations during prime time is the most conspicuous consequence of this continuing contest. The public stations provide a real service with their commercial-free quality offerings, but they lack the funds to consistently produce first-class programmes, and their relatively small audiences exclude many people who most need exposure to serious material.

Government regulation of media content is anathema in the American tradition. People who have seen what happens when governments completely control the media, as in the communist countries of Eastern Europe, do not advocate that for the United States. But Britain's two broadcasting organizations—one supported by licence fees and the other by commercial income—are closely supervised by the two public corporations set up by Parliament for that purpose. Therefore, despite strong advertiser pressures on the IBA, its overall programme balance is much better than that maintained by America's commercial broadcasters, and advertising interruptions are much better controlled.

The competition that resulted from the creation of ITV in 1954 was a good thing for British broadcasting. Not only did it make a programme choice available, but it led to many improvements in the BBC. News, politics, and current affairs are among the areas that benefited, precisely because competition caused both agencies to put a high premium on creativity, and to press for release from some of the restrictions that had retarded the growth of the BBC through the years. But this competition is controlled: although the BBC and IBA are encouraged to outdo each other, if this leads to lowered programme standards, their respective governing boards step in to curb any excesses. In the last analysis, it is not how large the audience is, or how much money the programme contractors earn, but programme quality and service to the entire public that determine policies and operational standards.

What really is important, though, is that these regulations have not brought with them any limitation on editorial independence. If anything, British broadcasters are freer and more outspoken than ours. The rough treatment given politicians in broadcast interviews may follow from Parliamentary traditions. But whatever the reasons, the fact of closer regulation certainly does not curtail freedom of expression on the British air.

It is in the American tradition for the media to regulate themselves, rather than having someone do it for them. Furthermore, successful self-regulation would provide one more example—at a time when it is needed—that the American system of free enterprise and free speech can meet its social obligations. Periodical furors over banal entertainment formats, poor programme balance, undue sex and violence, along with the continuing criticism of commercial excesses, give the broadcasters excellent opportunities to demonstrate—if they wish to do so—that they can regulate themselves.

By listening and viewing critically, and by offering constructive suggestions, members of the public can influence the broadcasters, both directly and indirectly. The FCC also is involved: it should be more concerned about the public to be served than about the industry it is appointed to regulate. Let us hope that the broadcasters will prove capable of slef-regulation, either by themselves or after outside pressure. But if not, then there is the British example to show that shortcomings and excesses can be curbed, and programme balance achieved, without sacrificing the basic freedom of expression so important to the free world.

Notes

1 INTRODUCTION

1. Quoted in Charles Curran, *Broadcasting from West of Suez*, p. 8.

2 CONSTITUTION OF THE BBC: HISTORICAL DEVELOPMENT

1. *Broadcasting: Memorandum on Television Policy* (Cmd. 9005) #2 (hereafter cited as *1953 White Paper*). Sir Charles Curran, BBC Director-General from 1969 to 1977, covers the items treated in this and the following chapter in *A Seamless Robe*, pp. 27–86.
2. *Report of the Committee on Broadcasting 1960* (Cmd. 1753), ##437, 915 (hereafter cited as Pilkington I); *Report of the Committee on the Future of Broadcasting* (Cmd. 6753), Recommendation 16, p. 476 (hereafter cited as Annan); Independent Television Companies Association, *The Annan Report: An ITV View*. Comment on Recommendation 16, p. 12; *Broadcasting* (Cmd. 7294), #42 (hereafter cited as *1978 White Paper*).
3. Paulu, *Radio and Television Broadcasting in Eastern Europe*, pp. 29–31.
4. The best summary of this period in British broadcasting is given in the first chapter of R. H. Coase, *British Broadcasting: A Study in Monopoly* (hereafter cited as Coase). The legal basis for the British Broadcasting Company was its Licence: *Wireless Broadcasting Licence: Copies of (1) Licence by the Postmaster-General to the British Broadcasting Company, Ltd . . . ; (2) Agreement with respect to the broadcasting of news and general information* (Cmd. 1822) (hereafter cited as *1923 Licence*). There is an outline of the company's structure on pp. 8–9 of *The Broadcasting Committee: Report* (Cmd. 1951) (hereafter cited as *Sykes Report*); Asa Briggs, *The Birth of Broadcasting* (*The History of Broadcasting in the United Kingdom*, Vol. I, Chap. 2 (hereafter cited as Briggs I; references to the second, third and fourth volumes in the series are given as Briggs II, Briggs III and Briggs IV).
5. *1923 Licence*, pp. 14–20.
6. For additional details on the structure of the British Broadcasting Company see Paulu, *British Broadcasting: Radio and Television in the United Kingdom*, pp. 9–10 (hereafter cited as Paulu, *British Broadcasting*). The problems encountered by the Post Office in bringing together the six principal stockholders, and some related Parliamentary reactions, are reviewed in Andrew Boyle, *Only the Wind Will Listen*, pp. 123–37 (hereafter cited as Boyle).
7. *1923 Licence*, ##2, 4, 5, 6.
8. The events leading to the committee's appointment are summarized in *The Broadcasting Committee: Report*. (Cmd. 1951), ##14–20 (hereafter cited as *Sykes Report*). Detailed information about this period of broadcasting is given in Briggs I, 147–97.
9. These changes were written into another agreement, which took effect 1 October 1923: *Wireless Broadcasting Licence: Copy of Supplementary Agreement . . . to Cmd. 1822 of 1923* (Cmd. 1976) (hereafter cited as *Supplementary Agreement*).
10. *Sykes Report*, ##4, 6, 21, 25 (a,b).
11. *Report of the Broadcasting Committee 1925* (Cmd. 2599), p. 2, ##5, 16 (hereafter cited as *Crawford Report*); Briggs I, 327–60).

12. J. C. W. Reith, *Into the Wind*, p. 102; Briggs I, p. 334.
13. *Crawford Report*, ##5, 16.
14. *Wireless Broadcasting: Drafts of (1) Royal Charter . . . for the Incorporation of the British Broadcasting Corporation and (2) Licence and Agreement . . . between His Majesty's Postmaster-General and . . . the British Broadcasting Corporation* (Cmd. 2756) (hereafter cited as *1927 Charter and Licence*).
15. For detailed information on the discussions of the Ullswater Committee, see Briggs II, pp. 476–516. *Report of the Broadcasting Committee 1935* (Cmd. 5091) (hereafter cited as the *Ullswater Report*).
16. *Ullswater Report*, pp. 48–51.
17. Briggs II, p. 504.
18. The results of the committee's work were published in two volumes: *Report of the Broadcasting Committee 1949* (Cmd. 8116), and *Report of the Broadcasting Committee 1949: Appendix H: Memoranda Submitted to the Committee* (Cmd. 8117) (hereafter cited as Beveridge I and II, respectively.) These two documents (327 pp. and 583 pp. in length, respectively) contain a wealth of documentary material about all aspects of British broadcasting up to 1950. For an intensive analysis of the Beveridge Committee's deliberations, see Briggs IV, pp. 291–420. Cf. E. G. Wedell, *Broadcasting and Public Policy*, pp. 80–7 (hereafter cited as Wedell); John Whale, *The Politics of the Media*, pp. 20–5 (hereafter cited as Whale).
19. *Broadcasting: Memorandum on the Report of the Broadcasting Committee 1949* (Cmd. 8550) (hereafter cited as *1952 White Paper*).
20. *Broadcasting: Copy of a New Charter of Incorporation granted to the British Broadcasting Corporation* (Cmd. 8605), and *Broadcasting: Copy of the Licence and Agreement Dated the 12th Day of June 1952, between Her Majesty's Postmaster-General and the British Broadcasting Corporation* (Cmd. 8579) (hereafter cited as *1952 Charter and Licence*).
21. 'Minority Report', Beveridge I, pp. 201–10, quotation from p. 203: Briggs IV, pp. 305, 366, 390–2.
22. Pilkington I, pp. 1–4, #124. For a discussion of the background and report of the Pilkington Committee, see Wedell, pp. 87–98.
23. *1952 Charter and Licence; House of Commons Debates*, 145:1402–6 (13 July 1960).
24. Pilkington I, ##77–111, 124, 289, 448, 485, 842–7, 901–5.
25. Hugh Greene, *The Third Floor Front*, p. 62.
26. *Broadcasting: Memorandum on the Report of the Committee on Broadcasting, 1960* (Cmd. 1770), ##20, 39, 49, 74 (hereafter cited as *July 1962 White Paper*).
27. *Broadcasting. Further Memorandum on the Report of the Committee on Broadcasting, 1960* (Cmd. 1893), #20, hereafter cited as *December 1962 White Paper*.
28. *Second Report from the Select Committee on Nationalized Industries: Report, Together with Minutes of Proceedings of the Committee, Minutes of Evidence, Appendices and Index Session 1971–72. Independent Broadcasting Authority (formerly Independent Television Authority)* (465), p. lxxii, Recommendation 29 (hereafter cited as *Nationalised Industries Report*).
29. *Second Report from the Select Committee on Nationalised Industries Session 1971–72. . . . Observations by the Minister of Posts and Telecommunications and the Independent Broadcasting Authority* (Cmnd. 5244), ##4, 5.
30. Annan, #1.1. The Committee's recommendations are summarized in Chapter 30, pp. 471–90. For some interesting observations on the report, see Whale, pp. 151–7; *Broadcasting. Presented to Parliament by the Secretary of State for the Home Department by Command of Her Majesty July 1978* (Cmnd. 7294) (hereafter cited as *1978 White Paper*). ##2, 48–9; *BBC Handbook 1980*, p. 39.
31. This analysis draws in part from Briggs I, pp. 67–8, 93, 101, 188 and 359, and on a manuscript copy of a talk given in Mexico City in 1968 by Sir Charles Curran, former BBC Director-General.
32. Eckersley, *The Power Behind the Microphone*, p. 48.

33. Briggs I, pp. 93–4, 96–7.
34. Briggs I, p. 347.
35. Reith, *Into the Wind*, pp. 99–101; 'Memorandum from Lord Reith', Beveridge II, pp. 363–6.
36. *1923 Licence; Sykes Report*, p. 35; *Supplementary Agreement*, #8; Briggs I, p. 188.
37. Coase, pp. 56–60, *Crawford Report*, #4.
38. Briggs I, pp. 359–60.
39. Hansard, *Parliamentary Debates*, Commons, Fifth Series, 199:1573 (15 November 1926) (hereafter cited as *House of Commons Debates*); Coase, pp. 46–60, 127.
40. Lord Elton, in Hansard, *Parliamentary Debates*, Lords, Fifth Series, 141:1184 (26 June 1946) (hereafter cited as *House of Lords Debates*).
41. Books by former employees included Paul Bloomfield, *B.B.C.* (1941); Maurice Gorham, *Sound and Fury: Twenty-one Years in the B.B.C.* (1948); P. P. Eckersley, *The Power Behind the Microphone* (1941); and R. S. Lambert, *Ariel and All His Quality: An Impression of the BBC from Within* (1940). Outside observers included Ernest Benn, *The BBC Monopoly* (1941); A. C. Turner, *Free Speech and Broadcasting* (1943); and 'A Plan for Broadcasting', *Economist*, **147**, 564–5, 597–8, 630–1, and 660–2 (28 October, 4, 11, and 18 November 1944).
42. Maurice Gorham, *Broadcasting and Television since 1900*, p. 193, Briggs III, pp. 646–7.
43. Coase, pp. 154–77.
44. Anthony Smith, *British Broadcasting*, pp. 84–6.
45. *The Times*, 26 June 1946.
46. For a review of this subject, see Paulu, *British Broadcasting*, pp. 374–80.
47. For a more detailed review of this subject see *ibid*., pp. 16–28.
48. Reith, *Into the Wind*, p. 99; see also his *Broadcast over Britain*, pp. 67–72.
49. 'Memorandum from the Right Honorable the Lord Reith', Beveridge II, p. 364.
50. Simon, *The B.B.C. From Within*, p. 50 (hereafter cited as Simon).
51. Beveridge I, p. 203.
52. Beveridge II, pp. 197–8.
53. Both subjects are well treated in Coase, pp. 69–123. Radio exchanges are discussed in Beveridge I, ##387–402; broadcasts from other countries, *ibid*., ##378–86. The BBC's comments on commercial broadcasts from abroad appear in Beveridge II, p. 106, and on relay exchanges, *ibid*., pp. 107–8. Cf. 'Wired Wireless', *Economist*, **173**, 1094 (25 December 1954). See also Briggs II, 346–67.
54. Coase, p. 76; Beveridge I, #388. Were it not for the fact that many cities, as well as some London boroughs, refused consent for the relay companies to lay their wires, the number of subscribers would have been much larger.
55. *Broadcasting in Britain*, p. 8; Ministry of Posts and Telecommunications. Report of the *Television Advisory Committee 1972*, ##38–40.
56. *Yearbook 1933*, p. 72.
57. *Ullswater Report*, #134; Beveridge I, pp. 113–14; *Broadcasting: Memorandum on the Report of the Broadcasting Committee 1949* (Cmd. 8291), ##36–8 (hereafter cited as *1951 White Paper*); *Broadcasting: Memorandum on the Report of the Broadcasting Committee, 1949* (Cmd. 8550), #33 (hereafter cited as *1952 White Paper*); *Yearbook 1933*, p. 71; *Licence for Broadcast Relay Stations*, #13; Pilkington I, ##939–48, p. 296, Recommendations 111–17. For a more detailed review of the relationships of the BBC with the relay exchanges and the foreign commercial stations, see Paulu, *British Broadcasting*, pp. 26–31.
58. *Licence for Broadcast Relay Stations*, ##5, 13 (1,2). An earlier form of the Licence is given in Beveridge I, pp. 277–81. The exchanges have always been subject to government regulation, because under the Wireless Telegraphy Acts the Post Office may, and does, require licences from both operators and subscribers.
59. On Radio Luxembourg see Paulu, *Radio and Television on the European Continent*, pp. 14–15, 96–8.

60. Coase, pp. 102–3, 108–9.
61. *Ibid.*, p. 116.
62. The Ullswater Committee condemned foreign commercial broadcasting (*Ullswater Report*, #114), with the approval of the government of the day (*Broadcasting: Memorandum by the Postmaster-General on the Report of the Broadcasting Committee 1935* (Cmd. 5207), #12. Ten years later the Labour Government's White Paper on broadcasting stated: 'The Government . . . intend to take all steps within their power . . . to prevent the direction of commercial broadcasts to this country from abroad' (*Broadcasting Policy* (Cmd. 6852), #47 (hereafter cited as *1946 White Paper*). But the Beveridge Committee in 1951 concluded: 'The problem of broadcasts to Britain from abroad is today of minor importance' (Beveridge I, #386).
63. *Representation of the People Act*, 1949, #80; *Representation of the People Act 1969*, #9 (5).
64. For a good analysis of the BBC's contest with the radio pirates and related matters, see Don R. Browne, 'The BBC and the Pirates: A Phase in the Life of a Prolonged Monopoly', *Journalism Quarterly*, **48** (Spring 1971), 85–99. See also Delbert D. Smith, *International Telecommunication Control*, pp. 77–98. *BBC Memorandum. Summary of Development 1962–1974*, #40 (hereafter cited as *BBC, Summary of Development*).
65. International Telecommunication Union. *International Telecommunication Convention . . . Montreaux 1965*, Art. 48 #422, Art. 28 #962 (hereafter cited as *Radio Regulations*).
66. British Broadcasting Corporation, 'Why No Continuous Pop?' *BBC Record 45*, pp. 1–3.
67. *Broadcasting* (Cmd. 3169), ##26–42 (hereafter cited as *1966 White Paper*).
68. Marine, &c., Broadcasting Offences Act. *A Bill to Suppress Broadcasting from Ships, Aircraft and Certain Marine Structures*.
69. For a review of the various methods by which broadcasting is financed, see Hans Brack, 'Theoretical Considerations on the Financing of Radio and TV', *EBU Review* (March 1968), Vol. 198, pp. 39–43. See also J. H. Askell, 'Broadcasting Finance: The Licence Fee System', Sydeney Carne, 'Broadcasting Finance: The Licence Fee System', and Sydney Carne, 'Broadcasting Finance: Some Possibilities', in E. G. Wedell, ed. *Structures of Broadcasting: A Symposium*, pp. 7–28.
70. *1969 Licence*, #16; *BBC Handbook 1977*, p. 290.
71. *1969 Licence*, #12.
72. Briggs I, p. 189. In these cases, the 'sponsors' provided the programme, the Company making no charge for air-time (*Sykes Report*, ##40–1; *Report of the Television Committee* (Cmd. 4793), #65 (hereafter cited as the *Selsdon Report*).
73. *1969 Licence*, #1 (a).
74. *Sykes Report*, ##34–43. For more information about the financing of British broadcasting prior to 1950, see Paulu, *British Broadcasting*, pp. 24–6.
75. *Crawford Report*, #9; *1927 Licence*, ##3, 18.
76. Briggs I, p. 359.
77. *Ullswater Report*, ##109–111.
78. Beveridge I, #197.
79. Beveridge I, ##194–8.
80. *Ibid.*, ##376–7, pp. 201–10, 213–28.
81. *Selsdon Report*, #65.
82. *Ullswater Report*, ##110–11.
83. *Report of the Television Committee 1943*, ##64, 71, 79 (Recommendation 18) (hereafter cited as *Hankey Report*).
84. *Sykes Report*, #40.
85. Beveridge II, p. 566.
86. *Committee on the Future of Broadcasting 1974. BBC Memorandum: Financing the BBC's Home Services*, pp. 5, 7, 8, 9.

87. Annan, #10.8.

88. Michael Swann, *The Autonomy of the Broadcasters: Constitution and Convention*, pp. 7, 9.

89. Annan, #5.7.

90. The *Guardian*, 6 January 1979.

3   CONSTITUTION OF THE BBC: OPERATIONS

1. There are examinations of the BBC's status as a public corporation in Lincoln Gordon, *The Public Corporation in Great Britain*; Ernest Davies, *National Enterprise: The Development of the Public Corporation*; William A. Robson, ed., *Public Enterprise: Developments in Social Ownership and Control in Great Britain*; Marshall E. Dimock, *British Public Utilities and National Development*; Terence H. O'Brien, *British Experiments in Public Ownership and Control*; John Coatman, 'The Constitutional Position of the B.B.C.', *Public Administration*, **29**; (Summer 1951), 160–72; 'Legal Background of Broadcasting', and 'Independence of the BBC', Beveridge I, pp. 6–9; 'BBC Memorandum: Constitutional Position', Beveridge II, pp. 90–3. Gordon (p. 3) defines a public corporation as 'an attempt to apply to public administration . . . the type of organization evolved for large-scale private commercial administration by the joint stock company.'

2. Briggs I, pp. 327–8.

3. *Sykes Report*, #6.

4. Briggs I, p. 328. Sir William Mitchell-Thomson, who was Postmaster-General at the time, also played an influential role in the decision to set up the BBC by Royal Charter. Boyle, p. 212.

5. *Crawford Report*, ##4 (d), 5, 16; Coase, pp. 55–60; Reith, *Into the Wind*, pp. 101–3. The British Broadcasting Company also supported these proposals.

6. *Crawford Report*, #20 (a, b).

7. Briggs I, pp. 352–3.

8. Pilkington I, #436.

9. Greene, *The Third Floor Front*, p. 56.

10. *BBC Handbook 1978*, pp. 254–5. (Hereafter, the annual volumes in this series, known variously as BBC *Yearbooks*, *Annuals* and *Handbooks*, are referred to by the title current in the year cited; e.g. *BBC Yearbook 1933*).

11. *BBC Handbook 1979*, p. 264.

12. *1964 Charter*, Preamble.

13. *Communications Act of 1934*, Section 307 (a): 'The Commission, if public convenience, interest, or necessity will be served thereby, subject to the limitations of this Act, shall grant to any applicant therefore a station licence provided for by this Act.'

14. *1964 Charter*, #14.

15. The *1964 Charter* said there 'shall be nine Governors or such other number as may from time to time be directed. . . .' The number appointed was raised to 12 in 1968; *1964 Charter*, #5 (1).

16. *Independent Broadcasting Authority Act 1973*. Chap. 19, Sched. 1, #1 (2) (hereafter cited as *IBAA 73*).

17. *1964 Charter*, ##8–11.

18. *1964 Charter*, #18.

19. *1964 Charter*, ##19–21.

20. *1969 Licence*, ##3–5.

21. *1969 Licence*, ##16–17.

22. *1969 Licence*, #12.

23. *1969 Licence*, #6; *IBBA 1973*, #24.

24. *1969 Licence*, #13 (1).

25. *1969 Licence*, #13 (2).

26. *1969 Licence*, #13 (3 and 4).

27. *BBC Handbook 1979*, p. 262; *1978 White Paper*, ##100–1.
28. *1969 Licence*, ##19, 23, 28.
29. Reith, *Into the Wind*, p. 133.
30. Boyle, p. 215.
31. *Ullswater Report*, #51.
32. Beveridge I, #202; *1951 White Paper*, #8; *1952 White Paper*, #18; Pilkington I, ##388, 395.
33. Annan, ##2.6, 2.7, 2.8.
34. *Third Report from the Estimates Committee . . . Appendices and Index, Session 1968–69*. ##10–12, 28–30 (hereafter cited as *Estimates Committee Report*).
35. *House of Commons Debates*, 199:1579–83 (15 November 1926).
36. The same Postmaster-General, discussing the BBC's first annual report in 1928, reiterated the same points. Pilkington I, #388; *House of Commons Debates*, 249:2229 (19 March 1931); *House of Lords Debates*, 218:368–71 (21 July 1959).
37. For a review of the role of Company during the strike, see Briggs I, pp. 360–84; Boyle, pp. 189–205.
38. Briggs I, pp. 376–7.
39. Briggs I, pp. 364–6.
40. Reith, *Into the Wind*, p. 112.
41. *Ullswater Report*, p. 49.
42. Briggs I, pp. 371–4.
43. Michael Tracey, *The Production of Political Television*, pp. 155, 230.
44. *Listener*, 13 May 1976, p. 597.
45. Greene, *The Third Floor Front*, p. 97.
46. Reith, *Into the Wind*, p. 304.
47. Briggs III, p. 600.
48. Reith, *Into the Wind*, p. 438.
49. Briggs III, p. 601.
50. Beadle, p. 29.
51. *BBC Handbook 1973*, p. 21.
52. Grace Wyndham Goldie, *Facing the Nation*, pp. 182–6 (hereafter cited as Wyndham Goldie). For her account of how the BBC—in her opinion—unnecessarily cancelled a projected programme on the Central African Federation in 1953, see pp. 157–61.
53. Article in *The Sunday Times*, 24 March 1968, quoted in Wyndham Goldie, p. 183.
54. Grisewood, *One Thing at a Time*, pp. 198–9.
55. *BBC Handbook 1973*, p. 25.
56. *House of Commons Debates*, 233:246 (10 December 1929). Similar rulings from this period are given in Lincoln Gordon, *The Public Corporation in Great Britain*, pp. 177–82.
57. *The Times*, 13 October 1950, p. 2; 16 December 1954, p. 9.
58. *House of Commons Debates*, 536:139 (26 January 1955).
59. *House of Commons Debates*, 874:31 (20 May 1974).
60. Annan, ##5.34–5.38; quotation from #5.37. For another review of this question see Stuart Hood, 'The Politics of Television', in Dennis McQuail, ed., *Sociology of Mass Communications*, pp. 406–34.
61. Greene, *The Third Floor Front*, p. 69.
62. Stuart Hood, 'The Politics of Television', in Dennis McQuail, ed., *Sociology of Mass Communications*, pp. 406–34; Wyndham Goldie, pp. 72–8, *passim.*; Hill, *passim*.
63. Ian Jacob, 'Television in the Public Service', *Public Administration*, **36** (Winter 1958), 315, 316–17.
64. Hugh Greene, 'Two Threats to Broadcasting: Political and Commercial Control', Supplement to *Ariel*, May 1959.
65. Gerald Beadle, 'Television in Britain', *The BBC and its Home Services*, pp. 10–12.
66. Jacob, 'Television in the Public Service', *Public Administration*, **36** (Winter 1958), 313.

67. Wheldon, *Competition in Television*, pp. 4–5.
68. *BBC Memorandum: Choice in Television*, #1.
69. Wyndham Goldie, p. 111.
70. Beveridge II, p. 198.
71. Pilkington II, p. 235.
72. Pilkington I, #147.
73. Briggs IV, pp. 977–8.
74. Milton Shulman, *The Least Worst Television in the World*, p. 140 (hereafter cited as Shulman).
75. Annan, ##8.7, 13.45.
76. *BBC Memorandum: Choice in Television*, ##2, 3.
77. *1969 Licence*, #6. In the United States, FCC Rules and Regulations prohibit an FM or TV licensee from enjoying the exclusive use of 'a particular site which is particularly suitable for broadcasting in a particular area', and this has stimulated the cooperative citing of FM and TV antennas. *FCC Rules and Regulations*, ##73.239, 73.635.
78. *1962 White Paper*, #8.
79. *Television Act 1954*, #3 (1) (1).
80. BBC Memorandum, July 1961, 'Coordination of BBC and Commercial Television', Pilkington II, pp. 275–83.
81. *BBC Memorandum: Choice in Television*, pp. 6–7, 11.
82. Paulu, *British Broadcasting in Transition*, pp. 219–20.

4   THE DEVELOPMENT OF TELEVISION IN THE UNITED KINGDOM

1. Some of the events reviewed in this chapter are presented in greater detail in Paulu, *British Broadcasting*, pp. 235–55.
2. Briggs II, pp. 520–2.
3. These early television years are described in John Swift, *Adventure in Vision* (which covers both technical and programme developments), pp. 19–66; Richard W. Hubbell, *4000 Years of Television*, pp. 54–84; Maurice Gorham, *Broadcasting and Television since 1900*, pp. 115–21; J. L. Baird, 'Television in 1932', *BBC Yearbook 1933*, pp. 441–6. Information about the early development of television in most of the countries of the world is given in UNESCO, *Television: A World Survey;* references in this chapter to early American television derive from pp. 57–9.
4. For a description of the disc see Edward Pawley, *BBC Engineering 1922–1972*, pp. 139–40, hereafter cited as Pawley.
5. Briggs II, p. 527.
6. Briggs II, pp. 526, 528; Pawley, p. 139.
7. Tyrone Guthrie, 'Future of Broadcast Drama', *BBC Yearbook 1931*, pp. 189–90.
8. Briggs II, pp. 563–5.
9. Briggs II, pp. 566–71.
10. Briggs II, pp. 574, 580–1.
11. *Selsdon Report*, p. 4.
12. For a more detailed discussion of this subject, see Paulu, *Radio and Television Broadcasting in Eastern Europe*, pp. 510–515.
13. *Selsdon Report*, ##41, 42 (a), 55; Briggs II, pp. 587–8. A description and appraisal of the Baird and EMI systems is given in Pawley, pp. 143–8.
14. Briggs II, p. 586.
15. *Selsdon Report*, #39.
16. Briggs II, pp. 587, 598.
17. *Selsdon Report*, #65; Briggs II, pp. 600, 617n.
18. *Selsdon Report*, #68.
19. *Selsdon Report*, ##66, 68, 70; Reith, *Into the Wind*, pp. 214–15.
20. Basic data about British television between 1936 and 1939 will be found in John Swift,

Adventure in Vision, pp. 72–91, 97–106. See also Pawley, pp. 143–56; Briggs II, pp. 594–622; *BBC Annual 1936*, pp. 142–50; *BBC Annual 1937*, pp. 146–57; as well as the Television Sections of the *BBC Handbooks* for 1938–40. To supplement the material in Pawley, there is a good technical description of the Alexandra Palace facilities in the *Report of the Television Committee 1943*, pp. 22–5, (*Hankey Report*). There are also frequent articles in the *Radio Times*, both then and later.

21. Alexander Kendrick, *Prime Time: The Life of Edward R. Murrow*, p. 116; Sydney W. Head, *Broadcasting in America: A Survey of Television and Radio*, third edition, p. 161.
22. A description of the Baird and Marconi–EMI transmission systems will be found in Paulu, *British Broadcasting*, pp. 240–2. The transmitters for the two systems are described in Pawley, pp. 154–55. For a contemporary account of the development of British television in this period, along with a description of the Baird and Marconi–EMI systems, see *BBC Annual 1937*, pp. 147–63.
23. *The Times*, 5 February 1937, p. 14.
24. Beveridge II, pp. 41, 52.
25. For additional details on BBC television programmes in those years, see Paulu, *British Broadcasting*, pp. 243–6.
26. Briggs II, p. 611. Technical details are provided in Pawley, pp. 151–2.
27. *House of Commons Debates*, 331:32 (1 February 1938).
28. Pawley, p. 156.
29. Briggs II, p. 622.
30. *Hankey Report*, p. 4. The committee's eight members were drawn from the government and the BBC. Information about this period of British television may be found in the following publications: Beveridge I, pp. 79–97; Beveridge II, pp. 40–56; Maurice Gorham, *Broadcasting and Television since 1900*, pp. 234–48; BBC *Yearbooks* and *Annual Reports*, 1946–56; Briggs III, pp. 723–5.
31. *Hankey Report*, ##17, 24–6.
32. *Hankey Report*, #16 (b,c). Some years later, a long-time member of the BBC engineering department, who published in 1972 a definitive volume on BBC engineering, answered the question of why Britain did not move immediately to a 625-line system by writing that the

> 625-line system was not standarized until July 1950. [To have waited for it] would have meant denying television to British viewers for at least a further four years. The public mood immediately after the war demanded reassurances that peace had really returned, despite the rigors of rationing, and the resumption of BBC-TV helped to meet this need. The 405-line service yielded pictures that were entirely acceptable to the public and it was to continue without a rival in this country until the 625-line service was opened in 1964 ... (Pawley, pp. 314–15).

on this question of line standards, Briggs wrote that Director-General

> Haley was anxious to see post-war television restored on the pre-war 405-line system: if there were protracted discussion of alternative line systems, he felt, then the BBC might not be invited to resume operations. He got his way, and the 405-line system was restored. Haley had been backed by BBC engineers, who pointed to the disadvantages of other line systems, including encroachment on VHF (Briggs IV, p. 176).

33. *House of Commons Debates*, 414:26 (9 October 1945); *House of Lords Debates*, 141:853 (18 June 1946); *The Times*, 25 August 1948, p. 3. In April 1950 the aspect ratio—the relative height and width of the picture—was changed from 5 : 4 to 4 : 3, to conform to world standards.
34. *Hankey Report*, ##19, 28; Pawley, p. 312.
35. *BBC Handbook 1959*, p. 205. In later years, a number of low-powered stations were added to bring the 405-line service to almost the entire country (*BBC Handbook 1976*, pp. 247–52).

36. Statement of Postmaster-General, *Observer*, 4 July 1954, p. 7. BBC plans are outlined in *BBC Annual Report 1954–55*, pp. 5–9 and in *BBC Annual Report 1955–56*, pp. 8–10, 67–8.
37. *Hankey Report*, #12.
38. William Haley, 'An Extension of Broadcasting', *BBC Quarterly*, 4 (October 1949), 131.
39. *Hankey Report*, ##68, 70–71.
40. *BBC Annual Report 1955–56*, p. 77.
41. Pawley, pp. 358–61.
42. Pawley, p. 355.
43. Pawley, p. 355.
44. *BBC Yearbook 1947*, pp. 77–80; *BBC Yearbook 1948*, pp. 37–40, 94–9; *BBC Yearbook 1949*, pp. 28–30, 93–5; *BBC Handbook 1955*, pp. 26–8. Cf. Briggs IV, pp. 208–11, 221–30.
45. Gorham, *Sound and Fury*, pp. 169–70.
46. Beadle, pp. 40–2, 59.
47. Simon, p. 140. Cf. Briggs IV, pp. 310, 453–56.
48. Beadle, p. 59.

5   THE INDEPENDENT BROADCASTING AUTHORITY

1. *Hankey Report*; Frederick James Marquis, first Earl of Woolton, *Memoirs*, Chap. 22; Briggs III, p. 721; Briggs IV, pp. 34–42.
2. *1946 White Paper*, p. 5.
3. *The Times*, 26 June 1946, p. 4; *House of Commons Debates*, 425: 1063, 1175–84 (16 July 1946).
4. Beveridge I, ##175–8, pp. 201–10; Beveridge II, pp. 316–43, 362, 367–85, 542–52.
5. Beveridge I, pp. 201–10, 226, 213–28.
6. *House of Lords Debates*, 172: 1236–7, 1213–32 (25 July 1951); Simon, p. 41.
7. *Broadcasting: Draft of Royal Charter for the continuance of the British Broadcasting Corporation for which the Postmaster-General proposes to apply* (Cmd. 8416). (Hereafter cited as *1952 Charter*.)
8. For much more detailed surveys of the subject, see H. H. Wilson, *Pressure Group: The Campaign for Commercial Television in England*, and Briggs IV, pp. 423–57, 883–936. Briggs refers to Wilson's monograph as a book of 'controversial quality', partly for 'its revelations of "cloak and dagger" detail', and also because 'it was something of a *livre d'occasion* which appeared at a time when both the BBC and its competitor... were under further official review by the Pilkington Committee' (Briggs IV, p. 907).
9. British Institute of Public Opinion data were consulted in their files. Cf. Briggs IV, pp. 888, 924.
10. Beadle, p. 82.
11. *1952 White Paper*, ##5, 7, 8, 9.
12. *1953 White Paper*, ##6, 17.
13. *Manchester Guardian*, 26 November 1953, p. 1; 15 December 1953, p. 1; *The Times*, 15 December 1953, p. 6.
14. *House of Lords Debates*, 184: 747–50 (26 November 1953); *Keesing's Contemporary Archives*, p. 13412. Additional details about the debates will be found in Paulu, *British Broadcasting in Transition*, pp. 36–7.
15. *House of Lords Debates*, 176: 1297 (22 May 1952). This and other excerpts from the Parliamentary debates are available in Smith, *British Broadcasting*, pp. 103–6.
16. *The Times*, 16 December 1953, p.6.
17. *The Times*, 15 June 1953, p. 2. Attlee's statement was made during a talk to an

audience of miners in Bedlington, Northumberland, on 13 June 1953. Two years later, at the time of the 1955 General Election, the Labour Party put an anti-commercial television plank into its platform, promising to repeal the Act if voted back into power.

18. After the 1951 General Election, the party division in the House of Commons was as follows: Conservative 320; Labour 296; Liberal 6. Most of the voting margins in the House were proportionate to this distribution. The government motion approving the 1952 White Paper, on 11 June 1952, was carried 297 to 269 (*House of Commons Debates*, 502: 335–42, 11 June 1952). The division on the 1953 White Paper was 302 to 280 (*ibid.*, 522: 526, 16 December 1953). Voting on the second reading of the television bill was 296 to 269 (*ibid.*, 525: 1553, 25 March 1954).

19. *IBAA 73*, #2 (1).

20. Sir Robert Fraser, 'Independent Television in Britain', *Public Administration*, **36** (Summer 1958), 1116. For a review of the subject-matter indicated by its title see 'The Formation and Management of a Television Company', Paper No. 251, *London School of Economics and Political Science, Seminar on Problems in Industrial Administration 1959–60*.

21. *IBAA 73*, Sched. 1, #1 (1).

22. *The Times*, 21 November 1955, p. 3; 22 December 1955, p. 4.

23. *IBAA 73*, sched. 1, #1 (3).

24. *IBAA 73*, ##3 (a), (2a), 3 (4).

25. *IBAA 73*, #3 (2a).

26. *IBAA 73*, ##10–11.

27. *IBAA 73*, ##25–31. *Television Act 1963*, #7 (a,b).

28. *Television Act 1963*, #15; *IBAA 73*, #33.

29. *IBAA 73*, #31 (5).

30. *Broadcasting Licence ... to the IBA*. (Cmd. 5413), #8 (2).

31. *IBAA 73*, #22 (1–4).

32. *IBAA 73*, #21. The original law (*Television Act 1954*, #9) authorized the ITA to state, if it so wished, that a specific announcement was being broadcast at government request, but unlike the BBC (*1952 Licence*, #15 (4), p. 9) it could not declare when a veto was being applied. However, the Television Act of 1963 (Sched. 2, #13) gave the ITA that right, and this was continued in the 1964 and the 1973 acts (*Television Act 1964*, #18 (4); *IBAA 73*, #22 (4)).

33. *IBAA 73*, #2 (2).

34. *Television Act 1954* (3) (1b).

35. *IBAA 73*, #2 (2).

36. *Television Act 1954* #3 (1a); *IBAA 73*, #5.

37. *Television Act 1954*, #3 (2); *Television Act 1964* #3 (2); *IBAA 73*, #4 (2).

38. *IBAA 73*, #4 (b).

39. *IBAA 73*, #4 (3). In the words of the law, programmes are to exclude 'any technical device which, by using images of very brief duration or by any other means, exploits the possibility of conveying a message to, or otherwise influencing the minds of, members of an audience without their being aware, or fully aware, of what has been done'. The NAB Television Code also prohibits subliminal messages (p. 6): 'Any technique whereby an attempt is made to convey information to the viewer by transmitting messages below the threshold of normal awareness is not permitted.'

40. *IBAA 73*, #4 (5).

41. Although the expressions 'proper proportions', 'British origins', and 'British performance' are not defined in the Act, the IBA considers a film to be British 'only when all the constituent elements in it are British'. (*ITA Annual Report 1958–59*, p. 23.)

42. *House of Commons Debates*, 523:621, 639–40, (27 May 1954).

43. *ITA Annual Report 1956–57*, p. 14.

44. *IBAA 73*, #4 (7d).

45. *Television Act 1964*, #3 (1d); *IBAA 73*, #4 (1d).
46. *An Alternative Service of Radio Broadcasting* (Cmnd. 4636), #5; *Sound Broadcasting Act 1972; IBAA 73*, #3 (1); *IBAA 73*, #4 (1e).
47. *IBAA 73*, #4 (4).
48. *IBAA* 73, #23.
49. *IBAA 73*, #3 (1), #13 (1).
50. *Television Act 1963*, #3; *IBAA 73*, #6.
51. *IBAA 73*, #13 (5).
52. *IBAA 73*, #8 (6). For a summary of the law and rules on advertising, see IBA, *Television and Radio 1979*, pp. 164–9.
53. *IBAA 73*, #8 (2); Sched. 2 (1–3).
54. *ITA Annual Report 1956–57*, p. 11; *The Times*, 28 January 1956, p. 8.
55. *IBAA 73*, #8 (3–5).
56. Annan, #12.18.
57. *ITA Annual Report 1957–58*, p. 15.
58. Portions of the American Code usually are reprinted in the *Broadcasting Yearbook*; references here, however, are to the NAB's official edition.
59. *IBA Code*, p. 3, ##1–3. Most issues of the *IBA Annual Report* contain a section on advertising control. For example, *TV and Radio 1977*, pp. 160–5.
60. *IBA Code* #17. The *NAB Television Code* (pp. 6, 11) also prohibits subliminal advertising as well as the advertising of 'fortune telling, occultism, astrology, phrenology, palm reading, numerology, mind-reading, character-reading, or subjects of like nature'.
61. The corresponding provision of the *NAB Television Code* reads (pp. 11–12): 'An advertiser who markets more than one product should not be permitted to use advertising copy devoted to an acceptable product for purposes of publicizing the brand name or other identification of a product which is not acceptable.'
62. *ITA Annual Report and Accounts 1962–63*, p. 35.
63. *ITA Annual Report 1963–64*, p. 62.
64. *ITA Annual Report 1964–65*, pp. 50–1.
65. *IBA Code*, #21. The American *Television Code* (p. 14) reads: 'Advertising should offer a product or service on its positive merits and refrain from discrediting disparaging or unfairly attacking competitors, competing products, other industries, professions or institutions.'
66. *IBA Code*, #18.
67. *IBA Code*, #18 (b). The American *Television Code* (p. 12) reads: 'Broadcast advertisers are responsible for making available, at the request of the Code Authority, documentation adequate to support the validity and truthfulness of claims, demonstrations and testimonials contained in their commercial messages.'
68. *IBA Code*, ##24, 27, 30, 31–2. The American *TV Code* (p. 11) reads: 'Advertising ... which ... [implies] promises of employment of make[s] exaggerated claims for the opportunities awaiting those who enroll for courses is generally unacceptable.' There are several provisions relating to mail order and direct sale advertising.
69. *IBA Code*, #33. The American *Television Code* (p. 5) states: 'The use of liquor and smoking in program content shall be de-emphasized. When shown, they should be consistent with thought and character development.' It also stipulates (p. 22) that 'commercials involving beer and wine [should] avoid any representation of on-camera drinking'.
70. *IBA Code*, Appendix 1, #1. The American *Television Code* reads (p. 12): 'The broadcaster and the advertiser should exercise special caution with the content and presentation of television commercials placed in or near programs designed for children. Exploitation of children should be avoided. Commercials directed to children should in no way mislead as to the product's performance and usefulness.'
71. *IBA Code*, Appendix 1, #1 (b, c, d).
72. *IBA Code1*, Appendix 1, #2.

73. *IBA Code*, Appendix 1, ##3–4.
74. *IBA Code*, Appendix 1, ##5–7. The American *Television Code* (p. 10) reads: 'Children shall not be represented except under proper adult supervision, as being in contact with or demonstrating a product recognized as potentially dangerous to them.'
75. *IBA Code*, Appendix 3.
76. *IBA Code*, #18 (b).
77. *IBA Code*, Appendix 3, ##2–4; IBA, *Annual Report and Accounts 1978–79*, p. 47.
78. *IBAA 73*, Sched. 2, #5 (1).
79. *IBAA 73*, Sched. 2, ##1–2.
80. *Television Act 1963*, #5 (4–5); *Television Act 1964*, #8 (3–4): *IBAA 73*, #9 (3–4). The Authority told the Annan Committee that it sought and received in the Television Act 1964 power so that it might 'assume a more formal and direct control over the acceptance of advertisements'. (IBA, *Evidence to the Committee on the Future of Broadcasting under the chairmanship of Lord Annan*, #74, hereafter cited as *IBA to Annan*. This and related matters are further discussed in, IBA, *Television and Radio 1976*, p. 162. The American *NAB Television Code* suggests (pp. 16–17) that on network stations, advertising 'not exceed 9 minutes 30 seconds in any 60-minute period' during prime time and 8 minutes at all other times. On children's programmes (p. 17), network stations are requested to limit advertisements to 12 minutes per hour Monday–Friday and 9 minutes 30 seconds periods on Saturdays and Sundays. During prime time the number of programme interruptions 'shall not exceed two within any 30-minute program, and at other times, up to four within any 30-minute program period'. Clearly, the number and length of programme interruptions allowed by the *NAB Code* is considerably greater than with the IBA.
    The FCC's requirements are even more generous, since its *Rules and Regulations*, in effect, permit 16 minutes of television advertising per hour, with some exceptions 'in excess of 20 minutes . . . during 10 percent or more of the station's total weekly hours of operation'. (#0.281 (7iii).)
81. *IBAA 73*, Sched. 2, #4.
82. *ITA Annual Report 1958–59*, p. 13; *House of Commons Debates*, 597:1108–11 (17 December 1958); 598:180–3 (21 January 1959); 602:373–8 (18 March 1959); *ITA Annual Report 1959–60*, pp. 11–12. Originally, some programme companies broadcast 'advertising magazines' or 'advertising features', consisting of from 12 to 14 minutes of solid commercial material in story or narrative form. Since many of these were preceded and followed by spot announcements for other products, some ITV stations at times carried as much as 21 minutes of advertising without intervening programme material. There was much criticism of this, even though such programmes were intended by the government when the TV Act was first introduced; in fact, the assistant Postmaster-General announced in the House of Commons in 1954 that, in addition to the time devoted to spot advertising, there also would be 'documentaries or the shoppers' guides, which might last for half-an-hour or so'. (*House of Commons Debates*, 542:554; 555 (14 June 1955); 542:1286 (22 June 1955); *ITA Annual Report 1957–58*, pp. 14–15). But in response to many complaints, they were eliminated in 1962.
83. IBA, *Independent Local Radio: The Acceptance and Presentation of Radio Advertisements*, pp. 4–5 (hereafter cited as *Radio Code*. The *NAB Radio Code* (p. 16) suggests that radio advertising time not exceed 18 minutes per hour, although 'for a good cause' the code authority might approve an increase. The FCC's *Rules and Regulations* permit as much as 18 minutes of radio advertising per hour, with 22 minutes or more under certain conditions (#0.281 (7 ii)).
84. *Radio Code*, p. 5.
85. *Visual Treatments*, No. 3 in a Series of Notes of Guidance on Television Advertising, p. 4.
86. *Nationalized Industries Report*, p. 33.
87. *IBAA 73*, #12 (5); #13 (4).

88. *Television Act 1963*, #8; *IBAA 73*, #14.

89. *IBAA 73*, #18 (6a).

90. *IBAA 73*, #12(2); *An Alternative Service of Radio Broadcasting* (Cmnd. 4636), #16.

91. *IBAA 73*, #12 (1); *Television Act 1963*, #11 (1).

92. *IBA to Annan*, #176, Appendix 1, ##12–13.

93. *Television Act 1963*, #10 (2); *IBAA 73*, #13 (6).

94. *IBAA 73*, #12 (3b).

95. *Television Act 1963*, #4; *IBAA 73*, #15.

96. *Television Act 1963*, #7 (1,2); *IBAA 73*, ##26 (1,2), 28.

97. Pilkington I, #563.

98. *IBAA 73*, #13 (2).

99. ITA Memo, 'The press and the Programme Companies', *Nationalized Industries Report*, pp. 318–19; Annan, #13.32. A table showing Press shareholdings in programme companies as of 1972 is given in *Nationalized Industries Report*, pp. 20, 320–2, and as of 1975 Annan, pp. 511–22. In its reply to comments on the Annan Report, the ITCA stated that the Committee's report on the extent of the Thomson organization's holdings in Scottish Television was in error, the correct data being that in 1965 its holding of non-voting shares was reduced to 55 per cent, and that since 1968 it has held 25 per cent of the voting shares and 24.5 per cent of the non-voting shares. (ITCA, *The Annan Report: An ITV View*, p. 56, see also *ibid.*, pp. 50–1.)

100. For the ITA's point of view see *ITA Annual Report 1954–55*, p. 16; Robert Fraser, 'Independent Television in Britain', *Public Administration* **36** (Summer 1958), 117–18; *ITA Annual Report 1959–60*, 24–5. For the opinion of two ITV parliamentary critics, Christopher Mayhew and Donald Chapman, see *The Times*, 30 January 1959, p. 7.

101. Annan, #13.43.

102. *ITA Annual Report 1954–44*, p. 6.

103. The principal interests represented in the programme companies operating in October 1960 are listed in Pilkington II, pp. 407–8. For frank appraisals of some programme company administrators, see 'Television's Tycoons', *Observer*, 20 September 1959, p. 7; 'Television Going West', *Observer*, 18 October 1959, p. 3. For descriptions of the two original London companies, Associated Television and Associated Rediffusion, see Paulu, *British Broadcasting in Transition*, pp. 62–5. Of the first nine contractors, newspapers were involved in six; cinema interests wholly owned two and had minority holdings in two others; theatrical organizations had interests in three; electronic manufacturers were involved in two; and various other big business groups had interests in four.

104. *Television and Radio 1976*, p. 36; *ITA Annual Report and Accounts 1967–68*, pp. 9–10.

105. The organization and its operation are described in Independent Television Companies Association, *ITV Evidence to the Annan Committee*, #460 ff. (hereafter cited as *ITCA to Annan*). See also IBA, *Television and Radio 1979*, p. 131.

106. *ITA Annual Report and Accounts 1963–64*, pp. 5, 7.

107. B. C. L. Keelan, 'Independent TV in Britain after 1968', *EBU Review*, 120B (January 1969), pp. 23–7; Pragnell, 'British Independent TV After 15 Years', *EBU Review*, 120B (March 1970), pp. 16–21. The IBA yearbooks from 1968 to 1977 provide information about ITV regions and companies; for example, *Television and Radio 1977*, pp. 113–29.

108. *ITA Annual Report 1966–67*, p. 4. The text also is available in *ITV 1968: A Guide to Independent Television*, pp. 11–12. Some groups applied for more than one franchise, hoping to get one or another grant. For further information about the companies receiving contracts, see *ITA Annual Report 1967–68*, pp. 3–13, 78–9.

109. Shulman, pp. 56–7.

110. Hill, p. 55; *ITV 1968: A Guide to Independent Television*, pp. 11–12. For stimulating

comments on the standards by which the programme companies were selected see Hood, pp. 177–81, and Wedell, pp. 114–19.

111. The five major contractors included two London companies (Thames Television and London Weekend Television); ATV Network in the Midlands (Birmingham); Granada Television in Lancashire (Manchester); and Yorkshire Television (Leeds). The large regional companies were Anglia in the East of England (Norwich); HTV in Wales and the West of England (Cardiff and Bristol); Scottish Television (Glasgow); Southern Television in the South of England (Southampton); and Tyne Tees in Northeast England (Newcastle upon Tyne). Small regional companies include Border Television in Northwest England, Southwest Scotland and the Isle of Man (Carlisle); Grampian Television in Northeast Scotland (Aberdeen); Ulster Television in Northern Ireland (Belfast); Westward Television in Southwest England (Plymouth); and Channel Television in the Channel Islands (St Helier, Jersey, and St Peter Port, Guernsey). (The current programme companies, together with information about their locations, studios, chief staff members, and principal programmes, are listed in each edition of the IBA handbook. For example, IBA, *Television and Radio 1979*, pp. 116–30.)

112. IBA, *Future Contracts and the Public*; IBA Press Announcement, 24 January 1980.

113. This description follows *IBA to Annan*, ##160–83; IBA, *Annual Report and Accounts 1975–76*, p. 32.

114. IBA, *Notes on Independent Radio*, Note F, ##2, 3, 5.

115. *IBA to Annan*, #176.

116. *Special Report and First, Second and Third Reports from the Committee of Public Accounts*, hereafter cited as *Public Accounts Report 1959*, ##3165–70.

117. *Public Accounts Report 1959*, p. 1, #113–15.

118. Pilkington I, ##159–60, 164.

119. Pilkington I, ##237–73, 571, 573.

120. Pilkington I, #1060.

121. Pilkington I, #579; p. 290, Recommendation 43.

122. Quoted in Wedell, pp. 88–9.

123. *July 1962 White Paper*, ##63–4. For an explanation of some of the factors which underlay the government first White Paper, see an account by the then Postmaster-General, Reginald Bevins, *The Greasy Pole*, pp. 85–6.

124. *December 1962 White Paper*, #14.

125. *December 1962 White Paper*, ##24, 30, 35, 37.

126. Reginald Bevins, *The Greasy Pole*, pp. 90–3.

127. *ITCA to Annan*, #21.

128. Shulman, p. 66.

129. *Nationalised Industries Report*, p. xi, #16. Various aspects of this are also discussed later in the *Report* pp. xvi–xix. For further comment on the London Weekend Television case, see Annan, ##12.27, 13.27, 13.31. For reactions and comments from the Minister and the IBA, see *Second Report from the Select Committee on Nationalized Industries.... Independent Broadcasting Authority... Observations by the Minister of Posts and Telecommunications and the Independent Broadcasting Authority* (Cmnd. 5244).

130. *Nationalized Industries Report*, pp. xviii–xxix.

131. *Nationalized Industries Report*, p. xxxviii, ##79, 82. In reply to this suggestion, the IBA told the Annan Committee that the European services following this procedure drew most of their income from licence fees or other non-advertising sources, and hence faced different problems. *IBA to Annan* #87.

132. *Nationalized Industries Report*, p. xxxviii, #81.

133. *Nationalized Industries Report*, p. xxxiii, #69; pp. xxx–xxxi, #65, pp. xxxiii–xxxiv, #70–2.

134. *Nationalized Industries Report*, p. xiix, #106.

135. *Annan*, pp. 478, 480, ##45–49, 73.

136. Annan, pp. 229–241. Quotations from ##15.3, 15.18, 15.19, 15.20, 15.21, 15.23, 15.30, 15.32.
137. *1978 White Paper*, #2.
138. *Broadcast* (14 May 1979), pp. 3–4; *Broadcast* (24 September 1979), pp. 4–5, 31–3.

6 THE TECHNICAL FACILITIES OF BRITISH BROADCASTING

1. For more information about the ITU, see Paulu, *Radio and Television Broadcasting on the European Continent*, pp. 9–17.
2. These include, among others: Aeronautical Fixed; Broadcasting; Mobile; Aeronautical Mobile; Maritime Mobile; Land Mobile; Radiodetermination; Radionavigation; Aeronautical Radionavigation; Radiolocation; Radar; Safety; Space; Earth–Space; Meteorological Aids; Amateur Standard Frequency; Time Signals; and Special. (*Radio Regulations*, Art. 1 ##24–84.)
3. Pawley, p. 515; *Radio Regulations*, Art. 5.
4. For a layman's analysis of the broadcasting spectrum, see Paulu, *Radio and Television Broadcasting in Eastern Europe*, pp. 509–15. A review of some of the international conferences and assignments mentioned above will be found in Pawley, pp. 65–70, 208–15; 408–16. See also Head, *Broadcasting in Africa*, pp. 375–94.
5. George Arthur Codding, Jr, *Broadcasting Without Barriers*, pp. 92–108 (hereafter cited as Codding).
6. For example, from 19 August 1953 to 2 February 1964 the United States operated in Munich a 1000 kilowatt station, then the most powerful in Europe, on 173 kilocycles, a frequency assigned by the Copenhagen Plan exclusively to Moscow with maximum power of 500 kilowatts (*EBU Review*, 83A (February 1964), p. 24. In 1979, in West Germany, the American Forces Network of the United States Army operated twenty-nine AM stations on four different frequencies and nine FM stations on eight frequencies. The United States used three frequencies on the AM medium band and one short-wave frequency for RIAS, plus one medium-wave and several short-wave frequencies for the Voice of America. Radio Free Europe and Radio Liberty operated a number of transmitters in Biblis, Holzkirchen and Lamphertheim. Still other transmitters were maintained by the Armed Forces Radio and Television of the United Kingdom, France, and Canada. *World Radio TV Handbook 1979*, pp. 102, 104–7 (hereafter cited as *WRTH 1979*).
7. The population figure for the United Kingdom is taken from the 1971 British census and the American data from the US Bureau of the Census and the Pennsylvania census estimates. In 1974, the population of the whole United States, according to official Census Bureau estimates, was 212 million.
8. Pawley, pp. 325–45; *An Alternative Service of Radio Broadcasting: The Developing Technology; Report of the Committee on Broadcasting Coverage* (Cmnd. 5774), ##78–127; BBC, *BBC Sound Broadcasting* (Cmnd. 4636), pp. 11–12; James Redmond, *Broadcasting: The Developing Technology; Report of the Committee on Broadcasting Coverage* (Cmnd. 5774), ##78–127; BBC, *BBC Sound Broadcasting: Its Engineering Developments*; E. L. E. Pawley, 'B.B.C. Sound Broadcasting 1939–60: A Review of Progress', *Proceedings of the Institution of Electrical Engineers*, Paper No. 3650, Vol. 108, Part B: 39 (May 1961), pp. 279–302.
9. *BBC Handbook 1980*, pp. 104, 106, 108.
10. Pawley, pp. 432–5.
11. *BBC Handbook 1978*, pp. 85–6, 209–10; IBA News Release, 9 June 1977.
12. *IBA Annual Report and Accounts 1974–75*, p. 60.
13. For details of the reasoning which led to this conclusion, see Pilkington I, ##734–84; General Post Office; *Report of the Television Advisory Committee, 1960*, ##19–49; Ministry of Posts and Telecommunications, *Report of the Television Advisory*

Committee 1972; Pawley, pp. 518–23. The Television Advisory Committee stated in 1961 that the

> extension of television into Bands IV and V would offer the last opportunity for making a change in line standards; and if television policy requires the use of Bands IV and V we recommend the use of 625-line standards with an 8 Mc/s channel in these Bands and ultimately their introduction into Bands I and III. (*Report of the Television Advisory Committee 1960*, #47 (e).)

14. General Post Office, *Report of the Television Advisory Committee 1967*, #19, and Appendix, pp. 25–6.
15. *1966 White Paper*, ##21–4.
16. Details about the transmitter and coverage areas of both BBC and IBA transmitters are provided in their annual yearbooks. For example, *BBC Handbook 1979*, pp. 61, 201–24; IBA, *Television and Radio 1978*, 189–93.
17. An explanation of the BBC's method of making such conversions is given in BBC, *Summary of Development*, #113, and in *BBC Memorandum. Engineering*, ##40–43 (hereafter cited as BBC, *Engineering Memo.*)
18. The BBC and the IBA shared the planning and the common facility costs. Alternatively, the BBC serves as landlord for the IBA and vice-versa, each with its own engineers.
19. BBC, *Engineering Memo*, #3.
20. For additional information about Broadcasting House and other BBC studio installations, see Pawley, pp. 101–25, *passim*.
21. For information about the BBC's World War II studio arrangements, see Paulu, *British Broadcasting*, p. 133.
22. *BBC Handbook 1976*, p. 197; E. L. E. Pawley, 'B.B.C. Television 1939–60: A Review of Progress', *Proceedings of the Institution of Electrical Engineers*, Paper No. 3588, Vol. 108, Part B: 40 (July 1961), pp. 375–97; F. C. McLean, H. W. Baker and C. H. Colborn, 'The B.B.C. Television Centre and Its Technical Facilities', *Proceedings of the Institution of Electrical Engineers* Paper No. 3786E, Vol. 109, Part B: 45 (May 1962), pp. 197–222; M. T. Tudsbery, 'The White City Site', *BBC Yearbook 1951*, pp. 7–11; H. W. Baker, 'Planning a TV Studio', *BBC Annual Report 1954–55*, pp. 7, 59; *BBC Annual Report 1955–56*, pp. 63–7; *BBC Yearbook 1951*, pp. 55–8.
23. *BBC Handbook 1980*, pp. 64, 194–5.
24. *BBC Handbook 1976*; p. 198, *BBC Handbook 1978*, p. 262; *BBC Handbook 1980*, pp. 172–3.
25. *ITCA to Annan*, p. 153.
26. IBA, *Television and Radio 1976*, p. 128.
27. IBA, *Television and Radio 1976*, p. 124.
28. IBA News Release, 26 January 1978; *Broadcast*, 6 June 1977.
29. BBC, *Engineering Memo*, #46; *BBC Handbook 1976*, pp. 14–15, 69, 306–7; *IBA to Annan*, ##329–35; IBA, *Television and Radio 1976*, pp. 173–4. IBA, *Television and Radio 1978*, p. 173; *BBC Handbook 1978*, pp. 81–2, 212, 304; *BBC Handbook 1979*, pp. 194, 238.
30. In more technical language the BBC told the Annan Committee:

> The rapid development of large-scale integrated circuits had made it possible to devise an alphanumeric character generator which would create at the receiver the necessary video signals to display text on the television screen. Digital signals included with the transmission of the regular television programmes can be extricated, stored and caused to operate the character generator which will then display pages of information about news, weather, sports results, and so on. A later development by the Independent Broadcasting Authority produced a very similar system called ORACLE, and since it was clearly undesirable to have incompatible systems being broadcast within the same country, a committee was set up to produce

a unified specification embodying the best features of both systems. This was rapidly achieved and although the two systems retain their distinctive names the technical specifications are identical.' (BBC, *Engineering Memo*, #46.)

For a technical description of the IBA's ORACLE, See N. W. Green and J. Hedger, 'ORACLE—the United Kingdom Independent Television Experimental Teletext Service', *EBU Review—Technical* **160**, 275–85 (December 1976).

31. *Broadcasting in Britain*, pp. 8, 24; 'The Cable Television Associations' Submission to the Annan Committee', reprinted in *Cablevision News*, March 1975; *Report of the Television Advisory Committee 1972*, ##38–48; *IBA to Annan*, ##343–6; several publications of the Council of Europe: James D. Halloran, *The Development of Cable Television in the United Kingdom: Problems and Possibilities*; J. D. Halloran, *Communication and Community: The Evaluation of an Experiment*; Ministry of Posts and Telecommunications, *Television Advisory Committee 1972: Papers of the Technical Subcommittee*, pp. 12–14, 60–81; *BBC Memorandum. Broadcasting in the Eighties and Nineties*, ##53–55.
32. *1978 White Paper*, ##173–82.
33. *BBC Memorandum: Broadcasting in the Eighties and Nineties*, ##51–2.
34. D. B. Weigall, *Satellites—Present Use and Future Ideas in Broadcasting; Report of the Television Advisory Committee 1972*, ##30–7; *IBA to Annan*, ##340–2, *Report of the Television Advisory Committee 1972: Papers of the Technical Subcommittee*, pp. 9–12, 32–59.

7 FINANCES IN BRITISH BROADCASTING

1. *ITCA to Annan*, #557.
2. *1964 Charter*, ##3, 16–18.
3. 1964 Licence, #16 (1).
4. For a comprehensive review of the subject, see Eugène Pons, *General Considerations on Licence Fees for Radio and Television Sets*.
5. *Third Report from the Estimates Committee together with part of the Minutes of Evidence taken . . . on 27th January 1969. . . .* (H.C. 387) #37, (hereafter cited as *Estimates Committee Report*); *Wireless Telegraphy Act 1967*, Part 1; Barrie Thorne, *The BBC's Finances and Cost Control*, p. 16 (hereafter cited as Thorne); Charles C. Curran, 'Supporting a Public Service', p. 6.
6. *Newspaper Press Directory 1976*. In 1975, the most widely circulated United States weekly magazine was *TV Guide*, with 19,168,096 copies. The second largest was *Time* (4,325,270), and then the *National Enquirer* (4,155,762) (Audit Bureau of Circulation).
7. *BBC Annual Report 1954–55*, p. 77; *BBC Handbook 1979*, pp. 71, 77; *BBC Handbook 1980*, pp. 70, 71, 89.
8. *BBC Handbook 1979*, pp. 71–4, 77.
9. *1964 Charter*, #3(u). Through the years, the borrowing limits have been successively raised.
10. *Observer*, 1 January 1978.
11. *The Times*, 28 October 1977.
12. *BBC Handbook 1980*, p. 92.
13. For a discussion of these points, see Paulu, *British Broadcasting*, pp. 79–83.
14. Thorne, p. 10.
15. Beveridge I, ##46–51, 238–45, 425; Beveridge II, pp. 69–70; *1951 White Paper*, #27; *1952 Licence*, #18–19.
16. *Estimates Committee Report*, ##83–8.
17. *1964 Charter* ## 16(b) 3(u), 17, 18 (2, 4).
18. *Estimates Committee Report*, p. viii.
19. The Standing Conference on Broadcasting, *Evidence to the Committee on the Future of Broadcasting*, p. 67 (hereafter cited as *The SCOB Papers*.)

20. Beadle, pp. 59–60.
21. *Annan*, #107.
22. *IBAA 73*, #25.
23. Memo, submitted by the ITA, *Nationalised Industries Report*, pp. 30–1, #3, 8.
24. *Television Act 1954*, #11. It was understood that this money was to come indirectly from the portion of the BBC's licence revenue retained by the government, although the law did not say so. For additional information, Paulu, *British Broadcasting in Transition*, p. 50.
25. *Sound Broadcasting Act 1972, Chapter 31*, #11 (hereafter cited as *Sound Broadcasting Act '72*); *IBAA 73*, #30; IBA, *TV and Radio 1977*, p. 215.
26. *Television Act 1963*, #7; *IBAA 73*, ##26–7.
27. *IBAA 73*, ##26, 28.
28. *Public Accounts Report 1959*, pp. 348–9.
29. National Board for Prices and Incomes. *Report No. 156. Costs and Revenues of Independent Television Companies* (Cmnd. 4524), #97 (hereafter cited as *Costs and Revenues*); *ITCA to Annan #19*. For a yearly summary of IBA finances, see the annual issues of *Television and Radio* (for example, *Television and Radio 1978*, p. 215), or, for more detailed information, the *Annual Report and Accounts* (for example, IBA, *Annual Report and Accounts 1976–77*, pp. 57–64).
30. *Costs and Revenues*, #68.
31. IBA, *Television and Radio 1977*, pp. 187–9.
32. *ITCA to Annan*, #18; *Television Act 1963*, #7.
33. ITA Memorandum, 'The Financial Position of Independent Television', Pilkington II, pp. 423–9, especially ##6, 7 and 19.
34. ITA Memorandum. 'Financial Arrangements in Independent Television After 1964', Pilkington II, pp. 581–5, especially ##3 and 6.
35. *December 1962 White Paper*, #27.
36. Reginald Bevins, *The Greasy Pole*, pp. 107, 110, 113–14.
37. *Costs and Revenues*, #1.
38. 'Memorandum Submitted by the Ministry of Posts and Telecommunications', *Nationalised Industries Report*, p. 366, #2.
39. *ITCA to Annan*, #58.
40. *Television Act 1963*, #7 (1b); *Television Act 1964*, #13 (4); *IBAA 73*, #26 (4).
41. *Nationalised Industries Report*, pp. 184, 187, #646.
42. *Nationalised Industries Report*, p. xxv, #53, pp. 366–369.
43. *IBAA 74*, #1.
44. Nationalised Industries Report, p. xxiv, #51, pp. 3–4, 12. The table is taken from *ITCA to Annan*, p. 156, although virtually the same material was reproduced in Annan, #12.33. The Annan Committee, after reviewing the history of the levy, supported it in principle. (Annan, #12.32–12.40.)
45. *IBAA 73*, #28; *Radio and Record News*, 13 April 1979.
46. *Nationalised Industries Report*, 'Appendix 3: Restrictions on I.T.A. Capital Expenditure', p. 318.
47. *IBAA 73*, #29; *Nationalised Industries Report*, 'Memorandum from the Ministry of Posts and Telecommunications, The Relationship of the Ministry of Post and Telecommunications with the Independent Television Authority', p. 4, #13.
48. IBA, *Television and Radio 1980*, p. 215.
49. *Costs and Revenues*, #31. As a consequence of the ban on cigarette advertising on American stations, which became effective at the beginning of 1971, American broadcasters lost over $211 million in revenues the first year. (*The New York Times*, 19 January 1972, p. 42).
50. From 1955 to 1963, ITV also had advertising magazines ranging from 5 to 15 minutes in length, which were nothing less than solid commercials, extolling the merits of one or more products without any intervening editorial or entertainment material. However, upon the recommendation of the Pilkington Committee, these were

eliminated in 1963. (Pilkington I, p. 293, #83; *December 1962 White Paper* (Cmnd. 189), #37.)

51. *IBAA 73*, Sched. 2, #7 (1).
52. Information supplied by the IBA.
53. Information supplied by the IBA, Thames Television, and Southern Television. Discounts for quantity purchase are not included in these figures.
54. IBAA 73, #15; *Nationalised Industries Report*, pp. 71–2; Annan, #12.24.
55. Annan, #12.41. The Annan Committee engaged Dr B. V. Hindley to look into the question of ITV profits, and his findings were published as Appendix G to its report. He concluded: 'Past rates of return on the ITA companies' capital have been very high, even after the introduction of the levy' (#10) since pre-tax earning rates often ranged from 28.6 per cent up to 85 per cent. 'Compared with almost any other industry, these figures are very high' (#11). Even after payment of the levy, but before the computation of taxes, the profit level of the contracting companies in 1974 ranged from 2 to 22 per cent (p. 79).

   In their comments on the Annan Report the programme companies questioned the Hindley data and the committee's conclusions on the grounds that they were based on an incomplete assessment of company assets. Further, said the companies, the committee 'takes insufficient account of the fact that more than £4 out of every £5 of profit goes to the Treasury in corporation tax and levy, thus alleviating the burden of the tax payer'. The companies also stated: 'The main industry rate of return in capital employed is no higher than that recommended by the National Board for Prices and Incomes.' (ITCA, *The Annan Report: An ITV view*, pp. 42–43.)

56. *Broadcast-Telecasting*, 11 June 1956, p. 27.
57. *Public Accounts Report 1959*, p. xlix, #109, p. 103; #1173.
58. Annan, ##12.46, 12.48, 12.50, 12.55.
59. *Variety*, 19 April 1978, p. 64.
60. IBA, *Television and Radio 1979*, pp. 213–14.
61. *ITCA to Annan*, ##496–502.
62. IBA, *Television and Radio 1977*, p. 129.
63. IBA data from IBA; *BBC Handbook 1979,* p. 71.
64. Data supplied by IBA.
65. *IBAA 73*, #8 (2).
66. *ITCA to Annan,* #547–53.
67. Data supplied by IBA.

8   BRITISH BROADCASTING PERSONNEL

1. *BBC Handbook 1980*, p. 240.
2. Information from the IBA.
3. *Crawford Report*, #8.
4. *Beveridge I*, #577; Pilkington I, ##396, 408, 409.
5. *BBC Memorandum. The Structure of the Board of Governors*, #15 (iv).
6. Annan, ##5.17–5.28; quotations from ##5.23–5.24; *1978 White Paper*, ##9, 43–9.
7. Pilkington I, #411.
8. Annan, #5.26.
9. Simon, pp. 63–64.
10. For an account of his experiences as Chairman, successively, of both ITA and BBC, see Charles Hill, *Behind the Screen: The Broadcasting Memoirs of Lord Hill of Luton* (hereafter cited as Hill.).
11. Wedell, p. 122.
12. *1964 Charter*, #5 (1).
13. The *Communications Act of 1934* stipulates: 'Not more than four members of the Commission shall be members of the same political party' (#4,b).

14. Annan, #5.23.
15. *BBC Memorandum, The Structure of the Board of Governors*, #15 (ii).
16. Pilkington I, #400; Hill, pp. 15, 69–70. For a review of the process by which governors and members were appointed in 1961, see General Post Office Memorandum, 'Appointment of BBC Governors and ITA Members', Pilkington II, pp. 49–53.
17. *1964 Charter*, ##5 (2, 3), 6 (2, 3).
18. *IBAA 73*, Sched. 1 (1).
19. *IBAA 73*, Sched. 1, #1 (3).
20. *IBAA 73*, Schedule, ##1 (2), (6).
21. Normanbrook, *Functions of the BBC's Governors*, pp. 9, 12. See also 'What Governors Do', Hill, pp. 213–16.
22. *BBC Memorandum. The Structure of the Board of Governors*, #3.
23. Michael Swann; *The Responsibility of the Governors*, p. 11.
24. Wedell, p. 120.
25. *BBC Memorandum, The Structure of the Board of Governors*, ##3, 5.
26. *Ullswater Report*, #12.
27. *Ullswater Report*, pp. 48–9.
28. For additional information on this point see Paulu, *British Broadcasting*, p. 96.
29. Henry Fairlie, 'The B.B.C.', in Hugh Thomas, ed., *The Establishment*, p. 191.
30. Howard Thomas, *The Truth About Television*, p. 144. On this point see also Wedell, pp. 125–7. Thomas also made some interesting observations about the development of the BBC, and the relationship between Directors-General and staff.
31. Hugh Greene, *The Third Floor Front*, p. 68.
32. Charles Stuart, ed., *The Reith Diaries*, pp. 56, 57, 413, 514. In its Reithian days, the BBC earned a great deal of justified criticism for attempts to control the personal lives of its staff. For a review of the famous 'Talking Mongoose' case, see Paulu, *British Broadcasting*, pp. 113–15.
33. Boyle, p. 224.
34. For a review of the situation facing Haley when he became Director-General, see Briggs III, pp. 714–26.
35. *Yorkshire Post*, 15 April 1977.
36. *Observer*, 6 July 1958, p. 7; Reith, *Into the Wind* p. 81. Briggs IV, p. 963, reproduces the advertisement for General Manager of the BBC which brought the position to John Reith's attention in 1922, and for ITA Director-General which led to Sir Robert Fraser's application in 1954.
37. This was the line taken by Beaverbrook's *Sunday Express*, always a bitter critic of ITV, in an article published 20 December 1959, entitled, 'Are these Men Fit to Run ITV?'
38. J. C. W. Reith, *Into the Wind*, pp. 88, 156, 260; Anthony Smith, *British Broadcasting*, pp. 60–1; Boyle, pp. 129, 245–6. For a description of Reith's relationship problems with the first Board of Governors, see Briggs II, pp. 424–39. Beveridge I, pp. 282–3; Simon, pp. 59–62; Beveridge II, p. 223; Beveridge I, ##554, 557; p. 191, Recommendation 11. The whole matter of the Whitley Document is reviewed in Paulu, *British Broadcasting*, pp. 100–1. Cf. Briggs IV, pp. 341–2, 403; Munro, *Television, Censorship and the Law*, pp. 17–18 (hereafter cited as Munro.)
39. *1951 White Paper*, #14; *1952 White Paper*, #17.
40. Hill, p. 261. In the last chapter of his book, Lord Hill reminisced about the role of the chairmen, (pp. 260–71). Cf. Shulman, pp. 37–54.
41. For a detailed and well-documented account, See Michael Tracey, *The Production of Political Television*, Chapter 9, 'The Retiring of Hugh Greene', pp. 157–81.
42. *BBC Memorandum, The Structure of the Board of Governors*, #2.
43. Annan, #9.66.
44. *1978 White Paper*, #9.
45. *1964 Charter*, ##8–11. Each issue of the BBC handbook lists current memberships. *BBC Handbook 1980*, pp. 39–44, 243–7. For additional details on the evolution of some BBC committees, see Charles J. Curran, 'The BBC's Advisory Bodies', *EBU*

Review 95ʙ (January 1966) pp. 10–15; Pilkington II, pp. 321–4. The papers the BBC submitted to the Pilkington Committee in 1960 review the range of activities of some of the BBC's advisory bodies at that time.

46. *1964 Charter* #8 (1); *Memorandum from the BBC General Advisory Council; BBC Handbook 1979*, pp. 37–8.

47. For example: in 1973, *A Study of Tastes and Standards in Programmes*; in 1974, *The Use of Broadcasting Frequencies in the UK*, and *The Coverage of Sport on BBC Television*; and in 1976, *The Task of Broadcasting News*.

48. *1952 Charter* #12; *1964 Charter* #10. In 1952 there was much disagreement over how Council members for Northern Ireland should be appointed. The Labour Government proposed that they be nominated by local authorities, but this suggestion was strongly opposed on the grounds that it would make them politically subservient. Arguments over this point were one of the reasons for the delay in the renewal of the BBC Charter in 1952 that led indirectly to the introduction of commercial television. (*1951 White Paper* ##18–22; *1952 White Paper* ##21–4; *House of Common Debates* 490:1446–51, 1455–8, 19 July 1951.)

49. *1964 Charter* #10 (4, 5).

50. *BBC Memorandum, The BBC and Regional Broadcasting*, pp. 11–13.

51. *IBAA 73* ##10–11; *Television Act 1954* #8; *December 1962 White Paper*, #18.

52. *IBAA 73*, #11; *IBA to Annan*, #222.

53. Pilkington I, #640, p. 291, Recommendation 49; *December 1962 White Paper*, #19; *Television Act 1964*, #9 (1); *IBAA 73*, #10 (1).

54. 'Report by the General Advisory Council', IBA, *Annual Report and Accounts 1975–76*, p. 134.

55. *Nationalized Industries Report*, ##119.

56. Annan, ##6.5–6.9.

57. *1978 White Paper*, ##51, 55.

58. BBC, *Summary of Developments*, #116. Diagrams showing BBC staff organization in 1927, 1933, and 1938 are given in Briggs II, pages following 663. Many editions of the *BBC Handbook* include a current diagram; e.g. *BBC Handbook 1977*, pp. 315–18. See also 'The BBC and Its Staff', and 'The BBC and Its Staff: Retirement Policy', in Pilkington II, pp. 261–75.

59. BBC, *Summary of Development*, #120; BBC, *BBC and Its Staff*, ##4, 8. For information about the way in which staff are recruited and promoted, W. O. Galbraith, 'Recruitment and Promotion in the BBC', *EBU Review*, 108ʙ (March 1968), pp. 22–7. Most issues of the annual handbook review some aspects of the Corporation's personnel policies. For example, *BBC Handbook 1979*, pp. 66–70.

60. BBC, *Regulations and General Information for Staff*. Appendix I in the Annan Report, a research paper written for the committee by A. Smith, 'The Relationship of Management with Creative Staff', examines practices in France, Canada, and Germany, and the section on Britain (pp. 139–46) contains much information about the working conditions of BBC and IBA producers.

61. BBC, *Regulations and General Information for Staff*, #4.28.

62. *BBC Handbook 1978*, p. 92.

63. BBC, *Regulations and General Information for Staff*, #4.14.

64. For a critical view of Corporation staff regulations as they were in December 1961, see 'A Supplementary Submission by The Association of Broadcasting Staff', Pilkington III, pp. 770–3.

65. Staff Instruction #206, supplied by the BBC.

66. BBC, *Regulations and General Information for Staff*, Outside Activities #4(c).

67. BBC Memorandum, *The BBC and Its Staff*, #24.

68. *BBC Staff Instruction*, #206 (4).

69. Annan, ##28.8–28.9.

70. IBA, *Television and Radio 1980*, p. 204.

71. Wedell, pp. 153–6.

72. IBA, *Television and Radio 1979*, p. 9; *ITCA to Annan*, ##325–9.
73. Beveridge I, #140.
74. *BBC Handbook 1980*, pp. 66, 93.
75. IBA, *Annual Report and Accounts 1977–78*, p. 68.
76. *1964 Charter*, #13 (1); *IBAA 73*, #32 (1).
77. *Ullswater Report*, ##37–8.
78. *1936 White Paper*, p. 9.
79. Beveridge II, p. 100.
80. Beveridge I, ##485–91; p. 199, Recommendation 93.
81. The main groups involved are: British Actors' Equity Association (actors and dancers); Variety Artistes' Federation (variety and music hall entertainers); the Incorporated Society of Musicians (vocal and instrumental solo music artists); The Musicians' Union (symphonic and dance-band musicians); the Incorporated Society of Authors (all types of writers); the National Association of Symphony Orchestras (six of Britain's principal symphony orchestras); and the Dance-Band Directors' Association (dance-band leaders and performers.) BBC Memorandum, 'Engagement of Artists and Speakers for Broadcasting', Beveridge II, pp. 164–73. The points of view of the several performers' groups are stated in their respective memoranda to the Beveridge Committee—Beveridge II, pp. 490–519.
82. 'Memorandum of Evidence by Musicians' Union', 13 May 1950.
83. Beveridge II, pp. 517; 211–12; Annan, #28.37. 'Commercial records' are such records as His Master's Voice, Columbia, RCA Victor, London, and others normally for sale to the public.
84. *BBC Handbook 1979*, p. 66.
85. *BBC Memorandum. The BBC and Its Staff*, #31.
86. *IBAA 73*, #16.
87. *ITCA to Annan*, ##489–95.
88. Annan, pp. 418–33. Quotations from ##27.2, 27.8, 27.20, 27.34, 27.41, 27.42.

9   PROGRAMMES: INTRODUCTION

1. *1964 Charter*, Preamble, #3(a).
2. *1969 Licence*, #13 (1, 2).
3. *IBAA 73*, #2 (1, 2).
4. Annan, #3.22.
5. *BBC Handbook 1928*, p. 71.
6. Beveridge II, pp. 24, 198. For other material on BBC objectives, see the discussion of the Corporation's constitution, pp. 5–45 above.
7. Pilkington I, ##114–15.
8. Pilkington I, ##156–64.
9. Bernard Sendall, 'Portrayal of Violence on Television', *Independent Broadcasting* (1 February 1975), pp. 4–6.
10. Pilkington I, #49.
11. Annan, ##4.1–4.13.
12. *Daily Telegraph*, 31 March 1969.
13. BBC Memorandum, *The BBC's Programme Policy*, ##22.25.
14. Charles Curran, *A Maturing Democracy*, p. 4.
15. Michael Swann, *Education, The Media and the Quality of Life*, pp. 9–10.
16. *ITCA to Annan*, #36.
17. ITCA, *The Annan Report: An ITV View*, p. 9, #14.
18. Brian Groombridge, *Television and the People*, p. 145; Paulu, *British Broadcasting in Transition*, p. 83.
19. Briggs III, pp. 125–40.
20. For a more complete description of the three programmes as they were in the decade

following World War II, see Paulu, *British Broadcasting*, pp. 146–54; Briggs IV, pp. 541–63.

21. William Haley, *The Responsibilities of Broadcasting*, pp. 10–11; Briggs II, p. 37.
22. *Broadcasting* (Cmnd. 3169), ##25–31 (hereafter cited as *1966 White Paper*).
23. BBC, *Broadcasting in the Seventies*. The theory behind the new alignment was explained in Gerard Mansell, 'The BBC's Radio Networks', *EBU Review*, 23:1 (January 1972), pp. 29–35. Lord Hill, BBC Chairman at that time, reviewed some of the accompanying controversy in Hill, pp. 126–40.
24. BBC, *Summary of Developments*, #45; Annan, #2.16.
25. BBC Memorandum, *The BBC's Programme Policies*, #17. See also Robin Scott, 'Radio One is One', *EBU Review*, 111B (September 1968), pp. 18–23; Ian Trethowan, 'Radio in the Television Age', *EBU Review*, 23.6 (November 1972), pp. 14–16. Most BBC handbooks review the current relationships of the four networks; for example, *BBC Handbook 1980*, pp. 12–16, 173–174.
26. BBC Memorandum, *The BBC's Programme Policies*, #18.
27. *Guardian*, 17 July 1978; *BBC Handbook 1980*, p. 24.
28. *1969 Licence*, #14 (10); *IBAA 73*, #21.
29. Pilkington II, p. 110, #108; Frank Gillard, 'The Local Broadcasting Experiment in Britain', *EBU Review*, 113B (January 1969), pp. 21–6.
30. *1962 White Paper*, ##74, 76; Pilkington I, p. 294, Recommendation 89; *1966 White Paper*, #38.
31. *An Alternative Service of Radio Broadcasting* (Cmnd. 4636), #6; BBC, *Summary of Developments*, ##29–61.
32. BBC Memorandum: *Local Radio*.
33. *An Alternative Service of Radio Broadcasting*, #5.13, 5.15.
34. *IBA to Annan*, ##148–200. John Thompson, 'Who Owns Independent Local Radio?', *Independent Broadcasting*, #6 (November 1975), pp. 15–19; John Thompson, 'The Shape of Local Radio', *Independent Broadcasting*, #7 (March 1976), pp. 15–22; John Thompson, 'The Development of Independent Local Radio in the United Kingdom', *EBU Review*, 27:4 (July 1976), pp. 10–18. Each issue of the IBA handbook—example, IBA, *Television and Radio 1977*, pp. 141–59—contains information about the radio companies, their directors, officers, something of their history, programme emphasis, members of their advisory committee, and their technical facilities.
35. *IBAA 73*, #2 (1).
36. BBC Memorandum, *Summary of Developments*, ##6–9; BBC Memorandum, *Choice in Television*, ##7–10; Paul Fox, *This is BBC*–1; David Attenborough, *BBC*–2.
37. Wedell (p. 132) says that in its early days, BBC 2 was competing with BBC 1 'in a manner which made "overall planning" in practice a dead letter'.
38. BBC Memorandum, *Summary of Developments 1962–74*, ##52–74; BBC Memorandum, *The BBC and Regional Broadcasting*.
39. Patrick Beech, *New Dimensions in Regional Broadcasting*.
40. BBC Memorandum, *The BBC and Regional Broadcasting*, pp. 16–17; *Report of the Committee on Broadcasting Coverage* (Cmnd. 5774), #1, p. 75, Recommendations ##12, 14. Wales is a good example of the problems encountered in developing national services. BBC, *Memorandum from the Broadcasting Council for Wales*, #1. See also BBC, *Memorandum from the BBC Northern Ireland Advisory Council*.
41. BBC Memorandum, *Summary of Developments 1962–74*, ##71–74.
42. *IBA to Annan*, #10, BBC Memorandum, *The BBC and Regional Broadcasting*, p. 3.
43. Annan, ##7.9, 13.43, Recommendation 47 on p. 478; *1978 White Paper* #53.
44. IBA, *Television and Radio 1977*, p. 5.
45. *Nationalised Industries Report*, #21.
46. IBA, *Television and Radio 1979*, pp. 11–12, 201.
47. *IBA to Annan*, #51; *Nationalised Industries Report*, pp. 357–8.

48. *IBA to Annan*, ##55–57; *ITCA to Annan*, ##388, 435, 190–4; Memorandum by ITA, 'Preparation of the Programme Schedules of Independent Television', *Nationalised Industries Report*, pp. 62–4; IBA, *Television and Radio 1979*, pp. 11–12. A review of the programme requirements written into the programme company contracts is given in *ITCA to Annan*, p. 152.
49. UNESCO, *Television: A World Survey*, pp. 24–5; Cecil McGivern, 'The Big Problem', *BBC Quarterly*, 5:144–6 (Autumn 1950); *BBC Handbook 1956*, p. 116.
50. *BBC Annual report 1958–59*, p. 8.
51. *IBA Annual Report 1958–59*, p. 2.
52. *Associated Rediffusion 2*, p. 9.
53. Pilkington I, ##191–5.
54. IBA, *Television and Radio 1979*, p. 12.
55. Christopher Rowley, 'ITV's Programme Balance, 1970–75', *Independent Broadcasting* (November 1975), p. 2.

10   PROGRAMME STANDARDS AND CODES

1. BBC, *Violence on Television*, p. v.
2. *89 Supreme Court Report 1797* (1969).
3. Federal Communications Commission, *The Communications Act of 1934 with the Amendments and Index Thereto*, Section 307 (a).
4. Annan, 16.3–16.4, 16.15.
5. *BBC Yearbook 1932*, p. 96; Briggs I, p. 374.
6. *The New York Times*, 16 September 1957, p. 33c.
7. *Daily Express*, 21 February 1959, p. 1; *Daily Herald*, 21,February 1959, p. 1; *The Times*, 21 February 1959, p. 6; 24 February 1959, pp. 7, 11; *The Sunday Times*, 22 February 1959, p. 4.
8. 'Television programme Guidelines', IBA, *Annual Report and Accounts 1976–77*, p. 110, #3.4.
9. AP Wire Report, 18 November 1973.
10. Annan, #16.9–16.16. Senior staff members from both BBC and IBA have written on the subject: Brian Emmett, 'TV and Real Life Violence: An Introduction for Broadcasters to the Relevent Research Findings', *EBU Review*, 123B (September 1970), pp. 25–30; Brian Emmett, 'TV and Violence—Two Years and a Million Dollars Later', *EBU Review*, 23:5 (September 1972), pp. 19–22; Joseph Weltman, 'The Independent TV Code on Violence and the Control of Violence in Programmes', *EBU Review*, 24:3 (May 1973), pp. 28–34.
11. Annan, #16.16.
12. Annan, ##16.1, 16.21, 16.51.
13. *Variety*, 3 December 1975, p. 35.
14. IBA, *The Portrayal of Violence on Television: Working Party Second Interim Report 1975*, p.6; IBA, *Annual Report and Accounts 1976–77*, p. 118, #10.2.
15. Shulman, pp. 101–2; Munro, pp. 132–133.
16. Mary Whitehouse, *Cleaning-Up TV: From Protest to Participation*, p. 23.
17. *Report to the Surgeon General of the United States Public Health Service from the Surgeon General's Scientific Advisory Committee on Television and Social Behavior*. A parallel campaign in the United States was developed by such groups as the League of Women Voters, and the National Citizens' Committee for Broadcasting.
18. Pilkington I, #168; p. 292, Recommendations 64, 65.
19. *December 1962 White Paper*, #38.
20. *IBAA 1973*, ##4 (1a), #5, (1a,b).
21. Annan, pp. 245–65; quotations from ##16.10, 16.46; *1978 White Paper*, #103.

22. IBA, *Guide to Independent Television '75*, p. 17; the Code, without the introduction, is printed in IBA, *Annual Report and Accounts 1976–77*, pp. 122–3; IBA, *Annual Report and Accounts 1978–79*, pp. 15–16. See also Neville Clark, 'A Policy on Violence', *Broadcast* (August 1975), pp. 7–10. The American *Television Code* states (pp. 4–5): 'Violence, physical or psychological, may only be projected in responsibly handled contexts, not used exploitatively.... The use of violence for its own sake and the detailed dwelling upon brutality or physical agony, by sight or sound, are not permissible. The depiction of conflict, when ... in programs ... for children, should be handled with sensitivity.... The presentation of techniques of crime in such detail as to be instructional or invite imitation shall be avoided.'

23. *Nationalised Industries Report*, pp. 65–8.

24. *NAB Television Code*, p. 5.

25. *Daily Mail*, 2 December 1976; *The Times*, 2 December 1976; *Daily Telegraph*, 3 December 1976.

26. *The Times*, 15 July 1977; *Daily Express*, 14 July 1977; *Guardian*, 14 July 1977; *Yorkshire Evening Post*, 19 August 1977

27. IBA, 'Television Programme Guidelines', *IBA Annual Report and Accounts 1976–77*, p. 110, #3.3.

28. 'Television Programme Guidelines', IBA, *Annual Report and Accounts 1976–77*, p. 109, #1.6; *Yorkshire Post*, 9 September 1978. In a California case, the mother of a girl who had been sexually assaulted with a soft drink bottle sued NBC for $11 million, charging that an NBC programme had given the idea of the crime to three girls. In September 1978, a British coroner announced that the hanging death of a 15-year-old boy had resulted from his seeing a film produced by Thames Television, although the programme company disputed the finding, saying that the scene took place after the boy had accidentally hanged himself.

29. Pilkington I, pp. 48–50. For a brief discussion of the BBC's 1960 code, which was written by Kenneth Adam when Controller of Television Programmes, see Hood, pp. 90–1.

30. 'BBC: The Focus of Controversy. Some Varying views', *BBC Handbook 1966*, pp. 11–19.

31. BBC, *Violence on Television*, pp. v; 7–8.

32. *Church Times*, 11 February 1977; *Daily Telegraph*, 6 April 1977; *Sun*, 6 April 1977.

33. BBC, *Tastes and Standards in BBC Programmes. A Study by the BBC for Its General Advisory Committee*.

34. Quotations from ##2, 3, 5, 8. There is a summary of this code, together with a discussion of tastes, standards, and language, in *BBC Handbook 1978*, pp. 286–9. See also, *BBC Handbook 1980*, pp. 4, 44, 231.

35. *London Daily Mail*, 15 April 1977; *The Sunday Times*, 17 April 1977; *BBC Handbook 1978*, p. 289.

36. *BBC Handbook 1977*, pp. 15–16; *BBC Handbook 1979*, pp. 2–3, 225–6.

37. For further discussions of these matters, see Paulu, *British Broadcasting*, pp. 273–6.

38. *Talking Points*, pp. 11–12.

39. Hill, pp. 115–18.

40. Hill, pp. 117–18. Cf. Munro, pp. 154–161. In its *BBC Handbook 1978* (P. 288) the Corporation observed:

> The use of swear words is undergoing a process of social change, but the BBC regards their gratuitous use in a script—perhaps to give force to lines or situations not otherwise lacking in it—as indefensible. Such intended use displays a lack of understanding of the audience and attempts to conceal what is a failure on the writer's part.

Producers in doubt about what to leave in and what to cut, the Corporation says, are to refer 'upwards', to the department head, and if necessary even to the Director-General himself, 'who is in effect Editor-in-Chief'.

11   NEWS PROGRAMMES

1. This paragraph is based on a statement provided by the BBC News Division. See also *BBC Handbook 1977*, p. 214.
2. *1964 Charter*, #3 (l). A similar clause was written into the first and all the subsequent charters of the BBC. *1927 Charter*, #3(e).
3. *1969 Licence*, #13 (2). The BBC began broadcasting daily accounts of Parliamentary proceedings in 1945, and the 1946 Licence made it a requirement. *Broadcasting: Copy of the Licence and Agreement dated the 29th day of November 1946 between H. M. Postmaster General and the British Broadcasting Corporation* (Cmd. 6975), #4 (2) (hereafter cited as *1946 Licence*).
4. *IBAA 73*, #2(a); #4(1,b) ##14, 18.
5. For a review of press opposition to news broadcasting, see the BBC's paper to the Pilkington Committee, 'The Effect of Broadcasting on Newspaper Circulation', Pilkington II, pp. 288–94, which also was submitted to the Royal Commission on the Press. Mitchell V. Charnley, *News by Radio*, pp. 1–39.
6. *1923 Licecce*, #2.
7. Briggs I, p. 130.
8. Briggs I, pp. 132, 210, 215.
9. Briggs I, pp. 264–5. Other examples of the pressure to limit BBC newscasting successfully brought by the press are cited by Briggs I, pp. 130, 172; Briggs II, pp. 153–9, 493.
10. 'BBC Memo, The Effect of Broadcasting on Newspaper Circulation', Pilkington II, p. 289.
11. *Crawford Report*, #12; Briggs I, pp. 153–5, 262–7.
12. The Corporation provided statistics to show that between 1937 and 1947, when news broadcasting most rapidly expanded, newspaper circulation increased by approximately 76 percent. Pilkington II, p. 292.
13. *Ullswater Report*, #80.
14. Briggs II, pp. 656–7.
15. Beveridge I, #493; Beveridge II, p. 5, #14.
16. Pilkington I, #315.
17. Charles Curran, *Broadcasting and Society*, p. 7; *idem., A Maturing Democracy*, pp. 4, 7, 10.
18. Information based on a statement from BBC News Division.
19. BBC, *The Task of Broadcasting News*, pp. 9–10; cf. BBC Memorandum, *The BBC's Programme Policies*, #31; 'A Case for Understanding', *Independent Broadcasting* (June 1976), pp. 1–13.
20. J. D. Halloran and P. Croll, 'Research Findings on Broadcasting', Annan, Appendix F, pp. 50, #113.
21. BBC, *The Portrayal of Violence in Television Programmes: A Note of Guidance*, p. 12; cf. *BBC Handbook 1978*, p. 287; 'Television Programme Guidelines', #4.4, p. 111; IBA, *Annual Report and Accounts 1976–77*.
22. *BBC Handbook 1977*, p. 32.
23. This paragraph is based on, and extensively quotes and paraphrases, notes provided by the BBC News Division. See also *BBC Handbook 1978*, p. 275; Briggs IV, pp. 567–78.
24. *BBC Handbook 1978*, pp. 273–4. The monitoring service is described further in Chapter 21 on External Services, pp. 390–1.
25. Greene, *The Third Floor Front*, p. 126.
26. For an extended explanation of BBC news policy as to editorial comment and impartiality, see BBC Memorandum, *BBC's Programme Policies*, pp. 28–40.
27. *BBC News Guide*, pp. 4, 25.
28. Briggs III, p. 202.
29. Wyndham Goldie, pp. 40–1, 192–4. See also, Briggs IV, pp. 588–605.

30. Simon, pp. 138–9

31. Anthony Davis, *Television: Here Is the News*, p. 11 (hereafter cited as Davis).

32. Greene, *The Third Floor Front*, p. 127.

33. *Daily Telegraph*, 31 August 1978.

34. BBC, *The Task of Broadcasting News*, pp. 19–25.

35. 'John Craven's Newsround: a BBC News Programme for Children', *EBU Review* 26:4 · (July 1975), pp. 14–16.

36. Davis, pp. 28–9.

37. *ITCA to Annan*, p. 153; IBA, *Television and Radio 1979*, p. 131.

38. IBA, *Television and Radio 1977*, p. 81.

39. Hill, pp. 29–32.

40. *ITCA to Annan*, ##201, 206.

41. IBA, *Television and Radio 1977*, pp. 131–39.; IBA, *Television and Radio 1979*, p. 153.

42. Annan, pp. 266–90. Quotations from ##17.6, 17.13, 17.17, 17.25.

43. Annan, ##11.10, 17.53.

44. Annan, Appendix F. pp. 50–68; quotation from #207 on p. 68.

45. These articles also generated a reply by David Glencross, the IBA Head of Programme Services: 'Birt and Jay: A Case for Understanding', *Independent Broadcasting*. (June 1976), pp. 10–13.

46. Sir Geoffrey Cox, 'Bad News—or Poor Scholarship?', *Independent Broadcasting* (December 1976), pp. 6–7.

47. Davis, p. 23.

48. For information about Eurovision, in addition to the citations given below, see Heinz-Dietrich Fischer, 'The Contribution of Eurovision and Intervision to Global Television', in Heinz-Dietrich Fischer and John Calhoun Merrill, eds., *International and Intercultural Communications*, pp. 350–71; '25 Years of the European Broadcasting Union. 'A Retrospect', *EBU Review*, 26:1 (January 1975), pp. 11–27 (the textual material in the EBU article is also available in Hans Brack, *The Evolution of the EBU Through Its Statutes from 1950–1976*, pp. 123–33); BBC Memorandum, 'Eurovision', Pilkington II, pp. 170–77; Paulu, *Radio and Television Broadcasting on the European Continent*, pp. 39–41: Briggs IV, pp. 474–505.

49. Jean-Pierre Weinmann, 'New York: The EBU's Television News Exchange Satellite Office', *EBU Review*, 26:3 (May 1975), pp. 23–5.

50. 'News Overhauls Sport on the Eurovision Exchanges', *EBU Review*, 91B (May 1965), pp. 12–13.

51. As used here, the word 'received' means that the BBC received 165 programmes from the EBU, but did not necessarily broadcast all of them.

52. For more detailed information about Eurovision news exchanges, see the May 1978 issue of the *EBU Review*, 30:3, all of which is devoted to Eurovision, on the occasion of its twenty-fifth anniversary. Data are from pp. 46–8.

53. Hors G. Jancik, 'The Exchange of News Between Eurovision and Intervision'. *EBU Review*, 26:3 (May 1975), pp. 26–7.

54. Barber, *Eurovision as an Expression of International Cooperation in Western Europe*, pp. 169–71, 'Grand Prix 1965 of the Eurovision Song Contest', *EBU Review*, 91B (May 1965), p. 78; 'Grand Prix 1966 of the Eurovision Song Contest', *EBU Review*, 96B (March 1966), p. 65.

12   CURRENT AFFAIRS, OPINIONS, AND CONTROVERSY

1. Wyndham Goldie has pointed out how Parliament (pp. 115–44) and party leaders resisted broadcasting—especially televising—ministerial, budget and party election programmes.

2. Briggs I, pp. 170–1, 268, 269.

3. *Crawford Report*, p. 15 (0). Briggs I, pp. 342–3. *Sykes Report*, #70.

4. Briggs II, pp. 128–9, *House of Commons Debates*, 199: 1581 (15 November 1926); Reith, *Into the Wind*, p. 128. By its famous Mayflower ruling in 1941, the FCC forbade American stations to editorialize, but in 1949 it reversed itself, permitting editorializing, provided stations gave equal time to other points of view.

5. Briggs III, pp. 508–621.

6. Manuscript copy of Curran talk, provided by the author. See also Curran, *A Seamless Robe*, pp. 105–34. For a learned discussion of legal barriers to press freedom in Britain, see Geoffrey Robertson, 'Television Seemliness and the law', *The Listener*, 27 September 1979, pp. 390–92.

7. Dennis Forman, then the Chairman and Joint Managing Director Director of Granada Television, told an ITV Consultation on News and Current Affairs Programmes in Bristol in 1972 that some programmes on ATV's *Free Speech* and Granada's *Under Fire* had violated the Fourteen-Day Rule before it was withdrawn in December 1956. (ITA, *News and Current Affairs Programmes*, p. 28.)

8. The text of the Aide-Mémoire, which concerned political broadcasting generally, and of which Paragraph 6 (iv) and Note 1 pertain to the Fourteen-Day Rule, will be found in Beveridge II, pp. 109–10, and in Wyndham Goldie, pp. 341–2. The latter source (pp. 123–5) also reviews the Aide-Mémoire's history.

9. Beveridge I, #264; Briggs IV, p. 606.

10. *The Times*, 28 July 1955, p. 8; *BBC Handbook 1956*, p. 16. The most complete description of the Fourteen-Day Rule's history is in *Report from the Select Committee on Broadcasting (Anticipation of Debates)*, pp. 23–31. See also Colin Seymour-Ure, *The Political Impact of Mass Media*, pp. 141–3 (hereafter cited as Seymour-Ure); Smith, *The Shadow in the Cave*, pp. 131–2.

11. *House of Commons Debates*, 537: 1277 (23 February 1955).

12. *House of Commons Debates*, 546: 235–2446 (31 November 1955).

13. *The Times*, 29 July 1958, p. 9.

14. *Report from the Select Committee on Broadcasting (Anticipation of Debates),...and an Appendix*, pp. ii–iii.

15. *House of Common Debates*, 562: 1095–97 (18 December 1956); *House of Commons Debates*, 574: 91–2 (written answers) (25 July 1957); *BBC Annual Report 1957–58*, p. 14.

16. ITA, *News and Current Affairs Programmes*, p. 14.

17. BBC Memorandum, *The BBC's Programme Policies*, #30.

18. 'Impartiality in Broadcasting' Pilkington II, p. 205.

19. 'Directions to Broadcasting Authorities,' Pilkington II, p. 15. *1979 White Paper*, #101 (3a). The Annan Report pointed out that the legislation then in effect might prevent an Authority Member or programme company director 'from broadcasting on any subject of public controversy', while the BBC—which has not been the subject of legislation on this point—got around the problem my making 'a distinction between the views of the Corporation on controversial issues and the views of individual governors'. Accordingly, the committee recommended

   that Members of Broadcasting Authorities and directors of organisations providing programmes under contract to a Broadcasting Authority should be allowed to broadcast on controversial subjects not related to broadcasting, on the services on which they have responsibilities. But they must inform the appropriate Broadcasting Authority in advance on each occasion (Annan, #7.16).

20. BBC Memorandum, *The BBC's Programme Policies*, #28.

21. Greene, *The Third Floor Front*, pp. 106–7. Lord Simon, BBC Board Chairman from 1947 to 1952, wrote in the same vein, a dozen years before Sir Hugh's talk:

   In practice it is found that there must be degrees of impartiality or of partiality. In matters where public opinion is practically unanimous—no impartiality. In matters where public opinion is overwhelmingly on one side, but there is an active and strong minority on the other side—acceptance of the majority view, with reservations. In matters of public controversy—complete impartiality. (Simon, p. 305.)

22. Annan, #17.7.
23. *BBC Handbook 1977*, p. 272.
24. *IBAA 73*, #4 (1b,f) (2); Joseph Weltmann, 'Impartiality in Broadcasting', *Independent Broadcasting* (August 1974), pp. 2–6, includes some interesting observations on the subject of impartiality.
25. *IBA to Annan*, #68. For the Authority's interpretation of this requirement to its programme companies, see 'Television Programme Guidelines', IBA, *Annual Report and Accounts, 1976–77*, pp. 111–13, ##5.1–5.6.
26. Quoted in Joseph Weltmann, 'Impartiality in Broadcasting', *Independent Broadcasting* (August 1974), p. 4. No broadcasting organization, of course, attempts to balance news bulletins, since their content depends upon the events of the day. Rather, by fair and honest reporting, it is hoped that over a period of time, news programmes will be self-balancing.
27. For a good general discussion of British news and current affairs programmes, see 'The Functioning of Identity', Tracey, *The Production of Political Television*, pp. 58–104.
28. Wyndham Goldie (p. 284) writes that broadcasting has always been more important to Labour than to the Conservatives, because Labour believes that the press, owned by capitalists, is pro-Conservative, and that broadcasting can be used to redress the balance.
29. *BBC Handbook 1980*, p. 20.
30. Annan, ##8.37–8.39.
31. *BBC Handbook 1977*, p. 34.
32. Programme descriptions are quoted from the *BBC Handbook 1977*, pp. 131, 133.
33. *Variety*, 4 May 1977.
34. *BBC Handbook 1978*, p. 145.
35. For a review of IBA current affairs broadcasts in 1978–9, see IBA, *Annual Report and Accounts 1978–79*, pp. 13–15, 83–89.
36. Davis, pp. 97–8.
37. *ITCA to Annan*, #180; cf. Gus MacDonald, 'Currents in Current Affairs', *Independent Broadcasting* (November 1975), pp. 5–9. See also, IBA, *Television and Radio 1980*, pp. 76, 83, 123.
38. Claudia Milne, 'With the Best Intentions', *Independent Broadcasting* (December 1977), pp. 4–6. Quotations from p. 6.
39. IBA, *Television and Radio 1977*, pp. 84–5.
40. *BBC Handbook 1977*, pp. 24, 30, 158; 'The EEC Referendum', *BBC Record*, #94 (March 1975), pp. 1–4. For data about public reaction to some of the referendum broadcasts, see J. G. Blumler, 'The Intervention of Television in British Politics', in Annan, Appendix E, pp. 18–20. BBC radio provided each organization three 10-minute broadcasts on Radio 4 and two 5-minute periods on Radio 2.
41. IBA, *Annual Report and Accounts 1975–76*, pp. 11, 35.
42. Davis, pp. 102–3; Rowan Ayres, 'Opening Doors', *EBU Review*, 25:2 (March 1974), pp. 27–31; *BBC Handbook 1977*, p. 28; Brian Groombridge 'Two Cheers for Access', *EBU Review*, 25:5 (September 1974); pp. 14–17; Francis Coleman, 'Speak for Yourself: A Speaker's Corner of the Television Air', *EBU Review*, 25:5 (September 1974), pp. 18–21; Whale, *Politics of the Media*, p. 58; *What's On in London*, 25 March 1977; *Morning Star*, 17 November 1977.
43. Rowan Ayers, 'Opening Doors, A personal Survey of the BBC's Venture into Public Access Television'. *EBU Review*, 25:2 (March 1974), p. 27; *BBC Handbook 1980*, pp. 172, 226.
44. Annan, #17.1.
45. Wyndham Goldie, p. 23.
46. Hill, pp. 99–101.
47. Hill, pp. 122–3.

48. Hill, pp. 220–2; Munro, pp. 14, 19, 146–152.

49. *Guardian*, 7 January 1977; *Daily Telegraph*, 8 August 1977; *Guardian*, 3 November 1977; *Sheffield Star*, 31 October 1977.

50. Shulman, pp. 25–54, quotations from pp. 25, 40.

51. 'Comeback', *Independent Broadcasting*, (November 1975), pp. 14–15.

52. IBA News Release, 8 June 1978; *Daily Telegraph*, 9 June 1978; *Guardian*, 10 June 1978; *The Sunday Times*, 11 June 1978; *The Listener*, 15 June 1978, p. 753; *The New York Times*, 9 May 1980, pp. 1, A1, A9; 11 May 1980, p. D37.

53. *BBC Handbook 1977*, pp. 215–16; 'Party Political Broadcasts: The Annual Series', IBA, *Annual Report and Accounts 1976–77*, p. 114, #6.2; BBC Memorandum, 'Political Broadcasting: Aide Mémoire', Beveridge II, pp. 109–10, quotations from ##(4), (6), (ii).

54. Reith, *Into the Wind*, pp. 151; cf. pp. 176, 216, 357; cf. Boyle, pp. 236–7.

55. Reith, *Into the Wind*, p. 181; Wyndham Goldie, p. 134. The problems encountered in political broadcasting during earlier years are reviewed in Paulu, *British Broadcasting*, pp. 163–8, 298–300. Each edition of the BBC handbook—for example, *BBC Handbook 1977*, pp. 31–2—lists the number and the length of party political broadcasts during the previous year.

56. Annan, #18.17; *BBC Handbook 1980*, p.19.

57. Annan, #18.21; *1978 White Paper*, #117.

58. *BBC Handbook 1980*, pp. 19, 185–6; 'Ministerial Broadcasts: the Aide-Mémoire', IBA, *Report and Accounts 1976–77*, pp. 114–15, #6.3; Annan, #18.19; Wyndham Goldie, pp. 92–3. Although ministerial broadcasts did not go on television until 1956, there were general election telecasts in 1951.

59. Almost every issue of the BBC handbook lists the ministerial broadcasts given during the previous year. See, for example, *BBC Handbook 1978*, p. 29.

60. Annan, #18.24; *1978 White Paper*, #118.

61. Briggs II, pp. 131–2, 134.

62. Programme details are given in the *Radio Times* and the *TV Times* for the week of 26 March–1 April 1977.

63. Briggs I, pp. 268–9; Briggs II, p. 132; Briggs IV, pp. 613–86; quotation from p. 636.

64. *IBAA 73*, Sched. 2, #8. The law reads: 'No advertisement shall be permitted which is inserted by or on behalf of any body the objects whereof are wholly or mainly of a religious or political nature, and no advertisement shall be permitted which is directed towards any religious or political incident or has any relation to any industrial dispute.'

65. IBA, *Annual Report and Accounts 1976–77*, pp. 113–14 (#6.1), 123–4 (Appendix 11), quotations from p. 114 (#6.11).

66. During the 1955 election, for example, the BBC cancelled plans to broadcast an Oxford University debate on the subject, 'Resolved that the Methods of Science are Destructive to the Myths of Religion', on the grounds that it might bear on some election issues. The debate was recorded, however, for presentation after the election. (*The Times*, 25 April 1955, p. 9.)

67. Greene, *The Third Floor Front*, pp. 127–8.

68. Examples of this confusion on the part of foreign governments are given by Reith, *Into the Wind*, pp. 171–2, 183–4, 273.

69. Wyndham Goldie, pp. 92, 122.

70. For a review of developments in party election broadcasting in the late 1950s and the 1960s, see Paulu, *British Broadcasting in Transition*, pp. 107–17; BBC, *The General Election: The Campaign and the Results on Television and Sound Radio*, p. 33; Edward R. Murrow, 'Television and Politics', in *Communication in the Modern World*, pp. 47–80 (available in abridged form in *The Twentieth Century*, **166**; 383–7 (November 1959); John Beaven, 'Television and Politics (II)', *The Twentieth Century*, **166**, 388–3 (November 1959); Joseph Treneman and Denis McQuail, *Television and the Political Image: A Study of the Impact of Television on the 1959 General Election*,

pp. 191, 233; Jay C. Blumler and Denis McQuail, *Television in Politics: Its Uses and Influence*, pp. 206, 263, 264.

71. *BBC Handbook 1980*, p. 186.
72. *Representation of the People Act 1969*, #915.
73. *BBC Handbook 1977*, p. 217, *BBC Handbook 1979*, pp. 12, 184. For an excellent treatment of this whole matter see Peter Hardiman Scott, 'Live from Westminster: Broadcasting the British Parliament', *EBU Review*, 29 (September 1978) pp. 16–20.
74. Seymour-Ure, p. 139.
75. Briggs I, pp. 342–3; *House of Commons Debates* (22 March 1926), 192, 866.
76. *Ullswater Report*, ##90–1.
77. Beveridge I, #264.
78. Wyndham Goldie, p. 244–5.
79. *BBC Handbook 1960*, p. 241.
80. *The Times*, 25 June, 1958 p. 6; 1 August, 1958 pp. 8, 9.
81. *First Report from the Select Committee on Broadcasting etc. of Proceedings in the House of Commons*, pp. v, 136–7, 147–54.
82. *BBC Handbook 1978*, pp. 278–9; *BBC Handbook 1979*, p. 184. See also the *First Report by the Select Committee on Televising the Proceedings of the House of Lords*, pp. iii–vi; *Ninth Report from the Select Committee on House of Commons (Services)*, p. v.
83. Seymour-Ure, p. 139.
84. James Bredin, 'Broadcasting Parliament: The British Radio Experiment', *EBU Review*, 26:5 (September 1975), pp. 17–19; Ed. Boyle and Mike Barton, 'The Parliamentary Broadcasting Experiment', *Independent Broadcasting* (August 1975), pp. 10–11; IBA, *Television and Radio 1977*, p. 175.
85. 'Memorandum by the Independent Broadcasting Authority', *First Report from the Select Committee on House of Commons (Services)*, pp. 41–52, quotation from pp. 44–5.
86. *BBC Handbook 1978*, p. 279; *House of Commons Debates*, 907: 1194, 1198 (16 March 1976); *BBC Handbook 1979*, pp. 184–5.

13   TALKS, FEATURES, AND DOCUMENTARIES

1. *BBC Handbook 1979*, p. 174. For background, see Briggs IV, pp. 578–86.
2. *BBC Handbook 1979*, p. 71. *The Listener* for 18 January 1979, reviewing its first 50 years of publication, reprinted a few outstanding items from earlier issues. Periodically the Corporation publishes anthologies of *The Listener* features.
3. For additional details about BBC radio talks during the 1950s, see Paulu, *British Broadcasting*, pp. 174–9; *Listener*, 4 May 1978, p. 561.
4. See any handbook, for example, *BBC Handbook 1978*, pp. 182–201, *passim*.
5. *BBC Handbook 1977*, pp. 336–7.
6. *BBC Handbook 1977*, pp. 28–28.
7. *BBC Handbook 1977*, pp. 133, 138.
8. Hugh Wheldon, 'The British Experience in Television', The Richard Dimbleby Lecture; *BBC Handbook 1979*, p. 260.
9. BBC Television, *Principles and Practice in Documentary Programmes*, p. 406. For some background material on BBC television documentaries, see Briggs IV, pp. 702–6.
10. BBC Memorandum. Summary of Developments, #22; Annan, #10.21.
11. Robin Scott, 'Going It Together: An Account of BBC Television's Experience with Co-Productions', *EBU Review*, 27, 1 (January 1976), pp. 6–10.
12. Time–Life Films—later Time–Life Television—'contributed vital co-finance (without any interference in editorial decisions)' (Robin Scott, *loc. cit.*, p. 7).
13. Kenneth Clark, *Civilisation*, pp. xv, xvii.

14. Jacob Bronowski, *The Ascent of Man*, p. 13.
15. Alistair Cooke, *Alistair Cooke's America*.
16. John Kenneth Galbraith, *The Age of Uncertainty*, pp. 7, 9.
17. *The New York Times*, 28 March 1977, p. 27. Patrick J. Sullivan, a professor of education at the University of Massachusetts, Amherst, writing in the *Public Telecommunication Review*, under the title 'Galbraith and His Predecessors; Notes on the New Television Teachers', referred in his opening sentence to 'the failure of John Kenneth Galbraith's *Age of Uncertainty* series'. After praising highly the preceding series by Clarke, Cooke, and Bronowski, the author said that it was 'evident from the first instalment . . . [that] the programme would be ludicrously embellished'. After observing that his 'negative assessment . . . needs to be tempered with the acknowledgement that, unlike the others, he was trying to present abstractions and ideas', he concluded by saying that 'as the series continued, Galbraith became paradoxically more accessible and more obscure'. (Quotations from pages 23, 24, 27.)
18. *The New York Times*, 2 March 1978, pp. 1, 12; *BBC Handbook 1979*, p. 160.
19. Norman Longmate, *If Britain Had Fallen*.
20. *Variety*, 22 April 1977, p. 63.
21. *Variety*, 31 August 1977, p. 42.
22. *ITCA to Annan*, ## 147– 51. For material generally about ITV documentaries, see the annual issues of the *Annual Report and Accounts* (for example, IBA, *Annual Report and Accounts, 1976– 77*, pp. 11–13) and of the IBA handbook (for example, IBA, *Television and Radio 1978*, pp. 18– 19).
23. On a repeat ITV telecast of *Genocide: 1941–1945*, on 16 May 1976, there were no commercial breaks, even though the rules permitted them. They were omitted so as not to interrupt the spell of the programme, which presented graphically the gruesome story of the murder of six million Jews at Auschwitz and elsewhere.
24. March Arnold-Forster, *The World at War*, p. i.
25. IBA, Television *and Radio 1976*, pp. 68– 9.
26. *The TV Times* for 14– 18 June 1976, devoted 4 pages to *Destination America*, but despite this, audiences were smaller than the programmes merited.
27. Maldwyn A. Jones, *Destination America*, p. 6.
28. Minneapolis *Star*, 26 August 1977, p. 1; *The New York Times*, 27 August 1977; AP radio wire, 26 August 1978. IBA, *Annual Report and Accounts 1977–78*, p. 15.
29. IBA, *Television and Radio 1976*, pp. 64– 5; *House of Commons Debates*, 896:2359– 90 (31 July 1975).
30. IBA, *Television and Radio 1976*, pp. 66–7.
31. IBA, *Television and Radio 1977*, pp. 68–9.
32. *TV Times*, 15– 24 May 1976, p. 49.
33. IBA, *Television and Radio 1977*, pp. 96– 7; IBA, *Television and Radio 1979*, pp. 27–9.
34. IBA, *Television and Radio 1977*, pp. 93– 4.

14 EDUCATIONAL BROADCASTING

1. *1964 Charter*, introduction; *IBAA 1973*, #2 (2, a).
2. BBC Memorandum, *Education and Broadcasting*, ##4, 6, 8.
3. *IBA to Annan*, #110; Annan, #19.5.
4. 'IBA Programme Requirements', *ITCA to Annan*, p. 152; Annan, #19.5.
5. Annan, ##19.2, 19.4.
6. BBC School Broadcasting Council, *BBC School Broadcasts: An Introduction*; Briggs II, p. 190. For a review of the early stages of educational broadcasting in Britain, see Briggs II, pp. 185– 226; and for the period 1945– 55, Briggs IV, pp. 804– 38. Much credit for the development of school broadcasting must go to the late Mary Somerville. Like Reith a Scot, her dedicated work provided the basis for British educational broadcasting. She also influenced broadcasting in the United States by counselling

visitors and by visiting American educational stations in the United States. For her account of 'How School Broadcasting Grew Up', see Richard Palmer, *School Broadcasting in Britain*, pp. 9–16.

7. School Broadcasting Council, *BBC School Broadcasts: Facts and Figures: A Statistical Digest*, pp. 52, 53 (hereafter cited as *BBC School Broadcasts: A Statistical Digest*).

8. *BBC Handbook 1980*, p. 188.

9. For further information about in-school programmes on the European continent, see Paulu, *Radio and Television Broadcasting on the European Continent*, pp. 163–72. The only substantial differences among continental countries in this respect are between East and West, and these follow from their different political concepts.

10. 'Memorandum, School Broadcasting Council for the United Kingdom', Pilkington II, p. 373, #29. The list of objectives given here is freely paraphrased and quoted from the School Broadcasting Council's memorandum to the Beveridge Committee (Beveridge II, p. 296.) See also BBC Memorandum, *Education and Broadcasting*, #5; *BBC Handbook 1977*, p. 221. These objectives are reviewed in more detail in Paulu, *British Broadcasting*, pp. 185–6.

11. *BBC, Summary of Developments*, #96. Cf. 'Memorandum. School Broadcasting Council for the United Kingdom', Pilkington II, p. 375, #35.1.

12. *ITCA to Annan*, #222.

13. *BBC School Broadcasts: An Introduction*, pp. 10–14.

14. Members are listed in each edition of the handbook; for example, *BBC Handbook 1979*, pp. 250–1. See also *BBC School Broadcasts: An Introduction*, pp. 20–1.

15. *BBC School Broadcasts: An Introduction*, p. 20.

16. BBC Memorandum, *Education and Broadcasting*, p. 23.

17. 'Memorandum, School Broadcasting Council for the United Kingdom', Pilkington II, pp. 371–2.

18. BBC Memorandum, *Education and Broadcasting*, #4.

19. Annan, #19.40. BBC Memorandum, *Education and Broadcasting*, #18(a).

20. *BBC School Broadcasts: Facts and Figures*, pp. 12, 13, 16, *BBC School Broadcasts: A Statistical Digest*, p. 36, BBC Memorandum, *Education and Broadcasting*, p. 23.

21. *BBC Handbook 1980*, pp. 116–7, 188–9, 231 BBC, *Education and Broadcasting*, #4.

22. *Guardian*, 17 July 1978; *BBC Handbook 1980*, p. 24.

23. BBC Memorandum, *Education and Broadcasting*, p. 23; *BBC School Broadcasts: An Introduction*, p. 6.

24. *BBC School Broadcasts: An Introduction*, p. 27; *ITCA to Annan*, #222.

25. More detailed information is available free of charge from the School Broadcasting Council, The Langham, Portland Place, London W1A 1AA. Information about the programmes described here is from BBC, *Radio and Television Annual Programme for Schools and Colleges 1977–78*, and BBC, *Radio and Television Annual Programme for Schools and Colleges 1978–79*. Lists of all BBC school radio and television series for the United Kingdom, Scotland, Wales, and Northern Ireland will be found in most editions of the BBC handbook. For example, *BBC Handbook, 1979*, pp. 23–5, 118–20, 189–90.

26. BBC, *Radio and Television Annual Programme for Schools and Colleges 1978–79*, pp. 8, 11; BBC, *Radio and Television Annual Programmes for Schools and Colleges 1978–79*, p. 25.

27. BBC, *Radio and Television Annual Programme for Schools and Colleges 1978–79*, pp. 6, 32.

28. Kenneth Fawdry and Charles Armour, 'A Broadcast Contribution to Sex Education in Primary Schools', *EBU Review*, 130B (November 1971), pp. 20–3; BBC, *Radio and Television Annual Programme for Schools and Colleges 1978–79*, p. 37.

29. BBC, *Radio and Television Programme for Schools and Colleges 1977–78*, p. 14.

30. Claire Chovil and Edwin Whiteley, 'Television and Backward Children', *EBU*

Review, 106ʙ (November 1967), pp. 34–8. See also Roy Edwards, 'Fool's Lantern or Aladdin's Lamp', *Independent Broadcasting* (November 1975), pp. 19–21. In this article a teacher reports favourably on the use of educational television programmes with slow-learning and otherwise handicapped children.

31. *ITCA to Annan*, #225.
32. *ITCA to Annan*, ##222–8; IBA, *Television and Radio 1979*, p. 51.
33. 'ITA Memorandum. Independent Television for Schools', *Pilkington II*, pp. 566–8.
34. *ITCA To Annan*, #237.
35. IBA, *Television and Radio 1977*, p. 61.
36. Data supplied by ITA.
37. IBA, *Television and Radio 1980*, 12.
38. Granada, *Independent Television for Schools and Colleges: Annual Programme 1976–77*, pp. 8–14.
39. *Independent Television for Schools and Colleges*, autumn term 1975; spring term 1976. *Exploration Man*.
40. IBA, *Television and Radio 1977*, pp. 64–5.
41. Anne Cuff, *A Study of the Use of Modern Language Broadcasts for Schools. With Particular Reference to Le Nouvel Arrivé*; quotations from p. 43.
42. 'Memorandum. Ministry of Education', Pilkington II, pp. 58–61. For data on programme use see BBC, *BBC School Broadcasts: Research and Evaluation Report No. 2*.
43. Annan, ##10, 19. For comments on ITV school broadcasting by the former director of BBC school television, see Kenneth Fawdry, *Everything But Alf Garnett: A Personal View of BBC School Broadcasting*, pp. 160–4.
44. Pilkington I, #372.
45. *July 1962 White Paper #37, December 1962 White Paper*, #43.
46. *ITCA to Annan*, #245. The EBU definition is given in Brian Groombridge and Jennifer Rogers, 'Using Adult Education Programmes', *EBU Review*, 24:2 (March 1973), pp. 17–23.
47. 'BBC Memorandum. Adult Education', Beveridge II, pp. 174–76. For additional details, see Paulu, *British Broadcasting*, pp. 191–2.
48. School Broadcasting Council, *BBC Further Education: An Introduction*, pp. 4–5 (hereafter cited as *BBC Further Education: An Introduction*.)
49. BBC Memorandum, *Education and Broadcasting*, #6.
50. BBC Memorandum, *Further Education: An Introduction*, p. 6.
51. BBC Memorandum, *Education and Broadcasting*, p. 23.
52. *BBC Handbook 1980*, p. 189.
53. *BBC Education: Programmes and Publications for Adult and Further Education. Annual Programme for 1977–78*, p. 1.
54. *BBC Handbook 1977*, pp. 140–63.
55. When some of these were first broadcast on Radio 3, the programme was called *Study on Three*, but in October 1975 the name was changed to *Lifeline*, in the hope of attracting more people who have 'seldom, if ever entered an educational centre since leaving school and who may be at a disadvantage because of unsatisfactory school experience'. (*BBC Handbook 1977*, p. 38.)
56. One consequence of the Pilkington Committee's recommendations was the setting up of a BBC Science Consultative Group in 1963 'to review the presentation of science and technology'. In a report to the Annan Committee, the group praised the Corporation's science output highly and referred particularly to *Horizons*, which it said 'commands the group's unanimous enthusiasm'. (BBC, *Report of the BBC Science Consultative Group*, p. 2.)
57. Lord Hill, who was successively IBA and BBC chairman, and was a medical doctor, had his first contact with broadcasting in the years before World War II, when he frequently broadcast as the *Radio Doctor*. At that time, policy prohibited identifying a practising physician by name when he was on the air.

58. James McCloy, 'The Postgraduate Education of Doctors on BBC Television', *EBU Review* 112B (November 1968), pp. 12–15.
59. *The BBC's Medical Programmes and Their Effects on Lay Audiences: A Study for the BBC's General Advisory Council*, pp. 25, 30–1, 40, 45.
60. IBA, *Television and Radio 1976*, p. 33; IBA, *Television and Radio 1977*, p. 63.
61. *ITCA to Annan*, ##249–52.
62. Charles Curran, *The BBC and Its Educational Commitment*, pp. 4–6.
63. *ITCA to Annan*, p. 152.
64. *ITCA to Annan*, ##242–3.
65. IBA, *Television and Radio1980*, p. 12; data supplied by IBA.
66. E. G. Wedell and James Wykes, 'The First Two Years: Activities in the Field of Adult Education by Two Independent Television Programme Companies', *EBU Review*, 93B (September 1965), pp. 20–2; Guthrie Moir and Edwin Whiteley, 'ETV and ITV: Educational Television in the Context of British Commercial Television', *EBU Review*, 112B (November 1968), pp. 25–8; *ITCA to Annan*, #239. For a thoughtful consideration of the subject, 'Using Adult Education Programmes', see the article of that name by Brian Groombridge and Jennifer Rogers, *EBU Review*, 24:2 (March 1973), pp. 17–23.)
67. IBA, *Television and Radio 1977*, pp. 64, 108.
68. IBA, *Annual Report and Accounts 1978–79*, p. 28; IBA, *Television and Radio 1977*, pp. 108–11; IBA, *Television and Radio 1979*, p. 56.
69. BBC, *The BBC and the Open University, An Introduction*, p. 3. Portions of this section are quoted and paraphrased from the article by Paulu, 'Europe's Second Chance Universities', *Educational Broadcasting Review*, 3:3 (June 1969), pp 75–82.
70. Walter Perry, *The Open University*, p.1 (hereafter cited as Perry). Perry's book is an excellent source of information about the Open University.
71. *A University of the Air* (Cmnd. 2992), #4. For additional information about the political genesis of the Open University, see Perry, pp. 10–30.
72. *The Open University: Report of the Planning Committee to the Secretary of State for Education and Science*, #18.
73. Perry, pp. 10, 18.
74. *BBC Handbook 1980*, pp. 24–27.
75. BBC, *The BBC and the Open University, An Introduction*, pp. 7–8.
76. BBC, *The BBC and the Open University, An Introduction*, pp. 3, 4 ff., 21, 25. These are 1974 data.
77. *BBC Handbook 1980*, p. 89.
78. BBC, *The BBC and the Open University, An Introduction*, pp. 16–19. See also Donald Grattan, 'The BBC and the Open University: A Broadcast Review', *EBU Review*, 23, 2 (March 1972), pp. 26–32.
79. BBC Memorandum, *Education and Broadcasting*, p. 24; *BBC Handbook 1980*, pp. 26–7.
80. *BBC Handbook 1980*, p. 107.
81. *The Open University in America*. Films and video-tapes are available through the Media Guild of Solana Beach, California.

15   RELIGIOUS BROADCASTING

1. Kenneth Lamb, *Religious Broadcasting*, p. 3; BBC, *Summary of Developments*, #102.
2. ITA Memo., *The Audience We Serve*, p. 26.
3. Reith, *Broadcast Over Britain*, pp. 195–6.
4. Annan, ##20.1–20.2.
5. *IBAA 73*, ##2 (2b), 4 (5a,b).
6. *Television Act 1954*, #8 (2a); *IBAA 73*, #4 (5a,b).
7. *IBAA 73*, Sched. 2, #8.

8. *IBAA 73*, Sched. 2, #5; IBA, *Television and Radio 1978*, p. 166. Before 1968, no advertising at all was allowed during the closed period on Sundays; beginning in 1968, advertisements could be run between programmes broadcast during the closed period; and at Easter time 1977, the Home Office approved advertisements within religious programmes. This was just in time for the *Jesus of Nazareth* film (see pp. 286–7), but still not within church services or programmes of a devotional character.
9. 'BBC Memorandum. Advice on Religious Broadcasting', Pilkington II, p. 302.
10. ITA, *Religious Programmes on Independent Television*, p.9.
11. 'BBC Memorandum, Advice on Religious Broadcasting', Pilkington II, p. 301, #2.
12. Pilkington I, p. 291, #50; *December 1962 White Paper*, #18, *IBAA 73*, #10 (2a). It may be that the recommendations for separate committees resulted from the unwillingness of either organization to discuss confidential business in the presence of the other. Since 1962 the Committee has met separately with BBC and IBA representatives, holding joint sessions only when taking up policy matters of mutual concern. In its evidence to the Annan Committee, CRAC strongly recommended 'entrusting to one Committee broad advisory duty over the whole range of religious broadcasting'. (Central Religious Advisory Committee, *Evidence to the Committee on the Future of Broadcasting*, #16.).
13. *Annan*, ##20.21–20.22; *BBC Handbook 1979*, p. 41.
14. IBA, *Television and Radio 1979*, p. 211; *ITCA to Annan*, #273. The programme company listings in each yearbook include the names of their religious advisors: for example, IBA, *Television and Radio 1979*, p. 211.
15. Annan, ##20.20, 20.24; *BBC Handbook 1979*, pp. 249–50.
16. BBC, *Summary of Developments*, #102.
17. *ITCA to Annan*, #286.
18. *Broadcasting, Society and the Church, #170.*
19. Reith, *Broadcast Over Britain*, pp. 191–2, 194.
20. Briggs II, p. 238.
21. Beveridge I, #246. The BBC's religious broadcasting policies and programmes from 1945 to 1955 are discussed in Briggs IV, pp. 763–804.
22. William L. Haley, *Moral Values and Broadcasting*. Address to the British Council of Churches on 2 November 1948, pp. 7–9.
23. Beveridge I, #252. The Pilkington Committee made a similar recommendation in 1962 (Pilkington I, ##277–8).
24. Simon, pp. 307–9.
25. Pilkington I, ##277–8.
26. Greene, *The Third Floor Front*, pp. 90–1, 95; Smith, *British Broadcasting*, pp. 182–4.
27. Central Religious Advisory Committee, *Evidence to the Committee on the Future of Broadcasting*, #11.
28. *ITCA to Annan*, #270.
29. CRAC, *Evidence to the Committee on the Future of Broadcasting*, #5; *BBC Handbook 1960*, p. 56; Pilkington II, pp. 95–6. The Corporation said about the same thing in *BBC Handbook 1978*, p. 284.
30. Annan, #20.12.
31. *Broadcasting, Society and the Church*, ##3.5.
32. Briggs I, pp. 273–4.
33. *The Times*, 9 July 1959, p. 4.
34. *ITCA to Annan*, #267; ITA, *Religious Programmes on Independent Television*, p. 8.
35. *BBC Annual Report and Accounts 1970–71* (Cmnd. 4824), p. 47.
36. *ITCA to Annan*, #267.
37. IBA, *A Historical Portrait of the Television Audience*, #5.10.
38. BBC *Annual Report and Accounts 1971–72* (Cmnd. 5111), p. 43.
39. IBA News Release, 'The Future of the Closed Period'; *BBC Handbook 1977*, pp. 34–5.

40. A review of some early religious programmes is given in Briggs I, pp. 273– 4.
41. Briggs II, pp. 233– 4.
42. Reith, *Broadcast over Britain*, pp. 195– 6: Briggs II, p. 227.
43. *BBC Handbook 1980*, pp. 105, 107.
44. IBA, *Television and Radio 1977*, p. 11; IBA, *Television and Radio 1980*, p. 12.
45. *BBC Handbook 1980*, pp. 22–23, 189– 90.
46. *BBC Handbook 1977*, p. 35.
47. *BBC Handbook 1980*, pp. 77– 8, 115, 190.
48. *The Times*, 17 April 1959, p. 6.
49. IBA, *Television and Radio 1976*, p. 103; IBA, *Television and Radio 1976*, p. 45.
50. IBA, *Television and Radio 1977*, pp. 43– 44.
51. *Independent Television for Schools and Colleges, Believe It or Not*. Spring Term 1976,
    p. 2.
52. IBA, *Television and Radio 1977*, p. 43.
53. Briggs III, pp. 626–31. For information on negative reactions to some other religious
    programmes, see *ibid.*, 621– 6.
54. BBC, *BBC Religious Broadcasting*, p. 3.
55. Charles Curran, *Code or Conscience? A View of Broadcasting Standards*, pp. 15– 17.
56. IBA, *Television and Radio 1977*, p. 47.
57. *Daily Express*, 19 March 1977; *Yorkshire Post*, 19 March 1977; *Daily Telegraph*, 18
    March 1977; *Daily Express*, 4 April 1977; *Daily Telegraph*, 4 April 1977; *Glasgow
    Herald*, 4 April 1977; *The Financial Times*, 4 April 1977; *Guardian*, 4 April 1977.

16   DRAMA, FILMS, AND LIGHT ENTERTAINMENT

1. *IBAA 73*, #2 (2).
2. Beveridge II, p. 24.
3. *BBC Handbook 1980*, p. 107. Comparable data may be found in all BBC handbooks.
   Although the exact figures vary from year to year, the general trend remains the same.
4. *BBC Handbook 1980*, p. 105. The percentage of dramatic material would increase if
   imported television programmes and cinema features on both BBC and ITV were
   included.
5. IBA, *Television and Radio 1980*, p. 12.
6. *BBC Handbook 1980*, p. 172.
7. IBA, *Radio and Television 1978*, p. 45. Most IBA handbooks include information
   about dramatic programmes. Thus *Television and Radio 1976* explains how Yorkshire
   Television did *Hadleigh* (pp. 17–31), and reviews how *Clayhanger* was developed by
   ATV into a twenty-six episode series. The 1977 handbook devotes several pages to
   how ATV produced six 1-hour plays about William Shakespeare's life in London (pp.
   15– 17), while succeeding pages review writing and production procedures for play
   anthologies, an afternoon serial, and other dramatic programmes.
8. BBC, *The BBC and the Arts*, pp. 16– 17.
9. Briggs I, pp. 280–1.
10. P. H. Newby, 'The BBC Third Programme: 20th Birthday.' *EBU Review*, 101B (January
    1967) pp. 26– 7. For additional details on BBC radio drama during the post war period,
    see Briggs IV, pp. 688– 99; also Paulu, *British Broadcasting*, pp. 204–5. Quotation
    from *BBC Handbook 1980*, p. 12.
11. *BBC Handbook 1976*, pp. 162– 4; *BBC Handbook 1977*, pp. 161– 2. Each edition of
    the handbook lists plays broadcast that year on radio and television.
12. *Variety*, 8 October 1975, p. 47, *BBC Handbook 1979*, p. 16.
13. For information about the Dales, see Paulu, *British Broadcasting*, pp. 205–7; '2,000
    Pages from Mrs. Dale's Diary', *Radio Times*, 11 November 1955, p. 5.
14. Shaum Sutton, *The Theatre in the Living Room*, pp. 6– 7.
15. Shaun Sutton, *The Theatre in the Living Room*, pp. 12–31.

16. *BBC Handbook 1976*, pp. 140–2; *BBC Handbook 1977*, pp. 141–5; *BBC Handbook 1979*, p. 7, *BBC Handbook 1980*, pp. 7–8, 128; Briggs IV, pp. 698–701.
17. Annan, #21.13.
18. IBA, *Television and Radio 1976*, p. 104.
19. IBA, *Television and Radio 1976*, p. 104.
20. A description of their production is given in IBA, *Television and Radio 1977*, pp. 15–17.
21. For comments on this production, see Cecil Clarke, 'Edward VII', *Independent Broadcasting* (August 1975), pp. 5–6.
22. *ITCA to Annan*, ##152–63.
23. IBA, *Television and Radio 1977*, p. 22.
24. IBA, *Television and Radio 1976*, pp. 107–9.
25. IBA, *Television and Radio 1977*, p. 24.
26. IBA, *Television and Radio 1976*, p. 112.
27. IBA, *Television and Radio 1979*, pp. 89–91; David Pryce-Jones, 'TV Tale of Two Windsors', *The New York Times Magazine*, 18 March 1979, pp. 40, 108–13.
28. *Variety*, 6 October 1976, p. 41; IBA, *Television and Radio 1977*, p. 27.
29. Annan, #21.14.
30. Associated Television, *Emergency-Ward 10; The Times*, 7 April 1959, p. 14.
31. IBA, *Television and Radio 1976*, p. 111; IBA, *Television and Radio 1979*, pp. 93–5.
32. For a general review of 'Films on Television', see Annan, pp. 336–43. An earlier view is in the chapter, "Canned Television', in *Television: A Critical Review*, pp. 119–30, written in 1963 by a former director of BBC Television, Gerald Beadle.
33. Annan, #22.6.
34. Pilkington I, #328–37; 'Memorandum of the British Actors Equity Association to the Pilkington Committee', *Pilkington III*, p. 785; Annan, #22.8.
35. Pilkington I, #109; Annan, #22.8.
36. *Television Act 1954*, Section 3 (1d); *IBAA 73*, Section 4 (1c.); ITA, *Annual Report and Accounts 1958–59*, p. 23.
37. *House of Commons Debates*, 528:621, 639–40 (27 May 1954).
38. ITA, *Annual Report and Accounts for the Year Ended 31st March 1957*, p. 14.
39. *ITCA to Annan*, #194; Annan, #22.3; IBA, *Television and Radio 1979*, p. 12; *Broadcast*, 3 July 1978.
40. *BBC Handbook 1980*, p. 105; Annan, #22.1.
41. IBA, *Television and Radio 1979*, p. 12.
42. Annan, #22.2.
43. IBA, *Television and Radio 1977*, p. 101.
44. Annan, #11.8.
45. *BBC Handbook 1980*, p. 6; IBA, *Annual Report and Accounts 1978–9*, p. 19.
46. Reith, *Broadcast Over Britain*, p. 18.
47. IBA, *Television and Radio 1977*, p. 49.
48. *ITCA to Annan*, ##187–8.
49. *BBC Handbook 1980*, pp. 105, 107; IBA, *Television and Radio 1979*, p. 12.
50. *BBC Handbook 1980* pp. 172, 174.
51. Each edition of the BBC handbook lists programmes broadcast during the previous year. For example, *BBC Handbook 1976*, pp. 164–5 *BBC Handbook 1977*, pp. 164–6, and *BBC Hand book 1980*, p. 14. For information on earlier programmes see Briggs IV, pp. 708–20.
52. *BBC Handbook 1976*, pp. 150–3; *BBC Handbook 1977*, pp. 151–4.
53. The ITCA submission to Annan said (#262): 'In light entertainment ITV's surrealist comedy "*Do Not Adjust Your Set*" (Thames) won a number of awards and led to the BBC's "*Monty Python's Flying Circus*".'
54. IBA, *Television and Radio 1977*, pp. 51–2.
55. IBA, *Television and Radio 1976*, pp. 54–5; IBA, *Television and Radio 1977*, pp. 56–7

56. *ITCA to Annan*, #189.
57. For many years BBC publications had an illustrated description of the programme entitled *The Black and White Minstrel Show*.
58. IBA, *Television and Radio 1976*, pp. 49–53.
59. *BBC Handbook 1976*, p. 150; IBA, *Television and Radio 1977*, pp. 58–9.

17   CHILDREN'S PROGRAMMES

1. Beveridge II, p. 23.
2. *Television Act 1954*, #8, (2c); *December 1962 White Paper*, #18. There is no BBC children's programme committee, although there is an Advisory Group on the Social Effects of Television. *BBC Handbook 1978*, p. 325.
3. *IBAA 73*, #5 (1a).
4. *BBC Handbook 1978*, p. 261.
5. Annan, #23.18.
6. Briggs I, pp. 258, 262.
7. Briggs III, pp. 626–8; see above, pp. 000–000.
8. *BBC Religious Broadcasting*, p. 3.
9. BBC, *Summary of Developments*, #34.
10. *ITCA to Annan*, #264, 465.
11. Doreen Stephens, *Television for Children*, pp. 3–5, 7, 8 (hereafter cited as Stephens).
12. These observations were reinforced several years later by a statement in a study of children's programmes made by the BBC for its General Advisory Committee in 1974:

    But children's programmes operate in as competitive a situation as the rest of television and it would be unrealistic to suppose that children would continue to watch in substantial numbers if they were simply offered what parents and teachers think they should have. It is the children themselves who must make the positive decision to watch. (BBC, *Children as Viewers and Listeners*, p. 5.)

13. Monica Sims, 'BBC Television Children's Programmes', *EBU Review*, 127B (May 1971), p. 21 (hereafter cited as Sims); *Children as Viewers and Listeners*, p. 6.
14. BBC, *Children as Viewers and Listeners*, pp. 12–13.
15. Sims, p. 25.
16. BBC, *Children as Viewers and Listeners*, pp. 9–10.
17. Sims, p. 24.
18. BBC, *Children as Viewers and Listeners*, p. 7.
19. BBC, *Children as Viewers and Listeners*, pp. 8–9.
20. *ITCA to Annan*, #254.
21. IBA, *Television and Radio 1976*, p. 80.
22. IBA, *Television and Radio 1977*, pp. 61, 104.
23. 'The ITV Code in Violence in TV Programmes', IBA, *Television and Radio 1976*, p. 16.
24. Sims, p. 21.
25. *BBC Handbook 1976*, pp. 22, 148, 155.
26. 'Appearances by children in programmes', IBA, *Annual Report and Accounts 1976–77*, p. 118; IBA, *Television and Radio 1976*, pp. 80–3.
27. *ITCA to Annan*, #263.
28. *BBC Handbook 1980*, pp. 105, 107.
29. IBA, *Television and Radio 1979*, p. 12.
30. BBC, *Children as Viewers and Listeners*, pp. 10–11.
31. IBA, *Television and Radio 1976*, p. 81.
32. BBC, *Children as Viewers and Listeners*, pp. 10–11.
33. BBC, *Children as Viewers and Listeners*, pp. 4–6; Sims, pp. 20–4.

34. Each BBC and IBA handbook contains sections on children's programmes which may be located through the index.
35. *BBC Handbook 1976*, p. 21.
36. *BBC Handbook 1976*, pp. 21–2.
37. Sims, p. 23.
38. *BBC Handbook 1976*, pp. 46, 148, 172, 18; *BBC Handbook 1977*, pp. 172, 183, 186.
39. IBA, *Television and Radio 1977*, p. 61.
40. IBA, *Television and Radio 1976*, p. 36.
41. IBA, *Television and Radio 1977*, p. 99.
42. IBA, *Television and Radio 1976*, pp. 86–87.
43. IBA, *Television and Radio 1977*, pp. 98–100.
44. *ITCA to Annan*, #261–2.
45. IBA, *Television and Radio 1976*, pp. 84–5.
46. *Annan*, #23.15.
47. BBC, *Children as Viewers and Listeners*, pp. 4, 16–35, provides detailed statistics about children's viewing and listening.
48. *BBC Handbook 1976*, p. 21.
49. *ITCA to Annan*, #266.
50. BBC, *Children as Viewers and Listeners*, pp. 19–25.
51. Mallory Wober, 'Children and Television', *Independent Broadcasting* (November 1974), pp. 4–7.
52. BBC, *The BBC's Programme Responsibilities Towards Adolescents and Young Adults*. Quotations from paragraphs 4, 8, 21.
53. Pilkington I, #207; 'Memorandum: Ministry of Education', Pilkington II, p. 65, #26.
54. Annan #23.16.
55. Stephens, pp. 10–11.
56. *ITCA to Annan*, #266.

18   OUTSIDE BROADCASTS AND SPORTS

1. *BBC Handbook 1979*, pp. 172, 174.
2. *ITCA to Annan*, #298–300.
3. IBA, *Annual Report and Accounts 1978–79*, p. 33; *BBC Handbook 1980*, pp. 105, 107.
4. *Broadcasting–Telecasting*, 19 September 1951, p. 26.
5. Peter Dimmock, *Television Outside Broadcasts*, pp. 3–5.
6. The broadcast of the coronation is most fully described in BBC, *The Year That Made the Day*; see also *BBC Handbook 1955*, pp. 75–81. (See also Paulu, *British Broadcasting*, pp. 262–5.)
7. *BBC Handbook 1976*, p. 146; *BBC Handbook 1977*, p. 163.
8. Briggs I, pp. 262–6; Briggs II, pp. 119–20.
9. BBC Memorandum, 'General Survey of the Broadcasting Service', *Beveridge II*, p. 8, #22. For a review of BBC sports programming from 1945 to 1955, see Briggs IV, pp. 838–82; quotation from page 844.
10. *Radio Times*, 17–23 April 1976, p. 16.
11. *ITCA to Annan*, ##291–7; IBA, *Television and Radio 1975*, pp. 74–5.
12. IBA, *Television and Radio 1977*, pp. 36–7.
13. BBC, *The Coverage of Sport on BBC Television*, pp. 2–4.
14. BBC, *The Coverage of Sport on BBC Television*, pp. 3–4.
15. IBA, *Television and Radio 1976*, p. 79; BBC, *The Coverage of Sport on BBC Television*, pp. 7–8.
16. For the current law see *IBAA 73*, #23. See also BBC, *The Coverage of Sport on BBC Television*, p. 8.
17. *Broadcast*, 4 December 1978, p. 2.

18. BBC, *The Coverage of Sport on BBC Television*, p. 9.
19. *ITCA to Annan*, #287–8.
20. IBA News Releases, 15 February and 19 October 1978; *The Times*, 5 October 1978, p. 2.
21. Annan, #23.7, p. 487, Recommendation 136; *1978 White Paper*, #122–3.
22. Annan, #10.58, 23.8.
23. Peter Dimmock, *Television Outside Broadcasts*, p. 12.
24. ITA, *ITV 2: A Submission to the Minister of Post and Telecommunications by the Independent Broadcasting Authority*, p. 10, cf. *ITCA to Annan*, ##289, 303.
25. Neville Wareham, 'The BBC and Advertising', *EBU Review* 27, 4 (July 1976), pp. 21–4; BBC, *The Coverage of Sport on BBC Television*, p. 9.
26. 'Coverage of Sponsored Events and Display Advertising on Independent Television', IBA, *Annual Report and Accounts 1976–77*, pp. 125–6.
27. The Annan Committee observed that 'every week viewers of sports programmes hear the names of commercial companies ... and see the names of firms and products emblazoned around sports arenas', and accordingly recommended that both BBC and IBA firmly 'control the arrangements for broadcasting the name of an event's sponsor'. Annan, #23.9, 23.13.
28. Peter Dimmock, *Television Outside Broadcasts*, p. 7.
29. Annan, #23.1, 23.13.

19   MUSIC

1. *BBC Handbook 1976*, p. 220. For other official statements on the BBC's music policy, see the following: William Glock, *The BBC's Music Policy*; Huw Wheldon, *Television and the Arts*; Howard Newby, *Radio, Television and the Arts*; Victor Hely-Hutchinson, 'Music Policy and Problems', *BBC Quarterly*, 1, 38 (April 1946); and Lionel Salter, 'The BBC as a Patron of Music', *EBU Review*, 107B (January 1968), p. 18.
2. IBA, *Television and Radio 1976*, p. 95.
3. Briggs I, pp. 42–3, 275–8, 344; Briggs II, pp. 175, 491. There is a review of BBC music broadcasting in the 1920s and 1930s in Briggs II, pp. 169–84, with pictures facing p. 200.
4. Some of this information was supplied in manuscript form by the BBC Music Department.
5. Quoted in Simon, p. 18.
6. *BBC Handbook 1978*, p. 264.
7. Information about television music up to the middle 1950s can be found in Kenneth Wright, 'Serious Music and Television', *BBC Quarterly*, **8** (Winter 1953–4), 299–324. Christian Simpson, 'The Artistic Use of Television', *BBC Quarterly*, **9**, 19–24 (Spring 1954); Christian Simpson, 'Presenting Music in Television', *Radio Times*, 25 November 1955, p. 3; *BBC Handbook 1956*, pp. 78–9, 121, 152; BBC *Annual Report and Accounts 1955–56* (Cmd. 9803), pp. 119–20.
8. *BBC Handbook 1978*, p. 261.
9. *BBC Handbook 1979*, pp. 41, 251; Briggs I, p. 244.
10. *BBC Handbook 1980*, pp. 188. The BBC Symphony Orchestra's permanent and chief conductors have included: Sir Adrian Boult, Sir Malcolm Sargent, Rudolph Schwartz, Antal Dorati, Colin Davis, Pierre Boulez, Rudolf Kempe, and Gennadi Rozhdestvensky. Its guest conductors have represented the world's best.
11. BBC, *Broadcasting in the Seventies*, pp. 11–12. *The New York Times*, 1 March 1980.
12. Annan, ##21.22, 21.24.
13. Each edition of the BBC handbook lists some of the principal music offerings for the previous year. For example, *BBC Handbook 1977*, pp. 156–8, *passim*.
14. Annan, #21.24.
15. *BBC Handbook 1977*, p. 160.

16. *BBC Handbook 1966*, pp. 220–1.
17. During a typical year, the Corporation broadcasts the premieres of thirty-five or forty works by British composers, of which ten or twelve are commissioned by the BBC itself. (*BBC Handbook 1977*, p. 159.)
18. *BBC Handbook 1976*, p. 222.
19. *BBC Handbook 1977*, pp. 160, 171; *BBC Handbook 1976*, pp. 175–7; *BBC Handbook 1979*, p. 15.
20. *BBC Handbook 1976*, pp. 26, 221; *BBC Handbook 1979*, pp. 13–16.
21. Annan, #21.8.
22. There are 600 versions of Strauss' *Blue Danube Waltz*, and over 100 of Beethoven's Fifth Symphony. The catalogue has four inches of cards for Bing Crosby recordings. The Collection's oldest records are wax cylinders made by phonograph pioneers Thomas Alva Edison and Emile Berliner in the 1880s. Along with Enrico Caruso's first 78 rpm discs are others with the voices of Robert Browning and Henry Irving, recorded in 1888. (AP Radio Wire dispatch, 16 July 1978.)
23. *BBC Handbook 1976*, p. 27.
24. *BBC Handbook 1976*, p. 165.
25. Robin Scott, 'Radio One is One', *EBU Review*, 111B (September 1968), pp. 18–23.
26. 'Relations with Performers' Unions', Beveridge I, #485–91; 'BBC Memorandum, Use of Commercial Gramophone Records in the U.S.A.'; 'BBC Memorandum, Restrictive Practices', Beveridge II, pp. 190–2; *BBC Handbook 1977*, pp. 314–15.
27. *BBC Handbook 1980*, p. 105. For additional information about serious music telecasts during the earlier years, see Paulu, *British Broadcasting*, pp. 312–16; Paulu, *British Broadcasting in Transition*, pp. 129–31.
28. *BBC Handbook 1976*, p. 144.
29. *The New York Times*, 21 November 1977, p. 62M; 4 January 1978, p 13c.
30. *BBC Handbook 1976*, p. 175.
31. For an overview of 'Independent Television and the Arts', by Derek Bailey, see *Independent Broadcasting* (March 1978), pp. 2–5.
32. IBA, *Television and Radio 1976*, p. 99; IBA, *Television and Radio 1977*, p. 35.
33. *BBC Handbook 1977*, pp. 138, 197–8.
34. IBA, *Television and Radio 1977*, pp. 31–3.
35. *BBC Engineering Division Monograph, #40: The Broadcasting of Music in Television* (February 1962). Although somewhat dated, this brochure shows the care taken by the BBC in televising both instrumental and vocal music, and explains some of the electronic and other devices used to solve problems encountered in television opera. See also Lionel Salter, 'Opera at Home', *EBU Review*, 96B (March 1966), pp. 12–18.
36. Kenneth Wright, 'Serious Music and TV', *BBC Quarterly*, **8** (Winter 1953–4), 233.
37. Bream also was seen during the year on broadcasts originated by Yorkshire television (IBA, *Television and Radio 1978*, p. 65).
38. IBA, *Television and Radio 1978*, pp. 63–4.
39. Annan, #8.1, 21.6, 21.7, 21.8, 21.26; Lord Redcliffe-Maud, *Support for the Arts in England and Wales*, p. 50; Roger L. Brown, 'Television and the Arts', in James Halloran, ed., *The Effects of Television*, pp. 105–37. Taken in full context, the Committee's judgement applied to drama, education, and other cultural areas, as well as music.

20 AUDIENCE RESEARCH

1. BBC Memorandum, *The BBC and the Public*. Much the same thing was said in a Lunch Time Lecture given in 1970 by Kenneth Lamb, the Director of Public Affairs for the BBC, under the title, *The BBC and Its Public*.
2. Annan, #6.1.

3. *1964 Charter*, ##8, 10, 11, and 15. For additional information about the BBC's councils and committees, see above, pp. 139–41.

4. Beveridge I, ##558–64; p. 190, Recommendation 7 (i); *1952 White Paper* #36; *1952 Charter*, #17; *1964 Charter*, ##8, 10, and 15.

5. *Television Act 1963*, #15; *Television Act 1964*, #26; *IBAA 1973*, #33.

6. *IBAA 1973*, ##10–11. See pp. 141–2 for additional information about the Authority's advisory committees.

7. Briggs I, pp. 240–5; Briggs II, pp. 67, 256–61.

8. Briggs II, pp. 70, 271, 363, 364. For information on the Reith Sunday, see above, pp. 282–3.

9. Briggs II, p. 261. For a review of the slow emergence of audience research, see Briggs II, pp. 256–80.

10. Harold Nicholson, 'Birthday of the Third Programme', *The Listener*, 7 October 1948, pp. 526–7.

11. Silvey's own story is charmingly told in his book, *Who's Listening? The Story of BBC Audience Research*.

12. BBC, *Audience Research in the United Kingdom: Methods and Services*. Fourth (revised) edition, pp. 3–5 (hereafter cited as BBC, *Audience Research in the United Kingdom*.

13. BBC, *Audience Research in the United Kingdom*, pp. 9–20; *BBC Handbook 1977*, p. 293. Each edition of the BBC handbook contains information about audience survey methods and results. See for example, *BBC Handbook 1978*, pp. 46–9, 290–2.

14. BBC, *Audience Research in the United Kingdom*, pp. 26–9; *BBC Handbook 1978*, pp. 291–2.

15. A selected list of such inquiries is given in BBC, *Audience Research in the United Kingdom*, pp. 35–41.

16. *BBC Handbook 1978*, p. 292.

17. *BBC Handbook 1980*, p. 223.

18. 'Fact-finding: The IBA's Audience Research Department', *Independent Broadcasting August 1974*, pp. 14–15.

19. Arthur C. Nielsen, *TV Audience Research for Great Britain*.

20. BBC, *Audience Research in the United Kingdom*, pp. 21–3; IBA, *Television and Radio 1976*, p. 210; IBA, *Television and Radio 1977*, pp. 206–7; IBA, *Television and Radio 1978*, p. 200. IBA, *Annual Report and Accounts 1978–79*, pp. 50–52.

21. Information provided by the IBA.

22. *Independent Broadcasting* (August 1974), pp. 14–15.

23. IBA, *Television and Radio 1978*, p. 201.

24. For a review of these differences by the former head of BBC Audience Research, see Robert Silvey, *The Measurement of Audiences*.

25. BBC, *Audience Research in the United Kingdom*, p. 23.

26. Annan, #29.3.

27. *The Financial Times*, 8 August 1976; *Variety*, 18 August 1976, p. 42.

28. *The Financial Times*, 19 August 1976.

29. *Broadcast*, 16 August 1976.

30. *Variety*, 20 October 1976, p. 169.

31. Annan, ##29.8, 29.4, p. 489, Recommendation 170.

32. *1968 White Paper*, #124.

33. Information from BBC and IBA. *BBC Handbook 1980*, p. 36.

34. *BBC Handbook 1979*, p. 103. Immediately preceding World War II, in August 1939, there were somewhere between 20,000 and 25,000 television receivers in the United Kingdom (Briggs II, p. 620).

35. BBC Memorandum, *The BBC and the Public: A Supplementary Statement. The Radio and Television Audience*, #3 (hereafter cited as BBC, *The Radio and Television Audience*).

36. These data, based upon information supplied by the Radio Advertising Bureau and A. C. Nielsen, are quoted from *Broadcasting Yearbook 1977*, p. b–176.

37. IBA Audience Research Department, *A Historical Portrait of the Television Audience: Evidence to the Annan Committee on the Future of Broadcasting*, #2.1–3 (hereafter cited as IBA, *A Historical Portrait of the TV Audience*); IBA, *Annual Report and Accounts 1978–79*, pp. 50–51.

38. Data from the BBC.

39. Information provided by the IBA.

40. Data from the BBC.

41. Roper, *Public Perceptions of Television and Other Mass Media: A Twenty-Year Review, 1959–78*, p. 4. A. C. Nielsen data indicate the average number of hours of television use in each home per week as follows: 1972—43 hours 28 minutes; 1973—42 hours 49 minutes; 1974—42 hours 42 minutes; 1975—42 hours 28 minutes; 1976—43 hours 10 minutes; 1977—42 hours 28 minutes. (*Broadcasting*, 24 October 1977, p. 47.)

42. W. R. Simmons, as quoted in Leo Bogart, *The Age of Television*, p. 375.

43. BBC, *Annual Review of Audience Research Findings*, Number 2, 1974–5, p. 8.

44. IBA, *A Historical Portrait of the Television Audience*, ##5.19, 5.23.

45. Data supplied by IBA.

46. IBA, *Annual Report and Accounts 1978–79*, p. 51.

47. *BBC Handbook 1980*, p. 35.

48. *BBC Handbook 1980*, pp. 34–5.

49. IBA, *A Historical Portrait of the Television Audience*, #4.12.

50. BBC, *Audience Research in the United Kingdom*, pp. 24–9.

51. BBC, *Annual Review of BBC Audience Research*, Number 1, 1973/4, p. 18.

52. BBC, *Annual Review of BBC Audience Research Findings* Number 1, 1973/4, pp. 26–35, quotation from p. 35. Pages 53–4 list other research reports. Some of these inquiries have been mentioned during the chapters on programming. For a description of *Till Death Do Us Part*, as a programme, see p. 365.

53. BBC, *Annual Review of BBC Audience Research Findings*, Number 2, 1974/5, p. 18.

54. BBC, *Annual Review of BBC Audience Research Findings*, Number 2, 1974/75, p 22.

55. BBC, *Annual Review of BBC Audience Research Findings*, Number 4, 1976/7, p. 22.

56. BBC, *Annual Review of BBC Audience Research Findings*, Number 2, 1974/5, pp. 36–64, quotation from p. 57.

57. BBC, *Annual Review of BBC Audience Research Findings*, Number 3, 1975/6, pp. 35–84.

58. BBC, *Violence on Television: Programme Content and Viewer Perception*, quotations from p. 58.

59. IBA, *A Historical Portrait of the Television Audience*, ##7.1–7.3, 7.5, 7.9–7.12.

60. IBA, *Attitudes to Broadcasting: A Survey of Public Opinion*, pp. 2–4.

61. Annan, ##29.6–29.7.

62. Advertising Association, *Public Attitudes to Advertising. A Survey. April 1972*, quotations from Foreword and p. 5.

63. *The Television Audience: Patterns of Viewing*, quotations from pp. vii, 125 and 126.

64. Television Research Committee, *Problems of Television Research: A Progress Report of the Television Research Committee*, p. 7, 10. The Authority provided £250,000 in five annual instalments for this project, centred at Leicester University, which led to several publications: *Attitude Formation, and Change* (1967); Television and Delinquency (1970); and *The Effects of Television* (1970).

65. Jay G. Blumler and Denis McQuail, *Television in Politics: Its Uses and Influences*.

66. Anthony Piepe, Miles Emerson and Judy Lannon, *Television and the Working Class*.

67. J. D. Halloran, in association with P. Croll, 'Research findings on Broadcasting', Annan, Appendix F, pp. 29–73.

68. Elihu Katz, *Social Research on Broadcasting: Proposals for Further Development*, p. 1.

69. Hill, pp. 193–203.
70. Hugh Greene, *The Future of Broadcasting in Britain*, p. 19; cf. Anthony Smith, *The Shadow in the Cave*, pp. 145–8.
71. *BBC Handbook 1978*, pp. 297–8.
72. IBA, *Television and Radio 1978*, p. 9; Neville Clarke, 'Talking Back', *EBU Review*, 24, 1 (January 1973), pp. 20–2.
73. *ITCA to Annan*, #311.
74. *The Listener*, 12 May 1977, pp. 622–3. The Leisure Arts case and six other complaints were reviewed in the Corporation's 1978 handbook (pp. 49–50).
75. *The Listener*, 29 July 1976, pp. 115–16.
76. Annan, ##6.11–6.18, quotation from #6.13; p. 474, Recommendation 5.
77. *BBC Response to Annan Committee Report*, p.6; ITCA, *The Annan Report: An ITV View*, p. 11; IBA, *Annual Report and Accounts 1976–77*, p. 106; *1978 White Paper*, #77.

21   EXTERNAL BROADCASTING

1. L. John Martin, *International Propaganda*, pp. 10–12.
2. Briggs I, pp. 322–4. Information about the historical background of Britain's present External Services is available in Paulu, *British Broadcasting*, pp. 382–97.
3. Sporadic short-wave broadcasts had begun in the United States in 1924, and Holland opened a regular three-day-a-week service in 1928 (Briggs II, p. 371n.).
4. *BBC Yearbook 1933*, p. 263. All the BBC handbooks for the period include data on the Empire Service. See especially 'The Empire Service', *BBC Annual 1935*, pp. 124–35; 'The Empire Service', *BBC Handbook 1939*, pp. 115–18; Cecil Graves, 'Ten Years of Empire Broadcasting', *BBC Yearbook 1943*, pp. 77–81; J. B. Clark, 'Through Twenty-one Years', *London Calling*, 10 December 1953, pp. 2–3, 5; H. V. Hodson, 'Broadcasting and the Commonwealth', *BBC Quarterly*, 6, 1–6 (Spring 1951).
5. *BBC Annual 1935*, p. 131.
6. Briggs II, pp. 156, 383, 385–6.
7. Briggs II, p. 386.
8. *BBC Annual 1935*, pp. 45–6; Felix Greene, 'Broadcasting Links with the New World', *BBC Handbook 1939*, pp. 51–4; Caesar Saerchinger, 'Broadcasting and Anglo-American Relations', *BBC Yearbook 1934*, pp. 299–302.
9. John B. Whitton and John H. Herz, 'Radio in International Politics', in Harwood L. Childs and John B. Whitton, eds., *Propaganda by Short-wave*, pp. 3–4; Will Irwin, *Propaganda and the News, or What Makes You Think So?*, pp. 129–32. For some generalizations about the role of, and a brief history of, international broadcasting, see Paulu, *Radio and Television Broadcasting in Eastern Europe*, pp. 196–99.
10. Briggs II, pp. 394–5; *Ullswater Report*, ##119, 121–2.
11. J. C. W. Reith, *Into the Wind*, pp. 290–1.
12. *House of Commons Debates*, 328:501 (29 October 1937); 328:674 (1 November 1937).
13. J. B. Clark, 'Through Twenty-one Years', *London Calling*, 10 December 1953, p. 3.
14. Briggs II, p. 404. Additional details about the Arab service are given in Briggs II, pp. 401–6, and about the Latin-American programmes on pp. 406–8.
15. Charles J. Curran, *Broadcasting from West of Suez*, p. 4.
16. The dates when some of these services were inaugurated are given below. In 1939: Hungarian, 5 September; Polish, 7 September; Czech, 8 September; Rumanian and Yugoslav, 15 September; and Greek, 30 September. In 1940, Bulgarian, 7 February; Swedish, 12 February; Finnish, 18 March; Danish and Norwegian, 9 April; Dutch, 11 April and Flemish, 28 September. In 1943, Japanese, 4 July. A limited wartime Russian service was begun 7 October 1943, and discontinued 26 May 1943, at the Russian government's request. Daily news bulletins in Morse code were transmitted

for the Resistance beginning 22 March 1942. *BBC Handbook 1956*, pp. 251–2. See also Briggs III, pp. 176–7, 397.

17. In January 1945 the Overseas Services were broadcasting in twenty-four languages to eighteen areas as follows: Pacific; Far East; India and South East Asia; Middle East; Near East; Eastern Mediterranean; Central Mediterranean; Western Mediterranean; East Africa; Central and South Africa; West Africa; North Africa; North America; North America West Coast; South America; Central America; West Indies; and South America south of the Amazon.

   The European services provided programmes for: Austria and Italy; Belgium, Czechoslovakia; Europe; South-Eastern Europe; France; Western France; Germany; Northern Germany; Holland; Poland; Portugal; Scandinavian countries; and Spain. The languages used included: Albanian, Bulgarian, Czech, Danish, Dutch, English, Finnish, French, German (and Austrian German), Greek, Hungarian, Italian, Luxembourg, Norwegian, Polish, Portuguese, Rumanian, Spanish, Swedish, and Yugoslav. (*BBC Yearbook 1945*, pp. 82–3, 129.)

18. Volume III, *The War of Words*, in Asa Briggs's *History of British Broadcasting*, deals at length with both the domestic and external programmes of the Corporation during World War II.

19. Edward R. Murrow, 'Transatlantic Broadcasting', *BBC Yearbook 1943*, pp. 82–6.

20. *BBC Yearbook 1946*, pp. 103–5.

21. R. D. A. Maurice and C. J. W. Hill, 'The Development of a Receiving Station for the B. B. C. Monitoring Service', *BBC Quarterly*, 2 (July 1947) 105–28; Briggs III, pp. 187–91.

22. Peter Fleming, *Invasion 1940: An Account of the German Preparations and the British Counter-Measures*, pp. 230–1.

23. Briggs III, p. 288.

24. Charles Curran, *Broadcasting from West of Suez*, pp. 11–12.

25. A little known but interesting aspect of Radio Luxembourg was its night-time 'Operation Annie', consisting of broadcasts in German on another frequency, which were announced as originating in Germany. (Brewster Morgan, 'Operation Annie', *Saturday Evening Post*, 9 March 1946, pp. 18–19, 121–4; Cabel Phillips, 'The Shadow Army that Fought in Silence', *The New York Times Magazine*, 7 October 1945, p. 12.

26. The BBC originally favoured independent broadcasting facilities for the several invading armies, while the Americans advocated an integrated operation. The latter procedure was agreed upon only after an appeal to Churchill by Eisenhower. The American side of the dispute is told by Edward M. Kirby and Jack W. Harris in *Star Spangled Radio*, pp. 137–62. On the American Forces Network in the United Kingdom, see *ibid*., pp. 58–60.

27. While stationed at Radio Luxembourg from April to September 1945, I talked with many civilians living in Central Europe who gave indisputable evidence of having listened to both BBC and OWI broadcasts.

28. I. A. Kirkpatrick, 'Calling Europe', *BBC Yearbook 1943*, pp. 103–5.

29. The complete text of his broadcast and other data about the campaign are given in Henning Krabbe, *Voices from Britain*, pp. 91–3; cf. *BBC Handbook 1942*, p. 25. The Germans tried unsuccessfully to annex the campaign by pointing out that 'V' also stood for the German *Viktoria*. For a more complete account of the 'V' campaign, see Briggs III, pp. 365–84.

30. Robert Silvey, *Who's Listening*, pp. 105–9.

31. Paulu, *Radio and Television Broadcasting in Eastern Europe*, pp. 79, 199, 509–15.

32. *BBC Handbook 1980*, p. 96. See also above, Chapter 6, 'Finances in British Broadcasting'. Additional information about British External Broadcasting from 1945 to 1955 is given in Briggs IV, pp. 137–61, 505–41.

33. Michael Swann, *The BBC's External Services Under Threat?*' p. 4; *BBC Handbook 1979*, pp. 3–4.

34. *Summary of the Report of the Independent Committee of Enquiry into the Overseas Information Services* (Cmd. 9138), pp. 4, 42; cf. Harold Nicolson, 'The Political use of Broadcasting (b) External', *BBC Quarterly*, **3** (April 1948), 14– 23.
35. *The United Kingdom's Overseas Representation* (Cmnd. 7308), #60.
36. Ian Jacob, 'The Voice of Britain in Europe', *BBC Quarterly*, **2** (January 1948), 211– 15.
37. Charles J. Curran, *Broadcasting from West of Suez*, pp. 3– 5.
38. *1964 Charter*, #3(a); *1969 Licence and Agreement*, #13 (5).
39. *1969 Licence and Agreement*, #13 (3), #13 (4).
40. *1946 White Paper*, #60. The Conservative Government in its *1949 White Paper* (#27), declared: 'The present division of responsibility between the Government and the Corporation for the Overseas Services will continue'. *The United Kingdom's Overseas Representation* (Cmnd. 7308), #60.
41. *Fourth Report from the Expenditure Committee*, #142.
42. 'BBC Memorandum. The Critical Control of Programmes in the BBC's Overseas Services', Beveridge II, pp. 193– 5; 'Memorandum of Evidence by the Colonial Office', *ibid.*, pp. 277– 8.
43. *BBC Handbook 1979*, p. 179.
44. In 1978, the last year for which the Corporation published comparative data, the USSR led the world in total external broadcasting output, with 2010 hours per week. Then came the United States with 1813 hours (including the VOA, RFE and RL), the Chinese People's Republic (1418 hours), the German Federal Republic (789 hours), and the United Kingdom (711 hours). (*BBC Handbook 1980*, p. 57.)
45. *BBC Handbook 1980*, p. 178.
46. *BBC Handbook 1978*, pp. 274– 5; *BBC Handbook 1980*, p. 182.
47. *BBC Yearbook 1978*, pp. 270–71.
48. These various services are described in the BBC handbooks; for example, *BBC Handbook 1978*, pp. 269– 72. See also the table of broadcasting hours on p. 137.
49. *BBC Handbook 1978*, p. 272.
50. Sir Ian Jacob in *BBC Handbook 1955*, p. 29.
51. In the Programme Review included in each handbook, there are lists of current World Service programmes; for example, *BBC Handbook 1978*, pp. 203– 5; *BBC Handbook 1979*, pp. 112– 14.
52. *BBC Handbook 1979*, pp. 53–4, 109– 11.
53. *BBC Handbook 1980*, p. 53; Christopher Dilke, *English by Radio and Television*, pp. 5–9.
54. *BBC Handbook 1978*, p. 272; *BBC Handbook 1980*, p. 53.
55. Paulu, *Radio and Television Broadcasting in Eastern Europe*, pp. 215– 19.
56. *The New York Times*, 31 January 1956, p. 4; *The Times*, 6 March 1956, p. 8; 1 August 1956, p. 7; *Annual Report and Accounts of the British Broadcasting Corporation 1955–56* (Cmd. 9803), p. 53.
57. Paulu, *Radio and Television Broadcasting in Eastern Europe*, pp. 218– 19.
58. James Monahan, *Broadcasting to Europe*, p. 6; Maurice Latey, *Broadcasting to the USSR and Eastern Europe*, pp. 4–7.
59. Briggs II, p. 403; Briggs III, pp. 187– 93.
60. John Campbell, *Listening to the World*, pp. 3– 4.
61. BBC External Services, *The Impact of Broadcasting*, Introduction; *BBC Handbook 1980*, p. 59.
62. *BBC Handbook 1978*, pp. 76–7. Each edition of the handbook contains comparable information; for example: *BBC Handbook 1979*, pp. 57– 8.
63. BBC External Services, *The Impact of Broadcasting*, ##7.4.3; 7.4.7; 7.4.8–7.5; RFE-RL, *Soviet Area Audience and Opinion Research*, Analysis Report #5–79, p. 7.
64. BBC External Services, *The Impact of Broadcasting*, ##1.2.1– 1.2.4, 4.7.1.
65. Annan, #8.5.

22   COMMENTARY

1. Portions of the final chapter are based on 'Western European Broadcasting in Transition/United Kingdom: Quality with Control', published in the *Journal of Communication* **28** (3), pp. 52–8, © *Journal of Communication*, 1978.

Bibliography

The literature on British broadcasting has grown greatly in both quantity and quality since I first wrote on the subject in the middle 1950s. Yet the main types of printed material used in this book are similar to those available then, with the noteworthy exception of *The History of Broadcasting in the United Kingdom* by Asa Briggs, of which the fourth volume was published in 1979. Government documents, and BBC and IBA publications remain the principal sources. The Corporation has consistently published much about itself, and the IBA now is producing some helpful material, although research into its work is complicated by the fact that much of its output is reported in the publications of its separate programme companies, which have widely varying publication policies.

This bibliography is divided into five categories: (1) British government publications; (2) BBC publications; (3) IBA (and IBA company) publications; (4) books and pamphlets from other sources; and (5) periodicals.

(Only materials cited in the footnotes are listed here. The BBC's bibliography, *British Broadcasting*, periodically revised, is the most complete general bibliography on the subject. The *Bibliography of Theses and Dissertations in Broadcasting; 1920–1973*, edited by John M. Kittross, contains over a dozen entries with 'BBC', 'British', or 'Britain' in their titles. Finally, the Bibliographical Note at the end of each Briggs volume and the footnotes in those volumes, cover a wide range of materials.)

1 BRITISH GOVERNMENT (HMSO) PUBLICATIONS

Publications of the British Government (Her Majesty's Stationery Office) are arranged by date of publication. The short titles in parentheses following some of the entries are the abbreviations by which they are cited in the Notes.

Wireless Broadcasting Licence: Copies of (1) Licence by the Postmaster-General to the British Broadcasting Company, Ltd., for the establishment of eight radio-telephonic stations and the transmission therefrom of broadcast matter for general reception; (2) Agreement with respect to the broadcasting of news and general information (Cmd. 1822), 1923 (*1923 Licence*).
The Broadcasting Committee: Report (Cmd. 1951), 1923 (*Sykes Report*).
Wireless Broadcasting Licence: Copy of Supplementary Agreement . . . to Cmd. 1822 of 1923 (Cmd. 1976), 1923 (*Supplementary Agreement*).
Report of the Broadcasting Committee 1925 (Cmd. 2599), 1926 (*Crawford Report*).

Wireless Broadcasting: Drafts of (1) Royal Charter . . . for the incorporation of the British Broadcasting Corporation; and (2) Licence and Agreement . . . between His Majesty's Postmaster-General and . . . the British Broadcasting Corporation (Cmd. 2756), 1926 (*1927 Charter and Licence*).

Committee on National Expenditure Report (Cmd. 3920), 1931.

Report of the Television Committee (Cmd. 4793), 1935 (*Selsdon Report*).

Report of the Broadcasting Committee 1935 (Cmd. 5091), 1936 (*Ullswater Report*).

Broadcasting: Memorandum by the Postmaster-General on the Report of the Broadcasting Committee 1935 (Cmd. 5207), 1936 (*1936 White Paper*).

Broadcasting: Drafts of (1) Royal Charter . . . for the continuance of the British Broadcasting Corporation; and (2) Licence and Agreement between His Majesty's Postmaster-General and the British Broadcasting Corporation (Cmd. 5329), 1936 (*1937 Charter and Licence*).

Report of the Special Board of Inquiry appointed by the Prime Minister to inquire into certain statements made in the course of the recent case Lambert v. Levita, affecting the British Broadcasting Corporation (Cmd. 5337), 1936.

Report of the Television Committee 1943 1945 (*Hankey Report*).

Broadcasting Policy (Cmd. 6852), 1946 (*1946 White Paper*).

Broadcasting: Copy of the Licence and Agreement dated the 29th day of November 1946 between His Majesty's Postmaster-General and the British Broadcasting Corporation (Cmd. 6975), 1946 (*1946 Licence*).

Representation of the People Act 1949. Geo. 6. c. 68.

Report of the Broadcasting Committee 1949 (Cmd. 8116), 1951 (Beveridge I).

Report of the Broadcasting Committee 1949: Appendix H: Memoranda Submitted to the Committee (Cmd. 8117), 1951 (Beveridge II).

Broadcasting: Memorandum on the Report of the Broadcasting Committee, 1949 (Cmd. 8291), 1951 (*1951 White Paper*).

Broadcasting: Draft of Royal Charter for the Continuance of the British Broadcasting Corporation for which the Postmaster-General Proposes to apply (Cmd. 8416), 1951 (*1952 Charter*).

Broadcasting: Memorandum on the Report of the Broadcasting Committee 1949 (Cmd. 8550) 1952, (*1952 White Paper*).

Broadcasting: Copy of the Licence and Agreement dated the 12th Day of June 1952, between Her Majesty's Postmaster-General and the British Broadcasting Corporation (Cmd. 8579), 1952 (*1952 Licence*).

Broadcasting: Copy of a New Charter of Incorporation granted to the British Broadcasting Corporation (Cmd. 8605), 1952 (*1952 Charter*).

Board of Trade. Report of the Copyright Committee (Cmd. 8662), 1952.

General Post Office. *First Report of the Television Advisory Committee 1952*, 1953.

Broadcasting: Memorandum on Television Policy (Cmd. 9005), 1953 (*1953 White Paper*).

General Post Office. *Second Report of the Television Advisory Committee 1952*, 1954.

Summary of the Report of the Independent Committee of Enquiry into the Overseas Information Services (Cmd. 9138), 1954.

The Television Act 1954, 2 & 3 Eliz. 2, Ch. 55, 1954.

Agreement Supplemental to a Licence and Agreement (Cmd. 9196), 1954.

Broadcasting: Copy of the Licence granted on the 6th Day of April 1955, by Her Majesty's Postmaster-General to the Independent Television Authority (Cmd. 9451), 1955 (*ITA Licence*).

Report from the Select Committee on Broadcasting (Anticipation of Debates) together with the Proceedings of the Committee, Minutes of Evidence and an Appendix. (H.C. 288), 1956.

Agreement Supplemental to a Licence and Agreement (Cmnd. 80), 1957.

Special Report and First, Second, and Third Reports from the Committee of Public Accounts together with the Proceedings of the Committee, Minutes of Evidence, Appendices and Index (H.C. 76-1, 93-1, 201-1, 248-1), 1959 (*Public Accounts Report 1959*).

Third Report from the Committee on Public Accounts (H.C. 248), 1959.

General Post Office. *Report of the Television Advisory Committee 1960*, 1960.

Report of the Committee on Broadcasting 1960 (Cmnd. 1753), 1962 (Pilkington I).

Report of the Committee on Broadcasting 1960. Volume I. Appendix E: Memoranda submitted to the Committee, Papers 1–102 (Cmnd. 1819) (Pilkington II).

Report of the Committee on Broadcasting 1960. Volume II. Appendix E: Memoranda submitted to the Committee, Papers 103–275 (Cmnd. 1819–I) (Pilkington III).

Broadcasting: Memorandum on the Report of the Committee on Broadcasting, 1960 (Cmnd. 1770), 1962 (*July 1962 White Paper*).

Broadcasting: Further Memorandum on the Report of the Committee on Broadcasting, 1960. (Cmnd. 1893), 1962 (*December 1962 White Paper*).

Television Act 1963, Eliz. 2, Ch. 50, 1963.

Television Act 1964, Eliz. 2, Ch. 21, 1964.

Broadcasting: Copy of Royal Charter for the Continuance of the British Broadcasting Corporation (Cmnd. 2385), 1964 (*1964 Charter*).

Broadcasting: Copy of the Licence granted on the 10th Day of June 1964, by Her Majesty's Postmaster-General to the Independent Television Authority (Cmnd. 2424), 1964.

A University of the Air (Cmnd. 2922), 1966.

Broadcasting (Cmnd. 3169), 1966 (*1966 White Paper*).

Marine, &c., Broadcasting (Offences) Act 1967, Eliz. 2, Ch. 41, 1966.

First Report from the Select Committee on Broadcasting of Proceedings in the House of Commons . . . in Session 1965–66, and Appendices (H.C. 146), 1966.

First Report by the Select Committee on Televising the Proceedings of the House of Lords . . . and Minutes of Evidence (H.L. 190), July 1966 and 1967.

Wireless Telegraphy Act 1967, Eliz. 2, Ch. 72, 1967.

General Post Office. *Report of the Television Advisory Committee, 1967*, 1968.

Ninth Report from the Select Committee on House of Commons (Services) . . . The Experiment in Radio Broadcasting (H.C. 448), 1968.

European Agreement for the Prevention of Broadcasts transmitted from Stations outside National Territories. Strasbourg, 22 January 1965 (Cmnd. 3497), 1968.

The Open University: Report of the Planning Committee to the Secretary of State from Education and Science, 1969.

Representation of the People Act 1969, Eliz. 2, Ch. 15, 1969.

Broadcasting: Copy of the Licence and Agreement dated the 7th Day of July 1969 between Her Majesty's Postmaster-General and the British Broadcasting Corporation (Cmnd. 4095), 1969 (*1969 Licence*).

Broadcasting: Copy of the Licence granted on the 24th Day of September 1969, by Her Majesty's Postmaster-General to the Independent Television Authority (Cmnd. 4193), 1969.

Representation of the People Act 1969, Eliz. 2, Ch. 15, 1969.

Broadcasting Supplemental Royal Charter Relating to the British Broadcasting Corporation (Cmnd. 4194), 1969 (*1969 Charter*).

Third Report from the Estimates Committee together with part of the Minutes of Evidence taken before Sub-Committee D on 27th January 1969 and following days, Appendices and Index, (*H.C. 387*), 1969 (*Estimates Committee Report*).

The Open University. Report of the Planning Committee to the Secretary of State for Education and Science, 1969.

Third Report from the Estimates Committee Session 1968–69 . . . Observations by the Minister of Posts and Telecommunications, the British Broadcasting Corporation and the Independent Television Authority (Cmnd. 4259), 1970 (*Third Estimates Committee Report and Observations*).

National Board for Prices and Incomes. *Report No. 156, Costs and Revenues of Independent Television Companies* (Cmnd. 4524), 1970 (*Costs and Revenues*).

Second Report from the Select Committee on Nationalised Industries, Report, together with Minutes of Proceedings of the Committee, Minutes of Evidence, Appendices and Index Session 1971–72. Independent Broadcasting Authority (Formerly Independent Television Authority. (H.C. 465) 1972 (*Nationalised Industries Report*).

An Alternative Service of Radio Broadcasting (Cmnd. 4636), 1971.

Ministry of Posts and Telecommunications. *Report of the Television Advisory Committee, 1972,* 1972.

Ministry of Posts and Telecommunications. *Television Advisory Committee 1972. Papers of the Technical Sub-Committee,* 1973.

Sound Broadcasting Act 1972, Eliz. 2, Ch. 31, 1972.

Second Report from the Select Committee on Nationalised Industries, Session 1971–1972. Independent Broadcasting Authority (Formerly Independent Television Authority). Observations by the Minister of Posts and Telecommunications and the Independent Broadcasting Authority. (Cmnd. 5244), 1973.

Broadcasting: Licence granted on the 1st Day of August 1973 by the Minister of Posts and Telecommunications to the Independent Broadcasting Authority (Cmnd. 5413), 1973.

Independent Broadcasting Authority Act 1973, Eliz. 2, Ch. 19, 1973 (*IBAA 73*).

Ministry of Posts and Telecommunications. Television Advisory Committee 1972: Papers of the Technical Sub-committee, 1973.

British Broadcasting Corporation: Supplemental Royal Charter (Cmnd. 5721), 1974.

Report of the Committee on Broadcasting Coverage (Cmnd. 5774), 1974.

Independent Broadcasting Authority Act 1974, Eliz. 2, Ch. 16, 1974.

Broadcasting in Britain, second edition 1975 (Central Office of Information Reference Pamphlet 111).

Report of the Working Party on a Fourth Television Service in Wales (Cmnd. 6290), 1975.

First Report from the Select Committee on House of Commons (Services) . . . The Experiment in Public Sound Broadcasting (H.C. 142), 1976.

Broadcasting Supplemental Royal Charter for the Continuance of the British Broadcasting Corporation (Cmnd. 6581), 1976.

Report of the Committee on the Future of Broadcasting (Cmnd. 6753), 1977 (Annan).

Report of the Committee on the Future of Broadcasting: Appendices E–I: Research papers commissioned by the Committee (Cmnd. 6753–I), August 1977.

Fourth Report from the Expenditure Committee . . . . The Central Policy Review Staff Review of Overseas Representation. Volume I (H.C. 286–1), 1978.

Broadcasting. Presented to Parliament by the Secretary of State for the Home Department by Command of Her Majesty July 1978. (Cmnd. 7294), 1978. (*1978 White Paper*.)

The United Kingdom's Overseas Representation (Cmnd. 7308), 1978.

2 BBC PUBLICATIONS

The British Broadcasting Corporation is the author and/or the publisher of the works listed below, unless otherwise indicated.

Annual Reports and Accounts of the British Broadcasting Corporation, 1927 to date, London: Her Majesty's Stationery Office, 1928 to date (*BBC Annual Reports*).

Annual Review of BBC Audience Research Findings, Number 1, 1973/4; Number 2, 1974/5; Number 3, 1975/6; Number 4, 1976/7.

Attenborough, David. *BBC-2*, 1966 (BBC Lunch-time lectures, 4th series—6).

Audience Research in the United Kingdom: Methods and Services, fourth (revised) edition, 1976.

The BBC and the Arts, 1968.

The BBC and the Open University: An Introduction, 1974.

BBC Education. Programmes and Publications for Adult and Further Education Annual Programme 1977–78, 1977.

BBC Engineering Division Monograph. Number 40 (February 1962). *The Broadcasting of Music in Television*, 1963.

BBC External Services: The Impact of Broadcasting, 1976.

BBC Handbooks, 1928 to date. These official handbooks contain much information about all aspects of British broadcasting. The titles vary: *Handbook*, 1928–9, 1938–42, and again beginning in 1955–6; *Annual*, 1935–7; *Yearbook* 1930–4, and 1943–4. (There were no publications in this series in 1953–4.)

BBC Memorandum. 'The Future of Sound Broadcasting: Network Expansion'. Pilkington II, pp. 213–16.

BBC News Guide, 1975.

BBC Programme Policy Governing Violence: A Code of Practice for the BBC Television Service, 1960.

The BBC's Programme Responsibilities Towards Adolescents and Young Adults, 1978.

BBC Regulations and General Information for Staff, 1975.

BBC Religious Broadcasting. With a Foreword by Sir Charles Curran, Director-General, BBC, n.d.

'BBC Response to Annan Report' (manuscript), 1977.

BBC School Broadcasts. Research and Evaluation Report No. 2: A Statistical Digest of BBC School Broadcasts 1974–75, 1975–75, and 1975–6, 1977.

BBC Sound Broadcasting: Its Engineering Development, 1962.

BBC Television: A British Engineering Achievement, 1958.

BBC Television Service: Principles and Practice in Documentary Programmes, 1972.

BBC Television, Television Centre, n.d.

The BBC's Medical Programmes and Their Effects on Lay Audiences: A Study for the BBC General Advisory Council, 1976.

The BBC's Programme Responsibilities Towards Adolescents and Young Adults. A Study for the BBC General Advisory Council, 1978.

BBC School Broadcasts. Research and Evaluation Report No. 2: A Statistical Digest of BBC School Broadcasts 1974–5 and 1975–6, 1977.

Bailey, K. V. *The Listening Schools: Educational Broadcasting by Sound and Television*, 1957.

Beech, Patrick. *New Dimensions in Regional Broadcasting*, 19 March 1970 (BBC Lunch-time lectures, 8th series—5).

British Broadcasting 1922–1972: A Select Bibliography, Jubilee edition, 1972.

Broadcasting in the Seventies: The BBC's Plan for Network Radio and Non-metropolitan Broadcasting [1969].

The Broadcasting of Music in Television, BBC Engineering Division Monograph, #40.

Bronowski, Jacob. *The Ascent of Man*, 1973.

Campbell, John. *Listening to the World*, 1967 (BBC Lunch-time lectures, 5th series—4).

Central Religious Advisory Committee. *Evidence to the Committee on the Future of Broadcasting*, 1975.

Children as Viewers and Listeners: A Study by the BBC for Its General Advisory Council, 1974.

Clark, Kenneth. *Civilisation: A Personal View*, 1969.

Committee on the Future of Broadcasting, 1974. BBC Memorandum. *The BBC and its Staff*, 1974.

Committee on the Future of Broadcasting, 1974. BBC Memorandum: *The BBC and Regional Broadcasting*, 1975.

Committee on the Future of Broadcasting, 1974. BBC Memorandum: *The BBC and the Public*, 1975.

Committee on the Future of Broadcasting, 1975. BBC Memorandum: *The BBC and the Public. A Supplementary Statement: The Radio and Television Audience*, 1975.

Committee on the Future of Broadcasting, 1974. BBC Memorandum: *The BBC's Programme Policies*, 1974.

Committee on the Future of Broadcasting, 1974. BBC Memorandum: *Broadcasting in the Eighties and Nineties*, 1975.

Committee on the Future of Broadcasting, 1974. BBC Memorandum: *Choice in Television*, 1975.

Committee on the Future of Broadcasting, 1974. BBC Memorandum: *Education and Broadcasting*, 1975 (*BBC, Education and Broadcasting*).

Committee on the Future of Broadcasting, 1974. BBC Memorandum: *Engineering*, 1975. (BBC, *Engineering Memo*).

Committee on the Future of Broadcasting, 1974. BBC Memorandum: *Financing the BBC's Home Services*, 1974.

Committee on the Future of Broadcasting, 1974. BBC Memorandum: *Local Radio*, 1975.

Committee on the Future of Broadcasting, 1974. BBC Memorandum: *The Structure of the Board of Governors*, 1975.

Committee on the Future of Broadcasting, 1974. BBC Memorandum: *Summary of Development 1962–1974*, 1974 (*BBC, Summary of Development*).

Committee on the Future of Broadcasting, 1974. *Memorandum from the BBC General Advisory Council*, 1975.

Committee on the Future of Broadcasting, 1974. *Memorandum from the Broadcasting Council for Wales*, 1975.

Committee on the Future of Broadcasting, 1974. *Memorandum from the BBC Northern Ireland Advisory Council*, 1975.

Committee on the Future of Broadcasting, 1974. *Report of the BBC Science Consultative Group*, 1975.

Cooke, Alistair. *Alistair Cooke's America*, 1973.

The Coverage of Sport on BBC Television: A Study for the BBC General Advisory Council, 1974.

Crawston, Richard *et al*. *Principles and Practice in Documentary Programmes*, 1972.

Curran, Charles. *The BBC and Its Educational Commitment*, 1972.

——. *Broadcasting and Society*, 1971.

——. *Broadcasting from West of Suez*, 1968. (BBC Lunch-time lectures, 7th Series—2).

——. *Code or Conscience? A View of Broadcasting Standards*, 1970.

——. *A Maturing Democracy: The Role of Broadcasting*, 1973.

Curran, Charles J. *Supporting a Public Service*, 1969.

Dilke, Christopher. *English by Radio and Television*, 1966. (BBC Lunch-time lectures, 4th Series—7).

Dimmock, Peter. *Television Outside Broadcasts*, 1968. (BBC Lunch-time lectures, 7th series—1).

Fawdrey, Kenneth. *Everything But Alf Garnett: A Personal View of BBC School Broadcasting*, 1974.

Fox, Paul. *This is BBC-1*, 1969. (BBC Lunch-time Lectures, 7th series—4).

Haley, William J. *Moral Values in Broadcasting: Address to the British Council of Churches on 2 November, 1948*, 1948.

The General Election: The Compaign and the Results on Television and Sound Radio, September–October 1959, 1959.

Glock, William. *The BBC's Music Policy*, 1963. (BBC Lunch-time lectures, 1st series—6).

Katz, Elihu. *Social Research on Broadcasting: Proposals for Further Development. A Report to the British Broadcasting Corporation*, 1977.

Latey, Maurice. *Broadcasting to the USSR and Eastern Europe*, 1964. (BBC Lunch-time lectures, 3rd series—2).

Lamb, Kenneth. *The BBC and Its Public*, 1970. (BBC Lunch-time lectures, 8th series—6).

——. *Religious Broadcasting*, 1965. (BBC Lunch-time lectures, 3rd series—5).

Longmate, Norman. *If Britain Had Fallen*, 1972.

Monahan, James. *Broadcasting to Europe*, 1963. (BBC Lunch-time lectures, 2nd series—1).

Newby, Howard. *Radio, Television and the Arts*, 1976. (BBC Lunch-time lectures, 10th series—4).

Normanbrook, (Rt. Hon. Lord). *The Functions of the BBC's Governors*, 1965 (BBC Lunch-time lectures, 4th Series—3).

Pawley, Edward. *BBC Engineering 1922–1972*, 1972. (Pawley).

Radio and Television Annual Programme for Schools and Colleges 1977–78, 1977.

Radio and Television Annual Programme for Schools and Colleges 1978–79, 1978.

Redmond, James. *Broadcasting: The Developing Technology*, 1974. (BBC Lunch-time lectures, 9th series—2).

School Broadcasting Council. *BBC Further Education: An Introduction*, 1974.

——. *BBC School Broadcasts: An Introduction*, 1974.

——. *BBC School Broadcasts: Facts and Figures: 1974 A Statistical Digest. Issued by the School Broadcasting Council for the United Kingdom*, 1974.

——. *The Organization of School Broadcasting in the United Kingdom*, n.d.

Silvey, Robert. *The Measurement of Audiences*, 1966. (BBC Lunch-time lectures, 4th series—4).

Stephens, Doreen. *Television for Children*, 1966. (BBC Lunch-time lectures, 5th series—1).

Sutton, Shaun. *The Theatre in the Living Room*, 1969. (BBC Lunch-time lectures, 8th series—1).

Swann, Michael. *The Autonomy of the Broadcasters: Constitution and Convention*, 1974.

——. *The BBC's External Services Under Threat?*, 1978.

——. *The Responsibility of the Governors*, 1974. (BBC Lunch-time lectures, 9th series—1).

Talking Points: A Series of BBC Comments on Questions that Viewers and Listeners Ask, 1968.

The Task of Broadcasting News, 1976.

Tastes and Standards in BBC Programmes: A Study by the BBC for Its Advisory Council, 1973.

A Technical Description of Broadcasting House, 1932.

Thorne, Barrie. *The BBC's Finances and Cost Control*, 1970. (BBC Lunch-time lectures, 8th series—3).

The Use of Radio Frequencies for Sound and Television Broadcasting in the United Kingdom, 1974.

Violence on Television: Programme Content and Viewer Perception. BBC Audience Research Department Report, 1972.

Weigall, D. B. *Satellites—Present Use and Future Ideas in Broadcasting*, 1968. (BBC Lunch-time lectures, 6th series—5).

Wheldon, Huw. *The British Experience in Television: the Richard Dimbleby Lecture*, 1976.

Wheldon, Huw. *Television and the Arts*, 1964. (BBC Lunch-time lectures, 3rd series—3).

'Why No Continuous Pop?', *BBC Record 45*, October 1966.

The Year That Made the Day: How the BBC Planned and Prepared the Coronation Day Broadcasts, 1953.

BBC SERIAL PUBLICATIONS REFERRED TO INCLUDE:

Ariel. London.

BBC Quarterly. A scholarly journal published in nine volumes from April 1946 to Autumn 1954.

Listener. Reprints talks, interviews, and other materials broadcast by the BBC. Also has reviews of broadcasts, films, books, and other items. Weekly since 1929.

London Calling.

Radio Times. Lists BBC domestic radio and television programmes. Weekly since 1927.

3 IBA PUBLICATIONS

The Independent Broadcasting Authority (or its predecessor, the Independent Television Authority) or one or more of the programme companies is the author and/or publisher of the works listed below, unless otherwise indicated.

ABC Television. *The Armchair Theatre*. (London: Weidenfeld & Nicolson, second impression, 1960).

Annual Reports and Accounts, 1954–55 to date. (London: Her Majesty's Stationery Office, 1955 to date).

IBA Annual Report. Reports published before 1973 appeared under the earlier name of the IBA, Independent Television Authority, and are cited as *ITA Annual Reports*.

Associated Television, *Emergency-Ward Ten*, 1958.

Attitudes to Broadcasting: A Survey of Public Opinion, December 1975.

Cuff, Anne. *A Study of the Use of Modern Language Broadcasts for Schools, with Particular Reference to Le Nouvel Arrive* (London: IBA, 1976).

Davis, Anthony. *Television: Here Is the News*, 1976.

Granada, *Independent Television for Schools and Colleges: Annual Programme 1976–77. Age 4–18*, 1976.

A Historical Portrait of the Television Audience: Evidence to the Annan Committee on the Future of Broadcasting, 1975.

Independent Broadcasting Authority. Evidence to the Committee on the Future of Broadcasting under the Chairmanship of Lord Annan (1974). (*IBA to Annan.*)

IBA Code of Advertising Standards and Practice, 1975. (*IBA Code.*)

Independent Local Radio: The Acceptance and Presentation of Radio Advertisements, 1976. (*Radio Code.*)

Independent Television Companies Association (ITCA). *The Annan Report: An ITV View. A Submission to the Home Secretary in response to the Report of the Annan Committee on the Future of Broadcasting*, June 1977.

——. *ITV Evidence to the Annan Committee* (London: Independent Television Books, 1975). (*ITCA to Annan.*)

ITV 2: A Submission to the Minister of Posts and Telecommunications by the Independent Television Authority, December 1971.

Independent Television for Schools and Colleges. Autumn Term 1975. Spring Term 1976. Exploration Man, 1975.

Independent Television for Schools and Colleges. Believe It Or Not. Spring Term 1976, 1976.

Independent Television News. *Some Problems of Television News and News Analysis: Evidence to the Annan Committee*, July 1975.

News and Current Affairs Programmes, January 1972.

Notes on Independent Radio (mimeographed), 1972.

The Portrayal of Violence on Television: Working Party Second Interim Report, 1975.

Religious Programmes on Independent Television, 1962.

The Structure and Pattern of Religious Television Now, 1973. (Includes the supplement, *Religious Broadcasting Now*, 1973.)

Television and Radio, 1963 to date. Before 1973, published by the ITA, with title: *ITV . . . [year] Guide to Independent Television.*

IBA SERIAL PUBLICATIONS FREQUENTLY REFERRED TO INCLUDE:

Independent Broadcasting, Miscellaneous information and short articles about IBA radio and television.

TV Times. Lists ITV television programmes. Weekly since 1955.

4 BOOKS AND PAMPHLETS

Advertising Association. *Public Attitudes to Advertising: A Survey*, 1972.

Arnold-Forster, Mark. *The World at War* (London: Collins, 1973).

Barber, Russell. *Eurovision as an Expression of International Cooperation in Western Europe* (Ph.D. thesis, Northwestern University, 1965).

Beachcroft, T. O. *British Broadcasting* (London: Longmans, Green & Co., 1946).

Beadle, Gerald. *Television: A Critical Review* (London: Allen & Unwin, 1963).

Benn, Ernest. *The BBC Monopoly* (London: Individualist Bookshop, 1941).

Bevins, Reginald. *The Greasy Pole: A Personal Account of the Realities of British Politics* (London: Hodder & Stoughton, 1965).

Bloomfield, Paul. *BBC* (London: Eyre & Spottiswoode, 1941).

Blumler, Jay G., and Denis McQuail. *Television in Politics: Its Uses and Influence* (Chicago: University of Chicago Press; London: Faber & Faber, 1969).

Board for International Broadcasting. *Fourth Annual Report 1978* (Washington: Board for International Broadcasting, 1978).

Bogart, Leo. *The Age of Television*, third edition (New York: Frederick Ungar Publishing Company, 1972).

Boyle, Andrew. *Only the Wind Will Listen: Reith of the BBC* (London: Hutchinson, 1972).

Brack, Hans. *The Evolution of the EBU through Its Statutes from 1950 to 1976* (Geneva: European Broadcasting Union, 1976; Legal and Administrative Series, Monograph No. 11).

Briggs, Asa. *The History of Broadcasting in the United Kingdom*. Vol. I: *The Birth of Broadcasting* (London: Oxford University Press, 1961). (Briggs I.)

——. *The History of Broadcasting in the United Kingdom*. Vol. II: *The Golden Age of Wireless* (London: Oxford University Press, 1965). (Briggs II.)

——. *The History of Broadcasting in the United Kingdom*. Vol. III: *The War of Words* (London: Oxford University Press, 1970). (Briggs III.)

——. *The History of Broadcasting in the United Kingdom*. Vol. IV: *Sound and Vision* (London: Oxford University Press, 1979). (Briggs IV.)

Broadcasting Yearbook 1978 (Washington: Broadcasting Publications Inc., 1978).

Butler, David E., and Richard Rose. *The British General Election of 1959* (London: Macmillan, 1960).

Charnley, Mitchell V. *News by Radio* (New York: Macmillan, 1948).

Childs, Harwood L., and John B. Whitton (eds). *Propaganda by Short-Wave* (Princeton: Princeton University Press, 1942).

Church of England, *Broadcasting, Society and the Church* (London: Church Information Office, 1973).

Coase, Ronald H. *British Broadcasting: A Study in Monopoly* (Cambridge: Harvard University Press, 1950). (Coase.)

Council of Europe. *European Agreement for the Prevention of Broadcasts Transmitted from Stations Outside National Territories* (Strasbourg: Council of Europe, 1965; European Treaty Series No. 53).

Crozier, Mary. *Broadcasting (Sound and Television)* (London: Oxford University Press, 1958).

Curran, Charles, *A Seamless Robe: Broadcasting—Philosophy and Practice* (London: Collins, 1979).

Davies, Ernest. *National Enterprise: The Development of the Public Corporation* (London: Victor Gollancz, 1946).

Dimock, Marshall E. *British Public Utilities and National Development* (London: George Allen & Unwin, 1933).

Eckersley, P. P. *The Power Behind the Microphone* (London: Jonathan Cape, 1941).

Emery, Walter B. *National and International Systems of Broadcasting: Their History, Operation and Control* (East Lansing: Michigan State University Press, 1969).

Federal Communications Commission. *The Communications Act of 1934 with Amendments and Index Thereto* (Washington: US Government Printing Office, 1971).

Fischer, Heinz-Dietrich and John Calhoun Merrill (eds.) *International and Intercultural Communication* (New York: Hastings House, 1976; Humanistic Studies in the Communication Arts).

Fleming, Peter. *Invasion 1940: An Account of the German Preparations and the British Counter-measures* (London: Rupert Hart Davis, 1957).

Frost, J. M. (ed). *World Radio TV Handbook,* Vol. 33 (New York: Billboard Publications, 1979).

Frost, J. M. (ed). *World Radio TV Handbook*, Vol. 34 (New York: Billboard Publications, 1980).

Funk & Wagnalls New Desk Standard Dictionary. [1948]

Galbraith, John Kenneth. *The Age of Uncertainty* (Boston: Houghton Mifflin, 1977).

Gans, Herbert J. *Deciding What's News: A Study of CBS Evening News, NBC Nightly News, Newsweek, and Time* (New York: Pantheon Books, 1979).

———. *Popular Culture and High Culture: An Analysis and Evaluation of Taste* (New York: Basic Books, 1975).

Goodhardt, G. J., A.S.C. Ehrenberg, and M. A. Collins. *The Television Audience: Patterns of Viewing* (Lexington, Massachusetts: Lexington Books, 1975).

Gordon, Lincoln. *The Public Corporation in Great Britain* (London: Oxford University Press, 1938).

Gorham, Maurice. *Broadcasting and Television since 1900* (London: Andrew Dakers, Ltd., 1952).

———. *Sound and Fury: Twenty-one Years in the B.B.C.* (London: Percival Marshall, 1948).

———. *Television, Medium of the Future* (London: Percival Marshall, 1949).

Great Plains National ITV Library, *The Open University in America* (Lincoln, Nebraska: Great Plains National ITV Library, n.d.)

Greene, Hugh C. *The Future of Broadcasting in Britain. The Granada Guildhall Lecture 1972* (London: Hart-Davis, MacGibbon, 1972).

——. *The Third Floor Front: A View of Broadcasting in the Sixties* (London: The Bodley Head, 1969).

Grisewood, Harman. *One Thing at a Time: An Autobiography* (London: Hutchinson & Co., 1968).

Groombridge, Brian. *Television and the People: A Programme for Democratic Participation* (Harmondsworth: Penguin 1972).

Halloran, J. D. *Communication and Community: The Evaluation of an Experiment* (Strasbourg: Council of Europe, 1975).

——. *The Development of Cable Television in the United Kingdom: Problems and Possibilities* (Strasbourg: Council of Europe, 1975).

Halloran, James D. *The Effects of Television* (London: Panther Books, 1970).

Hardy, Forsyth (ed.). *Grierson on Documentary* (Berkeley and Los Angeles: University of California Press, 1966).

Harris, Ralph, and Arthur Seldon. *Advertising in a Free Society* (London: Institute of Economic Affairs, 1959).

Head, Sydney W. (ed.). *Broadcasting in Africa: A Continental Survey of Radio and Television* (Philadelphia: Temple University Press, 1974).

——. *Broadcasting in America: A Survey of Television and Radio*, third edition. (Boston: Houghton Milfflin, 1976).

Hill of Luton, Charles Hill, Baron. *Behind the Screen: The Broadcasting Memoirs of Lord Hill of Luton* (London: Sidgwick & Jackson, 1974). (Hill.)

Himmelweit, Hilde T., A. N. Oppenheim, and Pamela Vince. *Television and the Child: An Empirical Study of the Effect of Television on the Young* (London: Oxford University Press, 1958).

Hoachlander, Marjorie E., *A Case Study Volume 1: Summary The Ascent of Man: A Multiple of Uses?* (Washington DC: Corporation for Public Broadcasting, 1977).

Hood, Stuart. *A Survey of Television* (London: Heinemann, 1967).

Hubbell, Richard. *4000 Years of Television.* (New York: G. P. Putnam's Sons, 1942).

International Telecommunication Union, *International Telecommunication Convention. Final Protocol to the Convention. Additional Protocols to the Convention. Resolutions, Recommendations and Opinions. Montreux, 1965* (Geneva: General Secretariat of the ITU, 1959).

Irwin, Will. *Propaganda and the News, or, What Makes You Think So?* (London: Whittlesey House; New York: McGraw-Hill, 1936).

Jones, Maldwyn A. *Destination America* (London: Weidenfeld & Nicolson, 1976).

Keesings, Contemporary Archives. (Bath, United Kingdom)

Kendrick, Alexander. *Prime Time: The Life of Edward R. Murrow* (Boston: Little, Brown & Co., 1969).

Kirby, Edward M., and Jack W. Harris. *Star Spangled Radio.* (Chicago: Ziff-Davis Publishing Co., 1948).

Krabbé, Henning (ed.). *Voices from Britain: Broadcast History 1939–45* (London: George Allen & Unwin, 1947).

Lambert, Richard S. *Ariel and All His Quality: An Impression of the BBC from Within* (London: Victor Gollancz, 1940).

——, and Harvey Price. *The Haunting of Cashen's Gap: A Modern 'Miracle' Investigated*. (London: Methuen & Co., 1936).

Lazarsfeld, Paul F., and Patricia L. Kendall. *Radio Listening in America* (New York: Prentice-Hall, Inc., 1948).

Lazarsfeld, Paul F., and Frank.; Stanton (eds.). *Radio Research 1942–1943* (New York: Duell, Sloan & Pearce, 1944).

Lean, E. Tangye. *Voices in the Darkness: The Story of the European Radio War* (London: Secker & Warburg, 1943).

Linebarger, Paul M. A. *Psychological Warfare* (Washington: Infantry Journal Press, 1948).

McLean, F. C., H. W. Baker, and C. H. Colborn, 'The B.B.C. Television Centre and its Technical Facilities', *Proceedings of the Institution of Electrical Engineers*, Paper No. 3786E, 109, Part B: 45 (May 1962), 197–222.

Manvell, Roger. *On the Air: A Study of Broadcasting in Sound and Television* (London: André Deutsch, 1953).

Martin, L. John. *International Propaganda: Its Legal and Diplomatic Control* (Minneapolis:University of Minnesota Press, 1958).

McQuail, Denis. *Sociology of Mass Communications: Selected Readings* (Harmondsworth: Penguin, 1972).

Munro, Colin Roy. *Television, Censorship and the Law*. London: Saxon House, 1979.

Murrow, Edward R. 'Television and Politics', *Communication in the Modern World: The British Association Granada Lectures* (London: The British Association for the Advancement of Science, and Granada TV, 1959).

National Association of Broadcasters. *The Radio Code*. Twentieth edition (Washington: National Association of Broadcasters, 1976).

National Association of Broadcasters. *The Television Code*. Nineteenth edition (Washington: National Association of Broadcasters, 1976).

Newspaper Press Directory (London: Benn Brothers, 1978).

Nielsen, Arthur C., *Television Audience Research for Great Britain* (Chicago: A. C. Nielsen Co., 1955).

O'Brien, Terence Henry. *British Experiments in Public Ownership and Control*. Lond: George Allen & Unwin, Ltd., 1937.

Paley, William S., *As It Happened: A Memoir* (New York: Doubleday & Co., 1979).

Paulu, Burton. *British Broadcasting in Transition* (Minneapolis: University of Minnesota Press, 1961).

——. *British Broadcasting: Radio and Television in the United Kingdom* (Minneapolis; University of Minnesota Press, 1956). (Paulu, *British Broadcasting*.)

——. *Factors in the Attempts to Establish a Permanent Instrumentality for the Administration of the International Broadcasting Services of the United States* (Ann Arbor: University Microfilms, 1949).

——. *Radio and Television Broadcasting in Eastern Europe* (Minneapolis: University of Minnesota Press, 1974).

——. *Radio and Television Broadcasting on the European Continent* (Minneapolis: University of Minnesota Press, 1967).

Pawley, E. L. E. 'B.B.C. Sound Broadcasting 1939–60: A Review of Progress', *Proceedings of the Institution of Electrical Engineers*, Paler No. 3650, 108, Part B: 39 (May 1961), 279–302; Paper No. 3588, 108 Part B: 40 (July 1961), 375–97.

Perry, Walter, *The Open University* (San Francisco: Jossey-Bass, 1977).

Piepe, Anthony, Miles Emerson, and Judy Lannon. *Television and the Working Class* (Lexington, Massachusetts: Lexington Books, 1975).

Pons, Eugène. *General Considerations on Licence Fees for Radio and Television Sets* (Geneva: EBU, 1964; Legal Monograph 1).

Redcliffe-Maud, Lord. *Support for the Arts in England and Wales. A Report to the Calouste Gulbenkian Foundation* (London: Calouste Gulbenkian Foundation, 1976).

Reith, J. C. W. *Broadcast over Britain* (London: Hodder & Stoughton, 1924).

——. *Into the Wind.* (London: Hodder & Stoughton, 1949).

——. *The Reith Diaries.* Edited by Charles Stuart (London: Collins, 1975).

Robson, William A. (ed.). *Public Enterprise: Developments in Social Ownership and Control in Great Britain* (London: George Allen & Unwin, 1937).

The Roper Organization. *Public Perceptions of Television and Other Mass Media: A Twenty-Year Review 1959–1978* (April 1979).

Rotha, Paul. *Documentary Film* (New York: W. W. Norton & Co., 1939).

Seymour-Ure, Colin. *The Political Impact of Mass Media* (London: Constable; California: Sage, 1974). (Seymour-Ure.)

Sharps, Wallace S. *Commercial Television: A Manual of Advertising and Production Techniques* (London: Fountain Press, 1958).

Shulman, Milton. *The Least Worst Television in the World* (London: Barrie & Jenkins, 1973).

Siepmann, Charles A. *Radio Television and Society* (New York: Oxford University Press, 1950).

Silvey, Robert. *Who's Listening? The Story of BBC Audience Research* (London: George Allen & Unwin, 1974).

Simon, Ernest Darwin. *The B.B.C. from Within* (London: Victor Gollancz, 1953).

Smith, Anthony. *British Broadcasting* (Newton Abbot: David & Charles, 1974).

Smith, Anthony, *The Shadow in the Cave: The Broadcaster, His Audience, and the State* (Urbana: University of Illinois Press, 1973).

Smith, Anthony (ed.,) *Television and Political Life. Studies in Six European Countries* (London: Macmillan Press, 1979).

Smith, Delbert D. *International Telecommunication Control: International Law and the Ordering of Satellite and Other Forms of International Broadcasting* (Leyden: A. W. Sijthoff, 1969).

The Standing Conference on Broadcasting. *Evidence to the Committee on the*

Future of Broadcasting (London: Standing Conference on Broadcasting, January 1976). (*The SCOB Papers.*)

Swift, John. *Adventure in Vision: The First Twenty-Five Years of Television*. London: John Lehmann, 1950.

Television Research Committee. *Problems of Television Research: A Progress Report of the Television Research Committee* (Leicester: Leicester University Press, 1966).

Thomas, Howard. *The Truth About Television* (London: Weidenfeld & Nicolson, 1962).

Thomas, Hugh (ed.). *The Establishment* (London: Anthony Blond, 1959).

Tomlinson, John D. *The International Control of Radio Communications* (Ann Arbor: Edwards Brothers, 1945).

Tracey, Michael. *The Production of Political Television* (London: Routledge & Kegan Paul, 1978).

Trenaman, Joseph, and Denis McQuail, *Television and the Political Image: A Study of the Impact of Television on the 1959 General Election* (London: Methuen, 1961).

Turner, A. C. *Free Speech and Broadcasting* (Oxford: Blackwell, 1943).

Webster's Third New International Dictionary of the English Language, Unabridged (1964).

Wedell, E. G. *Broadcasting and Public Policy*. (London: Michael Joseph, 1968).

——. (ed.). *Structures of Broadcasting: A Symposium* (Manchester: Manchester University Press, 1970).

Whale, John. *The Politics of the Media* (Glasgow: Fontana/Collins, 1977).

Whitehouse, Mary. *Cleaning-Up TV: From Protest to Participation* (London: Blandford Press, 1967).

Wilson, H. H. *Pressure Group: The Campaign for Commercial Television in England* (New Brunswick, N. J.: Rutgers University Press, 1961).

Woolton, Frederick James Marquis, First Earl of. *Memoirs* (London: Cassell, 1959).

Wyndham Goldie, Grace. *Facing the Nation: Television and Politics 1936–1976* (London: The Bodley Head, 1977).

UNESCO, *Television: A World Survey* (Paris: UNESCO, 1949).

5   NEWSPAPERS AND PERIODICALS

Broadcast (London).
Broadcasting (Washington).
Cablevision News (London).
Church Times (London).
Daily Express (London).
Daily Mail (London).
Daily Telegraph (London).
EBU Review (Geneva).
Economist (London).

Educational Broadcasting Review (Washington).

The Financial Times (London).

Guardian (formerly *Manchester Guardian*) (London).

Glasgow Herald (Glasgow).

IBA Technical Review (London).

Independent Broadcasting (London).

The Institution of Electrical Engineers, Proceedings (London).

Journal of Communication (Philadelphia).

Journalism Quarterly (Minneapolis).

The Minneapolis Star (Minneapolis).

The New York Times (New York). (Almost all *New York Times* references are to the (early) City Edition, so that date and page citations may differ from those in the Final Edition stocked by most libraries.)

Observer (London).

Public Administration (London).

Radio and Record News (London).

Saturday Evening Post (Philadelphia).

Sheffield Star (Sheffield).

The Sunday Times (London).

The Times (London).

Time Out (London).

Variety (New York).

Index